The
Psychosocial
Interior
of
the
Family

List
of
Contributors

Norman W. Bell
Linda A. Bennett
Peter Berger
Anni Bergman
Francesca M. Cancian
Dorothy Terry Carlson
E. J. Cleveland
Alice Cornelison
G. W. Elles
Diane Ehrensaft
Stephen Fleck
Else Frenkel-Brunswik
Richard J. Gelles
Gerald Handel
Jules Henry
Robert D. Hess
Hansfried Kellner
Ralph LaRossa
Hope Jensen Leichter
Oscar Lewis
Theodore Lidz
W. D. Longaker
Katharine McAvity
Margaret S. Mahler
Elizabeth Newson
John Newson
Fred Pine
Lee Rainwater
Edward J. Speedling
Helm Stierlin
Robert S. Weiss
Norbert F. Wiley
Ezra F. Vogel

The
Psychosocial
Interior
of
the
Family

Third Edition

Edited by
GERALD HANDEL

ALDINE
Publishing Company
New York

About

the

Editor

Gerald Handel is Professor of Sociology at the City College and Graduate Center, City University of New York. He is the author/coauthor/editor of: *The Apple Sliced: Sociological Studies of New York City; Social Welfare in Western Society; The Child and Society: The Process of Socialization; Workingman's Wife: Her Personality, World and Lifestyle;* and *Family Worlds.* He is former Associate Editor of *Journal of Marriage and Family.*

Aldine Publishing Company
200 Saw Mill River Road
Hawthorne, New York 10532

Library of Congress Cataloging in Publication Data

The psychosocial interior of the family.

  Includes bibliographies and indexes.
  1. Family—Addresses, essays, lectures.   2. Social psychology—Addresses, essays, lectures.   I. Handel, Gerald.
HQ728.P76   1985   306.8'5   84-18398
ISBN 0-202-30317-9
ISBN-0-202-30318-7 (pbk.)

Printed in the United States of America
10 9 8 7 6 5 4 3 2 1

The whole business of science does not lie in getting into realms which are unfamiliar in normal experience. There is an enormous work of analyzing, of recognizing similarities and analogies, of getting the feel of the landscape, an enormous qualitative sense of family relations, of taxonomy. It is not always tactful to try to quantify; it is not always clear that by measuring one has found something very much worth measuring. It is true that for the Babylonians it was worth measuring—noting—the first appearances of the moon because it had a practical value. Their predictions, their prophecies, and their magic would not work without it; and I know that many psychologists have the same kind of reason for wanting to measure. It is a real property of the real world that you are measuring, but it is not necessarily the best way to advance true understanding of what is going on; and I would make this very strong plea for pluralism with regard to methods that, in the necessarily early stages of sorting out an immensely vast experience, may be fruitful and may be helpful.

Robert Oppenheimer
The American Psychologist
(March, 1956, p. 135)

Contents

VI PATTERNING SEPARATENESS AND CONNECTEDNESS

VII STRESS, CRISIS, AND SEPARATENESS/CONNECTEDNESS

Introduction to the Third Edition

GERALD HANDEL

Family studies have been in an expansionist ferment since the 1960's. The women's movement led to widespread and deep questioning of the status and role of women, studies of how the family as an institution is organized were an inevitable part of this re-examination. The counterculture contributed to a new and more public discussion of sexuality, introducing notions of "alternative life styles." These, in turn, led to new discussions of "the future of the family." Rising divorce rates, increasing age of first marriage, and declining birth rates further contributed to assessments of the family's future. Whether because of these social changes or not, historians evinced a sudden interest in the history of the family, and a growing output of studies has resulted from their work. Psychologists who study child development began to expand their interest from maternal influences to paternal ones, leading to a new science of father–child relationships parallel to the established science of mother–child relationships. Psychiatrists, dissatisfied with the results achieved with individual therapies even in the 1950's and earlier, continued to proliferate family therapies, an effort in which some psychologists and social workers joined. Some sociologists, dissatisfied with what they felt was the excessively empiricist habit of family research in that discipline, expanded their efforts to develop theories of the family.

In the midst of this enormous expansion in family study is a glaring omission. It is an astonishing fact that no social science concerns itself with studying how families function. No social science discipline takes as its continuing task the study of family groups. For the most part, the field of family psychiatry (or, more broadly, family therapy) has taken on this task,

and the social sciences have apparently been content to allow this to occur. The study of family groups, insofar as it is practiced at all, is largely
carried on as a part of the field of mental illness and mental health. Within
the social sciences, the family is divided. Marriage is a central focus in sociology and anthropology, but only a minor one in psychology. In contrast,
parent—child relations are of major interest in psychology and human development, but only a minor one in sociology and anthropology. Sociology
conceptualizes marriage and the family as institutions, but not families as
groups. Anthropology conceptualizes the family as part of a society's kinship system, its larger interest. Mainstream developmental psychology thus
far has not found it possible to conceptualize a unit larger than a dyad.
When I remarked, not long ago, to the head of a doctoral program in developmental psychology that the field seemed to be moving toward the
concept of the family, the program head replied, "We're moving toward
the *context;* I'm not sure we're moving toward the *concept.*"

Clearly, there is a need to crystallize a field of study that has been
emerging for some time but which does not yet have a name of its own
and a community of scholars, teachers, and students who mutually interact
as members of a community with a shared focus. I suggest that there is a
need for a social psychology of the family. Families are naturally occurring
groups, just as are work groups, friendship groups, and others, although they
are more deeply and more widely consequential than other kinds of groups
for most people in modern society. Families are part of the social nature of
humanity and deserve and require to be understood, just as do other forms
of human organization and association—bureaucracies, communities, voluntary associations, social movements, and networks.

This book presents a set of papers that delineate a social psychology of
the family. It is based on the assumption that the study of families is not
and should not be solely a byproduct of family therapy and should not be
approached solely from the perspective of mental health and mental illness. There are other questions to ask than simply "Is this healthy?" or "Is
this sick?" As Robert Oppenheimer reminds us, there is an enormous work
of sorting out a field. We need to leave ourselves as open as possible to
new kinds of information and new answers to the question: What kinds of
things go on in families? What is their impact and importance? How does
the marital relationship affect the development of children? How does the
way children are developing affect the marriage? What kinds of ties can
develop among parents and children? What is the range of possibilities?

This book is based on a conception of the family and the human individual that emphasizes two characteristics: human beings are both *social*
and *imaginative.* The human must *interact* with others and must *interpret*
situation, self, and others. The book builds on these underlying concepts.
A family is an organization that creates meaning among its members. A
family is begun by two adults who bring with them certain meanings de-

rived from the culture and from their individual life histories. But they do not simply enact their culture and re-enact their individual histories. They create meaning through their interaction. When we say that a family creates meanings we refer to at least the following kinds:

- *persons* (the meaning of the self and of other family members in relation to the self)
- *goals* (the meaning of the future in relation to the present)
- *activities* (the meaning of effort in relation to time, space, energy, money, and other resources)

If we wish to understand families, we need to delineate how families create the meanings that govern their interactions and relationships. We need to understand how family members give meaning to each other and interweave these meanings; how they define the goals of family life; how they selectively endow activities with meaning that justifies particular kinds of effort and excludes other kinds.

This volume takes the view that families are not simple reflections of the society to which they belong and the culture in which they participate. Rather, families exert effects at their own level of organization, influenced by the specific resources and constraints affecting the particular family, and, further, influenced by the imaginative capacities of the members to interpret their individual situations and the family group situation in relation to the wider society and culture. This perspective is not offered as an alternative to the more traditional views in sociology and anthropology but as a supplement to them, a perspective that merits development in its own right. All of the papers in this volume exemplify this view that families must be understood as groups whose members construct their own group worlds through interpretive activity that underlies the interactions they undertake.

No single volume can attempt to do everything, even within its chosen domain. Therefore, a word should be said about the scope of this one. Clearly, the book is focused on the marriage and child-rearing years of the family developmental cycle. It does not deal comprehensively with courtship, dating, and living together—the activities preparatory to establishing a family—nor does it deal with the later stages of the family cycle—the postparental empty nest or relationships between parents and their adult children. It is also not possible in the space available to deal with the full range of family problems. The focus is on the stages of family life that deal with marriage and parent–child relationships during the child's developmental years.

The book is delimited also in terms of the type of work represented. The vast majority of papers are based on qualitative research methods: field observation, depth interviews, clinical study. This is the kind of work that seems to me most promising of deeper understanding, most productive of new ideas and insights and, not least, most interesting. I believe the reader—

whether student, professor, practicing professional, or interested nonspe-
cialist—will find here an array of extremely interesting studies and discussions. None is the final word on its subject, but all are illuminating and
thought-provoking. Taken together they deepen our insight into families.
They sketch the outlines of a social psychology of the family, a field that
has been gestating for at least 60 years since Ernest W. Burgess suggested
we recognize "the family as a unity of interacting personalities" and that
is now more than ready to be born.

The Psychosocial Interior of the Family

I

Orientation: Constructing Meaning and Organization

The selections in Part I present the basic orientation of this volume. Every family faces the task of constructing some kind of life among its members. Through social interaction they define their relationships to one another and to the world beyond the family. The members establish individual identities as well as a collective family identity. The selections in this first part open up the discussion of what tasks are involved and how they are approached.

The process of defining and constructing a family world most commonly begins with a married couple who inaugurate a new family by their marriage. Peter Berger and Hansfried Kellner introduce the concept of the marital conversation as the means by which the partners bring into some kind of order the two individual versions of reality they brought into the marriage. The authors' point of departure is Emile Durkheim's concept of anomie, a social condition of breakdown in norms with the result that people drift in confusion and bewilderment. They set out to explain how a social order is built in marriage so that anomie is forestalled.

Berger and Kellner's discussion has been widely esteemed. Norbert Wiley, acknowledging the continuing value of their conceptual approach, points out that social changes in the years since they wrote have rendered certain of their statements out of date. He sets forth the ways in which the marital conversation of the 1980's probably differs from that of the 1960's.

Sociologists and social psychologists have long studied marriage relationships. Psychologists have long studied mother-child relationships and, in recent years, they have begun to study father-child and sibling relationships. Hess and Handel took the step of conceptualizing the family as a group. A family is not merely the sum of its part-relationships. Once there are children, a family becomes a group, a unit that needs to be understood at its own level of organization. Hess and Handel offer concepts that focus attention on this group, engaged in psychosocial activity that encompasses all its members.

1

Marriage and the Construction of Reality

AN EXERCISE IN THE MICROSOCIOLOGY OF KNOWLEDGE

PETER BERGER AND HANSFRIED KELLNER

Ever since Durkheim it has been a commonplace of family sociology that marriage serves as a protection against anomie for the individual. Interesting and pragmatically useful though this insight is, it is but the negative side of a phenomenon of much broader significance. If one speaks of *anomic* states, then one ought properly to investigate also the *nomic* processes that, by their absence, lead to the aforementioned states. If, consequently, one finds a negative correlation between marriage and anomie, then one should be led to inquire into the character of marriage as a *nomos*-building instrumentality; that is, of marriage as a social arrangement that creates for the individual the sort of order in which he can experience his life as making sense. It is our intention here to discuss marriage in these terms. While this could evidently be done in a macrosociological perspective, dealing with marriage as a major social institution related to other broad structures of society, our focus will be microsociological, dealing primarily with the social processes affecting the individuals in any specific marriage, although, of course, the larger framework of these processes will have to be understood. In what sense this discussion can be described as microsociology of knowledge will hopefully become clearer in the course of it.[1]

Marriage is obviously only *one* social relationship in which this process of *nomos*-building takes place. It is, therefore, necessary to first look in more

Reprinted with permission from *Diogenes*, Summer, 1964, 46, pp. 1–23.
Peter Berger is Professor of Sociology, Boston University. Hansfried Kellner is Professor of Sociology, University of Darmstadt, West Germany.

general terms at the character of this process. In doing so, we are influenced by three theoretical perspectives: the Weberian perspective on society as a network of meanings, the Meadian perspective on identity as a social phenomenon, and the phenomenological analysis of the social structuring of reality, especially as given in the work of Schutz and Merleau-Ponty.[2] Not being convinced, however, that theoretical lucidity is necessarily enhanced by terminological ponderosity, we shall avoid as much as possible the use of the sort of jargon for which both sociologists and phenomenologists have acquired dubious notoriety.

The process that interests us here is the one that constructs, maintains and modifies a consistent reality that can be meaningfully experienced by individuals. In its essential forms this process is determined by the society in which it occurs. Every society has its specific way of defining and perceiving reality—its world, its universe, its overarching organization of symbols. This is already given in the language that forms the symbolic base of the society. Erected over this base, and by means of it, is a system of ready-made typifications through which the innumerable experiences of reality come to be ordered.[3] These typifications and their order are held in common by the members of society, thus acquiring not only the character of objectivity, but being taken for granted as *the* world *tout court,* the only world that normal men can conceive of.[4] The seemingly objective and taken-for-granted character of the social definitions of reality can be seen most clearly in the case of language itself, but it is important to keep in mind that the latter forms the base and instrumentality of a much larger world-erecting process.

The socially constructed world must be continually mediated to and actualized by the individual, so that it can become and remain indeed *his* world as well. The individual is given by his society certain decisive cornerstones for his everyday experience and conduct. Most importantly, the individual is supplied with specific sets of typifications and criteria of relevance, predefined for him by the society and made available to him for the ordering of his everyday life. This ordering, or (in line with our opening considerations) nomic apparatus, is biographically cumulative. It begins to be formed in the individual from the earliest stages of socialization, then keeps on being enlarged and modified by himself throughout his biography.[5] While there are individual biographical differences making for differences in the constitution of this apparatus in specific individuals, there exists in the society an overall consensus on the range of differences deemed to be tolerable. Without such consensus, indeed, society would be impossible as a going concern, since it would then lack the ordering principles by which alone experience can be shared and conduct can be mutually intelligible. This order, by which the individual comes to perceive and define his world, is thus not chosen by him, except perhaps for very small modifications. Rather, it is discovered by him as an external datum, a ready-made world that simply is *there* for him to go ahead and live in, though he modifies it continually in the process of living in it. Nevertheless, this world is in need of validation, perhaps precisely because of an ever-present glimmer of suspicion as to its social manufacture and relativity. This validation, while necessarily undertaken by the individual himself, requires ongoing interaction with others who coinhabit this same socially constructed world. In a broad sense, *all* the other coinhabitants of this world serve a validating function. Every morning the newspaper boy validates the widest coordinates of my world and the mailman bears tangible validation of my own location within these coordinates. However, some validations are more significant than others. Every individual requires the ongoing validation of his world, including crucially the validation of his identity and position by those few who are his truly significant others.[6] Just as the individual's deprivation of relationship with his significant others will plunge him into anomie, so their continued presence will sustain for him that *nomos* by which he can feel at home in the world at least most of the time. Again in a broad sense, all the actions of the significant others and even their simple presence serve this sustaining function. In everyday life, however, the principal method employed is speech. In this sense, it is proper to view the individual's relationship with his significant others as an ongoing conversation. As the latter occurs, it validates over and over again the fundamental definitions of reality once entered into, not, of course, so much by explicit articulation, but precisely by taking the definitions silently for granted and conversing about all conceivable matters on this taken-for-granted basis. Through the same conversation the individual is also made capable of adjusting to changing and new social contexts in his biography. In a very fundamental sense it can be said that one converses one's way through life.

If one concedes these points, one can now state a general sociological proposition: The plausibility and stability of the world, as socially defined, is dependent upon the strength and continuity of significant relationships in which conversation about this world can be continually carried on. Or, to put it a little differently: The reality of the world is sustained through conversation with significant others. This reality, of course, includes not only the imagery by which fellowmen are viewed, but also the way in which one views oneself. The reality-bestowing force of social relationships depends on the degree of their nearness;[7] that is, on the degree to which social relationships occur in face-to-face situations and to which they are credited with primary significance by the individual. In any empirical situation, there now emerge obvious sociological questions out of these considerations; namely, questions about the patterns of the world-building relationships, the social forms taken by the conversation with significant others. Sociologically, one must ask how these relationships are *objectively* structured and distributed, and one will also want to understand how they are *subjectively* perceived and experienced.

With these preliminary assumptions stated we can now arrive at our main thesis. Namely, we would contend that marriage occupies a privileged status among the significant validating relationships for adults in our society. Put slightly differently: Marriage is a crucial nomic instrumentality in our society. We would further argue that the essential social functionality of this institution cannot be fully understood if this fact is not perceived.

We can now proceed with an ideal-typical analysis of marriage; that is, seek to abstract the essential features involved. Marriage in our society is a *dramatic* act in which two strangers come together and redefine themselves. The drama of the act is internally anticipated and socially legitimated long before it takes place in the individual's biography, and amplified by means of a pervasive ideology, the dominant themes of which (romantic love, sexual fulfillment, self-discovery and self-realization through love and sexuality, the nuclear family as the social site for these processes) can be found distributed through all strata of the society. The actualization of these ideologically predefined expectations in the life of the individual occurs to the accompaniment of one of the few traditional rites of passage that are still meaningful to almost all members of the society. It should be added that, in using the term "strangers," we do not mean, of course, that the candidates for the marriage come from widely discrepant social backgrounds—indeed, the data indicate that the contrary is the case. The strangeness lies rather in the fact that, unlike marriage candidates in many previous societies, those in ours typically come from different face-to-face contexts; in the terms used above, they come from different areas of conversation. They do not have a shared past, although their pasts have a similar structure. In other words, quite apart from prevailing patterns of ethnic, religious and class endogamy, our society is typically exogamous in terms of nomic relationships. Put concretely, in our mobile society the significant conversation of the two partners previous to the marriage took place in social circles that did not overlap. With the dramatic redefinition of the situation brought about by the marriage, however, all significant conversation for the two new partners is now centered in their relationship with each other; in fact, it was precisely with this intention that they entered upon their relationship.

It goes without saying that this character of marriage has its root in much broader structural configurations of our society. The most important of these, for our purposes, is the crystallization of a so-called private sphere of existence, more and more segregated from the immediate controls of the public institutions (especially the economic and political ones), and yet defined and utilized as the main social area for the individual's self-realization.[8] It cannot be our purpose here to inquire into the historical forces that brought forth this phenomenon, beyond making the observation that these are closely connected with the industrial revolution and its institutional consequences. The public institutions now confront the individual as an immensely powerful and alien world, incomprehensible in its inner workings, anonymous in its human character. If only through his work in some nook of the economic machinery, the individual must find a way of living in this alien world, come to terms with its power over him, be satisfied with a few conceptual rules of thumb to guide him through a vast reality that otherwise remains opaque to his understanding, and modify its anonymity by whatever "human relations" he can work out in his involvement with it.

It ought to be emphasized, against some critics of "mass society," that this does not inevitably leave the individual with a sense of profound unhappiness and lostness. It would rather seem that large numbers of people in our society are quite content with a situation in which their public involvements have little subjective importance, regarding work as a not-too-bad necessity and politics as at best a spectator sport. It is usually only intellectuals with ethical and political commitments who assume that such people must be terribly desperate. The point, however, is that the individual in this situation, whether he is happy or not, will turn elsewhere for the experiences of self-realization that do have importance for him. The private sphere, this interstitial area created (we would think) more or less haphazardly as a by-product of the social metamorphosis of industrialism, is mainly where he will turn. It is here that the individual will seek power, intelligibility and, quite literally, a name—the apparent power to fashion a world, however Lilliputian, that will reflect his own being; a world that, seemingly having been shaped by himself and thus unlike those other worlds that insist on shaping him, is translucently intelligible to him (or so he thinks); a world in which, consequently, he is somebody—perhaps even, within its charmed circle, a lord and master. What is more, to a considerable extent these expectations are not unrealistic. The public institutions have no need to control the individual's adventures in the private sphere, as long as they really stay within the latter's circumscribed limits. The private sphere is perceived, justifiably, as an area of individual choice and even autonomy. This fact has important consequences for the shaping of identity in modern society that cannot be pursued here. All that ought to be clear here is the peculiar location of the private sphere within and between the other social structures.

In sum, it is, as a rule, only in the private sphere that the individual can take a slice of reality and fashion it into his world. If one is aware of the decisive significance of this capacity and even necessity of men to externalize themselves in reality and to produce for themselves a world in which they can feel at home, then one will hardly be surprised at the great importance the private sphere has come to have in modern society.[9]

The private sphere includes a variety of social relationships. Among these, however, the relationships of the family occupy a central position and serve as a focus for most of the other relationships (such as those with friends, neighbors, fellow members of religious and other voluntary associations).

Since, as the ethnologists keep reminding us, the family in our society is of the conjugal type, the central relationship in this whole area is the marital one. It is on the basis of marriage that, for most adults in our society, existence in the private sphere is built up. It will be clear that this is not at all a universal or even cross culturally wide function of marriage, which in our society has taken on a very peculiar character and functionality. It has been pointed out that marriage in contemporary society has lost some of its older functions and taken on new ones instead.[10] This is certainly correct, but we would prefer to state the matter a little differently. Marriage and the family used to be firmly embedded in a matrix of wider community relationships, serving as extensions and particularizations of the latter's social controls. There were few separating barriers between the world of the individual family and the wider community, a fact even to be seen in the physical conditions in which the family lived before the industrial revolution.[11] The same social life pulsated through the house, the street and the community. In our terms, the family and within it the marital relationship were part and parcel of a considerably larger area of conversation. In our contemporary society, by contrast, each family constitutes its own segregated subworld, with its own controls and its own closed conversation.

This fact requires a much greater effort on the part of the marriage partners. Unlike an earlier situation in which the establishment of the new marriage simply added to the differentiation and complexity of an already existing social world, the marriage partners now are embarked on the often difficult task of constructing for themselves the little world in which they will live. To be sure, the larger society provides them with certain standard instructions as to how they should go about this task, but this does not change the fact that considerable effort of their own is required for its realization. The monogamous character of marriage enforces both the dramatic and the precarious nature of his undertaking. Success or failure hinges on the present idiosyncracies and the fairly unpredictable future development of these idiosyncracies of only two individuals (who, moreover, do not have a shared past)—as Simmel has shown, the most unstable of all possible social relationships.[12] Not surprisingly, the decision to embark on this undertaking has a critical, even cataclysmic connotation in the popular imagination, which is underlined as well as psychologically assuaged by the ceremonialism that surrounds the event.

Every social relationship requires objectivation, that is, requires a process by which subjectively experienced meanings become objective to the individual and, in interaction with others, become common property and thereby massively objective.[13] The degree of objectivation will depend on the number and the intensity of the social relationships that are its carriers. A relationship that consists of only two individuals called upon to sustain, by their own efforts, an ongoing social world will have to make up in intensity for the numerical poverty of the arrangement. This, in turn, accentuates the drama and the precariousness. The addition of children will add to the density of objectivation taking place within the nuclear family, thus rendering the latter a good deal less precarious. It remains true that the establishment and maintenance of such a social world makes extremely high demands on the principal participants.

The attempt can now be made to outline the ideal-typical process that takes place when marriage functions as an instrumentality for the social construction of reality. The chief protagonists of the drama are two individuals, each with a biographically accumulated and available stock of experience.[14] As members of a highly mobile society, these individuals have already internalized a degree of readiness to redefine themselves and to modify their stock of experience, thus bringing with them considerable psychological capacity for entering new relationships with others.[15] Also, coming from broadly similar sectors of the larger society (in terms of region, class, ethnic and religious affiliations), the two individuals will have organized their stock of experience in similar fashion. In other words, the two individuals have internalized the same overall world, including the general definitions and expectations of the marriage relationship itself. Their society has provided them with a taken-for-granted image of marriage and has socialized them into an anticipation of stepping into the taken-for-granted roles of marriage. All the same, these relatively empty projections now have to be actualized, lived through and filled with experiential content by the protagonists. This will require a dramatic change in their definitions of reality and of themselves.

As of the marriage, most of each partner's actions must now be projected in conjunction with those of the other. Each partner's definitions of reality must be continually correlated with the definitions of the other. The other is present in nearly all horizons of everyday conduct. Furthermore, the identity of each now takes on a new character, having to be constantly matched with that of the other, indeed being typically perceived by people at large as being symbiotically conjoined with the identity of the other. In each partner's psychological economy of significant others, the marriage partner becomes the other *par excellence*, the nearest and most decisive coinhabitant of the world. Indeed, all other significant relationships have to be almost automatically reperceived and regrouped in accordance with this drastic shift.

In other words, from the beginning of the marriage each partner has new modes in his meaningful experience of the world in general, of other people and of himself. By definition, then, marriage constitutes a nomic rupture. In terms of each partner's biography, the event of marriage initiates a new nomic process. The full implications of this fact are rarely apprehended by the protagonists with any degree of clarity. There rather is to be found the notion that one's world, one's other relationships and, above all, oneself have remained what they were before—only, of course, that world, others and self will now be shared with the marriage partner. It should be clear by now that this notion is a grave misapprehension. Just because of this fact, marriage now propels the individual into an unintended and un-articulated development, in the course of which the nomic transformation takes place. What typically *is* apprehended are certain objective and con-crete problems arising out of the marriage, such as tensions with in-laws, or with former friends, or religious differences between the partners, as well as immediate tensions between them. These are apprehended as external, situational and practical difficulties. What is *not* apprehended is the subject side of these difficulties, namely, the transformation of *nomos* and identity that has occurred and that continues to go on, so that all problems and relationships are experienced in a quite new way, that is, experienced within a new and ever-changing reality.

Take a simple and frequent illustration: the male partner's relationships with male friends before and after the marriage. It is a common observation that such relationships, especially if the friends are single, rarely survive the marriage, or, if they do, are drastically redefined after it. This is typically the result of neither a deliberate decision by the husband nor deliberate sabotage by the wife. What happens, very simply is a slow process in which the husband's image of his friend is transformed as he keeps talking about this friend with his wife. Even if no actual talking goes on, the mere pres-ence of the wife forces him to see his friend differently. This need not mean that he adopts a negative image held by the wife. Regardless of what image she holds or is believed by him to hold, it will be different from that held by the husband. This difference will enter into the joint image that now must be fabricated in the course of the ongoing conversation between the marriage partners—and, in due course, must act powerfully on the image previously held by the husband. Again, typically, this process is rarely ap-prehended with any degree of lucidity. The old friend is more likely to fade out of the picture by degrees as new kinds of friends take his place. The process, if commented upon at all within the marital conversation, can al-ways be explained by socially available formulas about "people chang-ing," "friends disappearing" or oneself "having become more mature." This process of conversational liquidation is especially powerful because it is onesided—the husband typically talks with his wife about his friend, but *not* with his friend about his wife. Thus the friend is deprived of the de-fense of, as it were, counterdefining the relationship. This dominance of the marital conversation over all others is one of its most important char-acteristics. It may be mitigated by a certain amount of protective segrega-tion of some nonmarital relationships (say, "Tuesday night out with the boys," or "Saturday lunch with mother"), but even then there are powerful emo-tional barriers against the sort of conversation (conversation *about* the mar-ital relationship, that is) that would serve by way of counter definition.

Marriage thus posits a new reality. The individual's relationship with this new reality, however, is a dialectical one; he acts upon it, in collusion with the marriage partner, and it acts back upon both him and the partner, welding together their reality. Since, as we have argued before, the objectivation that constitutes this reality is precarious, the groups with which the couple associates are called upon to assist in codefining the new reality. The couple is pushed toward groups that strengthen their new definition of themselves and the world, avoids those that weaken this definition. This, in turn, releases the commonly known pressures of group association, again acting upon the marriage partners to change their definitions of the world and of themselves. Thus the new reality is not posited once and for all, but goes on being redefined not only in the marital interaction itself but in the various maritally based group relationships into which the couple enters.

In the individual's biography marriage, then, brings about a decisive phase of socialization that can be compared with the phases of childhood and adolescence. This phase has a somewhat different structure from the earlier ones. There the individual was in the main socialized into already existing patterns. Here he actively collaborates rather than passively accommodates himself. Also, in the previous phases of socialization, there was an apprehension of entering into a new world and being changed in the course of this. In marriage there is little apprehension of such a process, but rather the notion that the world has remained the same, with only its emotional and pragmatic connotations having changed. This notion, as we have tried to show, is illusionary.

The reconstruction of the world in marriage occurs principally in the course of conversation, as we have suggested. The implicit problem of this conversation is how to match two individual definitions of reality. By the very logic of the relationship a common overall definition must be arrived at, otherwise the conversation will become impossible and, *ipso facto,* the relationship will be endangered. Now, this conversation may be understood as the working away of an ordering and typifying apparatus—if one prefers, an objectivating apparatus. Each partner ongoingly contributes his conceptions of reality, which are then "talked through," usually not once but many times, and in the process become objectivated by the conversational apparatus. The longer this conversation goes on, the more massively real do the objectivations become to the partners. In the marital conversation a world is not only built, but it is also kept in a state of repair and ongoingly refurnished. The subjective reality of this world for the two partners is sustained by the same conversation. The nomic instrumentality of marriage is concretized over and over again, from bed to breakfast table, as the partners carry on the endless conversation that feeds on nearly all they individually or jointly experience. Indeed, it may happen eventually that no experience is fully real unless and until it has been thus "talked through."

This process has a very important result; namely, a hardening or stabilization of the common objectivated reality. It should be easy to see now how this comes about. The objectivations ongoingly performed and internalized by the marriage partners become ever more massively real, as they are confirmed and reconfirmed in the marital conversation. The world that is made up of these objectivations at the same time gains in stability. For example, the images of other people, which before or in the earlier stages of the marital conversation may have been rather ambiguous and shifting in the minds of the two partners, now become hardened into definite and stable characterizations. A casual acquaintance, say, may sometimes have appeared as lots of fun and sometimes as quite a bore to the wife before her marriage. Under the influence of the marital conversation, in which this other person is frequently "discussed," she will now come down more firmly on one *or* the other of the two characterizations, or on a reasonable compromise between the two. In any of these three options, though, she will have concocted with her husband a much more stable image of the person in question than she is likely to have had before her marriage, when there may have been no conversational pressure to make a definite option at all. The same process of stabilization may be observed with regard to self-definitions as well. In this way, the wife in our example will be pressured to assign stable characterizations not only to others but also to herself. Previously uninterested politically, she now identifies herself as a liberal. Previously alternating between dimly articulated religious positions, she now declares herself an agnostic. Previously confused and uncertain about her sexual emotions, she now understands herself as an unabashed hedonist in this area. And so on and so forth, with the same reality—and identity—stabilizing process at work on the husband. Both world and self thus take on a firmer, more reliable character for both partners.

Furthermore, it is not only the ongoing experience of the two partners that is constantly shared and passed through the conversational apparatus. The same sharing extends into the past. The two distinct biographies, as subjectively apprehended by the two individuals who have lived through them, are overruled and reinterpreted in the course of their conversation. Sooner or later, they will "tell all"—or, more correctly, they will tell it in a way that fits into the self-definitions objectivated in the marital relationship. The couple thus not only construct present reality but reconstruct past reality as well, fabricating a common memory that integrates the recollections of the two individual pasts.[16] The comic fulfillment of this process may be seen in those cases when one partner "remembers" more clearly what happened in the other's past than the other does—and corrects him accordingly. Similarly, there occurs a sharing of future horizons, which leads not only to stabilization, but inevitably to a narrowing of the future projections of each partner. Before marriage the individual typically plays with quite discrepant daydreams in which his future self is projected.[17] Having now considerably stabilized his self-image, the married individual will have to project the future in accordance with a maritally defined identity. This narrowing of future horizons begins with the obvious external limitations that marriage entails, as, for example, with regard to vocational and career plans. However, it extends also to the more general possibilities of the individual's biography. To return to a previous illustration, the wife, having "found herself" as a liberal, an agnostic and a "sexually healthy" person, *ipso facto* liquidates the possibilities of becoming an anarchist, a Catholic or a lesbian. At least until further notice she has decided upon who she is—and, by the same token, on who she will be. The stabilization brought about by marriage thus affects the total reality in which the partners exist. In the most far-reaching sense of the word, the married individual "settles down," and *must* do so, if the marriage is to be viable, in accordance with its contemporary institutional definition.

It cannot be emphasized strongly enough that this process is typically unapprehended, almost automatic in character. The protagonists of the marriage drama do *not* set out deliberately to re-create their world. Each continues to live in a world that is taken for granted—and keeps its taken-for-granted character even as it is metamorphosed. The new world that the married partners, Prometheus-like, have called into being is perceived by them as the normal world in which they have lived before. Reconstructed present and reinterpreted past are perceived as a continuum, extending forward into a commonly projected future. The dramatic change that has occurred remains, in bulk, unapprehended and unarticulated. And where it forces itself upon the individual's attention, it is retrojected into the past, explained as having always been there, though perhaps in a hidden way. Typically, the reality that has been "invented" within the marital conversation is subjectively perceived as a "discovery." Thus the partners "discover" themselves and the world, "who they really are," "what they really believe," "how they really feel, and always have felt, about so-and-so." This retrojection of the world being produced all the time by themselves serves to enhance the stability of this world and at the same time to assuage the "existential anxiety" that, probably inevitably, accompanies the perception that nothing but one's own narrow shoulders support the universe in which one has chosen to live. If one may put it like this, it is psychologically more tolerable to be Columbus than to be Prometheus.

The use of the term "stabilization" should not detract from the insight into the difficulty and precariousness of this world-building enterprise. Often enough, the new universe collapses *in statu nascendi*. Many more times it continues over a period, swaying perilously back and forth as the two partners try to hold it up, finally to be abandoned as an impossible undertaking. If one conceives of the marital conversation as the principal drama and the two partners as the principal protagonists of the drama, then one can look upon the other individuals involved as the supporting chorus for the central dramatic action. Children, friends, relatives, and casual acquaintances all have their part in reinforcing the tenuous structure of the new reality. It goes without saying that the children form the most important part of this supporting chorus. Their very existence is predicated on the maritally established world. The marital partners themselves are in charge of their socialization *into* this world, which to them has a pre-existent and self-evident character. They are taught from the beginning to speak precisely those lines that lend themselves to a supporting chorus, from their first invocations of "Daddy" and "Mummy" on to their adoption of the parents' ordering and typifying apparatus that now defines *their* world as well. The marital conversation is now in the process of becoming a family symposium, with the necessary consequence that its objectivations rapidly gain in density, plausibility and durability.

In sum: The process that we have been inquiring into is, ideal-typically, one in which reality is crystallized, narrowed and stabilized. Ambivalences are converted into certainties. Typifications of self and of others become settled. Most generally, possibilities become facticities. What is more, this process of transformation remains, most of the time, unapprehended by those who are both its authors and its objects.[18]

We have analyzed in some detail the process that, we contend, entitles us to describe marriage as a nomic instrumentality. It may now be well to turn back once more to the macrosocial context in which this process takes place—a process that, to repeat, is peculiar to our society as far as the institution of marriage is concerned, although it obviously expresses much more general human facts. The narrowing and stabilization of identity is functional in a society that, in its major public institutions, must insist on rigid controls over the individual's conduct. At the same time, the narrow enclave of the nuclear family serves as a macrosocially innocuous "play area," in which the individual can safely exercise his world-building proclivities without upsetting any of the important social, economic, and political applecarts. Barred from expanding himself into the area occupied by these major institutions, he is given plenty of leeway to "discover himself" in his marriage and his family, and, in view of the difficulty of this undertaking, is provided with a number of auxiliary agencies that stand ready to assist him (such as counseling, psychotherapeutic and religious agencies). The marital adventure can be relied upon to absorb a large amount of energy that might otherwise be expended more dangerously. The ideological themes of familism, romantic love, sexual expression, maturity and social adjustment, with the pervasive psychologistic anthropology that underlies them all, function to legitimate this enterprise. Also, the narrowing and stabilization of the individual's principal area of conversation within the nuclear family is functional in a society that requires high degrees of both geographical and social mobility. The segregated little world of the family can easily be detached from one milieu and transposed into another without appreciably interfering with the central processes going on in it. Needless to say, we are not suggesting that these functions are deliberately planned or even apprehended by some mythical ruling directorate of the society. Like most social phenomena, whether they are macro- or microscopic, these functions are typically unintended and unarticulated. What is more, the functionality would be impaired if it were too widely apprehended.

We believe that the above theoretical considerations serve to give a new perspective on various empirical facts studied by family sociologists. As we have emphasized a number of times, our considerations are ideal-typical in intention. We have been interested in marriage at a normal age in urban, middle-class western societies. We cannot discuss here such special problems as marriages or remarriages at a more advanced age, marriage in the remaining rural subcultures, or in ethnic or lower-class minority groups. We feel quite justified in this limitation of scope, however, by the empirical findings that tend toward the view that a global marriage type is emerging in the central strata of modern industrial societies.[19] This type, commonly referred to as the nuclear family, has been analyzed in terms of a shift from the so-called family of orientation to the so-called family of procreation as the most important reference for the individual.[20] In addition to the well-known socioeconomic reasons for this shift, most of them rooted in the development of industrialism, we would argue that important macrosocial functions pertain to the nomic process within the nuclear family, as we have analyzed it. This functionality of the nuclear family must, furthermore, be seen in conjunction with the familistic ideology that both reflects and reinforces it. A few specific empirical points may suffice to indicate the applicability of our theoretical perspective. To make these we shall use selected American data.

The trend toward marriage at an earlier age has been noted.[21] This has been correctly related to factors such as urban freedom, sexual emancipation and egalitarian values. We would add the important fact that a child raised in the circumscribed world of the nuclear family is stamped by it in terms of his psychological needs and social expectations. Having to live in the larger society from which the nuclear family is segregated, the adolescent soon feels the need for a "little world" of his own, having been socialized in such a way that only by having a private world to withdraw into can he successfully cope with the anonymous "big world" that confronts him as soon as he steps outside his parental home. In other words, to be "at home" in society entails, *per definitionem,* the construction of a maritally based subworld. The parental home itself facilitates an early jump into marriage precisely because its controls are very narrow in scope and leave the adolescent to his own nomic devices at an early age. As has been studied in considerable detail, the adolescent peer group functions as a transitional *nomos* between the two family worlds in the individual's biography.[22]

The equalization in the age of the marriage partners has also been noted.[23]

This is certainly to be related to egalitarian values and, concomitantly, to the decline in the "double standard" of sexual morality. Also, however, this fact is very conducive to the common reality-constructing enterprise that we have analyzed. One of the features of the latter, as we have pointed out, is the reconstruction of the two biographies in terms of a cohesive and mutually correlated common memory. This task is evidently facilitated if the two partners are of roughly equal age. Another empirical finding to which our considerations are relevant is the choice of marriage partners within similar socioeconomic backgrounds.[24] Apart from the obvious practical pressures toward such limitations of choice, the latter also ensures sufficient similarity in the biographically accumulated stocks of experience to facilitate the described reality-constructing process. This would offer additional explanation to the observed tendency to narrow the limitations of marital choice even further, for example in terms of religious background.[25]

There now exists a considerable body of data on the adoption and mutual adjustment of marital roles.[26] Nothing in our considerations detracts from the analyses made of these data by sociologists interested primarily in the processes of group interaction. We would argue only that something more fundamental is involved in this role-taking; namely, the individual's relationship to reality as such. Each role in the marital situation carries with it a universe of discourse, broadly given by cultural definition but continually reactualized in the ongoing conversation between the marriage partners. Put simply: Marriage involves not only stepping into new roles, but, beyond this, stepping into a new world. The *mutuality* of adjustment may again be related to the rise of marital egalitarianism, in which comparable effort is demanded of both partners.

Most directly related to our considerations are data that pertain to the greater stability of married as against unmarried individuals.[27] Though frequently presented in misleading psychological terms (such as "greater emotional stability," "greater maturity," and so on), these data are sufficiently validated to be used not only by marriage counselors but in the risk calculations of insurance companies. We would contend that our theoretical perspective places these data into a much more intelligible sociological frame of reference, which also happens to be free of the particular value bias with which the psychological terms are loaded. It is, of course, quite true that married people are more stable emotionally (*i.e.*, operating within a more controlled scope of emotional expression), more mature in their views (*i.e.*, inhabiting a firmer and narrower world in conformity with the expectations of society), and more sure of themselves (*i.e.*, having objectivated a more stable and fixated self-definition). *Therefore* they are more liable to be psychologically balanced (*i.e.*, having sealed off much of their "anxiety," and reduced ambivalence as well as openness toward new possibilities of self-definition) and socially predictable (*i.e.*, keeping their conduct well within the socially established safety rules). All of these phenomena are concomitants of the overall fact of having "settled down"—cognitively, emotionally, in terms of self-identification. To speak of these phenomena as indicators of "mental health," let alone of "adjustment to reality," overlooks the decisive fact that reality is socially constructed and that psychological conditions of all sorts are grounded in a social matrix.

We would say, very simply, that the married individual comes to live in a more stable world, from which fact certain psychological consequences can be readily deduced. To bestow some sort of higher ontological status upon these psychological consequences is *ipso facto* a symptom of the mis- or nonapprehension of the social process that has produced them. Furthermore, the compulsion to legitimate the stabilized marital world, be it in psychologistic or in traditional religious terms, is another expression of the precariousness of its construction.[28] This is not the place to pursue any further the ideological processes involved. Suffice it to say that contemporary psychology functions to sustain this precarious world by assigning to it the status of "normalcy," a legitimating operation that increasingly links up with the older religious assignment of the status of "sacredness." Both legitimating agencies have established their own rites of passage, validating myths and rituals, and individualized repair services for crisis situations. Whether one legitimates one's maritally constructed reality in terms of "mental health" or of the "sacrament of marriage" is today largely left to free consumer preference, but it is indicative of the crystallization of a new overall universe of discourse that it is increasingly possible to do both at the same time.

Finally, we would point here to the empirical data on divorce.[29] The prevalence, indeed, increasing prevalence of divorce might at first appear as a counterargument to our theoretical considerations. We would contend that the very opposite is the case, as the data themselves bear out. Typically, individuals in our society do not divorce because marriage has become unimportant to them, but because it has become so important that they have no tolerance for the less than completely successful marital arrangement they have contracted with the particular individual in question. This is more fully understood when one has grasped the crucial need for the sort of world that only marriage can produce in our society, a world without which the individual is powerfully threatened with anomie in the fullest sense of the word. Also, the frequency of divorce simply reflects the difficulty and demanding character of the whole undertaking. The empirical fact that the great majority of divorced individuals plan to remarry and a good majority of them actually do, at least in America, fully bears out this contention.[30]

The purpose of this article is not polemic, nor do we wish to advocate any particular values concerning marriage. We have sought to debunk the familistic ideology only insofar as it serves to obfuscate a sociological understanding of the phenomenon. Our purpose has been twofold. First, we wanted to show that it is possible to develop a sociological theory of marriage that is based on clearly sociological presuppositions, without operating with psychological or psychiatric categories that have dubious value within a sociological frame of reference. We believe that such a sociological theory of marriage is generally useful for a fully conscious awareness of existence in contemporary society, and not only for the sociologist. Second, we have used the case of marriage for an exercise in the sociology of knowledge, a discipline that we regard as most promising. Hitherto this discipline has been almost exclusively concerned with macrosociological questions, such as those dealing with the relationship of intellectual history to social processes. We believe that the microsociological focus is equally important for this discipline. The sociology of knowledge must be concerned not only with the great universes of meaning that history offers up for our inspection, but with the many little workshops in which living individuals keep hammering away at the construction and maintenance of these universes. In this way, the sociologist can make an important contribution to the illumination of that everyday world in which we all live and which we help fashion in the course of our biography.

NOTES

1. The present article has come out of a larger project on which the authors have been engaged in collaboration with three colleagues in sociology and philosophy. The project is to produce a systematic treatise that will integrate a number of now separate theoretical stands in the sociology of knowledge.

2. Cf. especially Max Weber, *Wirtschaft und gesellschaft,* Tuebingen: Mohr, 1956); Id., *Gesammelte aufsaetze zur wissenschaftslehre,* Tuebingen: Mohr, 1951; George H. Mead, *Mind, self and society,* Chicago: University of Chicago Press, 1934; Alfred Schutz, *Der sinnhafte aufbau der sozialen welt,* Vienna: Springer, 1960; Id., *Collected papers,* I, The Hague: Nijhoff, 1962; Maurice Merleau-Ponty, *Phénoménologie de la perception,* Paris: Gallimard, 1945; Id., *La structure du comportement,* Paris: Presses Universitaires de France, 1953.

3. Schutz, *Aufbau,* 202–220; Id., *Collected papers,* I, 3–27, 283–286.

4. cf. Schutz *Collected papers,* I, 207–228.

5. Cf. especially Jean Piaget, *The construction of reality in the child,* New York, Basic Books, 1954.

6. Cf. Mead, *op. cit.,* 135–226.

7. Cf. Schutz, *Aufbau,* 181–195.

8. Cf. Arnold Gehlen, *Die seele im technischen Zeitalter,* Hamburg: Rowohlt, 1957, pp. 57–69; Id., *Anthropologische forschung,* Hamburg: Rowohlt, 1961, pp. 69–77, 127–140; Helmut Schelsky, *Soziologie der sexualitaet,* Hamburg: Rowohlt, 1955, pp. 102–133. Also, cf. Thomas Luckmann, On religion in modern society. *Journal for the Scientific Study of Religion,* Spring 1963, pp. 147–162.

9. In these considerations we have been influenced by certain presuppositions of Marxian anthropology, as well as by the anthropological work of Max Scheler, Helmuth Plessner and Arnold Gehlen. We are indebted to Thomas Luckmann for the clarification of the social-psychological significance of the private sphere.

10. *Cf.* Talcott Parsons and Robert Bales, *Family, socialization and interaction process,* Glencoe, Ill.: Free Press, 1955, pp. 3–34, 353–396.

11. *Cf.* Philippe Ariès, *Centuries of childhood,* New York: Knopf, 1962, pp. 339–410.

12. *Cf.* Kurt Wolff (Ed.). *The sociology of Georg Simmel.* Glencoe, Ill: Free Press, 1950, pp. 118–144.

13. *Cf.* Schutz, *Aufbau,* pp. 29–36, 149–153.

14. *Cf.* Schutz, *Aufbau,* pp. 186–192, 202–210.

15. David Riesman's well-known concept of "other-direction" would also be applicable here.

16. *Cf.* Maurice Halbwachs, *Les cadres sociaux de la mémoire.* Paris: Presses Universitaires de France, 1952, especially pp. 146–177; Also, *cf.* Peter Berger, *Invitation to sociology—a humanistic perspective.* Garden City, N.Y.: Doubleday-Anchor, 1963, pp. 54–65.

17. *Cf.* Schutz, *Collected papers,* I, pp. 72–73, 79–82.

18. The phenomena here discussed could also be formulated effectively in terms of the Marxian categories of reification and false consciousness. Jean-Paul Sartre's recent work, especially *Critique de la raison dialectique,* seeks to integrate these categories within a phenomenological analysis of human conduct. Also, *cf.* Henri Lefebvre, *Critique de la vie quotidienne.* Paris: l'Arche, 1958–1961.

19. *Cf.* Renate Mayntz, *Die moderne familie.* Stuttgart: Enke, 1955; Helmut Schelsky, *Wandlungen der deutschen Familie in der Gegenwart.* Stuttgart: Enke, 1955; Maximilien Sorre (Ed.). *Sociologie comparée de la famille contemporaine.* Paris: Centre National de la Recherche Scientifique, 1955; Ruth Anshen (Ed.). *The family—its function and destiny.* New York: Harper, 1959; Norman Bell and Ezra Vogel, *A modern introduction to the family.* Glencoe, Ill.: Free Press, 1960.

20. *Cf.* Talcott Parsons, *Essays in sociological theory.* Glencoe, Ill.: Free Press, 1949, pp. 233–250.

21. In these as well as the following references to empirical studies we naturally make no attempt at comprehensiveness. References are given as representative of a much larger body of materials. *Cf.* Paul Glick, *American families.* New York: Wiley, 1957, p. 54. Also, *cf.* Id., The Family Cycle, *American Sociological Review,* April 1947, pp. 164–174. Also, *cf.* Bureau of the Census, *Statistical Abstracts of the United States,* 1956 and 1958; *Current Population Reports,* Nov. 1959, (Series P-20, No. 96).

22. *Cf.* David Riesman, *The lonely crowd.* New Haven: Yale University Press, 1953, pp. 29–40; Frederick Elkin, *The child and society.* New York: Random House, 1960, *passim.*

23. *Cf.* references given under Note 21.

24. *Cf.* W. Lloyd Warner and Paul Lunt, *The social life of a modern community.* New Haven: Yale University Press, 1941, pp. 436–440; August Hollingshead, Cultural factors in the selection of marriage mates. *American Sociological Review,* October 1950, pp. 619–627. Also, *cf.* Ernest Burgess and Paul Wallin, Homogamy in social characteristics. *American Journal of Sociology,* September 1943, pp. 109–124.

25. *Cf.* Gerhard Lenski, *The religious factor.* Garden City: Doubleday, 1961, pp. 48–50.

26. *Cf.* Leonard Cottrell, Roles in marital adjustment. *Publications of the American Sociological Society,* 1933, *27,* 107–115; Willard Waller and Reuben Hill, *The family—a dynamic interpretation.* New York: Dryden, 1951, 253–271; Morris Zelditch, Role differentiation in the nuclear family. In Parsons and Bales, *op. cit.,* pp. 307–352. For a general discussion of role interaction in small groups, *cf.* especially George Homans, *The human group.* New York: Harcourt Brace, 1950.

27. *Cf.* Waller and Hill, *op. cit.,* pp. 253–271, for an excellent summation of such data.

28. *Cf.* Dennison Nash and Peter Berger, The family, the child and the religious revival in suburbia. *Journal for the Scientific Study of Religion,* Fall 1962, pp. 85–93.

29. *Cf.* Bureau of the Census, *op. cit.*

30. *Cf.* Talcott Parsons, Age and sex in the social structure of the United States. *American Sociological Review,* December 1942, pp. 604–616; Paul Glick, First marriages and remarriages. *American Sociological Review,* December 1949, pp. 726–734; William Goode, *After divorce.* Glencoe, Ill.: Free Press, 1956, pp. 269–285.

2

Marriage and the Construction of Reality: Then and Now

NORBERT F. WILEY

In *Principles of Psychology* (1890, vol. II, chap. 21) William James introduces the paradoxical notion of multiple realities or worlds. There is the main, everyday, central reality, to which we always return. Then, to make his highly original point, there are spheres of reality outside the main one. These special realities include art, both making and enjoying, science, religious mysticism, sleep and dream states, chemical highs, sexuality, play, ritual, and other high ceremonies. Each reality is a sphere of meaning, containing its own kind of symbols and its own experiential space. We always return to the main one, and we tend to interpret the puzzles of other spheres, for example dreams, in relation to this central reality.

But the central reality is not itself a completely coherent and puzzle-free skein of meaning. This main reality includes not only the physical or natural world but also the sociocultural one. It is atom bombs ready to burst at a moment's notice, it is uncertainties about nations and economies, it is discontinuities in the flow of our lives, it is senseless suffering and meaningless loss, and it is emotion, too thick and smoky to be endured. Reality is a thing that fights itself and defies our glance. Even at its best, in victory and consummation, there are the seeds of trouble. Reality is a jigsaw puzzle with parts that do not keep the same shape. Reality is unsolvable, but it is livable. What you need to do is work at it, fit it together, downplay the parts that make the least sense, and find the emotions to oil up your fit.

Peter Berger and Hansfried Kellner's "Marriage and the Construction of Reality" (1964) argues that the reality-constructing and reality-maintaining process goes on primarily in the family. And within that family the process

Norbert F. Wiley is Associate Professor of Sociology, University of Illinois.

is centered, not on parent–child communication or sibling interaction, but on the "marital conversation" of husband and wife.

The article is extremely insightful, opening up the inner world of the family and its symbolic culture as few others have done. This is the middle class family to be sure: highly verbal, possessed of a rich vocabulary for emotion-talk, and mobilized to make use of every social opportunity. Making sense of everyday, socioemotional life is especially important for these couples, for they live off the world of interaction and symbolism. Meanings are particularly important for the white collar group, both in work and in family life. But even if the Berger-Kellner family is unusually talkative and sharp-eyed, their stance is merely an intensification of what goes on in all modern families. These families are adrift in highly privatized little worlds. Either the families themselves make sense of their worlds or no one does, and they then remain senseless.

The authors' contribution, then, is a major one, and its importance has been recognized by constant scholarly citation since it was published. On the other hand, the paper is very nestled in the time and family mentality of its period: that of the 1950's and early 1960's. This was a period typified by a stable family, a fixed foreign policy, a consistently working economy, and a clear route to success for the young. The social sciences of the time were building stability into the core of their theories—things were stable because they had to be stable—and family sociology was no exception. The reigning functionalists of the time pictured the family as tending by nature and inevitably toward the 1950's togetherness model. The sex roles, childrearing patterns and power arrangements were said to be those most healthy or functional for society. It was also strongly suggested that they would never change, except to become more so. This was the best there could be, and all research and theory on the family should take this as a premise.

In many ways Berger and Kellner bought that argument. Their cognitive steering device, the marital conversation, guides this boat toward functionality and need-fulfillment. Their argument explains, in a fine-grained way, how the 1950's family managed all that stability and togetherness. It shows the functioning family as a process in which the meaning of family success and failure was constantly shaped into an acceptable and understandable pattern. It is a brilliant article, but its portrayal must be redrawn for today.

It depicts a utopian, conflict-free world, which was not true even of the 1950's, and is considerably less true today. The backdrop is all changed: the stable economy, the black-and-white foreign policy, the nuclear family model and the clear route to success. Instead we have had the 1960's, with their intense politics and value changes; we lost the wrong war in Vietnam, we ran capitalism to some kind of ground in the 1970's and 1980's, and we shook the family up to such an extent that all bets are off. People now work out their family life with little traditional guidance and much internal conflict.

Berger and Kellner's world is long gone, and the tacit assumptions of their paper are now the wrong ones. Yet the marital conversation goes on, just as they said it would. People are still hammering out that main reality in primary group settings. Lovers, couples and marrieds still face each other and stitch together some kind of world. But the larger world has changed and family worlds have changed with it. The marital conversation is more struggle and less chitchat than in Berger and Kellner's base period. This sketch will discuss some of the major ways in which the original paper no longer applies and how it might be fruitfully redirected.

LAING'S EXISTENTIAL PHENOMENOLOGY AS A CONTRASTING CASE

Shortly after Berger and Kellner published their paper, a British psychiatrist, R.D. Laing, was writing papers that depicted a totally different and far less functional marital conversation. He was an "object relations" type of psychiatrist, picturing the personality, or rather the self, as based on the incorporation of others. These others, e.g., parents and siblings, were not necessarily placidly contained in the self. They could be at war with each other, within you, and uncongenial to your needs. Still, they were you.

Laing also used existentialist ideas from Jean Paul Sartre. Sartre (1956, 1976) emphasized not *what* I am but *that* I am, placing existence as prior to and "more real" than essence. This became, for Sartre, the ontological priority of self over others, all others, for existence was primarily one's own existence. The self was the point from which the world was organized and made sense. This was the comfortable world that we control. The "other" was also a point from which the world was organized, but it contradicted our organization. That world all belonged to another self, and it served that self's comfort. Even we, our own self, were positioned somewhere in that rival self's world, subordinate to those purposes and defined in relation to that other point. In other words, Sartre talked himself into seeing a huge chasm between any two persons. He thought relationships tended to be either conflict or enslavement of some kind (even though his actual life relationships appear to have been quite normal and healthy).

Laing had been working with extremely disturbed families, and he saw the chasm at its worst. He thought insanity was a casualty in the struggle over meaning, the loser losing his internal point and no longer having an organized world. The marital, or rather now the family, conversation, which, for Berger and Kellner constructed the reality of that group, is now a psychological battleground over how that world will be structured and whose meanings will prevail. Laing's books—*The Politics of Experience* (1967) and *The Politics of the Family* (1969)—use these ideas to analyze not the disturbed but the normal, ordinary family. They are perhaps an exaggeration on the pessimistic side, just as Berger and Kellner exaggerate on the functional, optimistic side. Yet the two models, taken together, are a good tool to bring to the analysis of the contemporary family (or other close relationship). Let us turn now to what happened between the 1950's and the 1980's, to set the context for finding the new conversation.

FROM THE 1950'S TO THE 1980'S

The 1960's brought us divorce and feminism, to mention two relevant changes. Divorce started increasing in the mid-1960's and continued at a high rate through the 1970's and into the 1980's. Feminism received its strongest push from left-wing radical women in various 1960's protest movements, and it stayed fairly strong in the subsequent years. Feminism shook up the definition of gender in the family and elsewhere. Clear gender roles had been assumed in Berger and Kellner's paper (and in the time period in which they wrote).

Divorce also affected gender styles, because it forced women, and sometimes men, into doing things that had been the preserve of the other sex. More women were raising children on their own, and these female-headed households would be having their own little family conversation, without Daddy, though he would be peripherally in the conversation and central to whatever world was being constructed in his absence.

In addition, the rising divorce rate gave us an increase in remarriage, a notoriously undefined form of family in which there was a lot more reality to be constructed and far fewer ready-made definitions with which to do it. Remarriage was a conversation in which other, earlier conversations loudly echoed, sometimes making it difficult to figure out who was saying what to whom.

The 1960's also brought a continued increase in the proportion of women holding jobs. To some extent the labor market participation caused, or conditioned, both divorce and feminism, though these variables were all influencing each other, with other factors in the mix as well. The jobs strengthened the position of women in the marital conversation and changed the script.

Another as yet poorly understood change of the 1960's was the liberalization of sexual behavior in matters such as premarital intercourse, masturbation, techniques of intercourse, extramarital sex and so on. The changes were primarily in the behavior of women rather than men. The college premarital sex surveys, for example, show that from the 1950's to the 1970's women became considerably more sexually active, but men only a little bit more. Typical is a study by King, Balswick and Robinson (1977), conducted at a large, southern state university, in which 65% of men and 28% of women said they were nonvirgins in 1965. That yields a gap of 37% between the genders. In 1975, at the same university, the men were 73% nonvirgins, an increase of 8% for that decade. Women, however, in the

1975 survey were 57% nonvirgins, an increase of 29% for that decade. Accordingly, the gap between the sexes shrunk from 37 to 16%. The same pattern is present in all the changes in sexual activity of the period, including extramarital intercourse (Hunt, 1974). Women, in other words, were catching up with men, and the double standard was diminishing. But what did this mean, apart from the numbers, in how men and women were encountering and engaging each other?

It seems obvious that men were switching from one kind of partner to another during this period. College boys, for example, were having sex with college girls rather than with prostitutes or lower-class girls. Their partners now were more likely to be marriageables and peers, and sex was becoming part of real, socioemotional life. The same kind of shift seemed to be occurring in extramarital affairs, from casual to more potentially serious encounters.

The result of all this is that sex is probably a more important ingredient in the couples' or marital conversation than before. Sex is a fast-changing, undefined area, and it is more likely to be the topic of the conversation, either explicitly or, perhaps more often, implicitly and nonverbally. Sex is probably a more important medium of the conversation, a way in which people can communicate emotions, nuances and meanings more effectively than with words (or with less egalitarian, pre-1960's sex). It is also a more important resource in the conversation for clarification, obfuscation, reward, punishment, getting closer and moving farther away.

The trends discussed so far are primarily internal to the couple and the family. In addition, there has been a major external trend in the 1970's—1980's economic downturn in world capitalism. The stable economic context, which permitted Berger and Kellner's couples to keep their world in repair, became unstable, and the magnitude of the uncertainties that the couples had to face became much larger and more threatening. No amount of talking it over would change the loss of American industry to other societies, the inflation that eroded spending power or the drastic reduction in state welfare benefits. Just when the internal emotional life of families was becoming more of a problem, the external economic structure was becoming more problematic as well. The marital conversation continued, but much more was at stake, it was an enormously more complicated encounter, and it was a far greater challenge to conduct effectively.

REEXAMINING BERGER AND KELLNER'S BASIC CONCEPTS

Having sketched the 1960's—1970's shake-up in the family, let us return to some of Berger and Kellner's ideas before trying to update them for the present.

These two sociologists are of the opinion that finding or constructing the "meaning" of life, including lives in couples and families, is just as important as the achievement of more practical goals. Even if life is being unkind to you, you are better off if you can fit things, including unpleasant things, together and make some sense of them. Without some blanket of meaning for existential protection, you are in the condition that Emile Durkheim (1951) called anomie or meaninglessness, which he thought made a person more vulnerable to suicide. Berger and Kellner refer to the couple's meaning system as a "nomos," the opposite of anomie.

They might also have used, but did not, Max Weber's notion of "theodicy." Weber (1968) thought that the main use of religion, at least for the ordinary believer, was to explain evil and thereby give sense to life (and death). The great world religions are each based on a unique theodicy: Judaism, the saving and rectifying messiah; Christianity, the afterlife; Hinduism, reincarnation; Zoroastrianism, the clash of two Gods—one good and one evil; Protestantism, predestination (eventually softened); Buddhism, thinking it all away, including the self; and Confucianism, his weakest case, a sense of optimism, order and cultivation that minimized the impact of evil. The theodicies explained misfortune, injustice and death by some belief that counterbalanced or evened things out in the long run.

Berger and Kellner's couples are presumably participating in these large scale or macro theodicies, i.e., they belong to the various mainline religious denominations. But they have to apply these theodicies to the details and specifics, the concrete setbacks and misfortunes of their private lives. This requires the construction and maintenance of what might be called micro or mini theodicies, tailored to the unique lives and personalities of these people. These little theodicies might combine elements from more than one of the macro theodicies, and would probably merge with the family's defense mechanisms, rituals, myths and buried secrets. They could vary from the pole of health and effectiveness all the way to group insanity and folie à famille (Wikler, 1980).

In making these analogies to Durkheim's nomos and Weber's theodicy, though, a certain amount of community and internal consensus is already being assumed for the couple. Berger and Kellner assumed a fairly clear set of family roles and have their couples more or less splitting the difference in whatever value discrepancy they entered the marriage with. This involves coming to working agreements in broad areas such as other people, their own "selves," the past, the present and the future. Specific puzzling or problematic events and characteristics would have to be interpreted in each area.

But if family roles and identities are unclear, these couples do not have the internal, psychological equipment with which to interpret the flow of events agreeably. Previously the family boat, so to speak, was sailing through the water and the couple was guiding its passage by keeping a sharp eye on the environment—rocks, waves, islands, weather, destinations and so on. The boat itself was all right. But now, in the 1980's, the attention has turned to the boat. It is leaky and falling apart and has to be repaired at the same time it sails through the water.

This point can also be made in relation to the distinction between the "two rules," made by John Rawls (1955) and John Searle (1965). Constituent rules are like game-defining rules, for they define the elements (players), their powers and the permissible areas of play. In other words, they state the nature or the "what is" of the group in question. Regulatory rules are the oughts and shoulds of good play. They assume the predefined constituent rules, without which they make no sense. Given a certain definition of what is, the regulatory rules state the behaviors that ought to be.

During the family 1950's and early 1960's, the culturally accepted definition or constitution of the family was so powerfully put together that it was almost invisible. This was how the family had to be, and the only issue was in tuning up the regulatory rules to fit this granite-like moral structure. To question the reigning constituent rules of the time, especially as they defined gender and generations, was to be dangerously deviant.

Now the constituent rules are themselves unclear and under challenge. What is a man (masculinity) or a woman (femininity), a parent or a child? And what has to be present for a family to exist at all or cease to exist? The current disagreement over these and other fundamental constitutive questions makes it difficult to have the conversation and sail the boat. The conversation turns inward, to the question of defining the makeup of the family. Such a conversation is no longer chitchat but the forging and fighting for identities. It is getting closer to R.D. Laing's families, struggling over what their internal meaning shall be.

In relation to the concept of identity we can also see the change in the family conversation. Erik Erikson invented the notion of identity to refer to the value reorganization a person must achieve sometime in the second or third decade of life. It involves disattaching some from parents, connecting to peers, and constructing or reconstructing a workable set of beliefs and values with which to face the future (1968).

Berger and Kellner had couples entering marriages with preexisting identities. They had already done the job. Now they had to adjust these identities toward each other to some extent, making the compromise, and in the process form a family or group identity. This would be the family beliefs-values, from which base the boat is sailed (and recurrent, puzzling events are explained and justified). Actually, a lot of people in the 1950's entered marriages not to combine two preexisting identities but to avoid the anguish of making one in the first place. They went into a "premature closure," to use Erikson's term, getting the temporary relief of forming a family identity before they had solid identities of their own. This evasion would cause trouble eventually. But let us assume these authors were right a lot of the time. People actually did combine preformed identities.

Today the forming of the adolescent or young adult identity is much mor difficult to do. And even if it is formed, it is kept more open, flexible and ready to change than was the case a couple of decades ago. The loosening up of the constituent rules of the family is partly behind this new flexibility. The world political-economic downturn, making jobs and world politics areas of uncertainty, is also a factor in making identities less fixed.

The result is that people go into couplehood and marriages without identities, with loose identities, or with highly changeable identities. Thus, forming a family or couple's identity is much more difficult. If the parts are unclear, the whole will be even more unclear. The conversation now is more a matter of "What are we?" and less "What are they?" or "What is it?"

THE MARITAL CONVERSATION IN THE 1980'S

With this background, let me sketch, in a general way, the qualities of the contemporary marital couple's conversation.

Multi-leveled Conversation

Berger and Kellner loaded up too much on the verbal dimension. They ignored the nonverbal and the behavioral as arenas or media of meaning. It is now clear that the couple's conversation goes on at several levels at once, and this is a complicating factor. The meanings being communicated at different levels can reinforce each other, but they can also contradict and cancel each other out. Fights jump levels, and peace may be made at one only to launch a surprise attack at another. The new couple's sexuality, discussed earlier, is a special problem in meaning, simply because it is new and undefined. The earlier, relatively clear rules of the double standard are declining, and people can now say whole new things with their bodies. But the new body language of egalitarian sex does not yet have a clear vocabulary, let alone rules of expression.

From Cognition to Emotion Conversation

The old conversation was primarily cognitive and verbal. It was over what is happening and how it fits into the accepted patterns; it followed the two rules, with the emphasis on the more superficial, regulatory level. Now, not only is the discussion more likely to proceed at the deeper level of constituent rules and identities, but it is also moving from the cognitive to the emotional.

The question now is often not what reality is happening but what emo-
Emotional unclarity has several aspects. It is over what the emotion is
at the mix is), whether people are experiencing the same emotion,

whether it is healthy emotion or indulgence, whether it is disguised as another emotion or true as it stands, whether blocked or expressed (or over-expressed). Generally we can say the emotional issue is over the labeling, over the power to affix one's preferred label, perhaps. The expression of, discussion of and clarification of feelings is very much a 1980's topic. This is the boat again. Now the power source and the fuel line are receiving the attention.

Loosely Coupled Systems

This notion appeared in the literature on organizations in the 1970's (Weick, 1976), and it refers to an organization with unusually autonomous parts. There are certain flexibility advantages to such a form of organization. It appears in the Israeli army, which allows unusual amounts of autonomy at lower officer levels.

The answer to the boat (or constituent) problem, as it seems to be emerging, is to reverse the 1950's kind of togetherness somewhat and shift into a loosely coupled system, an organizational looseness in the sense of decentralization (Vaughan, 1983). Part of this decentralization was brought about by feminism and the growth in the family power of (some) women. The old centralization assumed the old gender definitions. But the new stance is also a reasonable response to heightened uncertainty generally, and the heightened ambiguity about both kinds of rules. This uncertainty exists concerning the inner structure of the family as well as the outer, macro world of economies and wars. Hanging loose, so to speak, can have its advantages when the situation and surroundings are loose.

Decline in the Privacy of the Conversation

It is my impression that the long, historical rise in family privacy has crested and is sliding into reverse. Privacy continually increased from Colonial times until today, with changes in dwellings and facilities. Equally important were social and psychological changes that turned the family more into itself. Families in private residences are not as readily accessible to relatives, neighbors, economic actors and others who transact with the family (Laslett, 1973). Their privacy is respected, as we say, and this can sometimes make things quite lonely and unstable in that residence. Berger and Kellner assumed maximum privacy, and they thought it to be functional. It made it easier for that family to be mobile, geographically and occupationally, and it made them a good fit for a fast-changing market economy. But it also put a curtain around that conversation and made it quite isolated from other ears.

Part of Berger and Kellner's argument was that the couple had to distance themselves from their before-marriage friends to get the intimacy they would need. Actually, the intimacy of their couple looks like that between two, elderly philosophers speculating about the world parading by. It does not sound especially passionate or wild. But such as it was, you had to kick your friends to get it. Friends would diminish the purity, intensity and reality-creating power of the conversation. So you discussed them away, more or less behind their backs, as the authors describe it. I have the impression though that people in couples are doing, retaining and making friends more than their 1950's forebears did. This reduces the privileged nature of the marital conversation to some extent and makes it compete with other conversations. It cuts into the privacy like an open wall.

All the new, easy exiting from the family (divorce, old people able to live alone, older teenagers moving out) is also diminishing the privacy. Obviously it is scattering people and getting them out of those residences. That is direct deprivatization. But I think it is also changing the kind of coherence and unity, in the loosely coupled direction, in all-present families. There is less emotional concentration in the centripetal, center-seeking direction and more emotion going outward or kept in reserve. This decline in pitch and intensity is a decline in psychological privacy.

Rediscovering Children

In the 1950's and early 1960's children were taken for granted. Berger and Kellner implicitly assume that children would passively accept whatever beliefs their parents poured into their heads. In the late 1960's and 1970's children were not only taken for granted—they were ignored. The intense family discussion of that period was about adults, men and women, and the implicit assumption was that children were a nuisance. In the 1980's it is clear that children were central to the family conversation all along, although we are only now noticing their presence and power.

They inject intense, raw emotionalism into the conversation, largely as part of their resistance to parental power. They also participate in one of the two love-intimacy axes of the family, that of parent–child. This axis often competes with the flow of love on the other axis, that of man–woman. The "clash of the two loves" (Wiley, 1979) is central to most family problems, especially psychological ones.

It is not completely clear how the children's contribution influences the conversation (or how emotion shapes cognition), but it is clear that children have a major causal role in constructing the family meaning system. I think it is in the actual shaping of persons and selves that children have the most impact. The turn from cognition to emotion, as a major dimension of the conversation, also favors the children's influence. In any case children now appear to be full members of the family conversation.

CONCLUSION

Almost everything I have said shows the family conversation of today to be more subtle, complex and charged than in Berger and Kellner's version, right or wrong for its time. To understand this conversation, particularly its combination of emotion and cognition, the insights of phenomenology and clinical psychology need to be combined. Husserl and Freud both took a deep look at the human self, but the former concentrated heavily on the cognitive and the latter on the emotional. The key to understanding the family today, however, is largely in understanding the interpenetration of the cognitive and the emotional.

If understanding the current family conversation is difficult, engaging in it is even more so. Anthony Giddens once said, "Life is a skilled performance," and family life is no exception. Rules and recipes are hard to find and courage is much in demand. The conversation is a challenge all right, but it can be seen as a burden or an opportunity. Laing saw it as a burden, and his families were just not up to the game. But what could be more fun than a new frontier right in your own back yard?

ACKNOWLEDGMENT

I want to thank Christine Chambers and Deborah Wright for sharing the findings of their unpublished study of female friendships and also for advice on earlier versions of this paper.

REFERENCES

Berger, Peter L. and Kellner, Hansfried. Marriage and the construction of reality. *Diogenes,* 1964, *46,* 1–23.

Durkheim, Emile, *Suicide* Translated by John A. Spaulding and George Simpson. Ed. with Introduction by George Simpson. Glencoe, Ill: Free Press, 1951.

Erikson, Erik H. *Identity: youth and crisis.* New York: W.W. Norton & Company, 1968.

Hunt, Morton. *Sexual behavior in the 1970's.* New York: Dell, 1974.

James, William. *Principles of psychology.* New York: Dover Publications Inc., 1890.

King, Karl; Balswick, Jack O. and Robinson, Ira E. The continuing premarital sexual revolution among college females. *Journal of Marriage and the Family,* 1977, *39,* 455–459.

Laing, R. D. *The politics of experience.* New York: Ballantine Books, 1967.

Laing, R. D. *The politics of the family.* New York: Vintage Books, 1969.

Laslett, Barbara. The family as a public and private institution: A historical perspective. *Journal of Marriage and the Family,* 1973, *35,* 480–494.

Rawls, John. Two concepts of rules. *Philosophical Review,* 1955, *64,* 3–32.

Sartre, Jean Paul. *Being and nothingness.* New York: Philosophical Library, 1956 (originally published 1943).

Sartre, Jean Paul. *Critique of dialectical reason.* London: NLB, 1976 (originally published 1960).

Searle, John. What is a speech act? In Max Black (Ed.) *Philosophy in America.* Ithaca: Cornell University Press, 1965.

Vaughan, Diane. Uncoupling: the social construction of divorce. In Howard Robboy and Candace Clark (Eds.), *Social interaction,* second edition. New York: St. Martin's Press, 1983.

Weber, Max. *Economy and society.* New York: Bedminster Press, 1968 (originally published 1922).

Weick, Karl D. Educational organizations as loosely coupled systems. *Administrative Science Quarterly,* 1976, *21,* 1–19.

Wikler, Lynn. Folie à famille: a family therapist's perspective. *Family Process,* 1980, *19,* 257–268.

Wiley, Norbert F. Notes on self-genesis: from me to we to I. *Studies in Symbolic Interaction,* 1979, *2,* 87–105.

3

The Family as a
Psychosocial Organization

ROBERT D. HESS AND
GERALD HANDEL

However its life spreads into the wider community, there is a sense in which a family is a bounded universe. The members of a family—parents and their young children—inhabit a world of their own making, a community of feeling and fantasy, action and precept. Even before their infant's birth, the expectant couple make plans for his family membership, and they prepare not only a bassinet but a prospect of what he will be to them. He brings his own surprises, but in time there is acquaintance, then familiarity, as daily the family members compose their interconnection through the touch and tone by which they learn to know one another. Each one comes to have a private transcript of their common life, recorded through his own emotions and individual experiences.

In their mutual interaction, the family members develop a more or less adequate understanding of one another, collaborating in the effort to establish consensus and to negotiate uncertainty. The family's life together is an endless process of movement in and around consensual understanding, from attachment to conflict to withdrawal—and over again. Separateness and connectedness are the underlying conditions of a family's life, and its common task is to give form to both.

The ways in which a family is a unit and the ways it provides for being a separate person are, in one sense, what every family's life is about. We are concerned with developing a framework for understanding the nuclear

Reprinted from *Family Worlds*, pp. 1–19, by Robert D. Hess and Gerald Handel by permission of The University of Chicago Press. © 1959 by The University of Chicago.

Robert D. Hess is Lee Jacks Professor of Psychology and Education, Stanford University. Gerald Handel is Professor of Sociology, The City College and Graduate Center, City University of New York.

family as a group. Within the family, events occur in far from random fashion; even uncertainty is given a customary place in a family's scheme of things. While illustrating distinctness, we work toward a systematic view of the family as a psychosocial organization. How may one describe a family, taking account of all its members? The multiplicity of household events takes place in a round robin of interaction that is a shapeless swirl only to the casual observer. There are nodes of connection, points at which feeling is concentrated and significance declared. There are tracks to which the interaction returns again and again. A family has discernible pattern and form.

It is imperative to relate the nature of individuality to the form of the particular family group in which it occurs and to examine the participation of family psychological modes of interaction in the personalities of individual members. As a guiding principle we are proposing that the intrapsychic organization of each member is part of the psychosocial structure of his family; the structure of a family includes the intrapsychic organization of its individual members. For example, if separateness and connectedness constitute one of the most fundamental problems a family must solve, then it is necessary first to adopt a standpoint from which one can see both tendencies as parts of the same solution, and second to view this solution both as an extension of individual needs into the group interaction and as a significant determinant of individual personality.

An understanding of the relationship between individual dynamics and family interactional matrix may be furthered by a second principle: in his relationships in the family an individual member strives toward predictability of preferred experience, attempting to discover or create circumstances that fit his image of what the world around him should be—how it should respond to him and provide opportunity for expression of his own preferences. This principle indicates how one might examine the fashion in which individual uniqueness is transformed into family uniqueness as a result of his own and others' experience. It attends also to the impact upon the individual member of his success, or lack of it, in obtaining the emotional atmosphere he desires. Neither the ties that bind the members to one another nor the barriers that separate them are adequately indicated by overt social behavior alone. Connection to others is outward and inward in infinite variety. In the study of ordinary people, the inner connections and the inner enclaves must command attention no less than the external encounters and the occasions for social privacy. Taking for granted, then, that the members of a nuclear family have personalities of their own, that each has a psychobiological individuality, and that each is guided by cultural role expectations, how shall we understand how they fashion a life together?

It is our purpose herein to indicate some concepts that are useful in understanding and describing in nonpathological terms the complexities of ordinary family interaction. The major processes described give shape to the flux of family life, coherence to the extended array of events, perceptions, emotions, actions, learnings, and changes the members experience or undertake. The essential processes discussed below are:

1. Establishing a pattern of separateness and connectedness.
2. Establishing a satisfactory congruence of images through the exchange of suitable testimony.
3. Evolving modes of interaction into central family concerns or themes.
4. Establishing the boundaries of the family's world of experience.
5. Dealing with significant biosocial issues of family life, as in the family's disposition to evolve definitions of male and female and of older and younger.

THE EFFORT TO ACHIEVE A SATISFACTORY PATTERN OF SEPARATENESS AND CONNECTEDNESS

Two conditions characterize the nuclear family. Its members are connected to one another, and they are also separate from one another. Every family gives shape to these conditions in its own way. Its life may show greater emphasis on the one or the other; yet both are constitutive of family life. The infant is born from the womb into the limits of his own skin, with individual properties of sensitivity and activity. He possesses an irreducible psychobiological individuality that no amount or kind of intense socialization can abolish. His parents, too, remain individual persons no matter how deep their love, how passionate their desire for one another or how diffuse their individual identities. Through the wishes and capacities of its members, the family defines and gives shape to separateness so that it looms large or small in family affairs, gives rise to pleasure or unhappiness. The range of possibilities is wide. The autistic child or the psychotic parent represents the pathological extreme of separateness. The benign extremes are more diverse—emotional richness, ego autonomy, individual creativity. Perhaps Erikson's concept of a clearly delineated ego identity best conveys the benign meaning of separateness.[1]

Yet connectedness of family members is equally basic. No human infant survives without ties. Connectedness can range from physical proximity and rudimentary child care to an intensity of mutual involvement that all but excludes all other interests. Separateness remains always, yet it can be transcended. Love and passion do unite family members and can make separateness seem infinitesimal—or comfortable. The signs of being connected to one another that the members of a family seek differ greatly even within the middle range. In one family intense emotional exchange is sought; the members need to relax defenses and public façade, and they respond freely. In other families such confrontation is threatening, though the wish to feel themselves together in binding ties may be great. A family of this kind may be able to approach its desire only through much formalized or ritualized action, such as giving gifts, celebrating birthdays and holidays, making joint excursions.

This fundamental duality of family life is of considerable significance, for the individual's efforts to take his own kind of interest in the world, to become his own kind of person, proceed apace with his efforts to find gratifying connection to the other members. At the same time, the other members are engaged in taking their kinds of interest in him, and in themselves. This is the matrix of interaction in which a family develops its life. The family tries to cast itself in a form that satisfies the ways in which its members want to be together and apart. The pattern it reaches is a resultant of these diverse contributions. This dual condition of inevitable individuality and inescapable psychosocial connection is a dynamic condition; it requires a family to make some kind of life together, lest the family dissolve. The family and its members must meet these two conditions in *some* way. The investigator's effort to understand family life is facilitated insofar as he asks constantly, In what way does this event or tendency or action bring the members together or keep them apart?

CONGRUENCE OF IMAGES

It is useful to regard life in a family as the family's effort to attain a satisfactory congruence of individual and family images through the exchange of suitable testimony. This view initially directs attention to the family as a group of members. Family research must somehow face up to this very obvious fact. All the members of the nuclear household must be taken into account if we are to understand the family's life. Data must be obtained from each member. We do not understand a family if we know the spouses' roles as mates and as parents but nothing of their children, nor is our foundation adequate if we have firsthand materials from a mother and child in therapy but see the father and other children only through their eyes. Thus, this first implication is methodological. It says something of the range of data to be collected.

Living together, the individuals in a family each develop an image of what the other members are like. This image comprises the emotional meaning and significance that the other has for the member holding it. The concept of image is a mediating concept. Its reference extends into the personality and out into the interpersonal relationship. Referring to one person's emotionalized conception of another, an image is shaped by the personality both of the holder and of the object. The image emerges from the holder's past and bears the imprint of his experience, delimiting what versions of others are possible for him. It says something about him as a person. But it is also a cast into the future, providing the holder with direction in relating to and interacting with the object. While it represents the holder's needs and wishes, it also represents the object as a source of fulfillment.

Each family member has some kind of image of every other member and of himself in relation to them. This image is compounded of realistic and idealized components in various proportions, and it may derive from the personalities of its holder and its object, also in various proportions. It draws from cultural values, role expectations, and the residue of the parents' experiences in their families of origin. One's image of another is the product of one's direct experience with the other and of evaluations of the other by third parties. From this experience, from evaluations of it and elaborations on it in fantasy, a conception of another person is developed, a conception that serves to direct and shape one's action to the other and that becomes a defining element of the interpersonal relationship. *An image of a person is one's definition of him as an object of one's own action or potential action.*

In studying a family, then, it is necessary to investigate both the images the members hold of one another and the ways in which these images are interrelated. It is necessary to understand how the interaction of the members derives from and contributes to this interrelation of images. The implication of this stance is that interaction cannot be fully understood in its own terms, that, instead, it must be viewed in the context of how the participants define one another as relevant objects.

From this experience with the other members of his family and from experiences outside the family, an individual comes to have another kind of image—an image of his family which expresses his mode of relationship to the unit and which defines the kind of impact the family has on him. A woman may gratifyingly conceive of her family as dependents who need and reward her, or she may see them primarily as the group that enslaves her and for whom she wears herself out. A man may feel proud of his family as a demonstration of his masculinity, or his image may be of a group of perplexing people with emotions and reactions he does not understand, or his family may mean to him primarily a welcome retreat from and contrast with his workaday world. For a child, too, the family may have diverse meanings. To one it is the group he is happy to belong to. For another it consists of those he lives with because he has no place else to go. A person's image of his family embodies what he expects from it and what he gives to it, how important it is and what kind of importance it has.

The images held of one member by the others diverge in varying ways from one another and from the individual's image of himself. The intimate and constant exchange that characterizes the nuclear family makes such divergence far from a matter of indifference. The members of a family want to and have to deal with one another; from the beginning they are engaged in evolving and mutually adjusting their images of one another. This mutual adjustment takes place in interaction, and it is, in part, the aim of interaction. Since complete consensus is most improbable, life in a family—as elsewhere—is a process ongoing in a situation of actual or potential instability. Pattern is reached, but it can never be complete, since action is always unfolding and the status of the family members is undergoing change.[2]

If a family system of interpersonal relations is to have any continuity, the images that members have of the family and of one another must in some sense tend toward compatibility. This is only to say that they strive toward some sort of stability or predictability of preferred behavior. When a child is born, the parents entertain an image of the child—which will be altered and elaborated with time, to be sure—that the child cannot share. The concept of socialization refers to the parents' efforts to get the child to regard himself in substantially the same way they regard him. From birth, also, the child is engaged in acquiring conceptions of his parents, striving to form a view of them that accords with their self-images. In an absolute sense, neither goal can be attained, but the efforts to reach satisfactory approximations—or congruence—constitute one of the springs of interaction.

It seems useful to draw an analytic distinction between the actual image a person holds of another and his desired image. Not only does an individual have an ideal for his own behavior, an ego ideal, but he also forms conceptions of what he wants others to be. In some families the greatest discrepancies may occur among these ideal versions of each other. Such a discrepancy may be described as the discrepancy between a person's ego ideal (his own image of what he strives toward in himself) and another's desired image of him (what the other strives to realize in him).

In other families there may be relatively little strain of this order. Such a family's interinvolvement may be characterized as its effort to live as a satisfactory example of what is accepted as desirable. The "problems" of living in systems of this type are more likely to arise from "falling short" of what is consensually desirable and from the difficulties of living up to all desirable claims simultaneously rather than from disagreement about what is desirable.

Families also differ in their tolerance of incongruence of images. In some there is pressure toward closeness of fit in minute particulars. In others a looser relationship is accepted as satisfactory, or the system can deal with incongruence strains short of disruption.

The issue involved here is not one of how similar the members must be to each other; that is, whether a neat housekeeper requires her husband and children to be equally neat, or whether a serious man requires the other members of his family to be likewise. Rather, the issue is whether the differences and similarities among the members are mutually acceptable. Child guidance clinics echo with parents complaining that the offending child does as they do rather than as they say. The personalities of the parent and the child may be quite similar; yet they may hold images of each other that are discrepant and unsatisfactorily so. But personality dissimilarity—at whatever level—may provide a firm basis for a satisfactory congruence of images. If a serious man finds himself responsible but his gay wife frivolous, and if she feels that he is dull but she is sparkling, an incongruent set of images characterizes their relationship. Where the serious husband relishes his wife's gaiety as lively and stimulating, where she welcomes his sobriety as a form of strength and stability, and where both concur in what each should be, the images they hold of each other are satisfactorily congruent.

The commonality of experience in a family will conduce to some congruence of family images among the family members. The intrinsic distinctions of age, sex, birth order, and role in society conduce to divergence of images. The overlap and the divergences are expressed and acted out in family life, each member participating in terms of the definition incorporated in his image.

Even when the congruence of images is satisfactory, interaction still has reference to it. If exploration and testing diminish in importance, affirmation and reiteration of what has been established become the content of interaction. The family members demonstrate their agreement with the group and strive toward validation of personal worth in family terms. The positive features of the family image provide the criteria for evaluating individual behavior. The audience toward which testimony is directed may be primarily composed of the family itself, or it may be extended to nonfamily persons. Whatever its audience, validation is pursued through those dimensions of behavior that the family regards as significant.

A stable human relationship is one in which the members have reached a high degree of consensus about one another; the terms in which personal worth may be demonstrated are clear and shared. Their interaction is an exchange of testimony of what the members are to one another. The action of each person in his family testifies to his image of it, of himself, and of the others. The members realize or seek out in interpersonal encounters those kinds of experiences which seem meaningful to them and with which they are comfortable. Feelings and actions are responded to in terms of their felt suitability. *Responsive judgments and feelings are responsive first to inward images of self, other, and family. They then become responses to and for others, so that family life is shaped within the participants as well as between them.*

We have tried to summarize in a general statement how a family's life may be understood in terms of the images family members have of one another and themselves; the inevitable divergences and fluctuations of these images; the psychosocial task of relating to others and attaining viable stability amid this potential fluctuation; the image members develop of the family as a unit—its meaning to family members, the character of its emotional and social exchange; and the utilization of the positive features of the family image in affirming to each member and to the group their personal worth and their right to emotional acceptance and participation.

THE FAMILY THEME

Individual images and responses are interrelated. In any particular family the kinds of action we have called testing, exploring, and affirming take place in terms of a particular content, which may be termed a "family theme." A family theme is a pattern of feelings, motives, fantasies, and conventionalized understandings grouped about some locus of concern that has a particular form in the personalities of the individual members. The pattern comprises some fundamental view of reality and some way or ways for dealing with it. In the family themes are to be found the family's implicit direction, its notion of "who we are" and "what we do about it." In delineating a particular family theme, we may bring several criteria to bear.

First, the theme affects behavior in several important family areas and activities. It is a postulated mold that exerts a variable impress on the observable events and ascertainable consequences of a family life. Thus, a family's feelings about most of its activities can be construed as particular manifestations of a more inclusive organizing principle, which for one type of family might be stated in this way: The family feels itself to be essentially alone in the world. Individual members endeavor to communicate with one another. They strive to foster any symbol or semblance of communication. The process of communication itself is important to all family members, and attempts to achieve contact with one another must be pursued whenever possible. Failure or disruption in communication is a failure in meeting the family objective.

The theme is an implicit point of departure and point of orientation for this family's behavior. Father's return to the family at the end of the day stimulates a flurry of greeting and excitement; the family dinner becomes one of the most important events of the day. Chores around the home are seen as opportunities for conversation. Members are expected to be "considerate" of one another, avoiding the conflict and disharmony that might threaten communication. Independence or solitude is discouraged; the individual family member should keep himself ready and available for interaction; activities that take a member out of the group are discouraged.

This is a brief illustration of a theme. A fuller statement would take greater account of the forces that have to be contended with in holding to the direction of solution and integration actually followed.

Second, a theme is a significant issue in the life of the family, expressing basic forms of relating to the external world and of interpersonal involvement.

Third, all members of the family are involved in the psychosocial definitions and processes which enter into the theme, though each may be involved in a different way. Thus the theme arises from and has consequences for the personalities of all the members.

The theme, then, is a particularly useful unit for analysis of family life, for it provides a way of characterizing the family group in terms of broad and significant psychosocial and psychocultural dimensions. At the same time, it permits flexibility, since it is not an arbitrary unit and does not require that a family be understood in terms of a set of a priori categories. The investigator can assess the family in its own terms, responding to and following the saliences that center its life.[3]

The concept of the theme is advantageous in two other important ways. Since it is a characterization of the family in terms of a significant issue in its life, the concept provides a point of reference for understanding the individual members and particular interpersonal relationships as specific versions and expressions of the theme. The individual's place in the family— what he does and what happens to him there—can be understood as the way in which he participates in these broader currents that help to determine the quality of his family membership. If we understand a theme as consisting of some significant issue and the general direction of attempted solution or resolution of that issue, each member has some part to play in this larger configuration. His part is complexly determined, as is every role— in some measure assigned by others, in some measure self-created. By determining the salient themes in a family's life, we are able to see more clearly how any individual's fate is shaped, what opportunities he has for interlocking his life with others, and what pressures he must contend with.

The concept of the theme also makes it possible to compare one family with another. It provides a way of characterizing a whole group in a fashion that is relevant to the group's individual members; yet since it is a group-summary statement, it can be arrayed with other such characterizations.

ESTABLISHING BOUNDARIES OF THE FAMILY'S WORLD OF EXPERIENCE

The concepts we have suggested are oriented toward revealing not only the family's internal functioning but its stance, the position it has taken up vis-à-vis the outer, nonfamily world. The significant themes consequently not only subsume the psychic content of the family's life but also indicate something of the breadth of its world. A family constitutes its own world, which is not to say that it closes itself off from everything else but that it determines what parts of the external world are admissible and how freely. The family maps its domain of acceptable and desirable experience, its life space. The outer limits of life space for any family are fairly definite and reasonably well marked. There are signposts for goals and signals for danger. But these metaphors fail because the boundaries lie within persons, and however firm they may be, there are always areas of inexperience not adequately charted. As new experiences occur, as new feelings arise, new actions are taken and are brought to the internal limits of the person taking them and to the limits others help to set. In this back-and-forth of interaction is to be found the family members' mutual regulation. Each directs himself toward others by virtue of the representation they have in his mind; the others respond to him in terms of the way he is represented in theirs. Limits to experience—broad or narrow—are established in a variety of ways and along several dimensions. Some of the more important are these:

1. *The differentiation of individual personality.* How elaborated individual personalities of the family members are; how self-directing individuals are and are expected to become. From the gross categories of infantile experience, comfort and distress, incorporation and expulsion, personality develops to encompass a range of emotional experience and more mature ego mechanisms. The complexity and differentiation of personality can proceed further in some families than in others.

2. *The intensity of experience.* How deep or how shallow experience is; how detached or how involved family members are in their activities and one another; how controlled or how spontaneous their behavior is. The question involved here is how much of the self is made available to experience—the depth of intimacy or the enthusiasm of commitment to something.

3. *The extensity of experience.* The literal geographical scope—the range and variety of actions; the importance of neighborhood and locality as compared with communities of more abstract definition—"democratic society," "the legal profession"; how much of the world it is important to know about and be interested in; how far actual acquaintance extends. Thus, less literally, how many kinds of life and action are conceived of, known of, or understood.

4. *The tendency to evaluate experience.* Families differ in their inclination to permit members to make unique personal evaluations of and responses to stimuli. The constraints of evaluation—the internalization of criteria—modify and translate stimuli and experience. Values create in the individual member emotional positions on definable categories of experience—jazz, sports, "classical" art and music, comic books, politicians, science and scientists, literature—the broad range of stimuli available in our culture. The family also evaluates experience initiated by the individual member and evokes from him modes of responsiveness to his own behavior and the behavior of others. A prominent element of this dimension is the tendency toward moral evaluation of experience. The freedom from or constraint by guilt and the freedom to range inwardly in thought, impulse, and fantasy, to entertain unaccustomed possibilities, are involved here. Moral evaluation also affects the freedom to range outwardly, to be at home in

new circumstances, to find answers for oneself. The central issue is the need, or lack of it, to condemn and repudiate or even simply to shun what is traditionally not one's own.

These are at least some of the most important dimensions that describe the boundaries of a family's world and the kind of life that can be lived within it. The characteristics of this arena help determine for each member how multiplex his life is, how close to himself, how close to others, how close to home. Establishing the boundaries of experience, in the terms just enumerated, is one of the principal processes of family life. It continues not only while the members live together but even after they disperse—even influencing how far and in what direction they will go.

In a final sense, the predicated states are never reached. What turns a life may take cannot be known, so that the pattern-establishing processes do not result in changeless solutions. While it may be possible to predict how a family of a given type will weather economic privation if it should occur, the predicted kind of change will not take place unless the financial stress does. Similarly, in greater or lesser degree, the "establishing" processes are always in play, responding to the new elements introduced into the family's life. However, it is necessary to recognize that while in a literal, concrete sense, the boundaries of experience are never definitively established, it is possible to ascertain with high probability what they are likely to be for a given family. If the life of a family never reaches a final, unchangeable form—even for a delimited period of the family cycle, such as the child-rearing stage—it nonetheless gains a recognizably firm structure, as any human association must.

DEALING WITH SIGNIFICANT GIVEN BIOSOCIAL ISSUES OF FAMILY LIFE

The most essential structural characteristics of the nuclear family are well known and need not be extensively elaborated here. The fact that a family, unlike other voluntary groups, must be established by one member from each sex means that sex membership is a basic point of reference. In the study of any particular family it is necessary to investigate what it interprets male and female to be. What qualities are attributed to each sex? What is demanded of each? What is accorded to each? How important is the distinction felt to be? Is the sex difference minimized, or does it serve as a basis for proliferation of emotions and activities? Are the two sexes differentially evaluated so that rewards and penalties are distributed on the basis of sex membership? All of these questions have, of course, certain conventionalized answers provided by the larger social units to which a family belongs—social class, ethnic group, community. Yet each family also provides answers of its own; each family makes use of sex difference in structuring its own world.

While parents choose each other voluntarily in marriage, their children become family members without exercise of choice. This fact, together with the fact that they are helpless at birth and hence born into the care and authority of their parents, sets the question of how the differences between the two generations will be construed and handled. How much of family life is to be regulated by considerations of authority becomes an important dimension. Parental authority—its scope, the manner in which it is exercised—is one of the forces shaping the pattern of separateness-connectedness. Its potential is realized in consequences for the child such as self-direction, submissiveness, a sense of injustice, or a readiness to learn from those of greater experience.

In dealing with this gulf in power and capacity between themselves and their children, parents have to make a decision (not a conscious decision, in its essentials, but one arising from their own personalities) about how insistently they will impose their images upon their children. Families differ in how far parents interact with their children, amending or reshaping their own aims as their children become increasingly formed. Where they expect the children to do all the adapting, there is little room for negotiating, so that the process of self- and mutual discovery is compressed within narrow limits.

Families differ also in how the parents pace their children through childhood—whether they push, encourage, or restrain. Parents seek to shape their children in keeping with their own desire to achieve preferred experience. They stimulate the children in accordance with what they feel children should be, as a part of their activity in defining their own world. The nature of parental stimulation—its intensity, frequency, and diversity—expresses the aims of their care and authority. When we observe that one parent is eager for his child to behave as much like an adult as quickly as possible, whereas another regrets his child's loss of babyish ways, it is clear that different personal wishes or aims are operating in the two cases. But it would appear that different concepts of growth and different time perspectives also operate here. In some families there is an urgency to growing up, sometimes motivated by the parent's wish to be quickly relieved of what are conceived as the taxing aspects of child rearing, or by an anxiety that each "delay" or concession to impulsivity is threatening to ultimate development. This idea seems to include a notion of a fixed termination point, a time when development has reached its goal and is then essentially over. The happenings beyond this point are construed not as growth but simply as events, important or not, in the passing of time. In other families a sense of a long, indefinite time span prevails, together with a belief that growth cannot be compressed. Children are seen as moving slowly toward maturity, and it is felt that they have time enough to do so. Growth is intricate, not readily mechanized, and the forces of childhood are tamed rather than broken.

Implicit in these several aspects of parental feeling and action vis-à-vis their offspring is another decision: *how much of the child's world does not belong to his parents?* In part, this is a matter of authority. In exercising authority, parents not only choose among techniques of reward and punishment, they also may or may not restrict themselves from incursions into the child's domain. Whether a child is granted privacy in any sense—privacy of quarters, of possessions, of thoughts and emotions, of responses to others—or whether these are all felt to be subject to his elders' inspection and manipulation is a question decided according to how parents define themselves and children. Bound up in the decision is a conception of integrity, for the terms on which people have access to one another, while communicated earlier in the infant-care context, become increasingly defined and actualized during childhood.

The relationships that develop among the various members of a family do not follow simply the intrinsic lines of sex and age. They are shaped as well by the underlying family themes and images that impart meanings to sex and age and also to various other personal characteristics. On the basis of the meanings the members have for one another particular interpersonal ties evolve. The closeness between any two members, for example, or the distance between a group of three closely joined members and a fourth who is apart, derives from the interlocking meanings that obtain among them. Each family tends to have a characteristic distribution of ties or pattern of alignment (which may be negative or positive in emotional tone) among members. How these patterns are developed and sustained is, then, a matter of considerable significance in understanding life within families as well as the course of any one member's life.

In these concepts we have attempted to provide a framework for understanding the family as an intimate group of members that functions in systematic ways. We have focused on the interior of the family, so that the framework is somewhat less useful for analyzing the relationship between the family and society. The case studies in *Family Worlds* have been prepared in terms of the point of view advanced in the present chapter, though the concepts identified here are not reiterated with each detail of family life. At various points where it has seemed necessary, we have elaborated on some idea that seemed to us to illuminate the family being discussed. The frame of reference is intended to serve as just that—marking out the range of phenomena encompassed and the terms in which they are considered.

NOTES

1. Erikson, Erik. *Childhood and society.* New York: W. W. Norton, 1950.
2. George Herbert Mead gave theoretical significance to this uncertainty of future action in his concept of the "I." "It is because of the 'I' that we say that we

are never fully aware of what we are, that we surprise ourselves by our own action. It is as we act that we are aware of ourselves. . . . I want to call attention to the fact that this response of the 'I' is something that is more or less uncertain. . . . The 'I' gives the sense of freedom, of initiative." *Mind self, and society.* Chicago: University of Chicago Press, 1934, pp. 174, 176, 177.

3. The concept of the theme has been introduced into social science by Henry Murray in psychology and by Morris Opler in anthropology. See Henry A. Murray *et al., Explorations in personality.* New York: Oxford University Press, 1938, and Morris Opler, Themes as dynamic forces in culture, *American Journal of Sociology, 51,* 198–206. Though he does not use the word, Fritz Redl's approach to group structure makes use of similar logic. See his Group emotion and leadership, *Psychiatry,* 1942, *5,* pp. 573–96.

II

Research Methods

The social sciences, considered as a group, are beset by a deep tension about their research methods. Their subject matter is human activity. To some social scientists, this distinctive subject requires research methods specific to its nature. To others, the essentials of scientific method are the same for all subject matters in the social, biological, and physical sciences. Most essential, in the latter view, is the scientist's controlled manipulation of independent variables in order to determine causes of change or difference in dependent variables.

Psychology and social anthropology as disciplines represent fairly clearly these opposite positions. Psychology has developed primarily as an experimental laboratory science, although a minority of researchers in psychology do other kinds of research. Social anthropology has defined its task as understanding how people construct their lives in their actual life situations. The anthropologist's task is to understand how the people he is studying interpret their situations and one another. As anthropologist Clifford Geertz writes, ". . . what we call our data are really our own constructions of other people's constructions of what they and their compatriots are up to. . . . Analysis, then, is sorting out the structures of signification . . . and determining their social ground and import." (Geertz: 1973:9.)

The position taken in this volume is that the logic of procedure in social anthropology is a more useful logic for the development of a social psychology of the family than is the logic of experimental psychology. The basic task is to understand what the members of a family are "up to"—how they define their situations, one another, and themselves, and to follow the implications and consequences of these definitions. Let it be immediately said that in advocating the greater usefulness of the social anthropological over the experimental logic of procedure, we are not arguing that the understanding of families is to be accomplished specifically, only, or primarily in anthropological terms. The view that social science involves interpreting people's own interpretations of themselves is fundamental also in those major branches of sociology that follow in the paths of such leading thinkers as Max Weber, George Herbert Mead, and Alfred Schutz, as well as all those parts of psychology and social science influenced by Sigmund Freud. Diverse as these several streams of thought may be, they have in common the basic assumption that human action follows from people's interpretation of their life situation. The social scientist's task is to gather data focused upon the interpretations and interpretive schemes that underlie human action.

Anthropologist Jules Henry applied the anthropological method of field work to the study of American urban families. Field work affords the great advantage of seeing people in their own environment or habitat. Although it is sometimes objected that people being observed do not behave naturally, field workers generally discover that most people cannot sustain a presentation of self that is entirely alien or uncharacteristic. People observed with consent undoubtedly often engage in maneuvers intended to hide some conception of themselves or their situation, but they do not do so invariably or completely. Indeed, the manner and extent of their doing so are in themselves data about them, for people cannot help being fundamentally themselves. This does not mean that a field worker cannot be misled—undoubtedly this happens—but that does not make the method invalid. Rather, it means that the field worker faces a problem common to all research workers: finding ways of checking the observations, estimating the scope and limits of their applicability, judging the significance of what is observed.

Henry lived in the homes of families who had a psychotic child in a residential treatment institution. He published his results in a series of conceptually focused case studies (Henry: 1963, 1971). Here he describes how he gathered his data. Since the pioneering field work of Henry and of Oscar Lewis (Lewis: 1959, 1961), variations of the method have been used by sociologists (Howell: 1973; Speedling, 1982; Clark, 1983) and psychologists (Piotrkowski: 1979).

More commonly used in sociology is the interview. In the survey interview, the respondent selects a preformulated answer from an array of preformulated answers to each question. In the conversational interview, questions are open-ended; the inteviewee is encouraged to respond in his or her own words. The goal is to have the interviewee exemplify, in the responses, the categories and dimensions of meaning that he or she uses ordinarily in thinking and acting in everyday life. The selection by Hess and Handel describes their procedures in studying a group of nonclinical families. Their data-gathering relied primarily on conversational interviews and on projective techniques. They chose these relatively unstructured methods in the belief that they would afford the greatest opportunity for discovery of phenomena of which the researchers were unaware.

In the Hess and Handel study, each parent and each child was interviewed separately; each was assured of confidentiality. The two succeeding selections raise questions about this separate and confidential procedure. Bennett and McAvity set forth a strong case for interviewing husbands and wives together in a joint-interview format. They also provide useful suggestions for conducting such interviews. In the next paper, LaRossa, Bennett, and Gelles bring to attention some important ethical dilemmas in doing qualitative research on families. By its nature, such research seeks to penetrate family privacy in the interest of increased understanding of how families function. The full consequences of this effort cannot be known in advance either by the researchers or by the participants. The authors caution researchers to be sensitive to possible hazards to family members.

REFERENCES

Clark, Reginald M. *Family life and school achievement.* Chicago: University of Chicago Press, 1983.

Geertz, Clifford. Thick description: toward an interpretive theory of culture.'' In Clifford Geertz, *The interpretation of cultures.* New York: Basic Books, 1973, p. 9.

Henry, Jules. *Culture against man.* New York: Random House, 1963.

Henry, Jules. *Pathways to madness.* New York: Random House, 1971.

Howell, Joseph T. *Hard living on clay street: portraits of blue-collar families.* Garden City, N.Y.: Anchor/Doubleday, 1973.

Lewis, Oscar. *Five families.* New York: Basic Books, 1959.

Lewis, Oscar. *The children of Sanchez.* New York: Random House, 1961.

Piotrkowski, Chaya. *Work and the family system.* New York: Free Press, 1979.

Speedling, Edward J. *Heart attack: The family response at home and in the hospital.* New York: Tavistock, 1982.

4

My Life with the Families
of Psychotic Children

JULES HENRY

In 1957, under a grant from the Ford Foundation, Bruno Bettelheim asked me to study the families of some psychotic children by living in their homes. Since I had long wished to do this,[1] I was happy to accept the invitation. For many years it had been my conviction that the etiology of emotional illness required more profound study than had heretofore been possible, and that the best way to new discoveries in the field was through study of the disease-bearing vector, the family, in its natural habitat, pursuing its usual life routines—eating, loving, fighting, talking, taking amusements, treating sickness, and so on; in other words, following the usual course of its life.

It had been clear to me that by confining the search for causes to the prestigeful instruments of psychiatry and psychology—that is to say, to the interview and therapy sessions and psychological tests—we were shutting out, rather than revealing, important causal factors. A moment's reflection indicates why this is so. Human social life is made up of innumerable events initiated at birth and continued through life, and when they are not seen they sink into forgetfulness, for they are too many to remember; and always repression lets us forget what is necessary for us to forget.

It is difficult to communicate concretely what is meant by events so numerous as to be uncountable and unremembered, but if you try to recall all that you experienced between eating your dinner and arriving here tonight you will get some idea of what I mean. Who among you can recall

Jules Henry, now deceased, was Professor of Anthropology, Washington University, St. Louis. This paper was originally given at Forest Hospital, Des Plaines, Illinois, in February 1964.

all of the following: how often at dinner you and your wife picked up and set down your knife and fork; how much water or wine you drank; how many pieces of bread you ate; how fast you ate and how much you left on your plate; what you said to your wife and children and they to you and in what tone of voice; how much sugar you put in your coffee; whether or not you or your children stained the tablecloth or dropped food on the table and what happened then, and so on? Who can tell with certainty whether he kissed his wife and children good-bye and whether on the cheek or on the lips; what he said when he departed and what they said in return? And granted the improbability that you remember *all* these things today, would you remember them tomorrow, next week, or a year hence? Yet it is clear to you, I am sure, that many of the incidents I have mentioned are significantly related to your inner state and to the relationship between you and your family; and some, indeed, may leave an indelible mark on the relationship even though the event itself may be forgotten. Naturalistic observation of the families of psychotic children is not concerned with *all* such details; I presented them simply in order to give at the very beginning a rough idea of what is meant by an uncountable and unremembered series of events.

Since the Greeks it has been clear to Man-in-the-West that science advances by reflection on experience;[2] and it is clear also that the universe is endless and potent with new revelations that can constantly provide material on which reflection can operate to produce new insights. We know that the telescope, the microscope, and free association, revealing as they did, new dimensions of the universe, made new theory possible. Direct observation of families functioning in their native habitats should be the microscope that reveals new phenomena of family existence and so provides the possibilities of new theory.[3]

Given this reasonable assumption, the problem for me was to live with these families. Before describing *something* of my life in these households and *more* of my findings, it is necessary to answer in advance questions that have been raised wherever I have spoken of naturalistic observation. The questions in everyone's mind have been: (1) What was your entree into the family? (2) Didn't your presence distort the family way of life? (3) What did you do? (4) How did you stand it? (5) What did you record?

1. *Entree into the family* was obtained by explaining to husband and wife that science was of the opinion that their child's illness was somehow related to family life, and that the best way to discover the relationship was by having a scientist study their family. It was further explained that it was our hope that my findings might contribute to the treatment of their child; and if not to their child, surely to future generations of children.

2. *The problem of the distorting effects of the observer* may be treated under several headings.

(a) *The family as a culture.* Your experience as social beings and as therapists tells you that every family is different, and that this individuality maintains itself even in the presence of the determined efforts of the therapist to change it. Such stability, such resistance to change develops as a direct consequence of the social interaction of the members of the family with one another and of their mutual adaptation and conflict. Interaction, adaptation, and conflict, meanwhile, occur in relation to a set of values adapted by the family from the values of the culture. That is to say, if in one family the values of struggle, male dominance, female subordination, permissiveness, and so on have become frames of reference in terms of which all interaction takes place, these can arise only because they are present in the culture as a whole. If we put together the pattern of interaction and the value system we have the family culture.

The interaction that takes place in a family can be described accurately; it can be shown that the interaction may be examined in terms of specific interactional constellations, and it is possible to count the number of possible interactional constellations in terms of the equation:

$$I = 2^n - n - 1$$

This equation tells us that in a family of two parents and three children there is a total of 26 interactional constellations. Each system is relatively stable in its structure. That is to say, mother and father have a relatively fixed type of interaction, mother and child-one have another, father and child-one another, and so on. Since these patterns of interaction become standardized they change with great difficulty. All the features I have discussed contribute to an exceedingly stable social environment—however pathologic it may be—and we therefore accept with skepticism the hypothesis of ready modification in the presence of an observer.

Finally, it is useful to point out that since all biosocial systems tend to low entropy, and since an interactional constellation in a family is a biosocial system, the biosocially determined tendency is not easily disturbed.

(b) *The factors of custom and strain.* When an observer is in the home playing the role of a benign relative who, while making no demands and getting involved in no family disputes, at the same time makes himself useful, the family becomes accustomed to him. This factor of custom cannot, however, be considered apart from the problem of strain. Though a family may wish to protect itself from the eyes of the observer, its members cannot remain on guard constantly and everywhere, for the strain is too great. The problem of strain, however, is related to the pressure of impulses and fixed patterns of behavior.

(c) *Impulses and fixed behavior patterns.* Since behavior deriving from unconscious impulses cannot readily be controlled, often the members of a family cannot hide crucial dimensions of their behavior and feeling for the simple reason that they are unaware of them. In addition, we must take account of conscious impulses that, though conceivably socially unaccept-able, are not hidden because they are too violent to be controlled. There are, furthermore, many forms of overt behavior that though deemed so-cially acceptable by the subjects, have critical dimensions which, if known to the subject, might make him think twice before behaving as he does in the presence of an observer. For example, in one family studied in this re-search, the father detached himself completely from the family every eve-ning, slumped in a corner of the sofa watching TV or reading the paper. Such behavior, though belonging to the natural order of things in the fa-ther's eyes, may in the long run be disturbing to his family. As an example of a conscious, overt, though socially deplored attitude, I give the follow-ing: In one family the fat, balding, middle-aged father, when showing me photographs, handed me one of himself when he was young, slender and wavy-haired. I remarked, "You were a handsome dog in those days," at which his wife rasped sarcastically, "Lord Byron!" Thus, conscious and unconscious impulses and fixed action patterns of long standing in families reveal to an observer crucial dimensions of the family culture.

(d) *The position of the observer and the situation of the subject.* As scientists we are prone to imaginatively project our own learning and un-derstanding into our subjects' minds. In my experience, persons skilled in dynamic psychology are particularly apt to do this, thinking that my sub-jects understand the implications of their own behavior as well as a trained observer does. Since this is not so, it follows that much of the time the sub-jects do not even know what one should inhibit or conceal.

(e) *Participation of the subject in the research.* In the families studied so far, the mother and father were interested in participating in the research in the hope of helping emotionally disturbed children. Guilt because of their role in their own child's illness also played a role in helping them believe that what was discovered about their own family might help other chil-dren. Hence, we start in some cases with a reduced tendency to conceal.

(f) *The pressures toward habitual behavior exerted by children in the home.* The inner needs of children, especially young and disturbed ones, are so powerful that they tend to come out even when "company" is around, and when company is around the strong impulses of the young may be-come an embarrassment even in so-called normal families. Since, how-ever, I soon cease to be company, the children's needs dominate them, and the expression of these needs *pushes the parents into habitual modes of conduct* even though they might choose to avoid them. An example is the rage of a 13-year-old boy that forced his parents into a characteristic pattern of anxious, hostile response and culminated before my eyes in an incipient asthmatic attack in the boy.

(g) *Inflexibility of personality structure.* Since under ordinary circum-stances personality integration cannot readily change, this fact makes a massive contribution to the validity of naturalistic studies in the home. For example, a rough-and-ready extroverted individualist cannot suddenly become a passive, clinging conformist; nor can an unintelligent, ineffectual man be miraculously transformed into the opposite because an observer is in his home. Yet these personality integrations are precisely the target of observation in naturalistic observation, prevent distortion of the normal situation, and hence inexorably make their contribution to family life at all times.

Finally, with respect to validity, in the cases of the families of emotionally disturbed children it is usually possible to compare the naturalistic observations with different kinds of data obtained independently by other investigators: casework records, psychiatric treatment records, psychological tests, and so on.

3. *What did I do?* When I had a room in the home I got up when the family did, or maybe before, and retired when they did. If I was living outside I would get to the home around breakfast time and remain until the family went to bed. During the day I hung around the house. Since during the week the husband was away at work, I naturally spent my time with the wife and children. Most of the time I talked to the wife about whatever happened to come up: about her neighbors, about her concerns for her children, about food and how to cook it, about her husband and herself, and so on. When the mother was doing household chores or taking care of the children I watched. If she went shopping, took a child for a haircut, went to pick him up at school, I went along. If the family went out of an evening I went too. I went on picnics, to church, to Bible study, to a meeting of the chamber of commerce, and so on. With the husband I could talk about business, the state of the nation, politics, jobs, and the like. I was always in the role of a visiting friend or relative. If the children wished to come up on my lap, take me out to play, show me what they had done, they were welcome. I remained, on the whole, passive and compliant.

I intervened rarely in any activity, but I tended to follow one rule, which was to intervene when some accident seemed to have happened to a child, or when the parent asked me to hold a child. Thus one day Pete Portman, age 16 months, uttered a loud shriek, and going into the bedroom I discovered he had knocked against something and made his lip bleed. When Georgie Ross was about to receive a shot from the doctor, his mother asked me to hold him on my lap because, she said, she did not want him to undergo pain when in contact with her.

4. *How did you stand it?* If one makes a commitment to a scientific enterprise he thereby binds himself not to destroy the subject matter of his investigation. It would therefore have been preposterous to have hurled myself upon the parents every time I felt they were doing something pathogenic; and it would have been absurd also if I had become so overwhelmed by the pathogenic behavior I witnessed that I had to run screaming from the house. Having studied the Kaingang Indians of Brazil and the

Pilaga Indians of Argentina, and having spent months and years studying psychiatric institutions, I am long accustomed to the bizarre and the destructive. This being the case, I maintained calm at all times but one, and my sleep and my dreams were not unusually troubled. The one time I almost became angry was at the Browns when, while one of the boys was having an asthmatic attack brought on in part by the parents' hostility and stupidity, the father suggested we go for a walk. Case-hardened as I am, I am not proof against everything. My notes on this occasion read as follows:

> Mr. Brown asked me to go for a walk. This irritated me a great deal and I asked him, "Why am I here?" At first he didn't understand and I repeated it, implying that my purpose in being here was to be present at such situations, and that this was no time to leave. Mr. Brown dropped the subject.

I would say that for me this event represented the peak of strain, and that no other event approached its emotional impact in this sense, although, as you will see, living in the homes of these families, one constantly encounters situations that might be unsettling to an untrained observer. Experience and training, however, impose automatic restraints. I imagine it must be remotely akin to the experience of an officer watching his men die on the battlefield.

6. *What did I record?* I recorded everything I could remember. Whatever it was, whether a discussion with the mother on how to broil chicken, an observation of how the mother fed the baby, or what the father told me about his job, everything I could recall went indiscriminately into the record. The scientific study of human emotions has been hampered by decisions made long ago about what was important for the vicissitudes of the emotional life. Obviously if I was to start naturalistic observation with a preconception of what is important, no advance would be possible. I therefore took the position that everything was important, and as I dictated from memory I made no attempt to arrange the data in sequence or in categories. I felt it was scientifically unsound to "prethink" the data, and I felt sure that when the record was finished I would be able to make sense out of it. After all, I have behind me a great history of a science that made the confusing variety of the universe appear orderly. Why not profit by the tradition and its brilliant successes?

THE OBSERVATIONS

Since the title of this paper is "My Life with the Families of Psychotic Children," I want to find a way of communicating to you something of my *life* with them and something of my *observations*. This can be done only in part, for were I to limit myself to data that give you an idea of what *my* life was like the distortion would be too great, and the relatively *insignifi-*

cant datum (the observer) might tend to loom larger than the centrally *important* data, the families. In presenting this material to you I shall emphasize data rather than theory—although the latter will by no means be missing—because I want you to get a good idea of what can be seen in direct observation. Therefore I shall try to "let the data speak for itself," and to restrict interpretation.

The first selection is from the study of a family of father, mother, and three children living in a small town. Tommy, the fourth child, had just been admitted to the Sonia Shankman Orthogenic School as autistic. He was the firstborn and was nine years old on admission. His brothers, Bobby and Jackie, were six and three, respectively, and Harriet was a year and a half old. Dr. Jones, the father, was a very bright, vainglorious, ambiguous, distrustful, and violent man. Much of his thought was cast in terms of survival, competition, and defeat, and he scoffed at golf and praised tennis because in the latter you can feel the shock of the contending bodies. Dr. Jones was also disorderly, in the sense of lacking firm orientations in the fundamental categories of time, space, and objects. It is not that he is psychotically disoriented in the clinical sense, but rather than he has no feeling for time schedules, certain serious obligations, evident danger signals in the environment, and the usual notions of material order. He leaves his car door open in the pouring rain and is careless about his dress. His consultation rooms look as if they had been orderly a week ago. In the intake interviews Dr. Jones and his wife gave me a history of violent strife between them, and while I *witnessed* nothing as bad as they recounted, their behavior during my week's visit with them was witness to the probable truth of the case history. Dr. Jones' relationship to the two boys, however, seemed good. They were visibly fond of him and their relationship was rough-and-tumble, hypermasculine.

Superficially Mrs. Jones was gentle. She seemed to dissociate strong affect quickly, to push things out of her mind, so to speak, and to be fundamentally gentle and passive. Actually she could fight back with biting sarcasms, and her behavior not infrequently was provocative. She was also strikingly pretty. Thus superficially the family seemed polarized between the vicious, slashing extroversion of the father, and the quiet, cutting, deep introversion of the mother. Bobby was much like his father, except that where the father's depression had to be inferred, Bobby's was visible in his face. Yet he was bright, agile, and physically self-confident. He constantly, and even dangerously, tormented Jackie, however, and avoided his mother except to ask her for specific objects and to insult and provoke her. Jackie was a rather immature three-year-old of garbled speech and fantasy. He constantly sucked his thumb and made weeping, screaming demands on his mother. Caught between his fierce brother, his athletic father, and his displacement by the new baby, Harriet, Jackie seemed to have nowhere to go but backward. Harriet was her mother's refuge, for it was there that Mrs.

Jones was able to find surcease from the battering of Bobby and her husband, and it was there that what tendencies to gentleness and tranquillity yet remained to her could be fully expressed. Hence the relationship between Mrs. Jones and Harriet was unruffled and rather underprotective.

I turn now to an arrowhead hunting expedition, an event of the first day of my visit with the Joneses. Naturally, on the first day of my visit, Dr. Jones felt he had to entertain me, and therefore, in line with his stereotypic model of an anthropologist, he suggested an arrowhead hunt. The account, follows:

A SAMPLE OF INTERACTION WITHIN THE JONES FAMILY

Dr. Jones, Bobby, Jackie and I drove out into the country to find an Indian mound and search it for arrowheads. We came to a little stream and we all began to wade along it because Dr. Jones said that this was the way to the mound. There was broken glass in the stream and Dr. Jones said there was danger from snakes. Jackie, the three-year-old, got frightened and complained of the cold. He was also afraid that the water was too deep for him. Dr. Jones paid little attention to Jackie's fear. Occasionally Dr. Jones stopped and picked some broken glass out of the bed of the stream. We wandered along the stream, up on the bank, down into the stream, up on the bank again, and so on, as the stream became impassible from time to time. Several times I carried Jackie, but finally Dr. Jones carried him for a long distance as he continued to complain of the cold, and it really was quite chilly for that time of the year. At last we reached a point where it was no longer possible to go on in the stream because it was too deep. We climbed up the bank through poison ivy and encountered a barbed wire fence over which we climbed as Jackie whimpered. No one was scratched on the wire. Over the wire we found ourselves at the far edge of a wide field covered with weeds, brambles, berry bushes, and so on, and we had to walk across it, barefooted, of course, in order to reach the road that bordered its far side. I carried Bobby across the field and Dr. Jones carried Jackie. Dr. Jones was surprised when I offered to carry Bobby and tried to dissuade me, saying that Bobby was too huge and heavy. I found him neither huge nor heavy; as a matter of fact, I scarcely felt his weight even though the going was difficult. In the Jones case history Dr. and Mrs. Jones, but especially the former, frequently refer to Bobby as "huge," "strong" and so on. Because of this I was all prepared for a giant, but I found him an ordinary, rather good-looking kid. Throughout the entire "expedition" Bobby took matters very well, and it was only Jackie who complained. At last we reached the road and walked back to the car. We got in and drove about a quarter of a mile to an old dwelling where Dr. Jones spoke to the woman of the house about our desire to explore the mound that was just behind her home, and which we could have reached simply by driving that quarter of a mile instead of trying to wade to it along the stream. We climbed up a little on the mound and found no arrowheads or anything at all that looked as if it had ever belonged to an Indian. Actually, moderate scratching in the mound showed that it was not an archeological mound at all but a natural geological formation of rotten shale.

Analysis
Figure 1 may contribute to a clear understanding of this incident.

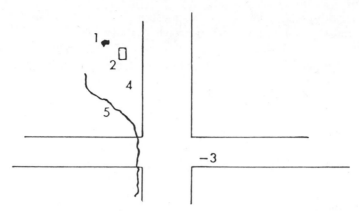

FIGURE 1. Probable relations of road, stream, field, house, and mound: (1) mound; (2) house; (3) car; (4) field; (5) stream.

It is not, of course, always necessary, especially when on a holiday, to take the shortest pathway between two points. Getting to a place by using a stream as the pathway can be fun: the pathway is defined by fun, which is the goal sought. The stream, however, was unknown, unsafe, ultimately impassable, and turned out not to be fun. As a matter of fact, Dr. Jones had misstated the case even in regard to the direction, for the stream was not *the* way to the mound, but a way, a piece of information Dr. Jones withheld from us. In the presence of accumulating inconvenience and even danger Dr. Jones did not for a long time turn back. Thus his misperception of the nature of the pathway was accompanied by an *inability to reverse himself*; and the entire venture was carried out *as if* the pathway were clear. We might say that Dr. Jones "forced the issue." It is well to bear these characteristics of the venture in mind: misperception, concealment of information, pathological as-ifness, and inability to reverse.

While wading in a stream can be fun, nobody was asked whether he wanted this kind of fun; and the enterprise was presented as if there was no alternative pathway. The result was that Dr. Jones endangered everybody. Such massive error of judgment, accompanied by the hiding of the alternative and an inability to reverse, suggests an obsessive process at work.

This brings us to the problem of depth. Obviously I perceive depth both in reference to myself and in reference to others; and if water is too deep, it can be too deep for me, for my child, or for both of us. Normally one reacts with anxiety to water that is too deep for one's child; and in a stream with unknown depth pockets the normal inclination would be to get out of the stream. Dr. Jones acted as if the danger from depth was minimal; yet he was at last *compelled* to abandon the stream because it really became too deep: *it thus took an acute and present danger, intruding upon him with overwhelming insistence*, to compel him to abandon the enterprise.

Such *extreme persistence* raises the question of how acute and present a danger must be for a person to perceive it as dangerous. We have been told repeatedly about the "overanxious" parent who sees danger where there is none. We need to know more about the "under-anxious" parent, who fails to see clear and present dangers. We need to know more about such *inappropriate composure.*

I have just described an event involving Dr. Jones and his two boys. Although I was part of the event I did not experience it as a member of the family did, yet since I was literally in it, I was acutely aware of all its objective features. Thus, in close proximity to the members of the family living in their native habitat, I was able to observe their actual life and arrive at some reasonably probable inferences. Because of the lack of space I do not, of course, give a complete theoretical analysis of the event. I believe it reasonably certain that the circumstances and spirit of this expedition could never be recovered from an interview. Thus naturalistic observation, by placing the observer in the midst of real family life, provides insights impossible to attain in any other way. Fundamentally, what it does is give *crucial behavior correlates of personality.*

RELATIONSHIP TO THE OUTSIDE WORLD

I turn now to another significant aspect of family life revealed by naturalistic observation: the family's relation to the outside world. This is important to us not only because the outside world reacts to the family and so conditions its existence, but also because observations of transactions between the family and the outer world enable us to test the validity of our formulations about the family and to explore more completely its potentialities for health and illness. Meanwhile, it is evident that an observer can give a better account of the family's transactions with the environment than a single member. It is also important that what seems critically significant to an observer might be withheld in an interview with a member of the family.

Keeping these points in mind let us turn to my record of the Jones' evening at a Bible study group. The Joneses, particularly Dr. Jones, consider themselves very religious; they feel close to God; they pray; Dr. Jones reads Martin Buber and on Sunday goes not only to church but also to men's Sunday school. The account follows:

> The Bible study group was made up of earnest and intelligent men who were searching for answers to questions like. What is faith? Can you trust people? Can you trust God if you don't trust people? What is the origin of faith? What makes a good religious leader? Can a religion be strong if leadership is weak? One of Dr. Jones' first acts was to attack St. Paul for what he considered Paul's pretentiousness—his pretense at humility while at the same time holding himself above everybody else. Nobody agreed with Dr. Jones. This reminds me of

the violent attack he made on a couple that left before the rest of us. Dr. Jones attacked them for being rigid and unwilling to look at themselves. Meanwhile Mrs. Jones kept saying, gently, "Oh, oh," as if she was not agreeing with her husband. But that is all she said. During the course of the discussion Dr. Jones argued that faith in man is impossible, and that faith in man is entirely different from faith in God. In this he opposed almost the entire group. In the course of the discussion Dr. Jones developed the following ideas: (1) It is completely impossible for man to become one with God because man can never achieve perfection. (2) It is totally impossible for man to be unified with man, because all men are basically individuals. (3) All men are weak and full of error and evil. It seemed to me that, though always logical, Dr. Jones was sometimes very pedantic. For example, he insisted on reading the authoritative interpretation of the word "faith"; and as he read he attempted to pronounce all the foreign words with a proper foreign pronunciation. For example, he attempted to pronounce the Hebrew word with the proper Hebrew pronunciation. The limelight was focused on Dr. Jones because he was in complete opposition to everybody and was really very threatening to them, because he said he didn't trust anybody; and one woman, passionately religious, apparently, said that if his position were correct it would DESTROY HER REASON FOR LIVING. When Dr. Jones said he had no faith in anybody his wife said, "You mean to say you wouldn't even trust me not to be unfaithful?" and right out in front of everybody, he said, "No." When Dr. Jones said he had no faith that his wife would not betray him, and when he later said people are weak and may change completely from one day to the next, Mrs. Jones said this was a signal for her to go out and have a good time. As we left the meeting, one of the women asked him to repeat his position. He then mentioned a series of persons who had tried to trick him. It is interesting that he mentioned nobody who had ever been loyal. There is no doubt that his wife took all this declaration of no faith, distrust, and so on, in a very personal way. During the meeting Mrs. Jones took an active part in the discussion. It was a very different kind of Mrs. Jones from the one I encounter in trying to get her to talk about personal matters. It is interesting that right out in public she challenged her husband to tell her whether he believed she would never betray him. As we emerged from the meeting Dr. Jones at once lit into his wife for not having told the baby-sitter where he was, and the two wrangled about this all the way home. The argument was about who was to take responsibility for telling the baby-sitter where he can be reached. He said Mrs. Jones should do the telling because she has the dealings with the baby-sitter; and she said they should both take the responsibility. However, he kept on insisting that she should do it; if two people took responsibility, nobody took responsibility. She responded that she's all concerned with telling the babysitter what to do with the children and is liable to forget the importance of his being in contact with his office and patients. She didn't give an inch in the argument. He was characteristically crude and she was characteristically resistant but not crude. His attack is very destructive, even when he doesn't use destructive words. His attitude is very brusque, as if talking to an inferior.

Eager to hear something about the aftermath of last night, I asked Mrs. Jones whether she and her husband had talked about it, and she said, "We only talked about it a little bit." I said, "It was quite a business," and in her usual way she made some comment that was off the main issue. So I brought the subject around directly to her husband's lack of faith in people, and she remarked that she believes this goes back to the fact that he spent a year in the hospital when he was an infant and got no real mothering. She says she believes this made it impossible for him to develop a relationship to people or any trust in them. When I raised the subject of his having said he couldn't trust her she said she *doesn't know* what it means.

As Dr. Jones and I were driving along, I brought up the subject of his lack of faith in people, and he said he raised the issue at the Bible study meeting yesterday primarily in order to test the people there, because he wants to know whether they will have faith in him should he make any mistakes in surgery. He said also that he is worried that if he gets too close to people he will become vulnerable, and this is somehow related to people's faith in him, and to his faith in them. When I reminded him of how concerned Ida was last night when he made statements about not trusting her, he laughed and affirmed that of course you can't absolutely trust anybody. After he had gone on for some time about all the people he couldn't trust and why, I asked, "Well, aren't there any people in your life who have been loyal?" and he said, "Yes, and one of them is Ida"; and then he mentioned one or two others. He said, however, that the cost of finding people you can trust is enormous; meaning that you use up a great many people trying to find a few you can trust. He said the people at the meeting were all confused—they talk about having faith in people but he doesn't believe that any of them really do.

We began to talk about the people at the Bible study meeting the other night, and Dr. and Mrs. Jones agreed that those people were entirely unrealistic about their own ability to have faith in others. Either Dr. or Mrs. Jones remarked that the husband of Sarah, one of the most active in protesting her faith in people, was a very hostile man. Dr. Jones said that Sarah's husband is the kind of man who will develop a coronary or a perforated ulcer later in life.

The Bible study group came together in order to examine the issue of faith in the light of the life and epistles of St. Paul. They hoped that in these they might, perhaps, find some basis for believing that faith of itself gives hope. However, the first thing they hear from Dr. Jones is a violent—a killing—personal attack on a sacred symbol of their religion. This is followed by an attempt by Dr. Jones to demolish by logic what hope remained: while the group hoped to come away with renewed hope, Dr. Jones tried to show there was none. Christianity rests on its sacred figures, on Jesus, Mary, and the Apostles. If the Apostles are degraded, much of Christianity becomes null, for their utterances become the mutterings of degraded men. What was threatening in what Dr. Jones had to say was not so much that St. Paul was "only a man," but that he was a pretentious one; and though pretense may lead, it can only betray. Dr. Jones' denials of the possibility of positive relations among human beings are clear from the record. Whoever does not agree with him is exposed to personal affront, like the couple that left before the meeting was over. Thus Dr. Jones attacked the group first by attacking the sacred foundations of its religion and then by attacking the premise of the meeting: that faith in man is possible. In this way he undermined the very possibility of a meeting. What became visible to the observer was the group's resentment and the anxiety and depression of one woman. It is reasonable to suppose that others felt anxiety and depression also.

In these various ways Dr. Jones turned the group, including his wife, against him and thus confirmed his underlying feeling that he could have faith in no one, and that he was therefore indeed a "lonely" man. If the intention of Dr. Jones had been to use the group to prove to himself once again that he stood alone, if it had been his intention to use it to *legitimize* his basic distrust, he could not have planned his strategy better.

Turning now to the last excerpt from the record, one finds Dr. and Mrs. Jones agreeing that the members of the group were "unrealistic about their own ability to have faith in others," as if "realism" had anything to do with the religiously motivated quest. When people in our culture engage in religious activity the real world is intuitively "suspended,"[4] and one commits one's self to intercourse with the ideal. A sincere person does not go to church, to Sunday school, or to Bible study groups to learn about reality, but to have spiritual intercourse with the ideal, in the hope that it will become part of him. When, therefore, Dr. and Mrs. Jones agree that the people at the group were unrealistic they render an *inappropriate* judgment based on an inappropriate perception of what was going on. I have called this kind of error lack of circumspection. The function of this evaluation of the group as unrealistic is to legitimize, even to glorify, in a way, Dr. Jones' attack. By this time, two days later, Mrs. Jones no longer counts herself among the unrealistic ones, but has joined the "enemy," her husband, in the interest of maintaining domestic tranquillity. Thus the *aftermath* of the quarrel with the group has been resolved.

Dr. Jones seems to have felt a certain expansiveness and pleasure as the group centered its attention on him. Thus his pleasure was gained at the expense of the group. The fact that even as the group was breaking up a woman asked him to explain his position again is one sign of the dismay Dr. Jones left behind him.

As a direct aftermath of *their* quarrel during the meeting, Dr. and Mrs. Jones had an angry encounter over the baby-sitter; but as an aftermath of *Dr. Jones'* quarrel with the *group,* husband and wife had reached an *entente:* through the doctrine of "realism" his position at the meeting was *legitimized* and *his* status raised while the group's was lowered. Family respect was stabilized by viewing the group with contempt. Thus Dr. and Mrs. Jones worked through his tensions with the group as a substitute for working through their tensions with each other: the fundamental issue was displaced in favor of permitting the domestic ambiguity to continue.

For my last example I have chosen to describe a home visit of a 16-year-old schizophrenic boy, hospitalized in a prisonlike state institution. We know that the reception a disturbed person receives on his return home often determines the outcome of his case, but all too often we can only guess what happens when he goes home. We will continue to know very little about the causes of recurrence of psychotic disturbance until we have a wide range of naturalistic observations of patients returned to their natural habitat.

Mrs. Burns is a histrionic woman who requires "oceans of love." It seems probable that because of a number of serious ailments she had in Eddie's early childhood he could not respond to his mother with anything approaching the flamboyant demonstrativeness she requires, with the result that she turned against him. On top of this Mrs. Burns is somewhat disoriented—just enough to complete the necessary pathogenesis. In contrast to Eddie, Mr. and Mrs. Burns are deeply involved in his sister, Trudy, now thirteen. The following announcement of the birth of Trudy gives the idea:

BURNS, INC.

Proudly Presents

GERTRUDE BURNS

in

HELLO WORLD

An original story of life based on Mother Nature

*   *   *

Executive Producer .... John Burns
Associate Producer .... Evelyn Burns
Directed by .... Dr. J. Commons
Assisted by the Cast of the
Mountain Hospital

Copywrited on April 6, 19—
By Burns, Inc.
Special Costumes .... Triangular Panties, all subject to change
Musical Arrangements by Evelyn's Sighs, accompanied by Gertrude's Cries.

COMMENTS

This production was nine months in the making. It is our prediction that this is a 4-Star Masterpiece, and all who see this production will recognize the exceptional performance of Gertrude Burns, and unanimously agree that she receive the coveted award.

Don't miss our 2nd great attraction! Premiere to be held at 1205 Mercer Street, Mansfield, Idaho. Admission—your very best wishes.

If there was such an announcement for Eddie, it was not shown me. The following extracts of my observations show the attitude of the mother toward Eddie on his home visit. I start with some of the preparations for his return.

After we had been in the five-and-ten for about twenty minutes Mrs. Burns came along and showed us immediately what she had bought. She had two very unattractive shirts for Eddie, but she said they were beautiful, one was reduced from $3.99 to $1. At this time I am reminded that as we were going around the five-and-ten looking for something for Eddie she said as we looked at the candy, "I want to buy some junk for Eddie." I can't remember what she ended up with. . . . Today in the supermarket the meat Mrs. Burns bought for Eddie's lunch tomorrow was the cheapest hamburger she could find.

Next day

Almost from the moment Eddie came into the house Mrs. Burns interfered with practically everything the boy did, in a yelling and very irritated way. As a matter of fact, it seemed to me that her whole pattern of behavior with the boy was so destructive and irritating that I constantly looked for effects of it in him, and by the end of the day I think that Eddie was in pretty bad shape, for he was depressed. His facial tics had increased and he started biting his fists. It is difficult to remember the many occasions upon which Mrs. Burns blocked and attacked the boy. I shall try to enumerate the ones I can remember. When Eddie came into the house, you could see from his behavior and from what he said that he wanted to soak up the house. He wanted to go around and look at all the rooms. He wanted to sit on the porch and relax. He wanted to go into his sister's room. Mrs. Burns would not let any of these things happen but insisted that he sit down and eat breakfast because everybody was hungry. She dragged him off the porch by scolding him when he was sitting out there just soaking the place up. He wanted to try on the new pants and she said no, he must eat his breakfast. As a matter of fact, Mrs. Burns was a completely transformed person the minute this boy set foot in this house. She became an irritated, nagging, destructive woman.

At the Beach

She was sitting on a raised platform at the back of the beach, this platform being the top of the staircase leading to the beach. Eddie, in order to reach her, could either have gone up the steps or climbed up. Only a boy, a young boy, would think of climbing up, so he climbed up and he was bawled out by Mrs. Burns; and when he tried to go down the same way she bawled him out. Mr. Burns blocked him too. On the platform there were seated with Eddie quite a number of people including Mr. and Mrs. Burns; three girls, one of them his sister, who had come along with us to go swimming, and also a couple of strangers, I think. Now Mrs. Burns loudly and irritatedly called attention to Eddie's penis. She loudly and irritatedly called attention to what seemed to her the fact that his very abbreviated trunks did not adequately cover him in that region and she said that he must not wear those same trunks again without a jock strap. This sort of behavior must have been terribly destructive and humiliating to the boy although he gave no sign. After supper the following situation developed in the living room. Eddie, who has sort of taken Elvis Presley as an ego ideal, wanted to sing in the living room. Now at about the same time he got the idea of singing his sister put on the record player and he scolded her for putting on the record player just when he started to sing. At this point Mrs. Burns tore into him for trying to get the limelight and yelled at him that he is not boss around here. I had gone into the other room, and later Mrs. Burns commented on this and told me what had transpired. But an almost identical incident developed a few minutes later when he started to sing again and Mrs. Burns scolded him for always trying to be in the limelight. She also scolded him for trying to sing that kind of song instead of other kinds of songs. She scolded him for trying to sing in Elvis Presley's voice instead of his own voice. All this was done in a very loud, irritated, scolding manner. When he started to sing she showed distracted attention. She also interrupted his singing to criticize his singing. He ended up not singing at all. At the table Mrs. Burns soon lost interest in Eddie and began to talk about other things, turning to me.

Even in the midst of Eddie's conversation she would change the subject. I'm reminded that at one point when Mrs. Burns was talking to Eddie, possibly scolding him, I heard him sing a bar of one song titled, "Oh, Why Was I Born." The bar he sang was, "Why was I born." All day long Eddie kept singing, if I may use the term, a song . . . a part line of which was, "Are you looking for trouble." Eddie roamed in and out of the rooms of the house, he could not sit still in any one place for as long as five minutes, and I think his mother bawled him out for not sitting still. Somewhere along the line she also bawled him out for being fidgety.

Here the observations speak entirely for themselves. All that is necessary to add, perhaps, is that there was scarcely an area of Eddie's behavior accessible to his mother in which she did not intervene in a disorganizing way. The result was that on the way back to the hospital, where we arrived almost too late because of Mrs. Burns' delaying tactics, Eddie's few shreds of self-confidence had disappeared, his facial tics were severe, he was biting his wrists and singing, "Why was I ever born?"

CONCLUSIONS

Naturalistic observation of the families of psychotic children is feasible because a scientist can be admitted to their homes and because for a variety of reasons distortions of the usual mode of life of the family are not serious enough to make observation fruitless. Whether we are observing the ongoing patterns of life or the return to the home of a psychotic individual, direct observation encounters almost the full drama of family existence. One should bear in mind, meanwhile, that unless direct observation is undertaken, important areas of etiology are concealed from us.

ACKNOWLEDGMENTS

I am indebted to Dr. Bettelheim and the Ford Foundation for the opportunity to do the studies on which this paper is based; and I am grateful to the Jewish Children's Bureau for obtaining the cooperation of some families for the study. I am also in the debt of those families that opened their doors to the research, and I regret that in their own interest they must remain anonymous in this paper.

NOTES

1. See J. Henry, Common problems of research in anthropology and psychiatry, *American Journal of Orthopsychiatry*, 1948, *18*, 698–703.
2. See, for example, Descartes, *Rules for the direction of the Mind.*
3. A more extended treatment is contained in J. Henry, L'observation naturaliste des familles d'enfants psychotiques, *La Psychiatrie de l'Enfant*, 1961.
4. Husserl's general term for excluding the usual world. See *Ideas*, pp. 155 *et seq.*

5

Some Comments on
Method

ROBERT D. HESS AND
GERALD HANDEL

BACKGROUND

The central aim of the research was to study families as groups of persons. This objective led us to formulate specific criteria for selecting families. The comments that follow refer not only to the five families presented in *Family Worlds* (see note below) but also to the total group of thirty-three from which data were collected and from which these were chosen. These are the defining characteristics of the families studied:

1. The unit of study is the nuclear family—parents living with their biological children. Families with adopted children were excluded, since our concern was with ordinary, intact families. Since, further, our interest lay primarily in understanding the interior organization of the unit made up of husband, wife, and children, we did not study the extended family—the unit that includes uncles and aunts, cousins and grandparents, as well as the nuclear family.

2. The children in these families are between the ages of six and eighteen. This criterion is based more on practical grounds than theoretical ones. Since all of our data-gathering techniques were verbal in nature, six seemed to us the youngest age at which we could obtain adequate data. We were not prepared to get involved with play or other nonverbal techniques because of the added complication these would entail. The upper age limit of eighteen was dictated by our intention of studying whole families. At

Reprinted from *Family Worlds*, pp. 287–297, by Robert D. Hess and Gerald Handel by permission of the University of Chicago Press. © 1959 by the University of Chicago. Robert D. Hess and Gerald Handel are identified in the footnote to Chapter 3.

this age some children leave home, if only to go to college, and are consequently often inaccessible. The basic framework of analysis that we have developed and presented in chapter 1 is applicable to families with children both younger and older than those of the present study, but its application would almost certainly require modifications in the data-gathering procedures.

The age range adopted is a wide one. The terms of our analytic framework are cast at a level of generality that does not tie them to particular age levels or forms of sibship. For our purposes, it sufficed to have some families with boys, some with girls, and some with boys and girls. The age span adopted had the distinct advantage of enabling us to develop a framework that was general and not age-restricted.

3. The families are northwest European in ancestry. This defining characteristic follows from our aim of studying a group of families relatively homogeneous in ethnic background and of minimal ethnic visibility in American society. Our interest was in understanding something of the differences that exist in that broad band of families who make up the core culture of the United States and who have no sense of tie to or inner conflict over minority group membership and tradition. The families selected are, in a broad sociological sense, not "special" in any way.

One may quarrel with the degree of homogeneity actually represented by the term "northwest European," if one wishes to press the point that only those of English ancestry have no "minority group" characteristics in this society. The objection hardly seems a serious one. There has probably been, in this country, more intermarriage within the northwest European group than between it and central or south Europeans. In addition, persons of Dutch or German or Scandinavian ancestry have on the whole lost their ethnic visibility much more rapidly than persons of, say, Slavic or Mediterranean ancestry.

4. The families are all resident in metropolitan areas, though in some instances the parents were born and spent their early years in small towns.

5. The families range, along the dimension of social class, from upper lower to upper middle. This variation was deliberate, since we expected that important differences in family life would exist along this dimension. Variation in social class membership was intended to assure a range of differences that might be expected to influence family life. Social class has been a background concept, rather than a focal point, of our analysis. At the same time, this breadth served us in the same way as did that of the children's age span: it facilitated developing concepts for family analysis that are not class-bound, just as they are not age-bound. A wide range of occupations was included.

6. The families are selected from the community at large and not from a clinic population. The significance of this criterion again derives from our basic objectives. We wished to study the "psychosocial interior" of fami-

lies, an area that has largely been the province of psychiatrists, psychologists, and social workers treating persons with psychoclinical disorders. Our study was directed to understanding psychosocial ties in ordinary families.

These, then, are the specifications for the families we set out to study. In the period allotted for field work, we succeeded in collecting data from thirty-three families. In the course of obtaining these, approximately twenty-five families who met our selection criteria and who were approached declined to participate in the study. In addition, one family that had agreed to be studied refused to continue, after half the data had been collected. This was the only dropout.

The names of potential families for study were obtained in two ways. Various people in the community who might be able to furnish names of families were approached. Our aims were explained to them in the same terms as they later were to the families themselves: "Everyone knows the saying 'like father like son,' and we also know that it isn't always true. We would like to know more exactly just how children are like their fathers and mothers, or if they are not, why not. We are interested in studying normal, typical American families. Much research has been done on unusual or abnormal families, but relatively little on the great number of normal families that make up a community. We hope that our work will contribute more information about the important matter of bringing up our children." Preservation of the anonymity of the families to be studied was, of course, stressed. We also indicated something of the range of topics our interviewing would cover and stated that we would not be probing into the most intimately personal aspects of family life but that our interviewing would deal with the ordinary events of daily living.

The names of the great majority of families contacted were obtained from those people in the community who were in a position to refer us to several. The second source of family names was the families actually studied. In response to our request, some referred us to families of their acquaintance. Of the total group of thirty-three, six were referrals from participating families.

The objectives of the study were explained to the husband or wife, or both, of each family contacted. It was also explained that the interviewer would want to talk with each member of the family privately and that what one member of the family said would in no instance be repeated to any other member of the family. The parents were told that all the procedures would require approximately fifteen to twenty hours of the family's time— no more than three or four hours with any one person.

In most instances the explanation of the objectives and time demands of the study were sufficient. In a few cases, families wanted to know what direct benefit they would derive from the study. For some of these, the question meant whether they would receive assistance with their own family problems. For others, the question was vaguer in intent. We explained that we could not offer counseling on family problems and that we would not in any way interpret the family to itself. To have done so would not have been consonant with the principal research condition we established—that each family member would talk about himself and his family in privacy with the interviewer and with assured confidentiality.

We explained that the only reward the family could expect was the satisfaction of knowing that, by their participation, they were contributing to scientific knowledge about family life and that, we hoped, this would ultimately be of benefit to other parents in bringing up their children.

The motives for participating in the study were not explicitly or systematically explored. Some of the parents, particularly but not exclusively the less sophisticated ones, voluntarily said they were pleased and even flattered they could make a contribution to scientific knowledge in this fashion. Some appeared to use the research as an occasion to express their satisfaction with what they had achieved in family living. Others seemed curious about what such a project could be like, or simply welcomed this novel addition to their lives. A few perhaps still hoped, despite our explanation, that they would receive some direct assistance with their immediate problems. We received only one such explicit request from a parent concerning a child; though declining to counsel directly, we did refer the parent to an appropriate agency.

In a few instances a parent attempted to find out how a child had conducted himself with or what he had said to the interviewer. Such probing was quickly discouraged by the interviewer, who made it plain that she would not violate the confidentiality that had been promised all the members of the family. Attempts to find out what a spouse had told the interviewer were even fewer in number and were handled according to the same principle.

OBTAINING THE DATA

After the family had agreed to participate in the study, the interviewing began with the obtaining of background information on the family. This initial session was most often held with both spouses present, but occasionally only with the wife. The former method was the one we preferred, but it was not always feasible because of the family's schedule. When this was the case, supplementary material was later obtained from the husband. This opening interview, in addition to serving as a warmup and allowing the parents to begin to feel at home with the interviewer, covered two main areas:

A. Face-sheet data
    1. Ages of all family members
    2. Birthplace of each member

3. Family's residence history
4. Education of husband and wife
5. Current and previous occupations of husband and wife
6. Nationality ancestry
7. Religious affiliation
B. Data on early life of husband and wife
1. What kind of people their parents were
2. Information about brothers and sisters
3. A characterization of what their home life was like

In retrospect, it seems that a fuller investigation of the early home life of the parents would have been helpful in further illuminating their contemporary motives in the family.

Several types of data were obtained from each family member: an interview, obtained sometimes in one session but often in two and occasionally in three; a TAT; a Sentence Completion; a brief essay from each child on "The Person I Would Like To Be Like"[1]; and an essay from each parent on "The Kind of Person I Would Like My Child To Be." The data gathering—all of which was conducted in the family's residence—was concluded with the administration of a set of five TAT-type pictures to the family as a group. These pictures were especially designed for this study. To each picture the family was asked to discuss and develop among themselves an agreed-upon story. The discussions as well as the story were recorded.

Each person was interviewed in privacy for periods of 1–1½ hours for children and for 2½–3 hours for parents. The number of sessions devoted to interviewing any one person depended upon the individual circumstances. Each member was interviewed on substantially the same topics. The questions were open-ended, designed to encourage the person to comment freely on general topics raised for discussion. Initial responses were followed by more specific probes where indicated. The interview guide covered these areas:

1. Each member's view of his family—what it is like, what the important things about it are.
2. The family's daily life—what they do and how they feel about it. The extent and variety of their activity, inside and outside the home. How the weekends differ from weekdays. The concrete happenings that occur and the kind of interaction among family members that is woven through them.
3. The work and responsibility roles of each member, including not only the earning role of the husband-father and others' feelings about it but also the assignment or assumption of household management responsibilities. Also extrafamilial responsibilities in school, church, civic organizations.
4. The course of the family's development, beginning with the parents'

own families of origin. What their parents and childhood homes were like. How the parents now see themselves in relation to their backgrounds—what their aims are for themselves and what they want for their children. Their goals, aspirations, regrets, and disappointments.

5. Related to the foregoing, the socializing of the children. Generally, how the parents deal with their children, how they construe the parent-child relationship. What behaviors they consider to be offenses and how these are handled.

6. How the family members perceive and feel about one another. In what ways they feel they resemble or differ from each other.

7. What problems each member feels he has in relation to himself or in relation to other family members. What he particularly likes about each of the other members. What changes he would like to see in himself and in others.

The progress of the interview generally followed this order of topics, though the procedure was a flexible one and was adapted to fit individual circumstance.

TAT stories to at least ten pictures were obtained from each person. Two of the pictures were from the specially drawn set mentioned above. The remainder were selected from the Harvard TAT. Parents and children were shown the same pictures. However, some of the pictures used with the first families studied were later dropped as not yielding material sufficiently useful to warrant inclusion. The pictures selected were those that seemed to promise useful material for family analysis. Some that we did not include might also have proved quite profitable.[2]

Two forms of the Sentence Completion were devised, one for use with younger children, the other administered to older children and parents.

With the group TAT procedure mentioned above, we sought to obtain concurrent projective and interaction data. We have not yet devised a satisfactory method of analyzing this material, though several have been tried. In *Family Worlds* we have occasionally drawn on the protocols for illustration. In none of the cases does an interpretation rest primarily on this material.

Supplementing the data obtained directly from the family members is the interviewer's record. The interviewer described the family's residence and each member of the family. She also described their demeanor during the interview and testing sessions.

ANALYZING THE DATA

The various techniques employed to gather the data for this study are all relatively unstructured. This research strategy was deliberate and was designed to maximize freedom in two directions. It was designed to allow our informants to express themselves as freely as possible about their families and themselves, and it was intended to allow the investigators a wide area of interpretive freedom. Our aim was clear: to find a way to describe and understand families as units while concomitantly relating the personalities of component members to the unit. This meant that we had to be prepared to work with concepts derived from psychology, anthropology, sociology, and social psychology—but in what combination we did not know in advance. Our task has been one of analysis and interpretation, as it is in any research. In carrying out this task, we have made three fundamental assumptions: (1) The data do not speak for themselves but gain coherence only as they are brought into relation with useful ideas about them. (2) The responses each informant gives us potentially convey much more than his words at face value indicate. He is also informing us about the implicit principles that guide his life and about how he organizes reality. He indicates something of his scope, his energy, his conventionality. Conclusions about such characteristics can be reached by attending not only to what is said but to how it is said. They can confidently be reached only from attending to a great deal of what a person has said, considered together. (3) What each family member says takes part of its meaning from what the other family members say.

These assumptions have guided the way we have handled the data. The essential procedure can be described as "movement"—of which there are three kinds. We have moved freely back and forth from one type of data to another, evaluating what each person has said on each instrument, utilizing it with whatever skill and understanding we could bring to bear. It was not part of our purpose to compare the various types of data.

We have moved back and forth from one family member's material to another's, looking for meanings in both that connect them to each other. Each member in succession was taken as a point of reference; examining every other member's view of him—as well as his view of himself—we then attempted to follow out the consequences of these congruences and incongruences of image. From any particular congruence, for example, we tried to describe how members were brought together or driven apart; what kinds of overt familial behavior were fostered and what kinds of feeling were discouraged; how each member defined his place in the family and how he was assigned a place by others. In reading across all the material from a family, we asked such questions as these: Is there a clear family image, or is it diffuse? How does the family set its boundaries? To what sources does it turn for stimulation? What experiences and feelings are urged upon the members and which are shunned? How does the family regulate behavior? What opposition is there between implicit and explicit tendencies? How are the distinctions of age, sex, and birth order being treated in this family?

Finally, we moved back and forth from one family to another, considering each as a unit and asking, What distinguishes this family from others?

Thus, the family as a group is placed in sharper focus, and the characteristics of particular individuals are assimilated to a more inclusive view. At this level of discourse, the various personalities and relationships within the family are expressed in the form of some group tendency. It is then possible to make statements such as: The Lansons provide no overt channels for intensity, which must then be contained in fantasy. The Newbolds demand intensity and assertion, and they react against evidence of its lack. Conclusions such as these are possible only if all the members of the family are studied and only if one family is compared with another.

In setting down the principles according to which the work proceeded, we are nonetheless obliged to say that their utilization cannot be made a matter of precise prescription. On two counts, the application of these principles remains at present beyond the reach of exact method and measurement. First, there is the issue of what the investigator is willing and able to conclude from his data. What he brings to bear and how far he is ready to carry his inference will determine the nature of his conclusions. Second, it is not possible to specify exactly where to look in the data for the answer to any particular question. Scrutiny of our data has taught us that we cannot predict where a person will most clearly and significantly declare himself. Presumably everything that one person says is of a piece, if we knew how to find its shape. In some cases this is easier than in others. But in any case, there is no substitute for sifting and analyzing until the investigator reaches a descriptive interpretation congruent with the data at his disposal.

NOTES

1. This technique is described in R. J. Havighurst, M. Z. Robinson, and M. Dorr, The development of the ideal self in childhood and adolescence, *Journal of Educational Research, 40,* (4), December, 1946.

2. For a systematic account of the nature of TAT data, see William E. Henry, *The analysis of fantasy: The thematic apperception technique in the study of personality.* New York: John Wiley and Sons, 1956.

6

Family Research: A Case for Interviewing Couples

*LINDA A. BENNETT AND
KATHARINE McAVITY*

Question: What kind of wedding did you have?
Answer: It was a traditional wedding.

If this response conjures up visions of Lohengrin's wedding march and a double-ring ceremony, read on for further enlightenment:

Owen: It was a traditional wedding.
Grace: Nontraditional.
Owen: Nontraditional?
Grace: Very nontraditional.
Owen: We made the arrangements. Friends helped us. Grace's parents came and so did mine.
Grace: Actually, everybody came. Just immediate family members. Owen has a lot of relatives, and they couldn't come. It was just a small house. There were about forty people at the wedding, maybe ten or twelve relatives, and the rest were friends. And everyone came in costume—dressed up. And it was like a nice big friendly family party. Which is sort of what we wanted it to be. And I think our relatives were shocked at the time. Everybody came in costume except the relatives; they came in suits. But that was part of the plan.
Owen: Well, not everybody came in costume; about four people came in costume.
Grace: I thought a lot of people did.
Owen: Well, you may think a lot of people did. But I remember four people.
Grace: Well, that's my memory of it.

Anthropologist Linda A. Bennett is Associate Research Professor in the Center for Family Research, Department of Psychiatry and Behavioral Sciences, George Washington University Medical Center. Katherine McAvity, M.S.W., is with the Washington Psychological Center, Washington, D.C.

75

Owen: Three or four or five people came in costume. And that's because they
   wanted to. We didn't tell people to dress up in costume.
Grace: I thought we did.
Owen: We did?
Grace: Yeah.
Owen: Did you go in costume?
Grace: Yeah, I wore a wedding gown. That's a costume.

This conversation is excerpted from an interview with a couple participating in a psychosocial study of alcoholism and family heritage.[1] Had only
the husband or wife been interviewed, a skewed and limited version of the
couple's nuptial event would have been recorded. Instead, a discussion of
differing recollections of the wedding is presented, leading to a fuller and
presumably more accurate depiction of the couple's view of the ceremony.
Our purpose in writing this paper is to demonstrate the advantages of the
joint couple interview in studies of family and kinship, as a means of obtaining shared perceptions of family life or varying perspectives on family
history.

Increasingly, anthropologists are becoming involved in interdisciplinary
studies that have the potential for clinical application, such as the one presented in this chapter. In the process, conventional assumptions about the
conduct of fieldwork are coming under review, and highly specific methodological questions are being raised. Whole volumes are devoted to the
consideration of anthropological research methods. Some authors focus on
the field work experience itself (e.g., Freilich, 1970; Jongmans and Gutkind, 1967; Powdermaker, 1966; Spindler, 1970; Wax, 1971; and Williams, 1967). Others address a wide range of methodological issues in anthropology, from selection of a research problem to the analysis of data
(e.g., Agar, 1980; Edgerton and Langness, 1974; Narroll, 1970; and Pelto,
1970). Still others deal with specific questions of methodology such as research design (Brim and Spain, 1974), use of statistics (Johnson, 1978), collection of data by way of life histories (Langness, 1965), interviews (Spradley, 1979), and participant-observation (Spradley, 1980).

FAMILY RESEARCH AND THE INTERVIEW FORMAT

Anthropology embraces a long-standing tradition of research on the family.
The classic work on cross-cultural patterns of family structure and kinship
terminology is Murdock's 1949 publication, *Social Structure.* Anthropological studies of family and kinship have been carried out in virtually all
culture areas, constituting a bedrock of British social anthropology and occupying a central position in American ethnology.

Morgan's work on consanguinity and affinity in 1871 is the first of a
number of field studies on family and kinship carried out among North
American Indian groups (e.g., Kroeber, 1917—Zuni; Parsons, 1923—La-

guna; Titiev, 1944—Oraibi; Eggan, 1950—Western Pueblos; and Lewis, 1970—Northwest Coast). Similarly, anthropological studies of African societies (e.g., Evans-Pritchard, 1945—Nuer; Fortes, 1949—Tallensi; and Colson, 1958—Plateau Tonga) and of Asian cultural groups (e.g., Geertz, 1961—Java; Freedman, 1970—China; and Potter, 1977—Thailand) explicate family organization and kinship systems.

In reviewing anthropological work on European and urban American societies over the last two decades, we note the proliferation of studies that focus on the family: for example, Greece (Campbell, 1964), Yugoslavia (Filipović, 1958; St. Ehrlich, 1966; Hammel, 1968 and 1972; Rheubottom, 1976; and Burić, 1976), Ireland (Arensberg and Kimball, 1940), England (Bott, 1957 and Firth et al., 1970), Mexico (Lewis, 1959, 1961 and 1964), Black Americans (Stack, 1974), New England (Fischer and Fischer, 1966), South Slavic émigrés in the United States (Simić, 1978 and 1979), Puerto Ricans (Lewis, 1965), and Japanese-Americans (Kiefer, 1974). Alcohol use and abuse among Irish and German families has been studied by Ablon (1980), kinship in American society by Schneider (1968), and intergenerational relationships in American families by Mead (1978). In contrast to studies of whole communities, urban family research is characterized by its focus on individual families as units of study and analysis. This is particularly the case in interview-based research.

Throughout this work, the interview has served as a critical data-gathering tool for anthropologists, especially in collecting genealogies, life histories, and linguistic materials. As we have adopted some of the more formal methods of related academic fields and carried out more of our work in urban contexts, the issue of who to interview becomes highly relevant. For example, the "alcoholism and family heritage" study is a joint venture between anthropology and psychiatry, with contributions from family sociology. As we began the project, we reviewed methodological questions about interviewing in some detail. Marital negotiation of family identity is the central theme of our research; therefore, the couple is the legitimate unit of study. This recognition led to the decision to interview husbands and wives together. Furthermore, we would interview them jointly in every case. Since we intended to compare all families studied along the same dimensions, consistency in data collection would be essential.

While anthropologists, social psychologists, and sociologists have paid considerable attention to the interview process itself,[2] little consideration has been given to the advantages of joint sessions, whatever the social unit under study. In contrast to the widespread acceptance of interviewing spouses together in therapeutic contexts,[3] the couple format is seldom adopted in a consistent fashion in research on family and kinship.

Anthropology provides a few striking exceptions. Bott, for example, interviewed each couple jointly in her study of social networks among twenty London families, but this decision is neither described nor defended. In contrast, the Six Cultures Series project on socialization (Whiting et al., 1966, pp. 75–91) incorporates a "parent interview" which, in fact, is a mother interview. The Maretzkis, who carried out the child rearing project in Okinawa, make this objection: "The major shortcoming of the Field Guide for the Study of Socialization is that it outlines only a mother interview and neglects a corresponding interview with the father or other primary socializers. We would suggest a separate but similar interview with the father, even though parents may wish to meet jointly for an interview" (Whiting et al., 1966, pp. 84–85). Frankel (1977) conducted couple interviews in her Philadelphia investigation of folk beliefs held by black women at the time of giving birth. Lewis, however, in his extensive interviewing with members of the Sanchez family in Mexico, draws upon individual accounts, "an approach which gives us a cumulative, multifaceted panoramic view of each individual [and] of the family as a whole" (1961, p. xi).

In Britain, Firth et al. relied upon individual interviews in a study of kinship among middle class London families. The field workers were inconsistent in the selection of husbands or wives for interviews covering specific types of information. They do note that "while husbands . . . were used whenever possible as informants, by far the greater proportion of data was obtained from women" (1970, p. 43). Whenever both spouses were interviewed, however, they found instances in which different points of view were expressed regarding their interest in kinship (1970, p. 101). In their New York City project on kinship and casework, Leichter and Mitchell (1967) intentionally chose to interview the wife to obtain certain types of information and the husband for other material. Even though they state that "interview data were obtained from both spouses whenever possible" (p. 315), it is not clear which interview data were so collected. Apparently, no couples were interviewed jointly.

Family sociology provides further examples of inconsistent collection of data from husbands and wives. Hill (1949) conducted research on families' response to the crisis of wartime separation and reunion. Expediency influenced the choice of respondents, since some of the husbands were still in military service at the time of the study. A two-hour interview was held with each wife; each husband, if available, was interviewed separately. In Hill et al.'s (1970) three-generation study of financial planning and consumer behavior in families, the choice of interviewees to represent the family is addressed more explicitly. Four interviews were conducted with each family: three held individually with the wife (who was considered to be the best spokesperson for the family, and the most accessible), and one held jointly with husband and wife. Young and Willmott (1957, p. 207) note their desire to interview husbands and wives separately in their East London family and kinship study, but found it difficult to conduct the individual sessions as planned. They arranged their schedule to see the husbands during the evening, but found that wives were nearly always present in the home when the husbands were interviewed. Nor were they always successful in getting husbands to participate, and some of their families were represented only by the wife.

Since interviews with one spouse are generally assumed to be the "normal" data collection procedure, there are few references to interviewing couples in the family and kinship literature. One exception is LaRossa (1977), a sociologist, who conducted a series of in-depth joint interviews with couples expecting their first child. He uses the joint session format in an attempt to gather data about the "mutually understood conceptions" of husband and wife. Similarly, sociologist Allen (1979) adopted this format for a study of patterns of sociability in British families. Collings and Nelson (1966), psychologists, discuss the relative merits of joint versus individual interviewing of spouses in regard to their research on the marital relationship of spouses, where one spouse is in treatment for mental illness. In a study of domestic violence, sociologist Gelles (1974) cites the potential for disruption of the session and accelerated marital conflict following the interview as his rationale for interviewing only wives.

In this paper we draw upon data forthcoming from a study of alcoholism and family heritage to demonstrate the advantages of the joint session and recommend some guidelies for successful research interviewing with couples. We argue that difficulties likely to be encountered by anthropologists and other researchers in conducting these sessions can be overcome with skillful and sensitive interviewing techniques.

ALCOHOLISM AND FAMILY HERITAGE STUDY

Conducted under a grant from the National Institute on Alcohol Abuse and Alcoholism, this research project is designed to explore alcoholism transmission over generations of families in the United States. In North American and western European societies, approximately one-third of alcoholics has an alcoholic parent (Cotton, 1979). Our work attempts to explain why some families evidence intergenerational recurrence of alcoholism while others do not, and why some children who have grown up in a family with an alcoholic parent develop drinking problems themselves while their siblings do not. We focus on family rituals—such as dinner time and holidays—and the impact of parental alcohol abuse behavior on those areas of family life. In addition, we explore the quality of relationships within the nuclear and extended family—the ethnic, religious, and family culture in the origin and present families of now-married children and their spouses, and the patterns of alcohol use and abuse over four generations of each family under study.

With a view to accounting for transmission of alcoholism from the parental generation to particular married children, we study the recollections of childhood experience reported by each interviewed child and his/her spouse, and the couple's perceptions regarding adult married life. This approach permits us to consider both origin family and present nuclear family development as potentially influencing the continuity or discontinuity of family pathology. Children from troubled families vary in their responses to the problems posed by a parent's abusive drinking, and they exhibit a variety of strategies for establishing their own families, from repeating to repudiating the model of the origin family.

For this study, begun in 1977, we have interviewed two or more grown siblings and their spouses from thirty extended families where at least one parent was alcoholic (see diagram). Sixty-eight couples have participated. Families volunteering to be interviewed live in the metropolitan areas of Washington, D.C.; Baltimore; Minneapolis-St. Paul; and Philadelphia, and in rural areas and small towns located in Virginia, Maryland, Delaware, Pennsylvania, and Tennessee. They were recruited through advertising, or referred by physicians and alcohol treatment counselors. A majority of the couples interviewed has one or two offspring and one-fifth is childless. For most of the couples interviewed (60) this is their first marriage. The average length of marriage is 11 years.

THE COUPLE INTERVIEW: PLAN AND PROCESS

Interview sessions usually took place in the couple's home and were relatively informal in tone. In a previously held interview with each spouse, they had been asked to read and sign a contract stipulating the rights and responsibilities of the participant and the research institution, following

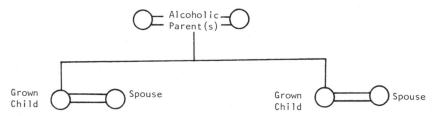

DIAGRAM 1. A Sample Family. The study group of 30 extended families is highly heterogeneous in terms of social and demographic characteristics. Ethnically, the families are predominantly German, Irish, English, Scots, or mainstream American (that is, they have been in the United States for so many generations that they have acquired a generalized "American" identity and have retained no specific ethnicity) according to self-ascription by interviewed children. Of the 30, 14 families were identified with a Roman Catholic parish, 14 families with a Protestant congregation, and 2 had no religious affiliation when the children were growing up. The mean age of the married children is 33 years.

federal regulations for Health and Human Services-funded research projects. In this session we repeated the assurance of confidentiality and explained that we would tape record the interview in order to obtain a verbatim transcript of the couple's dialogue.

The material covered was similar in subject matter and parallel in organization to that collected earlier in the individual sessions that focused on the husband's and wife's families of origin. After soliciting basic demographic information, we attempted to determine the structure and affective qualities of life in this nuclear family. We began with the history of courtship and description of the couple's wedding, then inquired about their relationship with each other and with their children. Extended family ties were explored in some detail: relationships with the couple's parents, siblings, and other relatives; the role non-nuclear family members play in the socialization of their children; and family mythology shared by the couple and being passed on to their offspring. The couple was asked to describe their drinking patterns over the years, and an alcoholic spouse's drinking history was probed extensively. In addition to details regarding the amount and frequency of alcohol consumed, special emphasis was placed on the consequences of a husband's or wife's abusive drinking. For example, what feedback did he/she experience at home or in the workplace? What family activities were most altered during intoxication?

We then posed questions that reflect our interest in family rituals and their continuity over generations. One area of ritual performance common to nearly all families is dinner time or the main meal of the day. We asked about their routines, their roles, any evidence of change in dinner customs over time, and the effect of alcohol abuse behavior on the families' meals. Another topic of investigation was holiday celebration. Again, we aimed for a description of current family traditions around the holiday occasions they identify as most important, a profile of their roles and routines, indications of fluctuation in the celebration from year to year, and assessment of the part played by the alcohol.

Last, we obtained information about the way family life was functionally organized in the home. Who takes which domestic roles and which financial and social planning responsibilities for the family?

This interview sequence is intentional. We begin with the least sensitive information, proceed to more emotional material—especially regarding the drinking and marital relationship—and conclude on a more neutral note.

In the session itself, we began with directions to the husband and wife jointly: "Either of you may answer any of the questions. If we hear from only one of you and the other doesn't answer, we'll assume that you're in agreement. So, if you don't agree, please let us know." The phrasing of our questions followed, but did not precisely duplicate the questions as they were formulated in the interview schedule. We would shift our attention from one spouse to the other, often focusing on the less talkative partner if no answers were forthcoming. We might ask if he/she saw things the same way as the more articulate spouse had described them, but only if more subtle, nonverbal cues provoked no response. In case of verbal disagreement, we allowed the couple considerable latitude for conversational back-and-forth before intervening. Such intervention took the form of a simple acknowledgment that the couple had failed to reach consensus on a particular issue.

As research interviewers, we generally took a neutral position: the subject's response was sometimes restated, but interpretations and evaluations were not made. If answers were incomplete, inadequate or contradictory, follow-up questions were posed only to amplify pertinent material, not to pursue new avenues of inquiry outside the scope of the research.

To conclude the questioning, we would ask if there was anything important that had been missed in respect to family history and family life: Couples' responses to this final initiative fall into three categories: "no," with some surprise at the extent of the material that had been covered in the interview; "yes," with the disclosure of additional evidence about the family that had no obvious relevance to the research questions (e.g., revelation of a family secret, such as an out-of-wedlock pregnancy); or "yes," with the interviewee offering supporting data about the family that was relevant to the study. This often took the form of "now I've figured out what you're after, so I can tell you something."

We ended the interviews in different ways, depending on each couple's needs. In every instance, we expressed appreciation for the couple's participation. If the session was emotionally stressful for either or both partners, this difficulty was acknowledged. When appropriate, we expressed our willingness to make referrals for counseling or alcoholism treatment. Formal follow-up in all cases consisted of brief notes of thanks sent to the participants, stating our intent to provide them with articles published from the study.

The sensitive nature of our project suggests that some interviewees hoped to obtain therapeutic benefit from their participation. Collings and Nelson report similar expectations on the part of subjects in a study investigating mental disorder in married couples (1966). In our experience, positive feedback from couples indicated that there was a quasitherapeutic aspect to the interview process. This effect probably resides more in the interviewee's perception of the research situation as a safe place for self-disclosure than in specific interventions by the interviewers.

ADVANTAGES OF THE COUPLE FORMAT

The couple interview generates *expanded information*. Such expansion, in turn, may lead to the *validation of agreement between husband and wife*, or result in the *clarification of differences*. We have not tested our thesis experimentally by posing the same questions to participants singly and then together with their spouses. However, we have collected both individual and couple interview data with each participating child and spouse covering parallel topics regarding origin family and the nuclear family experiences. On the basis of these two sessions, we observe that those interviewees who provide limited answers in the individual session become more forthcoming and involved in the couple interview. For example, many of the responses made by Peter Martin in his individual session have an air of finality:

Interviewer: Have you been given anything by anyone in the family that has special value to you?
Peter: No.
Interviewer: Were your mother's parents well known in their community, as far as you could tell?
Peter: As far as I could tell, yes.

Such responses force the researcher to take a more active role in formulating follow-up questions to obtain a fuller sense of what lies behind the immediate reply. Peter made a notable shift in the extent of his engagement from the individual to the couple session. The interchange with his wife replaced the need for the interviewer to extract further information.

Excerpts from interviews with two sisters and their spouses illustrate this process at work. Sandra and Peter Martin and Janet and Larry Jennings are in their early 30's and each couple has a young son. The Martins and the Jenningses have experienced marital problems in recent years, and the Jenningses were separated at one time. In the case of the Martins, Peter's drinking has become an issue of concern; he shows signs of developing a serious dependence on alcohol. There are no alcohol problems among the other three spouses: Sandra is an abstainer and Janet and Larry are moderate drinkers. All four are college-educated and work in professional positions in the Washington, D.C. area.

The expansion of information takes three distinct forms in the couple interview sessions: (1) the elaboration and clarification of the factual (objective) information being presented; (2) the elaboration from the initial factual responses toward more symbolic and emotional (subjective) material; and (3) the disclosure of more sensitive information that might not have been revealed if only one spouse had been interviewed. Many instances of *elaboration and clarification of objective information* occurred in our interviews:

Interviewer: What do you [Larry]call Janet's parents?
Janet: "Hey, you."
Larry: That's terrible. We've been married for nine years and normally I avoid calling them anything. They want me to call them Gerald

and Maggie, their first names, and that's what I normally call them
if I call them anything.

The back-and-forth nature of these interviews encourages further exploration, rather than the brief one-line or one-idea responses that occur so
frequently in individual interviews (Allen, 1980). In case after case, we noted
that the resulting dialogue not only unfolded naturally, but was also highly
relevant to the topic at hand. In the couple format, the interviewer is under
considerably less pressure to "pull out" pertinent information than he is in
individual session. Many reticent interviewees become more expressive as
they become accustomed to the setting. The presence of the other spouse
can stimulate greater involvement subtly or by demand, as when one spouse
commands the other to divulge more information or present his/her own
point of view (LaRossa 1978).

Further, when couples have the opportunity for discussion together, their
initial representation of "the facts" often leads to the presentation of more
symbolic and emotional material.

Interviewer: What kind of impact, if any, has Peter's drinking had upon your
dinner time?

Sandra: Friday night, for instance, I had a steak dinner made. He called at
five o'clock and said he was asking my permission to go out
drinking. And I said, "if you're looking for my permission, you're
not going to get it. But I can't stop you." And I'm panicking inside
because I've had all these negative experiences lately, and I'm kind
of on the edge of hysteria and I'm saying, "but, but, but I'm so
glad you called because I know one of the reasons you don't call
is because you know I disapprove. So I just ask that you would
tell me what time you would be home, please don't drink and
drive." and he said, "Well, I'll be home by eight o'clock." And I
said, "If you're going to be later, will you call?" And he said he
would. So I kept dinner, and he wasn't home. He finally got home
about one or one thirty. So our dinner hour has been disrupted.

Interviewer: How unusual is that, to happen around dinner time?

Sandra: Recently, pretty often. And I've repressed a lot of it. I don't know
what time you actually came in last Friday.

Peter: That's because you were on the phone for two hours.

Sandra: I had to talk to my support system

Peter: I would say that you missed the phone call.

Sandra: Yeah, but I don't feel that I had to miss a phone call. I think if I
wasn't there for one phone call there would have been an appropriate time to try another. So that's where I'm coming from. When
you were bowling with that league, that would be an unspoken
thing—that you weren't coming home for dinner those nights.

Peter: Well, I wouldn't get home until like seven o'clock anyway.

Sandra: So that might have been just a night when I might have been taking a class. We tried to coordinate things like that. I don't remember that being a problem then.

Interviewer: It's been more recent that . . .

Sandra: That's what I'm concerned about. That I see as neglect.

Interviewer: Is there anything that's still an unpleasant thing for the two of you to deal with? That you hope changes?

Janet: Yeah, the past. I was very much involved with somebody else. That's very unpleasant. More so for Larry. It's not so bad I guess now as it was because . . .

Larry: No, it still bothers me.

Janet: It bothers him, but it's not something . . . it's something . . . it's something we can talk about now. Whereas before it was something that we only yelled at each other about.

Larry: I think the thing is with something like that, though, it's not that you blame a person for doing that. But you feel it was your fault. Or I felt it was my fault, and that something's wrong with me.

Janet: But once you have become uninvolved and you find that little spark of whatever it was when we first got married, it's suddenly coming back to you. And it makes it a lot easier. And I live with the guilt and he lives with the—

Larry: Frustration.

Janet: The frustration of what happened, so you know, one is just as bad as the other. It's something we've worked out.

Finally, sensitive information may eventually be disclosed for the first time, including perceptions that might not have been expressed had only one spouse been interviewed.

Interviewer: Would you describe your relationship over the years, touching on the best times and the more difficult times?

Sandra: I would say that Peter and I get along very well. The area of greatest tension between us is what I call his overdosing in sports . . . I think socially we're pretty compatible, sexually we're pretty compatible, very compatible. We don't agree about discipline of our child. He thinks I'm too casual, and I think he's too strict.

Interviewer: Do you want to say anything more about the relationship?

Peter: Well, it's pretty even for the most part. Steady.

Sandra: We had a little turbulence.

Peter: On financing.

Sandra: Peter, you shock me. I don't see that as a problem.

Peter: One half wants to spend all the money.

Frequently, the verbal expansion consists of the validation by one spouse of what the other just said (Allen, 1980). Spouses who are basically in agreement, such as Janet and Larry, corroborate each other's point of view repeatedly:

Interviewer: How did you feel about your pregnancy?

Janet: Oh, I was, we were both happy about it.

Larry: I felt very happy.

Janet: But it took me—it wasn't one of these things that just happened. I had quite a hard time getting pregnant; so once I finally did, I was just ecstatic about it.

> *Interviewer:* Would the two of you do more drinking at Christmas time than other times of the year?
> *Larry:*   I don't think so. The only difference might be wine before the Christmas meal.
> *Janet:*   Yeah, the holiday meals we usually have wine or something with the dinner, but that's not something we do any other time.
> *Larry:*   I think that would be the only difference.

Couples such as Janet and Larry are "high agreement" couples. As interviewers, we feel greater confidence that they do, in fact, agree on a given topic when they confirm their accord in the session.

For other couples, expanded discussion concluded in the clarification of differences, as couples agree that they disagree on a particular issue or area of family life:

> *Interviewer:* How have the things you wanted at the time of your marriage worked out?
> *Peter:*   Giving space, we haven't really done that. Well, to a certain degree, we have. She says I do more than I should, and I say there's other people doing a whole lot more. I know people who bowl five or six times a week, and I bowl once.
> *Sandra:*   But he has twice.
> *Peter:*   I bowl up to twice a week.
> *Sandra:*   So, in that respect I feel that I give him a lot more space. I would say Peter gives me a lot of space to be my own person. And even, like with the religious business, Peter's not interested. But he doesn't ever give me any vibes that he thinks I'm crazy or I should pursue this. I'd say that area of space we need to work on. We don't agree, as it's been obvious in this conversation.

> *Interviewer:* What times do you feel closest, most like a family?
> *Sandra:*   Not much.
> *Peter:*   Ocean City.
> *Sandra:*   Yeah, that was really kind of an eye-opener for me because that's the first time we'd really taken a family vacation together. That was this summer. Yeah, we did go last summer, but Jimmy was too little. Like, then I was up at the condominium most of the time.
> *Peter:*   At the swimming pool.
> *Sandra:*   Yeah, or over at the swimming pool because he didn't like the sand. We went to Disney World this winter and I thoroughly enjoyed that, and that was fun. But on a consistent basis, nothing.

Such couples are often at odds over any number of issues. When their discord is openly acknowledged in the couple session, we can then comprehend the extent to which the couple maintains or lacks a shared perspective on the questions under study. This opportunity for clarification by the couples themselves—rather than ex *post facto* analysis of two individuals' interview transcripts by the researcher—is a primary justification for the couple format.

GUIDELINES FOR CONDUCTING COUPLE INTERVIEWS

Husbands and wives—once they have agreed to participate, and have developed some measure of rapport with the anthropologist or any other type of researcher—are better prepared to deal with the potential stress of the joint interview situation and more willing to answer fully and openly than many anthropologists would anticipate. We state this so boldly only because we approached couple interviewing with considerable trepidation, and developed a more optimistic view after a great deal of positive firsthand experience.

We acknowledge certain serendipitous features of our research situation that more than likely contributed to the couple's positive response to their interviews. First, spouses had each been interviewed individually in advance of the couple session, contributing to familiarity and perhaps a sense of trust in the researchers. Second, we had the good fortune to be able to conduct most of the sessions as cointerviewers. As we have noted, cointerviewing provided us the enviable opportunity for debriefing together after some sensitive sessions. We were congruent in our interviewing styles and felt entirely comfortable with sharing responsibility for the sessions, one adding questions while the other paused, and assisting each other in developing alternative strategies for exploring certain issues within the session. We presented ourselves as sympathetic researchers who knew the alcoholism field well and who had the expertise to refer couples to clinical sources, but made it clear that we were not there to do therapy of any kind. On the other hand, a number of our couple sessions were conducted by one interviewer, with no marked differences in process or in the data collected.

Thorough preparation is the best insurance toward establishing rapport and obtaining the desired information in these sorts of interviews. We offer these guidelines for conducting couple interviews:[4]

1. Know your underlying research questions and keep them squarely in mind throughout the interview. This may appear to be simplistic advice, but it is easy to get caught up in the dynamics of the session and forget. In our research, some issues were fundamental: "How similar or different is this nuclear family from either of the families of orientation?" and "How much has alcohol abuse intruded upon ritual performance in any of these families?" Though we had any number of questions in mind, we knew that in the analysis of interview data we would want to answer the crucial question about the carry-over of heritage from the origin families into the present generation, and to document the impact of drinking upon estab-

lished family rituals. Given the limited time and the sensitive situations in which we found ourselves, it was essential to establish a "mind set" that kept the primary research objectives in focus.

2. Become confident in the techniques of interviewing so that attention can also be paid to the dynamics of the session. Our interview schedule provided a moderate amount of structure, not simply to make the data more comparable across families, but to free the interviewer to attend to the couple's interactional process. For example, the researcher needs to have alternative ways to obtain information. When an initial question is misunderstood, ignored or resisted, back-up questions must be quickly devised. Moreover, a variety of strategies can be employed to encourage full responses, such as sustained pauses, partial restatement, or rephrasing of the initial probe.

In general, the goal is to facilitate the couple's dialogue with each other. We occasionally directed questions to the less talkative spouse, or asked for confirmation of a wife/husband's earlier answer to give the opportunity for amplification or the emergence of a slightly different point of view. Throughout the session, it is best if the researcher maintains an attitude of emphatic detachment, remaining neutral when spouses argue and resisting the impulse to provide answers or supply interpretations.

3. Set forth clearly the ground rules for the couple interview. If the objective is to hear from both husband and wife, it is important that neither be permitted to dominate the other. We began our sessions by noting that either spouse could answer any of the questions, but instructed them to let us know if they were not in accord with the response provided by their partner. We found that couples—whether they were in rural Virginia or Delaware or in urban Washington or Minneapolis—readily understood this instruction and took it to heart. There were many laughing acknowledgments that such disagreements would probably occur in the course of the session. We found couples' willingness to "agree to disagree" quite striking, and attribute this in part to our ability to tolerate verbal conflict.

4. Consider carefully the procedural aspects of couple interviewing. If at all possible, conduct the interview in the couple's home to maximize their comfort with the situation. Give them an estimate of the length of the session when the appointment is made. Upon arrival, make yourself at home without being intrusive. Tape the sessions whenever possible, since it is exceedingly difficult to keep up with the pace of a joint session through notes alone and since it is essential to focus your attention on the interview process and content.

5. Do not communicate ambivalence about your role as researcher or some couples will expect you to make clinical interpretations and interventions. Keep to the primary objective of collecting data during the interview, and deal with requests for treatment referral at the close of the session.

CONCLUDING REMARKS

The couple interview format is not suitable for all research objectives, nor is it workable in all situations. The desire to establish an alliance with one representative of a couple or a family, toward achieving greater rapport with that specific person, may dictate against the couple interview. Expediency may also be a consideration, if the anthropologist lacks the scheduling flexibility that is necessary when gathering data from husband and wife together.

This paper focuses on a specific research problem but raises a more fundamental issue: the logical selection of individuals to represent a group under study. Whatever the unit of research—the family, a school, a hospital, a community, an ethnic group—care should be taken in the choice of participants for field research and in the consistent application of an interview format. In research on the family, we urge researchers to consider the joint format whenever they seek information from married persons and whenever the following circumstances apply: when the topic at hand deserves— or demands—a contribution from more than one individual and when the question under study requires direct personal disclosure (LaRossa, 1978). These are situations in which one person cannot legitimately represent or assume to represent what another thinks or believes to be true.

In addition to the family heritage and alcoholism study, we have adopted the couple interview format for other research projects. In a current study of the consequences to young children of growing up in alcoholic families, the parents participate as couples in both structured and open-ended, unstructured sessions. Also, the couple format has been used in a study of Serbian-American families, with a focus on the negotiation and maintenance of their ethnic identity over generations.

We recommend the couple interview for the ease with which it can be combined with other research methods (such as individual interviews, participant-observation, projective tests, and questionaires) to confirm and expand information collected by other means. Furthermore, the technique of interviewing couples can be varied from structured to highly unstructured to fit the stipulations of the research design.

In essence, the joint interview permits and encourages spouses to portray themselves as a couple. Our opening excerpt illustrates this dynamic at work. Following the extended discussion of the "traditional" wedding, Grace and Owen describe their dinner time:

> *Interviewer:* What kinds of things do you talk about at the dinner table?
> *Grace:*   Work, work stories.
> *Owen:*   Work stories, customers, hoping it will snow, or . . .
> *Grace:*   . . . going skiing . . .
> *Owen:*   . . . talk about the dog; it's next to the yard.

Grace:	Pretty mundane things.
Owen:	Or we talk about the move sometimes.
Grace:	Oh, we talk about Wayne and Helen and the latest . . .
Owen:	. . . or friends.
Grace:	Gossip.

Interviewer:	Does anybody tend to dominate the conversation?
Grace:	I don't think so.
Owen:	No, definitely not.
Grace:	I don't dominate it, I don't think so.
Owen:	No, nobody does.
Grace:	No, it's a pretty well shared thing, coversation-wise.

In the course of their dialogue, Grace and Owen negotiate a sense of their own reality (Allan, 1980). Whether the inquiry is along substantive lines such as the impact of alcohol abuse behavior or the minor details of domestic life, the couple's conversational exchanges represent "the way we are." At its best, the couple interview is much the same—a "pretty well shared thing."

SUMMARY

The decision to interview husband and wife together is made infrequently in research on the family. Even when the couple interview is adopted, it is rarely used consistently throughout a study. The authors propose that the joint interview format is a productive means of gathering information from spouses when a goal of the research is to obtain a shared account of family culture. In the course of a couple's dialogue, objective information is clarified and expanded upon, and sensitive material is disclosed. Spouses present their perspective as a couple, which may differ from their individual accounts of the issues being studied. Data from a psychosocial study of the intergenerational transmission of alcoholism in American families is used to document the use of this procedure. Guidelines for conducting interviews with couples are proposed. The broader issue raised by this paper is the logical selection of individuals to represent a group under study. Whatever the unit of research—the family, a school, a hospital, a community, an ethnic group—care should be taken in the choice of participants for field research and in the consistent application of an interview format.

ACKNOWLEDGMENTS

The work upon which this publication is based is supported by a grant from the National Institute on Alcohol Abuse and Alcoholism (#2 RO1 AA 01454). The authors acknowledge the contribution of their colleague, Steven J. Wolin, M.D., principal investigator on the Alcoholism and Family Heritage Study, who provided a clinical perspective for the writing of this paper. They also express their thanks to Barbara Frankel, Richard Gelles, Ralph LaRossa, and Alvin Wolfe for their constructive comments. Earlier versions of the paper were presented at the Preconference Theory Development and Methodology Workshop of the National Council on Family Relations meetings, Philadelphia, 1978, and at the Society for Applied Anthropology meetings, Edinburgh, Scotland, 1981.

Linda A. Bennett, an anthropologist, is associate research professor in the Department of Psychiatry and Behavioral Sciences, George Washington University Medical Center and is coprincipal investigator on the Alcoholism and Family Heritage Study. Katharine McAvity, formerly research assistant on the project, was the family recruiter and cointerviewer.

NOTES

1. Like all other interviewee names referred to in this paper, Grace and Owen are pseudonyms.
2. Examples of those anthropologists who have discussed the interview process in respect to ethnographic research include Agar, 1980; Bott, 1957; Langness, 1965; Nadel, 1939; Paul, 1953; Pelto, 1970; Spradley, 1979; and Williams, 1967. Cannell and Kahn, 1967, Merton, Fiske, and Kendall, 1956, and Maccoby and Maccoby, 1954, sociologists and social psychologists, present extensive reviews of interviewing in social science.
3. Among the many people who have written about interviewing couples in clinical contexts are Belville, Raths, and Belville, 1975; Couch, 1969; Leslie, 1964; O'Connor, 1975; Sager, 1967; Satir, 1967; Skidmore and Garrett, 1955; Watson, 1963; and Weisberg, 1964.
4. While some of these guidelines also apply to interviewing in general, their importance and usefulness is heightened when interviewing spouses together.

REFERENCES

Ablon, Joan. The significance of cultural patterning for the "alcoholic family." *Family Process,* 1980, *19,* 127–144.

Agar, Michael H. *The professional stranger: An informal introduction to ethnography.* New York: Academic Press, Inc., 1980.

Allan, Graham. *The sociology of friendship and kinship.* London: George Allen and Unwin, 1979.

Allan, Graham. A note on interviewing spouses together. *Journal of Marriage and the Family,* 1980, *42,* 205–210.

Arensberg, Conrad M., and Kimball, S. T., *Family and community in Ireland.* New York: Macmillan, 1940.

Belville, V. P., Raths, O. N., and Belville, C. J., Conjoint marriage therapy with a husband and wife team. *American Journal of Orthopsychiatry,* 1969, *39,* 473–483.

Bott, Elizabeth. *Family and social network: Roles, norms, and external relationships in ordinary urban families.* London: Tavistock Institute of Human Relations, 1957.

Brim, John A., and Spain, David H. *Research design in anthropology.* New York: Holt, Rinehart, and Winston, 1974.

Burić, Olivera. The Zadruga and the contemporary family in Yugoslavia. In Robert F. Byrnes (Ed.), *Communal families in the Balkans: The Zadruga*. Notre Dame: University of Notre Dame Press, 1976.

Campbell, J. K. *Honour, family and patronage*. Oxford: Clarendon Press, 1964.

Cannell, Charles F., and Kahn, Robert L. Interviewing. In Gardner Lindzey and Elliot Aronson (Eds.), *The handbook of social psychology*, Reading, Massachusetts: Addison-Wesley Publishing Co., 1968.

Collings, J., and Nelson, B. Interviewing the married couple: Some research aspects and therapeutic implications. *British Journal of Psychiatric Social Work*, 1966, 8, 46–51.

Colson, Elizabeth. *Marriage and the family among the Plateau Tonga*. Manchester: Manchester University Press, 1958.

Cotton, Nancy S. The familial incidence of alcoholism; a review. *Journal of Studies on Alcohol*, 1979, 40(1), 89–116.

Couch, E. H. *Joint and family interviews in the treatment of marital problems*. New York: Family Service Association of America, 1969.

Edgerton, Robert B., and Langness, L. L. *Methods and styles in the study of culture*. San Francisco: Chandler and Sharp, 1974.

Eggan, Fred. *Social organization of the western Pueblos*. Chicago: University of Chicago Press, 1950.

Evans-Pritchard, E. E. *Some aspects of marriage and the family among the Nuer*. Livingstone: Rhodes-Livingstone Papers 11, 1945.

Filipović, Milenko S. Vicarious paternity among Serbs and Croats. *Southwestern Journal of Anthropology*, 1958, 14, 156–167.

Firth, Raymond, Hubert, Jane, and Forge, Anthony. *Families and their relatives: Kinship in a middleclass sector of London*. New York: Humanities Press, 1970.

Fischer, John L. and Fischer, Ann. *The New Englanders of Orchard Town, U.S.A.* New York: John Wiley and Sons, 1966.

Fortes, Meyer. *The web of kinship among the Tallensi*. London: Oxford University Press for the International African Institute, 1949.

Frankel, Barbara. *Childbirth in the ghetto: Folk beliefs of Negro women in a North Philadelphia hospital ward*. San Francisco: R and E Research Associates, 1977.

Freedman, Maurice (Ed.). *Family and kinship in Chinese society*. Stanford: Stanford University Press, 1970.

Freilich, Morris. *Marginal natives: Anthropologists at work*. New York: Harper and Row, 1970.

Geertz, Hildred. *The Javanese family: A study of kinship and social organization*. New York: Free Press, 1961.

Gelles, Richard J. *The violent home*. Beverly Hills: Sage Publications, 1974.

Hammel, Eugene. *Alternative social structures and ritual relations in the Balkans*. Englewood Cliffs: Prentice-Hall, 1968.

Hammel, Eugene. The Zadruga as process. In Peter Laslett (Ed.), *Household and family in past time*. Cambridge: Cambridge University Press, 1972.

Hill, Reuben. *Families under stress*. New York: Harper and Row, 1949.

Hill, Reuben, et al. *Family development in three generations*. Cambridge, Massachusetts: Schenkman Publishing Co., Inc. 1970.

Johnson, Allen W. *Quantification in cultural anthropology*. Stanford: Stanford University Press, 1978.

Jongmans, D. G., and Gutkind, P. C. W. (Eds.). *Anthropologists in the field*. Assen, the Netherlands: Van Gorcum and Company, 1967.

Kiefer, Christie. *Changing cultures, changing lives: An ethnographic study of three generations of Japanese Americans*. San Francisco: Jossey-Bass Publishers, 1974.

Kroeber, A. L. Zuni kin and clan. *Anthropological Papers of the American Museum of Natural History*, 1917, 39–205.

Langness, L. L. *The life history in anthropological science.* New York: Holt, Rinehart, and Winston, 1965.

LaRossa, Ralph. *Conflict and power in marriage: Expecting the first child.* Beverly Hills, California: Sage Publications, 1977.

LaRossa, Ralph. Conjoint marital interviewing as a research strategy. *Case Analysis* 1(2), 1978, 141–149.

Leichter, Hope Jensen, and Mitchell, William E. *Kinship and casework: Family networks and social intervention.* Russell Sage Foundation, 1967.

Leslie, G. R. Conjoint therapy in marriage counseling. *Journal of Marriage and the Family*, 1964, *26*, 65–71.

Lewis, Claudia. *Indian families of the northwest coast.* Chicago: University of Chicago Press, 1970.

Lewis, Oscar. *Five families.* New York: Basic Books, 1959.

Lewis, Oscar. *The children of Sanchez.* New York: Random House, 1961.

Lewis, Oscar. *Pedro Martinez.* New York: Random House, 1964.

Lewis, Oscar. *La Vida: a Puerto Rican family in the culture of poverty—San Juan and New York.* New York: Vintage, 1965.

Maccoby, E. E., and Maccoby, N. The interview: A tool of social science. In Gardner Lindzey (Ed.), *Handbook of social psychology* (Vol. 1), 1954.

Mead, Margaret. *Culture and commitment: The new relationships between the generations in the 1970s.* New York: Columbia University Press, 1978.

Merton, R. K., Fiske, Marjorie, and Kendall, Patricia L. *The focused interview.* Glencoe, Illinois: Free Press, 1956.

Morgan, L. H. *Systems of consanguinity and affinity of the human family.* Washington, D.C.: Smithsonian Contributions to Knowledge (Vol. 17), 1871.

Murdock, G. P. *Social structure.* New York: Macmillan, 1949.

Nadel, S. N. The interview technique in social anthropology. In F. C. Bartlett, et al., *The study of culture.* London: Routledge and Kegan Paul, 1939.

Narroll, Raoul, and Cohen, Ronald (Eds.). *A handbook of method in cultural anthropology.* New York: Columbia University Press, 1970.

O'Connor, P. A. A Model of power and coalition formation in conjoint marriage counseling. *The Family Coordinator*, 1975, *24*, 55–63.

Parsons, Elsie Clews. Laguna genealogies. *Anthropological Papers of the American Museum of Natural History*, 1923, *19*, P. 5.

Paul, Benjamin D. Interview techniques and field relationships. In A. L. Kroeber (Ed.), *Anthropology today.* Chicago: University of Chicago Press, 1953.

Pelto, Pertti J. *Anthropological research: The structure of inquiry.* New York: Harper and Row, 1970.

Potter, Sulamith Heins. *Family life in a northern Thai village.* Berkeley: University of California Press, 1977.

Powdermaker, Hortense. *Stranger and friend.* New York: W. W. Norton, 1966.

Rheubottom, David B. Time and forum: Contemporary Macedonian households and the Zadruga controversy. In Robert F. Byrnes (Ed.), *Communal families in the Balkans: the Zadruga.* Notre Dame: University of Notre Dame Press, 1976.

Sager, C. J. The conjoint session in marriage therapy. *American Journal of Psychoanalysis*, 1967, *27*, 139–146.

Satir, Virginia. *Conjoint family therapy.* Palo Alto: Science and Behavior Books, Inc. 1967.

Schneider, David. *American kinship: A cultural account.* Englewood Cliffs: Prentice-Hall, 1968.

Simić, Andrei. Winners and losers: Aging Yugoslavs in a changing world. In Barbara G. Myerhoff and Andrei Simić (Eds.), *Life's career-aging*. Beverly Hills: Sage Publications, 1978.

Simić, Andrei. White ethnic and Chicano families: Continuity and adaptation in the new world. In Virginia Tufte and Barbara Myerhoff (Eds.), *Changing images of the family*. New Haven: Yale University Press, 1979.

Skidmore, R. A., and Garrett, H. Van Steerer. The joint interview in marriage counseling. *Marriage and Family Living*, 1955, *17*, 349–354.

Spindler, George (Ed.). *Being an anthropologist: Fieldwork in eleven cultures*. New York: Holt, Rinehart, and Winston, 1970.

Spradley, James P. *The ethnographic interview*. New York: Holt, Rinehart, and Winston, 1979.

Spradley, James P. *Participant observation*. New York: Holt, Rinehart, and Winston, 1980.

Stack, Carol B. *All our kin: Strategies for survival in a black community*. New York: Harper and Row, 1974.

St. Erlich, Vera. *Family in transition: A study of 300 Yugoslav villages*. Princeton: Princeton University Press, 1966.

Titiev, Mischa. Old Oraibi. *Papers of the Peabody Museum*, 1944, *22*(1).

Watson, A. S. The conjoint psychotherapy of marriage partners. *American Journal of Orthopsychiatry*, 1963, *33*, 912–922.

Wax, Rosalie. *Doing fieldwork: Warnings and advice*. Chicago: University of Chicago Press, 1971.

Weisberg, M. Joint interviewing with marital partners. *Social Casework*, 1964, *45*, 221–229.

Whiting, John W. M., et al. *Field guide for a study of socialization*. New York: John Wiley and Sons, Inc., 1966.

Whyte, William F. Interviewing in field research. In Richard N. Adams and Jack J. Preiss (Eds.) *Human organization research*. Homewood, Illinois: Dorsey Press, Inc., 1960.

Williams, Thomas Rhys. *Field methods in the study of culture*. New York: Holt, Rinehart, and Winston, 1967.

Young, Michael and Willmott, Peter. *Family and kinship in East London*. London: Routledge and Kegan Paul, 1957.

7

Ethical Dilemmas in Qualitative Family Research

RALPH LaROSSA, LINDA A. BENNETT,
AND RICHARD J. GELLES

This chapter examines and analyzes the major ethical dilemmas in qualitative family research. While the ethical issues of conducting human subject research have previously been discussed and debated in the fields of medicine, social work, psychology, anthropology, and sociology (e.g., Diener and Crandall, 1978; Reynolds, 1979; Wolfensburger, 1967), and while there has been extensive discussion of the ethics of qualitative research (e.g., Barnes, 1963; Becker, 1964b; Cassell, 1978; Douglas, 1979; Jorgensen, 1971; Klockars, 1977; Rynkiewich and Spradley, 1976), there has been virtually no discussion of the ethical problems of conducting qualitative studies of families.

There are two important reasons to devote special attention to the ethics of qualitative family research. First, the private and intimate nature of the family imposes unique constraints and raises distinctive ethical issues for investigators using qualitative methods; and second, although qualitative techniques have been infrequently used in family research (Hodgson and Lewis, 1979; Nye and Bayer, 1963; Ruano *et al.*, 1969), the increased interest in system level analysis (e.g., Kantor and Lehr, 1975) has made it likely that more family studies will be employing qualitative designs (*cf.* Waxler, 1977).

Reprinted by permission from *Journal of Marriage and the Family,* May, 1981, pp. 303–313. Copyrighted 1981 by the National Council on Family Relations, 1219 University Avenue Southeast, Minneapolis, Minnesota 55414.

Ralph LaRossa is Associate Professor of Sociology, Georgia State University, Atlanta. Linda A. Bennett is Associate Research Professor, Center for Family Research, Department of Psychiatry and Behavioral Sciences, George Washington University Medical Center. Richard J. Gelles is Professor of Sociology, University of Rhode Island, and he is on the staff of Children's Hospital Medical Center, Boston.

The ethical dilemmas inherent in the data collection, analysis, and publication strategies of qualitative family research will be reviewed in light of two basic ethical issues that bear on all forms of human subject research: informed consent and the risk-benefit equation.[1] In discussing these dilemmas, we hope to encourage a more responsible approach to qualitative family research as well as to provoke debate on a variety of issues that require serious thought.

ETHICAL ISSUES: INFORMED CONSENT AND THE RISK-BENEFIT EQUATION

Students of the ethics of human subject research generally recognize two basic ethical questions that affect all investigations: (1) Do the subjects in the research fully understand what participation in the project entails and have they given their consent to participate? (2) How do the risks to the subjects involved in the research compare to the potential benefits of the study?

The first question centers on the principle of informed consent, "the cornerstone of all considerations of the welfare and protection of subjects" (Wolfensburger, 1967). In essence, the principle of informed consent requires that sufficient information be conveyed to allow the subjects to make decisions about the risks and potential benefits of participation, and that subjects be told that not only is their initial decision to participate voluntary, but also that they are free to withdraw from the project at any time (Diener and Crandall, 1978).[2]

Although most social scientific research does not place subjects in situations that directly and overtly jeopardize their health and well-being, most social research does involve some risk. Discomfort, anxiety, reduced self-esteem, and revelation of intimate secrets are all possible costs to subjects of becoming involved in a research project. No investigator should think that it is possible to design a risk-free study, nor is this expected of researchers. Rather, the ethics of human subject research require that investigators calculate the risk-benefit equation, or balance the risks of a subject's involvement in the research against the possible benefits of the project (both to the subject and to society).

Ethical Issues and Qualitative Research

The Federal regulations published by the Department of Health, Education, and Welfare have sensitized scientists to potential ethical problems in their research. However, the government guidelines, initially developed to protect subjects from major physical harm, contain an implicit medical and natural science model that makes it difficult, it not impossible, to apply the guidelines to qualitative or ethnographic research (Cassell, 1978). For example, the principle of informed consent assumes an investigator understands and can assess all the risks and possible benefits associated with the project because he or she sees the research in its totality. But qualitative research is conducted more as an *ad hoc* process whereby "the researcher usually does not know everything he is looking for himself when he starts out and structures his study to some extent as he goes along" (Roth, 1962, p. 283). Thus, it is nearly impossible in a qualitative study for a subject to be completely informed about the nature of the research at the outset of the project.

In terms of the risk-benefit equation, it is again assumed that this can be computed at the design stage of the research. However, the ad hoc character of qualitative research also makes calculating the risks and potential benefits of a project very difficult. Moreover, despite recent efforts to describe the range of potential benefits as well as risks of field work (e.g., Cassell, 1978), the assumption that risks and potential benefits can be measured and analyzed is viewed in some circles as "absurd" (Douglas, 1979).[3] While it is epistemologically meaningless to say that trying to balance the pros and cons of a study is hopeless, it is true that the task is more complex in qualitative than in quantitative research. As extreme as it is, Klockars's characterization of the risk-benefit equation in field work is not far from the mark: "When you hear a life historian talking about the benefits of his research outweighing the risks to his subject, somebody either has been, or is about to be, had" (1977, p. 223).

Ethical Issues and Qualitative Family Research

Qualitative researchers have traditionally been aware that there are extraordinary ethical problems in their type of research that warrant discussion outside the confines of methodological appendices. Thus, there are a number of articles devoted exclusively to the special ethical dilemmas in qualitative research. The illustrations used in these articles have, however, generally been from studies of deviancy or communities. None of the articles on the ethics of qualitative research examines the problems associated with doing qualitative studies of families. We see this as a significant oversight because, as we will soon demonstrate, the family setting and the nature of topics typically investigated in family research raise ethical dilemmas for the qualitative researcher that also warrant discussion outside the confines of methodological appendices. The sections that follow are devoted to an examination of the principle of informed consent and the risk-benefit equation in light of the special nature of qualitative family research.

INFORMED CONSENT

Four aspects of the family create special contingencies within which investigators must seek and maintain the informed consent of their subjects: (1) the pervasiveness of family life; (2) the inaccessibility of family life; (3) the physical setting in which qualitative family research is conducted; and (4) the resemblance of qualitative family research to therapy.

The Pervasiveness of Family Life

As briefly noted earlier, one of the most obvious difficulties in applying the DHEW guidelines of informed consent to qualitative research is that qualitative investigators approach their research settings with incomplete knowledge of what will transpire during a study. Rather than having a highly structured work plan, qualitative researchers consciously make an effort to remain flexible and receptive to the unexpected, since the aim of a qualitative study is to generate insights and theories from the data (Glaser and Strauss, 1967). In practice, this means that researchers will often conduct interviews and make observations that are essentially unstructured and nonstandardized.

The general problem of informed consent in qualitative research is more acute in qualitative family research because of the pervasiveness of family life. Since the family is often the hub for most, if not all, other activities in our lives, the range of issues that can emerge in a qualitative study far exceeds the range of issues that can become salient in other types of research. It is not uncommon, for example, for an unstructured interview with a husband and wife to include comments about fellow workers, in-laws, best friends, and so on. Nor is it unusual for seemingly unrelated issues, e.g., pregnancy and violence (Gelles, 1975), to merge during the course of a study. Thus, more than other investigators, a qualitative family researcher cannot know, nor can he or she explain to the subjects at the outset, just who or what will be examined as part of the research.

Many anthropologists and sociologists who engage in qualitative research become members of the groups they are studying. They either become "complete participants," not informing the group of their research, or they "participate as observers," joining the group but making it clear that they are field workers (Gold, 1958). Whether or not they conceal their true identities, as group members they acquire considerable methodological leverage in that they can legitimately "hang around" with their subjects, often for hours, days, or weeks, and get "bombarded" with data.

Such a strategy, taken for granted by most ethnographers, is less frequently available and more constrained in practice to the qualitative family researcher. One can sometimes make arrangements with a family to live in their house (e.g., Henry, 1965; Kantor and Lehr, 1975; Lewis, 1959), but one cannot become an actual member of the family. Thus, not only will the family field worker generally spend less time with a family group than other field workers spend with friendship groups (e.g., Whyte, 1955), religious cults (e.g., Lofland, 1966) and the like, but the qualitative family researcher will also not experience the same emotional or intense involvement in the group as will other researchers who choose the complete participant role.

The inaccessibility of the family partially explains why most qualitative family research involves unstructured interviewing, as opposed to the exclusive or predominant use of the observation method of data collection. Since most family behavior takes place "behind closed doors," in a nonpublic place, the interview remains the most efficient, and often the most feasible, method for the collection of data about families.

On the one hand, the unstructured interview approach means that the family field worker will not have to grapple with the ethical problems of undercover research (e.g., Douglas, 1976). On the other hand, the heavy reliance on interviewing poses ethical problems of its own. Interviewers who are placed in situations where they need to gather important and sensitive data *quickly* may wittingly or unwittingly shift from an interview to an interrogation. Sheehy (1974, pp. 158–160) illustrates this style of questioning.

> Why doesn't Ginny go to law school? Who "won't" let her? Or what is she afraid of?
> (Couple answers.)
> Suppose that Ginny were to talk about going to law school now?
> (Husband answers.)
> What do you think she would be really good at? As opposed to what it would be convenient (for you) to have her do?
> (Husband answers.)
> Was it threatening to you to have Ginny want to become what you are?
> (Couple answers.)
> Meaning, you can be successful without running away from me?
> (Couple answers.)
> Maybe what Ginny is hearing is the last part. That the major reason you work longer is not to provide her with luxuries, but to elevate yourself to the position where you can handle the more interesting cases?
> (Couple answers.)

Some researchers argue that Sheehy's style of questioning is what in-depth interviewing is all about (e.g., Douglas, 1976). But from the point of view of the principle of informed consent, the central issue is whether a family who divulges information under this kind of "cross-examination" is willingly offering that information or is being coerced. Respondents can, and do, refuse to answer some questions, but the unstructured nature of the interaction and the physical setting of the interview (discussed in the next section), together with other properties of qualitative family research (such as an ongoing relationship between investigator and family that may span several months or years), all combine to reduce the likelihood that such a refusal will occur.

Subject compliance, both in the general case of research and in the case of qualitative family research, is a function of relative powerlessness of the subject vis-à-vis the researcher. As Kelman (1972, p. 992) notes, "the power deficiency of the subject within the research situation derives from the structure of the situation itself, rather than from the subject's position in society or organization." Thus, the Sheehy interview segment reveals that although the husband may have thought, when he consented to be interviewed, that as "the man of the house" he would retain the right to judge the appropriateness of any question, the structure of the interview situation places him in a subordinate position to Ms. Sheehy. This means that, like it or not, he will probably answer the questions addressed to him.

Conjoint Interviewing. Unable to observe families on a day-to-basis, some qualitative researchers have resorted to using conjoint or group interviews to gather behavioral data on family life (e.g., Allan, 1980; Bennett et al., 1978; LaRossa, 1978a). However, as the excerpt from the Sheehy study shows, the ethical issues produced by the inaccessibility of the family are exacerbated by the use of the conjoint interview technique. Subjects in conjoint interviews have less control over what will be said during a session (and, thus, less of an opportunity to exercise "informed consent"). Of course, a family may try to decide before the interviewer arrives which topics are taboo, but the possibility remains that (1) the family will get their signals crossed (e.g., "I misunderstood you, George; I thought you said we *could* talk about our mythical son in front of our guests!"); or, (2) an unanticipated topic will come up during the interview (highly likely in qualitative interviewing), and rather than appear as if they are trying to hide something, the family openly discusses the issue—perhaps to regret it later when the interviewer leaves. A case in point is the husband in one study who, to his expectant wife's surprise and chagrin, decided on his own to bring up the topic of sex (LaRossa, 1978b, p. 11):

> *Husband:*   My physical desires have dramatically lessened but are by no means gone. . . . It's just that I have no overwhelming need to satisfy all the time. I get satisfied in other forms.
> *Interviewer:* How about you? (addressed to the wife).
> *Wife:*   (Obviously annoyed with her husband) Um, I've got nothing further to add (silence).
> *Husband:*   I thought we had to be at least honest and candid with this. . . .

Obviously, the problems of obtaining informed consent in conjoint interviewing can be quite vexing. Does the consent of one spouse "count" for the other? Should the interviewer curtail a line of questioning if one partner appears to be upset about what the other is saying about him/her, or the marriage?

Crisis Interviewing. The inaccessibility of family life has also produced strategies or "tricks" that are intended to make data collection more "efficient" (that is, maximize the amount of "useful" information per transcript page). Perhaps the most widely known strategy is that of studying a family during an actual or fabricated family crisis (Lewis, 1959, p. 18). But, while this strategy has its methodological advantages, there are clearly some ethical problems that need to be considered. During periods of stress and transition, a family is likely to be more vulnerable to the skilled and/or prying investigator. As a result, the vulnerable subjects may divulge more than they might otherwise reveal (Deschin, 1963). Furthermore, families under stress or in crisis may be more receptive to help (either financial or psychological) than less troubled families. This vulnerability can create a power-dependency relationship between field worker and family that is not unlike the unbalanced situation which generally exists between physicians and their subjects in medical research (Kelman, 1972; Cassell, 1978). When the subject is dependent—physically, emotionally, or financially—the informed consent rule stating that the subject should feel free to withdraw at any time is difficult to guarantee.

The Setting of Qualitative Family Research

Qualitative family research is almost always conducted in the home because it is assumed that natural geographic and social milieus provide the richest possible context for the study of family life (Kantor and Lehr, 1975; Henry, 1965). The home is also a popular location because it is often the only setting where an investigator can get a subject to commit a large block of time. But observing a family in their native habitat raises special ethical considerations.

First, by choosing to study a family in their home, the researcher is selecting an informal atmosphere and thus wittingly or unwittingly encouraging friendliness, trust, and self-disclosure (Douglas, 1976, p. 174). Anyone, for example, who has done home research is aware of the extent to which some families will "go all out" for a scheduled interview or observation; cookies, cakes, and coffee—made or purchased especially for the occasion—are not uncommon. It is obvious that the field worker is being treated as a guest as well as a researcher.

The ethical significance of the field worker's double role is that home interviews or observations may lull some families into disclosing more about themselves than they had originally planned. In other words, although the family members may not have intended to discuss certain topics, the ambience of a home setting may generate a "what the heck, we're all friends here" attitude, which may result in unanticipated disclosures.

Second, serendipity is more likely to play a role in home research. An unexpected visit or telephone call by a friend or relative (improbable in the researcher's office or lab and irrelevant in home survey research) can yield information that the family views as unimportant but that the investigator considers highly significant. For example, in one qualitative study, a couple is talking about the kind of relationship they have with the wife's mother when the telephone rings, as if on cue, and we become witnesses to a conversation that documents the paradoxical nature of that relationship (La-Rossa, 1977, pp. 92–93):

Wife:	I don't think my mother is going to butt in much.
Husband:	She will.
Wife:	You think so?
Husband:	In her self-affixing way. But this is something I can say, this is my territory. I can really put my foot down. Although I thought I could do that when it came to my house. I don't dare throw them out. I tell them to shut up. There's nobody else that I've been quiet for.
Telephone:	Ring . . . ring . . .
Husband:	Oh, we were just talking about you! Oh, only complimentary things.
Wife:	It must be my mother (addressed to interviewer).
Husband:	Ha! Ha! Ha! Behind your back is your chair, I'm sure. We have our shrink over here with us—the guy doing the survey on the marriage.
Wife:	The marriage? It's on pregnancy!
Husband:	The pregnancy, that's what it's all about. (pause) Very good. Bye.
Telephone:	Clunk.
Husband:	See how polite I was?
Wife:	Yes.
Husband:	She said, "You're lying. You're not saying nice things."
Wife:	She knows you don't like her.
Husband:	Does she? Why, did she ever tell you that?
Wife:	No, I can tell.

While the above interchange is a good advertisement for the methodological payoff of home research, the ethical question it raises cannot be ignored. Does the curious juxtaposition of the couple's comments and the telephone conversation—what some would call a "lucky break" (Loud with Johnson, 1974, p. 138)—constitute an invasion of privacy? Not only has the wife's mother, without her knowledge or consent, become a participant in the study, but the couple, sidetracked by the telephone call, may have provided more information than they had originally consented to when they agreed to be studied.

The ambience of the home and the serendipitous quality of the setting and interaction thus raise special ethical dilemmas for the qualitative family researcher. Should the field worker take advantage of the ambiguities inherent in this situation (Kelman, 1972)? Is the success of qualitative family research derived from exploiting the situations created by various role clashes, such as insider/outsider or stranger/friend (*cf.* Jarvie, 1969)?

The Resemblance of Qualitative Family Research to Therapy

The telephone conversation reported above reveals that the subjects have alter-cast the researcher as a therapist ("We have our shrink over here . . ."). The remark, stated in jest, could have, as all humor does, a deeper message: Investigators conducting qualitative family research are often perceived as therapists; and the subjects of qualitative family research often feel as if they are in therapy. The reason behind this is that qualitative family research does resemble a clinical diagnosis or assessment. While not employing the 50-minute hour, qualitative interviewers do use the same relatively nondirective form of interviewing to tap sensitive topics that therapists use to diagnose an individual or family problem. Moreover, it is not unusual for the field worker to conduct a series of "sessions" with his or her subjects; for example, the average number of interviews with each family in Bott's (1971) study was 13, with a range of 8 to 19.

If a subject casts the interviewer in the role of therapist, he or she may disclose much more intimate information than would have been forthcoming if the subject saw the interviewer as purely a researcher. Just as the home ambience creates role clashes between friend and researcher, the therapeutic ambience of qualitative family research creates role ambiguities that bear on the issue of informed consent.

This is, in fact, what occurred in Bott's study. Although her original plan was to proceed without an outline and without taking notes during the interview/observation sessions, as time went on, she was forced to abandon this procedure in favor of a more structured format. Both the families and the field workers in the study felt uncomfortable with the "confusion" over whether the field workers were supposed to act like researchers, therapists, or friends. When the interviewers began to use outlines, ask questions about specific issues, and take notes—in other words, when they began to look like researchers—"everyone was relieved" (Bott, 1971, p. 21).

The fact that both the subjects and the field workers felt uncomfortable about the confusion of roles raises the final point of this section. The ethical responsibilities of a project director under the principle of informed consent must be understood to include the research staff as well as the subjects. Without careful planning and supervision, qualitative family research can turn out to be more than the field workers bargained for when they signed on.

THE RISK-BENEFIT EQUATION

A second major ethical issue facing all researchers is an assessment of the risks and potential benefits associated with their research. In principle, if the known risks exceed the potential benefits, the investigation must be substantially altered so that either the risks are minimized or the benefits are increased, or the study should be cancelled.

Because it is difficult, if not sometimes impossible, to fully calculate a risk-benefit equation at the outset of a qualitative study, it is crucial that qualitative researchers understand and attempt to deal with the attendant risks of their studies as the research progresses. The two major risks in qualitative research are public exposure and self-exposure, or more specifically, the difficulty of masking identities and the problem of seeing one's personal life scrutinized and objectified. Two aspects of the family create special contingencies within which qualitative family researchers must achieve and maintain a balanced risk-benefit ratio: (1) the private or secret character of family life, and (2) the importance of family life to self-esteem.

Public Exposure of the Family's Private Life

Nearly all social scientists make commitments to ensure the confidentiality of their data. Researchers conducting quantitative investigations typically inform subjects that confidentiality will be maintained by presenting only statistical summaries of the data in research reports. Qualitative researchers enjoy no such luxury, since the data derived from qualitative studies are generally transformed into case analyses, in which lengthy quotations and descriptions from transcribed interviews or observations are presented.

Because qualitative researchers cannot promise confidentiality through statistical summaries, they must promise and rely on efforts to mask their subjects' identities by using pseudonyms and/or fictitious biographies (e.g., they change the age, occupation, or residence of their subjects in the case reports). However, these disguises are frequently not sufficient. Community researchers learned that a simple name change or oblique geographical reference—"Springdale is located in upper New York State, about twenty-five miles from three different commercial-industrial centers" (Vidich and Bensman, 1958, p. 12)—will not guarantee a town's anonymity. Family researchers should also be aware that although disguising a family may be easier than disguising a community, there have been instances where a family's anonymity was destroyed. For example, a researcher known to the authors was recently involved in a very serious compromising of a family's identity. This individual had carried out a study of family relations in which extremely sensitive material was revealed by a number of subjects. A few years after the study was completed, our colleague was interviewed by a newspaper reporter and, to illustrate a point, provided a brief description of one of the families in the study. In the newspaper story, the reporter identified the researcher, the small town in which the family lived, and some characteristics of the family. The study was conducted in a town of less than 10,000 people, and some of the characteristics of the family were so rare that the family was easily and immediately identified by friends and neighbors reading the news article. A tremendous furor arose, with threats of lawsuits and great damage done to the family members, some of whom had never heard of the episode discussed with the interviewer.

One might argue that this type of problem could be eliminated by having social scientists avoid all contact with representatives from the media. Erikson (1967) points out that the press is ready and able to translate technical reports into news copy and that this compromises social scientists' abilities to protect their subjects. But, avoiding the press is not a solution, since anyone—newspaper reporter, television producer, or neighbor of a subject family—can read professional journals or scholarly monographs. In her study of professional elite families, Harrell-Bond (1976) discovered that despite the care she took to conceal the identities of her 14 case studies, people who personally knew the families were able to recognize the subjects in her pre-publication report. (She decided to resolve the problem by discarding much of the illustrative-descriptive material in the published version of the study.)

Research subjects who are identifiable and identified by others are only one aspect of the public exposure problem that qualitative researchers must deal with. Subjects who publicly reveal themselves are another aspect. LaRossa (1977) found that while he struggled to write up case studies that protected his subjects from discovery, they were telling friends, relatives, and sometimes strangers about their participation in the research (cf. Klockars, 1977).

Although the ethical problem of public exposure affects all qualitative researchers, the private nature of the modern Western family (Laslett, 1973) puts even greater pressure on qualitative family researchers to protect the identity of their subjects. In family research, even the most "innocent" activities may be considered "treasured family secrets" by subjects. Thus, *everything* about a family's private life is potentially embarrassing, should the family's identity be revealed. This means that, in qualitative family research, it is especially imperative the subjects know that public exposure is a possibility (however small). The researcher should also explain to the families the kind of results typically generated by a qualitative study, perhaps by showing the families, in advance, sample case analyses (Becker, 1964b). This explanation would also warn subjects that they may regret having told their relatives and friends about their participation in the research once the study is published, and it would thus reduce the number of subjects who set themselves up for public exposure.

Some qualitative family researchers take a collaborative approach in their studies, permitting and encouraging subjects to coauthor their own case reports (Laslett and Rapoport, 1975). Although this may not be the most valid procedure in all research situations (and hence should not be used indiscriminately), a collaborative approach does reduce, to some degree, the harmful effects of public exposure, since the subjects are given the opportunity to remove potentially embarrassing data.

Self-Exposure and the Importance of Family Life to Self-Esteem

While public exposure is a problem with no simple solutions, there is yet another problem linked to publishing qualitative family research that is more complex. That problem is the exposure of a family to itself. Though the effect of having one's life translated into scientific (or media) jargon is deflating enough when statistical summaries are used (Becker, 1964b), the impact can be devastating when case studies are presented (Fichter and Kolb, 1953).

Obviously, concern over exposing research subjects to themselves through case analysis is not unique to family research. It becomes a particularly potent issue, however, when one considers the investment people have in their families. The fact that the family is a major source of self-esteem makes people all the more sensitive to criticism in this domain of their lives. An example of this is the reaction of Pat Loud, the wife/mother in the television documentary, *An American Family,* to her broadcast case study:

> Oh, no, this is more than I bargained for, I never asked to know this much. It wasn't just a case of truth or lies, or distortion or misinterpretation, or being unfairly treated. It was the enormity of evidence I couldn't bear, as though I'd asked for a little light to see by and been pounded by a thousand suns (Loud with Johnson, 1974, p. 139).

When breadth is sacrificed for depth in qualitative family research (*cf.* Lofland, 1971), virtually anything may become data for presentation. For example, if open-ended or conjoint interviews are used, investigators will probably examine not only what was said, but how it was said. Thus, a variety of nonverbal cues—tone, inflection, cadence, rhythm—will be used to analyze the expressions given and given off (Goffman, 1959). For example:

> *Liz looks matter-of-factly at Peter.* "I don't think Peter would be unfaithful to me."
> *Peter's response is to lean forward and say,* "I guess the thing I value most about our marriage is the combination of love and respect we have for one another." *He hasn't directly answered the question wrapped in Liz's statement. She chooses to ignore that* (O'Brien, 1977, p. 203; our italics).

Families may also be surprised to learn that field workers pay attention to how a family lives:

> The Canwin household is likely to be as cluttered with objects as it is with people. The hallway is typically strewn with clothes, yesterday's or last month's,

forcing people to pick their way, as through a gentle minefield (Kantor and Lehr, 1975, pp. 139–140).

One wonders what the "Canwins" reaction might be if they read this account.

As sensitive as the self-exposure problem is, when qualitative family researchers publish case studies, there is typically little mention of whether the families read or had the opportunity to read the results of the study (but see Piotrkowski, 1978; Rapoport and Rapoport, 1971; and Rubin, 1976). Hess and Handel, for example, emphasize that they told their subjects "that what one member of the family said (in a private session) would in no instance be repeated to any other member of the family" (1959, p. 290). They also told the subject families that the researchers "would not in any way interpret the family to itself" (1959, p. 291). But, suppose the families read the book published by Hess and Handel—would they not learn what others said, and would they not see their lives interpreted?

What was said almost 20 years ago is still true today: "We know almost nothing about the effects of (research) publication, negative or positive" (Barnes, 1963, p. 132).

Self-Exposure during Data Collection. Revelation through prepublication or published reports is the most obvious instance of the risk of self-exposure, but the problems can also arise during data collection. An interview session may sensitize a family to some aspect of their life that will be the subject of discussion long after the field worker has left. In a study in which one of us is presently involved, a husband remarked to the interviewer at the close of one session, "You'll be safe at home in an hour; we'll be up for the rest of the night arguing." This same husband said at the end of the study that on the basis of what he had heard and observed during the interview sessions, he had come to the conclusion that he and his wife needed therapy. Some investigators may feel such a request poses no ethical problem, and in fact one of the potential benefits to subjects of qualitative family research is that families with emotional difficulties will be discovered. But are there not risks associated with implicitly or explicitly suggesting to a family, who viewed themselves as healthy at the start of the research, that they now need help?

This dilemma is undoubtedly one of the most difficult in qualitative family research, and may in fact be "irreducible" (cf. Becker, 1964b). One thing does seem clear, however. Whether or not the field worker (or project director) is a trained therapist, the right to intervene in a family's life should not be assumed (Rubin and Mitchell, 1976). This is not to say that qualitative family researchers should ignore their responsibility to debrief a family at the end of a session and at the end of a study, and to talk with the family about some of the emotional issues that were raised. It does mean, however, that researchers themselves should not be confused by the resemblance of qualitative family research to therapy, and they should not assume that intervention is part and parcel of the research process.

CONCLUSION

Our objective in this paper has been to examine qualitative family research in order to identify and illustrate some of the major ethical problems that arise in this type of investigation. Although qualitative methods have been used with increasing frequency by family researchers, the discussions of ethical dilemmas have, for the most part, been relegated to appendices of published reports or hallway discussions at professional meetings.

At one time, we considered concluding this paper with a "code of ethics." We now believe, however, that a formal code would oversimplify and obscure some of the very complex issues that arise in qualitative family research (cf. Becker, 1964a; Friedson, 1964). Thus, our goal was to help build a more complete understanding of how and why qualitative studies of families are ethically problematic, so that intelligent decisions can be made when investigators find themselves confronted with the humanism versus science paradox.

In terms of informed consent, we see the major problem as one of balancing the need to penetrate the private, pervasive, and emotional back regions of family life against the tempting, and often easy, violation of a family's privacy and hospitality. Because qualitative researchers cannot possibly know where they will go with an interview or observation at the outset, the investigator must be concerned with holding to the informed consent rule, which says that the subject should be allowed to withdraw from the study or delimit an area of discussion at any time.

In establishing a risk-benefit equation, qualitative family researchers must consider the standard risks of human subject research and add to them the risk of public exposure and the delicate problem of exposure of a family to itself. The fact that many people consider their family both a sanctum and their most precious possession is something that qualitative family researchers should never forget and never abuse.

This paper has been but a first attempt to identify and organize the various ethical dilemmas in qualitative family research. Because the ethics of human subject research are an ongoing concern, where researchers are frequently confronted with basically irreconcilable, no-win situations, it is imperative that institutionalized forums for the discussion of research ethics be established and maintained both at professional meetings and in professional newsletters and journals.

SUMMARY

Two basic ethical questions—informed consent and the risk-benefit equation—are examined as they apply to the data collection, analysis, and publication strategies of qualitative family research. Although previous discussions of qualitative research ethics have focused almost exclusively on the difficulties of studying deviant groups or communities, it is our opinion that the distinctive features of family life warrant a special discussion of the ethical dilemmas inherent in the qualitative study of families. The increasingly important role which qualitative methods will play in the analysis of family systems underscores the need for a review of these ethical problems.

NOTES

1. It should be noted that the term risk-benefit equation is by definition asymmetrical. "Risk" implies possibility or probability and thus is not analogous to "benefit," which suggests certain payoffs (May, 1978). We decided to follow convention and use the risk-benefit equation rather than some alternative (e.g., harmbenefit equation) to avoid contradictions between quoted material and the main text of the paper. We do, however, generally refer to "potential benefits," rather than simply "benefits," for symmetry.

2. According to the U.S. Department of Health, Education, and Welfare's *Institutional Guide to DHEW Policy on Protection of Human Subjects* (1971), informed consent consists of six basic elements. Subjects must be given: "(1) A fair explanation of the procedures to be followed, including identification of those which are experimental. (2) A description of the attendent discomforts and risks. (3) A description of the benefits to be expected. (4) A disclosure of appropriate alternative procedures that would be advantageous for the subject. (5) An offer to answer any inquiries concerning procedures. (6) An instruction that the subject is free to withdraw his consent and to discontinue participation in the project or activity at any time."

3. Douglas gives two reasons why he believes that the "rationalistic" approach to the "morality of field research" is meaningless: "It is absurd first because the moral decisions we face in this research differ from those of our everyday, nonresearch lives only in small degree and must be dealt with in the same ways we deal with similar moral problems in the rest of our everyday lives, if they are to be moral and effective. It is absurd secondly because there is no possible way in which we can rationally calculate the costs and benefits of research" (Douglas, 1979, p. 27). We feel that Douglas' position is extreme. Our approach to the problem is closer to Cassell's (1978). Because of its differences from biomedical research, qualitative research needs special guidelines which can and must be developed through a concerted effort.

REFERENCES

Allan, G. A note on interviewing spouses together. *Journal of Marriage and the Family*, February 1980, *42*, 205–210.

Barnes, J. A. Some ethical problems in modern fieldwork. *British Journal of Sociology*, June 1963, *14*, 118–134.

Becker, H. S. Against the code of ethics. *American Sociological Review*, June 1964a, *29*, 409–410.

Becker, H. S. Problems in the publication of field studies. In A. J. Vidich, J. Bensman, and M. R. Stein (Eds.), *Reflections on community studies*, pp. 276–284. New York:John Wiley and Sons, 1964b.

Bennett, L.A., McAvity, K. and Wolin, S. J. Couple versus individual interviews: An issue in family research methodology. *Paper presented at the Pre-Conference*

Workshop on Theory Construction and Research Methodology, in conjunction with the annual meetings of the National Council on Family Relations, Philadelphia, October, 1978.

Bott, E. Family and social network: Roles, norms, and external relationships. In *Ordinary Urban Families.* New York:The Free Press, 1971.

Cassell, J. Risk and benefit to subjects of fieldwork. *The American Sociologist,* August 1978,*13,* 134–143.

Deschin, C. S. Some further applications and suggested principles (involved in interviews on sensitive subjects). *Social Work,* April 1963, *8,* 14–18.

Diener, E., and Crandall, R. *Ethics in social and behavioral research.* Chicago:The University of Chicago Press, 1978.

Douglas, J. D. *Investigative social research: Individual and team field research.* Beverly Hills:Sage Publications, 1976.

Douglas, J. D. Living morality versus bureaucratic fiat. In C. B. Klockars and F. W. O'Connor (Eds.), *Deviance and decency: the ethics of research with human subjects,* pp. 13–33. Beverly Hills: Sage Publications, 1979.

Erikson, K. A comment on disguised observation in sociology. *Social Problems,* Spring 1967, *14,* 366–373.

Fichter, J. H., and Kolb, W. L. Ethical limitations on sociological reporting. *American Sociological Review,* October 1953, *18,* 544–550.

Friedson, E. Against the code of ethics. *American Sociological Review,* June 1964, *29,* 410.

Gelles, R. J. Violence and pregnancy: A note on the extent of the problem and needed services. *The Family Coordinator,* January 1975, *24,* 81–86.

Glaser, B.G., and Strauss, A. L. *The discovery of grounded theory.* Chicago: Aldine Publishing Company, 1967.

Goffman, E. *Presentation of self in everyday life.* Garden City, New York: Anchor/Doubleday, 1959.

Gold, R. L. Roles in sociological field observation. *Social Forces,* March 1958, *36,* 217–223.

Harrell-Bond, B. Studying elites: some special problems. In M. A. Rynkiewich and J. P. Spradley (Eds.), *Ethics and anthropology: dilemmas in fieldwork,* pp. 110–112. New York:John Wiley and Sons, 1976.

Henry, J. *Pathways to madness.* New York:Random House, 1965.

Hess, R. D., and Handel, G. *Family worlds: A psychosocial approach to family life.* Chicago:University of Chicago Press, 1959.

Hodgson, J. W., and Lewis, R. A. Pilgrim's progress III: a trend analysis of family theory and methodology. *Family Process,* June 1979, *18,* 163–173.

Jarvie, I. C. The problem of ethical integrity in participant observation. *Current Anthropology,* December 1969, *10,* 505–508.

Jorgensen, J. G. On ethics and anthropology. *Current Anthropology,* June 1971, *12,* 321–356.

Kantor, D., and Lehr, W. *Inside the family.* San Francisco:Jossey-Bass, 1975.

Kelman, H. C. The rights of the subject in social research: An analysis in terms of relative power and legitimacy. *American Psychologist,* November 1972, *27,* 989–1016.

Klockars, C. B. Field ethics for the life history. In R. S. Weppner (Ed.), *Street ethnography.* Beverly Hills:Sage Publications, 1977, 201–225.

LaRossa, R. *Conflict and power in marriage: Expecting the first child.* Beverly Hills:Sage Publications, 1977.

LaRossa, R. Conjoint marital interviewing as a research strategy. *Case Analysis 1,* 1978a, *2,* 141–149.

LaRossa R. Negotiating a sexual reality during the first pregnancy: Language and marital politics. Paper presented at the annual meetings of the Southern Sociological Society, New Orleans, April 1978b.

Laslett, B. The family as a public and private institution: An historical perspective. *Journal of Marriage and the Family*, August 1973, *35*, 480–492.

Laslett, B., and Rapoport, R. Collaborative interviewing and interactive research. *Journal of Marriage and the Family*, November 1975, *37*, 968–977.

Lewis, O. *Five families*. New York:Basic Books, 1959.

Lofland, J. *Doomsday cult*. Englewood Cliffs, New Jersey: Prentice-Hall, 1966.

Lofland, J. *Analyzing social settings*. Belmont, California: Wadsworth Publishing Company, 1971.

Loud, P., with Johnson, N. *Pat Loud: a woman's story*. New York: Coward, McCann, and Geoghegan, 1974.

May, W. F. The right to know and the right to create. *Newsletter on Science, Technology, and Human Values*, April 1978, *23*, 34–41.

Nye, F. I., and Bayer, A. E. Some recent trends in family research. *Social Forces*, March 1963, *41*, 290–301.

O'Brien, P. *Staying together: Marriages that work*. New York:Random House, 1977.

Piotrkowski, C. *Work and the family system: A naturalistic study of working-class and lower-middle class families*. New York:The Free Press, 1978.

Rapoport, R., and Rapoport, R. N. *Dual-career families*. Harmondsworth, England:Penguin, 1971.

Reynolds, P. D. *Ethical dilemmas and social science research*. San Francisco:Jossey-Bass, 1979.

Roth, J. A. Comments on 'secret observation.' *Social Problems*, 1962, 9(3), 283–284.

Ruano, B. J., Bruce, J. D., and McDermott, M. M. Pilgrim's progress II: Recent trends and prospects in family research. *Journal of Marriage and the Family*, November 1969, *31*, 688–698.

Rubin, L. B. *Worlds of pain: life in the working class family*. New York:Basic Books, 1976.

Rubin, Z., and Mitchell, C. Couples research as couples counseling. *American Psychologist*, January 1976, *31*, 17–25.

Rynkiewich, M. A., and Spradley, J. P. *Ethics and anthropology: Dilemmas in fieldwork*. New York:John Wiley and Sons, 1976.

Sheehy, G. *Passages: Predictable crises of adult life*. New York:E. P. Dutton, 1974.

U.S. Department of Health, Education, and Welfare. *Institutional Guide to DHEW Policy on Protection of Human Subjects*. Washington, D.C.: U.S. Government Printing Office, 1971.

Vidich, A. J., and Bensman, J. *Small town in mass society*. Garden City, New York:Doubleday, 1958.

Waxler, N. E. Review of power in families edited by Ronald E. Cromwell and David H. Olson. *Social Casework*, May 1977, *58*, 315–316.

Whyte, W. F. *Street corner society*. Chicago:University of Chicago Press, 1955.

Wolfensburger, W. Ethical issues in research with human subjects. *Science*, January 1967, *155*, 47–51.

III

The Family As Mediator Of the Culture

The concept of culture is one of the most fundamental in anthropology. Its influence has spread not only to other social sciences but to many applied fields that increasingly recognize that behavior expresses attitudes and feelings held in common by a large social segment. Kroeber and Kluckhohn, two of the most distinguished American anthropologists, in stressing the importance of the concept of culture, state:

> . . . few intellectuals will challenge the statement that the idea of culture, in the technical anthropological sense, is one of the key notions of contemporary American thought. In explanatory importance and in generality of application it is comparable to such categories as gravity in physics, disease in medicine, evolution in biology. Psychiatrists and psychologists, and, more recently, even some economists and lawyers, have come to tack on the qualifying phrase "in our culture" to their generalizations, even though one suspects it is often done mechanically in the same way that medieval men added a precautionary "God Willing" to their utterances. Philosophers are increasingly concerned with the cultural dimension to their studies of logic, values, and esthetics, and indeed with the ontology and epistemology of the concept itself. The notion has become part of the stock in trade of social workers and of all those occupied with the practical problems of minority groups and dependent peoples. Important research in medicine and nutrition is oriented in cultural terms. Literary men are writing essays and little books about culture.[1]

The concept of culture was initially applied to relatively small, homogeneous groups that comprised multiple kinship units, usually a tribe or a village. Each of these groups was considered to have its own culture. When a tribe or a village is the unit characterized as having a culture, the culture is applicable to the entire unit. Although conflict stemming from acculturation—the adoption by some members of ideas, values, and practices learned from members of other societies but not acceptable to all members of the adopting society—may develop within the society, generally the tribal or village society is not thought to harbor more than one culture. Therefore, we have a concept that helps to explain the cohesion of the society. The variation in social activity and attitude that occurs between families is not attributable to culture difference but rather to culturally prescribed differential participation in the culture or to noncultural idiosyncrasy. For example, if one man works harder than his neighbor in the same village, the difference is attributable to noncultural idiosyncrasy rather than to their having two different cultures. If one man in the tribe is a priest while others are farmers, this, too, is not due to their having two different cultures but instead to culturally prescribed differential participation in the same culture.

When the concept of culture is applied to larger units such as the modern nation, a more complex version of the concept must be used. The social differentiation within such a large unit requires us to consider the members of different segments of society as having their own versions of the culture. Margaret Mead writes:

> After deciding what larger unit we wish to refer to . . .
> then smaller observations are considered in terms of
> the regularities which have been identified for the
> whole. The term *cultural regularities* includes the way
> in which the versions of the culture found in different
> classes, regions, or occupations are systematically re-
> lated to one another. So a member of the French

bourgeoisie who is also a Protestant will manifest behavior which is French, which has certain peculiarities in common with the behavior of French Protes-
tants, which has other peculiarities in common with
the French bourgeois, and still others in common with
his province, and others in common with his generation, etc., . . . when we are making a cultural analysis, we are interested in identifying those characteristics—including, if not specifying, the possibilities of
variation by class, region, religion, period, etc.—which
can be attributed to sharing in the tradition of the larger
group, whether that group be nation, tribe, province,
or some even larger unit with a common tradition, such
as the culture of an area like Southeast Asia.[2]

The concept of culture is, then, applicable to social
units of varying size and scope. It enables us to discern regularities in the behavior of large classes of
people, and also provides tools for understanding how
the people within the class (region, tribe, social class,
or whatever) govern their relationships with one another in a wide variety of contexts. In this usage of
culture, each individual and each family are *carriers*
of the culture, enacting the tradition and sustaining
it by socializing the young into it.

The articles in Part III show that families make
choices from the culture. One principal point made
by Oscar Lewis is that cultures are much less homogeneous than the traditional reports of anthropologists have seemed to imply, and he advocates the
study of representative whole families within a society as a corrective to this oversimplified view. Early
in the paper he indicates that a family can be studied
as though it were a self-contained culture, but he does
not take the position that each family is in fact an
independent culture. Indeed, he later justifies his ad-

vocacy on the ground that it provides a superior method for studying culture patterns of the society. Studying representative whole families provides more extensive information than reliance on a few informants for constructing an account of the society's culture pattern. Lewis here is committed to the anthropologist's traditional task, but offers what he feels is a superior tool for accomplishing it. However, midway between his discussion of families as "societies" and his discussion of them as more informative avenues to a description of the culture of the whole society of which they are a part, he advocates whole family study as the best way to observe the interrelation between the culture and the individual. "One of the advantages of studying a culture through the medium of specific families is that it enables one to get at the meaning of institutions to individuals." This statement is close to the concept of this section's title, the family as mediator of the culture.

Lest misunderstanding arise, it should be pointed out that studying families as selective mediators does not at all invalidate the anthropologist's traditional goal of describing a culture in terms applicable to the whole society sustaining it. That is a different problem from the one concerning us in Part III, not an old-fashioned way of studying the same problem. Studying Mexican culture is one problem. Studying the culture of a Mexican village is another problem, because the unit of analysis is different. Studying how individual families in one Mexican village utilize and interpret the culture of their village is still a third problem; it is more recent in formulation than the preceding two, but it does not render them obsolete. This third problem is important because it focuses on the family as a unit that more or less actively selects from an array of cultural alternatives those that seem most congenial.

The selection by Cleveland and Longaker is an account of what happens when a family selects mutually contradictory alternatives from the culture. Their goal was understanding why some families contribute several members as neurotic patients to a small town mental health clinic in Nova Scotia. They examine one family in detail, and, on the basis of their study of this family as well as of others not specifically reported here, they offer some concepts for understanding the pathology in the family. Fundamentally, they say, the family mediates the culture in a way that is damaging to some members, although they do not explain why some members escape the damage. The family adopts conflicting values offered by the culture, and these become internalized in the personalities of the members. Then one set of values is disparaged so that the members engage in self-disparagement.

NOTES

1. A. L. Kroeber and Clyde Kluckhohn, *Culture; a critical review of concepts and definitions*. Cambridge, Massachusetts: Harvard University. Papers of the Peabody Museum of American Archaeology and Ethnology, 1952, 47, 3.

2. Margaret Mead, in Margaret Mead and Martha Wolfensten (Eds.), *Childhood in contemporary culture*. Chicago: University of Chicago Press, 1955, Chap. 1, p. 10.

8

An Anthropological
Approach to Family
Studies[1]

OSCAR LEWIS

The field of family studies is one that has become identified with sociologists rather than anthropologists, and even among sociologists it is sometimes viewed as the highly specialized field of practical problems in applied sociology rather than the more general and theoretical treatment of cultural dynamics. One might ask, therefore, just what can anthropology contribute to this field, since anthropologists have, in fact, neglected the field of family studies? However, on the basis of my own experience with family studies in rural areas in Mexico and Cuba, I believe that anthropology can make a distinctive contribution by utilizing the family approach as a technique for the study of culture and personality. In this paper I describe an anthropological approach to family studies and the contribution of such an approach for at least two important methodological problems in anthropology and other social sciences; namely, how to arrive at a more reliable and objective statement of the culture patterns of a given society and obtain a better understanding of the relationship between culture and the individual.

The field work upon which this chapter is based was done in the Mexican village of Tepoztlán. It will be recalled that Robert Redfield studied Tepoztlán in 1926. Seventeen years later, in 1943, I returned to the village to do a study of culture and personality. This involved a broad ethnographic study of the community, an analysis of the many changes that had occurred in the village since 1926, a comparison of the total impression of

Reprinted from *American Journal of Sociology*, 1950, *55*, 468–75, by permission of the University of Chicago Press. Copyright 1950 by the University of Chicago.

Oscar Lewis was Professor of Anthropology, University of Illinois, at the time of his death.

Tepoztlán as revealed by our two studies, and finally, a study of Tepozte-cans as individuals and as a people.

At the outset there was the problem of method. Tepoztlán is a large and complex village with a population of approximately 3,500, with seven bar-rios or locality groupings, generation and wealth differences, and a rapidly changing culture. The traditional anthropological reliance upon a few in-formants to obtain a picture of the culture and the people, though perhaps feasible in a small, primitive, tribal society, was inadequate to this situa-tion. The question of sampling and of securing data and informants repre-sentative of all the significant differences in the village was just as pertinent here as in a study of a modern urban community. Sampling and quantita-tive procedures were therefore employed wherever possible, as were cen-sus data, local government records and documents, schedules, and ques-tionnaires.

But how could we best study the individual and understand his relation-ship to the culture? How might we reveal the great variety of practices and the range of individual differences to be found in such a complex village? How might we understand Tepoztecans in all of their individuality? Again, though we came prepared with the traditional anthropological techniques as well as with some of the psychologist's, such as the Rorschach and other projective tests, something more was needed, and we turned to the study of the family. We hoped that the intensive study of representative families, in which the entire family would be studied as a functioning unit, might give us greater insight into both the culture and the people. Family studies therefore became one of the organizing principles in the entire research.

The first problem was how to select the families to be studied. The first few weeks were spent in analyzing a local population census of the village taken a year before our arrival. The census data were reorganized first on a barrio basis. The seven barrios were still, as in 1926, the most important locality groupings. Barrio lists were drawn up and each family and house-hold was assigned a number, which thereafter was used to identify the family. In addition, alphabetical lists of both sexes were drawn up in each barrio with the corresponding number after each name. In this way we were able to identify all individuals in the village in respect to barrio and family membership.

As a preliminary to selecting families that would be representative of the various socioeconomic groupings in the village for special study, several informants were asked to rank the families in each barrio according to rel-ative wealth and social position. The criteria used in this tentative classifi-cation were items that seemed important in this peasant community, namely, the ownership of a house, land, and cattle. Thus we obtained a rough idea of the relative standing of all the families of the village. On this basis three families representing different socioeconomic levels were tentatively se-lected for study in each of the seven barrios.

At this point, after I had been in the village for about a month, student assistants from the University of Mexico began to come into the village one at a time. Soon there were six assistants for each of whom arrangements were made to live with a selected family in a different barrio. An effort was made to place these assistants with families representative of the different socioeconomic levels, as well as of differences in family size, composition, and degree of acculturation. However, we found that there was a greater willingness among the better-to-do and more acculturated families on our list to have one of the staff live with them. Some of the selected poorer families expressed willingness to accept a student but were unable to do so because of crowded living conditions.

We were now ready to begin to accumulate a great variety of information on every family in the village. Each assistant was made responsible for gathering the data in his barrio. In the three smaller barrios, none of which had over forty families, it was possible to get a few informants who knew of the families there quite intimately. In these smaller barrios practically any male adult knows who does or does not own land or other property. In the larger barrios no single informant was well acquainted with more than a small percentage of the families, and we therefore had to use many more informants. In effect we were doing a census in each barrio, with the number of items investigated progressively increasing as our rapport improved and as we felt free to ask more questions.

Among the items of information we eventually obtained by survey for each family were (1) ownership of property, such as house, land, cattle and other animals, fruit trees, and sewing machines; (2) occupation and sources of income; (3) marital status, number of marriages, barrio of origin or other birthplace of each spouse, kinship relations of all persons living on the same house site; (4) social participation and positions of leadership; (5) educational level and whether or not any of the children had attended school outside the village. These items were supplemented by a number of partial surveys on other items; we also utilized and checked much of the information contained in the population census of 1940.

In addition to this survey of the village as a whole, each assistant studied the individual family with which he was living. The family was treated as if it were the society. We learned that most of the categories traditionally used in describing an entire culture could be used effectively in the study of a single family. Thus, we obtained data on the social, economic, religious, and political life of each of the families observed. We studied the division of labor, sources of income, standard of living, literacy, and education. An area of special concentration was the study of interpersonal relations within the family between husband and wife, parents and children, brothers and sisters, as well as relations with the extended family and with nonrelatives. In addition, each member of the family was studied individually.

We applied to the single family all the techniques traditionally used by the anthropologist in the study of an entire culture—living with the family, being a participant-observer, interviewing, collecting autobiographies and case histories, and administering Rorschach and other psychological tests. A long and detailed guide was prepared for the observing and recording of behavior. Seven families were studied in this intensive manner.[2] Each family study runs to about 250 typed pages.

How does this approach compare with other approaches? Certainly the family case study is not in itself a new technique.[3] It has been used by social workers, sociologists, psychologists, psychiatrists, and others; but their studies invariably have centered around some special problem: families in trouble, families in the Depression, the problem child in the family, family instability, divorce, and 101 other subjects. These might be characterized on the whole as segmented studies in which one particular aspect of family life is considered, and generally the methodology has been of a statistical nature with emphasis upon large numbers of cases supplemented by interviews and questionnaires. Despite all the emphasis in the textbooks on the family as an integrated whole, there is little published material in which the family is studied as that.[4]

If the sociological studies of the family have tended to be of the segmental, specific problem type, the work of the anthropologist has been of the opposite kind; that is, generalized description with little or no sense of problem. In most anthropological community studies the family is presented as a stereotype. We are told not about a particular family but about family life in general under headings such as composition, residence rules, descent rules, kinship obligations, parental authority, marriage forms and regulations, separation, and so on. And always the emphasis is upon the presentation of the structural and formal aspects of the family rather than upon the content and variety of actual family life. Anthropologists have developed no special methodology for family studies and to my knowledge there is not a single published study in the entire anthropological literature of a family as a unit.

Despite all that has been written and the considerable progress that has been made, I believe it is still a challenge to anthropology and the other social sciences to devise new and better methods for studying the relationship between the individual and his culture. Most monographs on so-called "primitive" or "folk" cultures give an unduly mechanical and static picture of the relationship between the individual and his culture: individuals tend to become insubstantial and passive automatons who carry out expected behavior patterns. For all the pronouncements in theoretical treatises, little of the interaction between culture and the individual emerges in the monographs. Indeed, as theoretical concepts in the study of culture have increased and our level of generalization and abstraction has been raised, we have come to deal more and more with averages and stereotypes rather than with real people in all their individuality. It is a rare monograph that gives the reader the satisfying feeling of knowing the people in the way he knows them after reading a good novel. Malinowski, many years ago in his famous preface to the *Argonauts of the Pacific,* wrote of anthropological monographs as follows: " . . . we are given an excellent skeleton so to speak, of the tribal constitution, but it lacks flesh and blood. We learn much about the framework of their society but within it we cannot conceive or imagine the realities of human life. . . ."[5] More recently Elsie Clews Parsons wrote: "In any systematic town survey such detail is necessarily omitted and life appears more standardized than it really is; there is no place for contradiction or exceptions or minor variations; *the classifications more or less preclude* pictures of people living and functioning together."[6] (Italics mine.) Here we have it. Parsons, in her book on Mitla, has attempted to remedy this situation by writing a chapter on gossip, and in other monographs we sometimes get more insight into what the people are like from scattered field-note references or from chance remarks about the nature of the informants in the foreward than from the remainder of the study. These vivid and dynamic materials are too important to be treated in such a haphazard way.

Anthropologists have made some attempt to salvage the individual through the use of autobiographies and life histories. Such studies represent a great step forward but they also have their limitations, both practical and theoretical. Autobiographies by their very nature are based upon informants' verbalizations and memory rather than upon direct observation by the trained observer. Furthermore, autobiographies give us a picture of a culture as seen through the eyes of a single person.

Intensive family case studies might help us to bridge the gap between the conceptual extremes of the culture at one pole and the individual at the other. The family would thus become the middle term in the culture-individual equation. It would provide us with another level of description. And because the family unit is small and manageable, it can be described without resort to the abstraction and generalization that one must inevitably use for the culture as a whole. Likewise, in the description of the various family members we see real individuals as they live and work together in their primary group rather than as averages or stereotypes out of context.

It is in the context of the family that the interrelationships between cultural and individual factors in the formation of personality can best be seen. Family case studies can therefore enable us to better distinguish between and give proper weight to those factors that are cultural and those that are situational or the result of individual idiosyncrasies. Even psychological tests become more meaningful when done on a family basis. For example, using family Rorschach tests we can study the extent to which personality differences run along family lines and the range of differences within families, as well as what seems to be common among all families and can therefore be attributed to broader cultural conditioning.

One of the advantages of studying a culture through the medium of specific families is that it enables one to get at the meaning of institutions to individuals. It helps us to get beyond form and structure or, to use Malinowski's terms, it puts flesh and blood on the skeleton. The family is the natural unit for the study of the satisfactions, frustrations, and maladjustments of individuals who live under a specific type of family organization; the reactions of individuals to the expected behavior patterns; the effects of conformity or deviation upon the development of the personality. Certainly those problems can also be studied in other contexts. However, I am assuming that the more data we gather on a small group of people who live and work together in the family, the more meaningful does their behavior become. This is a cumulative process, especially important for understanding the covert aspects of culture.

Family case studies can also make a contribution to the study of culture patterns. The concept of culture and culture patterns is certainly one of the proud achievements of anthropology and other social sciences. But here again conceptualization has run far ahead of methodology. Kroeber writes of culture patterns: "In proportion as the expression of such a large pattern tends to be abstract, it becomes arid and lifeless; in proportion as it remains attached to concrete facts, it lacks generalization. Perhaps the most vivid and impressive characterizations have been made by frank intuition deployed on a rich body of knowledge and put into skillful words."[7] This point has been brought home clearly to most sociologists by the recent writings of anthropologists on national character. One of the results of these writings has been to make sociologists and others wonder about the reliability of anthropological reporting even in the case of so-called "primitive" or "folk" societies.

A real methodological weakness in anthropological field work has been too great a reliance upon a few informants to obtain a picture of the culture. The traditional justification of this procedure has been the assumption of the essential homogeneity of primitive or folk societies. But this very presupposition has often affected the methods used and therefore colored the findings. An account of a culture based upon a few informants is bound to appear more uniform than it really is. This became apparent in the restudy of the village of Tepoztlán, where we found a much wider range in custom and in individual behavior than we had been led to expect from Redfield's earlier work.

One of the virtues of the intensive study of representative families is that it can give us the range of custom and behavior and can serve as a more adequate basis from which we can derive culture patterns. In doing intensive studies of even two or three families, one must use a larger number of informants than is generally used by anthropologists in monographs on an entire culture. Furthermore, in studying a family, we get a deeper understanding of our informants than is otherwise possible. This intimate knowledge of them is extremely helpful in evaluating what they tell us and in checking the accounts of family members against one another. By the same token such intimate knowledge of informants can be used in checking the usefulness of Rorschach and other projective techniques developed in our own society.

In order to convey some idea of the range in custom and family life that can be found in even a relatively homogeneous peasant society like Tepoztlán, we present a brief summary of findings on two family case studies.

> The first family, the Rojas family, consists of the father, mother, four daughters, and one son. The children range in age from thirteen to twenty-six and all are unmarried. The second family, the Martinez family, consists of the father, mother, four sons, and two daughters, the elder of whom is married. The ages of the children range from eight to twenty years.
>
> Both families are close to average size for Tepoztecan families, which is about five members. In terms of family composition they are the simple biological family living alone on a house site. Over 70% of Tepoztecan families live in this way. Both cases represent families in an advanced stage of development, since neither has infants or very young children.
>
> The Rojas family is a relatively well-to-do landowning family in the upper economic group, which is made up of about 4% of the families in the village. The Martinez family is one of the poorer, landless families of the lowest economic group, which constitutes about 80% of all families. The latter exemplifies those families that practice hoe culture on communal lands primarily with family labor.[8]
>
> Whereas the Rojas family depends upon the communal lands only for firewood, charcoal, and the grazing of cattle, the Martinez' depend upon the communal lands for their basic food supply. Neither the father nor the son of the Rojas family works as day laborers for others in the village or on nearby haciendas. However, both the father and the older sons of the Martinez family do this as a regular practice to supplement their income. This pattern goes back to the days before the Mexican revolution of 1910, when the head of the Martinez family, as a youth, worked as a peon on the haciendas, while the head of the Rojas family worked only on his father's lands.
>
> These two families have sharply contrasting standards of living. The Rojas family is well housed, well fed and well clothed according to Tepoztecan standards. They can afford some luxuries and their home contains many modern articles such as beds, chairs, tables, a clock, flashlight, and sewing machine. The Martinez family, in contrast, lives close to a bare subsistence level; it has but a minimum of clothing and house furnishings and none of the luxuries found in the Rojas family. The Martinez' are reduced to a diet of tortilla, chili, and black coffee during several months of the year. The Rojas family has had more formal schooling than the Martinez' and, as a whole, shows a higher degree of literacy since every member of the family can read and write. Everyone in this family has had some formal education. The father and the two elder daughters have gone through the third grade; the mother through the second grade. In addition, the Rojas family is somewhat unusual in that the three younger

children are students preparing for a professional career. However, the father in the Martinez family, though a self-educated man, is much more literate than the father in the Rojas family, and one of the Martinez children has had an advanced education. Like most members of their generation, the parents of both families are bilingual and frequently use Nahuatl in speaking with older villagers but rarely with their children. Although the children of both families understand Nahuatl, the Rojas children have more occasion to use it because of their grandmother, who has only a limited Spanish vocabulary.

The question of what the two families represent in regard to social relations is more difficult to answer. In general, the Rojas family is the more respected of the two but this has less effect upon social relations than might be expected. Both families well exemplify the essentially atomistic nature of the social organization of the village, whereby the biological family constitutes the basic economic and social unit. Independence, self-reliance, and a strong sense of privacy, some of the most cherished values of Tepoztecans, clearly emerge in these two families. Both families are characterized by limited relations with the extended family and neighbors, a paucity of intimate friendships, minimal compliance with obligations to *compadres*, reticence in borrowing or calling upon others for help, and, by the same token, reticence in giving help. However, a closer comparison of the two families reveals some differences. The Martinez parents have even less contact with their relatives than does the Rojas family, principally because of the rift over the change of religion. The Martinez', due to the political activity of the father, have much wider contacts among nonrelatives than the Rojas'. However, the Rojas children, because of their greater freedom and higher status, have a more extensive social life among both relatives and nonrelatives than do the Martinez children, whose outside activities are minimal.

Both families are strong, cohesive units and represent relatively close ingroups. Each is held together by traditional bonds of family loyalty and parental authority, by common economic strivings and mutual dependence, by the stability of marriage between the parents, and, finally, by the absence of other social groups to which the family members can turn in time of need. The Rojas family is further bound together by the prospect of inheritance on the part of the children.

These families provide examples of different types of family situations and interpersonal relations, and in some respects represent two extremes of family organization in Tepoztlán. In the Rojas family the wife is the dominating figure, although the husband is the nominal head of the family and maintains some authority. The husband spends much of his time in his fields working tirelessly to support his wife and children and to provide them with their more-than-usual demands. He entrusts household affairs and family finances to his wife, who, in addition to these duties, carries on several gainful activities and substantially contributes to the family economy. Both the wife and children have an unusual amount of freedom and independence. However, interpersonal relations within the family are characterized by considerable conflict, tension, and maladjustment. There is much quarreling on the part of the wife, drunkenness and adultery on the part of the husband, difficulties with in-laws, strong mother-son ties and favoritism on the part of both parents, and competition, hostility, and feelings of rejection among the siblings.

In the Martinez family the husband is a dominating, authoritarian figure who rules his wife and children with an iron hand. The wife is completely submissive and, in contrast to the wife of the Rojas house, inactive and unable to contribute financially to the support of the family. The husband is unusual in the extent to which he supervises expenditures and household affairs. Both the wife and children are extremely restricted in their activities and have little freedom of expression. The older sons work under the direction of their father and frequently work to support the family while the father devotes himself to political activity. The chief conflicts in this household are between the father, on the one hand, and the mother, and children on the other. Under the father's repressions the mother and her sons and daughters have drawn closer together and often demonstrate mutual loyalty and consideration. There is little of the sibling rivalry to be found in the Rojas home and only occasionally do hostilities between the brothers flare up. In the past the father was extremely indulgent toward his eldest daughter, but he has recently broken off relations with her because he disapproves of her husband.

It can be seen from this summary that any statement of overall culture patterns would have to be made in terms of the range of differences rather than in terms of some abstract, hypothetical norm. It should be noted that the difference in the husband-wife relationship in these two families cannot be explained in terms of class or subcultural differences, since they cut across class lines in Tepoztlán.

A practical advantage of this type of approach to the study of culture and personality is that a reasonably complete family case study can be done within a relatively short time, about two or three months, and might be profitably carried on by anthropologists or sociologists who have only their summer vacation in which to do field work. Several intensive family case studies done in as many summers would be in effect a cumulative study of the culture.

The family case study also presents us with an excellent method of introducing anthropology students to field work. The family, small in size but reflecting at the same time almost all aspects of the culture, is a manageable unit of study well within the comprehension and abilities of the student—certainly much more so than an entire community. The traditional training field party too often spends itself in either a confused, pathetic scramble on the part of the students to gather and understand a large amount of data covering all aspects of the culture or in the limited pursuit by each student of a single problem or institution. From my own experience with groups of students in rural Cuba and Mexico, I have found the family approach to field work an invaluable aid. Furthermore, family case studies are very useful as a teaching aid in communicating a feeling for real people.

There is a need for intensive individual family case studies in cultures all over the world. The publication of such studies would give us a literature on comparative family life not now available and would be of use to many social scientists interested in a variety of problems concerning culture and the individual. Moreover, because individual families can be described without recourse to abstractions and stereotypes, the publication of case studies would provide us with some basis for judging the generalizations made by anthropologists and others concerning the total culture patterns of any community. The implication of the family case study for anthropological research is clear. It means that we have to go more slowly, that we have to spend more time doing careful and detailed studies of units smaller than the entire culture before we can be ready to make valid generalizations for the entire culture. These suggestions for individual family studies may seem excessively cautious at this time, when some anthropologists are writing with such abandon about the character structure of entire nations. Yet it may be necessary to take a few steps backward if we are to forge ahead on surer ground.

NOTES

1. This paper was read at the Midwest Sociological Society meetings, April 29, 1949, in Madison, Wisconsin.

2. Two of these family studies will be published in my forthcoming book on Tepoztlán.

3. Professor Thomas D. Eliot comments that Le Play used the family as a unit of research. However, the tradition he began has not been continued by American sociologists. I understand from Professor Florian Znaniecki that he and his students did family studies in Poland somewhat similar to those described here.

4. Professor Eliot's comment at a meeting of the American Sociological Society in December 1924 still applies today. He said, "Each feels and interprets only the small part of the problem with which he is in direct contact, and thinks he is describing the whole."

5. Bronislaw Malinowski, *Argonauts of the Pacific*. New York: E. P. Dutton and Co., 1932, p. 17.

6. Elsie Clews Parsons, *Mitla, town of the souls*. Chicago: University of Chicago Press, 1936, p. 386.

7. Alfred Kroeber, *Anthropology*. New York: Harcourt Brace & Co., 1948, p. 317.

8. Although about 80% of the families in the village fall in the lower economic group, about 20% of the families regularly work as *tlacololeros*. See Oscar Lewis, Plow culture and hoe culture—a study in contrasts. *Rural Sociology*, June 1949, *14*, (2), 116–27.

9

Neurotic Patterns in the Family[1]

E. J. CLEVELAND AND
W. D. LONGAKER

We shall here attempt to examine the impact of sociocultural factors on individual mental health by analyzing the transmission and mediation of values in a family setting. The focus of our effort is the elucidation of neurotic patterns in a single kinship group that contributed several patients to the caseload of a small-town clinic. Basic data were obtained during psychotherapy, and additional information was supplied by the psychologist on the clinic team who gave the results of his testing and the impressions from his own interviews. The data from patients were supplemented by home visits and interviews with various relatives, carried out for the most part by a social worker, though occasionally by a psychiatrist.[2]

It is thought that the occurrence of neurotic patterns in several members of a large family permits us to consider some aspects of etiology in this kind of mental illness, with particular reference to specific social circumstances. The approach complements and supplements an epidemiological research program being carried out in the same community (4).

Within the brief compass of this chapter it will be necessary to simplify the rich complexities of personality structure and the detailed web of val-

Reprinted by permission of the publisher from Alexander Leighton, John A. Clausen, Robert N. Wilson, (Eds.), *Explorations in social psychiatry.* New York: Basic Books, Inc., 1957, pp. 168–95. Copyright 1957 Basic Books, Inc.

Eric J. Cleveland is Executive Director, the Fundy Mental Health Centre, and is also research associate in clinical pastoral training, Acadia University, Wolfville, Nova Scotia, Canada. At the time of writing he was Executive Director, Stirling County Psychiatric Clinic, and Research Associate, Cornell University. William D. Longaker practices psychiatry in New York State. At the time of writing he was Associate Psychiatrist, Stirling County Study, and Research Associate, Cornell University.

uative influences that affect individual styles of behavior. In describing the transmission of neurotic patterns from one family member to another, we shall inevitably stress psychopathology and neglect the positive attributes that contribute to a rounded assessment of individual functioning. Again, the concentration on values held and expounded by members of the kinship system forces us to slight the many other agents of valuative transmission. Although the tenets of family members are thus given special prominence, we recognize the host of other value sources impinging on the individual's developing framework of choice and belief; peers, schoolteachers, religious leaders, and the various vehicles of the mass media all modify the family influence on any individual.

In many instances through this account, we shall be developing implications for a general statement of neurotic patterning in families. This tendency to discern the universal in the clinically particular may be as misleading as it is scientifically suggestive. Therefore, we must recognize that the description is really limited to a single family living in a specific cultural milieu. Clinical experience with several other families indicates that the phenomena are recurrent within the culture studied; nevertheless, the qualification of conclusions in terms of the context in which they have been derived should be understood even if it is not constantly reiterated.

The clinic from which the study was made is situated in a small town in a rural county. Both treatment and research are carried out, and the clinic is part of a larger program, the Stirling County Study, concerned with the relationships between mental health and social environment. Coordinated with the clinic for certain aspects of the work is a team of social scientists who have been studying the social and cultural processes in the same county for several years. In the present chapter, we have drawn on the social science team for a characterization of critical elements in the local culture.[3]

The population of Stirling County, which totals about 20,000, is divided into two major groups; a little over one-half is generally of English-Protestant background, the remainder is French-Acadian-Catholic and speaks French. The economy of the county is based mainly on fishing, lumbering, farming, and a combination of these, and wage work. There are over 93 named places in the county—some are rural communities with their own church, school, post office, and general stores, some are mere crossroad settlements or small neighborhoods, others are semiurban centers with all the utilities found in a small town. The clinic is located in the largest semiurban center of the county, Bristol, a town with a population of about 3,000.

FRAME OF REFERENCE AND MAJOR CONCEPTS

As a result of experience with certain cases at the clinic, we became impressed with patterns in the transmission of values from one generation to the next as being significant in the development of neuroses. In approaching this problem we have utilized the concepts of need, role, and value; in the cases considered here the data have all been reviewed with reference to these concepts. Each individual was examined in the context of his family of orientation and his family of procreation, and also in the context of those sociocultural stresses that seemed to us to be of primary etiologic significance in his disturbed functioning. Our aim was to see how the individual's problems may be related to certain important features of his personality (needs), to behavior expected of him by the society (role), and/or to difficult and conflicting patterns of cultural prescription (value).

The discussion of neurotic patterning in the family will emphasize two chief processes. Although these processes will be more fully defined after the presentation of some specific cases of disorder in a large family system, it may be useful to foreshadow them briefly. The first process is on the level of cultural value configurations and manifests itself most dramatically in the clash of incompatible orientations toward the ends and means of life in this semirural environment.

The second process is on the level of individual development and personality integration. It consists in a culturally recurrent mode of self-devaluation, which has roots in the methods of child rearing. Generated in the socialization process, this intense self-devaluation is linked to the failure of individuals to adjust to the incompatible orientations toward the ends and means of life noted above. It will be convenient to term the first process *value conflict*, the second process (a resultant neurotic maladaptation) *disparagement*.

Value conflict is most strikingly observed in the contrast between orientations that stress long-range gratification in individual achievement of material success, as symbolized by money and status, and those that tend to underline the virtues of adjustment to one's environment in a manner emphasizing the pleasurable rhythms of nature and the immediacy of gratifications. The individuals to be discussed in this paper have all been in some sense trapped by the conflicting tenets of these two broad paths of life. It may be supposed that the effort to choose between them, or to resolve them in some workable amalgam, is difficult—but not impossible and not inherently productive of individual disorder. Our hypothesis is that the way in which these value conflicts are mediated within the family setting is critical in the development or nondevelopment of many cases of psychoneurotic disorder.

The pattern of extreme devaluation, which heightens the vulnerability of certain aspects of individual personality, is, we suggest, a type of response to particular stresses learned during the socialization period. Self-disparagement can arise in the developing individual when the socializing agents, primarily the parents, hold out contradictory models of behavior (grounded on conflicting cultural values) or are so suffused with the burden of their own inferiority feelings that some areas of learning become either threatening or coldly nonrewarding to the child. Disparagement can become a fixed tendency in the child to devalue certain facets of his own personality. When an obstacle to learning develops in an area of life relevant to the already vulnerable and devalued segment (for instance, in the sphere of occupational achievement or sexual fulfillment), then the disparaging tendency is activated and may become so acutely negative that it constitutes a neurotic behavior disorder.

Disparagement is quite similar in some respects to Adler's concept of the inferiority complex (1). In both there is the core idea of deep personal unworthiness. Disparagement, however, is conceived to be more closely linked to the cultural context in its etiology, distribution, and consequences. It is tied to group values and is recurrent as a maladaptive pattern in the family. Moreover, the disparagement of self is often not confined to one's own individual capacities but radiates to disparagement of the defined behaviors and value systems of his culture. In short, it touches all that has been internalized by the individual, or with which he identifies.

In the following cases, the phenomena of value conflict and disparagement may be viewed as underlying themes. In each instance, our focus will be on the family as the scene of socialization in which cultural value conflict is translated into interpersonal patterns predisposing to individual illness via the path of disparagement.

THE DEAN FAMILY—A KINSHIP GROUP

As already noted, we have been able to examine, fairly extensively and intensively, a number of members in several large families or kinship groups. One of those will be presented here and will be called the Dean family. This kind of study makes it possible to cross-check data, since one case frequently corroborates information from another. In addition, the case material is enriched by the diverse viewpoints presented about one member of the family by several other members.

The Deans currently live in several neighboring crossroad settlements a few miles outside Bristol, and, although they consider themselves to be oriented toward the town, they also participate in their own small communities. Except for a few service stations and country grocery stores and small farms, there is little in the immediate neighborhoods to offer work or economic support. The people of the area turn for the most part to the town or the sea for employment. Many of them have small woodlots a few miles away, but these are usually cutover stands from which only a limited number of cords of wood are taken per year for fuel or pulpwood. Each house has a summer garden for vegetables.

The Deans provide services, such as sawyer, garage mechanic, and shopkeeper, which keep them in touch with their neighbors and ensure relatively good economic status. They are rather well regarded in the communities, and certain members are recognized for their inventive capacities with machinery, despite modest formal education. As a family they are not extraordinary in matters of religion and morality—they belong nominally to the predominant Baptist sect—and include behavior among different members that ranges from the unconventional to the conventional.

Three Patients

Three persons in the Dean family have been selected to serve as points of focus and reference in this presentation. They are Stan Davis, his son Ray Davis, and Stan's first cousin, Alice Mary Seeley. A brief abstract from the case history of each will be presented. Their relationship to other members of the family is shown in Fig. 1. The names of those who have been clinic patients are set in capital letters.

Stan Davis. Stan is tall and gives the impression, on casual contact, of being at ease and self-assured. Although he is in his mid 50s, he looks somewhat younger. Locally he is known as a man of parts, and he has been able to put his marked mechanical abilities to much productive use. He is separated from his wife, yet contributes a small amount toward her support.

Stan was first seen at the clinic some months following an illness that abruptly ended the very active type of life he had been leading. He did not accept bed rest easily, nor the uncertainty and fear engendered by his condition, and it was necessary for his doctor to use morphine and other sed-

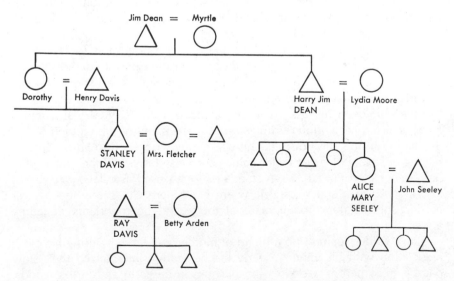

Figure 1. The Dean family.

atives in order to keep him at rest. Eventually, during convalescence, over-dependency on the drugs became a matter of concern to both the doctor and the patient. It was at this point that he came on his own initiative to the clinic.

His presenting complaints, in addition to concern about the drugs, were that he "felt jittery and trembling," had choking feelings and difficulty in breathing, had no appetite, and had "fluttering in the stomach." He also said that his legs got "trembly and shaky" when things upset him. Along with these complaints, there was a definite tendency to depression and self-blame. He expressed concern over the fact that he had to take things easy and was, therefore, unable to keep up his former standards of hard work. The diagnostic impression was that he suffered from depression and anxiety attacks and that both of these became worse when he tried to relinquish the drugs. There was much to suggest that the patient had anxiety attacks off and on since the age of six.

At the time of Stan's birth the family lived in a woodland area, and it was here that Stan spent most of his childhood and adolescence. As a child he was very close to his father, Henry Davis, who earned an adequate living in lumbering in the winter and farming in the summer, work he thoroughly enjoyed. Stan describes his father, now deceased, as kind and generous, but with little ambition for getting ahead or for education. They had much mutual enjoyment in working and hunting. In many things they sided against the mother, often playing practical jokes on her. Both liked working at a slow pace and for the pleasure of it. They enjoyed nature and the beauty of the woods and the farm. Personal ambition and a quest for money were kept in the background; sociability was valued. One might sum up this lifeway as physically vigorous, independent, lusty, generous, friendly, and geared to the even pace of the changing seasons.

The mother was different. She was a Dean, the sister of Harry Jim Dean, and lived according to a standard of values almost opposite to those of her husband. Stan describes her as not liking the life of the farm and said, "She would much rather be where there was more doing." The whole course of her life had been restless, including a move to the United States and a number of moves within Stirling County. Like many of the women of her generation in this rural district, she was strongly opposed to liquor and rejecting of sexual pleasures. Her values comprised much of the pattern that has been called Puritan. High standards (often used as a lever on others) and a sense of moral superiority were combined with strong feelings regarding social status, money, material goods, and the importance of getting ahead.

Stan's values seem to be a blend of mother and father. During his close association with his father in early life he readily internalized the "slow pace," enjoyment in working and playing on the farm and in the woods. With this went a thoughtfulness for other people, generosity, fairness, and a verbalized contempt for a money-oriented existence. However, the material values have been apparent too, as for instance in the driving, money-making kind of life he has led, in episodic feelings of guilt with regard to idleness and sexual pleasures, and in the strict kind of woman he selected for his wife.

When Stan was twenty-three he married a woman somewhat older than himself. It seems fairly clear on the basis of clinical evidence that this marriage represented an affiliation with an idealized mother figure. Certainly, there were striking similarities between the two women. We believe he was drawn to his wife because her values were similar to those of his mother and, at a deeper level, by a desire to secure a dependent-submissive relationship to a female who seemed inherently superior. Once he was married, however, Stan found that his wife was considerably more strict than his mother had been. Her demands that Stan be a "success," particularly in the area of goods and money, led to continual strain between the two. Under this pressure Stan was obliged to work harder and longer hours than before. The couple separated after twenty years of marriage, during which one child, Ray, had been born. The allegiance of the son has always been to the mother.

So far as his current anxiety and depression were concerned, Stan improved in the course of brief psychotherapy as he learned to accept lessened physical activity and a return to a slower pace, the "slow pace" that his wife and mother had decried, the "slow pace" that his father had inculcated in him during his boyhood. Fortunately, he had discovered that he could maintain his financial security while doing this.

Ray Davis. Although Ray, who is 32, resembles his father, Stan, in physical appearance, he is unlike him in manner. Ray is always on the go at a fast pace, and there is an evident high level of tension in all his restless movement. On the other hand, he does exhibit his father's inventive and mechanical aptitudes, although his restlessness and shifting goals, and a preoccupation with health, interfere with advancement. He is married and has three children.

Ray came to the clinic after contemplating the step at least a year. In the meantime, through his advice he was instrumental in the coming of his father, his mother, and his great-uncle, Harry Jim Dean. The presenting complaints given by Ray were mostly referable to his heart, and the diagnostic impression was of a severe cardiac neurosis that kept him from work six months out of each year. He had been to see many doctors who prescribed medicines and told him not to worry. The chief result of this was a conviction that the doctors knew he had a serious illness but out of mercy would not tell him the diagnosis.

There are indications in his history of severe neurotic disturbance from an early age. From seven to nine years his eyes troubled him, and he wore glasses for "wavy vision." At twelve he was treated by the family physician for "heart trouble," which he described as "pounding of the heart and nervousness." His job history to date has been extremely irregular. He is a perfectionist, restless and never satisfied with a job, seldom remaining in one for as long as a year. Each time he has approached the point of giving up a job there has been an increase in his physiological symptoms. For example, he quit his job as a taxi driver because pains in his heart kept getting worse as each work day wore on. It is noteworthy that his heart pains and palpitations correspond almost exactly to those presented by his mother. These symptoms occur particularly when he exerts himself in an occupation that does not satisfy him; he says, "then I get ugly and disagreeable." Insomnia and frightening dreams were other complaints.

Ray's parents have been sketched in Stan Davis' history. He grew up in an atmosphere of open hostility between his mother and father. As noted earlier, he sided with his mother, and she has dominated him all his life. He has shared her contempt for the father, especially in relation to his father's friends and associates. There has always been, in Ray, compliance toward his mother and an underlying fear that she might "blow up" in anger.

Getting ahead is important to Ray; he is very prejudiced against the local "slow" way of life and dreams of going to the United States. However, he is blocked by his restlessness, his overambitious goals, and his desire to achieve too much too fast. Advancement is also thwarted by his overinvestment in his body. He is afraid, for example, that close work will harm his eyes and that standing on the concrete floor of a garage will injure his health generally.

Ray married a daughter of Tom Arden (also a patient) when he was in his mid 20s. He had always admired the way Mrs. Arden looked after her husband. Her overprotectiveness and Tom's untroubled acquiescence appealed to Ray and influenced him in choosing their daughter for his wife. She is very much like her mother in that she is a good housekeeper and yet a person of level temperament.

Ray's treatment at the clinic was sporadic and he was not greatly improved.

Alice Mary Seeley. A first cousin to Stan Davis, Alice Mary Seeley is, like most of the family, tall and thin. She is also frail looking and appears worn and older than her actual age of 30. There is an external superficial cheerfulness that acts as a rather thin disguise for an underlying anxiety. When she speaks there is hesitation with frequent blocking. Perhaps this is an indirect expression of a strong undercurrent of resentment that frequently breaks through.

She was referred to the clinic by a physician because of a problem with one of her four children. The referral stated that she was "resentful and hated" this child. This presenting difficulty was, of course, only one expression of more widespread trouble. Most of her complaints centered

on her genito-urinary tract, and there was a long history of menstrual difficulties. Several operations had been performed in an attempt to treat this
problem. She was seen 12 times at the Clinic and, although she continues
to have most of her somatic complaints, she has been able to accept her
family problems much better.

Alice Mary's mother, Lydia Dean, was the wife of Stan Davis' uncle, Harry
Jim Dean (see Fig. 1). She had a hostile orientation toward childbearing
and children, especially female children. Moreover, this attitude seems to
have reached a high point at the time of Alice Mary's birth. Mrs. Dean
thoroughly disliked the rural, slow-paced way of life and showed little interest in her home. She had a fearful, rejecting attitude toward sexual activity, one expression of which was frigidity, and yet she had shown a marked
curiosity about the activities of her daughter and was overly suspicious of
her relations with boys.

Alice Mary's father is dominated by his wife, but their basic values seem
to be about the same. He has rejected the values of such persons as Henry
Davis (Stan's father) in that he has no use for farming, hunting, or fishing.
He is extremely antagonistic toward the way of life in the "backwoods"
farms, and refers to himself sarcastically as coming from "out there with
the rabbits and the deer." His major value constellation appears to be found
in money and he is known as a miser. He also values independence. This
is perhaps the affirmative alternative to hatred of the rural ways of life. He
is concerned about his body and worries in a hypochondriacal manner, yet
he mistrusts doctors and shops about for medical advice.

VALUE CONFLICT

In the crossroad neighborhoods where the Deans live there is no clear-
cut, obvious prestige hierarchy or power structure. Nevertheless, there are
prestige values, and two contrasting orientations seem to characterize the
persons who have been preeminent at certain times and in certain groups.
These orientations are by no means distinct and consistent, nor do they ex-
haust the range of behavioral variation. Hence, in order to describe them,
we offer constructed types that are represented with varying degrees of intensity and coherence in the lives of the Deans and their neighbors.

1. *Striving:* Personal ambition for substantial material success, especially as reflected in occupational striving, acceptance of the rational money
economy, the specialization of function and the technological innovations
so prominent in Western industrial society; emphasis on individual
achievement and self-development, on personal responsibility for success
and for failure.

2. *Being:* Preference for a rather slowly paced, traditional style of life
exemplified by physical labor in a natural environment, such as farming,
fishing, timbering, or hunting; absence of intense drives toward occupa-

tional or material achievement, yet a strong desire for independence and personal integrity; development of personal satisfactions and warm communal relatedness and of immediate gratifications rather than more abstract rewards of money and position; satisfaction with stable interpersonal relationships and currently meaningful activities.[4]

Older women, who have internalized the "Protestant Ethic" type of scheme marked by striving toward material success and toward the individual grace attested by that success, seem to include the more intensely ambitious persons following the first path. Perhaps even more important, they stake out this pattern of individualistic striving as a model for the men of the family. It involves, for these women, a strong component of felt moral superiority and the use of moral sanctions.

One might say that the first orientation tends to value the individual by his achievements and symbolic rewards of money and status, whereas the second assesses personal worth more nearly in terms of intrinsic features of the personality and expressive interpersonal effectiveness. The first emphasizes triumph over adverse features of the interpersonal or physical environment, the second stresses adjustment to the situation in which one finds himself.

The two types of orientation seem to correspond to a conflict of values in the culture of the group in which the Deans live. Factors in the specific situation of the individual are thought to be of primary influence in turning him to one or the other direction. Undoubtedly the interpersonal relations and socialization patterns of early childhood are of major importance here due to their role in personality development. However, it is probable that the circumstances of later life also play a part. Thus, the low-keyed, communal, accepting orientation is easier to maintain when there is not undue personal hardship and when intimate interpersonal bonds and strong group pressures are present to reinforce it.

Each of the two value orientations is exemplified in quite distinct form by different members of the Dean family. In an effort to explore the patterning and transmission of these values and their bearing on the appearance of psychoneurosis, the orientations of several family members have been examined. It should be noted that our conclusions are apt to be influenced by the fact that our contact with the family is uneven and we have worked with the material as it came to hand in the clinic or in home visits without endangering therapeutic relationships. Since no attempt was made to achieve either total coverage or a systematic sampling of the extended family, there are important individuals about whom we have very little information. For example, some of the presumably normal members might serve as controls or, at least, points of contrast. On the other hand, the Deans are only one of six families that have been studied in this manner and our impressions are thus based on work with approximately 30 cases. Furthermore, from the studies of the social science team and its anthropological appraisal of the county, it is evident that the patterns of value and communications exemplified by the Deans are widespread in the culture of Stirling.

Although we have assumed the primacy of value conflict in the etiology of neurosis, it is not yet clear how much weight should be attributed to this type of stress as compared with other stresses to which the developing individual is exposed. A number of questions might be asked about the relative potency of variously phrased threats to the personality. Does neurosis sometimes occur with no, or a very slight, background of cultural value conflict? For example, does organ inferiority, bodily illness, or disaster sometimes play the most critical part in the development of neurosis? In our cases, such obstacles seemed of importance only in the precipitation of neurosis, for example, the sudden illness of Stanley Davis which preceded the anxiety state that brought him to the clinic.

In what way are certain *situations* in a given society particularly threatening to the psychological functioning of the individual?[5] For instance, among people who have a striving background and strong upward mobility tendencies, is it particularly stressful to be in an area where the chances of fulfilling such ambitions are slight or where success, if it occurs, produces hostile attitudes and social disarticulation?

Turning now to our approach, we may ask: What are the relationships in problems of need, role, and value in the etiology of neurosis?

SIGNIFICANCE OF THE CURRENT SOCIAL SITUATION AND ROLE EXPECTATIONS

Modern trends of rapid technological change have had different effects upon persons of various value-orientation and of various age and sex within the same value orientation. These contemporary trends place emphasis on material advancement achieved within a complexly ordered society. The individualistic aspect of the striving pattern has made it easier for some to accept highly ambitious goals of material advancement and the modern means of achieving these goals. Our scientific heritage is also a reinforcing agent in terms of modern educational requirements.

The effect of such trends can be seen, for example, in particular areas emphasized in the value system of Stan's wife. She has impressed Ray Davis, her son, with tremendous upward mobility striving and a restless desire to emigrate to the United States. However, the importance of cooperation in the complicated division of labor characteristic of the modern West has been underestimated or ignored by her. Interpersonal responsiveness is incompatible with her interpretation of the "striving" orientation. This failure to stress the coordinative aspects of contemporary life is significant in Ray's inability to achieve his ambitions and in his development of neurotic substitute aims, and will be described later in this paper as the process of disparagement.

The situation of Mrs. Seeley is interesting in this connection. As a woman, and because she occurred late in a long line of siblings, she was subjected to somewhat different influences within the same general social situation. Her mother, like Ray's, had very strong upward mobility strivings and restlessness. However, the disadvantages of pregnancy and of children were particularly stressed in her case. Marriage was to be valued as a means to higher social status, but the male should be kept in subservience as an instrument of the female's ambitions. In no case was he to be allowed pleasures.

Mrs. Seeley rebelled and attempted to reverse these values, but she was never able to free herself from disgust with sexual pleasures, presumably acquired from her mother, nor to accept her husband and children on a basis of trust.

Thus her problem, like Ray's, can be traced to inconsistency and disarticulation in the values of the parents, particularly the mother. Later on we shall discuss the relationship of these antecedent events to a basic self-concept of inferiority and the appearance of neurotic symptoms.

TWO MAIN POSTULATES

In approaching our analysis we have made certain assumptions, or postulates, bearing on the development of concepts regarding the transmission of values through the family. The first is that man is a communicating animal, and communication with other persons is not just a means but is in itself one of his major goals. Man seems to take an active interest in joining in the pursuit of "agreed upon" goals as well as in the simple gratification of what are supposedly bodily instincts.[6] Following Harry Stack Sullivan (7), we conceive of the oral, anal, and genital erogenous zones as serving an important function in communication. In this connection the Freudian principle of unconscious motivation is also assumed—and, in general, the kind of symbolism that is described in such theory. We have focused especially on data that might give a better understanding, however, of the full meaning of such symbolism: for example, being interested in not only the early experiences that may give rise to castration anxiety but also the manifestation of castration symbolism in social living and how this is related to specific modes of role-learning in later life. Thus, the symbolism of Ray Davis, as described by him in his dreams, is suggestive of castration anxiety, and our interest includes the manner in which his mother has played a part in obstructing his learning of occupational roles.[7]

A second postulate is that a framework of common values underlies the process of communication, and these values are passed on by certain modes of behavior and techniques of socialization. Critical elements in this transmission are the mechanisms of reward and punishment, approval and disapproval, which create certain strongly held values and give them the dynamic impress of binding moral force. Such values are reinforced by a social technique, often termed sanctions, which dramatizes them and affords them a substantial potency in the lives of both transmitter and receiver.

The transmission of values and their supporting sanctions may be conceived as occurring at two main levels: they may be passed on without conscious effort, covertly conveyed by symbolic processes of gesture and intonation that elude deliberate recognition by either source or recipient; they may be inculcated by overt manifestations, as precept and example, recognized by both parties to the transaction.

On the basis of general observation it seems obvious that any personality incorporates elements of different value systems and rarely behaves according to a single consistent pattern. As a result, it is necessary to seek some way of formulating the inconsistency and fluctuation that often characterize valuative behavior. One ordering would emphasize that certain values are amenable to conscious selection and activation, whereas others are less susceptible to conscious expression and verbalization: this ordering might be described as the distinction between *manifest-overt* and *latent-covert* values.

Another conceptual distinction is necessary, however, to account for the *hierarchical aspect* of value systems—the fact that values are not all mobilized with equal potency at all times. That is, even within the distinction above between manifest and latent there are subdistinctions conditioned by time, place, situation, and personality state. Among the values amenable to conscious activation, for instance, some will be stressed at one time, some at another. This further refinement might be keyed to the words primary and secondary, or activated and dormant.

The first distinction advanced is one of *level,* dividing verbalized awareness from the behavioral forces that operate behind the curtain of the unconscious. The second distinction is one of *hierarchy* and *primacy* within levels, distinguishing more active and intensely held values from less active and weakly held values, recognizing that situational variation may condition the hierarchical alignment at any point in time.[8]

In the case of Stanley Davis, we may propose that he incorporated both paternal and maternal values in varying degrees but that their level of conscious realization and their situational order of primacy differed. He acquired his father's values by identification with the attractive paternal figure; and he was engaged in daily practice (and seemingly frequent verbalization) of the paternal orientation toward slowly paced, immediately gratifying activities. On the other hand, his mother's valuative pattern was obviously also impressed on him at a very deep level of personality integration. Had it not been so significant as a point of reference in their lives, Stanley and his father would presumably have had little reason to ridicule it and ally themselves against it. There seems little doubt that Stanley felt guilty about not showing more overt allegiance to the maternal orientation and that he was emotionally convinced of its moral superiority.

This formulation is further corroborated by the fact that he married a woman who expressed his mother's viewpoint and who dominated him in marriage. Although Stanley then exhibited the maternal values for many years and gave them behavioral expression, he has reactivated the paternal orientation in his more recent life. Since being separated from his wife, and especially since his recent illness, he has placed much more emphasis on the *being* pattern of his father. It has required therapy, however, and will undoubtedly require substantial reorganization of his personality for him to overcome the severe guilt generated by his failure to persist in the now covert but latently powerful maternal *striving* values.

Although one might assert that the father's values were more deeply internalized through the process of identification, as indicated by the eventual return to them, it is also apparent that different valuative patterns were mobilized in Stanley under different objective social conditions. One might then account for a large part of Stanley's realistic shifts in values as a functional adaptation to external conditions, partly conscious and cognitive, partly unconscious.

The idea of the Oedipus complex has always been considered crucial to the understanding of psychopathology. Perhaps the concept could well be extended to view the patient as internalizing a whole drama of parental interaction, not confined to sexual alliance but including the parents' total system of values.

DISPARAGEMENT AS A CONCEPT FOR LINKING SOME ASPECTS OF INDIVIDUAL AND GROUP PHENOMENA

Neurotic patterns contain elements that are largely nonrational and inaccessible to conscious formulation. The very potency of neurosis consists in hyperbolic, disproportionate affect, an emotional overinvestment in some area of life that does not square with a rational strategy of ends and means. Exaggerated emotional valences of a number of different types occur in neuroses, of course, but the one we shall delineate here is thought to be peculiarly enervating since it erodes portions of the individual's system of values, leading to self-defeating behavior. Further, it is damaging to society because not only does neurosis decrease the effectiveness of the disordered person, it also, in this particular pattern, weakens certain cohesive group values with resultant societal disability in adjusting to changing circumstances.

The pattern in question, which we term *disparagement,* has not yet been fully elaborated as conceptual orientation, especially with regard to its relation to other elements of personality theory and social theory. This is particularly true with reference to psychoanalytic schemes such as regression; but although the articulation of such different aspects of phenomena and constructs are as yet unclear, we do not feel that there is necessarily any conflict. Sullivan has proposed disparagement as the *sine qua non* of neurosis (7). On the sociological side, Merton speaks of disparagement as *the* characteristic of people in a state of anomie (5). We believe our use of the term has a similar, if not identical, meaning to that of Sullivan and Merton.

In our definition, *disparagement is an habitual choice of extreme devaluation as a pattern for coping with problems of an intrapsychic and interpersonal nature.* As such, it appears to be pervasive as an observed phenomenon in the cases seen at our clinic and to be, within limits, a useful explanatory link in describing the relationships between sociocultural environment and the evolution and perpetuation of neuroses in individuals.

Because man is a communicating animal and because he lives in a framework of values that have hierarchy and primacy, he must constantly make choices and express preferences. In this process, it is patently necessary that he exalt some alternatives over others; the act of choice always implies a relative devaluation of the alternatives not chosen. Devaluation may be a residual category to handle things not especially liked, and it may quite healthily assume the form of a sharp attack on *selected* targets. In the pattern of *disparagement,* however, the process is a global unselective attack on huge areas of both the self-system and the tenets of the social milieu. It is thus a disproportionate, more or less consistent, Stephen Dedalus type of nay-saying, at the extreme end of the arc of devaluative possibility; its corrosive implications stem from both the tendency to deny individual worth, with resultant crippling of selfhood, and the tendency to deny the worth of group values and thus to cripple interaction.

Disparagement as a concept raises a number of as yet unresolved questions. Two that are critical may be stated as follows:

1. How does the extreme devaluative tendency become activated, and what personal needs does it meet?
2. In what conditions does disparagement develop in a way that directs devaluation toward the self or, alternatively, toward others? Perhaps most important—are the depreciation of personal worth and of societal currency dynamically related, so that disparagement always involves elements destructive of both the self-image and certain societal value patterns?

Figure 2 is an effort to construct a model of the original course of the disparaging process in the individual. As can be seen, it takes origin in a sociocultural context, mediated by the parents, and is eventually passed on to the next generation if the patient has children of his own. Many elements in our previous account of the Dean family seem to become more

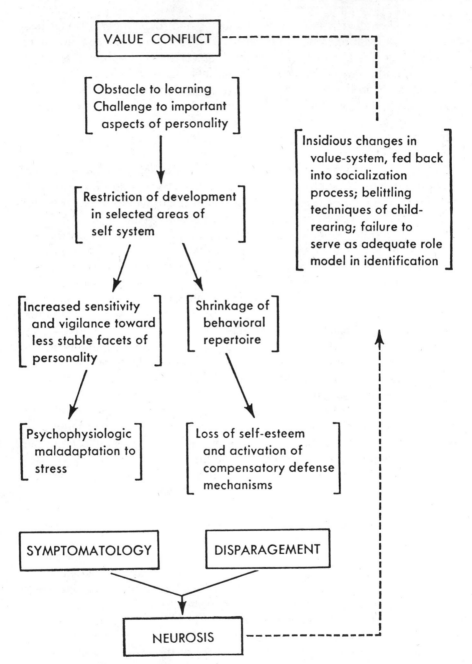

Figure 2. Disparagement in the neurotic process.

meaningful in this framework, and in the following discussion we shall attempt to use that family's neurotic anatomy in order to explicate disparagement and related concepts. To this end it may be helpful to essay a description of one individual, Alice Mary Seeley, as an illustrative example of the process sketched in the diagram.

Beginning at the upper left-hand corner and following the directions indicated by the arrows, we may note that Alice Mary Seeley began life as an unwanted child. Her mother was in rebellion against the feminine role and was vehement in her adherence to striving standards of moral superiority and self-denial combined with the pursuit of worldly success through the acquisition of money and status. These revulsions and aspirations were, however, futile and fruitless, since she had sexual relations with her husband, bore children, and never achieved either money or status.

The child, Alice Mary, grew up in an atmosphere of value conflict, without having available for identification a model of the normal female role. However, rather than internalizing wholly the maternal values in all their conflict and disjunction with reality, Alice Mary rebelled and added something of her own. The rebellion was no doubt in part a response to the mother's rejection. In other circumstances she might have turned to her father as the main figure for identification, but his values were similar to those of the mother and there is no indication that he was ever warm or accepting toward her.

Thus she developed an urge to be "different" from her parents. This urge, however, was from the beginning severely handicapped in two main dimensions. In the first place, she had already internalized her mother's values so that they were pervasive at both conscious and unconscious levels. Second, because of geographic and hence social isolation, she had no living model upon which to pattern the way of life toward which she aspired. Hence, she developed a fantasy of a not-too-realistic feminine role that would be sexually responsive, companionable, motherly, and calmly accepting. As is evident, this relates to the *being* pattern rather than the *striving* pattern of her parents. Other aspects of her fantasies so related were a desire for a stable existence close to nature, renunciation of economic and social ambition, together with more enjoyment of love, sharing, and interpersonal vivacity.

To sum up, she disparaged the values of her parents in a blind, all-or-nothing fashion; yet they were already within her and attempts to replace them only added fantasied unachieved contrasts of what life might have been. Thus it came about that, in devaluating her mother's tenets, she devalued herself.

This picture was well established by the time Alice Mary reached adulthood and has been further compounded by her marriage, since her husband turned out to be one who blocks her effectively from the outdoor existence and sensuous home life of her fantasies.

We find, then, disparagement, first of her mother's values and now of her own worth and role performance, as a critical feature of Alice Mary's psychic structure. This brings us to the box marked "Disparagement" in the lower mid-portion of the diagram. Alice Mary feels inferior and self-recriminatory; she is hostile toward her child, for he was conceived in the most fiercely rejected (and conflictual) portion of the feminine role—the sexual—and must be raised in an almost equally difficult portion, the maternal. She is beset by physiological complaints that are significantly centered on the genital organs, including postnatal difficulties and menstrual disturbances. These are relevant to the box in the diagram marked "Symptomatology." One may see in her case the grim determinism of inadequate socialization and thwarting objective social circumstance. The disparagement of the feminine role, so sedulously practiced by her mother, has continued to flourish; and her isolated social milieu and particular family situation have done little to mitigate this pervading devaluation. The total complex of symptoms and disparagement constitute her neurosis, the lowest box in the diagram; and it appears all too probable that this is exerting an influence on the development of her own children quite comparable to the kind of influence she experienced at the hands of her mother.

The life stories of Stan and Ray Davis and the evolution of their neuroses show a similar pattern, although with different items of specific content. The same diagram serves equally well to point up the relationships. In this case, however, it is possible to see in Ray the results of the process in a third generation, much as we predict it will be for at least some of Alice Mary's children.

It is impressive in our cases how regularly ideas of disparagement multiply when there is a major obstacle in the (social) learning situation, as for instance when there is a conflict of value systems, a demand to fill difficult roles, or any other inability to meet group expectations or carry out personal ideals.[9] It is as if for the patients any great discrepancy between goal and achievement is registered mentally in terms of absolute and final inferiority. The process seems to be sweeping, irrational, and accompanied by the arousal of powerful affect; the capacity for making finer discriminations seems incapable of functioning. Moreover, the process of disparagement tends to be self-perpetuating; this is due to the antagonizing or unresponsive behavior in relation to people that accompanies it, and it thus acquires a degree of self-fulfilling autonomy in the mentation of the individual, which interferes with his reality testing.

One of the social science team has studied the effect of widely shared personality factors on the failure of a trade union, many of whose members lived in the same geographic district from which our cases were drawn (6). The results of analyses of the life histories of several workingmen are presented, showing how their rejection of active union participation was related to personal apathy, self-disparagement and hopelessness. The author traces such feelings to insecure personal relations within the family of origin. His study thus supplements and to some extent confirms the picture we have drawn of a culturally pervasive pattern of self-devaluation. It is perhaps significant that inquiries into phenomena as seemingly diverse as union activity and individual neurosis should lead to similar explanatory patterns in this cultural setting.

Although we have illustrated our thesis in such a manner as to imply that the *striving* values are more noxious and hence more often linked to disparagement and neurosis than are the *being* values, we should like to state explicitly that we feel the crux of the matter to be in the value *conflict* and not in either *striving* or *being* per se. Furthermore, it is possible for a neurotic pattern to have the outer characteristics of either of the two main value systems. "Individualism" is the banner of Stan Davis' wife, but it is neurotic in its nature and context because it constitutes a means of establishing a sweeping, nondiscriminating disparaging relationship to others. On the other hand, it is just as possible to have verbalized attachments to the *being* way of life (as does Alice Mary Seeley) that are neurotically determined, unrealistic, and maladaptive. Unless one looks for the distorting factor of disparagement in stated systems of value, he is easily misled into mistaking a neurotic attachment for a normal adherence to important themes offered by the sociocultural matrix.

Neurotic problems are commonly expressed in terms of an apparently rational conflict of values. In fact, however, if they are neurotic they arise out of a previous state of personal feelings of inferiority and disparaging relationships with others. In such cases, avowed affiliation with a system of values may serve as a vehicle for the disparagement. For example, Ray Davis would say that he prefers modernism and efficiency, but the neurotic indicator in his pattern is the force of the contempt that he feels for "the old ways" of his father. We suspect that the irrational element of disparagement in his attitude is the effect of difficulty in his socialization, the impossible goals set by his mother, and his inability to deal with these factors realistically. He is, apparently, inculcated with ambition by the mother, yet remains emotionally and geographically close to her, so that there is no chance of taking effective steps toward fulfillment. To this must be added that, despite his hostilities toward his father, he has internalized some of the latter's *being* values and thus increased his psychic conflict. He stands disparaged in his own estimation, whether measured by his father's or his mother's standards.

DISPARAGEMENT AS A VARIABLE IN METHODS OF SOCIALIZATION

Child has reviewed the literature on methods of socialization.[10] The impression emerges that, in any particular area of learning, there is no one-to-one relation between effective socialization and such phenomena as punishment, love, reward, etc.

Adelaide Johnson (3) has pointed out that the regard of the socializing agent tends to become identical with the self-regard of the person socialized. Harry Stack Sullivan has made a similar point with respect to what he calls the development of the self-system. One might conjecture that an essential stimulus to given behavior in an interpersonal situation is the fact of being overtly regarded or estimated by another person. Manifest interest in the person being socialized on the part of the socializing agent may be just as significant as punishment or love in themselves. If this is so, then a critical factor could be whether the socializing agent regards the person being socialized with esteem or with disparagement. Where there is no regard and no expectation, there is probably little effective socialization.

Numbers of our patients reveal that their parents have used techniques in their upbringing that are relevant to these considerations. Included are excessive rejection, domination by threats, rules, bribes, and verbal or physical punishment. Of particular importance is the impression of the child that the parental example is inconsistent with their own explicit teachings.

It is clear that such techniques of socialization, if excessive, arise out of processes of disparagement and tend to inculcate disparaging tendencies in the person socialized. As Johnson notes, negative techniques of child rearing and of relating to others in general weaken the self-esteem and the capacity of the developing child to meet problems in the particular area in which they are used. In turn, they reflect an anxiety and incapacity on the part of the socializing agent to deal with these areas of interpersonal relations.

It would be interesting and most important to derive valid generalizations regarding relationships in the socialization process. Our cases afford some clues to possible general statements, but they are too few, and their cultural context too singular, to let us do more than pose a series of intriguing questions.

When there is extreme conflict within the value system, or between competing value systems, do certain methods of socialization become more prominent? For example, is there likely to be (due to anxiety on the part of the socializing agent) increased use of extremely repressive measures or even of rejection and withdrawal? How is parental rejection related to children's tendencies to withdrawal? Can we relate certain schizoid trends in the personality to the severity of social stress? Are specific behavior disorders induced by specific methods of child rearing?[11]

Does compulsiveness coupled with rejection provoke a kind of negative learning, so that the rules that are compulsively taught become systematically broken?

The person who forms a dependent relationship is of particular interest in the transmission of values. Stanley Davis, for instance, altered his values significantly when in a dependent relationship with his wife, and again later with a therapist. Perhaps the strength of the trend toward dependency, even though it may be regarded as a pathological way of relating, has the advantage of providing a means of flexibility in the individual that is important in his adjustment to changing circumstances. Its significance in the development of transference and of the reorientation in the early phase of therapy is acknowledged, but perhaps something of the sort that is also useful occurs in everyday life.

Precipitation of Neurosis

The precipitation of neurosis is very difficult to describe in causal terms. Almost certainly, in a given case, there are multiple determinants at physical, psychological, and social levels. However, it has frequently been observed that the appearance of frank neurotic symptoms—disturbances of affect, disturbance of physiology, obsessions, and other manifestations of pathological mental mechanisms—is intimately related to immediate events in the patient's life situation.

In the case of Stanley Davis, an organic illness was the apparent precipitant. It seems reasonable, however, to consider his physical impairment not only as a threat to life and hence affecting the equilibrium of personality, but also in the social context of a disease that renders one inactive and unable to work. His limited scope became a matter of great concern to Stanley Davis, and he continued to be bothered with thoughts of self-blame and obsessive worrying until he had at least partially worked through the problem with a sympathetic listener. This working through involved a trial consideration of possible shifts in role and a reorientation of values. Although the immediate effect of the organic disorder was to increase greatly his anxiety, disparagement, and self-blame, it became a choice-point from which, in the course of a few months, he evolved a new role for himself out of his total past experience.

Many factors seem to enter into the sort of crisis in the learning situation that occurred with the organic illness of Stanley Davis. Some of these might be listed as follows:

1. The role-taking facility that the person has developed throughout his life.
2. Intellectual capacity.
3. The difficulty of the presenting situation; in particular, the diverse pressures that are currently being exerted by various family members and acquaintances.
4. The manner of socializing exhibited by significant others—blame, threats, rewards, and other modes.

5. The severity of the person's previously developed tendencies toward disparagement.

The outcome for Stanley Davis might have been quite different if at the time of his illness he had still been living with his wife; she might have scolded him for his dependency on drugs and threatened him with various reprisals. This would probably have led to a perpetuation of his feelings of self-disparagement with further development of overt neurosis, depression, and obsessive thinking. In contrast, he was able to make arrangements that provided nursing attention, sympathy, and acceptance.

In the case of Ray Davis, neurotic symptomatology tended to be chronic. He continued to live near his mother even after his marriage. Whenever there was some slight disappointment in his ambitions, when he failed to make a good business deal or lost a little money, his ordinary worrisomeness would develop to the point of "unreasonable," completely unconstructive obsessional thinking. This would be accompanied by various physiological disturbances such as pain, rapid heartbeat "like my mother," and restlessness, so that he could not stick at his work. Frequently he felt so devalued that he took offense at minor or fancied slights.

Although much has been written about the symbolic significance of symptoms such as vomiting and diarrhea, Ray Davis and others of our cases suggest that psychophysiologic symptoms sometimes appear as a part of the process of identification with a person who has similar disturbances. It may be that certain physiologic symptoms have more social than personally symbolic meaning and can be better understood in terms of "transmission" of the same complaints from one person to another as part of identification, internalization, and learning.

In each case described in this chapter, there was a specific vulnerability to certain situations and to certain techniques through which others related themselves to the patient. The reactions of the potentially neurotic may be characterized as erring in the direction of dependency or withdrawal, among other pathological alternatives. In either of these cases any situation where disparagement is implied by others tends to be seen by the patient as either overprotection or rejection, depending to a great extent upon his previously learned patterns of value and perception rather than upon the actual situation.

New situations and new roles impose a particular stress upon the dependent or withdrawn individual who has been lodged in a family nucleus. This is because he does not have the outlets for his hostility that are accepted within the family. For example, the neurotic who threatens suicide as a hostile gesture toward his dominating mother will not find this an appropriate expression of hostility to a dominating employer.

We now have some clues to the critical questions raised in our earlier discussion of disparagement. The activation of extreme devaluative patterns has been partially located in the socialization process, as seen in segments of the Dean family. Disparagement seems to arise as a protective mechanism when two contrasting patterns of value are presented in incompatible form to the child; since they cannot both be fully incorporated, one may be harshly devalued in the interests of lessened tension and heightened psychic integration. Again, both parents may exhibit sweeping disparagement of broad areas of values (and persons who follow such values), thereby transmitting a habitual devaluing tendency to the child. In this instance, even a firm identification with parental models does not equip the child with a sufficiently flexible valuative repertoire to meet adequately the situations of adult life. Intense feelings of inferiority and self-deprecation appear to follow in two ways, or in some combination of them: when the parent of the same sex holds values distasteful to the developing individual (as for instance when that parent rejects the child) and the child fails to make a healthy identification with a mature sex role, yet involuntarily slips into the hated model for want of any other; and when the child at the edge of adulthood chooses an ideal role but almost entirely fails to fulfill it, so that an unmanageable gulf exists between aspirations and achievement.

The relation between disparagement of self and disparagement of others is, however, still unclear. Obviously there is an opportunity for the individual who disparages certain value orientations to generalize this negation toward holders of the detested orientation. These holders may in turn be categorized as suitable out-group targets of social prejudice, in conventional clusterings of religion, ethnicity, status, and so on. We suggest that expressed social prejudice is positively linked to neurotic behavior and that both are often based on disparagement. This is a strong clinical impression, but it requires much further exploration, particularly in the light of Adorno's contrasting findings (2).

SUMMARY

In the most general terms, this chapter has tried to view individual neurosis in its cultural and familial context. Numbers of members of several different large family groups have appeared as patients in a community psychiatric clinic, where a characteristic pattern of their relationships to one another, and to nontreated family members, has been perceived as a vitally predisposing element in neurotic development. Neurotic patterning in the family has been described in part as a reaction to cultural process through which family members experience their basic introduction to culturally-defined paths of behavior. Evidence from cases not described here, and from other types of study, tends to support the proposition that disparagement is a very widespread maladjustive mode in this culture and that the neurotic patient may represent an exaggeration of a phenomenon recurrent in the larger, nontreated population.

A divergence between two equally sanctioned sets of cultural values has been outlined. Persons growing up in this region are exposed to both orientations in such a way that they have difficulty in assigning clear-cut primacy to either one or in combining them into a satisfying coalescence. Failing such an adjustment, they often reject selected values on a superficial level but continue to deprecate themselves in areas of personality function related to those values. Opportunities for thoroughgoing fulfillment of either "striving" or "being" are seldom utilized, so that one finds a shared ambivalence toward occupational patterns, interpersonal behavior, and general style of life.

Cultural value conflict is most forcefully presented to the individual in early life through the socialization process. The family environment is the most obvious and important link between configurations of group value and the developing alignment of forces within the personality. Ambiguities in socialization, the conflicts, surfeits, and emotional starvations that distort normal functioning, are thought to be the most fertile source of neurosis. The child's parents, the primary agents of socialization, are in this series of cases at odds with one another over incompatible values or internally torn between the prescriptions for behavior generated by different value systems.

The child, then, suffering from difficulties in identification with a mature, consistent role model, and from poorly integrated patterns of value, develops severe vulnerabilities in one or more important phases of life. When these vulnerabilities and restricted facets of the personality are challenged by the need for new learning by the assumption of demanding role responsibilities, the neurotic process of disparagement is likely to be activated. Disparagement seems to be a favored mechanism among our cases and in this culture as a whole. It is really a denial of challenge, in the sense that the individual deprecates himself as unworthy of a serious effort and/or deprecates the values embodied in the challenge as undeserving of his best energies. He is not a failure because he did not try.

Our selected cases of neurotic patterning in one family can, of course, afford only slight evidence of the hypothesized relations between cultural value, family system, and individual disorder. A great deal of systematic research must be performed to substantiate specific correlations among group values, methods of socialization, personality development, and the employment of neurotic mechanisms such as disparagement. It is hoped that this chapter may be helpful as a step in that direction through the formulation presented and the questions raised.

NOTES

1. This chapter comes from the Stirling County Study, which is being conducted by Cornell University in collaboration with the Department of Public Health

of the Province of Nova Scotia and with the cooperation of Acadia and Dalhousie Universities. Invaluable help has also been provided by the Faculté des Sciences Sociales, Université Laval. Within Cornell, the Stirling County Study is attached administratively to the Social Science Research Center and is sponsored by the Department of Sociology and Anthropology and the Department of Psychiatry of the New York Hospital and Cornell University Medical College. Financial support is provided by the Carnegie Corporation of New York, the Department of National Health and Welfare of Canada, the Department of Public Health of the Province of Nova Scotia, and the Milbank Memorial Fund.

2. The staff of the project at the time the article was written consisted of the following, who are listed according to their functions in the study: Alexander H. Leighton, Director, and Allister M. Macmillan, Deputy Director; Eric J. Cleveland, Chief of the Psychiatric Clinic; W. D. Longaker, Associate Psychiatrist; Bruce Dohrenwend, Social Analyst; W. H. D. Vernon, Clinical Psychologist; M. Adelard Tremblay, Chief of the Social Science Unit; Jane M. Hughes, Administrative Assistant; Dorothea C. Leighton, Assistant to the Director. The authors wish to express appreciation for the assistance of Bernard Hebert, clinical psychologist, and Janice Ross, social worker.

3. Grateful acknowledgment is made for extensive and valuable help provided by M. Adelard Tremblay.

"Stirling" is a code name for the Canadian Maritime region under study.

4. Our categories of "striving" and "being" are extremely close in most essentials to the orientations "doing" and "being-in-becoming" originated by Florence Kluckhohn (Dominant and substitute profiles of cultural orientation, *Social Forces*, May 1950). There is also an apparent symmetry between the patterns sketched here and certain features of the many conceptual distinctions of life-style elaborated by Tonnies, Redfield, and others—e.g., "gemeinschaft-gesellschaft," "folk-urban," "sacred-secular." Ours is perhaps a local variation of a theme which runs through much of human culture and history, particularly since the Renaissance.

5. Many investigators have found the seeds of individual neurotic conflict in incompatible cultural prescriptions (cf. the writings of Horney, Fromm, and Frank). Yet the precise juxtaposition of cultural ambiguity and individual disorder remains unclear.

6. The organism's tendency to reach out for meaningful social relationships has been termed by Angyal, *The trend toward homonomy*, Chap. II.

7. The three cases of Stan, Ray, and Alice Mary exemplified anal-retentive, phallic-aggressive, and oral-incorporative symbolism, respectively, in their clinical interviews, particularly in their recounting of dreams. Stan has been more concerned with "holding his own," and his dreams included preoccupation with money, fears of being robbed or gypped by a woman. Ray's problem has been to put forth the initiative required to satisfy the maternal ambitions. His dreams reflect his deeper frustration and hostility, his fears of castration and, perhaps by a reversal, his fears that the mother might be killed. Alice Mary, on the other hand, is deeply convinced of the fact of maternal rejection, to which she reacts by a rather aimless rebellion that alternates with very marked "oral dependency" that makes her easily influenced by the pressures of others.

8. Cf. A. H. Maslow, *Motivation and personality*. New York: Harper & Brothers, 1954.

9. The importance of various types of discontinuity and inconsistency in the learning situation has been stressed by Child. See Irvin L. Child, Socialization. In *Handbook of social psychology*, Gardner Lindzey (Ed.). Cambridge: Addison Wesley, 1954, Chap. 8, p. 655; also, Jurgen Ruesch, Social techniques, social status, and social change in illness. In *Personality in nature, society and culture*, Kluckhohn, Murray, and Schneider (Eds.). New York, Knopf, 1953, Chap. 9.

10. *Ibid.*

11. Lack of realism in the value system or conflict between contrasting value systems may generate problems in trust, autonomy, and other areas. Different value systems, as Erikson points our (cf. Erik H. Erikson, *Childhood and society*. New York: Norton, 1950), are linked to different ways of conceptualizing a situation. Thus a sexual situation may be conceptualized in oral, anal, or phallic terms, and the mode of sanctioning seems to be the primary determinant of whether the problem is to center on dependency, autonomy, etc. For instance, it is perhaps not necessarily the method of bowel-training in itself that produces obsessive neurosis but the parents' treatment of many sorts of situations *as if* they were bowel-training situations.

REFERENCES

1. Adler, Alfred. *A study of organ inferiority and its psychical compensations.* Trans. Smith Ely Jelliffe. *Nervous and Mental Disease Monograph*, No. 24, 1917.

2. Adorno, T. W., Frenkel-Brunswik, Else, Levinson, D. J., and Sanford, R. N. *The authoritarian personality.* New York: Harper, 1950.

3. Johnson, Adelaide M. Sanctions for super-ego lacunae of adolescence. In K. R. Eissler (Ed.), *Searchlights on delinquency,* New York: International Universities Press, 1945, 1955, p. 225.

4. Leighton, Dorothea C. The distribution of psychiatric symptoms in a small town. *American Journal of Psychiatry,* 1956, *112,* (9).

5. Merton, Robert K. *Social theory and social structure.* Free Press, 1949.

6. Parker, Seymour. Union participation: A study in culture and personality. Unpublished Ph.D. dissertation, Cornell University, 1954.

7. Sullivan, Harry S. *The interpersonal theory of psychiatry.* New York: Norton, 1953.

IV

The Meanings of Family Boundaries

Part III was concerned with ways in which a family unit draws upon the culture and utilizes its selections in shaping its own particular life course. The culture offers a wide array of content from which families may choose.

Part IV considers in several ways how a family establishes boundaries for itself, boundaries that are more or less constraining and more or less permeable to relationships and experiences defined as extrafamilial. Norman W. Bell examines the boundary between the nuclear family and the extended family. Gillian W. Elles studies the boundary between the nuclear family and the larger world of community and institutions.

Bell studied two groups of urban working-class families. The families in one group, called disturbed families, each had a functionally disturbed child. The other group, designated well families, had children of whom none suffered from a clinically manifest disturbance. Bell found four aspects of the relationship between the nuclear family and the extended family, and disturbed and well families handle these four aspects differently.

Elles' concept of a family boundary is of a somewhat different order from Bell's. She refers to a system of interlocking fantasies among family members that causes the family to develop a resistance to what they perceive as the "invasion" of outside ideas and feelings. The family also resists, however, by withdrawing from contact with various extrafamilial agencies. Elles reports specifically on a highly disorganized family whose members form "a closed circuit" because of a fear of madness and because of criminal behavior that makes them vulnerable to the

intervention of police authority. Efforts to help this
family failed because the family could not allow itself to be open to any kind of outside power, however benign.

10

Extended Family Relations
of Disturbed and Well
Families

NORMAN W. BELL

It has long been recognized that the mental health of individuals is related to the family. However, until recently there has been a failure to conceptualize the family *qua* family; studies of individual pathology have usually reduced the family to individual psychodynamic terms (1). Beginning with Richardson's (2) pioneer attempts to characterize the family as a group with properties in its own right, considerable changes have taken place. Numerous investigators have developed conceptual schemes to describe the subtle and complex processes in families. Such reformulations involve a shift away from the view that mental illness is a characteristic of an individual toward the view that disturbance in one member is a symptom of the functioning of the whole family. Concomitantly, different therapeutic approaches to families as groups (3) or to individuals (4) as family members have been developed.

These reconceptualizations produce a needed corrective to earlier tendencies to overemphasize the significance of an individual's innate tendencies or of isolated segments of relationships in which he may be involved. However, to the family sociologist there appears a danger that the fallacies of oversimplification and reductionism characteristic of the focus on the individual are being repeated again at the family level. Family psychiatrists seem, by and large, to view the family as a self-contained, invariable unit (5) existing in a social and cultural vacuum. The significance of a

Reprinted by permission from *Family Process*, September 1962, *1*, (2), 175–93. Copyright 1962 by the Mental Research Institute of the Palo Alto Medical Research Foundation and the Family Institute.

Norman W. Bell is Professor of Sociology in the Department of Sociology and in the Clarke Institute of Psychiatry, University of Toronto.

grandparent[1] or an extrafamily activity of a parent may be recognized as incorporated in one member's pathology in particular instances. But systematic consideration of the interdependence of the nuclear family and related families of orientation, or of the nuclear family and the surrounding society as a universal structural principle, have been lacking.[2] Both on theoretical (7) and empirical (8, 9) grounds it is difficult to find justification for neglecting the frameworks within which families function.

PROBLEM

This chapter will explore only one segment of the total web of relationships in which families exist, namely relationships with extended kin. Every society recognizes and patterns the relations of successive generations (10). The breaking or changing of old ties and the formation of new ties through marriage are always transition points with potential stresses. As Radcliffe-Brown has expressed it ". . . Marriage is a rearrangement of social structure. . . . A marriage produces a temporary disequilibrium situation. . . . The establishment of a new equilibrium after a marriage requires that in certain types of kinship or family structure there is a need felt for emphasizing the separateness of the two connected families. . . . The principal points of tension created by a marriage are between the wife and the husband's parents and the husband and the wife's parents." (11, pp. 43–58 passim). The thesis of this chapter is that disturbed families are ones in which this "disequilibrium created by marriage" has not been resolved but continues to provoke and maintain conflicts and the underlying discrepancies that cause them, and that well families have achieved some resolution of the problems of ties to extended kin so that these kin are neutral or even positive forces in the resolution of family problems.

Before presenting data relevant to this thesis it may be helpful to review briefly the nature of family processes that lead to individual pathology and some features of the American kinship system, two domains not previously related to one another.

In common with various other family researchers, I assume that functional disturbances arise from and are maintained by family interaction, including the emotional dynamics associated with overt behavior. Different researchers have focused upon different aspects of the patterns of interaction, some emphasizing the persistent structural features, others the nature of communication processes, still others the discordance between overt behavior and inner feelings. Common to all appears to be some conception that, as a group, the family must try to adapt to the discrepancies within and between individuals and reach some equilibrium. Unless the underlying issues are resolved there will be a strong tendency to act out the problems by involving others in biologically, psychologically or socially inappropriate roles. Such processes lead to disturbances of ego identity. The disturbance, so dysfunctional for the individual, serves positive functions for the family in its efforts to secure or preserve some sort of integration (12). Removal of, or change in, the disturbed individual upsets the "pathological equilibrium" and leads to changes throughout the system. Much less work has been devoted to well families, but conversely it might be formulated that to cope with discrepancies they adopt mechanisms which actually resolve the discrepancies, or at least contain them in ways that are not pathogenic for individual members.

The family processes associated with mental illness or health have been described by others in some detail (13), with focus on the operations within nuclear families. But any nuclear family is part of a larger "family field" and must cope with the establishment and structuring of ties to two families of orientation. Some kinship systems stress the continuity of generations by subordinating the younger generation to the authority of the elder and stress the preference of one lineage over the other. The American kinship system (14) emphasizes the structurally isolated nuclear family and is bilateral. The emphasis on the isolated nuclear family means that there is discontinuity and relative independence of adjacent adult generations. The characteristic of bilaterality means that both the husband's and wife's families are potentially of equal importance in reckoning descent, controlling property, giving support and direction and so on. Since neither side of the family receives a culturally prescribed preference, each family must work out its own balance of the ties to, and independence of, two extended families. This task is further complicated by the tendency to define the maintenance of kinship ties as a feminine rather than masculine role.[3]

DATA

The data to be cited here are drawn from a long-term study of disturbed and well families. The broader project, directed by Drs. John Spiegel and Florence Kluckhohn, is concerned with the interrelation of cultural values, family roles and the mental health of individuals.[4] Details of the population studied have been presented elsewhere (1, 15, 16); here it is sufficient to note that intact working-class families with at least three generations available for interviewing were studied intensively for periods ranging from two to five years. The families were of varying ethnic backgrounds. Half of them had a functionally disturbed child (here called "disturbed families"); half had no clinically manifest disturbance (called "well families").

Contact with the "sick" families was mainly in the office setting; the child and both parents, at a minimum, were seen in weekly therapy sessions. Occasionally parents or a parent and child were seen jointly. Family behavior before and after interviews was observed. Eventually all families were visited in their homes on several occasions, and relatives were interviewed where possible or at least were met during visits. With the "well" families there was similarly extended, regular contact by teams of a child psychiatrist, a psychiatric social worker and a sociologist. The bulk of these contacts was in homes. Clearly the meaning of the contact for these well families was different, but we were reasonably satisfied that comparable data were obtained for both groups.

FINDINGS

Four aspects of how extended kin articulate with nuclear families will be discussed. The first two (extended families as countervailing forces and extended families as continuing stimulators of conflict) deal with the dynamics of intergroup relationships. The second two (extended families as screens for the projection of conflicts and extended families as competing objects of support and indulgence) deal more with the social-psychological qualities of the relationship. Distinguishing these four aspects is, of course, an analytic device; empirically they are intertwined.

Extended Families as Countervailing Forces

The ability of the nuclear family to contain its conflicts and control the impact of its discrepancies by means of a child is limited. Adult members in particular may experience guilt about the child, particularly when his condition is defined by outside agencies such as schools, courts and neighbors. But even short of this step, parents are capable of experiencing guilt or anxiety through identification with the child, a necessary but often neglected correlate of the child's identification with the parent.

> Mr. Costello, for instance, brought his younger son for medical attention when this son began to stutter seriously. The father had suffered from a speech problem himself in childhood. He "understood" his son's stuttering as something learned from an older brother, although it was more closely related to the chronic stool-retention problems this younger child had, the physical symptom for which medical attention was sought. The older son's stuttering had not affected the father deeply; this symptom in the younger son with whom the father was so closely identified was intolerable.

Aging of the child may shift the child's capacity to absorb family tensions so that he is able to escape parental pressures more and get support for himself from the peer group (17). Maneuvers within the family are not always adequate to restore the pathogenic equilibrium. At such times there may be a resorting to the extended family to shore up crumbling group defenses. Typically this process includes a seeking for support from the natural parents and an attack upon the in-laws. In the full form this becomes reciprocal with the other spouse drawing upon his family for reserves and attacking his in-laws. As the vicious circle progresses, the whole family becomes split. A day in the life of the McGinnis family will illustrate this:

> Mr. and Mrs. McGinnis lived in a state of armed truce. Mrs. McGinnis domineered the family in an irrational, active way. Her domination of their oldest son, perceived by herself as maternal devotion, was extreme. Mr. McGinnis had developed set patterns of schizoid withdrawal from the family and persistent needling of the 12-year-old son to grow up before he was drafted into the army or was thrown out of the family to go to work. The bane of Mr. McGinnis' life was his old, unreliable car, which in its weaker moments he used to kick and curse. For Mrs. McGinnis and her son this car was the proof of the father's stupidity and the family's low status. Mr. McGinnis was continually harassed to get a new car. One day, independently, he did go out and buy a second-hand station wagon. When Mrs. McGinnis was told of this she conjured up an image of a high, homely, small bus. In the telephone conversations with her family, which quickly followed, this distorted image was elaborated. They soon gathered around to "kid" Mr. McGinnis about running a jitney to New York. Their perverse pleasure was short-lived when they saw a quite ordinary station wagon. By this time Mr. McGinnis was bitterly attacking his in-laws and soon after paid a rare visit to his aged mother who was nearly indigent and in a nursing home. His visit reawakened Mrs. McGinnis' suspicions that her mother-in-law had money hidden away that should be given to them. When Mrs. McGinnis' spinster sisters came under fire from Mr. McGinnis, she defended them in exaggerated terms and returned with interest comments about Mr. McGinnis' paranoid sister.

For the McGinnises this schismogenic process was not conscious. Mrs. McGinnis called her various family members every day, so there was nothing unusual in her telling them of the "bus" her husband had bought. In other families the process is quite conscious and deliberate. The Manzonis, for example, knew that visits to their own families made their partners wildly jealous, and knew just at what point to call or visit a relative.

Even children become sensitive to the familial tensions regarding extended families and disappear to visit grandparents, insult visiting relatives, or engage in other operations to crystallize the parents', and eventually the whole family's, split feelings about in-laws.

The mechanisms by which extended families are brought into conflict situations may be conscious or, at least apparently, unconscious. Frequently the sequence is initiated by what seems to be a casual and innocent conflict. Until we are able directly to observe the initiation of this spreading of conflict, it is difficult to be specific about the mechanisms involved. I feel fairly sure that the process is a subtle one, that no direct reference to conflicts in the nuclear family or direct request for allies has to be made. Rather both or all parties to the relationship are sufficiently sensitized that the spreading process can begin, or flare up, through minimal cues in tone of voice, timing of contacts and so forth. In all, I believe these mechanisms are not different from those observed in the families of schiz-ophrenics, where therapy teams (18) and hospital staff can become drawn into family conflicts (19).

In light of Bott's findings (8) regarding the nature of the social network and intrafamilial role allocation, it is important to inquire into the relation-ships between the extended families. When they are drawn into family conflicts do they themselves echo those conflicts, as Brodey finds that ther-apy teams do? None of our families had been geographically mobile to any large extent, so most extended families did have superficial acquaintance with each other. The frequency of active relationships was low, being clearly present in only one out of eleven cases. Since the frequency of active re-lationships in the general population is unknown, it is difficult to be sure of the significance of this. Of course, in our society the respective parental families stand in no particular relationship to each other, and there is no term to denote it.[5]

Well families also have conflicts, but they differ in several respects. The open conflicts that occur are incidents on a foundation of basic integration, are self-limiting, and do not compromise a wide range of interaction in the future. In striking contrast to the disturbed families, active engagement in disputes was kept within the family by well families. This does not come about by the kin being unaware of the conflicts. Indeed, they often seem quite well-informed about them, but these kin groups are not drawn into the pattern of balancing off one side of the nuclear family against the other.

In some well families there was evidence that the extended families not only did not become drawn into and amplify the conflicts, but even acted in benign ways to reduce conflicts and restore family functioning. An in-teresting example of this occurred in the DiMaggio family:

> One summer Mr. DiMaggio's mother wanted to visit a nephew who had recently migrated to Canada from Italy. Over Mrs. DiMaggio's protests it was decided that the grandparents and four of their five sons, including Mr. Di-Maggio, would make the trip; Mrs. DiMaggio would stay at home with her youngest child. During the absence of her in-laws, Mrs. DiMaggio became mildly depressed, and developed fantasies that her husband was having a gay time. Though her own family was living nearby, her contact with them did not in-crease markedly. The night before arriving home, Mr. DiMaggio phoned his wife. Though she did not complain openly, he sensed her state of mind. He felt guilty and when they arrived home, managed to arrange it so that the rest of the family entered the apartment before he did. In their first contacts the brothers-in-law and parents-in-law were attentive to Mrs. DiMaggio. One brother-in-law, a priest, took her aside and talked to her about the obligations of mar-riage and informed her of how unhappy her husband had been while away. When Mr. DiMaggio did come in, his wife put aside her complaints, brightened up and was genuinely glad to see her husband. Mrs. DiMaggio remained aware of her reactions but resumed a normal, close relationship with her in-laws.

Extended Families as Stimulators of Conflict

Extended families are not always passive elements in the situation, and in some instances the initiative for provoking conflict seems to rest with them. Extended families may be responding to discrepancies in their family structure in the same ways, thereby inducing conflicts within the nuclear families we have in focus.

> The Mozzarellas had for some time had the father's unmarried brother living with them and their three children. At one point this brother took or stole a small amount of money from the Mozzarellas. Mrs. Mozzarella was furious and began to fight with her husband. The conflict grew and the brother moved out. Rather than abating, the conflict between husband and wife widened and deepened. Finally Mr. Mozzarella moved out for a few days, but did not stay with his brother. After a few weeks absence the brother also moved back in with the family.

In all such instances it is likely that the action of the extended family has to fall on prepared grounds in the nuclear family. Often these actions are appropriate—almost uncannily so—to the weak spots in the family organization. In themselves the actions of the extended family may appear innocent enough, but their effects are widespread. Frequently the triggering incident is a gift.[6]

> Mrs. McGinnis' mother gave her grandson gifts of money just at the times when Mr. McGinnis was berating his son for his failure to earn his own spending money. The money mitigated the economic problem but increased the father-son conflict, and eventually the whole family was at odds.

In some instances the precipitating incident seems to be more genuinely innocent, with the problem being the inability of the family to develop or employ mechanisms for insulating themselves or for controlling conflicts once they have begun.

> Mrs. Manzoni's brother was in an army basic training camp about 40 miles away. He often visited the Manzonis when on leave. His visits were agreeable to the Manzonis, who even looked forward to them since their uncontrollable son responded well to direction from this uncle. One weekend, however, he brought a buddy along with him. Mrs. Manzoni tried to be hospitable, but father and son both reacted sharply to this shift. Bitter arguments about the invasions and demands of Mrs. Manzoni's family ensued. Mrs. Manzoni retaliated with accusations that her husband did many favors for his family.

Whether conducted in an innocent or calculated way, extended families frequently do provoke conflicts in the nuclear families. The impact is not always the open conflict described in these examples. Often the impact is at the latent level, exaggerating the discrepancies that already exist.

At the well end of the continuum extended families do not intervene in their married children's lives in ways that set off the trains of reaction described above. The interventions that do occur do not cut to the bone and are not reacted to in a stereotyped way. To illustrate:

> Mr. McNally's brother was a heavy drinker and had served time for theft. Occasionally he would come around to the McNally home, presumably looking for food and money. Mrs. McNally would refuse to let him into the house. Mr. McNally, though he had some interest in and sympathy for his brother, supported such responses on the part of his wife. At times he sought out his brother and tried to help him, but these approaches were not timed and carried out so as to reflect on his wife or compensate for her rejection of the brother. On her side, Mrs. McNally did not interfere with her husband's attempts to rehabilitate his brother, though she expected little to come of them. Both husband and wife had mixed feelings about this relative but their attitudes toward him appeared to be appropriate.

Rather than acting as agents provocateurs, the extended kin of well families are able to remain neutral and respect the boundaries of the nuclear family. For their part, the well families are not hypersensitive to the actions of kin.

> Mrs. Flanagan's parents lived nearby. They were old and somewhat infirm. Periodically heavy demands for help were made on Mrs. Flanagan. Even though the whole family was preoccupied with being cared for and had much physical illness, these demands were accepted as a necessary sacrifice, even by the children. Mr. Flanagan accommodated himself to the demands on his wife by being helpful at home and at his parents-in-law.

Extended Families as Screens for the Projection of Conflicts

The extended family need not be an active or even potentially active element in the conflict situation. In all cases there was some evidence that the extended family served as a screen onto which a family member could project sentiments that referred more immediately to a spouse, child or parent. This process, which I have labeled the *overgeneralization of affect,* is mainly of negative sentiments. Positive sentiments are also involved as a reciprocal tendency, though they are not so conspicuous. The overgeneralization spreads over social space and time. In the extreme cases an impervious dichotomy of good and bad occurs and rationalizes a wide range of avoidance behavior and expression of dislike.

> Mrs. Donovan, in her first therapy sessions, painted a picture of the many deficiencies of her oldest son and her husband. She felt they were no good and were just like her husband's family, all of whom were no good and never had been any good. Her own father, who died in her adolescence, was completely different, having been intelligent, sensitive, liberal, sophisticated and unpre-

judiced. Her mother, concerning whom she had more mixed feelings, came in for little comment at this time. Mrs. Donovan had had, since her marriage, minimal contact with her husband's family. Contacts that did occur substantiated her view of her in-laws.

The families in which pathology was highly integrated tended to show a pattern of each spouse directing his or her negative sentiments toward the in-laws and directing positive sentiments toward the natural parents. Reality sometimes makes such splitting difficult. However, grandparents who can in calm moments (or in therapy) be evaluated realistically, tend to be defended when they are criticized by the partner, and part of the defense is an attack upon the partner's side of the family. The reverse picture, of one person directing negative sentiments to his own parents and positive ones to his in-laws, seems infrequent. In our cases it was noted only in one family, and in this case the tendency was mild.

This sort of conflict involves, naturally enough, parents more than children. Still, it is not restricted to them. The children are quite likely to assimilate the parental sentiments and to align with one rather than the other or "slide" between the two.

> Jackie McGinnis, for example, could echo all of his mother's feelings and suspicions of his paternal grandmother and condemn the paternal grandfather who had died many years before his birth. At such times he was positive about and in close contact with maternal relatives. To a lesser degree he could reverse the roles if he was in conflict with his mother and wanted to get something from his father.

Again, projection of feelings through space and time need not emerge in overt conflict. The projection may be a stable characteristic of an individual's psychological functioning within the family, which magnifies the discrepancies that do exist.

> Mrs. McGinnis occasionally used her suspicion that her mother-in-law had money secreted in a Canadian bank in her arguments with her husband, insisting it was money they had a right to. Even when she was not attacking her husband on this account, it was part of her fantasies about giving her son the education her husband was convinced he should not have and was incapable of getting. Buttressed by this projection, she was able to push her son and herself in directions that took them farther and farther from the father.

I hope it is clear that there is more to this pattern than the pathological functioning of individuals. Individuals, children as well as parents, utilize the structure of the family and the extended family as arenas in which to express their ambivalent feelings. Reciprocally the schisms of the family and the extended family reinforce and perhaps even stimulate complications in their feelings about parent figures. Individuals who may have been able to integrate their ambivalent feelings toward their parents reasonably well may have difficulty in adapting to the existence of parents *and* parents-in-law.[7]

Members of well families, as material cited earlier suggests, do not develop such polarized feelings about kin. There certainly were mixed feelings and, on occasion, strong negative feelings about kin, but these could be handled and even if not fully expressed, the tendency to split feelings and maintain them in a rigid fashion was not present. This lack of overgeneralization of affect was true of positive feelings as well as negative ones. In contrast to Epstein and Westley's (22) normal families, we did not meet the pattern of "adoration" that they observed in the wife-husband relationship. This difference in findings regarding normal families may be a genuine difference in the sample of families studied or may be a function of different methods of investigation used. In our group there was also no "adoration" spreading to the extended families.

Extended Families as Competing Objects of Support and Indulgence

I have chosen to treat separately a theme closely related to all the above. I feel that this theme is a central and basic one. It is this: extended families become competing sources for and objects of support and indulgence for the nuclear family. In American society the norm is for nuclear families to be independent.[8]

The disturbed families we have seen almost universally presented problems of this sort. When the loyalty and commitment of some menbers can no longer be implicitly assumed and are called into question, processes are set in motion to generate and amplify conflicts. In some instances the medium of conflict is money, as with Mr. McGinnis:

> He had an ambulatory paranoid sister who journeyed about the country taking skilled clerical jobs. Invariably she would develop suspicions that she was being watched and plotted against and quit her job. In desperate financial straits, she would wire Mr. McGinnis for money. Though recognizing her as ill, Mr. McGinnis would usually get money somewhere and send it to her. He maintained that he kept this secret from his wife, though she was well aware of what was going on. (Both, incidentally, silently assumed that all this was kept secret from the children, which was also inaccurate.) For Mrs. McGinnis this justified her suspicions that her mother-in-law was holding back and in derivative and half-recognized ways complicated the family fights over money.

The diversion of material goods as well as money to the extended family can be the precipitant of conflicts. For the Manzonis it was the cost of food that was consumed by Mrs. Manzoni's family. Mr. Manzoni felt the food served his in-laws was better than that served *his* family if they visited, and more of it was consumed.

In other cases the questioned commodity was affection and attention. Mr. McGinnis was preoccupied with the amount of time his wife spent talking to her family on the telephone and compared it to the neglect of his own mother, a neglect of which he himself was guilty. The Manzonis were continually suspicious that the other was seeing his own family and being influenced by them. Children too were perceived as liking one side of the family more, paying more heed to one side, and even of resembling, physically or in personality, one side of the family rather than the other.

> In the Costello family such a pattern was developed to the extreme. Their first son was a "mother's boy," the second a "father's boy," and they moved in largely separate interactional spheres. When Mrs. Costello wanted to visit her parents, which she felt obliged to do weekly, her older son would not tolerate being left behind while her younger son protested strongly about going. Each visit was thus a struggle for Mrs. Costello and sufficient proof to Mr. Costello that she should stay at home.

Whatever the resource under contention, the pattern of real or perceived favoritism for part of the extended family structure can arise. The pattern seems to serve multiple functions; it externalizes the internal conflicts of any given individual and allows him to rationalize his own shortcomings (as with Mr. McGinnis), for his own shortcomings pale into insignificance in the light of the others' misdeeds. At the same time it preserves the conflicts within the family. Being external, they are beyond influence of any one person of combination of people.

Once again well families stand in contrast. They too have problems about the allocation of resources, but diverting them to one family of orientation, as the earlier illustration of the Flanagans suggests, does not stimulate feelings of deprivation and resentment. Correspondingly resources from extended families, even when the differential between the contributions of the two sides of the family is considerable, do not become foci of conflict.

To summarize the material presented above, it may be said that disturbed families have difficulties in solving the problems of how to relate to two sets of "parents" and of establishing family boundaries. The absence of boundaries allows family conflicts to spread to extended kin and means a deficit in the ability of the nuclear family to insulate itself from the vagueness of the outside world. Thus, extended kin are drawn into or play into the conflicts of the nuclear family so that underlying discrepancies are not resolved but are spread and made more rigid. In this family setting individual members have difficulty in taking roles as representatives of the whole family. *Vis-à-vis* the outside world of kin they act as individuals; what they give to or receive from kin casts them as competitors with other members rather than as collaborators with the whole family. This interpersonal situation appears to foster the awakening and acting out of ambivalent feelings with a consequent circular effect.

IMPLICATIONS

The thesis has been advanced here that the extended families are, or become, involved in family pathology, and that different patterns of relationship with extended families are set up by disturbed families from those set up by normal or healthy families. In conclusion I should like to explore some of the implications of such findings for theories of the relationship between family processes and mental illness, and for therapeutic efforts at diagnosis and treatment.

Several years ago Ackerman complained of etiological theories in dynamic psychiatry, saying that they ". . . hypothesize a relation between a piece of the child and a piece of the parent." (25, p. 182) His evaluation was that these were inadequate and that we had to evolve theories which related to the integrity of the individual to the family as a whole. A great deal of progress in this direction has been made, but the question may be raised again with regard to family-centered theories. The point is not that they are incorrect but that they are only part of the picture. Families are seldom, if ever, isolated from kin. If ties to extended families are present and involved in the family processes, must we not at some level include this in our theory? The findings presented, though based upon a small and selected population and derived from studies of neurotic children rather than psychotic adults, seem to me to argue in this direction.

The issue can be posed in a more general form. The systems we deal with are not closed, they are always embedded in and to some degree derive their rationale and patterning from broader systems. For some purposes we may treat them *as if* they were closed, but we must never paint them as the whole truth. In this I have tried to look outward from the family system to its kin. One might equally well take cognizance of the fact that the family is involved in many other networks of relationships and that these too may function to stimulate and maintain conflicts or alternatively to contain and correct them.[9] Ultimately we must refer our finding to the general patterns of values that characterize cultures and subcultures and that have a pervasive influence in shaping personality, family role patterns, and the whole family field extending through space and time, indeed the whole fabric of society. Florence Kluckhohn has devoted her major attention to the analysis of these patterns of value orientations (26). It is, I believe, possible to show that the type of issue that comes up in this process of re-equilibrating the imbalance associated with marriage, the pathological ways of coping with discrepancies, and the available alternatives for resolving the issues can be deduced from the variations in value orientations characteristic of different groups.

Our work is vastly complicated by such a theoretical position, but I see no alternative to dealing with reality as it is. If a broader range of variables can be dealt with precisely and adequately, we may develop theories with more specificity than our current conceptions. In an earlier era it was popular to attribute mental disturbances to broken homes; I daresay there are 100 papers in the literature reporting such findings. It is only part of the problem of these studies that they report inconsistent findings and that they seldom have adequate control groups. A more serious problem is that broken homes seem to be related to delinquency, neurosis, schizophrenia, and various psychosomatic disorders. An agent so nonspecific is of little help, or at best is merely the first step. Most studies of families have also lacked control groups. It is not clear whether the presumably pathogenic processes detected in the families of schizophrenics are really absent in families with less seriously disturbed individuals and perhaps even families without disturbance. Tracing out how pathology is integrated in a broader network than the nuclear family may give some added specificity.

There might also be advantages to paying close attention to the history of families. It is striking that we have not developed models of the developmental processes of families that compare to our models of individual development. For example, in the Donovan family many shifts in group and individual dynamics coincided with changes in the closeness of the nuclear family to the wife's mother.

> After their marriage the Donovans lived with the wife's mother, and had a fairly happy marriage. Acute difficulties arose after they moved to their own dwelling; Mrs. Donovan's sentiments about her in-laws became more negative, and Mr. Donovan's contacts with his family, which were more rigidly pursued, became more threatening to the wife. The problems were heightened after Mrs. Donovan's mother remarried. During the course of therapy the two family units jointly purchased a two-family house and lived close to each other again. Many conflicts abated following this move.

If we can learn to listen to the histories patients give, not individual but familial, we can learn much about the dynamics of the group and how the family has gotten to its present state. Such findings as have been reported may also have implications for our therapeutic endeavors. To the extent that we misplace the causal forces that have led to and maintain pathology, we may misjudge the potential for change and how to bring it about. Systematic consideration of patterns of relationships with extended families can give us added leverage in a diagnosis of particular problems with which we are confronted.

Treatment strategies may need rethinking in the light of this view of pathology as a process broader than the individual family. In our research work we saw relatives, not because we had any systematic program or good rationale to intervene therapeutically with them, but in pursuit of our research interests. This was not always readily agreed to by members of the nuclear family, but in many cases it had a salutary effect for the family members, for the relatives, and for their relationships. Relatives were seldom ignorant of the difficulties in the nuclear families or of the involvement with the psychiatric clinic. Nuclear families often preferred to believe that their problems and attempts to get help were unknown to kin, but on close examination, this was another example of "open secrets."

In several cases it was a significant turning point when the person being seen could allow his relatives to be seen by the therapist.

> Mr. Donovan was resistant to therapy in many ways but dead set against his family being seen. After a year with very limited progress (and incidentally some time after the family had moved back into a house shared with Mrs. Donovan's mother), he was unable to discuss his discomfort with authority figures unless he could be on close friendly terms with them. A little later, Mr. Donovan offered to take the therapist to visit the rest of his family. Subsequent to this social visit, there took place meaningful discussions of Mr. Donovan's feelings of loyalty to and sympathy with his own family, and his resentment at his wife's depreciation of them, him, and his son.

While such techniques are regarded by many as unorthodox, dangerous and/or unnecessary, I believe a case can be made that there are instances in which therapy fails unless the therapist can understand and involve himself into the fabric of meanings and the network of relationships the patient knows as natural (4).

As for the relatives, seeing them legitimizes their interest in the nuclear family, but brings this interest under some control. We found they were sometimes able to neutralize their involvement in and get for themselves a broader perspective on the nuclear families. It was also profitable to get a fresh perspective on a case by seeing a relative. Just as Brodey sees the advantages of seeing married partners to get a "stereoscopic view" of the relationship, so seeing members of several families offers the advantages of a stereoscopic view of families.

We have not included relatives in therapy on a systematic and regular basis, and I can only conjecture about the advantages and problems that "kin group therapy" might bring. There are no logical grounds for stopping at the boundaries of the nuclear family, boundaries that are very permeable and shifting.[10] At one level, movement in therapy consists of changes in the sentiments about and interaction with extended families. To cite the Donovans once more:

> Mrs. Donovan's depreciation of her son, husband and all her husband's family gradually gave way during therapy. In the space of three years, they altered sufficiently to lead her to buy a small Christmas gift for her mother-in-law. Contact of the whole family with her husband's siblings increased. Eventually, she visited her mother-in-law and found that she had good qualities as well as bad, and that it was not unpleasant to visit her. As her sentiments were mitigated, her relationship with her husband expanded and changed and shifts even appeared in the whole family constellation.

It is possible that this central process in the whole family might have been speeded up if both partners could have been influenced simultaneously, as indeed occurs in the treatment of mother-child pairs.

SUMMARY

This paper has taken up the issue of whether our understanding of functional disturbances can afford to stop at the boundaries of the nuclear family. It has been argued, and some evidence has been presented, that disturbed families are distinguishable from well families in terms of their patterns of relationships with extended families. Disturbed families have a deficiency of family boundaries that leads them to involve extended kin in their conflicts and makes them sensitive to influence from extended kin. Directly or indirectly a considerable segment of kindred systems become part of a pathological drama, until pathology is a characteristic of the system, not of individual persons or families. Such findings require replication with larger samples, but do raise questions about the adequacy of our theories of family pathology and our treatment techniques.

NOTES

1. The first volume of *The Psychoanalytic Review* in 1914 includes abstracts of articles on the "grandfather complex" by Jones, Abraham, and Ferenczi.
2. Ackerman (6) is one of the few who have advanced into this area, and he puts the stress mainly on the emotional and attitudinal aspects.
3. I do not mean to imply that the American kinship system presents more, or more intense, problems than other kinship systems. Other systems engender problems too (e.g., the daughter-in-law in traditional Chins), but the focal problems are different.
4. Sponsored by the Laboratory of Social Relations, Harvard University, and the Children's Medical Center, Boston, and supported by grants from the National Institute of Mental Health and the Pauline and Louis G. Cowan Foundation.
5. Other languages do have a term for this relationship, e.g., the Jewish word *Machatenen*.
6. The gift, as Marcel Mauss has shown (20), creates an obligation of the receiver to the donor. Normally this cements the social structure. As I shall discuss presently, for conflicted families the assuming and discharging of obligations is problematic and tends to break down the social structure.
7. Cf. Parsons' (21) proposition that socialization involves the internalization not simply of separate parent figures but also the internalization of the *relationship between* the parents.
8. Legally the situation is confused. Marriage is recognized as a legal union that obligates the husband to support his family, and both parents to support their minor children. Similarly a legal marriage (and even in some circumstances a common-law union) entails the right to pass property onto family members and the right of family members to claim property of a deceased member. At the same time we still have laws, occasionally enforced, that children, even married children, are obligated to support indigent parents (23). This vagueness of our laws and our mores,

together with our bilateral kinship system, presents the possibility of conflict. Family resources—whether they be money, goods, affection or services—are not unlimited. There are always alternative directions in which they may be allocated. Even comfortably situated families may have problems in the allocation of wealth and contain "poverty-stricken" members (24).

9. For brief comments on how work associates, neighbors and professionals may be assimilated to pathological family patterns see (4, 12).

10. One wonders what family therapists would do if they attempted to treat matrifocal families such as exist in the south and around the Caribbean.

REFERENCES

1. Spiegel, John P. and Bell, Norman W. The family of the psychiatric patient. In Silvano Arieti (Ed.), *American handbook of psychiatry*. New York: Basic Books, 1959.

2. Richardson, Henry B. *Patients have families*. New York, Commonwealth Fund, 1945.

3. Bell, John E. Family group therapy. *Public Health Monograph*, 1961, *64*, U. S. Department of Health, Education and Welfare.

4. Bell, Norman W., Trieschman, Albert and Vogel, Ezra F. A sociocultural analysis of the resistances of working-class fathers treated in a child psychiatric clinic. *American Journal of Orthopsychiatry*, 1961, *31*, 388–405.

5. Leichter, Hope. Boundaries of the family as an empirical and theoretical unit. In Nathan W. Ackerman, Frances L. Beatman and Sandord N. Sherman (Eds.), *Exploring the base of family therapy*. New York: Family Service Association of America, 1961.

6. Ackerman, Nathan. Emotional impact of in-laws and relatives. In Samuel Liebman (Ed.), *Emotional forces in the family*. Philadelphia: Lippincott, 1959.

7. Bell, Norman W., and Vogel, Ezra, F. Toward a framework for the functional analysis of family behavior. In Norman W. Bell and Ezra F. Vogel (Eds.), *A modern introduction to the family*. Glencoe: Free Press, 1960.

8. Bott, Elizabeth. *Family and social network*. London: Tavistock Publications, 1957.

9. Zimmerman, Carle, and Cervantes, Lucius. *Successful American families*. New York: Pageant Press, 1960.

10. Apple, Dorrian. The social structure of grandparenthood, *American Anthropologist*, 1958, *58*, 656–663.

11. Radcliffe-Brown, A. R. Introduction. In A. R. Radcliffe-Brown and Daryll Forde (Eds.), *African systems of kinship and marriage*. London: Oxford University Press, 1950.

12. Vogel, Ezra F., and Bell, Norman W. The emotionally disturbed child as a family scapegoat. *Psychoanalysis and the Psychoanalytic Review*, 1960, *47*, 21–42.

13. Sanua, Victor D. Sociocultural factors in families of schizophrenics. *Psychiatry*, 1961, *24*, 246–265.

14. Parsons, Talcott. The kinship system of the contemporary United States. In Talcott Parsons, *Essays in sociological theory* (revised edition). Glencoe: Free Press, 1954.

15. Kluckhohn, Florence R. Variations in the basic values of family systems. *Social Casework*, 1958, *39*, 63–72.

16. Spiegel, John P. Some cultural aspects of transference and countertransference. In Jules H. Masserman (Ed.), *Individual and familial dynamics*. New York: Grune & Stratton, 1959.

17. Pitts, Jesse R. The family and peer groups. In Norman W. Bell and Ezra F. Vogel (Eds.), *A modern introduction to the family.* Glencoe: Free Press, 1960.

18. Brodey, W. M., and Hayden, M. The intrateam reactions: Their relation to the conflicts of the family in treatment. *American Journal of Orthopsychiatry,* 1957, *27,* 349–355.

19. Bowen, Murray, Dysinger, R. H., Brodey, W. M., and Basamania, B. Study and treatment of five hospitalized family groups with a psychotic member. Paper delivered at the American Orthopsychiatric Association Meetings, Chicago, 1957.

20. Mauss, Marcel. Essai sur le don. In Marcel Mauss *Sociologie et anthropologie.* Paris: Presses Universitaires de France, 1950.

21. Parsons, Talcott, and Bales, R. F. *Family, socialization and interaction process.* Glencoe: Free Press, 1955.

22. Epstein, Nathan B., and Westley, William A. Grandparents and parents of emotionally healthy adolescents. In Jules Masserman (Ed.), *Psychoanalysis and human values.* New York: Grune & Stratton, 1960.

23. Schorr, Alvin L. *Filial responsibility in the modern American family.* Washington, D. C.: U. S. Department of Health, Education and Welfare, 1960.

24. Young, Michael. The distribution of income within the family. *British Journal of Sociology,* 1952, *3,* 305–321.

25. Ackerman, Nathan W., and Behrens, M. L. Child and family psychopathy: Problems of correlation. In P. H. Hoch and J. Zubin (Eds.), *Psychopathology of childhood.* New York: Grune & Stratton, 1955.

26. Kluckhohn, Florence R., Strodtbeck, Fred, and others. *Variations in value orientations.* Evanston, Ill.: Row, Peterson, & Co., 1961.

11

The Closed Circuit: The Study of a Delinquent Family[1]

G. W. ELLES

The aim of this chapter is to show the way unconscious fantasies of various family members are interlocked. This enabled the individuals to make use of each other and to exploit each other's compulsive acting out in an attempt to gain relief from their own frightening fantasies. It had the effect of making the family unable to accept therapy, because this was experienced as an overwhelming threat to their own closed circuit.

In earlier research[2] at Henderson Hospital, a group of psychopaths and their families were followed through their treatment phase and rehabilitation up to five years after discharge. The research established that most of these families had complemental character disorders in the marriage pair. Members of such families broke down easily, and were severely restricted in the relationships they could make. Yet the family organization could be seen as having a therapeutic function, retarding and limiting the nature of the personal breakdown and offering a basis for rehabilitation. From our observations it was possible to work out various patterns of emotional balance in the families. The most important to the present subject was the balance between personal identity and family identity. This family-based identity, in its pathological form, represents the transfer into a central family body of many unacceptable thoughts, feelings and activities of individual adult members. At the same time, persons so shorn of their identity are more likely to be used as an organ or limb of such a family body. Yet survival depends on being surrounded by this family. For, unable to be aware of

Reprinted by permission of Sweet and Maxwell, Publishers from *British Journal of Criminology*, 1961, 2, 23–39.

Gillian W. Elles (now Mrs. Parker) is a psychoanalyst in private practice in London. At the time of writing she was research therapist at Henderson Hospital, Sutton, Surrey, England.

themselves to any degree, the *family* is then needed as a means of indirect communication, both with themselves and with the world outside. Thus, in the small group of families studied, four stages of family imbalance were worked out. At the bottom of the scale stood the family so threatened by disintegration that family needs took precedence over nearly all personal needs, even the need for individual psychotherapy. The family became a closed circuit, unable to allow any effective help to reach the family members. In this paper such a family is described, the whole family being seen as the "patient," and each individual but a limb of the family.

The Lukes have been married some six years, but Henderson Hospital has information going back to 1949, when Mr. Luke was first admitted for treatment. Furthermore, intensive home visiting on two occasions has given cross-sections of the family activities that could be compared to show apparent degenerative personal illness. Both the Lukes have been admitted twice to the mental unit—indeed it was at the unit that they met. Both have been in several other mental hospitals for short periods as a result of suicidal gestures. Here then is a ten-year period covered by the recollections of the Lukes, by clinical notes on them as individual patients, and by observations made within their home at two periods of considerable stress related to Mrs. Luke's pregnancies. Over the years this family has become less and less able to tolerate relationships of a therapeutic nature. At the same time, clinics, mental hospitals, special psychotherapeutic centers have all been unable to devise a treatment approach that can be accepted by the Lukes long enough to produce a change toward better functioning. Seen as a progressive failure between the Lukes and the Health Services, ten years ago Mr. Luke tolerated an eight-month's stay in the hospital. Eight years ago they both stayed about three and a half months, and six months ago the wife stayed three days. One month ago, having sought admission, neither of them could bring themselves to accept treatment, and so simply failed to arrive. Therefore, though the Lukes have been admitted many times to many hospitals for observation, there is a pattern of increasing intolerance of treatment leading to more precipitate discharge.

Certain points seem important in a family like the Lukes. First, that such a division of family experience into past, present and future really has little meaning. These families feel "futureless" because past memories and fantasies are experienced as action in the present. Family energy is mainly spent on seeing each day through and surviving. Secondly, because of this basic insecurity, such families find it more important to maintain the status quo—however unsatisfactory—than to allow change to take place. Change means insecurity greater than they can bear. Therefore, there is little learning by experience. Finally, the overwhelming fear of these families is that they will be invaded by other peoples feelings and ideas, and that they will be defenseless.

In order to discuss the unconscious activity of this family, material has been collected from various sources. The psychiatrist's report gives the family's immediate problem. The report of the research worker adds a picture of the relationships of such a family in its present setting. Information from two other sources is channeled in. There is a distillation from the hospital files on both the Lukes, dovetailed together into a family history of illness. Finally, there is the record of the research worker over six months, during which the Lukes worked with her to show how the family functioned under stress situations.

In collecting all this information, it is accepted that the various levels of abstraction are not comparable, but that each source of information has something to add to a total picture of a family functioning in difficulty. From it there emerges a picture of the Lukes dealing with three major themes: an oral theme (difficulties of eating, starving, addiction and drunkenness); a theme of violence (fighting, sexual attack); and a theme of death (not being able to stay alive—a passive state—or killing). The themes remain constant, though through the ten years there is both a change in symptomatology and a change of actors. But the drama repeats itself over and over again.

THE LUKES' PROBLEM*

Mrs. Luke had been admitted to Henderson Hospital for the second time in order that a growing addiction to tranquilizers be treated. At the initial interview with the psychiatrist, the whole family was present; that is, Mrs. Luke, her husband, and her three-year-old daughter, Mary. Mr. Luke was attentive and gentle with his wife, and the child was exceptionally well behaved. Mrs. Luke was thin, anxious and appealing. Mr. Luke, a quiet, serious man, looked more robust, and at the time seemed the more mature of the two. The story they told was a tragic one. After their marriage they had had an extremely difficult time. In the intervening seven years, Mr. Luke had had only twelve months' employment. Their son, born two years after the marriage, proved a difficult child to feed, apparently passing into a comalike condition after taking very little milk. He had suffered from colic, and this had kept everyone awake. In desperation one night, they had placed his cot outside their bedroom so as to get some rest, and the next morning they found that he was dead. The postmortem showed that he had suffered from bronchial pneumonia. At this time Mrs. Luke was again pregnant; she developed eczema first, and after Mary's birth was thought to have developed a gastric ulcer. A similar pattern of feeding difficulties showed up, and the child would not take her food, passing into a trancelike state. Mrs. Luke took an overdose of sleeping tablets on two occasions, leading to her admission for short periods into a mental hospital. On the first occasion, it was arranged that Mary be looked after by foster parents. During the nine

*As presented by them to the psychiatrist.

months that she was away from home, there appeared to be no feeding problem. On the other hand, Mrs. Luke became more and more distressed at not having the child and fought to get her back. Mrs. Luke got Mary back when the baby was about 18 months old. By this time Mrs. Luke was three months pregnant. Both the Lukes were thoroughly alarmed about the possible effect a second baby would have on Mrs. Luke, particularly as Mary had redeveloped all her eating difficulties, and now vomited her food easily. Therefore, it was particularly tragic for the couple when the third pregnancy resulted in a stillbirth. It confirmed their sense of guilt about not wanting the child, and their feelings of inadequacy. Both felt people were talking about them or shunning them, and Mr. Luke gave up his job to be with his wife.

This account of themselves was told to the psychiatrist on a Tuesday at the time of Mrs. Luke's admission. Three days later she came in great distress to the sister in charge of the unit, saying that she must return home immediately as her child was ill, her husband must go out to find work, and the two of them needed her at home.

RESEARCH WORKER'S REPORT

The Family and Its Environment

The Lukes live in a road of respectable, solidly built four-storied houses, most of which have been divided into flats and maisonettes. In the daytime the road appeared empty, but in the evening groups of neighbors could be seen gardening or tinkering with old cars and motorbikes. At one end of the road is a main thoroughfare and big shops; at the other end there is a small road leading to one-roomed shops.

The Lukes appear very isolated, even though they themselves have lived in the house for seven years and Mr. Luke's mother had the ground-floor flat until her death. Such relationships as the Lukes have appear to be "tainted," and are felt as likely to lead to trouble. For instance, on the first floor is Mr. Luke's sister and brother-in-law. She is seen by the Lukes as a lewd, jealous woman, very antagonistic to them both and aggressive toward Mrs. Luke. She is also felt to be dangerously seductive to Mary, who has to be watched to see that she doesn't get up to her aunt's flat. In the basement, which belongs to the Lukes, there is a young colored couple. They are described by the Lukes as nice people and in themselves friendly. Because they are illegally occupying the flat their presence, though lucrative to the Lukes, is also a threat. Mr. Luke seems to have cut himself off from most of his relatives since his mother's death. Mrs. Luke's kin live in the North of England, and for many years she had been estranged from them, until recently. With both there is a story of their parents' marriage breaking up and each parent marrying unhappily again. Neither of the Lukes seem to have any local friends. Indeed, they flinch from speaking to the neighbors. They hear the local gossip through Mr. Luke's sister.

At the level of formal relationships, the same pattern of tainted contacts is to be found. Mr. Luke has a long record of unemployment (17 jobs between 1946 and 1949, a prison sentence of eight months, and then just over a year's employment in the last ten years). High personal aspirations have all along been linked with inadequate performance. One job appealed to him; he would like to return to it, but it is no longer open to him because he took advantage of the kindness of his employer. With the landlord a similar pattern is developing. This old lady, who has been sympathetically inclined to Mr. Luke because she knew his mother over many years, let the young couple take on Mrs. Luke senior's flat when she died, thus with their basement flat giving them a maisonette. When the landlord visits there is great apprehension in case the tenants' secret is discovered. With the National Assistance Board they again fear discovery, this time the discovery of a false declaration about their income. To mitigate their guilty feelings Mr. Luke has stopped claiming other benefits, either for himself or for the child.

From every side the Lukes fear retribution. Put another way, the Lukes could be described as working with a system of values that has become split and highly conflicting. One half of it, immensely moralistic, rigid and retaliative, leads them to feel that they are forever doing wrong. This brings the expectation that in all their relationships they will never be allowed to keep the good things that they want for themselves. They expect to be forced to give up or offer back the things that have given pleasure. Therefore, in a family defense, they secretly operate by a different value system, one which allows them to steal, defraud and dispose. This system is the exact opposite of all the "oughts and musts" with which their conversation is peppered. The first set of values force them to judge these secret norms as "cheating," but at the same time this first set are felt as an external, coercing set of values, unintegrated into their family life, yet dictating it. It is in the presence of these conflicting sets of norms that gratifying emotional contacts outside the family become destroyed. The resultant isolation makes the Lukes desperately dependent upon each other. Each has come to label themselves as criminal, and also feels an accessory to the other's "bad" deeds. Each has involved the other in more unacceptable behavior as a way of lessening their own sense of wrongdoing. (The "bad" and "wrong" are judged by their first set of values, but at the same time they represent generally accepted social norms too.) Therefore, it becomes even more necessary for them to stay together as a family. Yet because they must be with each other all the time, neither can fulfill adequately the role tasks in the marriage relationship, so that each also despises the other. A vicious circle is established.

The Role Relationship Failure and Its Effect on Treatment

Mrs. Luke cannot let her husband go out to work; she is too frightened of her responsibility as a mother. On the other hand, she is ashamed of the poverty of her home, feels she can invite no one in, and therefore is very bitter toward Mr. Luke on this account. Mr. Luke cannot allow his wife to accept treatment because he then has to take full responsibility for the child, or else go out to work while she is at a nursery. If he goes out to work he feels exposed by his inadequate work skills and fears that people are laughing and talking about him. In this tangle of failed relationships there is a further twist. Because each feels a failure in his or her own right, both identify themselves with each other's failure and assume a protective role. Therefore, though Mr. Luke feels that Mrs. Luke needs treatment, he can also feel, on her behalf, the pain she might have to face in discussing her problems in a therapeutic group. Therefore, he finds it extremely difficult to adopt an attitude that might enable her to remain in treatment. Again, though Mrs. Luke feels her husband's work record is despicable, she is so aware of his problems at work that it is easier *for her* to have him unemployed.

It can be seen at this point that Mrs. Luke's reason for leaving treatment is grossly overdetermined. At the center of this family maze is Mary, aged three. Whoever undertakes to feed her then becomes so wrought up that they can scarcely feed themselves. She has to find a way of dealing with her parents' anxiety about her health, her diet, and even her sleep (for they nudge her to see if she is still alive). The child seems loving and obedient, neat and tidy in between not eating or being sick. The parents feel that she is preoccupied with ideas about biting, as she will only take liquid or mashed foods. At least a quarter of the day is spent over her meals. Through her behavior, Mary exerts an enormous control over her parents, who feel they are being driven to the point of breaking. Most of their day is spent in protecting and cherishing her, but at the same time there is much talk between them about the other two babies, particularly the eldest son, who is idealized. Mary, in her questioning, would seem to feel that this boy was more special and better than she. Therefore, she has to contend with a rivalry of two dead siblings who are so much in her parents' minds. At the same time she has to deal with her parents' anxiety that she too may suddenly die.

The total family problem can be seen in terms of a recurring unsatisfying parent–child relationship. There is a disbelief in a benign and competent authority who can feel like a good parent. Authority seems to mean forceful control or mad power. Things labeled "good" do not feel good, and therefore pleasant experience has to be secretly found, burdensome responsibilities secretly disposed of. As a result, Mr. and Mrs. Luke, though seeing themselves as essentially upright and law-abiding, find themselves a family pursued by the furies of their conscience externalized in formal authority figures—officials, employers, doctors in hospitals, landlords, and the police. There are propitiatory acts of self-denial, and these give way, at times, to crueler acts of self-punishment in suicidal episodes, which, in their turn, inflict more suffering on the other family members. As time goes by, more formal agencies stand to be involved in the behavior of this family. Parallel to this, the informal spontaneous and socially gratifying relationships become tainted, disordered, and are now practically nonexistent.

Basically the Lukes seem to have the capacity to interact with one another in a loving and ongoing manner, but inasmuch as the original marriage was a flight from facing what they feared was a "mad" part of themselves, so a large proportion of family energy must be deployed in keeping the marriage alive for purely defensive reasons. The intense care for Mary can stand for a family "acting out" of an inner individual fear that the child within each one of them may become overwhelmed by mad, cruel and driving parental standards.

THE FAMILY FUNCTIONING

If this report assessed the matter accurately, then a prediction could be made that the Lukes' system of family functioning precluded the possibility of formal psychotherapy. Indeed, this was demonstrated in the pattern of family behavior over the next half-year. The prediction was based on the Lukes' apparent assumption that there was no good powerful enough to help them, and, therefore, they had to do everything for themselves. The unconscious converse of this seemed to the research worker equally important; i.e., that the Lukes had to feel that they could act omnipotently as a way of avoiding their own intense feelings of chaos and failure. To feel that other people could help only highlighted their inadequacy and their guilt.

Shortly after the two visits on which the foregoing report was made, the Luke family engaged in a further drama. Mrs. Luke began to fear that she was again pregnant. In front of the research worker, and in earshot of Mary, the Lukes discussed how they could deal with this. Again both assumed that it would be a disaster for Mrs. Luke to have another baby. Over the weeks, various drugs were procured by Mr. Luke and swallowed by Mrs. Luke to terminate the pregnancy. At the same time, Mary became interested in the baby next door, wanted to know if she could have a baby to play with. During these two months no conclusive evidence came to light that a pregnancy had been established, yet a great deal of family energy was devoted to dealing with the fears relating to it. On two occasions Mrs. Luke made herself rather ill, and on both these occasions had to miss appointments with psychiatrists.

One way of looking at this episode would be to see it as a sort of "family dream." The family is acting out the theme of infanticide and, at the same time, exposing this to the research worker. Mr. and Mrs. Luke become the active people, treating themselves, while two psychiatrists and two treatment units are rendered impotent. The Lukes, recognizing that Mrs. Luke left one unit rather than discuss the problem of the death of two babies, now manipulate a situation where they again show their need to have treatment, but only from themselves. They demonstrate their need to be, at one time, patient, doctor and culprit, thereby closing the circuit.

This negative way of using medical services could be shown to the Lukes. It led, in this instance, to some small recognition of how each used the other's problems as ways of dealing with his or her own. Mr. Luke recognized that, so long as he felt he could not possibly leave his wife, he did not have to face persecutory feelings at work. Mrs. Luke recognized how she could use this situation as a way of avoiding being confronted with her very troubled feelings. For now she saw that some of her problems of feeding Mary represented a mirror image of a similar situation between her and her own mother. Here, for a fleeting instance, there was some slight increase in personal awareness. Both saw in themselves some small fragment of what ordinarily was felt to be a family experience. As a result, it seemed that for 24 hours they acted in an "unfamily" way. After this, a complex family maneuver took place so that the family equilibrium could remain steady. The threatening situation seemed to be one in which *simultaneously* there was an alteration in the balance of defensive projection in both the Lukes. Now Mrs. Luke kept in touch with the research worker, and Mr. Luke did not. Such a balance might have continued longer but for the fact that Mrs. Luke's father arrived to stay with them.

It so happened that Mrs. Luke's father met the research worker on the day he arrived. Shortly after, Mrs. Luke contacted Henderson Hospital asking for a home visit to discuss treatment. When seen by herself in the kitchen, Mrs. Luke poured out her despair about her behavior and her husband's reaction to it. She felt herself to be a bad mother and a bad wife. She felt her husband often accused her of taking tranquilizers when she hadn't. He did not trust her with any money. Indeed, he continually searched her and her belongings, in case she was hoarding. She painted a picture of herself wanting treatment, but of her *father and husband* making it impossible for her to go to the hospital. She felt their attitude was that she could pull herself together, and that no hospital could help. Yet later the father tried to get the active cooperation of the research worker to make his daughter go into the hospital, saying he was sure she needed help. When the three of them met in the presence of the research worker, the father maintained the attitude that his daughter needed and could get help. Mr. Luke took a neutral position, and Mrs. Luke now took the *opposite* attitude to her previous one in the kitchen two days before. The father had considerable drive and seemed deeply concerned about his daughter and son-in-law. Gradually they both agreed to ask for another interview at a hospital, which had been prepared to see the whole family. The out-patient interview took place, the date of admission was arranged, but this was never kept. It coincided with the father's return to his home. As an indication that this was going to happen, the research worker found, on her last visit, two pointers. First, that Mrs. Luke and her husband now felt that the whole problem "had to do with sex." All they felt was needed was that they should go into this themselves. In other words, the Lukes were going to be both patient and doctor once more. Second, Mr. Luke's sister was present for part of the time. Once she had left, the discussion turned on how the Lukes were trying to persuade *her* to get treatment, as they felt sure she needed it. At subsequent visits this tended to be the family attitude.

THE QUESTION OF THEME VARIATIONS

It was suggested earlier that families like the Lukes feel futureless. A sense of future depends, in part, on being able to separate past experiences from present, to become free of enacting, compulsively, massive blocks of such experience. With this family the frightening past had to be projected continually into the relationships around them. Paradoxically, this then tied them even further to those childhood experiences. Furthermore, it led them to become more and more dependent upon each other as a target for these projections and as a tool in their enactment. By looking at the early history of the Lukes, the central projective themes can be identified and their modification traced in the family experience.

Mr. Luke had always seen himself as shy, acutely self-conscious and impulsive. His parents were unhappily married and separated when he was about ten. His mother went to live with another man, and Mr. Luke could remember having "murderous" feelings toward him. His mother drank, and he frequently came home to very sordid scenes. He also feared his mother's suicidal tendencies, and on one occasion found her with her head in the gas oven. At one time he feared that he had wanted to kill her, and it was a great relief when she recovered. His school and early work record were poor, although he enjoyed reading and politics. In company he was afraid that people were laughing and talking about him. His most successful period was while serving the R.A.M.C. in a field-ambulance unit. After discharge from the army he had eight months' in-patient treatment as a result of a depressive episode in which he had suicidal ideas. He showed a marked improvement, but on leaving the hospital could not find suitable work. He joined with two brothers-in-law in breaking and entering barges and garages. Eventually he got an eight-months' prison sentence. Again he was admitted to the hospital for treatment, and on this occasion met his future wife and left precipitately after three-and-a-half months' treatment. The reason he gave was that he must get work and find a home so that he could marry. Shortly after he was admitted to another hospital, having made a suicidal gesture. At this point his mother seems to have found the young couple a flat under hers. The future young Mrs. Luke then left her treatment, and the two of them got married and settled into the flat.

Mrs. Luke, when discussing her early experiences, had none of the hesitancy and understatement of her husband. She talked about them as if they were happening at the moment. Again there was the history of unhappily married parents who separated and remarried—unhappily—when she was ten. The important things to her were having tonsils and appendix removed by the time she was four. She remembered her father telling her that at the time there was a further worry, a local lad had interfered with her. Later on, there was another occasion when she had been "taken up to the woods" by an older man. When she was five her father lost his job, became morose, and took to drink and going with other women. Her mother went out to work, she went to school and had to find her own midday dinner at home. The marriage of her parents finally broke up when her father developed venereal disease. Her mother got a divorce and then married another man, who was both a drunkard and had VD. The mother was infected, and Mrs. Luke was subjected to tests. When Mrs. Luke was 14, her mother died suddenly. Mrs. Luke was never clear about the cause, whether it was due to her mother's heart or to pills she had been taking at the time. Therefore, there was a fear that the mother committed suicide. Furthermore, Mrs. Luke became worried about her stepfather's sexual feelings toward her. At this time she had disassociative and hallucinatory experiences, and she also started drinking. After undergoing a short period of treatment, she left her home town and gradually worked her way to London, never holding any job for very long. She liked the work, but became frightened about the boss's feelings toward her. Eventually, she was admitted to Henderson Hospital after having lost consciousness for eight hours while working as a chambermaid in a hotel.

THE THEMES

The themes of child care has in some measure already been traced in the family history. One child dies at 3½ months, one at birth, and one is just an idea. Mary, in her relationship with her mother, typified an ill-remembered bad relationship between Mrs. Luke and her own mother—ill-remembered because Mrs. Luke has idealized her mother, who was the one safely loving person in her life. More easily, Mrs. Luke can recall her mother discussing her own childhood. The older woman was brought up by a crazy foster mother because her own mother had to be put into an asylum. The foster mother overfed the children at the beginning of the week and ran out of money at the end. To a certain extent this also fit into Mr. Luke's experience of his mother, who at one moment could be warm, protective and giving, and then at another withdrawn into depression or drunkenness.

Therefore, in mothering there is a significant theme for the Luke family: mothers can be overindulgent and at the same time driven mad by their children.

Again, in their experiences connected with drinking and taking drugs, each of the Lukes has some overwhelming memory that enables him or her to be used by the other as a way of disposing of these haunting experiences. For instance, Mr. Luke's need to save his wife from her excessive use of tranquilizers has this side to it: to save her is also connected with saving his mother from his own intense anger, and gas oven or the lover, while Mrs. Luke enacts both drunken parent and frightened child. The death of the babies (boys) can stand for Mr. Luke's need to find some way of acting out his feared impulses toward his mother's lover and the fear of retaliation associated with the mother's many pregnancies. On Mrs. Luke's side, her anxiety about having a sexual relationship and becoming pregnant is linked to desire for an incestuous relationship and her reaction to it. So long as she can feel like the small child being interfered with, she can avoid responsibility. When the Lukes were single, both at times were suspected of stealing. Mr. Luke's record showed several incidents of breaking and entering. Now the pattern is somewhat altered. Mr. Luke from time to time takes all his wife's money, breaking open cupboards, searching her and her belongings. Mrs. Luke counters this by taking from the housekeeping, while both of them feel they have defrauded formal agencies. Their sexual relationship also has the feature of breaking into a forbidden place.

Furthermore, in all their relationships there is the theme of death, sometimes active death, sometimes just not staying alive. For instance, before marriage Mr. Luke is twice admitted to a mental hospital following a suicidal gesture; Mrs. Luke's period of unconsciousness is similarly treated by admission. Once Mr. Luke is married, he abandons this form of communication, but his wife makes two suicidal gestures that get her into an observation ward. In all these episodes a gradual condensation of acting out has taken place, as with the other themes. It is suggested that such an act on Mrs. Luke's part represents not only her own reaction to an intolerable situation, but her unconscious reaction to her husband's need for her to respond in such a way to his expectation. This expectation is one to which Mrs. Luke responds, not only because she has many reasons for feeling suicidal, but also because, in such severely disturbed relationships, one person can make use of an unconscious countertransference in a way that leads to the enactment of their *own* secret impulse, here Mr. Luke's suicidal feelings being enacted by Mrs. Luke.

DISCUSSION

This paper has set out to describe some small section of the experience of a young married couple in a phase where the family had to remain in a closed circuit. Two pressures forced them to bring this about. The first one represented an unspoken fear of madness. As a family, they combined to defend themselves against this by boosting each other's apparent ego strength, by their own weakness, a defense against psychosis. The steps they then took led them to criminal behavior, criminal by their own harsh superego system, but also, at times, criminal by the social norms surrounding them. This, in turn, became the second pressure necessitating even more drastically closing the circuit. Treatment was felt as a seductive process that could only lead to *family* disaster and a return to seeing themselves as isolated individuals, the one with paranoid fears, the other with gross hysterical symptoms. Therefore, as the closing of the circuit became more effective, so the compulsive enactment of certain themes (associated in the first place with childhood traumata) became more determined. The family lived in a perpetual psychodrama, with themselves as both actors and audience. By operating a very complex system of fragmented identification, they could avoid the agony of responsibility. Because they could not accept, at a personal level, the guilt associated with it, they gained no relief of a permanent nature. On the other hand, through the six years of marriage, their use of each other became more "sophisticated," so that gradually a condensation took place. Now in the compulsive acting out, many of the themes originally experienced by both can be assumed by one actor and reacted to by the other. Each of these themes, fortunately, reaches its point of social danger at different times. There has been a movement from action that society might prosecute to one that it could condone, although the basic motivation remains unaltered. As Eissler has pointed out, society is only interested in behavior—not in motivation. Therefore, though this marriage has brought many grave problems, it also can be seen to have helped these two sick people, in a lopsided manner, from becoming chronic state pensioners, either as recidivists or inpatients. Nevertheless, they remain crippled by the limited relationships they are able to make, and this is now being passed on to the next generation.

The fact that families like the Lukes have had appalling childhood experiences that link closely to unconscious fantasy material makes repression an inadequate adult defense against anxieties and leads to the massive use of acting out. With this is associated fears about being invaded by ideas and feelings of others. The currents of projective identification, the waves of sustained acting out, drag and toss the family like a small boat on a turbulent ocean, an ocean of the dynamic unconscious of the individuals composing the family. To help these families remains a very big problem. Seen as individuals, they are very sick. As a family, however, they can be seen as developing their own treatment. So long as the movement of this treatment is in the direction of socially accepted behavior, that is from areas of prosecution to areas of condonement, it achieves something. However, medical and educational authorities must remain deeply concerned about the health of the children of such marriages, for from birth they are pressed into the service of the family, rather than being felt as individuals in their own right. However, while the family circuit remains closed, little direct treatment can reach them.

Finally, it is suggested that with severely disturbed people, usually labeled "character disorders" seen generation after generation, there may be two phases of the illness. The deviant behavior drawing down punitive feelings of society is well known. The second phase, as represented by what is here described as the closed circuit, quiescent from society's point of view, has both destructive and therapeutic factors in it. The balance between these negative and positive elements has to be studied before effective help can be offered to the family.

SUMMARY

1. This paper describes a family that, in the six years of its existence, gradually became a closed circuit, unable to make use of any psychiatric treatment unless self-administered.

2. The family is described in terms of the relationships that the members could make.

3. Following a diagnosis in terms of family functioning, the family experience of the next half year is described to support this diagnosis.

4. Three aspects of the family are discussed: (a) the futureless aspect of the family; (b) the need of the family to resist change in family members; (c) the family fear of being overwhelmed by the feelings and ideas of others.

5. Three main themes of compulsive behavior are linked to early childhood experiences, and the modification of these themes, in the family experience, is briefly traced. The changes in the themes are seen in terms of intensity, in social condonement, and also in changes in the actors.

6. The present family experience is seen as a perpetual psychodrama that brings no sense of catharsis. Yet, inasmuch as the compulsive behavior is moving in the direction of socially condoned behavior, it is seen as having a limited therapeutic value.

7. Concern for the children within a closed circuit family is mentioned.

NOTES

1. This study is taken from a pilot research into the after-care needs of patients discharged from the Social Rehabilitation Unit, now Henderson Hospital, Belmont, Surrey. It has been carried out with help from the S. W. Metropolitan Regional Board under Dr. Maxwell Jones and his Deputy, Dr. Fergus Stallard. To them, and to the clinical team, I would like to express my thanks for their interest and support.
2. This study was part of a much larger research project for Belmont Hospital Social Rehabilitation Unit, Director Dr. Maxwell Jones. The research team was di-

rected by Dr. R. N. Rapoport under the auspices of the Nuffield Foundation. Paper read at Psychotherapy and Social Psychiatry Section of Post Hospital Care of the Family, 1957.

REFERENCES

1. Eissler, Kurt. Some problems of delinquency. *Searchlights on delinquency,* International Universities Press, 1949.

2. Giovacchini, Peter L. Mutual adaptation in various object relationships. *International Journal of Psychoanalysis, 39,* (4).

3. Glover, E. On the Relation of the Total Ego to its Environment and the Concept of Adaptation, Concept of dissociation. *International Journal of Psychoanalysis,* 1943, *24.*

Glover, E. On the etiology of drug addiction. *On the early development of the mind,* 1956, Vol. I, Imago.

4. Heimann, Paula. Dynamics of transference interpretations. *International Journal of Psychoanalysis,* 1956, *37.*

5. Johnson, A. M. Sanctions for super-ego lacunae of adolescents. *Searchlights on delinquency.* New York: International Universities Press 1949.

6. Main, T. F. Presidential Address, The Ailment. *British Journal of Medical Psychology,* 1957, *30*(3), 127–145.

7. Money-Kyrle, R. E. Normal counter transference and some of its deviations. *International Journal of Psychoanalysis,* 1956, *37.*

8. Rapoport, R., and Rosow, I. An approach to family relationships and role performance. *Human Relations,* 1957, *10*(3), 209–221.

V

The Family as a Universe of Cognition and Communication

The marital conversation may, as Berger and Kellner argue, be the basis for constructing the family's world, but the birth of a baby brings about a certain amount of remodeling. No matter how well prepared parents are, no matter how set in their direction by their values and beliefs, the baby introduces novelty, challenge, and new tasks of interpretation.

The baby and its activities must be interpreted. The first selection, by psychologists John and Elizabeth Newson, makes clear how important parental interpretation is in defining the baby's human nature and the baby's role in the family. This portion of their study of 709 mothers of one-year-old children in Nottingham, England, focuses on mothers' interpretations of crying. To be sure, a one-year-old is not a newborn, but the difference is itself a matter of interpretation: some mothers emphasize the difference, while some consider that the one-year-old is not all that different. The diverse interpretations mothers give to their child's crying can also be seen as diverse ways of shaping separateness and connectedness to the child, a topic that we focus on in Part VI.

A family is a universe not only of communication but also of cognition. Family members teach and learn from each other, sometimes knowingly and intentionally, sometimes unknowingly and unintentionally. A family is an organization of many different kinds of functions, activities, and capacities. A family organizes its members' perceptions, focuses their attention, defines the subjects worth knowing about, shapes thinking. These aspects of family life have received some study, but not in a systematic way. Hope Jensen Leichter, a sociologist, presents an overview of the teaching and learning activities that occur in families and thus presents an agenda for research in this domain. She points to the "relative inattention to moment-to-moment processes of education within the family and to the more general processes by which the family mediates educational experiences elsewhere."

The paper by Else Frenkel-Brunswik dates from the 1950's and is based on work that began in the 1940's. The whole world was in crisis as a result of the destruction already caused by the totalitarian society in Nazi Germany. As part of a broad-range research effort to understand why some people are democratic in outlook while others are authoritarian, Frenkel-Brunswik turned to an examination of family processes. She presents contrasting case studies of two families, one of which produced a democratic personality in a daughter, the other an authoritarian personality in a son. By this contrast, she brings into focus some ways in which exercise of parental power influences children's thinking and learning. Although the Nazi period is past, Frenkel-Brunswik's paper retains relevance not only because families still produce authoritarian and democratic personalities but because, more generally, it suggests how intrafamilial processes can have broader social and political implications. A more recent study examined (among other factors) differences in family processes in the backgrounds of men who resisted the Vietnam war and men who joined an elite combat unit to fight in it (Mantell, 1974).

Finally, the paper by Theodore Lidz and his associates illustrates family education gone awry. The Lidz group was one of the pioneers in psychiatry, studying family processes that seemed to be generating or at least connected with schizophrenia. Among the most striking symptoms of this disorder are disturbances in thinking and communication such that the victim is severely impeded in entering into a consensually established definition of reality. The Lidz group finds evidence that the disturbance has some roots in the family processes of communicating and defining reality.

REFERENCE

Mantell, David Mark. *True Americanism: Green berets and war resistors*. New York: Teachers College Press, 1974.

12

The Roots of Socialization

JOHN NEWSON AND
ELIZABETH NEWSON

What the mothers told us about how they dealt with bedtime and wake-fulness gave us some indication of their attitude toward their babies' crying, and led naturally into a more general discussion of how they felt about crying and rebellion in situations other than bedtime. Since crying is the child's main means of expressing protest at this age, the feelings and responses it evokes in the mother are of considerable interest, for they will be closely related to the behavior she adopts on questions of discipline and sociali-zation. We were therefore concerned to find out something of the mother's own assessment of the significance of her child's crying and the quickness of her response to it; to investigate the incidence and the circumstances of that more emphatic form of protest, the temper tantrum, and the results it produced in the mother; and to inquire into the existence, at this stage in socialization, of sanctions other than generalized disapproval: the forms of punishment and the moral attitudes with which punishment was associ-ated.

In Nottingham, the baby who cries a good deal is usually referred to as a "mardy baby"; but this dialect word, which everybody understands, car-ries rather subtle variations of meaning, depending on the referent. Used of a very young baby, it merely indicates that the child cries rather a lot and implies no moral overtones; but of the older child, from a year on-ward, it almost always denoted a "cry-baby," a child who habitually whines and cries for little cause, or simply as a means of attracting sympathy and

Reprinted by permission from John and Elizabeth Newson, *Infant care in an urban com-munity*, pp. 85–99. London: George Allen & Unwin, 1964.

John Newson is Professor of Psychology and Elizabeth Newson is Senior Lecturer in Psy-chology, University of Nottingham, England.

attention, or to get his own way. Thus the adjective "mardy" seems to be directly derived from the verb to mar, or spoil, and a mardy baby is a spoiled baby;[1] indeed, the word is occasionally used as a verb, the exact equivalent of pamper or spoil: "I don't mardy them, you know, I don't mardy them up a lot. I mean, I love[2] them and that, but I don't make them *mardy*, if you know what I mean." Most mothers seem to feel that there is a danger of spoiling the child, either by fussing over him too much or by indiscriminately 'giving in' to his attention demands; but many also believe that some children are constitutionally difficult, and are therefore especially demanding from birth. A few mothers believe that playing with the child and generally making much of him may be overdone, and result in a spoiled child.

> She's a bit distempered, her great-uncle spoils her, you see. He's been off work a few weeks, and he's always picking her up and playing with her. He tells me I'm always nagging at her. But she's got to be checked. I think she's a bit spoiled really.

While most of these mothers appear to agree that spoiling is possible at 12 months, their opinions vary very widely as to how much attention is permissible and where to draw the line. Some are extremely permissive at this age, respond easily and quickly to the child's demands, allow any behavior short of that which will bring him into physical danger and, where danger threatens, divert rather than forbid. Others seem constantly aware of the child as a kind of moral predator, waiting to take advantage of any relaxation of principle; they bring up their children, even at this tender age, on what we came to think of as the 'give them an inch and they'll take an ell' philosophy. Others again are in theory restrictive, but in practice permissive: conscious of the risks they believe they run of spoiling the child, they yet give in much or most of the time for the sake of peace; one receives the impression of great inconsistency in the child's treatment, as the mother continually makes and breaks new resolutions not to spoil him.

These three general types of behavior are of course spread out along the permissive-restrictive continuum, so that one pattern shades imperceptibly into another, and one cannot rigidly categorize mothers nor give percentages for each type. Nevertheless, it is very easy to discern the three points of view—permissive, restrictive and inconsistent—having their effect in the behavior shown by mothers in individual areas of the child's upbringing: crying, tantrums, punishment and so on; and in this chapter we will try to show the different ways in which they find expression.

LEAVING THE BABY TO CRY

Against the background of what we had already learned of the mother's attitude toward crying at bedtime, we asked: "Do you think it does a child of this age any harm to be left to cry?" The main purpose of this question was to provoke discussion, and in this aim it was usually successful: few mothers answered with a simple "yes" or "no." The question was followed by a check: "How long would you leave him if you thought there was nothing wrong with him?" This we found was very necessary; many times we were told, "No, it doesn't do any harm at all," followed by, "Well, I wouldn't leave him more than a couple of minutes myself." Thus the question Does it do any harm? while useful for prompting discussion, was not successful in itself obtaining an accurate measure of the mother's attitude or practical permissiveness; and we often felt that the answer, "No, it does them no harm, but . . ." was a form of lip service paid to the prevailing medical advice. We also found it important for the interviewer to obtain a definite statement of the maximum time the mother would leave the crying child; the vague answer, "Oh, I wouldn't leave him for long," might be completed "—not more than five minutes," or, by another mother, "not more than an hour." The form of the question ". . . if you thought there was nothing wrong with him" is perhaps worth mentioning: it was intended to give the hardhearted mother an opportunity to tell the truth without feeling that she sounded unkind, and the softhearted mother the chance to say that if the baby was crying then she *would* think there was something wrong with him. We received plenty of both types of answer.

While we did not, unfortunately, deliberately investigate the point, several mothers stressed that there would be a difference in their attitude toward the crying of the one-year-old and that of the tiny baby, but the conclusions they arrived at were contradictory.

"Do you think it does a child of this age any harm to be left to cry?"

Ironworks laborer's wife:
Not at this age, I'd say. If he cried a lot younger I'd see to him, but not at this age—if he did cry, I'd leave him. Well, for a certain length of time anyway—he could carry on for an hour, maybe. Of course, it's partly the *way* he's crying, isn't it, and if he cries really hard you would go to him sooner, wouldn't you?

Baker's wife:
Now . . . well, in a way, yes. When they're babies they can cry for crying's sake. When it's a year, they *feel* more—they're beginning to know. There must be something wrong if they cry.

Foreman's wife:
No—I don't—not once they get to this age—I don't think it does them a bit of harm at this age, because I think if they *know*, like, that you're going to pick 'em up, they do it all the more; they do, yes. I'd leave her quarter of an hour, anyway. If she cried longer than that, I should pick her up, and if she stopped put her back again—you see—because there's nothing really wrong with her, because a baby *knows*, like, you know.

Lorry driver's wife:
I think it does do some harm at this age, because they're fractious at this age—you know—if I ever get cross with her, you know, and say, "I can't pick you up, like, just now, I'm too busy just now," she comes round you in such a pitiful way, you've got to in the end. Now she's older, you see, I know she doesn't cry for nothing. I used to leave her half an hour when she was tiny.

Minister's wife:
I don't like to leave them to cry. I don't suppose it does harm them, but I don't think it's a nice thing to do. I wouldn't do it to mine, just leave them to cry—no I wouldn't. I think a baby of *any* age will only cry for some reason. I think there must be something the matter, there *is* a reason. I don't think babies cry for fun.

Some also distinguished between different sorts of cry; sobbing was particularly mentioned as a type of cry that few mothers would resist, although one or two did say that they had attempted to ignore even this. The "mardy cry" and the "temper cry" were especially singled out by some as demands that it was safe, and indeed sensible, to ignore.

Brick laborer's wife:
Well, I don't leave her long to cry, because I can't stand to hear her cry; if she cries, you know, really brokenhearted, I go up, I don't like it, I think it does do her some harm, there's really something wrong with her. I let her cry if I think she's just mardy, like, I'd let her cry a good while until she got fed up herself, about quarter of an hour; I'd leave her till she got tired of it, and if she didn't do she'd get a smacked bum.

Chauffeur's wife:
I don't like to hear him cry—not unnecessarily, like. If it seems a mardy cry, I might let him cry a few minutes, but not for long.

Furniture dealer's wife:
For too long, yes, it might do him some harm; I think—certainly if I knew there was no reason for it, you know, if it was just probably a temper or something, I would leave him until he really *wouldn't* quieten, you know; but very often I've found that if he does cry it's either that he's dirtied his nappy or he's too wet, or something like that, and usually that does the trick; but I certainly wouldn't leave him for an awfully long time, you know. The longest I ever left him was about three-quarters of an hour, I think, and I knew then that there was nothing wrong with him, he'd been playing in here and we'd had visitors and he just didn't want to go back, you see. But I just left him, and eventually he did cry himself to sleep. But I think it was more a temper cry than anything, you know.

It was sometimes pointed out that you couldn't always be sure that the cry was "only temper."

Toolsetter's wife:
I don't think there's any harm as long as they don't cry for too long, I mean, I couldn't stand a child crying for too long, but they get crafty, you see. Perhaps if they're

being temperamental I'll take no notice; but . . . I mean . . . well, a little while back we found that she was crying, and took no notice, and it went on for about a quarter of an hour, and she was absolutely screaming; and I said to my husband, "Will you fetch her down, there must be something wrong"; and when he went up she was standing up and she couldn't get down, and she was tired out . . . and as soon as he laid her down she went right off.

Having specified that the question referred to the 12 months child, and discounting if necessary both sobbing and mere whining, there were still very wide differences of opinion. In the permissive group, a common response was that babies, especially at this age, do not cry for nothing. These mothers thought that crying, and unhappiness generally, should be avoided as much as possible, for the sake of the child's mental and physical well-being; the underlying attitude (not by any means universal among mothers) was that a crying child was an unhappy child; the possibility of naughtiness in connection with crying hardly arose; and, therefore, unhappiness had no moral value and was naturally to be prevented as far as possible. Particularly constructive in her approach and articulate about her ideas was Mrs. West, the 38-year-old mother of three children and wife of a craftsman just setting up his own business. Although she expected her little boy to "get over" his own temper crying, she seemed to take far more trouble than most mothers to avoid tempers in the first place, and they occurred very rarely.

> Yes, I think it does do them some harm, if they're unhappy. If he's not happy—if he's got a pain or any kind of trouble—then he *shouldn't* cry, he should be coaxed and loved. After all, it's not fair to just bung somebody in a room and shut the door on them and let them cry till they're unhappy—that's not right at all. And you find in the long run, if you coax them and love them, that they don't cry so long with their unhappiness as if you just pushed them away, that's making them *more* unhappy. But tantrums, yes, just let them cry them out, because they must learn to get over tempers; but not unhappiness cries I shouldn't—never. . . . If he's on the floor and he goes into things, into the books, and you want him to come out—it's no good just pulling him out and making him cry; you find something that attracts his attention over the other side of the room, which *brings* him out without causing tantrums. Because if you start them on tantrums—I know a good example of it, of a child who's been made to leave things alone while his mother got on with the work—he must always keep out of the way, the work must be done, it's the first thing; with the result that he's been pushed around while the housework's been done, and now he's full of tantrums; because nobody *loved* him out of a situation, he was *bullied* out of the situation. Yet they thought they was being kind to him, but I don't. You shouldn't *make* them do things that way.

"You don't know what damage you're really doing to a child's mind when you leave them to cry on their own," said the father whom we quoted in the last chapter; and his feeling was echoed by many other parents, some of whom specified the damage, mental or physical, that they believed might be done to the child.

"Do you think it does a child of this age any harm to be left to cry?"

Laborer's wife:
I don't like to. I don't believe in it. Even my husband don't believe in it. It's not
right. They don't feel secure.

Depot manager's wife:
I think so—they cry and they get worse as they go along. She perspires—her hair
gets quite wet, and I don't like to see her like that.

Bottling manager's wife:
Well, I do; I think it causes a lot of bed-wetting. My sister leaves hers to cry, and
they all wet their beds.

Laborer's wife:
Well, I don't know anything, but me mam says to me, don't let 'em cry too long,
because they say—if it's a boy—it can give him rupture, don't know how true it is.

Cabinetmaker's wife:
Yes—because at this age they're beginning to be aware of people, and they'd be
bewildered if you just left them.

Miner's wife:
You could leave them quarter of an hour—then they want a bit of love. You have
to let them know you're there. It frightens them if they think you're not there. I
don't believe in frightening children.

Chemical worker's wife:
It upsets their nerves. I've seen children tremble and shake after crying a lot. (This
baby is brought downstairs during the night, every night, and played with for two-
and-a-half hours, rather than let him cry.)

Cycle-packer's wife:
I've never left a child to cry. I can't do it. I can't do things if a child's crying—I
couldn't get on with my work if Anne was grizzling. I think they get thoroughly
disturbed. There must be some reason why they cry.

   The more restrictive, "give them an inch" mothers were convinced that
children must sometimes be left to cry as a matter of principle. In their view,
all children tended to be both willful and cunning—"crafty" was the usual
adjective—and at 12 months these traits were already well developed and
needed to be dealt with firmly; the child had to learn who was master, and
was not too young to understand that he couldn't always have his own way.
He must not be allowed to become addicted to indulgence, and any temporary relaxation of rules might bring about such an addiction: we were
often told how upsets in family routine, such as holiday periods, had forced
the parents to pick up the crying baby "for the sake of other people," with

deleterious results to his moral fiber. After such a setback, we were told, it was extremely difficult to make up the lost ground in the baby's training. For this group of mothers, then, crying was an inevitable part of the child's upbringing.

Salesclerk's wife:
I did want to go up to him, but at the same time it can become a regular habit, and it might go on for months. And of course you can't always let them rule the roost like that, even though they are so tiny. They've got a certain amount of will of their own, and I think they do learn even if you are inclined to think it seems hard-hearted at the time. (Do you think it does a child of this age any harm to be left to cry?) No. They are getting opinionated, they're self-willed, they find they can do things. I'd leave him twenty minutes, anyhow; a baby soon forgets at that age, he hasn't got any memory, or very little memory, and they soon forget, especially if there's something else to interest them.

Joiner's wife:
No, I think it does them good sometimes. If you pick them up, they seem to want it *every* night, don't they? They get used to it, and they play on you.

Departmental manager's wife:
They get to know if you give in, they start expecting it. You can't just leave your housework to attend to a baby's whims. If I was busy or we were having our lunch, well he'd just have to wait. I'm a hard sort of mother, you'll find that out.

Hauler's wife:
At the time now—at this age—they're trying to see who's master. I'd leave him an hour or so—then I'd begin to think there *was* something wrong.

Builder's wife:
(Do you think it does a child of this age any harm to be left to cry?) No, not really, not for a short time, you can spoil them. (How long would you leave her to cry if you thought there was nothing wrong with her?) Knowing Linda, about an hour, because she's so crafty, you know.

B.R. fireman's wife:
Not just for a little while. I wouldn't leave him for a long while; just for a little while, to see whether he's just trying to get attention. Most often it's not real tears, because when I walk into the bedroom he starts to laugh.

Caretaker's wife:
You find with children when they get to about one, you know, they get very crafty, and if they know that you're going to keep running up and down they do it all the more, and then they stop and they laugh at you.

These last two quotations, and that of the foreman's wife on the previous page, illustrate the attitude of the restrictive mother to a common enough situation. Baby cries; mother, sooner or later, picks him up; baby stops crying.

To this, the restrictive mother typically reacts: he stopped crying as soon as I picked him up—so there was nothing wrong with him at all, he was just having me on. The result is that the baby is put back again to cry it out, sometimes with a smack to drive home the lesson. The permissive mother's interpretation of the same situation is totally different. She will report it thus: he stopped crying as soon as I picked him up—so it must have been what he needed. The result in this case is that the baby is held and cuddled, and is given the comfort he has been demanding. Again and again we have encountered these two contrasting interpretations, both stemming from the same action on the part of the baby, and they seem to typify the basic attitudes of the two groups: the restrictive mother's suspicion of the baby as a small enemy in a continual battle of wits, the permissive mother's matter-of-fact assumption that the child's immediate happiness is her chief aim. We might perhaps go further, and say that the permissive mother looks upon crying not as a cunning attempt to obtain indulgence, but rather as a simple act of communication, which naturally requires a response. Two more examples will suffice. Mrs. Brown, the 29-year-old departmental manager's wife who called herself "a hard sort of mother," had always left the baby to cry on principle; but he had recently "got into bad habits" on holiday, when the family had been staying in a hotel and had had to pick him up to avoid disturbance. He was at the time of the interview under regular sleeping drugs in order to break him of the expectation of being picked up when he cried.

> We were worried it might rupture him, he cried so hard, and for two hours sometimes, just screaming; but the doctor said, "Rubbish, it can't do him any harm, just let him cry it out"; so I'm going by what he says. If there's something wrong with the child, you don't mind getting up to him, do you?—tummyache, or something like that. But him—well, you should see the change— *he can be screaming his head off for an hour, and then you pick him up and it's all sunshine. There's nothing wrong at all. That makes me cross.*

Mrs. Matthew, the 22-year-old wife of a long-distance lorry driver, made no claim to be a competent manager of children; with an uncooperative husband and two extremely active toddlers, she admitted that she was often at her wits' end. She had met us at the door with, "I don't know what good it'll be asking *me* questions. Honestly, if they do anything wrong I just shout at them!" All through the interview, however, she showed a warm sympathy with her children, talking of her 3½-year-old daughter particularly as of an equal.

> You don't know if they're frightened when they cry. I did let him cry once—I didn't know he was, I was in the other room, and when I came out I could hear him and *he was screaming himself blue; and as soon as he saw me he stopped, he was all right, so I thought he must have been frightened because he'd been left on his own.* It's a terrible thing to be frightened. I'm frightened

of the dark, and so is Michelle (3½), and I wouldn't like Julian to get like that, so I don't let him cry. No, I think that's cruel. (How long would you leave him to cry if you thought there was nothing wrong with him?) To tell you the truth, the minute I heard him crying I'd be up there with him.

There was a substantial group of mothers who thought that, although crying might not harm the baby, it would certainly harm *them*. Many of these mothers had been told by well-meaning outsiders that they ought to allow the child to cry and that they were "making a rod for their own back"; some had attempted to follow this advice, but had been too softhearted to keep it up, so that the child had been subjected to very inconsistent treatment; others had consistently followed their hearts rather than what they felt to be their better judgment.

Cycle-assembler's wife:
I'd let him cry half an hour maybe. You can't stand too much of it, can you—that's the point.

Printer's cutter's wife:
I just don't like to hear her you know—because I mean, the way she cries now—I didn't mind when she was younger, I let her cry a bit; but now, I mean, she really breaks your heart you know, if she is crying.

Furniture dealer's wife:
I can't bear to hear him—I don't suppose it does any harm really.

Laboratory technician's wife:
Well, yes, I think it does do them some harm, I proved that with Robin (older sibling) when *he* was a year old. You know what it is, they tell you to let them cry, oh, I got really fed up with it, all my neighbors were always on at me, leave him to cry, leave him to cry, they said; so one night I did; and he cried for an hour, and when I finally went up to him he was in hysterics, and after that he wouldn't go near his crib, he really took against it, he seemed frightened of it, and we had him in our bed every night for three months.

Cook's wife:
(Do you think it does a child of this age any harm to be left to cry?) Well, no, I don't, definitely not; it's just if you can stand it. I can't. I am one of those who can't stand to hear a kiddy cry. I mean, sometimes with *him* (older sibling) I've shut myself in the kitchen, you know—I've gone in there so I can't hear him, and then I kept going to the stairs to see if he was still on. You know, I just can't stand it, not for long. But with her I've stood it a bit more, because of course it's *use*, you see.

Miner's wife:
Oh no, no harm at all; I'd leave her indefinitely till she gave up. (Do you think you'd pick her up after an hour?) Well, yes, because it'd be getting on my nerves by then. (Would you be picking her up because it was harming her or because it was getting on your nerves?) Oh, because it was getting on my nerves! (laughed)

Other mothers could stand the noise of crying themselves, but had to consider the neighbors, other children or fellow-tenants; it was these considerations that prevented them following a firm line with a lusty one-year-old.

"It's a bit loud at this age, isn't it!"

"I don't like to leave her—I think it annoys the neighbors to hear a baby cry."

"The only reason I do bring her down is in case she wakes the others— if she was the only one, I'd just let her cry, if I knew there was nothing the matter with her. I'd leave her a good couple of hours, I should say, then if she *didn't* stop I'd gather really there *was* something the matter."

"She shouts so—folks'd think I'm killing her!"

"I don't think it's worth it to let them cry at this age, they just about blow the roof off."

Finally, there was a small group who believed that crying was positively beneficial to the child, and one mother who propounded the theory that the child enjoyed it, an argument we seemed to have heard before in relation to fox-hunting.

"Do you think it does a child of this age any harm to be left to cry?"

Depot manager's wife:
No—I think it does them good to have a cry now and again. I think it exercises all the lungs and that for them. Because if you let them cry, it gives them a deep voice and that. I think it does them good to cry.

Laborer's wife:
No. Makes them sleep better, a good cry does.

Lorry driver's wife:
They say it makes them a bit more strength, but I don't like to hear them cry.

Salesman's wife:
I don't like to hear her crying—not because it worries *her* so much, she seems to enjoy it once she starts—but because it worries *me* more. But I mean *she* thinks it's lovely, just opening her mouth and letting it come out, you see. And sometimes there are days when you *don't* know why they're crying; and I think it *must* be because they just *like* it.

Our general impression was, then, that the majority of mothers were aware of some kind of conflict over the problem of crying. They were frequently torn between the desire to be firm on principle and a natural inclination to be kind to the child. In consequence, some of them felt guilty whatever they did. A few of them were to some extent forced by pressure of circumstances to behave in a particular way, despite personal feelings and theories. For a variety of reasons, few mothers found it possible to adopt a wholehearted policy of being firm, and they could seldom remain unresponsive to prolonged crying in the one-year-old. Only 33% said that they would leave a child of this age longer than fifteen minutes, even if there were nothing obviously wrong, and less than 8% would leave him for more than half an hour.

Because a large number of mothers mentioned the theory that crying is all right for girls but might give a boy a rupture, we looked for a possible difference in the treatment of girls and of boys. We found none. Evidently, while the belief has wide currency, particularly among working-class mothers, it is not acted upon.

It was clear that many mothers were on the defensive against any implied suggestion that they might be spoiling their children. In replying to the health visitors, 16% admitted that they would leave the baby only for a very short while (five minutes or less) before going to him; but when the questioner was the university interviewer the proportion in this category rose significantly to 31%. Whenever the mothers reported receiving professional advice from doctors or nurses, it was in fact invariably in the direction of urging them not to "give in" to the child. They were often told that in the long run it was kinder to the child to be hardhearted than to give way; yet most of these mothers found the advice either impractical or incompatible with their attitudes and principles, and, in consequence, they either felt guilty or resented the source. It will be noticed, in the following quotations, that the assertion "crying does a child no harm" seems to have been presented with an authoritarian certainty that is hardly a good advertisement for the scientific humility of the medical profession.

"Do you think it does a child of this age any harm to be left to cry?"

"No, I don't think so. They leave them to cry in hospital. They leave them to cry for hours in hospital. Two hours I've seen babies cry there when I was there, he was a tiny baby then. They don't take a bit of notice. And it can't do them any harm, they must know, mustn't they?"

"Doctor told me to leave him; and if he cried, let him; if I put him to bed and he wouldn't go to sleep, to let him cry—to leave him an hour, and if he still cried to go up and slap him and leave him another hour; but I couldn't—not to let him cry like that."

". . . We were worried it might rupture him, he cried so hard, and for two hours sometimes, just screaming; but the doctor said 'Rubbish, it can't do him any harm, just let him cry it out'; so I'm going by what he says."

" 'Let her cry,' he said, 'she'll get over it.' "

"Well, I've been to the clinic—they say, 'leave her, mother, let her cry; it won't do her any harm, it'll do her the world of good—strengthen the lungs.' "Well," I used to say to them, "it's all right for you;" and they said 'Put her in a room on her own, turn the wireless up, do anything so you won't hear her.' "

". . . So I told the clinic about it, and they told me to just leave her, to let her cry it out. Well, that's what I do do, you see."

"Of course, the clinics say it does them no harm. . . . When she was born, she cried on and off for a whole day. I was worried, but the midwife said, 'Put her in the bathroom and shut the door so you can't hear her, it won't hurt her.' But I didn't."

NOTES

1. "Mardy" may also be used of the older school child, especially of the 'tell-tale-tit' type of child; one frequently hears derisive cries of 'mardy-baby!' being shouted after a retreating child during street play. It may even be used by an adult.

2. "Love" is probably used here in the very common sense of "cuddle." It is used in the same sense in the statement by Mrs. West on page 197; cf. an adult's direction to a child to "love dolly!"

13

Models of the Family as an Educative System

HOPE JENSEN LEICHTER

The complexity of possible family constellations inside and outside the household and the multiplicity of intertwined influences that inevitably enter into any thoughtful consideration of familial education soon begin to boggle the mind. Examining one set of paired relationships within the nuclear family is clearly too simple; but moving from one dyad to another in the hope of covering all possible combinations ends up an unmanageable task—one that those concerned with the consequences of sibling interaction have plainly backed away from. Thus, the need is apparent to reexamine the kinds of models that have been implicit or explicit in studies of family interaction, in the hope of discovering approaches that offer new promise of guiding fruitful educational research.

At the least, models of the family as educator need to meet the criterion that I have referred to as "contextual rigor"; that is, the rigor that derives from placing the analysis of specific relationships in the context of other significant relationships and influences and in the process considering cross-pressures that stem both from within the family and from without. Contextual rigor does not imply studying everything all the time, but it does imply a broad conceptual framework that can be systematically scanned for significant influences. The scanning will not necessarily produce identical in-

Hope Jensen Leichter is Elbenwood Professor of Education in the Department of Family and Community Education and is Director of the Elbenwood Center for the Study of the Family as Educator, Teachers College, Columbia University.

fluences in every instance—grandparents or cousins, for example, may or may not be important educative influences in particular families—but the framework for analysis should suggest a fairly extensive range of possibilities, so that external influences will not be overlooked and internal influences overemphasized.

If the family is to be understood as part of a wider social context, then it is no longer possible to view the family as a closed system. Rather, it must be conceived as a system open to a multitude of external influences. This point became clear some years ago to researchers concerned with family therapy. The initial argument was that the individual could not be understood in isolation, hence, the need to diagnose and treat families. But it soon became clear that families too could not be understood in isolation; families too could most usefully be seen as open rather than as closed systems.[1]

In addition, even if one can clearly specify an empirical unit defined as the family, the unit is not necessarily the most meaningful theoretical unit for all purposes. Thus, when one considers the time family members spend inside and outside the household, it is immediately clear that to assume the family is the source of all significant influences is fallacious. In effect, the theoretical unit that is meaningful for a particular analysis is a function of the purpose of that analysis. If one is attempting to understand an individual's behavior outside the home (however one regards the determining effects of the early years), there is sufficient reason to anticipate that external influences, such as peer relations, will be significant in understanding the behavior. Thus, if one wishes to explain school achievement, it is clearly fruitful to look for certain sources of that achievement in the home, but it is even more fruitful to do so in a way that considers how influences of the home, the school, and other contexts are continuously combined.

As Goode and others have pointed out, the accepted subunits of a science change with the degree of sophistication of the science. In some instances, the initial commonsense subunits, such as the family, which is, after all, a phenomenon of everyday experience, may cease to be regarded as serious units for analysis as the science advances. "When we deal with the family as one sub-system, we may simply be trying to relate the wrong variables to one another."[2] Since the experience of the individual cuts across numerous social groupings, family, peers, schoolmates, occupational associates, etc., and is undoubtedly influenced by all of these, it is important to have a model for analysis of the family that is open to the inclusion of numerous significant influences, a model that incorporates the family's external context. If one would focus on the individual, then a model is needed that permits a charting of the individual's lifespace and an exploration of the ways in which the individual combines experiences from various realms.

Because of the variability of the family as a social unit, in terms of both the composition of the particular household unit and the definition of what constitutes the family, one cannot presume that in studying something called the family one is studying a constant phenomenon. It is unreasonable, therefore, to presume that the experience in one unit called the family is necessarily similar in significant ways to the experience in other units called the family. Any such similarity (or lack of it) must itself be made a matter for investigation.

These arguments have profound theoretical consequences. They imply that research on the family or on dimensions of the family in terms of a model of "variables" may well be inappropriate. As Blumer has pointed out in a classic critique, variable analysis is an appropriate procedure *only* for those realms of social life that are "not mediated by an interpretive process" or in which "stabilized patterns of interpretation" prevail.[3] Too often, however, investigators assume stabilized patterns where they do not exist. Thus, measuring the educational consequences of being an eldest child makes little sense when such measurement assumes, without investigation, that the definition of being eldest is comparable from one family to another or from one social group to another. The significance of being eldest may vary enormously from one social setting to another, for example, in relation to patterns of inheritance. Similarly, analyses of sex roles sometimes fail to take into account differences in definition from one social circumstance to another, assuming rather that being male or female has identical meanings in all situations. In short, one needs to base analyses of the family as educator on concepts that take into account the processes by which family interactions are defined by their participants and by significant others outside the family.

A fruitful model of the family as educator should facilitate an understanding of these interpretive processes, encouraging sensitivity to the multiplicity of meanings that any event may have for different individuals within a particular family and to the shift in meanings that can occur from one moment to another. It should also make room for the continuous changes in character and composition that derive from maturational and personal changes in family membership, and it should not assume that the family itself is a constant entity. Individuals clearly differ in their susceptibility to change and the ways in which they initiate and react to change.[4] Even if one believes that basic personality characteristics remain fairly constant over time, it can scarcely be argued that no change is possible. Thus, the measurement of a mother–child relationship at one moment in time cannot be assumed to represent the relationship at another moment in time. Even in a case where the mother is comparatively insulated from change in her style of mothering, the same personal characteristics of the mother may have very different consequences for the child at different ages. The mother who controls and organizes her child's environment with detailed attention may have one effect when the child is an infant and a very different effect when the child is a teenager. Thus, no model of the family can effectively guide research that does not take into account the shifting character of interactions throughout the life cycle.

CONCEPTS OF EDUCATION WITHIN THE FAMILY

If educational encounters within the arena of the family are to be studied in ways that will contribute more generally to an understanding of the nature and processes of education, the questions investigators bring to such study must be enlightened by a thoughtful consideration of educational theory, so that wooden and oversimplified conceptions of teaching and learning and of one-to-one cause-effect connections can be laid aside. As Cremin has remarked: "What is taught is not always what is desired, and vice versa; what is taught is not always what is learned, and vice versa. Moreover, there are almost always unintended consequences in education; indeed, they are frequently more significant than the intended consequences. Hence, educational transactions are often marked by profound irony."[5] The lesson is basic, but much of the family literature to date, even where the concept of the unconscious is usefully employed, has ignored the lesson.

It is also necessary in scrutinizing educational encounters within the family to assume a perspective that takes multiple levels of experience into account. Even if one considers education to be a deliberate effort—an effort that is the focus of aware attention—experiences at the margins of consciousness or at the level of peripheral awareness (which are not the same as the unconscious) remain part of the educative process. Much of the activity within the family is of a repetitive, moment-to-moment nature. Such interaction is very different from even the most immediate recollection of it, since even short-term memory is highly selective.[6] Yet, to understand those moments of intentionality and awareness that one might wish to regard as educational—those moments when events that go on at the margins of awareness are lifted into focal attention—it is essential to have a framework that sets those deliberate moments in the context of multiple levels of awareness, so that the investigator can examine those realms in which the explicit shades off into the indistinct, the intentional into the incidental, and the focal into the peripheral. Research on educational encounters within the family, even when it focuses on those moments of education in which intentionality is readily apparent, must also include experiences that pass into and out of awareness on a fleeting, moment-to-moment basis. In fact, the insistence upon a framework that embraces multiple levels of awareness constitutes one important element of contextual rigor.

One can also fruitfully extend the range of possible outcomes that are assumed to result from familial education. As has been indicated, the literature to date, at least that which has dealt with the American situation,

has tended to focus fairly narrowly on specific types of educational outcome, notably school achievement. Even where the concern of the investigator has broadened to include more general personality characteristics
as outcomes, such as independence or assertiveness, these too have been
seen in terms of their relation to the ability to function in the student role,
as measured, for example, by achievement on school tests. Apart from the
questions one might raise about success in schooling as the sole measure
of educational outcomes, it is clear that the conception of the outcomes of
familial education can fruitfully be enlarged. If one defines education as
the deliberate, systematic, and sustained effort to transmit, evoke, or acquire knowledge, attitudes, values, skills, and sensibilities,[7] numerous suggestions come to mind. Knowledge, for example, may be viewed from the
family's point of view rather than the school's, with private or specialized
knowledge, such as information about ethnic customs or languages not used
in the school, taking on particular importance. Attitudes and values can be
associated with religious beliefs, which are often deliberately excluded from
the school curriculum. An almost limitless list of skills can become relevant, depending on the traditions, the interests, and the concerns of particular families. Some of these skills, for example, the ability to organize materials in space or activities in time, may have useful carry-over into
schooling, while others, for example, the ability to clean fish in a family of
fishermen, will assume their value whether or not they carry over into
schooling.

Even in analyses of familial education primarily concerned with outcomes, the loci of these outcomes can be broadened and viewed from a
variety of perspectives. Thus, most educational outcomes have been examined from the vantage point of children. Yet outcomes can also be examined from the vantage point of parents, or even of grandparents and other
relatives. It is also possible to extend the concept of outcome itself to include the individual's more general approaches to education. I have suggested elsewhere, in formulating the concept of "educative style,"[8] a number of components of such general approaches that might usefully be
considered as outcomes of familial education: the manner of criticizing and
appraising; the mode of integrating experiences over time; the level and
rate of activity; the ways of combining and segregating particular tasks; the
character of response to cues from others; the ways of appraising and syn-
thesizing knowledge, values, and attitudes of others; the mode of scanning
and searching for information; the approaches to embarrassment in learning situations—the list is illustrative rather than exhaustive. I have also pointed
to the ways in which components of educative style interact as an individual engages in, moves through, and combines diverse educative experiences over a lifetime.

Finally, as the idea of educative style suggests, the concept of outcomes
can be usefully extended to include not only the immediate effects of ed-

ucation at a particular moment, but also the "ripple effects" or chain of reactions to a given outcome.[9] Thus, one experience of success may serve to trigger additional experiences of success. From such a perspective the concept of outcome begins to merge with the concept of process.

THE PROCESSES OF EDUCATION WITHIN THE FAMILY

One result of the emphasis on outcomes in the recent literature on familial education has been a relative inattention to moment-to-moment processes of education within the family and to the more general processes by which the family mediates educational experiences elsewhere. In this respect, differences in fundamental conceptions of human nature have distinct importance. If one regards personality as basically fixed during the first years of life, then the need to search beyond early experience—both within and outside the family—is substantially reduced. If, on the other hand, one regards personality as subject to continuing modification over time, then it becomes necessary to look at education as it occurs throughout life. Beyond this, it is important to examine the processes by which the individual combines educational experiences that occur in different arenas. In this respect, it is interesting to note that the emphasis in the literature on the family and other systems varies with the stage of the individual's life cycle. For the very young, the family is seen as the central arena of education; for older children, the focus shifts to the school; for adults, the focus shifts to the occupation. Yet as the life cycle progresses, the fact that multiple arenas of education coexist may be as significant as the fact that the focus shifts from one arena to another; and even if the several arenas do not have equal importance at all times, their interrelationships require careful examination, both in their own right and with respect to the ways in which various aspects of education are combined in the life of the individual.

If education is conceived as a lifelong process, then the process itself bears scrutiny. Even if one can show correlations between indices of education inside the home and indices of educational achievement outside the home, the indices themselves remain summary statements, or what Blumer has called "truncated" factors;[10] to establish the relationships leaves open the question of the processes by which the relationships come to be. Moreover, where "intervening variables" have, in fact, been examined, they have themselves often been treated as outcomes rather than as processes of connection. Thus, to cite one example, the characteristic of independence is commonly seen as a result of parental behavior that in turn positively affects school achievement; but the process by which independence actually links with school achievement is left vague. In the absence of information about the process itself, about the context in which the variables being measured by the index arise, the ways in which one variable influences another are, in the words of Blumer, "both concealed and misrepresented by the statement of the relationship between the two variables."[11] Thus, a shift in the focus of inquiry is needed, to what Blumer has referred to as the "complexes of activity" and the "processes of interaction in which human group life has its being,"[12] or alternatively, to what Dewey once called "working adaptations of personal capacities with environing forces."[13]

We have seen the strategic difficulties of attempting to understand educational encounters within the family by examining the outcomes of particular paired relationships, for example, the influence of parents on children or of children on parents. It is quite possible, however, to examine educational activities as they occur on a moment-to-moment basis across a variety of relationships, focusing on the processes of interaction and on the patterns these processes assume over time and at different times. The approach has been used in a number of "natural history" investigations of social phenomena, of which Jackson's studies of classroom interaction are a noteworthy example.[14] The potential value of the approach with respect to an understanding of education within the family would seem considerable, as perhaps the following few illustrations will indicate.

Language Interaction Within the Family

Language interaction offers one example of the promise of a process oriented analysis of familial education. Actually, much of the recent research on outcomes with respect to the educational functions of the family has dealt with language usage and language development. Virtually every child in our society learns a language before entering school, and although many influences mediate the process, for example, television, that language is acquired largely within the household. The situation is a natural for outcome analysis. The characteristics of the parents' language, such as their proficiency, their enunciation, or their grammar, can be measured independent of family interaction; those measures can be correlated with measures of the children's school achievement; and both the variable measures and the correlations can in turn be considered in light of indices of racial, ethnic, and social class background (though there has been considerable disagreement over the findings in this last area).

Yet some of the recent research on the language usage of adults and children illustrates the possibilities of focusing more directly on the processes of family interaction as they relate to language interchange. Gleason, for example, has described the ways in which very young children engage in "code switching," or modifying the modes of their talk with adults, peers, and infants. The phenomenon seems to reflect the fact that adults themselves shift their verbal styles when talking with infants and with younger children (indeed, they sometimes fail to move sufficiently far from "baby talk" when conversing with toddlers and thereby incur resentment).[15] The ability of the child to switch codes appears to develop with age. Thus,

Gleason points out that "infants are selective about whom they talk to at all. Four-year-olds may whine at their mothers, engage in intricate verbal play with their peers, and reserve their narrative, discursive tales for their grown-up friends. By the time they are eight, children have added . . . the politeness routines of formal adult speech, baby-talk style, and the ability to talk to younger children in the language of socialization."[16] In similar fashion, Schneider and Homans have noted the intricacy with which kinship terms of reference and address are varied in different situations, depending on the individuals who are present during the conversation.[17] Thus, the term for one's father may shift from "my father" to "your son" to "our father," depending on the company. Through a recent study of conversational rhythms, Jaffe and Feldstein have also pointed to the significance of language interaction, examining the processes by which the "switch" from speaking to listening roles takes place.[18] These subtle and intricate modes by which adults and children shift their language usage, depending on the particular relationships and functions involved in given conversations, highlight the value of scrutinizing the processes of language usage within the family rather than merely assessing linguistic outcomes in individuals and the relation of those outcomes to academic achievement.

In addition to switching, there is also the fascinating area of questioning and answering behavior. An elaborate complex of linguistic and social codes (codes that vary significantly from one society and setting to another) surrounds the ways in which questions are asked and answered—one might think of it in the way Sapir described the process by which gestures are recognized; namely, as an elaborate and secret code "written nowhere, known by none, and understood by all."[19] Even a glance at current research on the "grammar of questioning" suggests the extraordinary intricacy of the questioning process and its importance in understanding social and educational relationships.[20] Indeed, how questions are asked and answered and the ways in which answers are sought and then appraised, for example, the amount of questioning that is seen as acceptable and the extent of embellishment or simplicity that is seen as appropriate in an answer, may be considered highly significant components of educative interaction in the family.

The observation that children as young as the age of four have already learned to "switch codes" when talking with individuals in different roles suggests that they have also learned a rich repertoire of questioning and answering behaviors, a repertoire so subtle that (as Sapir's description of gesture suggests) it cannot be acquired by explicit instruction alone.[21] Since much of this learning undoubtedly takes place in the home—indeed, the mother's response to the child's questions has been noted as a significant variable in some of the educationally oriented research on the family—and since the school is also concerned with questioning and answering, an examination of these processes holds promise not only for an understanding of education within the family but also for insight into the relationship between familial and school education.

The Organization of Activity in Space and Time

The processes by which space and time are dealt with in the home offer another example of the possibilities of a process oriented analysis of familial education. Spatial organization has been seen as a basic dimension of social interaction, and cultural and situational variations in the definition of personal space (or the distances that people maintain from one another), in the kinds of comfort and discomfort occasioned by different spatial arrangements, and in the ways in which the organization of space itself conditions social interaction have been observed.[22] Some recent investigations have used videotaping in the home as a device for obtaining data on the relations between spatial organization and familial interaction.[23] There is little doubt from the reports of these investigations that behavior with reference to space, ranging from the distances observed in personal interaction to the modes of arranging objects in relation to space (the "messy" playroom versus the "neat" playroom), represents an important realm of familial education, one that occurs at least partially at the margins of awareness.

The element of time enters into the family's activities in a variety of ways, most of which are of considerable educational significance. First, the family's activities are organized in time, and this organization offers a clear example of an interactive process. Some of the recent research on outcomes has suggested the importance of such variables as "proper" scheduling and time management in the home for the child's success in school, treating scheduling and time management as if they were dimensions of parental (or more often maternal) behavior. Yet as anyone can attest who has waited for others in the family who are late (or who has been hurried by others who see themselves as prompt), scheduling is clearly a matter of interaction, a process by which family members coordinate, modify, and pace their activities in relation to one another.

The family's organization of activity in time involves numerous levels of individual and interactive timing. Some recent research, for example, that of Chapple, has indicated the possibility that individuals differ in fundamental biological activity levels and that various biological rhythms and time clocks are combined and fitted together in social interaction. The extent to which "synchrony" results or fails to result in the coordination of activity levels varies considerably from one relationship to another.[24] Awareness of and response to differences in individual activity levels are reflected in the fact that children are often evaluated in terms that refer to the pacing of their behavior, for example, "lethargic" or "high-strung" or "hyperactive." At least one recent study has examined the ways in which children's behavior contributes to the coordination of their own activity with that of their parents.[25] When individual activity rates are combined within the family, differences in amount and pacing of activity can also be observed at the level of the family as a unit, where some families appear to carry out extraordinary amounts of activity in a given time period, while others by contrast appear to lead slow-moving lives.

Finally, there are concepts about time and orientation in time that can be considered to affect the nature of planning and organizing with reference to the future. Like scheduling, planning has been noted as a variable in familial organization that relates to the child's success in school.[26] But the process by which time definitions are acquired is itself a significant aspect of education. Here, cultures have been shown to differ markedly in their emphasis on past, present, and future, and indeed a recent commentary on the experience and organization of time by Cottle and Klineberg points to the connection between anticipation of the future and forms of fantasy.[27]

As with behavior relating to space, behavior relating to time represents an important area of familial education, again one that occurs at least partially at the margins of awareness. It can also be examined at multiple levels. Golden, for example, has gathered a fascinating set of videotapes that demonstrate similarities in rates of interaction across three generations of a family from the northern United States and three generations of a family from the southern United States, along with the adaptations that occurred when a man from one of the families married a woman from the other.[28] At a related level, studies that have concerned themselves with the "micro" analysis of social interaction suggest the fruitfulness of examining time as an element in particular verbal interchanges within the family, for example, the matter of what constitutes an interruption, what constitutes a pause, and what constitutes a legitimate invitation for entry into a discussion.[29] In such analysis the process of managing time merges with the process of language, in ways that have considerable educational significance. At still another level, timing may be examined in the organization of explicit learning activities in the home, such as homework, or self-study, or preparation for tests. Since processes of timing, such as delaying gratification and "taking turns," have been seen as significant in the school,[30] this emphasizes, once again, the numerous possibilities of insights not only into the role of the family as educator but also into the educational relationships between family and school.

Memory as an Interactive Process

The social triggering of memory and its reinforcement by others provide a further example of an educational process that can be systematically investigated within the family. Individuals differ greatly in their modes of remembering, and the differences enter significantly into family interaction. Memory itself can be seen as a social process that is not only influenced by the icons and symbols present in the social settings but also triggered and reinforced by other individuals. As such, it affords an intriguing illustration of familial interaction of the sort that frequently transcends particular dyadic relationships.

In observations of family discussions at mealtime, for instance, one notes that several members of a family may join in fitting diverse bits and pieces into a conversational mosaic. This process was exemplified in a recent interview during the course of my own research in which a mother, two daughters, and a young son in a Puerto Rican family were discussing the problems of gangs in their neighborhood. While the mother and the older daughter were talking, the son moved in and out of the conversation, contributing additional information that was apparently not known or not initially remembered by the mother or the daughter. (The interview, incidentally, was with a family in which neither parent had completed a high school education, indicating that the process of memory triggering and reinforcement is by no means confined to those who are highly educated.)

It is quite possible that families sometimes develop a division of labor in the realm of memory. This may occur with respect to subject matter as well as types of remembering. Thus, a wife with a factual memory may recall dates and places of family events, while the husband recalls visual images or the things people said. In family discussions or especially in the telling of family stories, one can often observe the various members requesting assistance in filling in details or in embellishing particular themes.

The role of family stories and myths in relation to the social process of memory bears special attention. Myths, of course, are not necessarily false (Leach defines a myth as a story considered to be divinely true by those who believe it but a fairy tale by those who do not).[31] Nor, indeed, are they necessarily true. But true or false they undoubtedly have educational substance and influence in their own right. Even gossip and critical stories about the experiences of family members and others can provide opportunities for formulating and clarifying values. In short, then, family discussions can be viewed as a highly important process by which family members transmit, evoke, and acquire knowledge, values, and attitudes via one another. Myths and legends as told and retold within a family convey the knowledge, values, and attitudes in a special (and often unique) form, at the same time that they offer explanations as to why particular viewpoints are held.

It is probable that childhood memories represent some melding of what might be called direct personal recollection and recurring stories of events as remembered by others. One may even argue that memory includes a category of "nonremembered" or "semiremembered" events—events embedded in family myth and lore that are from time to time recalled or returned to the center of awareness in discussions within the family. The social process by which memory is thus reaffirmed and reinforced by others is essential in the phenomenon of individual recall (as well as modes of relating to others in recall), and an examination of the process will doubtless shed considerable light on the more general dynamics of education within the family.

The Processes of Evaluating and Labeling

Yet another realm of interaction within the family that illustrates the potential of a process-oriented approach is the way in which family members evaluate and label one another. Evaluation is unquestionably part of the individual's experience from birth to death; even a day-old baby may be described as cuddly or tense. Moreover, virtually every aspect of social life is subject to evaluation. Everyone evaluates others and is in turn evaluated by others. Evaluations are summarized by labels that become part of a complex imagery. Some evaluations are fleeting, others are assigned greater importance and reinforced over time, coming to have lasting significance. The process of evaluation may be raised to the level of an explicit and formal statement, as, for example, in a parent's discussion with a child about a teacher's appraisal of the child's schoolwork; but it may also proceed in more subtle and continuous ways, by indirection, by innuendo, and via nonverbal communication. Teasing, name-calling, and other forms of joking are examples of less formal interactions that commonly embody elements of evaluation.

The family may be considered a primary reference group with respect to evaluation, in that its members, even where the continuity of household arrangements is brief, know each other over considerable spans of time and observe and appraise each other's abilities in a variety of spheres. Moreover, familial evaluations are likely to be subjective and laden with emotion, and they are apt to be recurrent.

Evaluation in its very nature takes place with reference to values and beliefs. Here the importance of differing beliefs and experiences on the part of different family members becomes critical. Whatever the content of the evaluation, the processes by which it is made and the effects it has on both the individual making it and the individual being evaluated (as well as others who know of it) are of crucial importance in understanding the family as educator. The impact that evaluative labels may have has been indicated in studies of the ways in which particular family members may be categorized, labeled, and even scapegoated by others,[32] and by the research of Hobbs and his colleagues showing how labels deriving from outside agencies, especially labels of children with special problems, are experienced and mediated within the family.[33]

The process by which individuals are evaluated by others undoubtedly has significance for their concepts of themselves. This is not to argue that any one-to-one correspondence prevails between self-image and images held by significant others—often this would be impossible because significant others hold divergent views of the individual. But it does imply that the continuous process of evaluation warrants serious attention, particularly attention to the ways in which the individual undergoes and responds to consistent and discrepant evaluations.

One of the basic features of interaction within the family is that all aspects of life are subject to what Heider has called "naive wisdom,"[34] or what anthropologists have sometimes referred to as "folk wisdom." There is invariably an immense body of lore in the common domain about how to rear children, the nature of child development, the nature of abilities, and the ways in which ability manifests itself. This body of lore has doubtless been infiltrated by psychological, sociological, and anthropological concepts in recent years, but it exists (and always has existed) independent of the behavioral sciences and needs to be considered in its own right.

One area in which the family's naive wisdom will be of special significance to the student of familial education is the family's beliefs and assumptions concerning the existence and sequence of developmental stages. Quite apart from whether the investigator accepts Piaget's, Erikson's, or Spock's formulations, or indeed none of them, what the members of the family being studied believe requires systematic scrutiny; for, paraphrasing Merton's statement of the so-called Thomas Theorem, if family members define situations as real, they are real in their consequences.[35] The fact is that children's development is continually evaluated by parents and other adults in the family with respect to assumptions about age-appropriate achievement. Children also continually appraise each other in terms of concepts of appropriate behavior for given age levels (the subtle awareness that children have of developmental stages is indicated by the research on code-switching in language). In families with several children, concepts of appropriate behavior are undoubtedly affected over time by memories, often blurred, of what the older children did at particular age levels. In sum, the ways in which the family sees any particular child, behaves with respect to that child, and conceives of that child's future are inevitably set against a backdrop of developmental notions.

One interesting and important aspect of sibling relationships involves the ways in which siblings evaluate one another. Thus, it has been suggested that siblings, particularly when close in age, may evaluate each other's behavior in terms that differ markedly from those employed by parents. Evaluations among siblings, once again, are part of a continuing process of moment-to-moment interaction within the family. One can, for example, observe that children talk to each other about school in a way that sometime verges on the scandalous, having a backstage quality[36] that differs substantially from the way they talk with their parents about school.

The process of evaluation is also conditioned by values concerning evaluation itself. Parents doubtless have ideas about what constitutes legitimate and illegitimate criticism on the part of one sibling of another, as well as ideas about ways of fostering or diminishing competition among siblings (encouraging intrafamilial sports, for example, versus selecting different instruments for music lessons in the family to avoid invidious comparisons). Children, too, have their own ideas about what constitutes legitimate and illegitimate criticism, which can readily be detected by observing their conflicts and differences of opinion, as well as their moments of protective solidarity.

The process by which family members evaluate and appraise evaluation offers a fascinating realm for further research of educational significance. Not only does the process of evaluation have continuing influence as the various members of a family develop concepts of their own abilities and attributes, but the evaluation of evaluations becomes a vehicle by which family members learn to learn; that is, learn about the process of criticism itself and develop strategies for accepting or discounting the views of others. Thus, in a painfully vivid portrayal, Coles describes the ways in which children of migrant farm workers learn to appraise the evaluations that those in outside institutions, for example, hospitals, make of them as these affect their life chances.[37]

There is a close relationship between evaluations and the social process of triggering memory. Parents relive their own experiences through their children, and this is important not only in its own right but also as part of the process of appraisal. Vicariously reliving one's own ambitions and failed ambitions through one's children has sometimes been seen as an instance of pathology within the family. Yet reliving and reenacting previous experience is not necessarily pathological. It is part of the basic process by which parents formulate aspirations for their children. Examination of interview materials readily reveals that family discussions move continuously back and forth between past, present, and future, interweaving time periods, basing evaluations of the present on past experiences and, at the same time, seeing the present in terms of future aspirations.

Examination of the processes of evaluation in the family becomes an especially useful vehicle for getting at the ways in which interpretations of the world proceed (or, in the terms of Berger and Luckmann, the ways in which "social constructions of reality" are developed and applied).[38] Although such interpretations of reality may become fixed and stable, it is especially important in comprehending the subtleties of educational interaction within the family to see interpretation as "a formative and creative process in its own right."[39] Interpretation constructs meanings that are not yet determined, shifts meanings where differences in situations require it, and transforms meanings where social change has transformed situations.

Particularly in an era in which social change has become pervasive, it is an exceedingly important area of interaction in which to "ferret out lines of definition and networks of moving relation."[40]

Finally, since families consist of numerous individuals in moving and multiple associations, each with differing—although sometimes overlapping—values, perspectives, and interpretations of the world, there is much to be gained from an approach to the family as educator that leaves ample room for a multiplicity of meanings. Some of the more psychoanalytically oriented family therapy literature, for example, has tended to search for an "underlying" or "dynamic" or "true" meaning in family interaction, one that is discernible to the analyst but not necessarily to the participants. While such an approach may have its therapeutic uses, any prejudgment of the meaning of family interaction can preclude an understanding of the richness and diversity of educational encounters within the family. In studying the processes by which family members interact with respect to broader interpretations of reality, the full range of shadings and variations can be of considerable significance to the investigator.

The Process of Educational Mediation

In all of the processes that have been discussed thus far as illustrative of a process-oriented approach to the family as educator, mediation may be considered an element. Parents evaluate not only their children but also their children's friends, and they thereby mediate peer influences. Parents may attempt to influence the family's selection of television programs, and they also react to the content of programs, thereby mediating the influence of television. Siblings mediate each other's experiences in school, both through a continuing process of mutual evaluation and through the direct conveying of information and expectations. Children in turn mediate their parents' knowledge of child development, and grandparents mediate images of the past and the future.

Mediation includes the variety of processes whereby family members translate and interpret educational experiences for one another. The parent, for example, may reappraise the teacher's interpretation of a particular historical event, suggesting alternative points of view. The husband may attempt to place the wife's experience in a particular job in a broader or different perspective. One sibling may criticize another for his gullibility with respect to television commercials. Or one sibling may discount the appraisal another has received from a particular teacher, contending that the teacher is "an easy grader" or "always says things like that." Report cards, physicians' and social workers' recommendations, evaluations of job performance—all are cast into the crucible of family discussion and become subject to its transformation. Whatever the motivations involved in any particular instance of mediation—and the question of motivation must not be equated with interactional consequences[41]—the process of educational interpretation and translation remains to be understood in its own right.

The process of educational mediation includes deliberate and explicit coaching that has the function of adding to or assisting (and inevitably also interpreting) educational experiences elsewhere; but it also includes the variety of concurrent processes that are always the backdrop of deliberate instruction. The process encompasses not only response to and interpretation of educational events that originate elsewhere but also the triggering and setting off of new educational encounters within the family. Here, incidentally, the way in which siblings stimulate and set the stage for one another in a continuous round of activities offers a fruitful area for examination.

Deliberate and systematic instruction within the family needs to be understood in the context of this continuing whirlpool of interaction that takes place on a recurrent and repetitive basis, in the context of events that have momentary impact as well as events of lasting significance. The process of evaluation needs to be understood in the same context. Any family is subject to a continuous barrage of evaluations of its members from external individuals and agencies.

At times there is a tendency for these evaluations to be attributed more significance than intended by the evaluator (they are "over-read"), particularly when the evaluator is assumed to have professional competence to make the evaluation. In such instances special pressures are placed on the family in appraising the evaluation. Even when evaluations are not attributed undue significance, the process by which family members mediate in the selection, acceptance, transformation, and rejection of evaluations is exceedingly important. Ultimately, it will affect in one way or another both the self-images and the world views of those who are involved.

These several processes that have been suggested as exemplary of a process oriented approach to the study of the family as educator are by no means exhaustive, although each is profoundly important in its own right. Each brings together the influences of different individuals within the family, but each at the same time can be studied as a process, for example, in terms of its step-by-step sequencing, without necessarily focusing on its outcomes from the perspective of a particular individual. Moreover, each involves interactions that are significant for what Bateson has referred to as "deutero-learning" or learning to learn.[42] Thus, learning how to ask questions, learning how to organize activities in time, learning how to appraise external evaluations—all involve learning to learn, and all thereby become doubly important for an understanding of education, even if they are not explicitly seen by participants as educational and even if they do not necessarily involve "teaching" or "learning."

A CONCLUDING NOTE ON VALUES AND CONTEXTS

The methodological issues in research on the family as educator take on added significance when one considers the ambience in which the research proceeds. The family has always been an exceedingly difficult subject for inquiry, in part because it is so much an aspect of everyone's experience that it becomes difficult to avoid projecting one's own values, beliefs, and attitudes onto the experience of others. As Levy has pointed out, "down through the years no organization has been the focus of greater moralizing or musing."[43] The moralizing and musing have no doubt been associated with the numerous instances in which the values of investigators unwittingly intruded themselves into their formulations. Maccoby has illustrated the problem by pointing to the ways in which projections of beliefs concerning sex differences can color hypotheses about verbal differences between boys and girls.[44] The moralizing and musing have also been associated with the fact that study of the family has sometimes been held in dubious repute as an area of serious scholarship. Even experienced and determined family researchers have despaired at times when reviewing the literature of their subject; in this area, as Levy has remarked, "in the scientific realm . . . we seem to have taken leave of our senses in handling this whole field."[45] Interestingly, where the tendency to moralize about the family is reduced by social and cultural distance, as in anthropological studies of kinship, research on the family has more readily taken its proper place as an enterprise of serious scholarship.

Associated with the tendencies to moralize and to project one's own values is the tendency to view the family in terms of simplified notions of cause and effect. Particularly when the family is studied with the goal of finding solutions to social problems, the tendency to overstate the impact of family relationships is much in evidence. There is the search for deficits in the home that by implication places heavy responsibility on those who fail to perform their family roles in just the right way, and there is the search for the elixir of motherhood—the formula that will strike just the right balance between the twin perils of maternal overprotection and maternal neglect. Underlying such search is the assumption that specific behaviors (particularly on the part of the mother) produce wide-ranging consequences and that these consequences can be modified by "correction" of the specific behaviors, even without other changes in the family or in the social environment.

The tendency to moralize is also reflected in an overly solemn and grim emphasis in the research itself. The therapeutically oriented literature, for example, while necessarily concerned with problems and pathologies, has virtually ignored the lighter side of family experience, the fun and exhilaration that can occur even in difficult circumstances. Even the recent search for "strengths" in the family has at times been heavy-handed. Humor has often been taken as a clue to hidden pathology rather than as a basis for integration and solidarity, while ritual has been viewed as a form of obsession rather than a pleasurable activity associated with sentiments of continuity. Not surprisingly, the same grimness has marked the educationally oriented literature, where one notes a somber preoccupation with absent fathers and insufficiently verbal mothers.

One need not get caught up in platitudinous romanticism about the family to suggest that any fruitful program of research on the family as educator must embody a fuller and more balanced approach, one that ranges over the entire gamut of familial experience. There are serious difficulties with the contemporary family, to be sure. There is need for alternative arrangements under certain conditions; there is widespread demand for reformulation of female and male roles; and there are the persistent problems of poverty and the unspeakable conditions it creates for people of all ages in families throughout the world. These problems need to be addressed and attacked with determination. But a narrowly conceived, subtly moralistic approach to familial experience is not likely to result in the broad understanding required for effective intervention.

Precisely because of the difficulty of examining the family without intruding premature external judgments, the argument for a contextual approach to the study of the family as educator becomes the more compelling. To lift specific segments or dimensions of experience out of the context of the interpretations and meanings that surround them is to increase the risk of unwittingly imposing ill-fitting external evaluations. The need is for methods that will facilitate the study of the family and its members in contexts sufficiently complex and subtle to take into account multiple levels of meaning and experience both within and outside the family.

Finally, the approach to the family as educator needs to take full account of the continuous process of change and development within the family, both for adults and children. Dewey often remarked that the goal of education is growth and that the process of growth has no end beyond itself, and furthermore, that the ideal of growth results in the conception of education as a constant reorganizing and reconstructing of experience.[46] His ideas apply as surely to the family as to the school. To understand the processes of education and growth within the family, one must focus directly upon those processes, with full scientific precision.

NOTES

1. Leichter, "Boundaries of the Family as an Empirical and Theoretical System," *op. cit.;* for a general discussion of these issues, see Yehudi A. Cohen, Social boundary systems, *Current Anthropology,* 1969, *10,* pp. 103–125.

2. William J. Goode, Sociology of the family. In Robert K. Merton, Leonard Broom,

and Leonard S. Cottrell, Jr. (Eds.), *Sociology today*. New York: Basic Books, 1959, p. 185.

3. Herbert Blumer, Sociological analysis and the "variable." In Jerome G. Manis and Bernard N. Meltzer, *Symbolic interaction: A reader in social psychology* (2nd ed.). Boston: Allyn and Bacon, 1972, pp. 101–102.

4. For one discussion of individual differences in the process of change, see Herbert Spiegel, An operational perspective on concepts of change, self and identity. *The American Journal of Psychoanalysis*, 1962, *23*, (1), 1–4.

5. Lawrence A. Cremin, Notes toward a theory of education. *Notes on Education*, Spring 1973, No. 1, p. 5. Institute of Philosophy and Politics of Education, Teachers College, Columbia University.

6. The selectivity in short-term memory of educational experiences within the family has been vividly demonstrated in my own research interviews.

7. Lawrence A. Cremin, Further notes toward a theory of education. *Notes on Education*, March 1974, No. 4, p. 1, Institute of Philosophy and Politics of Education, Teachers College, Columbia University.

8. Leichter, The concept of educative style, *op. cit.*

9. This concept of the "ripple effect" has been applied to examination of the therapeutic process by Herbert Spiegel and Louis Linn, The 'ripple effect' following adjunct hypnosis in analytic psychotherapy. *American Journal of Psychiatry*, 1969, *126* (1), 53–58.

10. Blumer, *op. cit.*, p. 99.

11. *Ibid.*, p. 101.

12. *Ibid.* Although coming from a different tradition, Blumer's statement is consistent with Wolf's argument for studying what parents actually do in their interactions with children; he, too, is concerned with problems arising from overgeneralized measures.

13. John Dewey. *Human nature and conduct.* New York: Henry Holt, 1922, p. 16.

14. Philip W. Jackson. *Life in classrooms.* New York: Holt, Rinehart & Winston, 1968.

15. Jean Berko Gleason, Code switching in children's language. In Timothy E. Moore (Ed.), *Cognitive development and the acquisition of language.* New York: Academic Press, 1973, pp. 159–167.

16. *Ibid.*, p. 167.

17. David M. Schneider and George C. Homans, Kinship terminology and the American kinship system. *American Anthropologist*, 1955, *57*, 1194–1208.

18. Joseph Jaffe and Stanley Feldstein. *Rhythms of dialogue.* New York: Academic Press, 1970.

19. Edward Sapir, The unconscious patterning of behavior in society. In David G. Mandelbaum (Ed.), *Selected writings in language, culture and personality.* Berkeley: University of California Press, 1949, p. 556.

20. Lindsey Churchill, *The grammar of questioning.* Unpublished paper, Ph.D. program, Department of Sociology, City University of New York Graduate School and University Center, New York, 1972.

21. Gleason, *op. cit.;* also Sapir, *op. cit.*

22. Edward T. Hall. *The hidden dimension.* Garden City, N.Y.: Doubleday, 1966; also Robert Sommer. *Personal space: The behavioral basis of design.* Englewood Cliffs, N.J.: Prentice-Hall, 1969.

23. This research is exemplified by the recent work of Adam Kendon, particularly the materials presented at the 1973 meeting of the American Anthropological Association.

24. Eliot D. Chapple. *Culture and biological man: Explorations in behavioral anthropology.* New York: Holt, Rinehart & Winston, 1970.

25. Daniel N. Stern, A micro-analysis of mother–infant interaction: Behavior regulating social contact between a mother and her 3½-month-old twins. *The Journal of the American Academy of Child Psychiatry,* 1971, *10* (3), 501–516.

26. Wolf, *op. cit.*

27. Thomas J. Cottle and Stephen L. Klineberg. *The present of things future: Explorations of time in human experience.* New York: Free Press, 1974.

28. Videotapes developed by June Golden.

29. One example of the "micro" level of analysis of interaction may be seen in Paul Byers, *From biological rhythm to cultural pattern: A study of minimal units.* Unpublished Ph.D. dissertation, Columbia University, New York, 1972.

30. Jackson, *op. cit.*

31. Edmund Leach. *Claude Levi-Strauss.* New York: Viking Press, 1970, p. 54.

32. Ezra F. Vogel and Norman W. Bell, The emotionally disturbed child as the family scapegoat. In Norman W. Bell and Ezra F. Vogel (Eds.), *A modern introduction to the family* (rev. ed.). New York: Free Press, 1968, pp. 412–427.

33. The research of Hobbs and his colleagues is of particular interest in this connection; Nicholas Hobbs, *Summary: The project on classification of exceptional children.* Unpublished mimeographed document, October 28, 1972.

34. Fritz Heider. *Psychology of interpersonal relations.* New York: John Wiley, 1958.

35. Robert K. Merton. *Social theory and social structure.* New York: Free Press, 1968 ed.; also for another discussion Robert K. Merton, Social knowledge and public policy: Sociological perspectives on four presidential commissions. *Center for Advanced Study in the Behavioral Sciences,* 1974, mimeographed, especially p. 19. The other side of the argument, namely, that something that is not believed to be true can nevertheless have consequences, does not take away from the importance of knowing about belief systems.

36. Concepts that point to the ways in which presentations of self are modified in different social situations can be found in the work of Erving Goffman. *The presentation of self in everyday life.* Garden City, N.Y.: Doubleday, 1959.

37. Coles, *Uprooted children, op. cit.*

38. Peter L. Berger and Thomas Luckmann. *The social construction of reality: A treatise in the sociology of knowledge.* Garden City, N.Y.: Doubleday, 1966.

39. Blumer, *op. cit.,* p. 98.

40. *Ibid.,* p. 101.

41. Merton's classic distinction between intention and consequence is relevant here. See Merton, *Social theory and social structure, op. cit.*

42. Gregory Bateson. *Steps to an ecology of mind.* New York: Ballantine Books, 1972.

43. Marion J. Levy, Jr. Some hypotheses about the family. *Journal of Comparative Family Studies,* 1970, *I* (1), p. 119.

44. Maccoby, Sex differences in intellectual functioning, *op. cit.,* p. 41.

45. Levy, *op. cit.,* p. 119.

46. John Dewey. *Democracy and education.* New York: Macmillan, 1916, pp. 59–60, 89.

14

Differential Patterns of Social Outlook and Personality in Family and Children

ELSE FRENKEL-BRUNSWIK

Most investigators who have written about the American family agree that at present we witness a weakening of the family as an institution and that this change runs parallel to the weakening of many other institutions. It is pointed out by these writers, especially by Ogburn,[1] that the dilemma of the modern family is due to the loss of some of its functions, such as the economic, the educational, or the religious function. But in the interpretation of this loosening of the older, more rigid forms of family organization the writers disagree. Some, such as Zimmerman,[2] see in this change signs of disintegration and point to divorces, delinquency, revolt of youth, and increased individualism as proof of their contention. Others, such as Burgess,[3] find that the increased relaxation of authority and regimentation within the family leads to greater stress on companionship and affection. Instead of regarding it as a sign of disintegration, he sees in the replacement of old-time family structures a phenomenon of growth and increased adaptability, brought about by greater democracy, freedom, and opportunity for self-expression within the family. A cogent analysis of the American family can be found in Mead.[4] In view of such comprehensive collections of the different views on the American family as that by Winch and McGinnis,[5] we need not expand on the subject further.

Although the trend toward democratization of the family is, without doubt, an outstanding development in this country, the old-type authoritarian fam-

Else Frenkel-Brunswik until her death was lecturer in psychology, University of California, Berkeley.

ily with its unquestioned parental rule, even though deviant by modern standards, has not vanished altogether. In the present chapter one example of each of the two opposite extremes of American families is presented. In each case the presentation is centered about one of the children. It was the children who were the basis of the selection of the two families; they represent the authoritarian and the democratic attitude and personality structure in their purest form. Neither of them can be considered representative in the statistical sense. To paraphrase a statement of Woodworth, they are so typical that they can be considered to be atypical. They exhibit most of the trends found statistically to be prevalent in their respective groups, to be introduced below, but rarely present in such completeness in a single individual. In accordance with our general findings, existing differences, if any, in sex, intelligence, or size of family may be considered of but secondary importance in the choice of paradigms for our present purpose, which is the concrete demonstration of the authoritarian versus the egalitarian syndrome. As will become evident to the reader, there are rather striking differences in the educational and intellectual levels of the two families. The question as to whether these differences are primary or whether they are secondary effects of the general inaccessibility to experience that is so characteristic of even the more intelligent authoritarian individuals cannot be fully discussed here, although some light will be thrown on this issue by the present material.

The first of the two families belongs to a pattern obviously less frequent in the present American culture than the second. It mirrors the old-fashioned authoritarian type of family structure in its most rigid form. Our second, democratic-minded example, even though by no means free of internal tensions, represents an orientation geared toward the realization of basically egalitarian principles; these are pursued in this family with relentless devotion and without compromise. It must be stressed that neither of the two families presents an ideal from the standpoint of perfect adjustment, as generally both the authoritarian and the nonauthoritarian personality are sometimes associated with their own particular brands of neuroticism.[6]

Since we are describing two individual families, we cannot generalize to the culture as a whole. In fact, our examples stress the variety rather than the uniformity of family life and the variety of individuals that can be found within one and the same culture. Furthermore, in the present context we are not primarily interested in social and economic determinants and, therefore, in the origin and structure of such social institutions as the family; rather, our main emphasis is on the influence of such institutions upon the outlook and personality structure of children and adolescents. However, we shall not neglect to point out the ways in which the family patterns described here seem to be rooted in some aspects of the complex institutional structure of our society.

Although our start is from the children and other individuals concerned and our method is a clinical one, with special emphasis on depth interviewing, our eventual concern is with general problems of social psychology. Under this aspect we explored the ways in which parents and children relate themselves to shared norms and values, their feelings of belongingness, their conception of parent-child relationships, of occupational roles and sex roles, and their religious and social outlook in general. Over and above this we tried to probe into the underlying patterns of motivation and emotions.

In a child-family study begun in 1944 and still under way at the Institute of Child Welfare, University of California,[7] approximately 1500 children and adolescents, most of them between the ages of 10 and 15, were given questionnaire-type tests dealing with attitudes toward minority groups as well as attitudes toward political and economic issues in general. From some of these instruments an overall ethnic prejudice or "ethnocentrism" score was derived. Among those scoring extremely "high" and extremely "low" on ethnocentrism (that is, scoring within the uppermost or lowermost 25%), 161 were interviewed and given a specially designed variant of the well-known Thematic Apperception Test.[8] The interviews, conducted in 1946 and 1947, concerned attitudes toward minority groups and the social scene in general, toward school, discipline, work, parents, friends, and the opposite sex, as well as the child's conception of the self. With respect to these procedures, our methods and results are analogous to those of a separate project on "The Authoritarian Personality,"[9] of which this writer was one of the authors and in which the relationship between ethnocentrism and a more generalized authoritarianism was ascertained for the case of adults. Over and above these procedures, one or both of the parents of 43 of our children were also interviewed concerning their attitudes and child-rearing practices; in addition, the socioeconomic family history was gathered. A further distinguishing phase of our child-family study consisted of an exploration of the children's cognitive mastery of reality by having them perform various experimental tasks in perception, memory, and thinking.[10]

The use of children as subjects in the study of social beliefs offers both advantages and disadvantages. Children are generally more direct and uninhibited; they openly express attitudes and feelings which, though no doubt still alive in adults, are manifested by them with greater reserve and restraint. On the other hand, children's attitudes are less structured and less consistent than those of adults. But even in children we found that the social beliefs held by an individual, though varying in degree of crystallization, tend to fall into a coherent pattern, and that this pattern seems to be related to the personal "fate" he had met in his early interpersonal relationships within the family.

A body of data has now been accumulated by various investigators which shows that different socioeconomic classes vary a great deal as to the pattern of child rearing. Since our study was not primarily oriented toward class differences, we tried to select two families that are not too different as far as their economic locus is concerned. In fact, the two families are even matched in the sense that both are objectively moving downward on the economic ladder when compared with the grandparents; yet we find a profound difference in the reaction to the loss of objective status. Although approximately matched economically, the two families differ widely with respect to many other social indices, such as education and prestige. These differences, without doubt, in addition to the differences observed in the personalities of the parents, will explain a good part of the radically different atmospheres prevailing in the respective homes.

CASE STUDY OF AN AUTHORITARIAN FAMILY AND CHILD

One of the most ethnocentric child subjects is an 11-year-old boy whom we shall call "Karl."

Parents and Home Atmosphere

Karl's father comes from an authoritarian family and is a mechanic. Karl's father and paternal grandfather were born in this country, whereas the child's paternal grandmother came from Germany. The paternal grandparents died when Karl's father was four years old, and the father was reared by the great-grandparents, who owned a large farm and a wholesale store and "who were rich but not generous with their money."

Karl's mother was born in this country, and so was her father, while her mother was born in Scotland. Karl's maternal step-grandfather was a notary. Karl's maternal grandmother had divorced her husband shortly after Karl's mother was born. In fact, Karl's mother had a succession of stepfathers, one of whom, a combination of musician and laborer, also played an important role for her. She finished the eighth grade, whereas Karl's father's education stopped even before he had reached this level.

The interviewer describes the home as crowded with overstuffed and dreary oak furniture, with lace doilies on the tables. All this perhaps represents a concerted effort on the part of the parents to stress their middle-class identification and to avoid the possibility of being grouped with the underprivileged. This anxiety stems at least partially from the fact that the socioeconomic history of the family is unstable and there was some loss of status as compared to the previous generation. There is, however, no evidence of poverty. The family lives in a six-room flat and owns a car and two radios.

The mother's background has much less stability than the father's. "I grew up in big cities and in one hotel after another." Generally, such geographical instability seems relatively common in ethnocentric homes. Both parents, furthermore, report their own parents as foreign-born. This, too, is significantly more often the case with parents of prejudiced than of tolerant children. As a group trend, it may be taken to indicate that the parents still see themselves entangled in the process of assimilation. Apparently as a counterbalance, they stress their "belonging" through both their social aspirations and the rejection of what is considered socially inferior.

Both of Karl's parents had been exposed to strict discipline. The father does not like to talk about his own father, whom he describes as a drunkard and psychopath who deserted his family. He is much more ready to discuss his grandfather, by whom he was raised:

> My grandfather was really strict. He had thirteen children, and even when they were grown up, there wasn't one of them that would talk back to him, and he could handle any of them.

The father of our boy grew up knowing little but work. His grandfather was anxious to see his grandson go to school and even to have his voice trained. Karl's father did not live up to any of his grandfather's ambitions, doing relatively simple work, although he still believes he will one day accomplish a great deal by an invention. He asserts that his occupation is only temporary, since he is likely to make a big mechanical invention soon. This aspiration remains on a fantasy level, since there is little evidence of any concrete work toward the goal.

The idea of achieving fame someday is still alive in the fantasies of Karl's mother as well. Though having worked mainly in factories and being a waitress at the time of the interview, she prides herself on her talents, such as photography, composing, and writing. There is here the same kind of unrealistic fantasy to which attention will be called in discussing Karl himself.

In discussing their children, Karl's parents emphasize that they made rules for them that had to be strictly obeyed. For instance, the children had to be in bed "sharp at six without fail." Asked whether the children ever have tantrums, the mother says:

> I should say not. They had better not. If they got mad, I just sat them on a chair and said to stay there until they could behave. I guess they never really had tantrums.

This is at variance with Karl's own statements, according to which he has outbursts of temper. Either this is mere boasting on his part, or the mother's denial of his ever deviating from what she considers good behavior is a distortion of fact; we are inclined to favor the latter interpretation. Apparently along the same line is the mother's statement about Karl, who is obviously a rather weak child, that "he has a strength but he hides it."

Both parents also report that they have used spanking as a disciplinary measure. To quote the mother: "The boys are more afraid of their father than of me; I guess because he is stronger." She seems not to realize that her children are overtrained and welcome the more severe punishment by their father. The father appears considerably worried about what the interviewer might have guessed about the children's relation to him: "It seems like Karl is afraid of me."

It is the father who represents in the family the rigid dichotomizing of the sex roles, which is, as we shall see, one of the characteristics of the authoritarian milieu: "Boys shouldn't do work in the home, though it's all right for a man to be a chef or a baker. The best of them are men." He apparently feels that it is considered appropriate for a man to be a chef and thus to enter the field of women only if there is assurance that he will excel.

The mother, in explaining her children's personality, relies heavily on astrology. She tells us that the personality of Karl's brother, whom we shall call Bill, can be explained by the fact that "he was born under the sign of The Twins." About Karl she says, "He is a dreamer of far places. He will go far and wide. The stars show that." The dependence on fate and the feeling of a mystical connection with supernatural forces has been found typical of the ethnocentric milieu,[11] the exaggerated ideas of self-importance going hand in hand with an underdeveloped self-reliance.

Both parents are ethnically extremely prejudiced. They consider the Negroes America's biggest problem, and the father adds, "Dig up Roosevelt and let him help settle it." He is concerned that the Negroes "want to go everywhere." The mother tells how, at the time she was a waitress, she personally took it on herself to put Negroes in their place. She would give them a glass of water and then ignore them:

> When they went out, we smashed the glass behind the counter good and hard so they were sure to hear it. The Chinese and Japanese should be separate too.

About the Jews the mother says:

> The Bible says they will always be persecuted. You know it wasn't a small thing they did—crucifying Christ—God said they would be punished till the end of time.

This line of argument is the more surprising because in the discussion about religion it is not the mother but the father who stresses its importance, as does Karl himself.

Karl's Social Beliefs

Karl is an unusually fat and passive boy with a history of many illnesses. The parents' ethnocentrism is shared by Karl, who in many other respects mirrors fascistic attitudes. We begin with quotations from that part of his interview record that deals with attitudes toward minority members. Karl says about Negroes:

> They make trouble, start wars. I wouldn't mind having all the Negroes in Oakland and all the white people in a different state. I would like to have a couple for good fighters. They are good fighters when they fight with a knife. Like somebody starts a fight and you have a gang with some Negroes to fight with you on your side with knives and guns.

Like most of the ethnocentric children, Karl is in favor of segregation of the outgroups, and, like some of them, his statements show implicit envy of characteristics ascribed to minority groups. Karl admires the physical power, strength, and aggressiveness of the Negroes. He rejects them and does not want them to mix with his own group, but he wants them as pro- tectors—we might almost say as bodyguards—in fights against other boys. His passivity and relative immobility also give direction to the stereotype he has about the Jews:

> They think they are smart and go anywhere they please. They think they are hot. They dress up in all kinds of jewelry. Some just kidnap girls and boys and use them for slaves.

Some characteristics of this image of the Jews, such as their alleged social dominance and their exhibitionism of wealth, are common in ethnocentric children. We find, however, in Karl's statements some emphases and elab- orations that, as we shall see, are rooted in his own specific conflicts. Thus the mobility and the enslaving motif is very personal with Karl. We have just heard him express the desire to use Negroes as his fighting slaves. The theme of fighting recurs again and again in Karl's description of minority groups. Although children not uncommonly ascribe aggressiveness to Ne- groes, it is most unusual for them to mention this quality in descriptions of the Chinese. Karl, however, stresses the point that Chinese are "good fight- ers"; and about the Filipinos he says, "They are good fighters and defi- nitely good to go through jungles with." As we shall see, the preoccupa- tion with jungles, where one can be lost and subject to deprivation, and the preoccupation with animals dominate Karl's fantasy in general.

Like many of the ethnocentric children, Karl sees general avarice and acquisitiveness as the cause of the last war, while the democratic-minded children specify in greater detail the wants of the different countries. Most of the children in our study think that there will be wars in the near future, but Karl, along with a great many of the ethnocentric children, takes this fact as natural and inevitable. "I think so because there's always going to be a war." As do over two-fifths of the high-scoring and a considerably smaller proportion of the low-scoring children, he thinks that we won the last war because of the atom bomb, ascribing a magical quality to its destructive potential. Egalitarian children refer more often in this context to better resources and the better equipment of America in general.

It is evident that Karl is at least in partial sympathy with Hitler and that his concern is only about the wrongs Hitler might have done to Americans. He states, "He was a little bit O.K. Sometimes he got a little bit too mean and did dirty stuff like putting lighted matches in the toenails of Americans." This partial sympathy with Hitler does not prevent Karl from exercising his extreme punitiveness toward the Germans. "We should put all the Germans and Japs on an island and put an atom bomb to it."

He considers America's biggest problem the fact that "a lot of people are getting mad because everybody is starting war against each other." Here is the recurrent fighting theme, this time in the form of an assumption of an almost chaotic war of all against all.

In Karl's response to another interview question we find a further dominant theme—fear of deprivation, especially food deprivation. Karl is against strikes because "if grocery stores go on a strike, we won't have no food. Farmers can go on a strike, and there will be no food, and we will have to grow our own food." Ethnocentric children frequently manifest this particular fear. It is especially exaggerated in Karl but has, as we have ascertained, no basis in real food deprivation.

Karl's attitude toward the social scene and his role in it is best characterized by the one-sidedness of his answer to the interview question, "How would you like to change America?":

> I would like to have a filling station every couple of blocks or so and palm trees and grass along the streets and lawns in front of people's houses and have the back yards all cleaned up and flowers growing. Every store should have all kinds of candy and bubble gum. They wouldn't have no fights in the neighborhood. The cops would take them all in. At Fleishacker's [an amusement park] have nice warm water [in the swimming pool] and the zoo cleaned up. Every day there would be hay for the animals that eat hay and the lions would have lots of meat every day for breakfast and lunch.

As are many of our ethnocentric children, Karl is concerned with cleanliness and external beautification, the removal of aggressive groups, and with having a constant flow of supplies. The only beings for which he shows concern are, characteristically, animals rather than people. His emphasis on rigid order as well as on the regularity in the appearance of streets and other objects contrasts sharply with his emphasis on, and even open advocacy of, turmoil and chaotic aggression, as noticed above.

Egalitarian children, on the other hand, are better able to remove themselves from the pressure of overanxiety about immediate needs. They are more likely to penetrate to such underlying and more general aspects of human welfare as justice and equality, lower prices and higher wages, and moral and ethical values in general.

Before leaving the topic of Karl's beliefs, we should like to point to the similarity between his statements on this subject and those of his brother Bill, older by one year. These differences exist in spite of the fact that the boys had no opportunity to discuss the subject between the respective interviews. Like Karl, Bill thinks that "we should kick out the colored people from San Francisco" because they get drunk and kill people. He feels that the German war criminals "should all have been hanged and not put in prison." Like his brother, he wants to put "the Japs on an island and throw bombs on them." He considers food to be America's biggest problem, and his main concern in this context is the problem of the rationing of sugar.

Karl's and His Brother's Attitudes Toward School, Family, and Sex Roles

The stereotypical approach to social and ethical challenges, with all its inherent inhibitions, carries over into such related, more specific areas as the conception of teachers, parental roles, sex roles, and so forth. The ambivalent submission to authority, found to be typical of ethnocentric children, is revealed in Karl's statement about teachers. An initial stereotyped denial of criticism, "I like everything about teachers," is followed by the mention of victimization and unjust treatment by teachers: "A lot of them make you go to the principal's office or out of the room for something you didn't do. I had that happen lots of times."

When asked in another context to describe the perfect boy, Karl starts off with a request for obedience to teachers. The craving for a complete surrender to authority is also exhibited in his brother Bill's statement about the kind of teacher he doesn't like: "Those who tell you in a nice way instead of being strict and then don't make you mind." Bill's ideal teacher would be "a man who would be strict," or, as second choice, a woman if "she was very strict." While the emphasis on negative aspects or on strictness seems to be a specific characteristic of ethnocentric children, the tolerant, by contrast, tend more often to emphasize positive traits in the ideal teacher, such as being helpful, laughing at jokes, and the like.

The attitude of ethnocentric children to the teacher appears to be but one of the aspects of a more generalized hierarchical conception of human relations, according to which the weak are expected to exhibit a self-negating surrender to the strong. Karl seems unaware of the fact that he himself succeeds only very partially in fulfilling the strict requirement of submissive obedience. Obviously, he is possessed by destructive and by no means dormant forces that are in part directed toward the very authorities to which he demands allegiance but that are, to an even larger extent, diverted to objects considered by him as underdogs.

In discussing the pupils he likes and dislikes, Karl seems exclusively concerned with the possibility of being attacked by one of the other boys, whereas his brother Bill stresses conventional values, such as politeness and obedience, values also emphasized by Karl in other contexts. Egalitarian children, such as our second major case, Peggy (see below), on the other hand, stress companionship, fun, common interests, and understanding as traits desired in friends.

Both Karl and his brother Bill stress, as do a relatively large proportion of the ethnocentric children, that money helps one to have friends. For Bill, money possesses magical evil attributes:

> It is the root of all evil. It's bad luck to be born with money. If your parents tell you to put it in a bank and you keep it until you are grown up, it's bad luck.

Bill proceeds to describe the disaster which befell several of his acquaintances after they saved their money. This is in line with the general tendency prevalent in the ethnocentric subjects to subscribe to all manner of superstitious statements, to see evil forces at work everywhere, and readily to anticipate doom and catastrophies.

Karl is one of the very few children who would prefer to have a private tutor rather than go to school. He explains that he would like to avoid the effort involved in getting ready to go to school, "to have to pack a lunch and hop a bus." Bill, however, rejects the idea of tutors as "just for rich people, and they are no good." This latter quotation exemplifies the resentment, frequent in ethnocentric subjects, against what they consider oppressors from above, a view that goes along with their fear that those below, such as the minority groups, may rise someday and take over in a fearful revenge.

Both boys have a rigid conception of sex roles, stressing politeness in girls. As Bill points out, "If a boy is talking, they shouldn't butt in." For him the best friend for a boy is a boy, for a girl, a girl. They both reject girls who are discourteous or aggressive toward boys, for example, "If she pulls a boy by the arm and tells him to take her to a show or someplace." Although dichotomizing of sex roles is to a certain extent general at this age, children scoring low on ethnocentrism do so to a much lesser degree, stressing more the point that boys and girls should behave naturally with each other. They also do not differentiate their descriptions of a perfect boy from that of a perfect girl as much as do the prejudiced children.

Asked what he would consider a perfect father, Karl, in line with many of the ethnocentric children, speaks mainly of the material benefits this kind of father would provide: "He will let you do anything you like and let you get any kind of food you like and let you take a girl out. Will give you about two dollars every day." Asked how he would like to change his own father, he states emphatically that "my father is good to me," but then goes on immediately to say that he would like to get more money from him to be able "to go to a show or dinner or any place I want." In almost every context he manifests this exploitive-manipulative approach to people.

As is often the case in ethnocentric boys, Karl's hostility is more directly expressed toward the mother than toward the father. When asked how he would like to change his mother, he starts off with "to make her nice," then proceeds to tell what he wants from her, such as "a car." That he is, on the whole, more oriented toward his father is probably related to the fact that the father is more powerful, in a position to provide more goods, and also better able to protect. This kind of dependency is often found to reduce open feelings and expressions of hostility.

While Karl sees people, and especially those in authority, primarily as "deliverers of goods," to use a term of Fenichel's,[12] Bill expects mainly regimentation from them. Thus a perfect father is for him one who, if asked for something, "ought not to give it to you right away." Bill denies that he has any desire to change his parents. There is ample evidence, from his interview and especially from his Thematic Apperception Test stories, of Karl's underlying hostility toward the parents. On a "blind" overall interview rating of attitudes toward parents, Karl earns the extreme rating of "6" with respect to both parents, representing the rater's impression that he is obsessed by the feeling of being threatened and victimized by their hostility. Bill receives a rating of "5"; this is only one step closer to the opposite extreme, "1," which would indicate an affectionate, secure, companionable relationship as seen by the child.

Both boys are assigned an extreme rating on "externalization of values," a category covering opportunism, conventionality, status-concern, and explicit condemnation of those who do not conform.

Both boys tell of corporal punishment at home, and both of them prefer to have their father rather than their mother punish them. Bill comes out with the explicit explanation that his mother "is a little too softhearted." In discussing this topic in general, both boys favor very severe punishment of children for relatively minor misconduct and seem only too ready to advocate intervention of the juvenile court in such cases. According to Karl, children should be punished for "talking back to grownups" and for breaking windows: "You should go to Juvenile one year for that."

In Karl a greater readiness toward explosive fits of aggression is revealed in his descriptions of how he reacts in anger: "I do anything I can—bite, pull hair, kick, tear into them." Bill, however, reports that he tries to control his anger as well as he can, mostly by going out of the field. Both explosive outbursts and frantic efforts of control are typical of our ethnocentric children.

Though both boys have shown some tendency to idealize their parents stereotypically and to stress their goodness, neither of them chooses any of the members of the family as companions on a desert island. Karl, of course, stresses first food and water, and also that he would take along a girl. From the dreams that Karl relates, as well as from the Thematic Apperception Test, it is evident that he connects the idea of a girl with feeding her or being fed by her, and, furthermore, that a girl means to him safety and absence of possible threats felt in connection with boys or men.

Along the same line are Karl's recurrent dreams, "It's about going with a girl for dinner," and about people getting murdered and hanged. The childhood memories he relates are full of mishaps and catastrophes. He remembers having fallen in a pond, recalls seeing his father kill a chicken that ran about without its head, seeing men killing turkeys, and seeing a crate of eggs broken under a truck.

Among his fears he lists his fear of wild animals, of high buildings, of drunken men, of "death in some dark night." He mentions that usually it is the girls who are especially afraid of the dark. When asked whether he wants to be a girl, he denies it but adds the stock projective answer, "Some guys want to be girls." The feminine identification that can be discerned behind much of the aggressive façade is apparent in the interviews and is especially evident in the Thematic Apperception Test.

Karl's Thematic Apperception Test Stories

The rigidification of the child's personality originally induced by the stress on self-negating submission and on the repression of nonacceptable tendencies not only leads to stereotypy; eventually the inherent pattern of conflict may result in a more or less open break between the different layers of personality and in a loss of control of instinctual tendencies by the individual. This contrasts rather sharply with the greater fluidity of transition and intercommunication between the different personality strata that are typical of the child in the more permissive home. The emotional makeup and the rigidity of defense, lack of insight, and narrowness of the ego of the authoritarian personality even carries over into the purely cognitive domain. Here, too, ready-made clichés tend to take the place of realistic spontaneous reactions.

Karl's TAT stories are full of murder and gore, much more so than the usual stories of children of his age. In practically every story a murder is committed under quite extraordinary circumstances. For example, a man who won in a race is "shot in the back five times" while he was "laying in bed, tired from his hard job." Two of the stories, to be further interpreted later, follow:

> It looks like murder. I saw a couple of murder pictures. A girl is down at the dock at night watching them unload freight. There is a man with a cane that is the girl's friend, and he is walking behind her. She had been gambling and won $200. This other man was trying to get the money off her. It was hid somewhere on her. The man with the cane presses on the cane, and a knife comes out. He stabs the man with the gun in the wrist, and the girl calls the cops, and they come and take him away in the patrol wagon to jail. He tries

to break away but can't. That night he went to the electric chair, and the girl had the money safe to keep the rest of her life.

Oh, gads: Sure is murder [cheerfully]. The man was in gambling. He believed the gambling table was crooked. He said it was, and the man behind the gambling table said it wasn't, and he had a whip and started whipping the other in the face. The U.S. Navy guy came in. It was a friend of his. He had a gun, and he shot the bullwhip out of the man's hand. The cops came, and the Navy guy told the cops what happened. The guy that owned it was arrested for having a crooked place, and it was turned into a big Safeway store and people went there and bought stuff. And the army guys got $250 for finding out the man had a crooked wheel. The guy in the middle died from bleeding too much.

Usually it is the men who are shot, and only in one story "a lady is hit in the back with a knife." In this case the woman is killed because she betrayed a man. In most of Karl's stories, however, the women manage to be safe and to get food and money.

In almost every one of Karl's stories food is mentioned in a general way or specifically; for example, peanuts, waffles, double-decker cones, etc., and there is reference to specific amounts of money, such as $200, $25, $250, $550,000, $400, 10¢. Usually the person who has the money is in great danger of being deprived of it and of being killed in the process.

Neither the role of the aggressive man nor that of the passive man seems to be workable in these stories. The man who is passive and in possession of some fortune is usually attacked in some surprising way, from behind or while asleep, and is destroyed. The aggressive man, on the other hand, is regularly caught by the police and sentenced at the least to life-imprisonment; more often, he is executed in the electric chair. The earlier story, in which the "crooked place was turned into a big Safeway store," obviously reveals Karl's deep-seated longing that all the dangerous men will be removed and that he will be allowed to be passive and surrounded by food, without fear of aggression and without the ensuing necessity for being aggressive himself. This is also the way he imagines girls to be. Even though the girls are, in the stories, in the more enviable position, not even they are always safe.

Here again we find the preoccupation with animals. In the stories they are being fed, as they were in Karl's projected ideal of America, which was quoted earlier. The feminine identification is apparent in the description of the "mother ape that had just laid a baby." Not even the animals and not even the baby ape are safe, since a man tries to "sock the baby ape with his gun."

Of the two types of men, the passive and the aggressive, Karl basically seems to feel closer to the former. In one story he describes in detail how a passive boy who always is being hit by a tough boy "had taken exercises from a guy that helps you make muscles." It is this same passive boy who feeds the animals. We thus have evidence both of insecurity about masculinity and of feminine identification, also manifested in the occurrence of many phallic symbols and castration threats and in an apparent embarrassment about body build and genital organs. In a swimming scene described by Karl he is careful to point out that the boys have swimming suits under their clothes and thus do not have to undress. Karl's stories are not only exaggerated versions of the stories common in ethnocentric boys in general, but also share similarites with the stories of overt homosexuals.

Concerning the formal aspects of Karl's stories the following can be said. They are long and flowing, presenting no necessity for probing on the part of the examiner. In spite of this fluidity, however, the form level of the stories is very low. They are neither coherent nor structured, and what seems like imagination is really a kind of ruminative repetition of the same themes over and over again. Karl is at times aware of this repetitiveness, and he starts one of his stories with the words, "another murder story." One of our foregoing stories begins, "Sure is murder," and the interviewer comments here that Karl makes this introduction with evident cheerfulness. The repetitiveness extends even to such details as numbers: the number $250 occurs in several stories, and other numbers are similar to it. The stories are, furthermore, utterly unrealistic as far as general plausibility is concerned, and they stray to a marked degree from the content of the picture, which, after the first few sentences, is frequently lost from sight entirely.

The image of the world found in Karl and in most of our ethnocentric subjects—the projection of the hostility they feel toward their parents, and their feeling that the world is a dangerous and hostile place—coincides with the image of the world Wolfenstein and Leites[13] found in American movie melodramas. This may represent a common fantasy which, in the more "typical" Americans for whom the powerful father is more imaginary than actual, is present at the most archaic levels only.

Bill's stories contain topics similar to those of Karl, such as quarreling, food, money, ambivalence toward the mother, catastrophes, and unhappy endings. But he is at the same time more constricted, and a great deal of encouragement and probing are necessary to lead him away from a mere description of the picture.

Remembering the evidence from the interviews, it appears that Bill is the more disciplined, not to say regimented, of the two boys and the more cautious, even though perhaps the one who will put his biases more readily into action if the opportunity is offered. On the other hand, social upheavals of a major order may be necessary to bring an individual such as Karl to the fore. Lacking these, he may very well lead an inconspicuous, unsuccessful life, ridiculed and baited by his fellows and possibly even passing over into a state of slow disintegration.

Discussion of Family Influence

From this material we gain the impression that the total outlook, just described, seems to a very appreciable extent to have its root in the authoritarian home. Family relationships in such homes are commonly based on roles clearly defined in terms of demands and submission. Execution of obligations rather than affection is the basis of smooth functioning in such homes. Furthermore, there is a stress on stereotyped behavior and on adherence to a set of conventional and rigid rules. The intimidating, punitive, and paralyzing influence of an overdisciplined, totalitarian home atmosphere may well exert a decisive influence upon the thinking and creativity of the growing child. The impoverishment of imagination seems to be analogous to that apparent under totalitarian social and political regimes. At the same time, the consideration of the responses to threats in childhood may reveal much about the ways in which individuals react to threats in adult life.

Intensive experiences in later life are undoubtedly in themselves capable of superseding both earlier influences and the individual predispositions to a certain extent, however, so that no direct or exclusive causal relationship between family structure, attitudes of children, and rise of totalitarianism may be assumed. We must also bear in mind that social conditions and institutions have, in turn, an impact of their own on the family structure.

It is primarily the fact that the home discipline in authoritarian homes is experienced as overwhelming, unintelligible, and arbitrary, demanding at the same time total surrender, which makes for the apparent parallelism with authoritarian political and social organizations. The similarity becomes even more evident if we consider that the child, by virtue of his objective weakness and dependence, is entirely at the mercy of the parental authorities and must find some way to cope with this situation. We found that parents in the authoritarian group frequently feel threatened in their social and economic status and that they try to counteract their feelings of marginality by an archaic and frequently unverbalized need for importance. It is noteworthy that what seems to matter is not so much the actual status on the socioeconomic ladder or the objective marginality within a certain class; what seems decisive in this respect is, rather, the subjective way in which these conditions are experienced and allowed to build up to certain vaguely conceived aspirations. Recent data further suggest that the status concern of individuals susceptible to authoritarianism is quite different from a realistic attempt to improve their position by concerted effort and adequate means-goal instrumentality. An example was given earlier by the rather naïve hope of Karl's father of becoming an "inventor." In addition, we frequently find such aspirations taking the form of an unspecific expectation that help will come from a sudden change in the external situation or from an imaginary person who is strong and powerful.

Authoritarian disciplinary rules seem to have one of their major roots in such vaguely anticipatory, yet inefficient, states of social unrest on the part of the parents rather than in the developmental needs of the child. The parents expect the child to learn quickly certain external, rigid, and superficial rules and social taboos. At the same time they are impatient, demanding a quick execution of commands that leaves no time for finer discriminations and in the end creates an atmosphere comparable to acute physical danger. The rules to be enforced are largely nonfunctional caricatures of our social institutions, based on a misunderstanding of their ultimate intent. In many ways one may even speak of a defiance of culture by external conformity. In any event, the rules are bound to be beyond the scope and understanding of the child. To compel the child into an obedience of the rules that he is thus unable to internalize may be considered one of the major interferences with the development of a clear-cut personal identity.

The authoritarian form of discipline is thus "ego-destructive," in that it prevents the development of self-reliance and independence. The child, being stripped of his individuality, is made to feel weak, helpless, worthless, or even depraved. Parents and parental figures, such as teachers or other authorities, acquire the threatening, distant, and forbidding quality that we have observed in the case of Karl. Disciplining, controlling, and keeping one in line are considered to be their major role. It seems to be largely the resultant fear and dependency that discourage the child in the authoritarian home from conscious criticism and that lead to an unquestioning acceptance of punishment and to an identification with the punishing authority. As we have seen, this identification often goes as far as an ostentatious glorification of the parents. As we have learned from psychoanalysis, however, repressions of hostility cannot be achieved without creating emotional ambivalence, at the least. Thus, children who seem most unquestioningly to accept parental authority at the same time tend to harbor an underlying resentment and to feel victimized, without becoming fully aware of this fact. The existing surface conformity that lacks genuine integration expresses itself in a stereotypical approach devoid of genuine affection, so that the description of the parents elicited by interview questions is more often characterized by the use of exaggerated clichés than by expressions of spontaneous feelings. In ethnocentric subjects the range of responses tends to be generally rather narrow and without the variations commonly found in the description of real people. Only the more palpable, crude, and concrete aspects are mentioned.

CASE STUDY OF AN EGALITARIAN FAMILY AND CHILD

For contrast, we shall present the case of a 12-year-old girl whom we shall call Peggy. She scores extremely low on the ethnocentrism scale and generally exhibits the democratic outlook upon life and society in a particularly clear-cut form. The fact that she is of the opposite sex seemed of little bearing on our comparison; our material shows that boys and girls generally seem to be distributed over the same patterns so far as sociopolitical outlook and its relation to personality and family are concerned. Just as Karl manifested almost all the traits we find prominent in the highly ethnocentric group as a whole, Peggy exhibits a similar concentration of features characteristic of the low-scoring group, thus highlighting the syndrome under discussion.

Parents and Home Atmosphere

The socioeconomic backgrounds of the two families show certain similarities. The difference between the present economic situation of Peggy's and of Karl's parents is not very great. And in both cases there is indication of higher social position and greater wealth in the case of the grandparents as compared with the parents. But the two families react very differently to this change. In addition, there is an appreciable difference in the purely social situation of the two families. There is a radical difference between the personalities of Peggy's mother and Karl's mother and certain differences in their social background, including a much greater stability in the family of Peggy's mother.

While Peggy's mother is American born and of American-born parentage, the father was born in Italy, the son of a small-town doctor. At the time of our interview he had just sold a small restaurant that he had come to consider a bad investment. His professional history includes being a salesman, a clerk, and a waiter. He is a college graduate, as is his wife, who is a social worker. Peggy's maternal grandfather was first a small-town lawyer and "a dictator and patriarch to the population. He entered the army. . . and liked the opportunity it gave him for expressing authority." Peggy's mother apparently received a great deal of warmth from her own mother, but she rebelled against her father.

Although the father's occupational history, especially as compared with that of his parents and that of the parents of his wife, could have led to a feeling of socioeconomic marginality, this family actually does not seem to be dissatisfied with its present status; much of the time of its members is devoted to pursuits such as supporting the causes of the community, participating in discussion groups, and so forth. Both parents are interested in reading, music, and art, and the mother has even written some poetry. Instead of resenting their marginality, the family makes constructive use of the greater freedom given them by their position. They have more time to follow the pursuits in which they are really interested, and they enjoy a great deal of respect among their friends. Although Peggy's parents are divorced, they are on good terms and see each other frequently.

Both parents feel strongly about equality between racial groups, and the father described how shocking the discovery of racial prejudice was to him when he came to this country "after reading Lincoln and Jefferson and men like that." Both parents declare in their interviews that greater tolerance and more education are the direction in which they would like to see America changed. At the same time, they are explicitly opposed to any radical movement.

Affection rather than authority or the execution of obligations dominates the general attitude of Peggy's parents toward the child. The perceptiveness and psychological insightfulness of Peggy's mother are reflected in her answer to the question concerning the positive ideal she holds for her daughter:

> I do hope that she will do something that will make her happy and at the same time be constructive. I hope the girl will have experience early enough that she can integrate it and lead an outgoing, constructive life; that she won't have to spend so long working out her aggression that she finds herself no longer young—not that I wish to spare my daughter the suffering and experience necessary for development, but I hope she may get it early and fast. I feel that I can help by giving a lot of trust and confidence in the girl. I do feel that at times in the past I may have expected too high a performance for the sake of my own gratification, and that may have troubled Peggy. The child has always been given more responsibility than the average, but as a rule it hasn't seemed to be a strain.

This quotation reflects the mother's concern with the inner life of her daughter, with her internal satisfactions, and it reveals how far removed she is from espousing a conventional ideal for her daughter. This absence of stereotyped conventionality becomes even more evident in the mother's response to the question as to what she considers the negative ideal for her daughter. She states that she would hate to see her daughter take a job she didn't like for the sake of money or caring too much for the acquisition of material things so that her ideals would be sacrificed.

Along similar lines are the statements of Peggy's father, in his separate interview. He wants his daughter "to grow up to have an all-around personality in such a way that she can get the best out of herself, be happy with herself and with other people. Whatever work she wants to choose— that is her business. If we can bring her up with self-assurance and not to give up at the first obstacles, we will be doing something."

Both parents stress again and again in varying formulations how much they enjoy the child. The mother considers as the strongest traits of her daughter "her sensitivity and receptivity to artistic things and to people. . . . She has a philosophical interest in people and seems to have a good idea of the interrelationship of people and nations." The father thinks Peggy's strong points are "strength of character and being intelligent and liberal." At the same time, he is aware of some weaknesses in his daughter, such as her insecurity, her exhibitionism, and her interest in boys; the latter he considers as typical of adolescent girls, however.

The Handling of Authority in the Egalitarian Home

The idea has been promoted in many homes and in some educational systems and political circles that, in order to avoid authoritarianism, all authority must be forsworn. Against this excessive view it must be held that total permissiveness would verge upon anarchy. Respect for the authority of outstanding individuals and institutions is an essential aspect of a healthy home and society. It does not as such lead to total surrender to, or to an absolutistic glorification of, the given authorities. This is especially true if their leadership is limited to specialized fields or to special functions. Rather than authoritarianism or anarchy, there must be "guidance," especially when this is combined with acceptance, thus strengthening the moral functions of the child and helping him to overcome the impulses toward selfishness and aggression. By guidance, therefore, we mean the encouragement of the child to work out his instinctual problems rather than repress them, thus avoiding their later breakthrough; this encouragement, in turn, must be rooted in a frank understanding of the child's particular needs and developmental steps. The child is treated as an individual and is encouraged to develop self-reliance and independence. His weakness is not exploited. He is allowed to express his likes and dislikes without the threat of losing love and the basis of his existence.

The statistical data we gathered on adults[14] as well as on children[15] suggest that the way of handling discipline is indeed a crucial factor in the laying of the foundation for an authoritarian or a democratic outlook in children. As we have just said, the way in which parents handle discipline reveals the constructive use or misuse of parental authority and the degree to which a genuine socialization of the child and his adoption of cultural values are made possible.

According to Peggy's mother, everything was explained to the child and very little active exercise of discipline was necessary. The mother still feels quite guilty that she spanked the child on a few occasions and thinks now that it was because she herself was angry. The father's independent statement, very similar to that of the mother, is as follows:

> I don't know that we ever tried to discipline her very much. I was guilty of spoiling her when she was a baby sometimes, but I don't remember ever trying to discipline her. Oh, I have given her a few times a spat on the rear when I was mad. I shouldn't do that, I know. I think the girl is a little obstinate, hot-headed, and not disciplined as much as she should be now, but maybe that's because she is an adolescent.

In reading the interview of the mother it becomes quite evident that she has, and always has had, a warm and unconditional acceptance of her child. In fact, she is quite outstanding in this respect as far as our total group is concerned.

However, she confesses that in her eagerness to do the right things she has used many techniques that she now would reject. She feels that she had been "too much influenced by Watson." Thus she thinks it was wrong to have started toilet training as early as she did. Further inquiry reveals, however, that all she did was to hold the child on a pot after meals when the child was six months old; but no pressure was used, and the child was allowed to regulate her own training, which was complete at two years of age. Furthermore, nursing was discontinued after three months, since the mother's milk failed. When the child was put on the bottle, she began to suck her fingers and continued to do this at bedtime until she was six or seven years old. The child never had tantrums, but she did express her objections and wishes emphatically. This is just the pattern of aggression that has been described as typical of individuals scoring low on ethnocentrism. There was never any evidence of nightmares, and the child called her mother during the night when she needed her. The mother always answered these calls because she remembered so keenly her own childhood fears at night. These details reveal that Peggy's mother, who tends toward intrapunitiveness, has not followed Watson as closely as she thinks she has. Apparently she also remembered well how comforting it was to have her own mother when she called for her.

Concerning the family atmosphere in the childhood home of Peggy's mother, she reports that her own mother had a similar attitude toward her child as the latter has toward Peggy. There seems never to have been any gross punishment. However, the father of Peggy's mother is described by her as a stern and authoritarian person. She thinks that her struggle for independence from her father played an important part in her development. She explains the fact that she, unlike her brothers, was able to rebel against her father by virtue of her being away from her father during the first years of her life. We would add that, as the only girl in the family, Peggy's mother had a better opportunity to identify with her mother than with her father. On the whole, her identification with her mother, whom she describes as "loving and gay when my father was gone," was a positive one. However, in one respect her mother furnished her with a negative example. She considers her mother "completely cowed by my father, whom she never opposed."

Thus the negative identification of Peggy's mother with her own mother seems to have led to an attempt to have a more independent life, which would not imply submission to an authoritarian husband. She realized these aims by attending college, pursuing a profession, which consisted in work with subnormal children, and marrying an utterly unauthoritarian man. As we have said, the marriage did not work out, however, and she blames this at least partially upon the difficulties she had had with her own father. Peggy's mother needed a long time and the help of a psychoanalyst to work out her problems of feminine identification. In spite of the fact that Peggy's parents are divorced, they and the child do many things together as a family. The parents speak with a great deal of respect about each other, and the father credits the mother with the satisfactory development of their daughter.

Peggy's Social Beliefs

Concerning minority groups, Peggy emphasizes in her interview that no one race is better than another:

> The Chinese can do really beautiful art work, the Germans have really intelligent and well-known scientists, and things like that. Every race has a certain amount of skill. They are pretty well equal. I go to parties at a Negro girl's house. I wouldn't mind going with a Negro boy to a party, but it would probably be better to go with a white one because the other kids would tease me, and the Negro boy and I would both feel funny.

This opinion is in sharp contrast to what the majority of the children feel along these lines. In the interviews, a staggering 96% of the children scoring high on the ethnic scale, 83% of the middle scorers, and even as many as 22% of the low scorers express ethnocentric attitudes toward Negroes by ascribing negative traits to them and by favoring segregation[16]; about 60% of the high scorers and middle scorers and 18% of the low scorers express similar attitudes toward the Chinese. Peggy, as we have seen, goes all out for an egalitarian view of the various ethnic groups.

While Karl thought that most of the foreign countries are against us, Peggy thinks that America is "really very friendly with many countries," except for Russia, which "doesn't understand our ways and she doesn't understand us." While Karl was at least partially sympathetic toward Hitler, Peggy thinks that "he was crazy with power." Asked what a regular American is, Peggy answers that everyone who has citizenship papers "is an American in his own way. There is some foreign blood in every one of the Americans. The first people were foreigners."

To an interview question, "How would you like to change America?" Peggy responds with the following statement:

> Try to have people be more understanding about the Negro problem. . . . Another thing is to have better schools and teachers; nice schools that kids would really like. Give them a chance to change the subject often so it wouldn't be boring. Also a better department for juvenile delinquents. Not treat them as if they did it on purpose; and a better home for these kids. They really don't want to be bad, but they just don't know what else to do.

Note the contrast with Karl's emphasis on the beautification of streets and on a plentiful supply of food in response to the same question.

Peggy's concern for the welfare of the population is also expressed in her ideal of the President of the United States, whom she considers to be a man who "really thinks of others, not of himself; thinks of them as friends; is always kind and works hard for the people."

Peggy's Attitude Toward School, Parents, and Sex Roles

In discussing her teachers, Peggy does not show much evidence of an exaggerated submission to authority. She does not demand strictness and supervision from the ideal teacher. Rather, she thinks that the ideal teacher is one who can "understand you, be a friend to you, someone you can confide in, someone you like." The unprejudiced children tend to emphasize positive things in the ideal teacher, whereas the prejudiced children more often offer negative formulations, such as not playing favorites. The teachers whom Peggy doesn't like she describes as "dumb, and scream at the kids and tell them to shut up," and she adds very perceptively, "The kids always answer this kind of teacher back."

In discussing the girls she likes, Peggy stresses companionship and mutual liking. She dislikes girls who are "silly, stupid, giggle all the time and never get their work done but say they do."

The pattern of Peggy's aggression is one that is mild and not repressed, in contrast to that of the prejudiced children, in whom we find suppression of aggression interspersed with violent breakthroughs. Thus, Peggy confesses that she really tries to like everyone, but she just can't do it. "Nobody can." She seems to have some mild guilt about her occasional hostile feelings that alternates with a readiness to accept them as unavoidable.

These guilt feelings may also be connected with the feeling of acting against her mother's apparent wish to imbue the child with a far-reaching tolerance toward everybody. Peggy reports that the only occasion on which she and her mother disagree is "when I criticize someone who looks stupid and funny. My mommy and daddy both think that I shouldn't do this, since people don't know any better, but I think they really do." Her strong identification with the underdog is revealed by the type of occasions on which she reports that she tends to get angry:

"When people pick on someone, even dogs or animals, or when they tease Negroes and call them dirty names."

Peggy thinks of a perfect father as one who "is a good friend to you, understanding and nice. Just a person." We recall here that prejudiced children tend to think of the ideal father mainly in terms of punishment, as either being too little strict or too much so, whereas unprejudiced children tend to stress companionship, as Peggy does. She describes her real father pretty much in the same words as she does the perfect father, and the same holds for her description of her mother. She reports (and this is substantiated in the direct interviews with her parents) that she has never been punished or scolded: "My mother just talks to me. Children should never really be punished, but have things explained to them."

Peggy's flexibility is also carried into her conception of the sex roles. Like the unprejudiced children in general, she does not tend toward a dichotomous conception of sex roles. To the question, "How should girls behave around boys?" she answers, "Not silly but act like herself. Having a boyfriend is just like having a good friend." She also thinks that boys "should not try to show off, should not try to show the girls how strong they are so the girls will be impressed." Furthermore, unlike most ethnocentric children, she does not make any marked differentiation between the best profession for a man and the best profession for a woman. Her description of the best profession for a man shows absence of hierarchical thinking in terms of social status: "Whatever he wants to do, whether it is a shoe clerk or a chemist or anything at all. Nobody else should decide for him." Concerning the worst profession for a man, she replies, "To have his life planned, to be what he doesn't want," and to the question about the best or worst profession for a woman she answers, "Same as for a man." Incidentally, Peggy's own professional ambitions are to be "an artist, a poet, a writer, and a dancer."

In spite of Peggy's egalitarian orientation in relation to authority and sex roles, she is far from being uninterested in boys. When asked about her daydreams, she reports that they are concerned with the wish to have a boyfriend and that her real dreams are also mainly concerned with boys. She usually dreams about one special boy and that he takes her to the movies. In fact, in a fond and understanding way, her father calls her "a little boy crazy," and he adds that Peggy occasionally shows exhibitionistic impulses. We have evidence for that in Peggy's childhood memories also. Asked for her earliest memories, she reports one, according to which—at the age of about three—she ran to the top of a nearby hill before her mother had finished dressing her, with only her pants and her shoes on. "The people were shocked by that kind of thing." This may be a projection, since she probably was too small at the time to shock people by her scanty clothes. She also reports that when she was a year and a half or two years old, she "ran out naked to say good-bye to Daddy." These slightly erotically tinted early memories are in decided contrast to Karl's early memories, which are preoccupied with death and violence and carry a distinctly sadistic flavor.

Peggy's Thematic Apperception Test Stories

Peggy's creativeness and imagination are reflected in her TAT stories. While Karl is obsessed with primitive, archaic themes, as evidenced by his rumination about the topics of food and destruction as if flooded by his unconscious, Peggy seems to be at ease with her unconscious trends, which find expression in stories possessing an artistic flavor. In her case the unconscious problems seem to contribute to imagination in a positive manner. Her stories flow freely and at the same time are cognitively disciplined. While Karl's stories were stereotyped and at the same time chaotic, Peggy's stories show a colorfulness of thought that can come only from ease of communication between the different layers of her personality. Although

she is by no means aware of all her problems, she possesses an unre-
pressed approach to life. Her basic self-acceptance has a disinhibiting effect on her productions, without leading to disintegration.

There are several distinct themes in Peggy's stories. The major motif is
the same we encountered in the interviews; that is, a protective feeling toward those who are different or who appear weak. While Karl is contemptuous of the weak and the "sissy," Peggy reveals considerable psychological insight in trying to demonstrate that he who is considered a sissy is
often the real hero. She describes, in one of her stories, a 9-year-old boy

> whom all the kids in school used to tease and say he was a sissy. Tommy cried
> when he went home. Next day the boys dared him to fight the biggest bully of
> the class. The bully hit Tommy in the face, and it made him mad. Tommy had
> to fight, and he licked the bully. After that he was liked. There was one boy
> that was a leader that hadn't liked him before that invited him to have a soda.
> And after that all the boys liked Tommy.

The picture to which Peggy refers here, and which was specially selected
for our study, is that of a cruel-looking white boy hitting a Mexican boy.
While Karl has nothing but derogatory statements to make about this boy,
some children—mainly the egalitarian ones—express some pity for him. But
it is only Peggy for whom he becomes a hero.

Here are some passages from Peggy's story in response to the picture of
a Negro boy who is being maltreated:

> He [the Negro boy] wondered why people could be so ignorant and not
> know that everybody is created equal, and that people could believe what people
> say that isn't true. Someone threw something at him and blinded him. Two
> kids from the army started beating up on him. Yet in the army you are sup-
> posed to learn to stand for what is right. . . . He went back to where he came
> from and thought that someday he would do something about all this.

Another story deals with two young Japanese men, approximately college
age:

> Well, there was a Sunday school in San Francisco and, uh, this boy is named
> Bill. Well, he came here many years ago when he was a little boy. He has
> grown up here and is proud of it and liked everyone and everyone liked him.
> Several years later he planned to go to college and get an education as a doc-
> tor. When he enrolled for college, people became very prejudiced. They thought
> he shouldn't go to the same school as white people. Bill felt bad because he
> liked everyone. So he dropped out of school. A few years later a cousin came
> from Japan to visit him. The cousin had just started his college education in
> Japan. He asked Bill why he wasn't going to college. Bill told him why. The
> cousin wasn't so sensitive as Bill and said the way to lick it was to show peo-
> ple you don't care. And so both of them enrolled for a four years' term, and
> Bill made friends with several of the professors and some boys and girls, and
> so did his cousin.

No one knew Bill was a very good pianist. One night at a dance the pianist walked out on them, and Bill offered to play. Everyone was surprised and liked him after that. Finally Bill finished medical school and became an M.D.

This story is quite typical of the way Peggy manages to give a constructive turn to almost every situation. In her reactions to her fellowmen she is generally and genuinely imbued with the spirit of Christian ethics. Thus, in still another story she describes a man who was entirely devoted to his success and almost "went to Hell' but was given an opportunity to change his ways, and so being finally saved:

Well, there was this man named Mr. Benson. He was hard working and very successful, but was not liked by many because he was an old crab. One day his son got mad at him because he was so mean, and the son told him so. When the man went home, he felt bad and lay down. He fell asleep and dreamed he went down to Hell—to the middle of the world. They go either there or to Heaven. The spirit in charge looked in the book and said he was not registered in either place. Mr. Benson told the spirit what he had done— thinking only of his business. The spirit said, "I think if you go back and change your ways, you can then go to the other place." He woke up on the floor. Next morning he went to his office and did something he never did before. He said a plesant "Good morning" to everyone in the office. Pretty soon his son came in, expecting the father to be mad when he told him about his plan to marry one of the secretaries. His father surprised him and said, "I hope you will be happy and have many children." He gave his son a present, and the father and son were friends after that, and it all turned out well. When Mr. Benson died, he went to Heaven. Though I don't believe there is any Heaven—we just stay in the earth and turn into little pieces."

Aside from Peggy's consideration for the weak, there is another outstanding theme in her stories—love. Significantly, Peggy often uses a fairy-tale type of approach in these stories, not losing her grip on the structure of the story, however. Oedipal conflicts are revealed in these stories, although she is obviously not aware of them. In one of her stories she tells about a "giant" who wants to keep a beautiful girl for himself while the girl wishes for a "prince." At the same time the two male figures are mixed in her fantasy:

A giant found her and took her to his cave and raised her. She grew up to be beautiful. Finally a prince came along and said he would rescue her from the giant. She told the prince that the only way to do that was to go down the river and rescue the giant's heart, which he lost there long ago. . . . The prince found the heart and took it to the cave and put it in the giant's supper. When the giant ate his supper, the heart went into his body and he became kind. He let the girl go and the prince married her. And they lived happily ever after.

While most of Karl's stories end in disaster, murder, or death, all of Peggy's stories end well. Every one of them constitutes an attempt to demonstrate positive ways of overcoming external or internal obstacles, including

prejudice, selfishness, and possessiveness. It is difficult to say whether Peggy's aggression is merely repressed or whether it is not very strong to begin
with. We are inclined to believe the latter. In any event it must be stressed
that there is very little discrepancy between the overt level of Peggy's verbalized self-perception and her personality as revealed in the projective
stories.

RELATIONS TO PERCEPTION AND THINKING

Perceptual patterns, especially the mechanism of projection, were brought
into the foregoing picture by the Thematic Apperception Test. But the relationship between social attitudes, personality, and the general cognitive
mastery of reality seems to go far beyond that. Experiments in perception,
memory, and cognition were thus added in order to investigate more systematically the matter of how far basic personality trends found in the emotional and social sphere may be reflected in this area. Their purpose was
to investigate the pervasiveness of ways of functioning within the authoritarian personality. The shift from the social and emotional to the cognitive
area has the added advantage of removing us from the controversial social
issues under consideration. As long as we remain under the potential spell
of certain preconceived notions, the evaluation of what is reality-adequate
or reality-inadequate may be difficult. The authoritarian may accuse the
egalitarian of distorting reality, and vice versa. Some of the experiments are
as yet in a preliminary stage, while others have already led to statistically
significant results.

In a memory experiment,[17] the children were read a story that described
the behavior of pupils in a school toward newcomers to their class. In the
fighting that developed, some of the older pupils were described as being
friendly and protective of the newcomers, while others were pictured as
aggressive. The children were then asked to reproduce the story in writing.

Ethnocentric children tended generally to recall more of the aggressive
characters, and the democratic-minded, tolerant children more of the friendly
characters. In addition, 43% of the former, as contrasted with only 8% of
the latter, recalled the fighting theme exclusively, without mentioning any
of the other themes of the story.

It is further to be noted that in the tolerant children the ratio of friendly
to aggressive individuals was closer to the ratio occurring in the story as first
presented. That is to say, the tolerant children adhered, in this respect at
least, more closely to "reality" than did the ethnocentric. A general tendency on the part of the ethnically prejudiced children to stray away from
the content of the story is combined with a tendency to reproduce faith-
fully certain single phrases and single details of the original story. Thus, the
stimulus is in part rigidly adhered to, while its remaining and perhaps major aspects are altogether neglected in favor of subjective elaboration. This

odd combination of accuracy and distortion also characterizes Karl's general cognitive approach as presented earlier in this paper.

Another experiment consisted in presenting the picture of a familiar object, such as that of a dog, and then leading through a number of vague or transitional stages to the picture of, say, a cat. The subjects were asked to identify the object in each picture. If tentative results with small groups are borne out, the stimuli less familiar and lacking in firmness and definiteness would seem to be more disturbing to the ethnocentric than to the unprejudiced children. Ethnocentric children tend to persist in using the name of the familiar object shown in the first picture, ignoring the changes in the successive pictures. Or they seem to fall more often into a spell of guesses, trying to inject known and structured objects into the vague stimulus, again relatively little concerned with reality. It is probably the underlying confusion and anxiety that compel these children to make a desperate effort to avoid uncertainties as much as possible, resulting in "intolerance of ambiguity."[18] The nonethnocentric children, on the other hand, being generally more secure, are apparently better able to afford facing ambiguities openly, even though this often may mean facing, at least temporarily, increased conflicts.

In another preliminary experiment a picture was presented showing four vertically striped zebras standing together and facing a lone, horizontally striped zebra left in a corner by itself. An inquiry as to the cause of the isolation of the horizontally striped zebra brought out interesting material about the attitude of some ethnocentric children to what is "different." Among other things, it appears that any difference setting off a minority from a majority of objects—even though the given difference may not in itself be emotionally tainted—tends to be conceived of by them as automatically establishing a barrier against social contact.

Rokeach[19] has investigated rigidity as related to intolerance of ambiguity. He used a problem in thinking developed by Luchins,[20] which involves the manipulation of three water jars. A mental set was first established by presenting the subjects with a series of problems solvable only by a relatively involved method. There followed problems that could be solved either by maintaining the established set or by using more direct and simple techniques. The ethnocentric children tended to persist in using the first, more complex method rather than shift to the more direct approach.

In recent years, experiments of the types described have multiplied in number and kind and generally have borne out the earlier findings.

We have already noted that Karl's cognitive makeup can be fitted into some of the categories found typical of ethnocentric children in these experiments. Karl's material further reveals that he tends to alternate in his perceptual and cognitive approach between sticking to the familiar and being overly concretistic, on the one hand, and adopting a chaotic, haphazard approach, on the other. Peggy, by contrast, shows considerable flexibility in her perceptual and cognitive approach, although it must be added that she did exhibit rigidity on the water-jar test just described. Here she used an established set without changing to the more functional, faster method. This may well be due to her general weakness in handling arithmetic problems. We have found that even flexible children may be rigid on tasks in which they show little ego involvement. Such tasks remain peripheral for them, and they do not bring out the best of their ability, so that there is regression to a more mechanized approach. There can be no doubt that everyone has areas of rigidity. In some cases we just find rigidity more pervasive than in others.

SUMMARY AND CONCLUSION

Out of a sample of children and their families studied by a variety of methods, two cases were selected that represent opposite extremes as to ethnocentric, as contrasted with democratic, outlook, other social beliefs, cognitive organization, personality, and family structure and atmosphere.

In describing the minority groups and the social scene in general, our paradigm of an ethnocentric, authoritarian child, Karl, exhibits rigid dichotomizing, aggressiveness, fear of imaginary dangers or threats of deprivation, and exaggerated adherence to conventional values, such as cleanliness and order. The same themes also occur in his stated attitudes toward parents and friends as well as in the projective material, especially his Thematic Apperception Test stories.

Our example of a democratic-minded, egalitarian child, Peggy, is much less given to dichotomizing and other forms of rigidity and intolerance of ambiguity than is Karl. This is evidenced, among other things, in her attitude toward minority groups and in her view of sex roles. In both cases differences are deemphasized, quite in contrast with Karl. While at the surface level Karl emphasizes rugged masculinity and is very much concerned with what is masculine and what is feminine, he is covertly engrossed in passivity and dependency; Peggy, with her lesser insistence on the dichotomy of sex roles, is basically much more feminine than Karl is masculine. A similar discontinuity between the manifest and the latent level had been found in Karl's attitude toward his parents; Peggy, on the other hand, reveals a genuine, personalized love for her parents that is not endangered and undermined by occasional eruptions of deep-seated aggression. Karl and his parents had been found to manifest an odd combination of unrest and predilection for chaos and total change with an uncritical, distorted glorification of existing institutions and social conditions; Peggy and her parents, on the other hand, show a certain healthy medium distance to these institutions in the sense of basically identifying with their aim, yet being concerned with seeing them properly executed, as in the case of ethnic equality. They would like to see some improvement and progress, but total upheavals and radical changes of the social scene do not have the same appeal for them that they do for Karl's parents. All these differences are related to the fact that the definition of an American is much more narrowly conceived by Karl and his parents than it is by Peggy and hers and that the former exhibits some preoccupation with what they consider American values, which at the same time presents a shrinkage and oversimplification of these values.

Toward parents, teachers, and authorities in general, Karl at the surface demands total submission, and he approves of whatever they do; but underlying resentment and hatred against them are only too apparent in the projective material. This discrepancy is but one of the many breaks and discontinuities found in Karl and in ethnocentric children in general. Another discrepancy is evident in Karl's explicit stressing of conventional values, which is combined with an implicit leaning toward destructive and chaotic behavior. In fact, there seems to be vacillation between a total adoption and a total negation of the prevalent values of our society.

Still another conflicting set can be discerned between Karl's strained effort to appear as a masculine boy interested in girls and his underlying identification with the opposite sex. Instead of being oriented toward girls as objects of cathexis, he envies them because he thinks of them as less in danger of being attacked and as being fed and given other material benefits. As becomes apparent, especially in the Thematic Apperception Test, to be a boy or a man means to him to be in danger. If a man is passive, he may not get the necessary supplies and is helplessly exposed; if he is aggressive, he is punished. Doom is thus inevitable for him. All through the material produced by our ethnocentric children there is evidence of panic lest food or money run short. In persons possessed by such fears, human relations are liable to become unusually manipulative and exploitive. Other persons, authorities, and even the magic forces of nature will, of necessity, be seen mainly as deliverers of goods. Aggression against those considered strong and powerful must then be repressed; at least in part, this aggression will be diverted toward those who can neither deprive nor retaliate.

While Karl thus shows many discrepancies and discontinuities in his personality makeup, Peggy is obviously more integrated. Karl fails to face some of the important emotional tendencies within himself, such as ambivalence toward the parents, passivity, and fear. His conscious image of himself contradicts the tendencies that are revealed in the projective material and that he projects onto others, such as minority groups. Peggy, on the other hand, accepts hers more fully, although this does not mean that she is not critical of herself. This basic acceptance of herself makes it possible for her to face her own weaknesses; it also leads to a greater acceptance and tolerance of other persons and peoples, although again she is very free in expressing her dislikes. But, on the whole, the world is for her a benevolent one, interesting and challenging, whereas for Karl it is a dangerous and hostile place, to be viewed with distrust, suspicion, and cynicism.

In spite of the ready flow of fantastic ideas about a wide range of topics, Karl's story productions show little evidence of creative imagination. His repetitive rumination in stereotypes, general diffuseness, and distortion of reality are obviously in the service of warding off anxiety.

This rigidity and lack of imagination is in line with results obtained on ethnocentric children in the experiments on perception and other cognitive functions. Ambiguous and unfamiliar stimuli often seem to be disturbing to these children. They tend to respond either with a spell of haphazard guessing, imposing something definite and definitive upon the indefinite, or with a clinging to a response once established. Both these reactions seem to mirror frantic efforts to avoid uncertainty; that is, an "intolerance of ambiguity," even though the price is distortion of reality. In addition, the recall of given stories by ethnocentric children shows distortion in the direction of greater emphasis on aggressive themes.

In analyzing and interpreting our material, extended use has been made of psychoanalytic hypotheses. Depth psychology has challenged the dominance of the phenotype and has sharpened our eyes to the underlying dynamic patterns. Because of this shift, we can discern in Karl the passivity behind his aggressive violence, the feminine identification and latent homosexuality behind the protestation of his heterosexual interests, the chaos behind his rigid conformity. But since the façade is also an essential part of the psychological makeup, we must think of personality in terms of "alternative manifestations."[21] These are quite self-contradictory in Karl, as they are in most prejudiced children. It is the inherent conflict and anxiety concerning the social, sexual, and personal role of the individual that must be seen at the root of the ensuing desperate avoidance of all ambiguity, with its dire consequences for the fate of man.

It should be kept in mind that while our chosen paradigms exhibit nearly all the traits which were found statistically prevalent in the respective groups as a whole, such marked personality consistency is not the rule. Furthermore, the overall immaturity Karl, our paradigm of an ethnocentric child, has been found to exhibit is to a certain extent shared with younger children, both authoritarian and egalitarian; some of the trends connected with ethnic prejudice or authoritarianism must be considered natural states of development, to be overcome if maturity is to be reached. Some of the test items correlated with ethnocentrism are at the same time subscribed to more often by the younger children than by the older ones. The difference is that our ethnocentric children continue to exhibit many trends that in egalitarian children are limited to the younger age levels and are later outgrown. To a notable extent this is independent of the purely intellectual aspects of development. Other factors, such as especially social background, are modifiers of the distinction between ethnocentric and egalitarian children. Important subtypes may thus be identified in both groups. For example, in ethnocentric children coming from distinctly upper-class backgrounds there is more genuine conformity to society, combined perhaps with a certain rigidity in the total outlook, but little of the psychopathic, destructive, and manipulative coloring that characterizes Karl and many other prejudiced children rooted in the lower social strata.

Karl's parents reveal the feelings of "social marginality" that are so common in the ethnocentric family. It is obviously in defense against the possibility of being grouped with the underprivileged that they rigidly identify with the conventional values of the class to which they try to hold on. The strict home discipline they are trying to enforce is in part in the service of these narrow social goals; beyond this, it is perhaps a revengeful repetition of the situation to which they themselves were exposed in the unstable socioeconomic history of the family. We have also seen how much more constructively an objectively similar socioeconomic family history is handled by the parents of Peggy.

Both the families we have discussed in this paper are American families. At the same time, they are so different that in many ways they appear as opposite ends of a psychological continuum, a continuum that ranges from rigidity and authoritarianism to affectionate guidance and acceptance.

In the context of American culture, Karl and his family are deviants. Fat, fearful Karl is certainly the opposite of the ideal American boy. Most of his and his family's attitudes are counterpoints to prevailing or consciously espoused American attitudes. Externalization and hostile exclusion are features they adopt from the wide variety of possibilities, offered within the culture as a whole. Other features contrasting with the major American pattern are their emphasis on hierarchical rather than egalitarian relations, their anxiety about the availability of material goods, and their belief in mystical forces and apprehension about catastrophes as against confidence in one's own efforts and in the collaboration of the environment.

To understand all this, we remember that Karl and his family are caught in an unsuccessful struggle for social status, a status they cannot achieve through their own efforts. Thus, they adhere rigidly to some absolute status values that oversimplify the social and cultural realities of our civilization. This renders them helpless and perverts their view of the social scene, making them susceptible to totalitarian propaganda.

It must be specially emphasized that the compulsive type of conformity with its all-or-none character, which we have observed in the family of Karl, differs in several ways from genuine and constructive conformity. It is excessive, compensating as it does for feelings of marginality and the attendant fear of becoming an outcast, and serving the function of covering up the resentment toward the social system as a whole, unconscious as this resentment may be. The lack of a genuine incorporation of the values of society in the authoritarian milieu accounts for the rigidity of the conformity. At the same time it accounts for a certain unreliability, the readiness to shift allegiance altogether to other authorities and other standards. The adherence to the letter rather than to the spirit of the social institutions, which further characterizes the compulsive conformist, issues from his distortion and simplification of the system of norms and commands in the direction of what one may call unidimensional interpretation.

Evidently, Peggy and her family are infinitely closer to the real values of the American civilization in the ways in which parental authority and child-parent relationships are handled, and the democratic outlook is being realized in word and action. They are in search of intrinsic and flexible and at the same time basically more consistent principles. Understanding, emphasis on internalization, thoughtfulness, empathy, compassion, insight, justice, individualism, reason, and scholarship are the values they admire. The core of the human institutions inherent in our culture that must be called upon to explain Peggy and her parents is the democratic tradition, with its protective attitude toward the weak.

NOTES

1. Ogburn, 1953.
2. Zimmerman, 1948.
3. Burgess, 1948.
4. Mead, 1949.
5. Winch and McGinnis, 1953.
6. Frenkel-Brunswik, 1954.
7. Frenkel-Brunswik, 1949a; Frenkel-Brunswik and Havel, 1953.
8. Murray et al., 1938.
9. Adorno et al., 1950.
10. Frenkel-Brunswik, 1951.
11. Adorno et al., 1950; Frenkel-Brunswik, 1949a.
12. Fenichel, 1945.
13. Wolfenstein and Leites, 1950.
14. Adorno et al., 1950.
15. Frenkel-Brunswik and Havel, 1953; other reports in preparation.
16. Ibid.
17. For details see Frenkel-Brunswik, 1949b.
18. Ibid.
19. Rokeach, 1943.
20. Luchins, 1942.
21. Frenkel-Brunswik, 1949b.

REFERENCES

1. Adorno, T. W., Frenkel-Brunswik, E., Levinson, D. J., and Sanford, R. N. The authoritarian personality. New York: Harper & Bros., 1950.
2. Burgess, E. W. The family in a changing society. American Journal of Sociology, 1948, 13(6), 417-23.

3. Fenichel, O. *Psychoanalytic theory of neurosis.* New York: W. W. Norton & Co., 1945.

4. Frenkel-Brunswik, E. A study of prejudice in children. *Human Relations,* 1949a, I(3), 295-306.

5. Frenkel-Brunswik, E. Intolerance of ambiguity as an emotional and perceptual personality variable. *Journal of Personality,* 1949b, *18*(1), 108–43.

6. Frenkel-Brunswik, E. Patterns of social and cognitive outlook in children and parents. *American Journal of Orthopsychiatry,* 1951, *21*(3), 543–58.

7. Frenkel-Brunswik, E. Social research and the problem of values: A reply. *Journal of Abnormal and Social Psychology,* 1954, *49*(3), 466–71.

8. Frenkel-Brunswik, E., and Havel, J. Prejudice in the interviews of children: Attitudes toward minority groups. *Journal of Genetic Psychology,* 1953, *82*(1), 91–136.

9. Luchins, A. S. Mechanization in problem solving: The effect of "einstellung." *Psychological Monographs,* 1942, *54*(6).

10. Mead, Margaret. *Male and female.* New York: William Morrow Co., 1949.

11. Murray, H.E., and Workers at the Harvard Psychological Clinic. *Explorations in personality.* London: Oxford University Press, 1938.

12. Ogburn, W. F. The changing functions of the family. In R. F. Winch and R. McGinnis (Eds.), *Marriage and the family.* New York: Henry Holt & Co., 1953.

13. Rokeach, M. Generalized mental rigidity as a factor in ethnocentrism. *Journal of Abnormal and Social Psychology,* 1943, *48*(2), 259–78.

14. Winch, R. F., and McGinnis, R. (Eds.). *Marriage and the family.* New York: Henry Holt & Co., 1953.

15. Wolfenstein, Martha, and Leites, Nathan. *Movies: A psychological study.* Glencoe, Ill.: Free Press, 1950.

16. Zimmerman, C. C. *Family and civilization.* New York: Harper & Bros., 1948.

15

Intrafamilial Environment of the Schizophrenic Patient: The Transmission of Irrationality[1]

THEODORE LIDZ, ALICE CORNELISON, DOROTHY TERRY CARLSON, AND STEPHEN FLECK

One of the distinctive features of schizophrenia lies in the disturbed symbolic functioning—in the paralogic quality of the patient's thinking and communicating that alters his internal representation of reality. We are following the hypothesis that the schizophrenic patient escapes from an untenable world in which he is powerless to cope with insoluble conflicts by the device of imaginatively distorting his symbolization of reality. Such internalized maneuvers do not require action, or coming to terms with other persons, or altering their attitudes. The patient can regain the mastery that he once possessed in childhood, before his reality was firmly structured, and it could still give way before the power of his wishes. It can be an alluring way because it is self-contained. It is a bitter way because it is isolating.

The present chapter will focus on this critical characteristic of schizophrenia, and, therefore, must neglect many other aspects of the developmental forces active during the childhood and adolescence of schizophrenic patients, even though these other aspects can be separated from the forces distorting mentation only artifically.

The distortions of mentation, the core problem of schizophrenia, have been relatively neglected of late because of interest in "borderline cases"

Reprinted by permission from *Archives of neurology and psychiatry,* 1958, 79(3), 305–16. Copyright 1958 by the American Medical Association. This article also appears in Theodore Lidz, Stephen Fleck, Alice Cornelison, et al., *Schizophrenia and the family.* New York: International Universities Press, 1965.

Theodore Lidz is Sterling Professor of Psychiatry, Emeritus; Alice R. Cornelison was a research assistant; Dorothy Terry Carlson was Assistant Professor of Psychiatry; and Stephen Fleck is Professor of Psychiatry, Emeritus—Yale University School of Medicine.

and in "pseudoneurotic schizophrenia" and in the similarities of the underlying psychopathology of certain psychosomatic conditions to that of schizophrenia. Patients suffering from these conditions are not clearly schizophrenic, because they remain sufficiently well integrated to permit a consensus between their thinking and that of others, and effective social communication remains possible. Such patients are potentially psychotic, and when their communication breaks down and becomes instrumentally ineffective, they are psychotic. Some never need this solution, but others may be unable to utilize it. It is possible for many persons to break under extreme conditions and achieve flight into irrationality, sacrificing reality to the demands of id impulses or to preserve some semblance of ego structure of self-esteem. A theory of schizophrenia must explain not only the patient's need to abandon reality testing but also his ability to do so. We must seek to understand why some persons can escape through withdrawal into unshared ways of experiencing the world around them more readily than others.

The thinking disorder in schizophrenia has been taken by some, and perhaps classically, to indicate dysfunction of the brain—dysfunction caused by lesions, deficiency, or metabolic disorder. The search for this brain dysfunction has been pursued for over 100 years. Each advance in physiology or neuroanatomy brings new hope, and each new form of physical therapy tantalizingly provokes prospects of leading to definitive knowledge of the malfunctioning of the brain. However, careful studies, and even casual observations, show that the thought disorder in schizophrenia differs markedly from any produced by a known organic deficit or a toxic disturbance of the brain. This is not the place to enter upon the nature of such differences. Although it is true that schizophrenic patients tend to concretize, they are also obviously capable of high degrees of abstraction, and may tend to abstract all too readily. More pertinently, unless a patient is permitted to become dilapidated by social isolation, the irrationality either remains or becomes more or less circumscribed. This girl who writes violently invective letters filled with delusions to her parents will in the next minute write a letter to a friend without a trace of delusional material, and then sits in her room and correctly composes inordinately complex music. No defect of thinking due to dysfunction of the brain permits such highly organized conceptualization.

There have been many approaches to the search for a genetic predisposition to schizophrenia. Our studies do not turn away from such consideration, but consider that a meaningful approach would focus upon a predisposition to symbolic distortion. Although our emphasis leads in another direction for theoretical reasons, which we shall seek to indicate briefly, we wish to point out that neither our theory nor our interpretations of data are of primary concern at present. We are attempting to present data derived from our study which we believe reliable and highly pertinent.

We consider that man is not naturally endowed with an inherent logic of causal relationships, but, rather, that the surroundings in which he is raised influence his ways of perceiving, thinking, and communicating. What makes "sense" at different periods of history and in different cultural settings (and, to a less extent, from one family to another) varies greatly. The Hindu way of regarding life in this world and life after death is irrational to us—and our way is just as meaningless and confused to the Hindu. Still, a trend toward a type of rationality exists in all cultures and in all groups. It is not that any of us has some particular ability to perceive reality as it is, for the actuality of reality—the *Ding an sich*—is never attainable by our senses. There is, however, a pragmatic meaning concerning what is fact—what is reality. It is measurable in terms of how our perceptions lead to effective action: if what we tell ourselves about events in the world around us leads to a degree of mastery over our environment and to workable interaction with the persons with whom we live. The effectiveness of reflective mentation is measured by how it helps the individual master his environment and achieve sufficient consensus with other persons to enable collaborative interaction. Communication, the outward manifestation of symbolic activity, measures the efficacy of mentation by the degree of consensus attained with others concerning what we perceive and what events mean. However, matters are not so simple. A large portion of mental activity is autistic rather than reflective; and autistic reverie is closer to primary process thinking, and to a great extent in the service of the wish of instinctual drives. The permeation of reflective thought, by the autistic processes, provides a major key to the understanding of schizophrenic thinking. Then, too, schizophrenic regression can reintroduce elements of perceptions and thought processes of early childhood that interpenetrate with more mature reflective and autistic mentation. Further, not all shared ideas need be reasonable and effective for purposes of controlling the environment. Man's need for emotional security, while he lives in this world of contingency, leads to systematization of ideas that actually may run counter to experience. Such systems, based upon unproved and untestable axioms, can direct our perceptions and understanding. As they are culturally approved, they are termed "beliefs" rather than "delusions." They result in compartmentalization of experience into segments that are kept from conflicting and challenging one another. Adherence to an axiom into which the perception of experience must be fitted almost requires distortion of perception of the environment. The issue is raised because a similar situation may be found within the family. If a parent must protect his tenuous equilibrium by adhering to a rigidly held need or self-concept, and everything else must be subsidiary to this defense, distortions occur that affect the rest of the family.

The family is the primary teacher of social interaction and emotional reactivity. It teaches by means of its milieu and nonverbal communication more than by formal education. The child's sources of identification and self-esteem derive from the family and markedly influence the developing patterns of symbolic functioning. However, the child is also exposed to the parental interpretation of reality and the parents' ways of communicating. Parental interpretations may have limited instrumental utility when they primarily serve to maintain the parents' own precarious equilibrium. The topic is very complex, and this paper will deal only with some of the more obvious influences of parental instability upon the children's thought processes.

We shall pursue the hypothesis that the schizophrenic patient is more prone to withdraw through distortion of his symbolization of reality than other patients, because his foundation in reality testing is precarious, having been raised amidst irrationality and chronically exposed to intrafamilial communications that distort and deny what should be the obvious interpretation of the environment, including the recognition and understanding of impulses and the affective behavior of members of the family.

The material that we present is derived from an intensive study of the family environment in which 15 schizophrenic patients grew up, which has now been in progress for over three years (3, 4, 8–11). The selection of cases required that the patient be clearly schizophrenic, be hospitalized in the Yale Psychiatric Institute, and have the mother and at least one sibling available for repeated interviews and observation, as well as for projective testing. It turned out that the father was also available in all but two families. With one or two exceptions, these families were uppermiddle or upper class, capable of supporting an offspring in a private psychiatric hospital for prolonged periods. In contrast with many other samples, there is a bias toward intact families with some degree of prestige in the community. The basic means of gaining information has been the repeated interviewing of all members of the family, and the observation of interaction of family members with each other and the hospital staff for periods ranging from six months to three years. Projective tests of all members of each family have been interpreted to yield information about the individual as well as concerning family interaction. Diaries, old family friends, former nursemaids, and teachers have been drawn into the study when possible and home visits made when feasible. The study has been carried out despite obvious difficulties and methodologic shortcomings, because any concept of schizophrenia as a developmental difficulty requires careful scrutiny of the family in which the patient grew up. Any effort to reconstruct a family environment as it existed over a period of 15 to 25 years will contain grave deficiencies. Still, the effort appears essential, and we believe that it has been highly rewarding, furnishing new leads and perspectives, if not clearcut answers.

Primarily, we are seeking to describe these families and find common features among them, rather than compare them with other types of families. We are, so to speak, describing the terrain of a country we are exploring, not comparing it with the geography of other countries. We have been skeptical, holding aloof from accepting too readily many current and past theoretical formulations. We have, for example, found many reasons to question hypotheses that seek to focus solely on the mother-child relationship during the early oral phase of development, noting the absence of clear-cut evidence of a type of rejecting or destructive mother-infant relationship that would differentiate the development of schizophrenic patients from persons with certain other psychiatric and psychosomatic conditions. The nature of the psychopathology or the relative health of the patients may well be determined by later events. In general, rather than focusing attention upon one phase of development or any single interpersonal relationship, we have been more interested in studying the forces that interfere with the emergence of a reasonably independent and integrated personality at the end of adolescence—the critical period in the development of schizophrenia, even if the onset is later in life.

We shall discuss in this paper two closely interrelated aspects of the family environment—the rationality of the parents and the nature of the communication within the family.

We shall first consider the rationality of the parents in the grossest terms. The findings are unexpectedly striking when compared with data from larger statistical studies (5, 12). However, Terry and Rennie found comparable figures, though their data are difficult to evaluate clearly (14). None of the parents of our patients was ever hospitalized in a mental institution and thus probably would not have been indexed as psychotic in any broad epidemiologic survey of psychoses in the parents of schizophrenic patients. Minimally, nine of the fifteen patients had at least one parent who could be called schizophrenic, or ambulatory schizophrenic, or clearly paranoid in behavior and attitudes. The finding is difficult to express explicitly, for the shading between what one terms schizophrenia and what bizarre behavior and ideation is arbitrary, and the line between psychosis and a paranoid outlook is equally fne. Although the proportion of families with more or less schizophrenic parents is very high, minimally 60%, it will become apparent that the cutoff point was quite arbitrary and other families could have been included. The classification is made difficult because of parents who maintain a reasonable degree of social presence and yet display seriously distorted thinking and motivation. Some of the mothers are seriously scattered and confused, particularly when anxious and under pressure. Fathers may be eminently successful but display behavior to their families that is pervaded and dominated by paranoid beliefs. Brief illustrations will clarify these statements.

We shall say little about the two mothers, A and B, who were frankly schizophrenic, except to say that despite delusions, hallucinations, and very confused reasoning they had continued to be the parent with the major responsibility for raising the children. [For further details and elaboration, see

Lidz *et al.* (10).] The husband of one was somewhat grandiose, if not paranoid, and spent most of his time away from home, while the other couple was divorced. Although a third mother, Mrs. C, sounded frankly schizophrenic, she ran the family business after her husband had suffered a "nervous breakdown" (before the patient was born), after which he had become passive and subservient to her. She openly expressed belief that her telephone was tapped and that the neighbors might burn down the home.

There were two mothers, Mrs. D and Mrs. E, who completely dominated the lives of their passive husbands and children. We consider these women typical "schizophrenigenic" mothers in needing and using their sons to complete their own frustrated lives. Their sons had to be geniuses, and any faults in them or anything that went wrong with their lives was consistently blamed on others—classmates, doctors, teachers, and society in general. They believed that only they understood their sons. We could never really understand these mothers, for their incessant talk was driven and mixed up, displaying unbelievable obtuseness to any ideas not their own. While we have hesitated to call these women schizophrenic, they are certainly not reality-oriented and are very close to being psychotic. Brief descriptions may convey the problem.

Two major private psychiatric hospitals had refused to keep Son E, not because of his behavior but because they could not stand his mother's incessant interference. Such behavior had plagued the boy and his teachers throughout his school years. Mrs. E talked incessantly about some fixed idea of the cause of her son's illness. When her ideas were questioned, she counterattacked; and if forced to abandon a theme, she would relinquish it only temporarily, retreating to her next, equally unreasonable idea. When the family had wished to build a home, she exhausted four or five architects, and the house was never built. When the daughter eventually gave up attempting to inform her mother that she intended to get married and simply announced her engagement, Mrs. E steadfastly ignored the daughter's intent. While the girl was seeking an apartment, the mother would only talk about reengaging her college room for the next academic year. The mother ignored the need to make plans for the wedding until the father, an unusually passive man, finally intervened shortly before the date that had been set for the wedding.

Mrs. D's life was dominated by the idea that her twin sons were geniuses whose development must not be hindered by setting any limits except in defense of her own extreme obsessiveness. Delinquent acts of the twins while still in grade school, such as breaking into and robbing a house and setting a dock on fire, were ignored and blamed upon other children. She insistently regarded a move from a suburb to the city, required because the twins were ostracized, and which disrupted her husband's business and social life, as a move to give her twins the superior education they required. Mrs. D fell into violent rages because of trivia that interrupted her obsessive cleanliness but gave inordinate praise for acts that the twins knew were nonsense. The household under her domination was a crazy place, and description could not be attempted without provoking the charge of gross exaggeration. For example, both twins claim that for many years they thought that constipation meant disagreeing with mother. Whenever one of them would argue with her, she would say they were constipated and needed an enema; both boys were then placed prone on the bathroom floor naked while the mother, in her undergarments, inserted the nozzle in each boy, fostering a contest to see which could hold out longer—the loser having to dash down to the basement lavatory. The projective tests of these last two mothers were judged frankly schizophrenic.

Only one of the four or five fathers who were considered psychotic or paranoid was as disorganized as these mothers. [For further material on fathers see Lidz et al. (8).] Mr. F, though a steady provider and a man with an ingenious turn of mind, was constantly engaged in working out one or another of his many inventions, which never materialized. He was vaguely suspicious and paranoid, fostering suspicion in his children; but it was his incessant talk, in which he jumped from one topic and one idea to another in driven fashion, that seemed most disturbing to the family. Like Mrs. E, he would hammer away at a fixed idea, and an hour with Mr. F thoroughly exhausted either of the two interviewers who tried to cope with him. The other fathers were more capable and less disorganized but more fixed in their paranoid ways. Mr. G was also an inventor, but a successful one, for a single ingenious invention had made the family wealthy. He spent much of his time steeped in the mysteries of an esoteric Asiatic cult, believing that he and a friend who shared these beliefs were among the few select who would achieve salvation in reincarnation. Whether he believed in his divinity or whether it was his wife who deified him is not clear, but this family lived in what we have termed *folie à famille,* which centered about the father and his esoteric beliefs, and according to a social pattern that was widely divergent from the society in which they actually lived. [Fuller details of the family are combined in an article by Fleck et al. (4).] Mr. H and Mr. I may be mentioned together as being competent businessmen who expressed many paranoid beliefs that did not interfere appreciably with their business activities but seriously upset family life. Among other things, Mr. H was paranoidly bitter against all Catholics, not an unusual situation, but here the paranoid bigotry focused upon his wife, who was a devout Catholic. At times he feared going to work because he felt people were against him. His wife, who has not been counted as psychotic, probably as a matter of relativity, was an extremely immature, scattered woman. [See Lidz et al. (11) for further description.] Mr. I was so suspicious that people were taking advantage of him that the hospital staff could not establish any relationship with him over a six-month period. His major concern at all interviews was to prove to the staff that his wife, who was actually a seriously obsessive woman, had been a malignant influence and had ruined his daughters, and also to make certain that the hospital was not lying, misrepresenting, or somehow taking advantage of him. Both men were hostile and contemptuous of women, and both had only daughters. The material offered here concerning these parents has been sparse, but we have abundant information which permits us to be certain that all nine have been virtually psychotic or markedly paranoid at least from the time of the patient's birth until the onset of illness. We are more interested in scrutinizing the situations in the remaining six families, in which the parents cannot be labeled so readily.

We can extract some generalizations from the study of these more disturbed parents that seem to apply to most, if not all, of the remaining six families, as well as to parents of many other schizophrenic patients. The struggles of these parents to preserve their own integration led them to limit their environment markedly by rigid preconceptions of the way things must be. The parents' precarious equilibrium will tumble if the environment cannot be delimited or if the parents must shift from the one rigid role they can manage. Mrs. D must see herself as the mother of twin geniuses. We understand something of how this came about. She, too, was a twin, but the deformed ugly duckling of the family, who dreamed of the phallus that would turn her into a swan. The birth of twins was her triumph, and their accomplishments her means of outshining her dominant twin sister. Mrs. B had written of how she had given birth to a genius, or perhaps a Messiah. She kept a diary of the child's development for 15 years, presenting an idyllic picture of the home life, which we learned from the sons and husband had little resemblance to reality. In a somewhat different sense, Mrs. H, the rejected Catholic wife, could only raise her daughters as Catholics, for she could not live according to any pattern except the one established for her by the church. Mr. I had to dominate his household and maintain his narcissistic esteem through admiration from all the females around him—his mother, wife, and two daughters. The slightest challenge to his imperious and unreasonable demands provoked a storm of fury.

These people must retain the necessary picture of themselves and their family. Some will fight to retain it; but others adhere to their conceptualization, which reality cannot alter or a new situation modify. They perceive and act in terms of their needed preconceptions, which they relinquish only under extreme pressures, and then with all sorts of maneuvers to explain through projection or ignore through isolation. We should like to take an example from outside the series of 15 families—from a case in which the sibling of the schizophrenic patient was in analysis. The father had left home when the children were very young to gain justice and revenge against a rival firm that had ruined his business by publicly accusing him falsely. Nothing mattered to him except to reestablish his power and prestige and gain revenge. He pursued his course for over 15 years without even visiting his family, though always writing that he would return home the following week. He was markedly grandiose and paranoid, however just his cause. Still, his attitude was scarcely more pathologic than the mother's. All through the years of separation, she insisted that nothing was wrong with the marriage, maintaining a shallow, euphoric attitude and telling her children that their concerns were groundless—the father was just attending to his business and would be back next week. Penelope was finally rewarded, but she could not unravel the fabric she had woven. Her son became schizophrenic within a month of her husband's return.

The parents' delimitation of the environment, and their perception of events to suit their needs, result in a strange family atmosphere into which the children must fit themselves and suit this dominant need or feel unwanted. Often the children must obliterate their own needs to support the defenses of the parent whom they need. They live in a Procrustean environment in which events are distorted to fit the mold. The world as the child should come to perceive or feel it is denied. Their conceptualizations of the environment are neither instrumental in affording consistent understanding and mastery of events, feelings, or persons, nor in line with what persons in other families experience. Facts are constantly being altered to suit emotionally determined needs. The acceptance of mutually contradictory experiences requires paralogical thinking. The environment affords training in irrationality.

The domination of a parent's behavior and attitude by rigid defensive needs clarifies other traits often noted among these parents. "Impervious" is a word we find ourselves using frequently to connote a parent's inability to feel or hear the child's emotional needs. The parent may listen but does not seem to hear and, further, seems oblivious to unspoken communications. These parents cannot consider anything that does not fit in with their own self-protecting systems. Indeed, as Bowen and his co-workers have also noted (2), such parents may respond to the child only in terms of their own needs displaced to the child, thus building up an entire pattern of maladaptive interactions. Bateson et al. have recently studied a related aspect of parent–child interaction (1). The parent conveys the impression of being cold or rejecting, and, of course, may be, but imperviousness is not simply a consequence of rejection of the child, but more a rejection of anything that threatens the parent's equilibrium or self-image.

These parents often talk in clichés, conveying a false impression of limited intelligence. Clichés and stereotypes serve to simplify the environment to enable the parents to cope with it in terms of their set needs. Such parents not only label a child as "the selfish one" or "the quiet one," but actually perceive the child only in terms of the stereotype. The fixed notions of an etiology of the illness, which may drive the psychiatrist to the verge of desperation, is a related phenomenon.

"Masking," which also confuses communication, refers to the ability of one or both parents to conceal some very disturbing situation within the family and to act as if it did not exist. Masking usually contains a large degree of self-deception as well as an effort to conceal from others; but it involves a conscious negation, as well as unconscious denial. The parent, unable either to accept or to alter the situation, ignores it and acts as though the family were a harmonious and homogeneous body that filled the needs of its members. Although some degree of masking may exist in all families, in some of our families the masking of serious problems dominated the entire family interaction. Problems that family members will not or cannot recognize are unlikely to be resolved. Children who grow up in such homes are aware that something is not right. They may become deeply resentful that the more intact parent takes no action to protect them from the situation. The children are puzzled, but may also learn to mask or ignore the obvious. Their efforts to explain away the situation, or to accept or convey pretense of affection and devotion, which has no resonance or real meaning, distorts their value systems.

The following two cases illustrate rather extreme degrees of imperviousness in which the parents appear severely rejecting.

The J's impressed the hospital and research staff as strange people, but they were one of the few couples in our series who were reasonably happily married. The younger of two daughters was severely hebephrenic. Mrs. J sought to blame the sex talk of the girl's college roommates. However, both parents could convince themselves to an amazing degree that the daughter was not really ill but merely being contrary and refusing to behave normally. This tendency increased as their financial means for retaining the girl in the hospital diminished, bearing little relationship to her condition. However, after some months of intensive therapy, the patient improved considerably. She repeatedly expressed her hopelessness that her parents would ever listen and understand her unhappiness over her school and social problems. As the patient could not be kept in the hospital for a long period and as the psychiatrist who was interviewing the parents found it impossible to get them to focus upon any meaningful problems that might be upsetting, a therapeutic experiment was undertaken, with great trepidation. The patient and the parents would meet together and, with the help of both psychiatrists, would try to speak frankly to one another. The daughter carefully prepared in advance what she wished to convey, and we tried to prepare the parents to listen carefully and to reply meaningfully. The patient, to the surprise of her psychiatrist, freely poured out her feelings to her parents and, in heartrending fashion, told them of her bewilderment and pleaded for their understanding and help. During the height of her daughter's pleas, the mother offhandedly turned to one of the psychiatrists, tugged at the waist of her dress, and blandly remarked, "My dress is getting tight. I suppose I should go on a diet." The mother had fallen back upon her habitual pattern of blocking out anything that would upset her bland equanimity. The next day the patient relapsed into incoherent and silly behavior.

Mrs. K, a cold and highly narcissistic woman, has been the other mother who did not wish to visit her offspring in the hospital. She said, "Wouldn't it upset Billy too much to have his mother see him in a place like this"; this clearly meant: "I couldn't stand visiting my son in a mental hospital." Mrs. K's intense dependency upon and attachment to her older sister, a very masculine woman, had contributed greatly to ruining her marriage. The sister had developed an intense dislike for the patient when he was still a small boy. After her husband's death, Mrs. K lived with her sister, but her 12-year-old son was not allowed in the house and had to live in a boarding room nearby. One Christmas Eve the mother stood by while the sister turned her son away from the home and from spending the evening with them. Later, when they were all going to visit relatives in a distant city, the sister refused to take the son along, and the mother remained blandly in the car while they passed the boy trying to hitchhike in a snowstorm. Mrs. K's dependency upon her sister took precedence over her son's needs. (Literary and dramatic illustrations of many features of these families can be found in Eugene O'Neill's *Long Day's Journey into Night,* Tennessee Williams' *The Glass Menagerie,* and August Strindberg's *Easter* and *The Father.*)

Another type of imperviousness existed in the cases of D and B. The mothers were solicitous enough, but the vision of the genius child who would complete and justify their lives made them oblivious to the actual needs, abilities, and deficiencies of their children. Mrs. C was so caught up in a struggle with her elder, psychopathic son that she scarcely noted anything that occurred in the life of the younger son, who eventually became schizophrenic, even though she was very controlling of much of his life.

Masking also distorts the communication within the family severely. Mr. L had been an eminent attorney who supported his family at a lavish level and basked in the light of his legal prestige and his associations with prominent persons. After his partner, the contact man for the firm, committed suicide, his income fell off disastrously. Mr. L was an obsessive brief writer and researcher who could neither gain clients nor plead cases. Gradually, he withdrew into his office and into his study at home, spending his time making scholarly analyses of legal matters, which earned him almost nothing. The need to consider himself a great legal mind and a prominent person took precedence over the needs of his family. He could not admit his failure to himself or anyone else, and could not alter his ways. His wife, who, fortunately, was a competent woman, went to work and, with the help of her relatives, managed to support the family as well as her husband's law office. For over ten years she helped maintain the pretense to the world and to her children and even managed to keep herself from recognizing the resentment she felt toward a husband who let her shoulder the entire burden of the family. She had to maintain the myth of a successful marriage to a strong father-figure. The children could not help but know that it was all fraudulent. The situation required consistent falsification, and all the communications between members of this household had a high degree of pretense concerning the feelings they felt obligated to express in order to retain the front. The daughter, as a patient, kept protesting the expense of her hospitalization to her father, though she was well aware that he had earned nothing since her early childhood.

Mr. and Mrs. M both strove to mask a situation they could not hide successfully. Mr. M, a successful businessman and once an athlete of renown, needed to be the center of considerable adulation. Mr. M could not tolerate the rivalry of his son and required the help of alcohol and numerous affairs to maintain his feeling of masculinity. He pretended that he was not an alcoholic, and that he spent most of his time traveling in order to provide well rather than to alleviate his anxiety and prevent open conflict. His wife also tried to maintain the pretense that they were happily married. Unable to consider separation seriously, she strove to blind herself to the seriousness of his alcoholism; his noxious influence on their son, whom he constantly belittled; and his extramarital affairs, which were highly embarrassing to the family.

Mrs. M appeared to accept her husband's obnoxious behavior but sought to establish altogether different standards in her son, in whom she fostered esthetic interests. A son, in such situations, gains confused concepts of what his mother cherishes in a man. The many other problems that beset this family are outside the immediate interests of this chapter, but we should note that the highly sensitive mother often became impervious to her son's needs because she had to center her attention on her husband and support his infantile needs.

Habitual masking may then be viewed as an irrational form of communication, but another feature that often affects the child's mental functioning is complete breakdown of communication between parents, especially when the child is caught between different value systems and attitudes that cannot be integrated. Mrs. N resented the daughter who was born after she and her husband had become emotionally estranged, whereas Mr. N sought from his daughter the affection he could not receive from his wife. The parents had quarreled before the patient's birth over their respective attachments to their families, attachments that took precedence over the marital relationship. Mrs. N's family had accused the husband's oldest brother of ruining their father's business. When Mrs. N had seemed to side with her family, her husband considered her disloyal and never forgave her. Indeed, they never spoke of the matter again, but never became reconciled and were openly hostile, though continuing to live together. Communication between them was largely vengeful and undermining. The father, for example, perhaps partly to punish his wife and partly to escape her vituperative temper, spent his evenings in his office reading, but, to conceal his own impotence, let his wife and family believe that he had a mistress with whom he spent much of his time. Many of the family quarrels centered on this nonexistent situation. In addition, the father's seductive use of the daughter to bolster his narcissism, while seeking to ignore his wife, further confused communication and meaning in this family.

We could properly place the O's, the remaining family, in the large category of psychotic or borderline parents, even though the parents were not so clearly psychotically disturbed. Mrs. O, particularly when anxious, spoke incessantly and said very little, and even less that was pertinent to the situation. She asked questions endlessly, but constantly interrupted with another question before anyone could answer her. This woman might be termed obsessive, but her obsessiveness was extremely scattered and disorganized when she was anxious. In contrast, her husband's ritualized obsessiveness led to behavior that often seemed highly irrational. He would go into rages if a toothpaste cap was not replaced, throw his wife's entire wardrobe on the floor because it was disorderly or her fur coat into the bathtub because she left it lying on the bed. Although frequently complaining and worried about money, he could not keep from making unnecessary purchases. When seriously concerned about meeting the cost of his son's hospitalization, he bought a third car and could not understand why his wife was angered by his fine present for her, even though his purchase of a second car had precipitated a violent quarrel just a month before. Mr. O saw nothing hostile in the purchase. We wish to call attention to the irrational atmosphere produced in a family when the parents are obsessive-compulsive, particularly when the two obsessive patterns are in direct conflict. The covert, hostile, and symptomatic behavior of each parent challenges the defensive pattern of the other. Neither makes sense, but both parents find rationalizations for their own behavior that neither the spouse nor the children can really understand. Although Mrs. O, along with Mrs. J, Mrs. K, and Mrs. H, could not be considered overtly psychotic, they all were strange, disturbed persons. The defensive structure of all these women led to a type of behavior that created great difficulty in communication within the family, because what they said was more in defense of their fragile equilibrium than a communication pertinent to the given situation.

Before ending this initial survey of the irrationality present in the family environment in which schizophrenic patients grow up, we wish to direct attention to the conscious training of children to a paranoid orientation that takes place in some families. Both Mr. H and Mr. I sought not only to make their daughters distrustful and suspicious toward their mothers, but to share their own paranoid suspiciousness of almost everyone. In a different vein, the G parents inculcated a system of religious belief that was aberrant and virtually delusional in the society in which the family lived.

COMMENT

The study of the irrationality and defective communication in these families presents a complex task. A fairly complete picture of each family would be required to bring out the many frustrating problems involved. Here, we have merely sought to convey an impression of the broad sweep of the distorting influences present in all of the families studied, which have also been apparent in most, if not all, of the families of the many other schizophrenic patients treated in the Yale Psychiatric Institute during the past several years. Other less obvious and subtler influences require attention that we shall consider in subsequent articles.

Although our studies encompass only 15 families, they form a good random sampling of middle- and upper-class families with schizophrenic offspring. The marked disturbances in instrumental utility of communications that can readily be noted in all of these families cannot be ignored in the search for reasons why these patients may be prone to withdraw from a reality orientation when unable to cope with their serious interpersonal problems.

We are not pointing to such defects in communication and the presence of an irrational milieu as a cause of schizophrenia. We are concerned with multiple factors distorting personality development rather than seeking a "cause." Other papers from this study emphasize the importance of the personalities of both parents, the confused family environments provided the children, and the faulty and conflicting model for identification offered by the parents; and still other facets of the family milieu await scrutiny. Here we simply, but significantly, indicate that our patients were not raised in families that adhered to culturally accepted ideas of causality and meanings, or respected the instrumental utility of their ideas and communications, because one or both parents were forced to abandon rationality to defend their own precarious ego structure. We are, therefore, concerned here with factors that may differentiate the genesis of schizophrenia from the genesis of other psychopathologic syndromes, in that persons who grow up in such families, having had their symbolic roots nourished by irrationality in the family, are less confined by the restrictions of the demands of reality when means of escape and withdrawal are required.

Of course, the presence of poorly organized or disorganized parents can just as well be taken as evidence of a genetic strain that transmits schizophrenia. Indeed, we have probably found more evidence of mental illness among parents and in other relatives than any study of the genetic factors of schizophrenia. At this time we are describing what exists in the family rather than explaining how it came about. According to our concepts of human development, such distortions of reasoning are more explicable through extrabiologic transmission of family characteristics than through genetic endowment. However, we need not seek a solution with an "either-

or," for, as with many other conditions, both genetic and environmental factors may well be involved.

SUMMARY

In an earlier paper we suggested that a theory of schizophrenia must explain not only the patients' needs to withdraw regressively and through abandonment of the restrictions of reality but also their ability to do so. The accumulating data in our intensive study of the intrafamilial environment in which schizophrenic patients grow up suggested the hypothesis that these persons are prone to withdraw through altering their internal representations of reality because they have been reared amidst irrationality and intrafamilial systems of communication that distort or deny instrumentally valid interpretations of the environment. The role of the family in transmitting instrumentally useful perception and mentation is discussed to provide a basis for the study. Markedly aberrant ways of thinking were present in most families; in at least nine of the fifteen families one or both parents were schizophrenic or paranoid, and in all the others less pronounced degrees of irrationality, with seriously disturbed ways of communications, would seriously affect the children's foundation in rational processes. We present these findings, along with an analysis of some of the more obvious difficulties, as but part of our studies of the influence of the family upon the developmental processes in schzophrenic patients.

NOTES

1. Read in abbreviated form at the 113th Annual Meeting of the American Psychiatric Association, Chicago, May 13–17, 1957. This research is supported by grants from the National Institute of Mental Health and from the Social Research Foundation, Inc.

REFERENCES

1. Bateson, G., Jackson, D. D., Haley, J., and Weakland, J. Towards a theory of schizophrenia. *Behavioral Science*, 1956, *1*, 251.

2. Bowen, M., Dysinger, R. H., Brodey, W. M., and Basamanie, G. *Study and treatment of 5 hospitalized family groups each with a psychotic member*. Presented at the Annual Meeting of American Orthopsychiatric Association, Chicago, March 8, 1957.

3. Cornelison, A. Case work interviewing as a research technique in a study of families of schizophrenic patients. To be published.

4. Fleck, S., Freedman, D. X., Cornelison, A., Terry, D., and Lidz, T. The intrafamilial environment of the schizophrenic patient: V. The understanding of symptomatology through the study of famly interaction. *Read at the Annual Meeting of the American Psychiatric Association*, May, 1957.

5. Kallmann, F. J. *Heredity in health and mental disorder: Principles of psy-*

chiatric genetics in light of comparative twin studies. New York: W. W. Norton & Company, 1953, p. 144.

6. Lidz, R. W., and Lidz, T. The family environment of schizophrenic patients. *American Journal of Psychiatry,* 1949, *106,* 332–345.

7. Lidz, R. W., and Lidz, T. Therapeutic considerations arising from the intense symbiotic needs of schizophrenic patients. In E. B. Brody and F. C. Redlich (Eds.), *Psychotherapy with schizophrenics.* New York: International Universities Press, 1952, pp. 168–178.

8. Lidz, T., Parker, B., and Cornelison, A. The role of the father in the family environment of the schizophrenic patient. *American Journal of Psychiatry,* 1956, *113,* 126–142.

9. Lidz, T., Cornelison, A., Fleck, S., and Terry, D. The intrafamilial environment of the schizophrenic patient: I. the father. *Psychiatry,* 1957, *20,* 329–342.

10. Lidz, T., Cornelison, A. R., Fleck, S., and Terry, D. The intrafamilial environment of the schizophrenic patient: II. Marital schism and marital skew. *American Journal of Psychiatry,* 1957, *114,* 241–248.

11. Lidz, T., Cornelison, A., Fleck, S., and Terry, D. Parental personalities and family interaction. *American Journal of Orthopsychiatry,* to be published.

12. Pollock, H. M, Malzberg, B., and Fuller, R. G. *Hereditary and environmental factors in the causaton of manic-depressive psychoses and dementia praecox.* Utica, N. Y.: State Hospitals Press, 1939, pp. 98–145.

13. Spiegel, J. P. The resolution of role conflict within the family. *Psychiatry,* 1957, *20,* 1–16.

14. Terry, G. C., and Rennie, T. A. C. Analysis of parergasia. *Nervous and Mental Disease Monograph Series No. 64.* New York: Nervous and Mental Disease Publishing Company, 1938, pp. 67–70.

VI

Patterning Separateness and Connectedness

The psychosocial interior of a family is created through interpretation of reality and through construction of social relationships. The papers in this section focus on processes of relationship construction, or, as we prefer to emphasize, construction of patterns of separateness and connectedness. Issues of dependence, independence, and interdependence are central and take various forms. Power and autonomy are negotiated and struggled over. Intimacy and distance are explored. Issues of power and intimacy become intertwined and both are intertwined with definitions of gender and definitions of age.

Francesca Cancian examines husband-wife conflict over intimacy. Her basic point of departure is the cultural definition of gender roles. She shows how these become the bases for conflict within the family as husband and wife struggle to implement their diverse conceptions of what love is.

Any person's capacities for separateness and connectedness originate in the separateness and connectedness that the baby achieved with the mother. Margaret Mahler, Fred Pine, and Anni Bergman present the fruit of years of work in delineating the stages of the newborn in negotiating its way from early attachment to establishment of a sense of separateness.

In the rethinking of family relationships that has been underway since the 1960's and continues today, increased importance of the father in child rearing has received some attention. Diane Ehrensaft reports on families she has studied that have tried to implement a concept of dual-parenting.

Everyone has heard of sibling rivalry. Most people also know that in some families the rivalry seems bitter and enduring, while in others it is overcome and the siblings become friends. Not much is known about how and why these different outcomes occur. Handel presents an analysis of some central issues that enter into the construction of sibling relationships, and he suggests that how these issues are handled and resolved over the course of the childhood years of the relationship affects its outcome in later years.

Mahler, Pine and Bergman show how the infant moves from a psychological state of fusion with the mother to establishment of a sense of separateness. The child as a separate person is also, of course, connected to the family. In the adolescent years, the task of separating from the family unit presents itself. Stierlin, basing his analysis on work with runaway (and troubled non-runaway) teenagers, presents an analysis of styles of separation.

16

Marital Conflict Over Intimacy

FRANCESCA M. CANCIAN

It is in marriage and sexual love that most Americans expect to find their major attachment to an adult. The very word "relationship" has come to mean a sexual, couple relationship. But expectations for marital intimacy are often frustrated, in part because of our system of gender roles. Love and the family are identified with the feminine role, while achievement and work are the core of masculinity. Love is seen as an activity that women control, and something that women need more than men; work is the focus of men's lives, and men monopolize higher paying jobs. This feminization of love and the relations of power and dependence between men and women produce one of the major conflicts in marriage: the struggle between wives who demand more love and husbands who withhold.

CONFLICTS OVER LOVE

According to the lore of clinical psychology, the traditional complaint of wives is that they do not get enough attention from their husbands, while the traditional complaint of husbands is that they feel trapped and suffocated. A recent popular psychology book by Pierre Mornell describes a contemporary version of this conflict among middle-class patients, the struggle between *Passive Men* and *Wild Women*.

This paper is part of a book, *Attachment and Freedom,* forthcoming. I am indebted to Steven Gordon, Gerald Handel, Arlie Hochschild, Barbara Risman, Lillian Rubin and Ann Swidler for helpful comments on earlier drafts of this paper.

Francesca Cancian is Professor of Sociology, School of Social Sciences, University of California, Irvine.

The husband arrives around 7 o'clock exhausted from his day at the office.
. . . He pays only token attention to his wife, maybe a little more (or less) to
the kids, and then withdraws behind TV's Monday night football. . . . (But)
most wives—at least a majority of those who seek my help for their troubled
marriages—do want "something more" from their husbands in those hours when
they come together.

This need for "something" more is directly or indirectly conveyed to the
man.

. . . He, in turn, experiences her demands (for longer talks, or an honest
expression of feelings, or spending more time with the kids or her, or his being
more active in sharing the domestic load, or her desire for better sex) as MORE
PRESSURE. . . . And in the face of that pressure, direct or indirect on his wife's
part, he withdraws . . . and she comes back at him with greater demands for
"something he's not giving her."[1]

There is considerable evidence that this type of conflict is frequent among
both working- and middle-class couples. Studies of working-class marriages by Mirra Komarovsky and Lillian Rubin found that the wives' unful-
filled longings for more communication and more emotional closeness were
major causes of marital dissatisfction. A laboratory study of 48 newlyweds
concluded that wives used more emotional pressure while husbands were
more conciliatory and tried to avoid conflict. A survey of middle-class couples found that husbands more than wives wanted their spouse to be less
emotional and create less stress, while wives more than husbands wanted
their spouse to be more responsive and receptive.[2]

Lillian Rubin describes how new cultural ideas of intimacy and communication in marriage lead working-class wives to feel lonely and discon-
tented. So they push for change but are confused:

I'm not sure what I want. I keep talking to him about communication, and he
says, "Okay, so we're talking; now what do you want?" And I don't know
what to say then, but I know it's not what I mean.

The women feel frightened and unsure about their demands:

I sometimes get worried because I think maybe I want too much. He's a good
husband; he works hard; he takes care of me and the kids. He could go out
and find another woman who would be very happy to have a man like that,
and who wouldn't be all the time complaining at him because he doesn't feel
things and get close.

The men are also unsure and afraid:

I swear, I don't know what she wants. She keeps saying we have to talk, and
then when we do, it always turns out I'm saying the wrong thing.
    I get scared sometimes. I always thought I had to think things to myself; you
know, not tell her about it. Now she says that's not good. But it's hard. You
know, I think it comes down to that I like things the way they are, and I'm

afraid I'll say or do something that'll really shake things up. So I get worried about it, and I don't say anything.[3]

Sometimes it is the husband who wants more contact and closeness, and the wife who withdraws. A 29-year-old housewife that I interviewed seems happy with her marriage to a sensitive and emotionally expressive carpenter, but would like more space.[4] "Couples need a lot of time alone and also a lot of time together," she comments; "I am glad to get away from him sometimes." She would like another child, but he opposes the idea: she would also like to visit with other couples more, but "he loves to keep us to himself." In a study I designed to find out how many couples fit the pattern of demanding woman-withholding man, about one-half the couples fit the pattern, one-third reversed roles, and the remainder said that this type of conflict over intimacy did not occur in their relationship.[5]

THE FEMINIZED DEFINITION OF LOVE

This conflict between the woman who wants "more love" and the man who withholds is the direct result of gender roles and the split between feminine attachment and masculine achievement. If love is a feminine specialty, then she will pursue closeness and he will not respond. Three related aspects of gender roles contribute to this conflict: the feminized definition of love, the allocation of marital love to women's sphere, and the dependency of wives on husbands.

One reason that wives want "love" more than husbands is that love is usually defined in terms of feminine styles of attachment, such as intimate talk, while masculine styles such as sex and practical help are seen as unessential. Researchers who study love, intimacy or close relationships usually emphasize qualities that are stereotypically feminine, like emotional expression, verbal self-disclosure, and tenderness. Thus, Lillian Rubin's recent book on marriage focuses on intimacy, which she defines as the "reciprocal expression of feeling and thought."[6] The general public also tends to define love as the expression of feelings, not as instrumental help. In 1980 I interviewed 130 adults from a wide range of social backgrounds and asked about the qualities that make a good love relationship. The most frequent response referred to honest and open communication.[7] If love is defined as talking about personal troubles and feelings, there will be frequent marital conflicts in which wives seek more intimacy and husbands withhold. Moreover, with this definition, women will usually be superior to men in being intimate, since women are typically more interested and skilled in intimate talk.

However, if intimacy were defined in terms of sexual relations, the tables would be turned, and there would be frequent conflicts in which husbands seek more intimacy and wives withhold.[8] Some excerpts from Rubin's study of working-class marriages illustrate this type of conflict. One husband commented, "I think sex should be that you enjoy each other's bodies. Judy doesn't care for touching and feeling each other though." Another husband said, "She complains that all I want from her is sex, and I try to make her understand that it's an expression of love. I'll want to make up with her by making love, but she's as cold as the inside of the refrigerator." According to the wife, "He keeps saying he wants to make love, but it just doesn't feel like love to me. Sometimes I feel bad that I feel that way, but I just can't help it."[9]

It is somewhat surprising that sex remains much less important than communication in public and expert opinion about the components of love, given the growing emphasis on sexual pleasure in marriage for women as well as men. Part of the answer may be that entreating another person for love implies being dependent and powerless. In our culture men are believed to need or want sex more than women, and typically they do. If this need were defined as a need for love and acceptance from their wives, the power advantage of husbands would be threatened. Husbands would no longer seem so strong and independent. This may be one reason that sexuality is not closely identified with love, and male sexual images emphasize power or aggression and not attachment or warmth. For example, a man with sexual problems is called "impotent," while a woman with such problems is called "frigid."

Giving practical help is another way of loving that men usually prefer but that is defined as not essential to love, especially by middle-class couples.[10] Most men seem comfortable giving help to someone they like, probably because giving help reinforces their power; it does not imply dependency or neediness. For couples that included giving help as a major aspect of love, I would expect much less of the conflict between the demanding wife and the withholding husband.

MARRIAGE AND LOVE IS PART OF WOMEN'S SPHERE

A common view of marriage in our culture is reflected in a 1966 Reader's Digest article, which argues that men give up more than women for marriage. Although women also make sacrifices, her sacrifices "were made for *her* marriage, *her* home, *her* family. Rightly or wrongly, the average man believes that while his wife may 'belong' to him, the marriage belongs to his wife."[11]

Love and marriage have been part of women's sphere since the 19th century. In the past decades, there has been some weakening of the split between feminine attachment and masculine achievement, as more women work and have fewer children, and as more men become interested in their personal life. Yet intimacy in marriage remains primarily women's concern and responsibility. For example, magazine articles on how to improve marriage remain directed primarily to women.[12]

What are the consequences of this division of labor for marital conflict? Insofar as marriage, love and the home are defined as the wife's "turf," an area where she sets the rules and expectations, men are more likely to feel threatened and controlled when she seeks more intimacy. If the couple believes that love is shown through the activities that women prefer and in which they are more skilled, i.e., intimate talk as opposed to sex, his negative feelings will be aggravated.[13] Talking about the relationship, as she wants, will feel like taking a test that she made up and he will fail. The husband is likely to react with withdrawal and passive aggression. He is blocked from straightforward counterattack insofar as he believes that intimacy is good and should not be opposed.

From a woman's perspective, since love and marriage are in her sphere of responsibility, she is very highly motivated to have a successful relationship with her husband. As the same Reader's Digest article comments, "When a woman marries, her home, her children and her husband become the most important things in her life. . . . She is at last taking on the task she has been aiming for since she first understood the difference between boys and girls."[14]

A more contemporary version of the separation of spheres is described in *Final Analysis,* a novel by Lois Gould. Several professional women in a consciousness-raising group are discussing the heroine's love affair with Dr. Foxx when a woman explodes:

> "What are we analyzing *him* for?"
> ". . . all *we* do is sit around worrying about some nut named Dr. Foxx! What about her *work,* damn it? What about. . . ."
> "Oh, Laurie," sighed Wanda. "Who cares about work when their love life stinks?"
> "*Men* do," said Tess. "Doris Lessing said she never met a man who'd fuck up his work for a love affair, and she never met a woman who wouldn't."[15]

For these women, love is still the first priority.

When there are problems in a marriage or a love affair, the woman wants to take steps to make things better. The man takes little initiative, beyond proposing sex, in suggesting ways to get closer; this is her sphere and he is unskilled and ambivalent about dyadic intimacy. A passive woman may accept this situation and retreat into tearful helplessness. A more active woman is likely to propose solutions such as discussing their problem or taking a vacation; he is likely to respond with passive resistance and act as if she were pushy, demanding and unfeminine. Thus, she is doubly blocked from succeeding in one of the main goals of her life—attaining a happy marriage. Not only is the relationship strained, but her efforts to improve the situation make her feel unfeminine and guilty.

The connection between love being in women's sphere and men withdrawing from love is supported by the contrast between courtship and marriage. In courtship men are more in control of love. Until the 1970's, there was a strong norm to the effect that the man should arrange dates, initiate sex, and propose marriage, and most couples probably still follow this pattern.[16] Men also seem to be less withdrawn during courtship and much more interested in talking about feelings and personal experiences. After marriage, love becomes primarily a woman's responsibility, and the conflict between withholding men and demanding women is much more likely to develop.

Differences in social class and in the life cycles of men and women also contribute to the conflict over love. Most couples marry while the partners are in their 20s, and in the following years the man is absorbed in work while the woman becomes absorbed by child rearing or the hectic schedule of combining children with a job.

Working-class men who have tedious or insecure jobs usually do not identify strongly with their work; they are more likely to be unavailable to their wives because they are anxious about supporting the family or numbed and exhausted by their jobs.[17] Middle-class husbands who provide a steady income but are not very involved in work may have the best relationship, on the average, with their wives—they are successful providers but still have plenty of time and energy to devote to their families.[18]

It is in the upper middle class that the conflict between demanding wives and withholding husbands might be most intense. The husband's career becomes his first priority, and he has little time for his wife or any attachment. Moreover, she becomes increasingly dependent on him as his earning potential moves far ahead of hers. He becomes obsessed with his work and she becomes obsessed with her marriage—a pattern that was found among British businessmen and their wives, and many other studies of affluent Americans.[19] If she also has career aspirations, she may feel not only rejected by her husband but also angry about her blocked ambitions and her conflicted and messy life compared to the focus and importance of her husband's career.[20] A woman biologist, Ann Gerrard, reflected on her unhappiness early in her marriage, when her career was floundering and her children were young:

> I was starting to get restless. I remember when we first went to Boston (where her husband had a job and she did not) just getting in the car and driving, thinking I'm just going to drive forever and I'm not ever coming back. . . . I thought there was something wrong with my husband because my life wasn't, I didn't like my life, so it must have meant there was something wrong with the marriage. . . . I thought what I needed was another man.

What Ann did with her restlessness was to press her husband to talk to her more, and to have long arguments about their relationship. Ann's anger at her blocked career, which she blamed on her husband, was probably one of the reasons he withdrew from her demands for more closeness.

Ann also became less interested in sex and more allied with her children. After commenting that her husband was "not terribly involved" with the children when they were small, she adds:

> Ann: I remember I kind of liked it that way. I guess it was my revenge.
> Interviewer: You mean, this is mine, you have yours?
> Ann: That's right, something like that. I remember that our sex life turned kind of sour after David (her second child) was born. That was the same time that my career was the total pits. . . . It wasn't what I had planned.

Controlling or attacking one's husband as a reaction to the burdens of the wife and mother role are also suggested by Lyn Gilmore, a woman who has just returned to school after 14 years of being a housewife. "I think what it was before was I wanted control over everybody else's life without trying to control my own. Now that I have control over my life, the control over my children's and my husband's life has kind of floated away. . . ."

The early years of marriage are when the conflict between the demanding wife and the withholding husband is probably most intense. It is the stage of life when couples of all social classes tend to be most unhappy with their marriages, sociologists have found, the period where he will probably be most preoccupied with work and she is most dependent on him for money and emotional support.[21] In later years (if the marriage survives), the conflict may abate if the husband becomes less absorbed in work and the wife can focus on her own projects and develop a network of friends as the children leave home.

DEPENDENT WIVES AND POWERFUL HUSBANDS

A woman's dependency on her husband for love, for money, and for her sense of identity is the third aspect of gender roles that leads wives to want "something more" from their husbands. She is more concerned with the relationship than he is, and less sure that she could survive without him. Therefore, she feels neglected and jealous of his work and other interests, and needs him to reassure her of his commitment by spending time and emotional energy on her. An extremely dependent wife may develop an insatiable need for more attention and closeness, like dependent children or sick people; they often focus all their attention on what they get from the person they depend on, and feel abandoned and deprived even if they seem to be receiving a lot of care. Similarly, in marriages where the husband is very dependent on his wife, he may develop an insatiable demand for attention from her, for example, men who are retired or unemployed.

Extreme dependency may also produce chronic anger, both because the husband will inevitably fail to meet some of his wife's needs, and because her dependency implies that he has a great deal of power over her and that he is responsible for what is wrong with her life. The anger of dependent and powerless wives may explain Mornell's observation that even when the husband agreed to talk more or do what the wife wanted, many wives rejected his offer and continued to criticize him for not being a good enough husband. It also explains the tendency of wives to blame their husbands for problems in the marriage, while husbands tend to blame themselves.[22]

This interpretation suggests that a woman is less apt to want greater intimacy from her husband if she is economically independent and has a job or other involvements that provide her a sense of identity. Thus, the trend to more women working may alleviate this type of marital conflict.[23]

The other side of the wife's dependency is the husband's power over his wife, his responsibility to be the breadwinner and provider for his wife and children, and his overt independence. He is supposed to provide for his family with little help from his wife. In our individualistic, capitalist system, if he fails as a provider it is his fault. Therefore, he is likely to feel burdened by his marriage and family; it is yet another externally imposed task that he must master.[24]

Thus, if a husband is a real man his wife will be satisfied. If she is not and says she wants something more from the relationship, he feels that he has failed, that he is being accused of being inadequate and not measuring up. He may also feel that what she is proposing is some new test of his manhood. Either reaction may lead him to defensively reassert his masculinity and become more aggressive and rational; or, if he believes that aggression and "intellectualizing" are wrong, he may close up and withdraw.

At the overt, explicit level, wives are usually more dependent on their husbands than their husbands are on them. This contributes to the conflict between demanding women and withholding men. It is also essential to maintaining a sexist or male-dominated society: men cannot maintain power over women unless women are dependent on them. Many aspects of our society besides the feminization of love maintain the husband's power and the wife's dependency, as feminist scholars have documented.[25] Both men and women prefer a marriage where the man is older, smarter, better educated and earns a higher income, which gives the husband a considerable power advantage, as Jessie Bernard has pointed out.[26] A wife who needs comfort may sit in her husband's lap in public, but if he were observed sitting in her lap, the couple would probably be very embarrassed. Female dependency is accepted and encouraged, while male dependency or a situation of equal interdependence is denied.

On a less overt level, it is not so clear who is more dependent, who has more power, and who needs whom the most. I assume that all people depend on others, and that people who are strongly attached to each other, like married people, by definition depend on each other. Thus, men who appear independent are probably covertly dependent on their wives. For example, the play *I'm Getting My Act Together, and Taking it on the Road* included a man married to an apparently helpless and neurotic woman. One of the ways he tried to keep her happy was to rent her an art studio— where she met her lovers. In a conversation with a feminist friend, the man said, "If my wife were strong like you I'd leave her." In other words, he was highly dependent on her needing him, and she had a lot of power in the relationship.

But overt and covert dependency seem to have quite different consequences. It is overt dependency that undermines power and results in a preoccupation with the relationship and a desire for more closeness.

PSYCHOLOGICAL CAUSES OF THE CONFLICT OVER INTIMACY

There are also psychological foundations to the conflict over love, besides the more sociological aspects of gender I have just discussed. Psychoanalytic theories argue that as long as infants are raised by women, men and women will have different attitudes to intimacy. For example, according to Nancy Chodorow's influential theory, the conflict over love is based on the fact that as infants, both boys and girls have a strong identification with and intimate attachment to their mother (or female caretaker). Since boys must grow up to be men, they repress this early identification and in the process repress their capacity for intimacy. Girls retain their early identification since they will grow up to be women like mother, so they continue to see themselves as connected to others. Women have difficulty separating from their original relationship with their mothers, and try to re-create an intimate, symbiotic relation with their husbands. Men, in contrast, are fearful of intimate ties with a woman that remind them of their early feminine identification.[27]

Theories of gender role socialization focus on the many social pressures that shape males and females into very different kinds of people. From the reactions of their parents and peers, from the toys they are given and the television programs they watch, girls learn that they are expected to be emotional and dependent while boys are encouraged to be assertive, emotionally controlled and independent.

Both types of psychological theories imply that men's and women's orientation to love becomes part of their personality, a built-in disposition that is impossible or very difficult to change in adulthood. But evidence that people change their orientation to love in different circumstances indicates that the current situation is sometimes more important than personality. The conflict over intimacy does seem to change between courtship and marriage; it seems to be most severe among young couples, and declines in middle age. Both personality and social structure, both the past and the present, contribute to the conflict between demanding wives and withholding husbands.

LYN AND TOMMY GILMORE

The conflict over love often follows the same pattern and grows out of the social organization of gender. But for each couple the conflict takes a somewhat different form, and the reality of their daily life is much more complex and contradictory than my sociological analysis suggests. The following portrait of a marriage is intended to convey some of this complexity and to strengthen the link between my analysis and our daily individual experience.

Lyn and Tommy Gilmore have been married for 14 years and have three daughters between the ages of five and eleven. They are in their mid-30s and seem to have a secure and lively relationship.

The Gilmores are moving away from a marriage based on highly differentiated gender roles, where she was the compliant housewife and mother and he was the dominant breadwinner. Now she is a full-time student and is becoming more assertive about trying to improve communication with her husband; he is participating more in housework and child care, and is becoming more interested in communication himself. Despite these changes, Lyn remains responsible for family relationships and the nonsexual aspects of marital intimacy, while Tommy still makes all the money and remains the dominant partner.

To Lyn, love means communication, especially since she took a course on "A Helping Relationship" at the local community college and had therapy with the instructor of the course. When asked how she would like to change the marriage, Lyn responded, "I'm working on changing our intimacy level," and the change is progressing very very slowly. For several years, she felt that sex was the only channel of communication open in her marriage, "and I don't like that. It was enough for him, or so he said, but it wasn't enough for me. . . . And that's where some of our problems came in when I first started to get him to talk with me." Lyn stopped initiating sex and "turned off." In her interview, she considered whether she was withholding sex to punish Tommy for not talking. "I don't want to hurt him either, but it's a two-way street."

Lyn is the one who works on improving marital communication. She encourages Tommy to talk about his work at a chemical plant where he has received several promotions and is now being pressured to move on to a managerial position. At first, Tommy said, he started talking about work because Lyn "expressed a desire to share more things like that . . . and because she needed somebody other than the children to talk to." But now he enjoys it, although she seems to need it less. "There's less of a demand, less of a need to get into my work," he comments, "now that she has school and other contacts outside the house."[28]

From Lyn's perspective, she is still the one who initiates most conversations, and he is rarely responsive or empathic when they do talk. In her first interview, Lyn described an incident that had occurred the night before, when she was making supper, her children were underfoot, and Tommy came out to the kitchen:

> I said, "While I'm making supper, why don't you unload the dishwasher and talk to me, just stand here and chat." And he proceeded to tell me what had happened with his day, then said, "I'm tired" and went in to lie down, and I never got to share my end of it.

An interview six months later reveals the same conflict over communication. Lyn reported mentioning to Tommy that she missed their old routine of talking together every evening, "looking at each other and listening."

> And he said, "Yeah, I've missed it too." I almost dropped dead, because a year ago he never would have said that. . . . and I said one of the reasons we haven't done it is that I got tired being the one hundred percent initiator of it.

In other aspects of love besides talking, Tommy is far from withdrawn or resistant. Lyn reports that he was quick to change when she asked him for help with "physical" and not "emotional" things, like "help me with the kids, help me with the shopping; at one point he used to do the shopping every week. . . ."[29] Tommy apparently has always been more interested in sexual intimacy than she, and in the past few years she has rarely taken the initiative. When he recently bought the book *How to Make Love to a Woman,* she was delighted that he was interested in "something beside just the physical end" and was willing to admit that he didn't know everything. But when he suggested that she read *How to Make Love to a Man,* her reaction was a vague "I might." Both Gilmores seem to accept a feminized definition of love according to which Lyn is deprived of the kind of love she wants but not Tommy. Thus, Tommy's only response to how he would like to change the relationship is "I would change it so we have more time together. I look forward to that as the kids get older." He made no reference to sex.

The Gilmores' tendency to treat their emotional relationship as Lyn's domain is probably reinforced by their belief that Tommy is a rational "loner" who is focused on his work, and that Lyn is a "feeling person" who is skilled at relating to people.[30] Lyn has several close friends; Tommy has none, and even reports getting "real itchy" at work when he has to be "one-on-one talking to people." Lyn seems to have a good relationship with her daughters and tries to be attuned to their unspoken troubles and needs. Tommy seems uncomfortable with his children, and Lyn says he is an "authoritarian" father. "He's always been one of these people who says, 'Do what I say or I'm going to slug you,' which he never does, but . . . they don't really react to that very well."

The imbalance of power and overt dependency in their marriage also contributes to their conflict. Lyn not only is completely dependent on Tommy financially, but she believes she could not survive economically without him, even though she was a registered nurse before marriage. She often expresses her fear about "what could happen if anything ever happened to him." As Tommy commented:

> It seems to be an underlying thought that she always expresses. "If you die, I'm not going to have any way to take care of the kids." I don't think she is so much afraid of my dying as she is of fending for herself in a situation like that. . . . So right now she's expanding and she's trying to move out into a self-sufficient, stand-by-herself-type person.

Except for the sphere of intimate communication, Lyn defers to Tommy's authority. Before returning to school last year, she comments:

> I used to just care about what he thought, not what I thought. . . . I was just a housewife, mother, Mrs. Gilmore . . . never Lyn, a person, and I allowed that and never did anything about that. I never said, "Hey, pay attention to me, I'm a human being," and when I would get put down in different ways, I would just go around and be depressed periodically.

Lyn still seems fearful about confronting her husband directly. Thus, to get him to agree to be interviewed, she thought about how to approach him for a few days. Then one evening,

> I said something like, "Boy, you've really given me so much support. I have a friend who is doing a study comparing people who give each other support and some who don't. . . ." Then I presented him with the questions . . . and dropped it.

This is her usual strategy for persuading him to do something "if it doesn't come from his mind, and it comes from mine." To avoid threatening him, she has learned to "just bring it up, mention it, and drop it. And when he's ready he'll bring it up again or maybe I'll wait a week and if he hasn't mentioned it, I'll bring it up again."

Lyn is also cautious about trying to change the division of labor at home, and Tommy seems successful in resisting primary responsibility for housework or child care. Although he does a lot of the work at home, it is defined as "babysitting" or "helping Lyn," and she is careful to appreciate his efforts. For example, he agreed to do the shopping, but insisted that she decide on the shopping list.

Lyn describes what happened last Monday when Tommy was in charge of the children and didn't notice that one of them was very sick.

> Tuesday, Loren had to stay home from school. Monday night, I came in from here and found Loren had a hundred and two fever, and he felt terrible because he hadn't realized it. Then he asked me what classes I have on Tuesday. I told him one class from eleven to twelve . . . and he said, "Well, I'll come home from work. I'll babysit Loren so you don't have to miss your class." I mean I said, "Oh, you doll." I complimented him, I try not to be too gushy with the compliments because that turns him off. . . . He was a real doll about it when I was a little nervous about how he'd accept it.

While Lyn's interviews convey her deference to her husband and "nervousness" about his reactions, Tommy talked as if there was no power imbalance. In fact, he complained about her attempts to dominate him by getting him to do more around the house. "She tries to put bounds on me that I don't see myself putting on her,"and tries to set up "a dominance-type thing" instead of a "sharing balance." But when asked how he handled her attempts at dominance he said with a laugh, "I just ignore it," suggesting that at some level he is aware of his power.

Lyn's dependency on her husband probably intensifies her need to get emotionally closer to him and improve their communication. Her powerlessness also leads her to suppress her feelings of being overburdened at home, and produces underground anger that comes out in periodic fights with her husband. Lyn describes a "really bad argument about communication":[31]

> It happened right in the middle of the restaurant and I ended up leaving the restaurant. What really bummed me out was that he said, "When all you think about is yourself . . ." and that was all he needed to say. . . . I had just spoken to him about the fact that I make sure every day before I leave for class that all the children are taken care of. . . . I write notes to the sitter and to the kids about what to do, and usually the dinner is set out, and five hundred other things . . . and all he has to do is take care of Tommy and leave . . . and then he calls me only thinking of myself.

One of the interesting aspects of this fight is that it began when Lyn tried to change the family's plans so she could have her weekly breakfast with her best friend. Tommy's jealousy about Lyn's friend seems to have ignited his anger. Tommy seems quite dependent on Lyn; perhaps just as dependent as she is on him, but his dependency remains covert, hidden from both himself and his wife. Therefore, it does not undermine his power advantage.

Despite these strains, the Gilmores have a strong attachment that will probably survive this stressful period of their lives when they are adjusting to Lyn's new life and are pressured by the demands of children, his career and her school. Lyn remains eternally hopeful that their communication will improve. "I think it will get easier, especially if we both sit down and talk, just a little bit every night, and practice some of these things we both need to work on." Tommy loves to watch her develop, "in spite of it's being aggravating at times." "She's coming into her own," he observes, growing "beyond the confines of responding to other people's needs into responding to her own needs." For him, "it's like watching a new person blossom. And I'm excited for her, as much as I am for us." Tommy himself is showing signs of "blossoming" recently, and has just enrolled in the course, "A Helping Relationship," at the community college.

NOTES

1. Pierre Mornell, *Passive men, wild women.* New York: Ballantine Books, 1979, pp. 2–3.

2. Mirra Komarovsky, *Blue-collar marriage.* New York: Random House, 1962; Lillian Rubin, *Worlds of pain.* New York: Basic Books, 1976. The laboratory study is described in Harold Rausch et al., *Communication, conflict & marriage.* San Francisco: Jossey-Bass, 1974. The couple survey is reported in Ronald Burke, Tamara Weir and Denise Harrison, Disclosure of problems and tensions experienced by marital partners. *Psychological Reports,* 1976, *38,* 531–542.

3. Rubin, op. cit., pp. 120–121.

4. This quote and all others that are not attributed to published studies are from open-ended interviews about close marriage and friendship conducted by myself, Eileen Pinkerton and Cynthia Garlich. Eileen Pinkerton interviewed the Gilmores. Most interviews lasted several hours, and the respondent's spouse and friends were also interviewed in most cases.

5. The data are from a nonrandom sample of 106 people who were acquaintances of the undergraduates who did the interviewing, including 46 married or long-term couples and 14 individuals. The mean age was 37, and 69 of the people were married. The findings I reported are from a question that presents a hypothetical conflict, where the first person wants to work on the relationship and needs more closeness, while the second person wants to leave things be and needs more freedom. Respondents were asked if such situations came up in their relationship, and whether they sympathized with the first or the second person. 33 women and 25 men identified with wanting closeness, 10 women and 17 men identified with wanting freedom, and 9 women and 12 men said the situation never came up in their relationships and they did not sympathize with either person.

6. Lillian Rubin, *Intimate strangers.* New York: Harper and Row, 1983, p. 90.

7. The next most frequent responses referred to being caring and supportive, and being tolerant and understanding. Ann Swidler reports similar findings from her interviews in *Ideologies of love in middle class America.* Paper read at Annual Meetings of the Pacific Sociological Association, San Diego, 1982.

8. Another parallel is that husbands typically seem to control the amount of talking, by vetoing or going along with their wives' efforts to talk. Wives control the frequency of sex, by vetoing or going along with their husbands initiative, at least in the middle-class couples examind in several studies. For an analysis of husbands and wives' preferences for sex, see Judith Long Laws, A feminist review of the marital adjustment literature. *Journal of Marriage and the Family,* 1971, *33,* 483–517.

9. Rubin, 1976, pp. 136 and 146.

10. For an excellent review of research on men's and women's styles of love, see Letita Peplau and Steve Gordon, Women and men in love: Sex differences in close relationships. In *Women, gender, and social psychology,* Virginia O'Leary, R. Unger and B. Wallston (Eds.), Hillsdale, New Jersey: Erlbaum, in press.

11. James L. Collier, When a man marries. *Reader's Digest,* October 1966.

12. Paul Rosenblatt and Robert Phillips, Jr., Family articles in popular magazines. *Family Coordinator,* 1975, *24,* 267–271.

13. Similarly, if the couple believes that love is shown by an activity which is usually defined as men's turf, such as sex, wives are likely to feel controlled when he wants to "be intimate." She may then respond with withdrawal and passivity.

14. Collier, op. cit.

15. Lois Gould, *Final analysis.* New York: Random House, 1974, p. 26.

16. Also, if the couple begins their relationship by "falling in love," then they will both be very dependent on each other and very concerned with maintaining their love. Being in love seems to make it acceptable for men to be emotionally dependent and powerless in relation to a woman.

17. For excellent descriptions of the negative effects of their economic position on working-class couples, see Lillian Rubin, 1976, and Mirra Komarovsky, 1962. Melvin Kohn shows how alienating jobs that allow workers little self-direction have negative effects on family life in *Class and conformity,* Homewood, Illinois: Dorsey Press, 1969.

18. Joan Aldous and colleagues make this interpretation on the basis of several studies of marriage in different social classes. See Joan Aldous, Marie Osmond, and M. Hicks, Men's work and men's families. In Wesley Burr, Reuben Hill, F. Ivan Nye, Ira L. Reiss (Eds.), *Contemporary theories about the family,* Vol. I, pp. 227–256. New York: Free Press, 1979.

19. For example, J M. Pahl and R. E. Pahl, *Managers and their wives.* London: Allen Lane and Penguin Press, 1971, and Daniel Levinson, *The seasons of a man's life.* New York: Knopf, 1978.

20. Arlie Hochschild describes how a young woman professor with a young child and successful husband experiences this situation, in her brilliant essay, Inside the clockwork of the male career. In Florence Howe (Ed.), *Women and the power to change.* New York: McGraw-Hill, 1975.

21. See for example R. Blood and D. Wolfe, *Husbands and wives.* New York, Free Press, 1960; and Norval Glenn and Sara McClanachan, Children and marital happiness. *Journal of Marriage and the Family,* 1982, *44,* 63–72.

22. This pattern was reported by the national survey described in Gerald Gurin, J. Veroff and S. Feld, *Americans view their mental health.* New York: Basic Books, 1960.

23. If this argument is applied to men, it suggests that men are less apt to want more sex from their wives if they are successful at and identified with their work.

24. Men may have more difficulty than women in experiencing work as intrinsically gratifying, because being successful at work is required of a man.

25. The power difference between the sexes has been the major focus of feminist research. For a sampling, of this work, see Barrie Thorne (Ed.) *Rethinking the family.* New York: Longman, 1982; and Marcia Millman and Rosabeth Kanter (Eds.), *Another voice.* Garden City, N.Y.: Doubleday, 1975.

26. Jessie Bernard, *The future of marriage.* New York: Bantam Books, 1972.

27. Nancy Chodorow's theory, which I have greatly simplified, is presented in her book, *The reproduction of mothering.* Berkeley: University of California Press, 1978, and a similar theory is presented in Dorothy Dinnerstein, *The mermaid and the minotaur: Sexual arrangements and human malaise.* New York: Harper & Row, 1976. Lillian Rubin gives an excellent short summary of Chodorow and uses the

theory to explain men's incapacity for intimacy in marriage, in *Intimate strangers,* op. cit.

28. Tommy went on to add, "So I think that now I am starting to share more with her, there's less of a need for it. So it's almost like the boomerang came back and there's no one for it to hit, or now that it's come back the target's moved." This is one of several comments in his interview suggesting his dependence on her and his sense of being rejected by her in favor of her new interests.

29. She goes on to mention the nonphysical things she also needed. "I guess I never knew I needed emotional support and connections. I always tried to find that with other friends, other women, when in fact I would like some from him. . . ."

30. This is a nice example of how couples establish a shared definition of reality, or congruent images of each other, as discussed in Robert Hess and Gerald Handel, *Family worlds: A psychosocial approach to family life.* Chicago: University of Chicago Press, 1959.

31. This is from an interview done six months after those quoted previously.

17

Stages in the Infant's Separation From the Mother

MARGARET S. MAHLER, FRED PINE,
AND ANNI BERGMAN

The biological birth of the human infant and the psychological birth of the individual are not coincident in time. The former is a dramatic, observable, and well-circumscribed event; the latter a slowly unfolding intrapsychic process.

For the more or less normal adult, the experience of himself as both fully in, and fully separate from, the "world out there" is taken for granted as a given of life. Consciousness of self and absorption without awareness of self are two polarities between which he moves with varying ease and with varying degrees of alternation or simultaneity. But this, too, is the result of a slowly unfolding process.

We refer to the psychological birth of the individual as the *separation-individuation process:* the establishment of a sense of separateness from, and relation to, a world of reality, particularly with regard to the experiences of *one's own body* and to the principal representative of the world as the infant experiences it, the *primary love object.* Like any intrapsychic process, this one reverberates throughout the life cycle. It is never finished; it remains always active; new phases of the life cycle see new derivatives

From *The psychological birth of the human infant: symbiosis and individuation,* by Margaret S. Mahler, Fred Pine, and Anni Bergman. © 1975 by Margaret S. Mahler. New York: Basic Books, 1975, pp. 3–119. Reprinted by permission of Basic Books, Inc., Publishers. The material presented in this chapter represents the main concepts relevant to the present volume. Material has been deleted in order to achieve continuity.

Margaret S. Mahler, a psychoanalyst, is Director of Research, Masters Children's Center, New York. Fred Pine is Associate Professor of Psychology and Director of Psychology, Bronx Municipal Hospital and Albert Einstein College of Medicine. Anni Bergman is Adjunct Professor of Psychology, City University of New York.

of the earliest processes still at work. But the principal psychological achievements of this process take place in the period from about the fourth or fifth month to the thirtieth or thirty-sixth month, a period we refer to as the *separation-individuation phase.*

The normal separation-individuation process, following upon a developmentally normal symbiotic period, involves the child's achievement of separate functioning in the presence of, and with the emotional availability of, the mother (Mahler, 1963); the child is continually confronted with minimal threats of object loss (which every step of the maturational process seems to entail). In contrast to situations of traumatic separation, however, this normal separation-individuation process takes place in the setting of a developmental readiness for, and pleasure in, independent functioning.

Separation and individuation are conceived of as two complementary developments: separation consists of the child's emergence from a symbiotic fusion with the mother (Mahler, 1952), and individuation consists of those achievements marking the child's assumption of his own individual characteristics. These are intertwined, but not identical, developmental processes; they may proceed divergently, with a developmental lag or precocity in one or the other. Thus, premature locomotor development, enabling a child to separate physically from the mother, may lead to premature awareness of separateness before internal regulatory mechanisms (cf Schur, 1966), a component of individuation, provide the means to cope with this awareness. Contrariwise, an omnipresent infantilizing mother who interferes with the child's innate striving for individuation, usually with the autonomous locomotor function of his ego, may retard the development of the child's full awareness of self-other differentiation, despite the progressive or even precocious development of his cognitive, perceptual, and affective functions.

From the observable and inferred beginnings of the infant's primitive cognitive-affective state, with unawareness of self-other differentiation, a major organization of intrapsychic and behavioral life develops around issues of separation and individuation, an organization that we recognize by terming the subsequent period the separation-individuation phase. We will describe the steps in this process (the subphases), beginning with the earliest signs of differentiation, proceeding through the period of the infant's absorption in his own autonomous functioning to the near exclusion of mother, then through the all-important period of rapprochement in which the child, precisely because of his more clearly perceived state of separateness from mother, is prompted to redirect his main attention back to mother, and finally to a feeling of a primitive sense of self, of entity and individual identity, and to steps toward constancy of the libidinal object and of the self.

We wish to emphasize our focus on *early* childhood. We do not mean to imply, as is sometimes loosely done, that every new separation or step toward a revised or expanded feeling of self at any age is part of the separation-individuation process. That would seem to us to dilute the concept and erroneously to direct it away from that *early intrapsychic achievement of a sense of separateness that we see as its core.* An old, partially unresolved sense of self-identity and of body boundaries, or old conflicts over separation and separateness, can be reactivated (or can remain peripherally or even centrally active) at any and all stages of life; but it is the original infantile process, not the new eliciting events or situations, to which we shall address ourselves.

In terms of its place in the larger body of psychoanalytic theory, we consider our work to bear especially on two main issues: adaptation and object relationship.

ADAPTATION

It was rather late in the developmental history of psychoanalysis that Hartmann (1939) began to bring a perspective on adaptation into psychoanalytic theory. Perhaps that is because, in the clinical psychoanalysis of adults, so much seems to stem from within the patient—from his long-standing character traits and dominating fantasies. But in work with infants and children, adaptation impresses itself forcibly on the observer. From the beginning the child molds and unfolds in the matrix of the mother–infant dual unit. Whatever adaptations the mother may make to the child, and whether she is sensitive and empathic or not, it is our strong conviction that the child's fresh and pliable adaptive capacity, and his need for adaptation (in order to gain satisfaction), is far greater than that of the mother, whose personality, with all its patterns of character and defense, is firmly and often rigidly set (Mahler, 1963). The infant takes shape in harmony and counterpoint to the mother's ways and style—whether she herself provides a healthy or a pathological object for such adaptation. Metapsychologically, the focus of the *dynamic* point of view—the conflict between impulse and defense—is far less important in the earliest months of life than it will come to be later on, when structuralization of the personality will render intra- and intersystemic conflicts of paramount importance. Tension, traumatic anxiety, biological hunger, ego apparatus, and homeostasis are near-biological concepts that are relevant in the earliest months and are the precursors, respectively, of anxiety with psychic content, signal anxiety, oral or other drives, ego functions, and internal regulatory mechanisms (defense and character traits). The *adaptive* point of view is most relevant in early infancy, the infant being born into the very crest of the adaptational demands upon him. Fortunately, these demands are met by the infant's ability, in the pliability and unformedness of his personality, to be shaped by, and to shape himself to, his environment. The child's facility for conforming to the shape of his environment is already present in early infancy.

OBJECT RELATIONSHIP

We feel that our contribution has a special place in the psychoanalytic study of the history of object relationship. Early psychoanalytic writings showed that the development of object relationship was dependent upon the drives (Freud, 1905; Abraham, 1921, 1924; Fenichel, 1945). Concepts such as narcissism (primary and secondary), ambivalence, sadomasochism, oral or anal character, and the oedipal triangle relate simultaneously to problems of drive and of object relationship (cf. also Mahler, 1960). Our contribution should be seen as supplemental in showing the growth of object relationship from narcissism parallel with the early life history of the ego, set in the context of concurrent libidinal development. The cognitive-affective achievement of an awareness of separateness as a precondition of true object relationship, the role of the ego apparatuses (for example, motility, memory, perception) and of more complex ego functions (such as reality testing) in fostering such awareness are at the center of our work. We try to show how object relationship develops from infantile symbiotic or primary narcissism and alters parallel with the achievement of separation and individuation, and how, in turn, ego functioning and secondary narcissism grow in the matrix of the narcissistic and, later, the object relationship to mother.

SOME DEFINITIONS

We have found, in discussions and presentations over the years, that three of our basic concepts are misunderstood often enough to warrant clarification. First, we use the term *separation* or *separateness* to refer to the *intrapsychic* achievement of a sense of separateness from mother and, through that, from the world at large. (This very sense of separateness is what the psychotic child is unable to achieve.) This sense of separateness gradually leads to clear intrapsychic representations of the self as distinguished from the representations of the object world (Jacobson, 1964). Naturally, in the normal course of developmental events, real physical separations (routine or otherwise) from mother are important contributors to the child's sense of being a separate person—but it is the sense of being a separate individual, and not the fact of being physically separated from someone, that we will be discussing. (Indeed, in certain aberrant conditions, the physical fact of separation can lead to ever more panic-stricken disavowal of the fact of separateness and to the delusion of symbiotic union.)

Second, we use the term *symbiosis* (Mahler and Furer, 1966) similarly, to refer to an intrapsychic rather than a behavioral condition; it is thus an inferred state. We do not refer, for example, to clinging behavior, but rather to a feature of primitive cognitive-affective life wherein the differentiation between self and mother has not taken place, or where regression to that self-object undifferentiated state (which characterized the symbiotic phase) has occurred. Indeed, this does not necessarily require the physical presence of the mother, but it may be based on primitive images of oneness and/or scotomatization or disavowal of contradictory perceptions (see also Mahler, 1960).

Third, Mahler (1958a,b) has earlier referred to infantile autism and symbiotic psychosis as two extreme disturbances of identity. We use the term *identity* to refer to the earliest awareness of a sense of being, of entity—a feeling that includes in part, we believe, a cathexis of the body with libidinal energy. It is not a sense of *who* I am but *that* I am; as such, this is the earliest step in the process of the unfolding of individuality.

A PRELIMINARY NOTE ON OBSERVATION AND INFERENCE

The question of the kind of inferences that can be drawn from direct observation of the preverbal period is a most controversial one. The problem is complicated by the fact that not only is the infant preverbal, but the verbal means of the observer-conceptualizer lend themselves only very poorly to the translation of such material. The problems of psychoanalytic *recon*struction here find their parallel in the problem of psychoanalytic construction—the construction of a picture of the inner life of the preverbal child, a task in which coenesthetic empathy, we believe, plays a central role. Although we cannot ultimately prove the correctness of such constructions, we nonetheless believe that they can be useful, and we are committed to attempting their formulation.

Analysts have taken positions that vary along a broad spectrum regarding efforts to understand the preverbal period. At one extreme stand those who believe in innate complex oedipal fantasies—those who, like Melanie Klein and her followers, impute to earliest extrauterine human mental life a quasi-phylogenetic memory, an inborn symbolic process (Mahler, 1969; Furer, quoted by Glenn, 1966). At the other end of the spectrum stand those Freudian analysts who look with favor on stringent verbal and reconstructive evidence—organized on the basis of Freud's metapsychological constructs—yet who seem to accord preverbal material little right to serve as the basis for even the most cautious and tentative extension of our main body of hypotheses. They demand that these hypotheses also be supported by reconstruction—that is to say, by clinical and, of course, predominantly verbal material. We believe that there is a broad middle ground among analysts who, with caution, are ready to explore the contributions to theory that can come from inferences regarding the preverbal period (Mahler, 1971).

Generally, in making inferences regarding th preverbal period from clinical psychoanalytic data, analytic theorists are asserting their right always to ask "Why?" "How did it come about?" and to answer by tracing earlier and earlier verbalizable memories, and ultimately to connect these memories to preverbal (but manifestly observable) phenomena of infancy that are isomorphic with the verbalizable clinical phenomena; for example, Freud's (1900, p. 271) comments on dreams of flying and the infant's experience of being swooped up by adults (cf. also Anthony, 1961). That is, we study phenomena of the preverbal period that appear (from the outside) to be the kinds of experience that match up with what patients are only later able to report during analysis, in their verbalizable recollections (that is, free associations), without at that point being aware of their origins.

As in clinical psychoanalysis, our method of working was from beginning to end characterized by "free-floating attention" in order to take in the usual and the expectable, but more particularly the unexpected, surprising, and unusual behaviors and transactional sequences. As the psychoanalytic instrument, especially the ear (see Isakower, 1939), functions during analysis, so, in psychoanalytic infant observation, the psychoanalytic eye lets itself be led wherever the actual phenomenological sequences lead (cf. A. Freud, 1951b).

But beyond these general modes of psychoanalytically derived observations, the observer of the child in the preverbal period has a special observational opportunity: the opportunity to observe the body in movement. To explain one of our major bases for making inferences from nonverbal behavior, let us briefly refer to the significance of the kinesthetic function and the function of motility in the growing child. As set forth in a number of papers in the 1940's (Mahler, 1944; Mahler, Luke, and Daltroff, 1945; Mahler and Gross, 1945; Mahler, 1949a), the observation of motor, kinesthetic, and gestural (affectomotor) phenomena of the entire body can have great value. It permits one to infer what is going on inside the child; that is to say, the motor phenomena are correlated with intrapsychic events. *This is particularly true in the first years of life.*

Why? Because the motor and kinesthetic pathways are the principal expressive, defensive, and discharge pathways available to the infant (long before verbal communication takes their place). We can make inferences from them to inner states because they are the end products of inner states. One cannot be certain of the inner state, but, in the effort to infer it, multiple, repeated, and consensually validated observations and inferences offer some safeguard against total error.[1] Furthermore, in the preverbal period, by definition, speech has not yet assumed the major expressive function it will later serve, thus leaving the task of communication predominantly to the mimetic, the motor, and the gestural spheres. And finally, in the very young child, changes like modulation, inhibition, stylization, and defensive distortion of bodily expression have not yet been learned.

The young child's rich and expressive affectomotor (gestural) behavior of his entire body, as well as the back-and-forth movement of approach and appeal behaviors and distancing behaviors between infant and mother— their frequency, amplitude, timing, and intensity—served as important guidelines, furnishing many clues to phenomena we encounter through verbal communication at later ages. We watched the infant's expressive motility as it progressed beyond immediate discharge of instinctual drive, by way of the detour functions provided by the primitive ego's abilities to delay, to learn, and to anticipate. We observed and assessed the infant's autonomous and conflict-free motor functioning, with special regard to progressive steps in his separation-individuation process. In short, the observation of motor-gestural behaviors gave us important clues to intrapsychic events, and the substantive formulations to which we shall soon turn have been influenced by such observations (see Homburger, 1923; Mahler, 1944; Mahler, Luke, and Daltroff, 1945).

Instead of entering further into the general controversy regarding observation of preverbal infants and the legitimacy of inferences about the evolution of intrapsychic phenomena, we would like to present the tentative results of one such effort.

THE FORERUNNERS OF THE SEPARATION-INDIVIDUATION PROCESS

The Normal Autistic Phase

In the weeks preceding the evolution to symbiosis, the sleeplike states of the newborn and very young infant far outweigh the states of arousal. They are reminiscent of that primal state of libido distribution that prevailed in intrauterine life and that resembles the model of a closed monadic system, self-sufficient in its hallucinatory wish fulfillment.

Freud's (1911) use of the bird egg as a model of a closed psychological system comes to mind: "A neat example of a psychical system shut off from the stimuli of the external world, and able to satisfy even its nutritional requirements *autistically* . . . is afforded by a bird's egg with its food supply enclosed in its shell; for it, the care provided by its mother is limited to the provision of warmth" (p. 220n.; italics added).

In the normal autistic phase there is a relative absence of cathexis of external (especially distance-perceptual) stimuli. This is the period when the stimulus barrier (Freud, 1895, 1920), the infant's inborn unresponsiveness to outside stimuli, is clearest. The infant spends most of his day in a half-sleeping, half-waking state: he wakes principally when hunger or other need tensions (perhaps what David M. Levy [1937] meant by the concept of affect-hunger) cause him to cry, and sinks or falls into sleep again when he is satisfied, that is, relieved of surplus tensions. Physiological rather than psychological processes are dominant, and the function of this period is best seen in physiological terms. The infant is protected against extremes of stimulation, in a situation approximating the prenatal state, in order to facilitate physiological growth.

During the first few weeks of extrauterine life, a stage of absolute primary narcissism, marked by the infant's lack of awareness of a mothering agent, prevails. This is the stage we have termed *normal autism*. It is followed by a stage of dim awareness that need satisfaction cannot be provided by oneself, but comes from somewhere outside the self (primary narcissism in the beginning symbiotic phase)—Ferenczi's stage of absolute or unconditional hallucinatory omnipotence (1913). Paraphrasing Ferenczi, we might term this stage of primary narcissism the *conditional* hallucinatory omnipotence.

The Beginning of the Symbiotic Phase

The newborn's waking life centers around his continuous attempts to achieve homeostasis. The effect of his mother's ministrations in reducing the pangs of need-hunger cannot be isolated, nor can the young infant differentiate them from tension-reducing attempts of his own, such as urinating, defecating, coughing, sneezing, spitting, regurgitating, vomiting—all the ways by which the infant tries to rid himself of unpleasurable tension. The effect of these expulsive phenomena, as well as the gratification gained from his mother's ministrations, helps the infant in time to differentiate between a "pleasurable"/"good" quality and a "painful"/"bad" quality of experience (Mahler and Gosliner, 1955). (This seems to be the first quasi-ontogenetic basis of the later splitting mechanism.)

Through the inborn, autonomous perceptive faculty of the primitive ego, memory traces of the two primordial qualities of stimuli occur within the primal undifferentiated matrix, which Jacobson calls the primal psychophysiological self (in the same sense used by Fenichel and by Hartmann, Kris, and Loewenstein). We may further hypothesize that these are cathected with primordial undifferentiated drive energy (Mahler and Gosliner, 1955).

From the second month on, dim awareness of the need-satisfying object marks the beginning of the phase of normal symbiosis, in which the infant behaves and functions as though he and his mother were an omnipotent system—a dual unity within one common boundary. This is perhaps what Freud and Romain Rolland discussed in their dialogue as the sense of boundlessness of the oceanic feeling (Freud, 1930).

At this time, the quasi-solid stimulus barrier (negative because it is uncathected)—this autistic shell which kept external stimuli out—begins to crack.[2] Through the aforementioned cathectic shift toward the sensoriperceptive periphery, a protective, but also receptive and selective, positively cathected stimulus shield now begins to form and to envelop the symbiotic orbit of the mother-child dual unity (Mahler, 1967a, 1968b)

It is obvious that whereas the infant is absolutely dependent on the symbiotic partner during the symbiotic phase, symbiosis has quite a different meaning for the adult partner of the dual unity. The infant's need for the mother is absolute; the mother's need for the infant is relative.

The term *symbiosis* in this context is a metaphor. Unlike the biological concept of symbiosis, it does not describe what actually happens in a mutually beneficial relationship between two separate individuals of different species. It describes that state of undifferentiation, of fusion with mother, in which the "I" is not yet differentiated from the "not-I" and in which inside and outside are only gradually coming to be sensed as different. Any unpleasurable perception, external or internal, is projected beyond the common boundary of the symbiotic *milieu interieur* (cf. Freud's concept of the "purified pleasure ego," 1915b), which includes the mothering partner's gestalt during ministration. Only transiently—in the state of the sensorium that is termed alert inactivity (cf. Wolff, 1959)—does the young infant seem to take in stimuli from beyond the symbiotic milieu.

The essential feature of symbiosis is hallucinatory or delusional somatopsychic *omnipotent* fusion with the representation of the mother and, in particular, the delusion of a common boundary between two physically separate individuals. This is the mechanism to which the ego regresses in cases of the most severe disturbance of individuation and psychotic disorganization, which Mahler (1952; Mahler and Gosliner, 1955) has described as "symbiotic child psychosis."

Patterns of the "Holding Behavior" of Mothers. A description of various holding behaviors will suggest why we call them the symbiotic organizers of psychological birth. We observed many different kinds of holding behaviors during the symbiotic period. Breast feeding, though important, did not necessarily result in optimal closeness of the mother and her infant. One mother, for instance, proudly breast-fed her babies, but only because it was convenient (she did not have to sterilize bottles); it made her feel successful and efficient. While breast feeding her child, she supported her on her lap with the breast reaching into the baby's mouth. She did not support or cradle the baby with her arms because she wanted her arms free to do as she pleased, independent of the nursling's activity. This baby was unsmiling for a long time. When she did develop a smile, it was an unspecific, all-too-ready smiling response. This unspecific smiling response lasted well into the differentiation period and appeared in situations when, under similar circumstances, other children might show apprehension or at least sober curiosity. Another mother breast-fed her little girl, but her puritanical upbringing prevented her from feeling comfortable with a nursing infant, and she did not like to be seen nursing.

On the other hand, there was a mother who thoroughly enjoyed her children when they were infants but did not breast feed them. During feeding she held them close, supporting them well. She smiled and talked to them, and even when her baby was lying on the diapering table, she had her arms underneath him to support and cradle him. This was a mother who was particularly good with her children while they were lapbabies. Her baby son was not only very happy and content, but developed first an unspecific and then a specific smiling response very early.

One of the mothers harbored unusually high ambitions for her child in all areas of functioning. Her favorite word was "success." Her sturdily endowed baby, Junie, had to cope with the stresses of the mother's narcissistically tinged symbiotic relationship to her.

The mother's characteristic interaction with the young baby seemed to be motivated by her pride in Junie's early patterns of muscular-skeletal maturation. Junie could stiffly maintain a standing position on mother's lap, and mother would clap Junie's hands as if she were already at the pat-a-cake age. Keeping the little body erect on her lap did not leave Junie's hands free to pat or explore her mother; she would undoubtedly have done so if left to her own devices. This pattern of standing Junie erect,[3] of which her mother was inordinately proud, became, of course, greatly libidinized and preferred by the young infant. The highly invested pattern of erecting herself on mother's lap and other surfaces became very marked in Junie's first motor patterns. Later, at the beginning of the practicing period, the impulse to stand up seemed to be a most prominent pattern in Junie's locomotor repertoire, *interfering* (that is, competing) for a relatively long time with the desirable, more mature motor pattern of *propelling oneself forward toward a goal* (which dominates most infants' subsequent motor behavior). Junie's inclination to stand up interfered with her ability to move her arms and legs forward, to make them work together to approach the mother, to crawl forward. Crawling was one of the motor achievements that Junie's mother impatiently encouraged and expected her baby to attain.

In observing that favorite patterns of mothering were taken over by the infant (see Tolpin, 1972), we noted that this seemed to be especially true if the pattern signified some frustration or some particular gratification. For example, during the weaning process, after a period of happy breast feeding, Carl's mother warded off and tried to deny her infant's clamoring for her breast, his clawing and tearing at her blouse to get to the breast. She comforted him by bouncing him up and down in her lap. The little boy later actively took over this bouncing up and down pattern and eventually converted it into a peek-a-boo game (see Kleeman, 1967). In this case, the mother's "bouncing pattern" was subsequently used by the boy in a game that was related to his mother, and later he sought social contact with his parents and visitors through his own rendition of the lovely peek-a-boo pattern that became the hallmark of his socializing rapprochement behavior. Thus, in Carl's case, the pattern served a constructive, adaptive, developmental purpose.[4]

Another little girl actively took over her mother's rocking pattern. The mother was an immature, highly narcissistic woman whose caretaking patterns had a mechanical quality. She would rock the baby in her lap in a tense, unrelated way. When the pattern was taken over by the child, it was not used in the mother-child relationship. The rocking was used in this case for self-comforting and for autoerotic self-stimulation, as if the child were playing mother to herself. During the subphase of differentiation, this little girl would try to augment the pleasure of rocking herself by rocking in front of a mirror, thereby adding a visual feedback to the kinesthetic pleasure. In contrast to Carl's case, the pattern taken over by this little girl served no adaptive, developmental purpose, but only contributed to her narcissism.

FIRST SUBPHASE OF THE SEPARATION-INDIVIDUATION PROCESS: HATCHING

The "hatching process" is, we believe, a gradual ontogenetic evolution of the sensorium—the perceptual-conscious system—which enables the infant to have a more *permanently alert* sensorium whenever he is awake (cf. also Wolff, 1959).

In other words, the infant's attention, which during the first months of symbiosis was in large part *inwardly* directed, or focused in a coenesthetic vague way *within the symbiotic orbit,* gradually expands through the coming into being of outwardly directed perceptual activity during the child's increasing periods of wakefulness. This is a change of degree rather than of kind, for during the symbiotic stage the child has certainly been highly attentive to the mothering figure. But gradually that attention is combined with a growing store of memories of mother's comings and goings, of "good" and "bad" experiences; the latter were altogether unrelievable by the self, but could be "confidently expected" to be relieved by mother's ministrations.

Observing the infants in our setup, we came to recognize at some point during the differentiation subphase a certain new look of alertness, persistence and goal-directedness. We have taken this look to be a behavioral manifestation of "hatching" and have loosely said that an infant with this look "has hatched." This new gestalt was unmistakable to the members of our staff, but it is difficult to define with specific criteria. It is probably best described in terms of state (cf. Wolff, 1959). The child no longer seems to drift in and out of alertness, but has a more permanently alert sensorium whenever he is awake.

At about six months, tentative experimentation at separation-individuation begins. This can be observed in behavior on the part of the infant such as pulling at mother's hair, ears, or nose, putting food into the mother's mouth, and straining his body away from mother in order to have a better look at her, to scan her and the environment. This is in contrast to simply molding into mother when held (cf. Spock, 1963). There are definite signs that the baby begins to differentiate his own from the mother's body. Six to seven months is the peak of manual, tactile, and visual exploration of the mother's face, as well as of the covered (clad) and unclad parts of the mother's body; these are the weeks during which the infant discovers with fascination a brooch, a pair of eyeglasses, or a pendant worn by the mother. There may be engagement in peek-a-boo games in which the infant still plays a passive role (Kleeman, 1967). These explorative patterns later develop into the cognitive function of checking the unfamiliar against the already familiar.

THE SECOND SUBPHASE: PRACTICING

The child's first upright, independent steps mark the onset of the practicing period par excellence, with substantial widening of his world and of reality testing. Now begins a steadily increasing libidinal investment in practicing motor skills and in exploring the expanding environment, both human and inanimate. The chief characteristic of this practicing period is the child's great narcissistic investment in his own functions, his own body, as well as in the objects and objectives of his expanding "reality." Along with this, we see a relatively great imperviousness to knocks and falls and other frustrations, such as a toy being grabbed by another child. Substitute familiar adults within the setup of our nursery are easily accepted (in contrast to what occurs during the next subphase of separation-individuation).

The smoothly separating and individuating toddler finds narcissistic solace for the minimal threats of object loss, which probably each new step of progressive development entails, in his rapidly developing ego functions. The child concentrates on practicing and mastering his own skills and autonomous (independent of other or mother) capacities. He is exhilarated by his own abilities, continually delighted with the discoveries he makes in his expanding world, and quasi-enamored with the world and his own grandeur and omnipotence. We might consider the possibility that the elation of this subphase has to do not only with the exercise of the ego apparatuses, but also with the elated escape from fusion with, from engulfment by, mother. From this point of view we would consider that, just as the infant's peek-a-boo games seem to turn from passive to active, the losing and regaining of the need-gratifying object and then the love object, so too does the toddler's constant running off until he is swooped up by his mother turn from passive to active the fear of being reengulfed by mother.

This behavior also reassures him that mother will *want* to catch him and swoop him up in her arms. We need not assume that such behavior is intended to serve these functions when it first emerges, but only that it produces these effects and can then be intentionally repeated.

Quite late in our study, we came to realize that it is the rule rather than the exception that the first unaided steps taken by the infant are in a direction away from the mother or during her absence; this contradicts the popular belief (reflected by Kierkegaard, among other poets) that the first steps are taken toward mother. The significance of this phenomenon bears further study.

Many of the mothers seemed to react to the fact that their infants were moving away by helping them move away, that is, by giving them a gentle or perhaps less gentle push, as the mother bird would encourage the fledgling. Mothers usually became very interested in, but sometimes also critical of, their children's functioning at this point. They began to compare notes, and they showed concern if their child seemed to be behind. Sometimes they would hide their concern in a pointed display of nonconcern. In many mothers, concern became especially concentrated in eagerness for their children to walk. Once the child was able to move away some distance, it was as if suddenly the mother began to worry about whether the child would be able to "make-it" out there in the world where he would have to fend for himself. Upright free locomotion seems to become for many mothers the supreme proof of the fact that the infant has "made it."

In summary, walking seems to have great symbolic meaning for both mother and toddler: it is as if the walking toddler has proved by his attainment of independent upright locomotion that he has already graduated into the world of independent human beings. The expectation and confidence that the mother exudes when she feels the child is now able to "make it" out there seems to be an important trigger for the child's own feeling of safety and perhaps also the initial encouragement for his exchanging some of his magic omnipotence for pleasure in his own autonomy and his developing self-esteem.

THE THIRD SUBPHASE: RAPPROCHEMENT

General Considerations

With the acquisition of upright, free locomotion and with the closely following attainment of that stage of cognitive development that Piaget (1936) regards as the beginning of representational intelligence (which will culminate in symbolic play and in speech), the human being has emerged as a separate and autonomous person. These two powerful "organizers" (Spitz, 1965) constitute the midwives of psychological birth. In this final stage of the "hatching" process, the toddler reaches the first level of identity—that of being a separate individual entity (Mahler, 1958b).

By the middle of the second year of life, the infant has become a toddler. He now becomes more and more aware, and makes greater and greater use, of his physical separateness. However, side by side with the growth of his cognitive faculties and the increasing differentiation of his emotional life, there is also a noticeable waning of his previous imperviousness to frustration, as well as a diminution of what has been a relative obliviousness to his mother's presence. Increased separation anxiety can be observed: at first this consists mainly of fear of object loss, which is to be inferred from many of the child's behaviors. The relative lack of concern about the mother's presence that was characteristic of the practicing subphase is now replaced by seemingly constant concern with the mother's whereabouts, as well as by active approach behavior. As the toddler's *awareness* of separateness grows—stimulated by his maturationally acquired ability to move away physically from his mother and by his cognitive growth—he seems to have an increased need, a wish for mother to share with him every one of his new skills and experiences, as well as a great need for the object's love.

The need for closeness had been held in abeyance, so to speak, throughout the practicing period. For this reason we have given this subphase the name of *rapprochement.*

The shadowing and darting-away patterns. Two characteristic patterns of the toddler's behavior—the "shadowing"[5] of mother and the darting away from her, with the expectation of being chased and swept into her arms—indicate both his wish for reunion with the love object and his fear of reengulfment by it. One can continually observe in the toddler a "warding-off" pattern directed against impingement upon his recently achieved autonomy. On the other hand, his incipient fear of loss of love represents an element of the conflict on the way to internalization. Some toddlers of rapprochement age already seem to be rather sensitive to disapproval; still, autonomy is defended by the "No," as well as by the increased aggression and negativism of the anal phase. (One is here reminded of Anna Freud's classic paper on negativism and emotional surrender, 1951a.)

In other words, at the time when the junior toddler of 12 to 15 months has grown into the senior toddler of up to 24 months, a most important emotional turning point has been reached. Now the toddler begins to experience, more or less gradually and more or less keenly, the obstacles that lie in the way of what he evidently anticipated at the height of his "practicing" exhilaration would be his "conquest of the world." Concomitant with the acquisition of primitive skills and perceptual cognitive faculties, there has been an increasingly clear differentiation, a separation, between the intrapsychic representation of the object and the self-representation. At the very height of mastery, toward the end of the practicing period, it had already begun to dawn on the junior toddler that the world is *not* his oyster, that he must cope with it more or less "on his own," very often as a relatively helpless, small, and separate individual, unable to command relief or assistance merely by feeling the need for it, or even by giving voice to that need (Mahler, 1966*b*).

The quality and measure of the wooing behavior of the toddler toward his mother during this subphase provide important clues to the normality of the individuation process. Fear of losing the love of the object (instead of fear of object loss) becomes increasingly evident.

Incompatibilities and misunderstanding between mother and child can be observed, even in the case of the normal mother and her normal toddler; these are to a great extent rooted in certain contradictions of this subphase. The toddler's demand for his mother's constant involvement seems contradictory to the mother: while he is now not as dependent and helpless as he was only a half year before, and seems eager to become less and less so, nevertheless he even more insistently indicates that he expects the mother to share every aspect of his life. During this subphase, some mothers cannot accept the child's demandingness; others, by contrast, are unable to face the child's gradual separation—the fact that the child is becoming increasingly independent of and separate from her and can no longer be regarded as a part of her (cf. Masterson, 1973; Stoller, 1973).

In this third subphase, that of rapprochement, while individuation proceeds very rapidly and the child exercises it to the limit, he also becomes more and more aware of his separateness and employs all kinds of mechanisms in order to resist and undo his actual separateness from mother. The fact is, however, that no matter how insistently the toddler tries to coerce the mother, she and he can no longer function effectively as a dual unit— that is to say, the child can no longer maintain his delusion of parental omnipotence, which he still at times expects will restore the symbiotic status quo.

Verbal communication becomes more and more necessary; gestural coercion on the part of the toddler or mutual preverbal empathy between mother and child will no longer suffice to attain the goal of satisfaction— that of well-being in Joffe and Sandler's sense (1965). The junior toddler gradually realizes that his love objects (his parents) are separate individuals with their own personal interests. He must gradually and painfully give up the delusion of his own grandeur, often by way of dramatic fights with mother—less so, it seemed to us, with father. This is the crossroads that we term the "rapprochement crisis."

The mother's attitude in the toddler's rapprochement period. Depending upon her own adjustment, the mother may react to the child's demands during this period either with continued emotional availability and playful participation or with a gamut of less desirable attitudes. It is, however, the mother's continued emotional availability, we have found, that is essential if the child's autonomous ego is to attain optimal functional capacity, while his reliance on magic omnipotence recedes. If the mother is "quietly available" with a ready supply of object libido, if she shares the toddling adventurer's exploits, playfully reciprocates, and thus facilitates his salutary attempts at imitation and *identification,* then internalization of the relationship between mother and toddler is able to progress to the point where, in time, verbal communication takes over, even though vivid gestural behavior—that is, affectomotility—still predominates (Homburger, 1923; Mahler, 1944, 1949a). Predictable emotional involvement on the part of the mother seems to facilitate the rich unfolding of the toddler's thought processes, reality testing, and coping behavior by the end of the second or the beginning of the third year. On the other hand, as we learned rather late in our study, the emotional growth of the mother in her parenthood, her emotional willingness to let go of the toddler—to give him, as the mother bird does, a gentle push, an encouragement toward independence—is enormously helpful. It may even be a sine qua non of normal (healthy) individuation.

Danger signals in the rapprochement subphase: increased separation anxiety. The toddler's so-called "shadowing" of the mother (or the opposite "darting away" phenomenon often encountered in the beginning of this subphase) seems obligatory to a degree. (Some mothers, by their protracted doting and intrusiveness, rooted in their own anxieties and often in their own symbiotic-parasitic needs, become themselves the "shadowers" of the child.) In normal cases, shadowing by the toddler gives way to some degree of object constancy toward the second half of the third year. However, the less emotionally available the mother is at the time of rapprochement, the more insistently and even desperately does the toddler attempt to woo her. In some cases, this process drains so much of the child's available developmental energy that, as a result, not enough energy, not enough libido, and not enough constructive (neutralized) aggression are left for the evolution of the many ascending functions of the ego.

Culling from our data and their processing, we found that we could subdivide rapproachement into three periods: (1) beginning rapprochement; (2) the rapprochement crisis; and (3) individual solutions of this crisis, resulting in patternings and *personality characteristics* with which the child enters into the fourth subphase of separation-individuation, the consolidation of individuation.

We arrived at these subdivisions through comparing month by month the nine most thoroughly studied children—the last group in our study— with regard to the development of their object relations, their moods, their psychosexual and aggressive trends, as well as their cognitive development. As we describe rapprochement in more detail, we shall be drawing on examples from the detailed studies of these children.

Beginning Rapprochement

At around 15 months, we noticed an important change in the quality of the child's relationship to his mother. During the practicing period as described, mother was the "home base" to which the child returned often in times of need—need for food, need for comforting, or need for "refueling" when tired or bored. But during this period mother did not seem to have been recognized as a separate person in her own right. Somewhere around 15 months, mother was no longer just "home base"; she seemed to be turning into a person with whom the toddler wished to share his ever-widening discoveries of the world. The most important behavioral sign of this new relating was the toddler's continual bringing of things to mother, filling her lap with objects that he had found in his expanding world. They all were interesting to him, but the main emotional investment lay in the child's need to share them with her. At the same time, the toddler indicated to mother by words, sounds, or gestures that he wished her to be interested in his "findings" and to participate with him in enjoying them.

Along with the beginning awareness of separateness came the child's realization that mother's wishes seemed to be by no means always identical with his own—or contrariwise, that his own wishes did not always coincide with mother's. This realization greatly challenged the feeling of grandeur and omnipotence of the practicing period, when the little fellow had felt "on top of the world" (Mahler, 1966b). What a blow to the hitherto fully believed omnipotence; what a disturbance to the bliss of dual unity!

Parallel or concomitant with his sensing that mother was a person "out there in the world" with whom he wanted to share his pleasures, we noted that the toddler's elated preoccupation with locomotion and exploration per se was beginning to wane. The source of the child's greatest pleasure shifted from independent locomotion and exploration of the expanding inanimate world to *social interaction*. Peek-a-boo games (Kleeman, 1967), as well as games of imitation, became favorite pastimes. Recognition of mother as a separate person in the large world went parallel with awareness of other children's separate existence, their being similar yet different from one's own self. This was evidenced by the fact that children now showed a greater desire to *have* or to *do* what another child had or did—that is, a desire for mirroring, for imitating, for identifying to an extent with the other child. They wanted the toys or the cup of juice and cookie that were handed to the other child. Along with this important development there appeared specific goal-directed anger, aggression if the desired aim definitely could not be attained. We are not, of course, losing sight of the fact that these developments take place in the midst of the anal phase, with its characteristics of anal acquisitiveness, jealousy, and envy.

The discovery of the anatomical sexual difference during this period will be discussed in a later part of this chapter; suffice it to say here that for girls, the penis seems to become the prototype of a wished for but unattainable "possession" of other children. For boys and girls alike, this discovery enhanced a more distinct awareness in the child of his own body and its relation to other persons' bodies. Increasingly, the toddler seemed to experience his body per se as his own possession. No longer did he like it to be "handled." Most noticeably, he resisted being kept or held in a passive position while being dressed or diapered. He did not even seem to like to be hugged and kissed, unless he was ready for it. We felt that this claim to the body's autonomy was more accentuated in boys.

Social expansion and the importance of the father relationship. The child's desire for expanded autonomy not only found expression in negativism toward mother and others, but also led to an active extension of the mother-child world: *primarily, to include father.* Father as a love object from very early on belongs to an entirely different category of love objects from mother. Although he is not fully outside the symbiotic union, neither is he ever fully part of it. The infant, in addition, probably very early perceives a special relationship of the father to the mother, the significance of which, during the separation-individuation phase and in the later preoedipal phase, we are barely beginning to understand (Abelin, 1971; Greenacre, 1966; Mahler, 1967a).

The Rapprochement Crisis: 18–20 to 24 Months and Beyond

Grandeur and fear of loss of love. Around 18 months our toddlers seemed quite eager to exercise their rapidly growing autonomy to the hilt. Increasingly, they chose not to be reminded that at times they could not manage on their own. Conflicts ensued that seemed to hinge upon the desire to be separate, grand, and omnipotent, on the one hand, and to have mother magically fulfill their wishes, without their having to recognize that help was actually coming from the outside, on the other. In more cases than not, the prevalent mood changed to that of general dissatisfaction, insatiability, a proneness to rapid swings of mood and to temper tantrums. The period was thus characterized by the rapidly alternating desire to push mother away and to cling to her—a behavioral sequence that the word "ambitendency" describes most accurately. But already at that age there was often a simultaneous desire in both directions, that is, the characteristic *ambivalence* of children in the middle of the rapprochement subphase.

It was characteristic of children at this age to use mother as an *extension of the self*—a process in which they somehow denied the painful awareness of separateness. Typical behavior of this kind was, for example, pulling mother's hand and using it as a tool to get a desired object, or expecting that mother, summoned by some magical gesture alone rather than with words, would guess and fulfill the toddler's momentary wish. An unexpected and strange phenomenon appeared, seemingly a forerunner of the projection of one's negative feelings: this was the child's sudden anxiety that mother had left, on occasions when she had not even risen from her chair! There occurred, more or less frequently, moments of a strange, seeming "nonrecognition" of mother after a brief absence on her part.

Separation reactions during the rapprochement crisis (18 to 21 months). During the period of the most acute rapprochement crises, all the children were aware of and at times highly sensitive to mother's whereabouts when she was absent from the room. On the cognitive side, the ability to realize that mother could be elsewhere and could be found (cf. Piaget's "object permanence") was now well established. This knowledge did suffice at times to reassure the toddler when he experienced the emotion of missing his mother. In general, however, the toddler at this age did not like to be passively "left behind." *Difficulties with the process of leave-taking itself began to develop,* expressed in the reaction of clinging to mother. Usually these reactions were accompanied by a depressive mood and an initial inability, brief or prolonged, to become involved in play.

Often, during these times of intense emotional anguish after being left, the toddler would attach himself closely to one of the observers, wanting to sit on the observer's lap and occasionally even regressing into sleepy drowsiness. At such times, the observer was clearly neither another love object nor merely some person in the other-than-mother world, but rather a kind of symbiotic mother substitute, an extension of the self. Yet splitting the object world had also begun (see Kernberg, 1967). The "observers" lent themselves particularly well to the child's exercise of this defense, becoming the target of his impotent rage reactions in order to protect the good mother image from his destructive anger. This was observable particularly in those children who had had a less than optimal relationship with their mothers during the earlier subphases.

"Splitting" mechanisms at this time could take various forms. If the observer in mother's absence became the "bad mother," she could not do anything right, and a mood of general crankiness prevailed. The "good mother" was longed for, yet she seemed to exist in fantasy only. When the actual mother returned, she might be greeted with "What did you bring me?" as well as with a spectrum of angry, disappointed, and other negative reactions. Or else the observer, as the subtitute mother, might become temporarily the "good symbiotic mother," and the toddler might passively sit on her lap and eat cookies like a small infant. Yet when the actual mother returns, there might be the impulse to get to her as fast as possible, and at the same time an impulse to avoid her, as if to ward off further disappointment. The toddler might ignore mother upon her return, or go toward her and then veer away, thereafter rejecting mother's overtures. In the latter instances, it would seem that the absent mother had become the "bad" mother and thus was to be avoided. Another variation was that the mother substitute was treated ambivalently as both the "good" and the "bad" mother, like the ambivalently loved mother herself when she was present.

By about the children's twenty-first month, we made the important observation in our month-by-month comparisons that it was no longer possible to group the toddlers in accordance with the general criteria hitherto used. The vicissitudes of their individuation process were changing so rapidly that they were no longer mainly *phase specific, but individually very distinct, and different from one child to the other.* The issue in question was not so much that of realization of separateness, but rather how this realization was affected by, and in turn affected, the mother-child relationship, the father-child relationship (the latter now being clearly different from the former), and the integration of the individual child's total personality. We also observed that there seemed to develop at this time a rather significant difference in the development of the boys as compared with the girls. In our comparatively small sample of cases, the boys, if given a reasonable chance, showed a tendency to disengage themselves from mother and to enjoy their functioning in the widening world (see Greenson, 1968). The girls, on the other hand, seemed to become more engrossed with mother in her presence; they demanded greater closeness and were more persistently enmeshed in the ambivalent aspects of the relationship. This seemed connected with the realization of the sexual difference. Very importantly, the narcissistic hurt experienced by the girls of not having a penis was almost without exception blamed on the mother (see p. 313).

The beginning of gender identity. Mothers often commented that the bodies of their girl babies felt different from those of the boys, that girls were softer and more cuddly. We do not wish to argue whether this feeling of the mothers was culturally determined or whether it was due to the fact that baby girls actually mold in a more pliable way than do boys; probably both. In any case, the feeling of the mother about her child's body may well have some early patterning influence. On the whole, we did observe boys to be more motor-minded than girls and more stiffly resistant to hugging and kissing beyond and even during differentiation; we also saw that the boys were interested earlier in moving objects, such as cars and trains.

Whatever sexual differences may have preexisted in the area of innate ego apparatuses and of early ego modes, they certainly were greatly complicated, and generally compounded, by the effects of the *child's discovery of the anatomical sexual difference.* This occurred sometimes during the 16- to 17-month period or even earlier, but more often in the twentieth or twenty-first month.

The boy's discovery of his own penis usually took place much earlier. The sensory-tactile component of this discovery may even date back into the first year of life (see Roiphe and Galenson, 1972, 1973); but there is uncertainty as to its emotional impact. Around the twelfth to fourteenth month, however, we have observed that the upright position facilitates the visual and sensory-motor exploration of the penis. Possibly in combination with a maturational advance in zonal libidinization, this led to a greater cathexis of this exquisitely sensuous, pleasure-giving organ.

At any rate, the little boy's exploration of his own penis during the practicing subphase seemed at first an experience of unmitigated pleasure; several mothers reported their boy's frequent quiet masturbation at home. This differed from our observation later in the separation-individuation phase (at the end of the second and the beginning of the third year) of boys clutching their penises for reassurance.

The girls' discovery of the penis confronted them with something that they themselves were lacking. This discovery brought on a range of behaviors clearly indicating the girls' anxiety, anger, and defiance. They wanted to undo the sexual difference. Therefore, it seemed to us that in girls, masturbation took on a desperate and aggression-saturated quality more often than in boys and at an earlier age. In some of our girls, early penis envy may have accounted for the persistent predominance of this affect.

In short, we found that the task of becoming a separate individual seemed, at this point, to be generally more difficult for girls than for boys, because the girls, upon the discovery of the sexual difference, tended to turn back to mother, to blame her, to demand from her, to be disappointed in her, and still to be ambivalently tied to her. They demanded from mother that she settle a debt, so to speak. As the girl is hit with her own imperfection, she may become imperfect in the unconscious of the mother as well. Boys, on the other hand, seemed to become faced with castration anxiety only later; during the second and third year, they seemed to find it more expedient than girls to function separately; they were better able to turn to the outside world, or to their own bodies, for pleasure and satisfaction; they also turned to father as someone with whom to identify. They seemed somehow to cope with their castration anxiety in a phase of quasi-preoedipal triangulation (Abelin, 1972); in our setup, this could not be easily followed.

THE FOURTH SUBPHASE: CONSOLIDATION OF INDIVIDUALITY AND THE BEGINNINGS OF EMOTIONAL OBJECT CONSTANCY

From the point of view of the separation-individuation process, the main task of the fourth subphase is twofold: (1) the achievement of a definite, in certain aspects lifelong, individuality, and (2) the attainment of a certain degree of object constancy.

As far as the self is concerned, there is a far-reaching structuralization of the *ego*, and there are definite signs of internalization of parental demands indicating the formation of superego precursors.

The establishment of affective (emotional) object constancy (Hartmann, 1952) depends upon the gradual internalization of a constant, positively cathected, inner image of the mother. This, to begin with, permits the child to function separately (in familiar surroundings, for example, in our toddler room), despite moderate degrees of tension (longing) and discomfort. Emotional object constancy will, of course, be based in the first place on the cognitive achievement of the permanent object, but all other aspects of the child's personality development participate in this evolution as well (see McDevitt, 1972).[6] The last subphase (roughly the third year of life) is an extremely important intrapsychic developmental period, in the course of which a stable sense of entity (self boundaries) is attained. Primitive consolidation of gender identity seems to take place in this subphase as well.

But the constancy of the object implies more than the maintenance of the representation of the absent love object (cf. Mahler, 1965a; Mahler and Furer, 1966). It also implies the unifying of the "good" and "bad" object into one whole representation. This fosters the fusion of the aggressive and libidinal drives and tempers the hatred for the object when aggression is intense.

The slow establishment of emotional object constancy is a complex and multidetermined process involving all aspects of psychic development. Essential prior determinants are: (1) Trust and confidence through the regularly occurring relief of need tension provided by the need-satisfying agency as early as in the symbiotic phase. In the course of the subphases of the separation-individuation process, this relief of need tension is gradually attributed to the need-satisfying whole object (the mother) and is then transferred by means of internalization to the intrapsychic representation of the mother. (2) The cognitive acquisition of the symbolic inner representation of the permanent object (in Piaget's sense), in our instance to the unique love object: the mother. Numerous other factors are involved, such as innate drive endowment and maturation, neutralization of drive energy, reality testing, tolerance for frustration and for anxiety, and so forth.

It is only after object constancy is well on its way, which according to our conceptualization does not seem to occur before the third year (see Mahler, 1965b), that the mother during her physical absence can be substituted for, at least in part, by the presence of a reliable internal image that remains relatively stable irrespective of the state of instinctual need or inner discomfort. On the basis of this achievement, temporary separation can be lengthened and better tolerated. The establishment of object permanence and of a "mental image" of the object in Piaget's sense is a necessary, but not a sufficient, prerequisite for the establishment of libidinal object constancy. Other aspects of drive and ego maturation and development take part in the slow transition from the more primitive ambivalent love relationship, which exists only as long as it is need satisfying, to the more mature (in the ideal and rarely attained instance postambivalent) *mutual give-and-take love-object relationship* of the schoolchild and the adult.

This fourth subphase of the separation-individuation process is not a subphase in the same sense as the first three, since it is open-ended at the older end.

We see a prominent, though still only relative, shift from phenomena of the rapprochement subphase with more or less difficulty in leave-taking and increased capacity to play separately from mother, with indications that the child can increasingly hold on to the image of her ("the good mother") automatically in her absence. But these changes reach no single, definite terminal point.[7]

We have found that as this subphase proceeds, the child is in general able gradually to accept separation from the mother once again (as he did in the practicing period); in fact, when he is engrossed in play, he seems to prefer staying in the toddler room without the mother to leaving the toddler room with her. We regard this as a sign of the beginning achievement of emotional object constancy. Yet many complex conflictual and conflict-free processes seem to go on in the child in the course of the third year, rendering object constancy a still rather fluid and reversible achievement.

The Achievement of Individuality

Because the child learns to express himself verbally during this period, we can trace some of the vicissitudes of the intrapsychic separation process from the mother, and the conflicts around it, through the verbal material that we get from him, along with the phenomenology of his behavior. Verbal communication, which began during the third subphase, develops rapidly during this, the fourth subphase of separation-individuation, and slowly replaces other modes of communication, although gestural language of the whole body and affectomotility still remain very much in evidence. Play becomes more purposeful and constructive. There is a beginning of fantasy play, role playing, and make-believe. Observations about the real world become detailed and are clearly included in play, and there is an increasing interest in playmates and in adults other than mother. A sense of time (and also of spatial relations) begins to develop, and with it an increased capacity to tolerate the delay of gratification and to endure separation. Such concepts as "later" or "tomorrow" are not only understood but also used by the child of this age: *they are experimented with, polarized by his mother's comings and goings.* We see a lot of active resistance to the demands of adults, a great need and a wish (often still unrealistic) for autonomy (independence). Recurrent mild or moderate negativism, which seems to be essential for the development of a sense of identity, is also characteristic of this subphase. (The child is still mainly in the anal and early phallic phase of zonal development.)

Thus, the fourth subphase is characterized by unfolding of complex cognitive functions: verbal communication, fantasy, and reality testing. During this period of rapid ego differentiation, from about 20 or 22 months to 30 or 36 months, individuation develops so greatly that even a cursory description of it exceeds the scope of this book (Escalona, 1968). Suffice it to say that establishment of mental representations of the self as distinctly separate from representations of the object *paves the way* to self-identity formation.

In ideal cases, during the second half of the third year, the libidinal investment persists regardless of the absence of immediate satisfaction and maintains the child's emotional equilibrium during the object's temporary absenses.

During the period of normal symbiosis, the narcissistically fused object was felt to be "good"—that is, in harmony with the symbiotic self—so that primary identification took place under a positive valence of love. The less gradually, the more abruptly, intrapsychic awareness of separateness occurs, or the more intrusive and/or unpredictable the parents are, the less does the modulating, negotiating function of the ego gain ascendancy. That is to say, the less predictably reliable or the more instrusive the love object's emotional attitude in the outside world has been, the greater the extent to which the object *remains* or *becomes* an unassimilated foreign body— a "bad" introject, in the intrapsychic emotional economy (cf. Heimann, 1966). In the effort to eject this "bad introject," derivatives of the aggressive drive come into play, and there seems to develop an increased proclivity to identify the self-representation with the "bad" introject, or at least to confuse the two. If this situation surfaces during the rapprochement subphase, then aggression may be unleashed in such a way as to inundate or sweep away the "good object," and with it the good self-representation (Mahler, 1971, 1972a). This would be indicated by early severe temper tantrums, by increased attempts to coerce mother and father to function as quasi-external egos. In short, great ambivalence may ensue, which continues to mar smooth development toward emotional object constancy and sound secondary narcissism. These are the consequences for those children in whom the too sudden and too painful realization of their helplessness has resulted in a too sudden deflation of their previous sense of their own omnipotence, as well as of the shared magical omnipotence of the parents, in Edith Jacobson's (1954) sense. These are the toddlers who, in the third year in particular, show a tendency to split the object world into "good" and "bad," and for whom the "mother in the flesh" (Bowlby, 1958), "the mother after separation" (Mahler, 1971), is always disappointing, and whose self-esteem regulation is most precarious.

We have observed many of our normal children recoiling from mother or showing other signs that had to be interpreted as a kind of erotized fear upon being cornered by the mother who wanted playfully to seek bodily contact with the child. At the same time, romping games with the father were often sought and enjoyed. These behaviors, we feel, were signs of the fear of reengulfment by the narcissistically invested, yet defended against, dangerous "mother after separation," in whose omnipotence some of these children still appeared to believe, although they felt that their mothers no longer let them share in her magic powers (Mahler, 1971).

The principal conditions for mental health, so far as preoedipal development is concerned, hinge on the attained and continuing ability of the child to retain or restore his self-esteem in the context of relative libidinal object constancy. In the fourth open-ended subphase both inner structures—libidinal object constancy as well as a unified self-image based on true ego identifications—should have their inception. However, we believe that both of these structures represent merely the beginning of the ongoing developmental process.

The "internal mother," the inner image or intrapsychic representation of the mother, in the course of the third year should become more or less available in order to supply comfort to the child in mother's physical absence. The first basis for the stability and the quality of this inner representation is the actual mother-child relationship as we saw it unfolding in the day-to-day interaction between mother and child. It seemed to be the result of the preceding three subphases. This, however, is by no means an end point. This new little being, in his third year, is ready to put into action his independent functioning in his relatively greatly widened world, and tries to weather, without the physical presence of his mother, the new storms that at times threaten or even do sweep away that delicate, newly formed inner structure of relative emotional object constancy.

The threats to libidinal object constancy and separate individual functioning originate from various sources. First of all, there is the pressure of drive maturation, which confronts the child with new tasks as he goes through the anal phase, with the demands that toilet training entails. Then, upon entering the phallic phase, the child becomes much more aware of the sexual difference, and along with it he experiences castration anxiety of varying intensity.

Psychoanalysts are well aware of the great variety of negations, fantasies, accusations, and fears with which the child tries to cope with these problems. For us, it is important here to see how these affect a budding, libidinal object constancy and libidinal investment of the individuating self.

We have described how castration anxiety, from as early as the second part of the second year on, may counteract the development and sound integration of self-representations (probably the body image in the first place) and may also counteract the libidinally cathected identificatory processes. Cumulative (developmental) traumata (cf. Khan, 1964) in the anal and especially in the phallic phase may constitute a roadblock in the way of object constancy, as well as in the way of a preliminary consolidation of the child's individuality.

These preceding and ongoing events decisively determine the three-year-old's style and degree of integration of his individuality. Both achievements—consolidation of individuality and emotional object constancy—are easily challenged by the struggle around toilet training and by the awareness of the anatomical sexual difference, a blow to the narcissism of the little girl and a great danger to the little boy's body integrity.

By the third year, there is in the life of each child a particular constellation that is the result of the hitherto experienced optimal or less than optimal empathic personality of the mother, her mothering capacity, to which he responds. This response branches out to the father and to the entire psychosocial constellation of the child's family. His reactions are greatly influenced by accidental, but sometimes fateful, happenings such as sicknesses, surgical interventions, accidents, separations from mother or father, that is to say, by experiential factors. Accidental events of this sort in a sense constitute each child's fate and are the substance from which are formed the endlessly varied, but also endlessly recurring, themes and tasks of his particular life.

NOTES

1. Kestenberg's important work bears witness to how much we may learn from movement patterns of mother and infant (1965a, 1965b, 1967a, and 1971). Unfortunately, it was beyond the scope of our research methodology to create a general guideline by which the motor, especially the expressional or affectomotor, phenomena could be more specifically and teachably used as referents to intrapsychic processes. Hopefully, future researchers will undertake such a project.

2. Benjamin and his co-workers (1961) noted an interesting physiological crisis at around 3 to 4 weeks. At that age a maturational crisis occurs. This is borne out in electroencephalographic studies and by the observation that there is a marked increase in overall sensitivity to external stimulation. "Without intervention of a mother figure for help in tension reduction, the infant at that time tends to become overwhelmed by stimuli, with increased crying and other motor manifestations of undifferentiated negative affect."

3. This is also a glaring example of what Phyllis Greenacre (1959) emphasizes, namely, that the child's body represents a penis in the mother's unconscious. We seem to have seen this in our mothers time and again, but we did not choose to point it out in each particular instance of our study.

4. When father came home or when guests arrived, Carl, even at 16 months of age, would hide behind a chair or banister, ducking his head or crouching; suddenly he would lift his head and stand up, indicating with sounds and grunts that he wanted the adults to exclaim, "Here he is!"

5. By "shadowing" we mean the child's incessant watching and following every move of the mother.

6. J. B. McDevitt, in his as yet unpublished papers and discussions, has significantly elaborated the criteria for libidinal object constancy in the sense used in this book.

7. Among psychoanalytic writers, Jacobson (1964) is one who makes clear the continuance of problems of merging of self and object images well into the third year.

REFERENCES

Abelin, E. L. The role of the father in the separation-individuation process. In J. B. McDevitt and C. F. Settlage (Eds.), *Separation-individuation: essays in honor of Margaret S. Mahler.* New York: International Universities Press, 1971.

Abelin, E. L. Some further observations and comments on the earliest role of the father. Paper read at the Margaret S. Mahler Symposium on Child Development, Philadelphia, May, 1972,

Abraham, K. Contribution to the theory of the anal character. *Selected papers of Karl Abraham.* (Translated by D. Bryan and A. Strachey). New York: Basic Books, 1953. (1921)

Abraham, K. The influence of oral erotism on character formation. *Selected papers of Karl Abraham.* (Translated by D. Bryan and A. Strachey). New York: Basic Books, 1953. (1924)

Anthony, E. J. A study of "screen sensations." *The psychoanalytic study of the child.* Vol. 16. New York: International Universities Press, 1961.

Benjamin, J. D. The innate and the experiential in child development. In H. Brosin (Ed.), *Lectures on experimental psychiatry.* Pittsburgh: University of Pittsburgh Press, 1961.

Bowlby, J. The nature of the child's tie to the mother. *International Journal of Psychoanalysis,* 1958, *39,* 350–373.

Escalona, S. *The roots of individuality: normal patterns of development in infancy.* Chicago: Aldine, 1968.

Fenichel, O. *Psychoanalytic theory of neurosis.* New York: Norton, 1945.

Ferenczi, S. Stages in the development of the sense of reality. *Sex in psychoanalysis: the selected papers of Sandor Ferenczi,* Vol. 1. New York: Basic Books, 1950. (1913)

Freud, A. Negativism and emotional surrender. *International Journal of Psychoanalysis,* 1952, *33,* 265. (1951a)

Freud, A. Observations on child development. *The psychoanalytic study of the child,* Vol. 6. New York: International Universities Press, 1951. (1951b)

Freud, S. Project for a scientific psychology. In J. Strachey (Ed.), *Standard edition,* Vol. 1. London: Hogarth Press, 1950. (1895)

Freud, S. The interpretation of dreams. In J. Strachey (Ed.), *Standard edition,* Vol. 4/5. London: Hogarth Press, 1950. (1900)

Freud, S. Three essays on the theory of sexuality. In J. Strachey (Ed.), *Standard edition,* Vol. 7. London: Hogarth Press, 1950. (1905)

Freud, S. Formulations on the two principles of mental functioning. In J. Strachey (Ed.), *Standard edition,* Vol. 12. London: Hogarth Press, 1950. (1911)

Freud, S. Mourning and melancholia. In J. Strachey (Ed.), *Standard edition,* Vol. 14. London: Hogarth Press, 1950. (1915)

Freud, S. Beyond the pleasure principle. In J. Strachey (Ed.), *Standard edition,* Vol. 18. London: Hogarth Press, 1950. (1920)

Freud, S. Civilization and its discontents in J. Strachey (Ed.), *Standard edition,* Vol. 21. London: Hogarth Press, 1950. (1930)

Greenacre, P. On focal symbiosis. In L. Jessner and E. Pavenstadt (Eds.), *Dynamic psychology in childhood.* New York: Grune and Stratton, 1959.

Greenacre, P. Problems of overidealization of the analyst and of analysis. *The psychoanalytic study of the child,* Vol. 21. New York: Intern. Universities Press, 1966.

Greenson, R. R. Dis-identification. *International Journal of Psychoanalysis,* 1968, *49,* 370–374.

Hartmann, H. *Ego psychology and the problem of adaptation.* New York: International Universities Press, 1958. (1939)

Heimann, P. Comment on Dr. Kernberg's paper. *International Journal of Psychoanalysis,* 1966, *47,* 254–260.

Homburger, A. Zur gestaltung der normalen menschlichen motorik und ihre beurteilung. *Zeitschrift Gesamte Psychiatrie,* 1923, *75,* 274.

Isakower, O. On the exceptional position of the auditory sphere. *International Journal of Psychoanalysis,* 1939, *20,* 340–348.

Jacobson, E. The self and the object world: vicissitudes of their infantile cathexes and their influence on ideational and affective development. *The psychoanalytic study of the child,* Vol. 9. New York: International Universities Press, 1954.

Jacobson, E. *The self and the object world.* New York: International Universities Press, 1964.

Joffe, W. and Sandler, J. Notes on pain, depression, and individuation. *The psychoanalytic study of the child,* Vol. 20. New York: International Universities Press, 1965.

Kernberg, O. Borderline personality organization. *Journal of the American Psychoanalytic Association,* 1967, *15,* 641–685.

Kestenberg, J. The role of movement patterns in development. I. Rhythms of movement. *Psychoanalytic Quarterly,* 1965a, *24,* 1–26.

Kestenberg, J. The role of movement patterns in development. II. Flow and tension and effort. *Psychoanalytic Quarterly,* 1965b, *24,* 517–563.

Kestenberg, J. The role of movement patterns in development. III. The control of shape. *Psychoanalytic Quarterly,* 1967, *36,* 365–409.

Kestenberg, J. From organ-object imagery to self and object representations. In J. B. McDevitt and C. F. Settlage (Eds.), *Separation-individuation: essays in honor of Margaret S. Mahler.* New York: International Universities Press, 1971.

Kleeman, J. A. The peek-a-boo game. Part I: Its origins, meanings, and related phenomena in the first year. *The psychoanalytic study of the child,* Vol. 22. New York: International Universities Press, 1967.

Levy, D. M. Primary affect hunger. *American Journal of Psychology,* 1937, *94,* 643–652.

Mahler, M. S. Tics and impulsions in children. *Psychoanalytic Quarterly,* 1944, *13,* 430–444.

Mahler, M. S. A psychoanalytic evaluation of tic in psychopathology of children. *The psychoanalytic study of the child,* Vol. 3/4. New York: International Universities Press, 1949.

Mahler, M. S. On child psychosis and schizophrenia. *The psychoanalytic study of the child,* Vol. 7. New York: International Universities Press, 1952.

Mahler, M. S. Autism and symbiosis: two extreme disturbances of identity. *International Journal of Psychoanalysis,* 1958a, *39,* 77–83.

Mahler, M. S. On two crucial phases of integration of the sense of identity: separation-individuation and bisexual identity. *Journal of the American Psychoanalytic Association,* 1958b, *6,* 136–139.

Mahler, M. S. Symposium on psychotic object-relationships. *International Journal of Psychoanalysis,* 1960, *41,* 548–553.

Mahler, M. S. Thoughts about development and individuation. *The psychoanalytic study of the child,* Vol. 18. New York: International Universities Press, 1963.

Mahler, M. S. On early infantile psychosis. *Journal of the American Academy of Child Psychiatry,* 1965a, *4,* 554–568.

Mahler, M. S. On the significance of the normal separation-individuation phase. In M. Schur (Ed.), *Drives, Affects, behavior,* Vol. 2. New York: International Universities Press, 1965b.

Mahler, M. S. Notes on the development of basic moods. In R. M. Loewenstein, L. M. Newman, M. Schur, and A. J. Solnit (Eds.), *Psychoanalysis—a general psychology: essays in honor of Heinz Hartmann.* New York: International Universities Press, 1966.

Mahler, M. S. On human symbiosis and the vicissitueds of individuation. *Journal of the American Psychoanalytic Association,* 1967a, *15,* 740–763.

Mahler, M. S. Child development and the curriculum. *Journal of the American Psychoanalytic Association,* 1967b, *15,* 876–886.

Mahler, M. S. On the first three sub-phases of the separation-individuation process. *International Journal of Psychoanalysis,* 1972, *53,* 333–338.

Mahler, M. S. and Furer, M. Observations on research regarding the "symbiotic syndrome' of infantile psychosis. *Psychoanalytic Quarterly,* 1960, *29,* 317–327.

Mahler, M. S. and Gosliner, B. J. On symbiotic child psychosis. *The psychoanalytic study of the child,* Vol. 10. New York: International Universities Press, 1955.

Mahler, M. S. and Gross, I. H. Psychotherapeutic study of a typical case with tic syndrome. *Nervous Child,* 1945, *4,* 359–373.

Masterson, J. F. The mother's contribution to the psychic structure of the borderline personality. Paper read at the Margaret S. Mahler Symposium on Child Development, Philadelphia, 1973.

Piaget, J. *The origins of intelligence in children.* Paris: Delachaux and Niestle, 1936.

Roiphe, H. and Galenson, E. Early genital activity and the castration complex. *Psychoanalytic Quarterly,* 1972, *41,* 334–347.

Spitz, R. A. *The first year of life: a psychoanalytic study of normal and deviant development of object relations.* New York; International Universities Press, 1965.

Spock, B. The striving for autonomy and regressive object-relationships. *The psychoanalytic study of the child,* Vol. 18. New York: International Universities Press, 1963.

Tolpin, M. On the beginnings of a cohesive self. *The Psychoanalytic study of the child,* Vol. 26. New York: Quadrangle, 1972.

Wolff, P. H. Observations on newborn infants. *Psychosomatic Medicine,* 1959, *21,* 110–118.

18

Dual Parenting and the
Duel of Intimacy

DIANE EHRENSAFT

> If we had a girl child now, I think Carol would have killed me a long time ago. She says that if she saw me making love to a girl as I do to Aaron, she would be extremely jealous.

> The quality of the attention Ben gives Aaron compared to the quality of attention he gives me is only bearable because I don't really see Aaron as a competitor.

And so unfolds the unexpected drama between the man and woman who "mother" together. The above statements are from a father and mother of a 15-month-old son. Prior to his birth, they made a firm commitment to each other to fully share the everyday care and upbringing of their child. The sentiments they express are not atypical, but reflect a repeated phenomenon reported by heterosexual couples who, on the basis of personal and ideological convictions, have committed themselves to a shared parenting arrangement. The phenomenon involves the blossoming of intimacy between father and child, a less tension-laden relationship between a child and a mother freed from the burdens of full-time mothering, but a new gender-related tension between men and women as to who is getting the father's intimacy—mother or child. How did this come to pass?

We are talking about a particular population of heterosexual parents, most in their 30s or 40s, from middle-class backgrounds, and now involved in professional occupations. I have interviewed five of these families in depth and had extensive discussions with many more.[1] They emerged from the era of the 1960's, questioning the norms of mainstream culture. Many of

Diane Ehrensaft is Professor of Psychology, The Wright Institute, Berkeley, California.

them, particularly the women, were either involved in or influenced by the rising tide of feminism. In that context, these men and women balked at the structures of traditional American parenting, in which women were primary caretakers and men primary breadwinners, and opted for a child-rearing arrangement in which both would be the "primary caretaker" and take over what has historically been the mothering functions. But given gender divisions in this society and given the acculturation of these women and men within these gender arrangements, we predicted that "it would be easier said than done" to actually share mothering. As late as 1980 I was writing:

> Often the sharing of physical tasks between mothers and fathers is easily implemented. . . . What is left at least partially intact is the sexual division of the *psychological* labor in parenting. There is the question, "Who carries around in their head knowledge of diapers needing to be laundered, fingernails needing to be cut, new clothes to be bought?" Answer: Mother, because of years of socialization to do so (Ehrensaft, 1980, p. 53).

THE UNEXPECTED PHENOMENON

Of the many women I have either interviewed or engaged in discussions, their original stance, prior to the birth of their child, is often yet more extreme and suspicious than the above. Each partner comes to the shared parenting arena with a mixture of excitement and fear: excitement about their innovative parenting experiment, both in gender relations and in parenting, and hesitation that it will never work. They are fighting upstream against a system in which they often believe that "the sexual and familial division of labor in which women mother and are more involved in interpersonal, affective relationships than men produces in daughters and sons a division of psychological capacities which teaches them to reproduce this sexual and familial division of labor" (Chodorow, 1970, p. 7). The woman often comes with a chip on her shoulder. "I'll have to see it to believe it.":

> Practically, I always had the idea that the only way to end up with anything near fifty-fifty was to have the man sign up for eighty to ninety percent of the job and then *maybe* if you were lucky you would come up somewhere near equal.

Women particularly doubt men's emotional capacities to mother and their willingness to stick to the drudgery, tediousness, and intrusion into one's work and personal life that a long-time commitment to a child entails. They had already discovered it no mean feat to reorganize household responsibilities. But what was forgotten was, as stated eloquently by a shared parenting father: "It's very hard to compare them because you get such wonderful feedback from a kid. You get no feedback from the dishes or the laundry or the grocery store."

This is not to say, however, that men themselves had no anxieties about their forthcoming life as a sharing parent. In every family interviewed, even though both parents, prior to their child's birth, were committed to sharing the parenting, it was the woman who either pushed harder or pushed deeper to raise the particular concerns and issues of "mothering" together. Given the ideology and norms that women mother, this reason was quite simple: "I certainly had a very strong feeling from the beginning of not wanting to be strapped with the child. I know that impetus to want to share time, continue to work, to have my own life, was really there and strong." In response, the men were often nervous. Given their own gender-specific preparation (or rather lack of it) for mothering and the ire of their partner's suspicion, they too worried they would not come through:

> I always felt I wouldn't have the kind of commitment to an infant that people talked about.

> And I was, although I never said it verbally, nervous about how willing I'd be to spend fifty percent of the time.

> Carol is the one who's empathetic, emotional, and everyone tells about their stuff. And I'm not particularly interested in that. Carol has a hypertrophied sense of looking out for someone else. That was a standard that I didn't think I could live up to.

What these fathers *did* know is that they wanted to be with their child.

The actual outcome, as is often the case, has been more complicated than anticipated, with an unexpected punch line. The difficulty of dividing up the "mental baggage" of parenting, mentioned earlier, was as predicted. In each situation the mother more likely was psychological-task manager, carrying the daily burden of the child's day-to-day needs in her head and wishing the father did it more. But this is only one aspect of the psychological phenomenon of "mothering." There is also the emotional bonds, the empathy, the primary identification, the ability to regress while remaining an adult, the capacity to "hold" not just in the physical but in the emotional sense. While the reality remains that parenthood appears more embedded in the woman's daily consciousness, and begins earlier in her life as a parent, the father's *emotional* commitment and involvement in the child go far beyond what either he or his female partner ever expected:

> Aaron is important to me, but I think he's more central to Ben. There's a certain level of intensity that I think is unusual in Ben. In fact, in some ways I think the baby matters more to Ben than anything in his life, but not in terms of how much of his day he wants to spend on it. There isn't a direct correspondence between the pleasure and joy and intensity of emotion and the allotment of time for either of us. (Mother)

> Now my favorite activity in the world is staying home with Michael. I do it every time I get a chance. I cancel appointments so I can have a whole day with him. (Father)

I've never had any question of the sharing of the emotional responsibilities with Chuck. The nurturing, the emotional, the psychological have been completely shared from the very beginning. His investment in parenting is as strong as mine. (Mother)

I thought that it would be much more a struggle than it is and I thought my wife would turn out to be more primary, that it would be seventy-thirty or at best sixty-forty. (Father)

Far from throwing in the towel after a short stint in parenting, these men demonstrate an ongoing, intense, and intimate connection with their child. They may still forget to change their baby's diapers often enough or think about next week's supply of clean clothes, much to their female partner's legitimate irritation. But they worry about their child's development, encourage close physical contact with their child, often find it difficult to separate from him or her. They form a permanent and intimate primary relationship with their child which, as an above respondent alerts us, cannot be assessed on the measuring rod of time and tasks alone. Our culture has a tendency to reduce parenthood to an ascribed or assigned set of "roles" with attendant responsibilities and duties. What gets forgotten is the emotional bonding, the unconscious and conscious transmission between two selves, parent and child, that are essential in the developmental task of child rearing. It is in this arena, contrary to prior doubts and suspicions, that the father is able to carry his weight in a 50–50 arrangement. This does not mean, however, that what he develops is equal or the same as that which develops between the mother and child. Instead, it is the very uniqueness of his intimacy with his child that sets the stage for a new dynamic and tension in the shared parenting mother-father-child triangle.

THE LOVE AFFAIR AND THE NEW TRIANGLE

I'm absolutely in love with her. Just passionately in love with her. On occasion that's almost frightening.

I'm totally in love with A—I'm in love.

It was at that moment that I realized that R—was the person I was most honest with and who understands me, and was able to look at the lines on my forehead and say, "What are you worried about?" To this day she can read my worry lines.

The sounds of a fine romance, the intimate murmuring of two lovers under the stars. Except that these are men talking about their relationships with and feelings toward their own children, both male and female. In the words of one mother, they have gone "ga-ga" over their children. In contrast, not one mother described her relationship with her child in comparable terms. She would talk about her attachment, her endearing feelings, her sense of closeness to her child, but never in the discourse of a love affair. Whereas all the women interviewed had taken trips or extended time away from their children, the men more likely expressed difficulty in separating from their children, in bearing to be apart from her or him for more than a moment's time. In fact, a subtle or overt tension is often played out between mother and father as father feels himself the committed and love-stricken parent:

> I've only been away on one overnight since Aaron's been born. Carol's gone to two conferences, at least. And I actually would not feel comfortable doing that, not out of any worried sense, but I wouldn't want to leave him that long. I joke about Carol being able to leave her kid and what kind of lousy mother she is.

> If anything I did more than Andrea did. She really got into school and being out, and there was a period when she was not very much into the house. She was just out a lot. We had lots of struggles, lots of fights and lots of heavy times with my accusation that she was running away.

There are several issues to be teased out and understood in this phenomenon. First, how is it that men, surprising both themselves and their female partners, become so "ga-ga" over their children and what are the underlying dynamics of this love affair? Second, what is it that women are bringing to the parenting relationship that *does not* manifest itself as an unbridled love affair? Lastly, what, then, is the new relational dynamic between shared-parenting men and women?

The first reality to be addressed is that men enter the shared-parenting situation hungry for intimacy, whereas women embark on shared parenting with a healthy skepticism and openly stated ambivalence about the accoutrements and entrapments of traditional motherhood. According to both Dinnerstein (1977) and Chodorow (1979), men, mothered themselves by women, have been early on pushed out of the nest to become a heterosexual "other" to a mothering figure. They are forced to repudiate the very early, preverbal merging between mother and child as they move on to be a gendered other (without heterosexual norms) who will ultimately relate to women not as caretaker but as object of sexual desire: "Boys are more likely to have been pushed out of the preoedipal relationship, and to have had to curtail their primary love and sense of empathic tie with their mother" (Chodorow, 1979, p. 133). In subsequent years the boy develops an ambivalent relationship toward women as he both desires to re-create the early intimacy but fears the reengulfment by maternal omnipotence. He internalizes himself as more "boundaried" than his female cohorts, also raised by female mothers. But he never gives up that *longing* for close intimacy. That hunger for intimacy fulfills itself in his new-formed opportunity to mother a child. As we will explore, this becomes a much safer arena in which to gratify his intimacy needs than the adult world of heterosexual love relationships. Let it suffice at this point in our exploration to say that shared

parenting allows men to turn passive into active, where instead of the regressive longing for the caretaker of their earliest years, they themselves become that "maternal" parenting figure in another child's life. It may be true,
as Chodorow and Dinnerstein argue, that these men do not have the same
internalized relational *capacities* as women due to past socialization, but
this is something quite different from the *desire* for relationship, the focusing of attachment and commitment in another person, in this case, their
child. As stated by one father: "But I must say I felt that way (totally in love
with my child) from early on, before his personality developed. So part of
it has to do with this hunger I've had for a kid for so long."

Let us look at the woman's needs in relation to the man's hunger for
intimacy. As mentioned earlier, the particular women under consideration
enter the shared parenting situation with a strongly stated repudiation of
traditional motherhood. More accurately, they allow themselves the *conscious* expression of ambivalence toward motherhood that is commonly
experienced but not so easily accessible to most women in our culture who
have internalized socially prescribed and ascribed female motherhood. The
shared parenting mother greets her first child with a feeling of push—pull
regarding the structure and position of motherhood. She, who herself has
most likely been raised by a female mother, faces in her own life a struggle
for separateness, for independence, stemming from her first boundaryless
relationship with her mother. In almost all cases women express a fear of
entrapment in motherhood.

Report from mother:

> I have always felt selfish for having a child but wanting time to myself, wishing
> I wasn't a parent sometimes. There are many times when I'd much rather be
> involved in work without interruption. This creates a tension.

Report from father:

> She felt like there was much greater potential for her to get trapped. She hadn't
> finished college yet. When we had this baby, she had this image of having no
> skills and no training and no profession and locked into baby.

If a woman has a fear of boundarylessness, there is no place more ripe for
the flourishing of that fear than in an intimate relationship with a child. At
a conscious level shared parenting mothers express the desire not always
even affordable at the level of fantasy for many women in our culture—the
desire to have the best of both worlds, immersion in the joys and intima-
cies of motherhood with a simultaneous adult identity outside that institution and experience. But they often feel perched on a precipice—the slightest push, as in their male partner's unwillingness to come through, might
send them over the edge back into the position of *single* primary parent.
That push can also as easily come from within. After all, the woman has

from early on incorporated a sense of self as "mother" or has had to spend much of her childhood disidentifying from this internalization, which is pushed so strongly inside by the norms of the outer culture. Why these particular women choose to disidentify from the normative structures of motherhood is a complex combination of class and educational backgrounds, relationship to their own mothers and fathers and family and community culture and values, their identification in adulthood with the women's movement, and their gradual desire in de Beauvoir's (1952) term for "transcendence." The purpose here, however, is not to unravel the causality but to state the uniqueness of these women's position. Whereas many women feel ambivalent about mothering, the shared parenting mother consciously expresses her ambivalence and also has the opportunity to act in a different mode and yet still be a mother. Most significantly, the shared parenting mother has another partner to fall back on, and she has the privilege of sometimes "stepping out" from the institution of motherhood, a privilege that she at times allows herself even more than the shared parenting father:

> I might want to escape from family for a while. There's no flexibility in my life. There's no spontaneity. I always have to account for my movements. Everything has to be so carefully premeditated and structured and planned and scheduled. I think he has less need to break away from family. (Mother's report)

There then may develop a superb choreography of a *pas de deux* between the shared parenting father and mother. As stated by one interviewee, "We're products of this particular historical group and movement that validated this project and let Ben do something that clearly he wanted to do anyway. And it gave me space, in fact, too, to not have to do something I always thought I had to do completely and therefore has certainly made it more enjoyable to me." The two pieces of the puzzle fit nicely together, and the shared parenting couple has the capacity for increased unity and harmony between them as they embark on the joint project of raising their children together. However, history is not so easily made over in a day. In addition to the "easier said than done" tensions around the psychological division of parenting tasks and power structures (cf. Ehrensaft, 1980), there is an unexpected twist: the convolution of the mother-father-child triangulation observed in traditional nuclear families. It is often reported in these traditional families that Father feels left out as he experiences his spouse's or partner's unlimited love and attentiveness, which he has grown accustomed to having, withdrawn from him and transferred onto the primary caretaking of their child. This is particularly true in the child's earliest months, where the mother demonstrates a "maternal preoccupation" (cf. Winnicott, 1971) with her infant. Remarkably, we find the jealousy and "cut-off" feeling in the exact opposite direction, albeit more subtle, in the shared parenting family. The mother often feels jealous and resentful as she witnesses the quality of intimacy *she has never had* with her male partner now so easily given by him to his child. First, she may see their child or children as somewhat more central to him than to her. Then, subsequently, she may report her jealousy or resentment, not just toward the intimate attachment between father and child but for the ease of that closeness. It is this very closeness that is so problematic in their adult love relationship, where the woman experiences the man as withholding or not capable of the intimacy she desires (cf. Chodorow, 1979 and Rubin, 1983). These men, on their part, are gleeful and delighted by their new specialness in their child's eyes:

> Carol is a little jealous of Aaron's greater attachment to me. She keeps it under wraps, but she's jealous. I love it, I absolutely love it.

> There's a small amount of competition between Ben and me around Aaron. Aaron is now more attached to Ben than he is to me. And it makes me jealous sometimes. Ben's really enjoying it. In other words, he's very pleased. He's really delighted.

> Renee and I have a much more intense, magical space together than Joan and she have, a lot more fantasy worlds that we go through together.

And the men concur that the intimacy is in fact more easily bestowed on their child than on an adult:

> I still have a lot of passion in me that I enjoy having Renee (daughter) available to share with me. And who Joan (mother) is, at times that's not available to me. That kind of romance. Renee and I have the metaphor of what it means to have a cozy place.

> It (the nurturance and intimacy) easily came out in a way with Aaron that I just couldn't imagine. The anxiety around it not being there was around *adult* relationships.

Why should it be that a man, so unprepared from his history, can apparently experience with his child the empathy, the primary identification, the nurturance, the emotional committedness that are part and parcel of what we have come to call the "capacity for mothering"? Are these not the same capacities that enter into any adult relationship and yet become so problematic between adult men and women? And why does this intimacy between man and child specifically take on the discourse of a love affair?

WHY SHOULD A FATHER BE ABLE TO MOTHER?

Traditional psychoanalysis, sociobiology, and contemporary conservative social forces all argue for the unique capacities of a woman over a man, stemming from her biological status, to mother a child. But according to recent psychological studies, anyone who can provide frequent and sustained physical contact, soothe a child when he or she is distressed, be sensitive to the child's signals, and respond promptly to the child's distress can mother a child. Beyond these immediate behavioral indices, anyone who has personally experienced a positive parent–child relationship that allowed for the development of both basic trust and individuation in his or her own childhood has the emotional capabilities to parent. On the other hand, years in female-dominated parenting situations and in gender-differentiated cultural institutions can and do differentially prepare boys and girls for the task of mothering. Adulthood, social forces in the labor market, schools, media, etc., buttress these differential abilities.

One would assume, then, that men would have a specific set of handicaps in their relational abilities to "mother." Specifically, because of the need in his development to separate earlier than girls do from an opposite-sex mother in becoming a male "other," boys would experience less of the fusion, projection, narcissistic extension, and primary identification that prepare girls later for the emotional tasks of mothering. It is what Margaret Mahler (1975) refers to as "libidinal availability," and Winnicott (1971) as "good-enough mothering" and the "holding environment." Yet it is this very emotional giving and responsiveness that both mother and father agree the shared parenting father is able to experience and express, despite his relative lack of preparation for concrete child-rearing tasks or psychological management of daily activities. If we think back again to the earliest experiences of the man from his own childhood, I believe we can find an explanation for this phenomenon.

In discussing the preparation of the man for *traditional* fatherhood, psychoanalyst Veronica Machtlinger observes, "Considerations of the factors held to be important in the male's psychological preparation for becoming a father usually begin with the well-known psychoanalytic observations of the small boy's wish to have and to bear children. . . . An assumption of the father's role in reproduction and relation to caretaking helps an adult man come to terms with his hitherto repressed and disquieting 'maternal desires' " (Machtlinger, 1981, p. 140). The shared parenting father is not willing to acquiesce to this back-seat role as the *secondary* parent. Instead, he "comes to terms" in a more active manner, by actually *unleashing* those maternal desires in full force. Whereas Machtlinger recognizes the boy's early wishes to have and to bear children as doomed to failure, the stated outcome of men's envy of women's active procreation functions is not inevitable. The shared parenting father instead can translate this early desire into a full participation in the *social* functions of mothering.[2]

Once throwing himself into the arena, can the shared parenting father actually deliver the primary identification and lack of separateness not under the sway of reality that is the requirement for "good enough mothering"? According to Chodorow (1979), "The early relation to a primary caretaker provides in children of both genders the *basic capacity* (italics added) to participate in a relationship with the features of the early parent—child one and the desire to create this intimacy" (p. 206). However, because both men and women have been mothered by a female, the subsequent difference in object relational experiences and the internalization and organization of this experience for girls and boys creates a gender divided phenomenon. "The relational basis for mothering is extended in women (with like-sex mothers) and inhibited in men, who experience themselves as more separate and distinct from others" (Chodorow, 1979, p. 207). The fact that shared parenting fathers, even to their own surprise, are able to open up those avenues of intimacy with their own children speaks to the underestimation of the primacy of these *earliest* relatively "genderless" mother—child relationships that all infants, both male and female, experience. Even if, because of the acculturation into "manhood," that experience lies dormant or repressed throughout much of a man's childhood and early adulthood, he is able to call it forth once again as he chooses to "mother" a child himself.

There is nothing apparently consistent in the constellation of family structure or dynamics across the group of shared parenting fathers discussed herein that could account for the choice to call forth their early experiences and mother rather than accept the traditional route of fatherhood. What *is* consistent in every father's report is their discomfort with or repudiation of traditional "boy culture" as they were growing up and as adult men. They reported a desire to do "sissy stuff," to hang out with girls rather than with boys, to play house and dolls, to avoid the "macho competition" of the male social world:

> I played house and I was a sissy. I really related mainly to girls. I hung out and played jump rope and hopscotch, and Tuesday nights was hanging out with the girls and getting into pajamas and having milk and cookies and playing with dolls.

> I related mainly to girls and played fantasy stuff around being a parent. Played a lot of house games.

> I'm not your basic macho male. I've always been kind of a loner, and very uncomfortable in a man's world. I have always spoken and communicated with women. It's hard to communicate with men beyond a competitive, gamey kind of conversation. Always backslapping and tooting our horns. And it feels like a role I'm not comfortable with.[3]

One could expect, then, that these are a group of boys that remained closer to that early experience and to the "feminine" sides of themselves than is true for most boys in our culture who from early on are pushed out of the nest.

So, then, in terms of emotional capacities, does the man mother just like a woman? On two counts, the data indicate not in regard to his sense of "otherness" from the child and in his notion and experience of "intimacy." In their reports the men did not reflect the same sense of identification or extension of self in relationship to their child as was evident in women's reports. The child, for the father, was much more likely to be an other, a lone object, than an extension of self. The same man who is so intensely involved with his child emotionally is still more willing than his female partner to "buy" extensive child care, send the child to a sick child-care program rather than stay home from work with a sick child. He does not as easily worry that an ill-dressed child will be a reflection of himself as a bad parent.

The shared parenting father, as I have demonstrated, definitely goes beyond the role of "doing" child-rearing tasks. He has an "intimate" relationship with his child. Yet he recapitulates a relationship that still has a ring of "other" to it. This recalls his early, but not *earliest*, childhood, when he was pushed out of his "preoedipal nest" in his relationship with his own mother, to whom he was a distinct "other" and with whom he had to accomplish certain developmental tasks to develop his own identity. He had to "disidentify" from his mother, turn to his father. Even in the shared parenting father who may (by volition) not have fully accomplished this task of adapting to culturally prescribed norms of maleness, this phenomenon likely occurred. Therefore, for many years adult-child love for him has had a more distinct flair of "otherness" than for the woman, as she calls her own child-rearing history with a female primary parent into play in her own parenting.

This leads to the second, gender-divided uniqueness in shared parenting mothering: the type of intimacy expressed and experienced. Let us recall again the tone of the love affair revealed in the father's (and not the mother's) description of his feeling toward his child:

> I go out with Renee. Go dancing together. Renee and I get all dressed up and go out for dinner.

> When we were alone together in the country when she was first born there was a kind of chill running through me of closeness, of real loving.

It is not that the father's relationship with the child is more "sexualized" than the mother's. At a surface level, one can explain the man's expression as the only mode of verbal discourse of intimacy accessible to him in the description of love for his child. Underlying this, however, is the deeper explanatory root, the bifurcation of intimacy into two types for women versus the unidimensional mode of intimacy for men in our culture.

The *desire* for intimacy is based in the boy's *earliest* experience with his own parent. But the form that it takes is subsequently shaped by the heterosexual norm of intimacy as developed throughout his childhood. Boys are not primed to be "mothers" in the same way their sisters are. Their major anticipation of intimacy in adulthood will not be with a child but with a woman who will be their lover or spouse. The main discourse of intimacy with which a boy is familiar is the discourse of heterosexual intimacy—not just with a love partner but with his own primary parent mother of the past.

The woman, on the other hand, has a very different history of intimacy. She has grown up in a culture that expects motherhood from her and instills her with those "virtues" from a very early age. She has grown up with a like-sex primary caretaker, which is her first exposure to intimacy. She is accustomed to a bifurcation in intimacy from very early on—the kind you have with mother and with females and the kind you have with men as you are directed down the course of heterosexual relations. The fusion of intimacy and sexuality will have different outcomes for different women. Some eliminate the bifurcation by bringing sexual and intimate love together in a relationship with a woman. More often, the woman maintains the bifurcation of heterosexual love relationships and same-sex intimate friendship. She is thus well prepared to divide intimacy between lover and child. Each requires a different kind of intimacy.

Men are not so well prepared. This is not to say men do not experience intimacy with other men, particularly their own fathers. However, having grown up in traditional nuclear families, father took the secondary position in the early mother-father-child intimacy triangle. He was meant to represent the rational discourse of the real world (Abelin, 1971). Men have close relationships with one another, but not with the same quality of preverbal merging, the mirroring, the regressive psychological interdependency that characterizes the parent–child or the lover relationship or the intimate friendships experienced between women. Therefore, when a heterosexual man calls forth a mode of intimacy in his relationship to his child, he has only one mode to call on—the heterosexual intimacy begun with his mother but transformed into a more mature form where woman is *other* and object (sexual) of desire. He does not have one mode of intimacy for lover and another for child.

In this light we can decipher a striking phenomenon, the shared parenting father's desire for a female child. This has been reported by one father after another. The consciously expressed explanations by the father are twofold: the excitement of raising a female child in the context of the woman's movement, and, more significantly, the father's abhorrence of young boy culture: that is, the *desire not to have a boy child*. It would recall the pain of their own boyhood and their early alienation from that boy culture. The fathers also worried about the management of their own hostile reactions as they watched their own male child be aggressive, teasing, and insensitive.

Women, too, expressed a desire for a daughter. But for a woman it has a very different meaning. For a woman, there is the desire for a reproduction of self, becoming the mother to a daughter, so that one can also relive and reconstruct her own history as a daughter. In that sense, she becomes mother to herself.

As we see, the father does not express the same desire for a same-sex child. There is not the same longing to re-create the self. In fact, there is a disidentification with his own gender not just in his repudiation of male culture but in his adult statement that "I will not be like other men. I will mother a child." The woman does a parallel act as she says, "I will not be primarily a parent. I will share that with a man and I will also have an identity outside the home." But it is more extraordinary for a man to be a mother than for a woman to work outside the home. Women have always been in the work force. Men have seldom been found by the crib.

The man, in his desire for a female child, also reveals an unconscious holdover from his early child-rearing years: the desire to hook up with a *female* in a parent-child dyad. Thus, both the man and woman search for a re-creation of their earliest attachment—with a female. Only this time, the female is their own infant rather than the mother of their primal memories and dreams. The man's desire for a girl also speaks to his notion of intimacy with an "other." Gurwitt (1976) addresses a clinical case in which a man's desire to have a girl and *not* to have a boy was to avoid reactivating old conflicts with his father. I think it is more likely with this father and with the shared parenting fathers that the desire for an opposite-sex child is because *heterosexual* intimacy is the only kind a man knows. It is much more difficult to *imagine* such preverbal intimacy with another male (even though in actuality the father is delighted and emotionally involved if that imagined child is in fact born male). The father–child relationship in which the man likely grew up is often referred to as a rational, verbal one, not built of primordial fantasies and dreams as with the mother. Men are not supposed to touch (cuddle, fondle) other males in a way women are given permission to do with females. Again, heterosexual intimacy is the only mode available to the man in his "mothering," in contrast to the woman's bisexual modes of intimacy.

FATHERS AS MOTHERS AND LOVERS: THE DUEL OF INTIMACY

The woman feels jealous as she watches her male partner "fall in love" with their child. She has entered a relationship with this man longing for the kind of closeness and merging she once knew a long time ago with her own mother. It is often asserted that women search for love partners not like their own fathers but like their own mothers. They may then discover, however, that in contrast to the intimacy they desire, their lover is withholding, "impermeable," unable to disclose, less "relational." For the shared parenting mother, insult is added to injury if she then witnesses her male partner unleash that desired intimacy, but not with her, with their child. The female partner sees the ease with which the man "cathects" to the child, becomes devoted to the child, is able to get into the psychological layers of the child's mind, frets about his or her happiness and well-being, becomes totally engrossed with the child, and at times has eyes for no one else. He can call forth a preverbal and nurturing interdependence with relative ease and grace—but relative to what? Relative to the ease and grace with which he can do the same thing with his female lover. Children, then, become the father's inroad to intimacy, but the potential source of heterosexual jealousy and tension as the child gets the intimacy so easily from the father that the woman wishes she could have and often struggles hard to get.

Why should it be so much easier for the man to be intimate with his child than with his wife or lover? As Dinnerstein (1977) has pointed out so graphically in *The Mermaid and the Minotaur*, because of their own female-dominated child rearing men develop a strong ambivalence toward women and toward intimate relations. They are dreadfully afraid of falling back into the hands of woman's perceived primitive powers, a devouring and all-encompassing giant who can swallow him up alive, leaving him like mush. It is very dangerous to open up to women. Men have spent a good deal of their childhood, adolescence, and adulthood shoring up defenses against the regressive pulls back to a relationship with a female in which they are helpless and woman is the life-giver. But they also *long* for this kind of intimacy. And it is right smack in the shared parenting relationship that they get to fulfill this longing—with their *child*. What is so hard to give their female lover is so much easier to give their child . . . the merging, the connection of two unconsciouses, the delights of mutual play, the mirroring, the en-face maternal gazing. Their child cannot swallow them alive. In their wildest fantasies their female lovers can.

SUMMARY AND CONCLUSION

We have learned that contrary to both the woman's, the man's, and outsiders' expectations, the shared parenting father is capable of a strong sense of emotional commitment and intimacy with his child. Although this intimacy manifests itself differently than in the female mother—child relationship, it speaks to the man's basic relational capabilities to "mother." The optimal outcome would be that in experiencing this longed-for intimacy with his child, man's fears and defenses against intimacy in general would get broken down or at least reduced. In other words, he would become more "relational." Chodorow argues that men do not have the same relational capacities to mother. But we have also demonstrated that all children, male and female, are afforded the basic opportunity for that intimacy in their earliest relationship with their primary parent. This raises an alternative possibility that a man does have the emotional capabilities to mother, but that in his socialization he has defended against them. The capacity is developed in the earliest months of life and only later defended against as the boy must separate and become a gendered other. The desire for that intimacy is never lost. Shared parenting thus can be viewed as a "compensatory" experience. If psychotherapy can cure the neurotic, then could not mothering and the opportunity for a "corrective emotional experience" structurally alter the expression of a male's relational capacities? If this is so, even in this generation of female-reared shared parenting men and women, we can expect a change in men from traditional fathers toward empathic, intimate mothers.

NOTES

1. The parent interviews involved separate interviews with mother and father. Criterion for being considered a "shared parenting family" was the self-definition by both parents as being mutually and equally involved in the child's primary care.
   Both members of each couple were also involved in a professional job or work commitment.
2. At the same time, shared parenting fathers *do* express their envy and frustration at the limitations of *full* sharing dictated by the unique capacity of women to bear and breast feed children.
3. This interview was not from my own study, but a quote from an interview conducted by Rick Sapp as part of his doctoral dissertation research on shared parenting fathers at The Wright Institute, Berkeley.

REFERENCES

Abelin, E. L. The role of the father in the separation-individuation process. In J. B. McDevitt and C. F. Settlage (Eds.), *Separation-individuation*. New York: International Universities Press, 1971.

Chodorow, N. *The reproduction of mothering*. Berkley, CA: University of California Press, 1979.

de Beauvoir, S. *The second sex*. New York: Knopf, 1952.

Dinnerstein, D. *The mermaid and the minotaur*. New York: Harper and Row, 1977.

Ehrensaft, D. When women and men mother. *Socialist Review*, spring, 1980, No. 49.

Gurwitt, A. Aspects of prospective fatherhood. *The Psychoanalytic Study of the Child*, 1976, *31*, 237–270.

Machtlinger, V. J. The father in psychoanalytic theory. In M. E. Lamb (Ed.), *The role of the father in child development*. New York: Wiley, 1981.

Mahler, M. S. , F. Pine, and A. Bergman. *The psychological birth of the infant*. New York: Basic Books, 1975.

Rubin, L. *Intimate strangers*. New York: Harper and Row, 1983.

Winnicott, D. L. *Playing and reality*. New York: Basic Books, 1971.

19

Centripetal and Centrifugal Forces in the Adolescent Separation Drama

HELM STIERLIN

To grasp the drama of separating parents and children, I developed the concept of *transactional modes*. These modes reflect the interplay and/or relative dominance of centripetal and centrifugal pushes *between the generations* rather than those between marital partners. In the intergenerational interplay, the transactional modes operate as the covert organizing transactional background to the more overt and specific child-parent interactions.[1] When age-appropriate transactional modes are out of phase, too intense, or inappropriately mixed with other modes, the negotiation of a mutual individuation and separation between parent and child is impeded.

The transactional modes reflect salient contributions of the parents and of the children to the interpersonal process. The modes are *transitive* and *reciprocal*. They are transitive in that they denote the active molding of an offspring who is still immature, dependent, and hence remains captive to parental influences. This accords with the fact that parents, from the beginning, impress on their child their "stronger reality" (Stierlin, 1959). They do this often unconsciously by using covert and subtle signals and sanctions. To this "stronger reality" a child must adapt lest he perish. In addition, these modes are reciprocal in the sense that there is always a two-way exchange. In this exchange, the children mold and influence their parents as much as the latter mold and influence them.

We can distinguish between the three major modes of *binding, delegating,* and *expelling*. As I shall try to show, all these modes reflect how ad-

Reprinted with permission of the publisher from Helm Stierlin. *Separating parents and adolescents.* New York: Jason Aronson, 1981.

Helm Stierlin is Professor of Psychiatry and Director of Research in Family Therapy, University of Heidelberg, West Germany

Table 19.1. Transactional Modes (Transitive and Reciprocal)

Centripetal forces dominant	Centripetal and centrifugal forces strong	Centrifugal forces dominant
(Reflected mainly in *nonrunaways* and *certain abortive runaways,* including *lonely schizoid runaways*)	(Reflected mainly in *crisis runaways*)	(Reflected mainly in *casual runaways*)
A. Binding	B. Delegating	C. Expelling
1st Level: affective binding (Id binding) Exploitation mainly of dependency needs with emphasis on regressive gratification (infantilization of adolescent)	Adolescent sent out yet held back by "long leash of loyalty." A limited and qualified autonomy is allowed or encouraged, depending on which mission the delegate is expected to fulfill	Enduring neglect and/or rejection of children who are pushed into premature and foreclosing autonomy. Weak loyalty bonds
2nd Level: cognitive binding (ego binding) Interference with differentiated self-awareness and self-determination. Mystification; violation of cognitive integrity; injection and/or withholding of meaning	Missions can be classified according to how they serve the parent's id, ego, or superego primarily (cf. Table 19.2)	
3rd Level: binding through the exploitation of loyalty (superego binding) Excessive breakaway guilt instilled; children turned into lifelong, self-sacrificing victim-adjuncts		

olescents do or do not run away. Table 19.1 may serve as a guide to the exposition that follows.

THE MODE OF BINDING

When this mode dominates, the family is gripped by centripetal forces. Parents and children operate under the unspoken assumption that essential satisfactions and securities can be obtained only within the family, while the outside world looks hostile and forbidding. This assumption then resonates in the attitudes of parents who, when faced with *their* developmental crisis, see only one avenue open to them: to tie their children ever more closely to themselves and to the "family ghetto" and to delay or prevent the children's separation at all cost.

While examining the runaway or nonrunaway status of my troubled adolescents, I saw binding chiefly in those disturbed adolescents who *did not* run away or who ran away abortively. The very abortiveness of their runaway attempts clarifed what was involved in binding.

The nonrunaways and abortive runaways shared one feature—*they tended to avoid peers*. This resulted from three interrelated factors: (1) they showed little or no drive to seek out and invest themselves in peers; (2) they feared excessively being "unmasked," being ridiculed, or being beaten up by peers; and (3) they lacked many of the relational skills needed to survive in a peer group.

I then looked more closely at this group of troubled non-runaways and abortive runaways and their families, and reflected on the transactional dynamics involved in such avoidance of peers. As a result, I came to distinguish three (more or less interrelated) levels on which the binding mode operates. There is a first "affective" level on which the parent exploits his children's needs for elementary satisfaction and dependency; this I term "id binding." A second level exists on which mainly "cognitive processes" are involved; this I label "ego binding." And at a third level the child's loyalty is exploited; I call this "superego binding."

On each level the parents provide transactional nutriment inappropriate to their adolescent's age and needs.

Affective Binding

On the first—need-satisfying and affective—level, the parent infantalizes his (or her) child by offering undue regressive gratification. The motives for such parental action vary. An overgratifying parent may need to be confirmed as being giving and bountiful by a continuously dependent adolescent. Or such a parent may unconsciously need to repair past losses and deprivations that he or she suffered. Here we typically find a mother who tries to give her child all the love she herself missed as a child. In order to make up through active mastery for what she had once to endure passively, namely, deprivation and abuse, she now recruits her child and gives to him as she had needed to be given to. The more compelling her need for reparative gratification, the more likely she becomes an intrusive and indulging juggernaut, unable to see what the child needs in his own right. Her child cannot help becoming deprived and psychologically exploited in the very process of the mother's giving.

Further, a parent, by offering infantile gratifications, may try to forestall and subdue the adolescent's maturing sexuality that threatens him (or her) directly or indirectly—directly because it stirs up frightening incestuous desires and indirectly because it threatens to shatter his precarious equilibrium of sexual wishes, fears, and inhibitions.

Still further, by regressively gratifying offspring, a parent may try to cope with ambivalent, hostile, and rejecting impulses toward the child. The child serves as a living proof of his parent's lovingness. Such a child is exploited insofar as he is not allowed to experience and define his parent's feelings and motivations for what they are: hostile and rejecting.

Whatever the specific motivations that impel parents to bind their child, the stage is now set for a particular developmental drama. Its major force is the awakening of the child's libidinal and aggressive drives during adolescence. Under these circumstances, the parent cannot but contribute to dangerously reactivated preoedipal and oedipal conflicts. Because the child's awakened drives have no other objects, the parents (particularly the opposite sex parent) become the target of renewed symbiotic and/or incestuous pulls, replete with anxieties and conflicts. Short of engaging in murderous battles and actual incest, the binding parent must attempt to either divert or subdue the child's awakened libidinal and aggressive drives. If he (or she) manages to divert them away from himself, he will, in fact, loosen the bind. If not, he will have a tiger on his hands. Whether the interaction revolves around relatively harmless, "pregenital" activities such as eating, arguing, swearing, etc., or whether it is more openly sexual and sadomasochistic, heightened conflict (overt or covert) is inevitable. The more a binding mother gratifies, indulges, and spoils her child, the more insatiable and monsterlike the child becomes.

This dynamic interchange explains some of the features of the group of disturbed nonrunaways and abortive runaways. It suggests why some of these adolescents actually run away, yet return home quickly. They cannot find any peer or other adult who accepts their excessive demands for regressive gratification. Some of these adolescents resort to drugs with the covert encouragement of one or both parents. Drugs seem to offer the easiest way out of the aforementioned dilemma, because they curb the intensified libidinal and aggressive drives and lessen the dilemma, at least for a while.

I was impressed with how spoiled, infantile, and demanding this subgroup of adolescents appeared. One girl threatened her mother with a knife when the latter refused to drive her somewhere. A son in this group, according to his doting mother, had "the table manners of a disgusting cannibal," and unendingly showered her with four-letter words for not sufficiently attending to him, relishing his oral onslaughts.

Two other adolescents in this group had long histories of unspecified somatic complaints or illnesses such as low-grade fever and stomach pains. Both girls had frequent hospitalizations and diagnostic workups. Much of the family interaction centered around these illnesses and symptoms, accompanied by underlying rage, suffocating clinging, demands for nurturance, and manipulation by guilt. The illnesses and symptoms promised "legitimate regressive gratification" in a transactional setting that had become agonizing to both the parents and children. I was tempted to think of these somatizations as runaway equivalents.[2]

Binding on the Cognitive Level

A second binding mode operates on a cognitive rather than an affective level. When this happens, the binding parent interferes with his child's differentiated self-awareness and self-determination. The ability to perceive and articulate one's own feelings, needs, motives, and goals as against those that others attribute to oneself is crucial in order for the child to cope with any conflicts over his separation. Therefore, his parents' cognitive binding stratagems reduce his chances to master such conflicts.

H. Bruch, among others, described the paradigm of a cognitively binding parent (1961, 1962, 1966). She noted that a mother, by being intrusively interpretative, prevents her child from perceiving and differentiating his basic bodily needs or states such as hunger, thirst, or fatigue. She cognitively binds her child when she imposes on him her own definition of his feelings, needs, or intentions; thereby she substitutes her own for the child's regulatory and discriminating ego. She misdefines the child to himself. Such cognitive binding operates also when a mother trains her child to perceive her as loving, whereas in reality she is hostile, rejecting, or at least ambivalent. A mother will very likely resort to cognitive binding when she must justify her own failure in life depicting herself as victimized by overpoweringly bad and persecuting outside forces, a view her child needs to share and confirm. The child's ego is deformed in the process. As a result of such maneuvers, the child is mystified about what he feels, needs, and wants. G. Bateson (1969), G. Bateson et al. (1956, 1963), L. Wynn & Singer (1963a, b), M. Singer & Wynne (1965a, b), J. Haley (1959), and R. Laing (1965), among others, have elucidated various aspects of this transaction.

I am inclined to call cognitive binding "ego binding," as the binder forces the bindee to rely on the binder's distorted and distorting ego instead of using and developing his own discriminating ego.

Cognitive—or ego—binding, thus understood, reveals important features: it implies devious communications that mystify (Laing, 1961, 1965), interfere with the sharing of a common focus of attention (Wynne and Singer, 1963a, b), and disaffirm one's own or the other's messages (Haley, 1959). Such devious communications strain and unsettle the partner in the dialogue and they throw this dialogue off the track. Insofar as they unsettle the partner, they are *transitive* and *violent*. They violate his or her "cognitive integrity"; they wound him; they cause him to lose trust in his inner signposts, in his perceptions of himself and others, and in his most basic feelings. Such feelings—for example, feelings relating to our loving or being lovable—are always vulnerable to contrary attributions, i.e., to assertions that the person does not "really" feel this way or that he is only covering up, deceiving himself, etc. For these experiences cannot be confirmed by ordinary logic, by simple proof or disproof, or by recourse to an impartial arbitrator. To be validated, they must be subjectively asserted yet also be shared and exposed. But such sharing and exposure imply vulnerability to the violence of a cognitive binder.

L. Wynne (1972) has recently shown that such violence of cognitive binding can take two principal forms. It can occur either as an *injection of meaning* or a *withholding of meaning*. Where meaning is injected, the binder, may label the bindee for example, a spouse, as overworked and "nervous," while the latter sees herself as "merely" (yet justifiably) angry. The meanings "overworked" and "nervous" are here injected in order to substitute for the meaning "angry" as offered by the spouse. The latter is violated because the meanings "overworked" and "nervous" impute a self-image of weakness and helplessness while the meaning "anger" does not or does so less. This makes further understandable why attributions of weakness such as statements that the other is "sick," upset, sexually frustrated, or dependent generally have a stronger binding impact than attributes of badness—statements that the other is, for example, rebellious, cruel, mean, angry, etc. Attributions of weakness, much more than attributions of badness, impute as well as reinforce a continuing dependency on the supposedly stronger or healthier binder. Attributions of badness imply that the other person can eventually separate via rebellion and defiance, even though this may have to be achieved at the expense of a negative identity (cf. Stierlin et al., 1971).

Where binding operates mainly through the withholding of meaning, the binder remains essentially silent. Anyone who has treated families with silent members is likely to have experienced this binding stratagem. This member's silence increasingly unsettles all other participants. They seem anxiously glued to him and try to decipher his every grunt and blink while communication among themselves is paralyzed. When the silent member finally talks, frequently in brief and cryptic statements, his every word becomes the subject of the others' enduring, obsessive rumination and attention.

"Obedient" Self-Determination

The more dependent and immature the bindee, the more fateful the violence of the cognitive binder. The paradigm here is the parents' relationship to a dependent and immature child. We can speak of this child's cognitive thralldom to his stronger parent's reality (Stierlin, 1959).

The stronger binder can be violently coercive and yet can depict himself as well meaning and caring. Recently, M. Schatzman (1971) described how Daniel P. Schreber, whose paranoia was analyzed by Freud, was subject to such coercive binding by his father. The latter, a highly reputed educator and author, of whom even Freud spoke respectfully, acted as a sadist and persecutor while he trained his son to perceive him, the father, as loving and benevolent.

The same happened to countless victims of the Inquisition who were tortured by benevolent sadists who believed—and caused their victims to believe—that they acted out of concern for their victims' salvation. It also happened to those faithful victims of Stalin's purges, described by A. Koestler (1941) and others, who obediently accepted their stronger persecutors' definition of Marxist reality as well as of their (the victims') own motives and needs, including the need to let themselves be willingly executed. Such boundness of the victim reflects what we may call "obedient" self-determination, expressed succinctly by the heroine Iphigenie in Goethe's famous play of the same title, who states: *"Und folgsam fühlte sich meine Seele am schönsten frei"* ("Being obedient, my soul felt most blissfully free"). Here the cognitive binding seems complete. All awareness of having been bound, violated, and coerced has been abolished. Although he is wax in the binder's hand, the bindee believes himself to be free; and the coercive binder, the possessor of the stronger reality, instead of being (overtly) hated or feared, is venerated and loved.

Mutual Cognitive Thralldom

Although it makes sense to speak of a dependent and immature person's thralldom to the stronger person's reality, in practice such cognitive thralldom becomes mutual or transactional. There develops a circular, reinforcing yet highly restricting system of relationships, according to Wynne et al. (1958), wherein parents and children tend to act intermittently as binders and bindees to each other, thereby strengthening the binding bond. After a while, such a binding bond becomes nearly unseverable. Seriously cognitively bound couples and families therefore present the greatest challenge to therapy. Any intervention and any interpretation on the part of the therapist merely becomes material for further binding and leaves these patients as bound as before.

Where cognitive binding prevails, interpersonal conflicts as commonly understood are made difficult if not impossible. For there is lacking that articulated separateness and distinctness of positions that is the *sine qua non* for the subjective experience of conflicts. Conflicts, instead, appear pushed underground and blotted out by a mutual retreat into what D. Reiss (1971) has called "consensus sensitivity." This is a seemingly conflictless yet regressive and muddy way of relating wherein it is more important to somehow atune oneself to the partner's emotional needs and wavelengths than to confront the partner via an individual and articulated separateness.

The Separation Drama of Cognitively Bound Adolescents

The stage is thus set for a particular type of drama. In this drama the adolescent's newly accruing reasoning skills, which were described earlier, become the critical element. These intellectual skills could become potent forces in liberating him from his parents. They could help him to critically compare his own feelings, motives, and goals with those of his parents. But, as matters stand, any such attempt to exert his ego assertively and discriminatingly is bound to raise the titer of his parents' anxiety, thereby redoubling their efforts to bind their child to them even more than before. Such an adolescent, hampered by an uneven development yet more or less at ease with feeling cognitively bound (and with cognitively binding others), most likely will not be able to let his cognitive skills serve his drive toward autonomy. Rather, he will pervert his ideas into chains that bind him even more closely to his parents.

This happened to be the case with Max, a 16-year-old boy of superior intelligence. As he grew up, he became more inquisitive and started to read philosophical and psychological texts. His intellectual curiosity disturbed his mother. When he talked once at the breakfast table about ideas of C. G. Jung, she alluded to bookworm types who fail in life. Thus, she defined his intellectual and philosophical interests as weak, escapist cravings. Whenever she found him reading those "heavy books," she conveyed this message—more through her apprehensive, disapproving looks than through what she said. Occasionally, though, she lectured Max on the degenerate intellectuals in his father's family who had either killed themselves or ended up in madhouses. She told him this, she said, only reluctantly, out of her concern for his growth and well-being. When Max subsequently secluded himself to read or just to think, he noticed his pulse was hammering and his concentration waning. Was not this proof that reading and thinking were harmful, that they were evidence of his weakness and self-destructive streak, and that his mother (a somewhat high-strung woman, to be sure, but basically loving and concerned) was right? When he ventured timidly into the peer world, his apprehensions were confirmed. Being hypersensitive to being perceived as bookwormish, awkward, and inept, he acted awkwardly and ineptly and thereby invited confirmatory feedback. Increasingly, he avoided books as well as peers and spent more and more solitary hours in his room, simultaneously watching TV and numbing himself with rock music. His room was adjacent to that of his mother, who did not mind the noise.

Again, this dynamic constellation is bound to affect and reveal whether and how an adolescent runs away. It explains why a number of disturbed adolescents could not run away at all or could run away only abortively.

Having become accustomed to being bound, they were simply not up to the task of successfully relating to peers and other adults. When they tried to separate even temporarily, they were heading for a rude awakening because they could not deal effectively with the interpersonal peer reality that prevailed outside their family orbit. Like Max, they appeared deeply unsettled when they tried to move from the family culture into the peer culture. All seemed to badly lack skills needed for a life in a peer group or for dealing effectively with alternate adults.

For example, Emily, an attractive, relatively silent girl of 16, suddenly ran away from home, yet froze into a mute panic when a young man in the street asked her a question. A policeman eventually took Emily by the hand and led her home safely.

Emily had no friends at school and had never dated a boy. However, she could animatedly chat away with her family when no observer seemed present. All her cognitive skills seemed to serve her survival within an unusually binding and mystifying family field. When she tried to move outside, she experienced the equivalent of a "culture shock." She seemed totally at a loss when she had to deal with "normal," nonmystifying strangers.

Other adolescents seemed to "run away inwardly," to use a term of L. Wynne (1971). This indicates a deflection of cognitive growth into the buildup of a fantasy world that replaces the real world of living peers and alternate adults, and becomes *the* valued reality in these children's lives. This fantasy world, however, on closer inspection continues to interdigitate more or less with the fantasy world of other family members, despite its seeming idiosyncratic cast. I. Boszormenyi-Nagy (1965a), in particular, has described such interweaving of the family members' fantasies.

Abortive runaways of this type may run away in response to parental hassles. More frequently, they run off with little or no apparent overt parental provocation. While thus running away abortively, they appear mainly guided by their idiosyncratic introjects—offshoots of their fantasy world. Invariably, they strike us as very lonely runaways who nonetheless seem to be held on a long leash by their parents. In a precarious way, these children seem to try to make themselves at home in their fantasy world while they remain tied to their parents. They seem to unbind themselves in one sense while they remain bound in another. They appear both separated and unseparated, living in their own world and that of their parents, and yet not following the normal separation course of adolescence.

Binding Through the Exploitation of Loyalty

Certain parents contribute to yet another type of drama. This drama centers around the shift and modification of loyalties that the adolescent must achieve. At stake is the adolescent's successful final resolution of the Oedipus complex. Such a resolution would imply a successful, though relative, transfer of loyalty *away* from his parents and *toward* his friends, sexual and marital partners. This transfer of loyalty is dependent upon the adolescent modifying and/or attenuating his parental introjects so that he can cathect persons and values outside his family of origin in a relatively guilt-free manner. Parents can interfere with this process, however, by turning their children into lifelong, self-sacrificing victim-adjuncts, a phenomenon described well by Boszormenyi-Nagy (1972). Adolescents who are chiefly bound on this level are likely to experience any thought of, not to mention attempt at, separation as the number-one crime for which only the harshest punishment will do. I am inclined to speak here of "superego-bound" adolescents. Attribution of weakness, as described earlier, is here an important element. But much more is involved. These parents convey—sometimes overtly, but more often covertly—that they have totally sacrificed themselves for their child, that they lived only *for him*. Also, they convey, through their actions and apprehensions, that they can live only *through him*, i.e., that they need him to supply their life's blood, as it were, that they cannot exist without him. Therefore, leaving his parents in either thought or action becomes the adolescent's worst crime. For leaving is now tantamount to the murder of his parents.

These adolescents are prone to suffer maximal primitive "breakaway guilt," a guilt that operates mainly unconsciously and gives rise to acts of either massive self-destruction or heroic atonement. Primitive breakaway guilt, as intended here, intermeshes with, but also differs from, the type of guilt seen in many classically depressed patients who, while also bound and binding, try primarily to extract regressive gratifications.

Such archaic loyalty binding, too, colors any "separation conflicts" in adolescence. The threat of intense "breakaway guilt" operates here as a signal that warns the adolescent not to attempt to separate in either thought or action. Where he attempts such a separation, his "breakaway guilt" makes his conflicts unbearably intense. He can then resolve this conflict only by either destroying himself or ruefully returning to the parental orbit.

Such guilt-induced self-destruction appeared characteristic of certain of our abortive runaways of the "lonely schizoid" group. Roy is a case in point. One night Roy began to drift around town in a lonely and bizarre manner. He was carrying a camera, which made him a desirable target for muggers. None bothered him that night, however. He finally entered the fifth-floor apartment of a strange woman, again a dangerous undertaking these days, with the result that he was arrested and then hospitalized in a psychiatric institution before the night ended. He is currently institutionalized in a psychiatric sanatorium with his mother living close by. She thinks almost constantly of Roy and tries to see him as much as she can, although she seems to court only rebuff and agony from him. Apart from Roy, there is little that could give meaning and direction to her life; she has few, if any, interests and friends and feels suffocated in her marriage to an unloved, retiring husband whom she cannot consider divorcing.

In general, we expect the loyalty-bound adolescent not to run away at all. However, certain adolescents seem to suffer so much from intensified conflicts and ambivalences that, at one point or another, they run away regardless. When they do, they are, according to my observations, likely to fail spectacularly, as their guilt will sabotage any chance of runaway success. We can therefore expect these adolescents to resume their conflicted and ambivalent ties with their parents at the end of their abortive runaway attempts—yet often under circumstances that further confirm them as victims *and* as failures. Rather typically, as the case of Roy demonstrates, they become hospitalized as psychiatric patients and as such remain the targets of their parents' unending, intrusive, though ambivalent, concern. Here again we find that the separation of the adolescent remains pathologic and incomplete.

THE MODE OF DELEGATING

This transactional mode is found in parents who react to their own developmental crisis with ongoing, unresolved ambivalence and conflict. Instead of settling on either a centripetal or centrifugal solution, as described earlier, these parents appear torn between centripetal and and centrifugal forces of seemingly equal strength. At one point they seek their salvation within the family; at another, they seem driven to flee the family orbit. They seem bent on consolidating existing relations and jobs, and yet also seem compelled to make new starts. As their ambivalence intensifies, they turn to their children with conflicting expectations. They need to bind their children, but also to send them out. They want to benefit from them, but also need to be left alone and unhampered.

The term "delegate" denotes that the parents subject their children to these conflicting tendencies and hence to centrifugal as well as centripetal pressures. By making their child into a delegate they *send him out,* that is, encourage him to leave the family orbit. This meaning is conveyed by the Latin verb *"de-legare."* But also, while sending him out, they *hold onto him.* They entrust him with a mission, they make him into their proxy, their extended self. This second meaning, too, is contained in the original Latin word.

To the extent that parents succeed in recruiting their child as a delegate, it becomes his task to bear *their* ambivalence. He both takes it upon himself to cope with parental ambivalence and makes himself *their* reconciling agent. He fulfills this function often with ingenuity and skill, but always at the expense of his own genuine growth and separation.

If we turn to the dynamics of this delegating mode, we find that they include dynamics of the binding mode, yet with characteristic modifications and changes. Binding comes into play to the extent that the delegate, in addition to being sent out, must be induced to return home. The binding must be strong enough to counterbalance the "sending-out" component in the parent's behavior. But such binding also must operate more selectively and with a low profile, as it were. The parents must rely heavily on exploiting the delegate's unconscious loyalty, while they must relatively play down stratagems that bind the child on the affective and cognitive levels. For neither the affectively bound child who remains unduly captive to regressive parental gratification and hence lacks the motivation to move out, nor the strongly cognitively bound child whose distorted ego does not equip him to move into the peer group, has what it takes to become a "good" delegate.

The "good" delegate is not devastated by unconscious guilt should he move into the world of peers or alternate adults. He is not loyalty-bound in the sense that breaking away from the family becomes his number-one crime. His loyalty implies that he should become autonomous and skilled enough to carry out his special mission (or missions) and that he should experience guilt only when he fails, doubts, or rejects this mission. The phenomenology of his "loyalty boundness" differs therefore from the one found in more primitively loyalty-bound adolescents. We can speak of a selective and differentiated bond of loyalty that ties the delegate to his sender.

In addition to relating the dynamics of delegating to the dynamics of binding, we can consider them from another angle. Instead of focusing on how the parents' contributions bind the child, we can focus on the *mission* the delegate must fulfill. This further clarifies those dynamic aspects that seem central to the delegating mode. In characterizing this mission we can again give transactional meaning to well-known psychoanalytic concepts.

The delegate's mission is dictated by his parents' needs. Typically, these needs would give rise to intensified internal conflict and ambivalence for the parent should he try to fulfill them without enlisting the service of the delegate.

The Conflicts of the Delegate

In taking it upon himself to carry out his parents' wishes and to resolve their problems and ambivalences, the delegate can become subject to two main types of conflict: *loyalty conflicts* and *mission conflicts*. These types of conflicts distort any other—more or less age-appropriate—conflicts he may experience over his individuation and separation.

Conflicts of loyalty arise when the delegate, in trying to remain loyal to one parent, is pitted against the other parent. Hamlet presents the paradigm of a loyalty conflict. He remained loyalty-bound to his dead father and was commissioned to destroy his mother. This embroiled him in deep and tragic conflict. The conflict of loyalties can also pit the adolescent's loyalty to the family as a whole against the loyalty he feels toward individual members.

Ordinarily, a child will align himself with the parent he perceives to be dominant (i.e., represents the stronger reality), similar to the way a medieval vassal would try to align himself with the most powerful feudal lord. This explains why loyalty conflicts in a family are bound to become most fierce when the two parents are nearly equally dominant or when the balance of parental power shifts.

Conflicts between incompatible missions are also common. If the adolescent tries to execute them both, his conflicts deepen. Such conflicts of missions are aggravated by a conflict of loyalties. This occurs when a delegate feels beholden to both parents, each of whom exposes him to his or her brand of incompatible missions. The different types of delegated conflicts become clearer when we consider, next, the various missions a delegate might have to fulfill. Table 19.2 may serve as reference.

Table 19.2. Major Missions of Delegates

A. Missions serving the parent's elementary (affective) needs	B. Missions serving the parent's ego	C. Missions serving the parent's superego
Delegate must supply "id nutriment," i.e., must become a "thrill provider," thus often fulfilling a repair function for parents. Thrills may be shaped by exigencies of oral, anal, or phallic period	1. Simple helping or ego-support missions Delegate must run errands, work in the house, etc. 2. Fighting missions Delegate must support embattled parent 3. "Scout missions" Delegate serves as parent's experimenter 4. Complex ego-support missions Delegate must protect parent's fragile ego by sparing him heightened conflict and ambivalence	1. Missions serving the parent's ego ideal: Delegate must fulfill parent's own unrealized aspirations 2. Missions serving the parent's self-observation: Delegate must externalize (embody) the parent's disowned "badness" 3. Missions serving to alleviate the parent's conscience: Delegate must atone for the parent's disowned "badness"

The Delegate Who Serves the Parent's
Elementary (Affective) Needs

It is the foremost mission of certain delegates to provide a parent with "id nutriment"—perceived to lie outside the family orbit—which the parent, for one reason or another, views as unobtainable by his own efforts. Therefore, the delegate is sent out and expected to bring back to the parent the coveted nutriment, which is then enjoyed by proxy. The parent experiences vicarious thrills, elicited by hints or vivid descriptions coming from the child, which stimulate the parent's imagination. These thrills, though avidly sought, can also conveniently be disowned by the parent. The child is scolded and punished for the very things he has been delegated to do. The thrills can be primarily sexual. In this case, the parent covertly goads the delegate to engage in various sexual activities, including perversions and orgies, on which the parent wants to feed. Or these thrills may have a more oral, pregenital flavor. In this case, the parent may covertly instigate and vicariously enjoy his child's drug or drinking parties. In other cases, these thrills chiefly involve wanting to do the forbidden and wanting to defy authorities. Such pleasures conceivably relate to vicissitudes of the anal period. In this case a parent covertly encourages and enjoys delinquent behavior in his child. But strong parental dependency needs of the clinging type, which play an important role in the binding mode discussed earlier, cannot be fulfilled by a delegate who is sent out and thereby allowed to loosen his ties to the parent. Therefore, if such parental dependency needs are strong, they will conflict with parental needs for having a thrill-providing delegate. In this case, the binding mode will most likely dominate over the delegating mode.

The delegate enlisted to provide vicarious satisfactions must often fulfill a repair function. He must provide his parents with experiences the latter missed when *they* were adolescents. He must now make up for his parents' aborted and frustrated adolescence and come up with a double dose of adolescent excitement sufficient for his own and his parents' consumption.

The Delegate Who Serves the Parents' Ego

H. Hartmann (1950), building on Freud's basic discoveries, called the ego an "organ of adaptation and organization." In sticking to this broad definition, we can outline several types of missions for adolescents that strengthen or support their parents' ego.

All these missions imply that the child is allowed and pushed to develop limited individuation, autonomy, and skills (or ego functions, if you wish), those required to carry out his missions. He is sent out and, held on a long leash of loyalty, he is also expected to come back.

A first type of ego mission can be called *simple helping or supporting.*

A child or house slave is expected to help in the kitchen or in the field and, for this purpose, is allowed and trained to wash dishes, pick cotton, or run errands.

A second type of helping mission implies more complex dynamics. Here the parent seeks ego support and protection from the adolescent in his on-going battles with other persons. These persons may be a hated spouse, an in-law, or an outside figure whom the parent perceives as persecuting and malevolent. It becomes the adolescent's mission to serve this parent as a faithful, unswerving ally in his battles, similar to the medieval bondsman who unwaveringly served his feudal lord. It is this mission for which Hamlet provides the paradigm, a mission most likely to embroil the delegate in loyalty conflicts.

This type of mission, like the others, ordinarily requires that the adolescent be sent out of the family orbit. If a mother enlists her son for the purpose of showing up her husband as a professional failure, she needs to encourage the son to move out and study hard so that he can become a professional success. Such recruitment of a son as a delegate ally may be prompted by the mother's ambivalent wish to break away from a marriage she finds distasteful and stifling. She exploits her son's sense of loyalty and uses him as part of a strategy designed to devalue and defeat her husband.

A third type of ego mission helps the partner to gather certain kinds of vital information. Such a parent may use the delegate as experimenter. This adolescent is expected to test out new solutions to his parents' conflicts or problems. These usually reflect the parent's ambivalent wish to break away from an existing job and family situation and to make a new start in life. In order for him to fulfill this type of mission, it becomes necessary that he be sent out (and be coerced to return). D. Reiss (1970) spoke here of the "scout function" of the adolescent. This adolescent is delegated to do something that the parent feels too afraid or to embarrassed to do himself. For example, a parent who wants to break out of the family and divorce his spouse but is afraid of doing so can use his adolescent for the purpose of obtaining firsthand information about what it is like to live by oneself. A shy and retiring father who is afraid of dealing with authority figures can covertly delegate his son to battle with such figures. After having observed the son's more-or-less successful battling, he can conceivably dare to do it himself.

Finally, closely related to the mission of providing id nutriment and of serving the parent's self-observation (to be discussed in the following section) is the mission to support and complement the parent's defensive system. For example, a delegate who must provide his parent with id nutriment (e.g., must engage in orgies or smoke pot on his parent's behalf) may also have to alleviate his parent's anxiety, guilt, and conflict about needing such nutriment. His task becomes now more difficult as he, in addition to becoming profligate, embodying and enacting his parent's forbidden impulses, must also offer himself as a living screen for his parent's punitive projections. His major mission becomes, then, to maintain the parent's defensive organization, i.e., to "protect" and support his parent's fragile ego by sparing the latter heightened conflict and ambivalence.

This delegating mode comes into play when a parent enlists an adolescent son to resolve his own conflicts over delinquent tendencies. This parent covertly encourages his son to become a delinquent and then attacks him for doing so. He allows him to associate with delinquent peers and permits him to move out of the family orbit temporarily, yet awaits his return to mete out punishment. The delegate must be a delinquent and willingly submit to punishment as well.

The Delegate Who Serves the Parent's Superego

The mission here can pertain to any of the three functions that Freud (1933) attributed to the superego: to serve as ego ideal, to self-observe, or to be a conscience.

If the adolescent is delegated mainly to serve his parent's ego ideal, he will be sent out into life in order to fulfill those parental aspirations the parent himself cannot realize. The adolescent is burdened with his parent's exaggerated and frustrated wishes to become an actor, scientist, physician, financial tycoon, etc.

If support of the parent's self-observation and self-confirmation becomes the adolescent's main mission, he will be delegated to provide a living contrast: to be bad. He is to be mischief-maker, troubled, crazy, and so on, in order for the parent to be reassured that he himself is not bad, crazy, etc., after all. This delegate must fulfill a function similar to that which the "inferior" southern Negroes performed for their white masters; the latter found their own inwardly doubted superiority confirmed by constantly observing and confirming the Negro's "inferiority."

Finally, a delegate's main mission can be the alleviation of the parent's often excessively strict conscience. In this case, the adolescent will be covertly encouraged to commit and seek punishment for those delinquent acts about which the parent himself harbors (chiefly unconscious) guilt. Here the term "superego lacunae," as suggested by A. Johnson and S. Szurek (1952), seems useful. The delegate is used to blot out these parental lacunae by making himself into the unwitting perpetrator of mischief and receiver of punishment. Here we typically find the adolescent who starts to steal in the same manner and at about the same time as did his father when the latter was an adolescent. The father can now comfortably tell himself that his own stealing as an adolescent could not have been so bad after all, as it is obviously an adolescent thing to do. Whatever residual guilt was left in the father will now be expiated by proxy, and he will continue to prompt his son to further punishment seeking.

This adolescent delegate becomes recruited to atone for his parent's assumed or actual wrongdoing. One can think here of certain German students who went to work in Israel in order to atone for their parents' crimes, crimes that these parents themselves could not consciously acknowledge. The youngsters called their action "sign of atonement" *(Aktion Sühnezeichen)*. Their parents seemed to have succeeded in delegating—i.e., sending out to Israel—and unloading the pain of their guilt and repair work on to their adolescent children.

Delegates Who Run Away

I found that most runaways in our sample exemplified to varying extents certain of the dynamics of delegating outlined above. Those runaways whom I have called "crisis runaways" particularly reflect these dynamics.[3] They differed from the abortive runaways in that they were more successful in their runaway attempts. They managed to get away from their homes for rather extended periods and, at the same time, were able to become more persistently involved with their peers than were the abortive runaways. Yet these runaways seemed to differ also from the group of more casual runaways which, as we shall see, chiefly reflect the expelling mode. The "crisis runaways" under discussion here typically seemed to run away in response to some manifest crisis within the family. These youngsters, like the abortive runaways, appear subject to conflicting forces from their parents and from within themselves, which affects the manner and style of their runaway ventures. They tend to relate more successfully to peers and therefore know where to run; namely to some group or peer hangout, occasionally to distant relatives. Thus, they manage to stay away longer than the abortive runaways.

Increasingly I came to see these crisis runaways as fulfilling various delegated missions that often conflicted with each other yet nonetheless held the adolescent in their grip. Those runaways who chiefly served their parents' elementary and affective needs were delegated to bring back to their parents thrills and excitements the parents could vicariously enjoy.

Lorraine, a crisis runaway, is here a case in point. The more Lorraine developed into an attractive, well-built, and slightly precocious teenager, the more her mother, grimly and excitedly, warned her of those wanton boys who were bent only on sexual mischief. This mother seemed obsessed with the possibility of Lorraine spending her nights with disreputable and orgy-prone young men. Not surprisingly, Lorraine confirmed her mother's apprehensions. She ran away repeatedly, first to a nearby abandoned house, later to a distant metropolitan area where she, indeed, slept around with strange boys. This came to a halt after the family and Lorraine entered therapy (conjoint therapy for the whole family and individual therapy for Lorraine). Mainly through Lorraine's individual therapy it became apparent how much the girl had served as her mother's unwitting, thrill-providing delegate.

Bob, a boy of 16, provides an example of a delegate who acted out his father's unconscious delinquent wishes and tendencies. While away from home, Bob kept his father agonized and excited by one daring exploit after another. He engaged the police in reckless car chases, stole money by the most ingenious methods, outwitted pool sharks, etc. Johnson and Szurek (1952) have well described the manner in which parents instigate and recruit delegates for such delinquent missions.

Gary, also 16 years old, demonstrated how an adolescent, in the very act of running away, can fulfill a parent's unconscious repair needs; that is, live out belatedly a part of this parent's own aborted adolescence. Gary, more than most other runaways in our sample, seemed motivated by wanderlust and roadside adventurism. After he returned home from a runaway episode of almost a month's duration, his parents—as well as his fellow patients and nurses on the ward—listened spellbound to the story of his exploits. He had gone to Mexico, had met many interesting people, had worked and slept at the most diverse places, making pale, so it seemed, the experiences of a Kerouac or "easy riders." Gary's father, I learned subsequently, had been deprived and pushed into a premature restrictive independence by his own parents and had never had a chance to satisfy *his* wanderlust. In the main, his adolescence had consisted of drudgery and study. He had dreamed of taking off, however, and visiting a certain area of the Mexican wilderness that for him was imbued with the romance of Indians and adventurous horsemen. It was this place that Gary, as if steered by a hidden, unerring gyroscope, had made the target of his runaway venture.

Tracy, another 16-year-old runaway, in response to her father's covert messages, became self-destructively promiscuous and, in so doing, offered herself as a target for her father's punitive projections. In this way she took upon herself not only the mission of providing her father with exciting sexual id nutriment, but also that of keeping operational her father's ego defenses of denial and projection. Typically, Tracy would run away in response to some allusion or covert expectation of the father that she, Tracy, was a whore at heart. One evening, for example, the father read Tracy's diary, which he was not supposed to read but which was ingeniously placed in his way. It referred to her sexual interests in several boys. He immediately "confronted" Tracy with this evidence of evil proclivities. Tracy, then not quite 13 years old, ran away later that night. Between the ages of 13 and 16 she ran away nine times. Each time she ran further away and stayed away for a longer period. Each time, also, she left some clue that made it possible for her father, by employing a detective's ingenuity, to trace her whereabouts—usually a hippie community in some metropolitan area—and eventually to rescue her. After the last rescue attempt, in which the father made use of police connections and underworld contacts, the family got into family therapy and Tracy received residential treatment. Family therapy revealed how much the father, a paranoid and potentially murderous man, had delegated Tracy to provide sexual excitement that he could also fight with sadistic righteousness.

Karen was another runaway in the crisis group. Her chief mission was to provide ego support to her embittered mother. This mother, who was the dominant parent, recruited the girl for the purpose of devastating her husband and thereby possibly breaking up a marriage that to the mother had become repulsive, stifling, and insupportable. Karen's mother hated, above everything else, what she considered her husband's restricted and restricting conventionality. In order to defeat him, she enlisted Karen as an ally. Karen ran away from home and—in the fulfillment of her mission—became sexually involved with a young black man who made his living from panhandling and pimping. The father, as was to be expected, perceived in his daughter's runaway escapade the ruin of everything he had worked for and believed in, while the mother praised Karen's daring unconventionality and inner freedom. As though to infuriate her husband even more, she invited Karen's lover into her home, where she treated him approvingly and flirtatiously. She continued to support her daughter's "honest experimental relationship" as long as it crushed her husband.

We turn now to the ways in which the runaways in our sample appeared to serve their parents' superegos. Here we have to deal, first, with the possibility of a delegate representing and fulfilling a parent's frustrated ego ideal. Dean and Donna, two runaway siblings aged 14 and 15, respectively, demonstrate how precipitous running away may become linked to the vicarious achievement of a certain type of parental ego ideal. Mr. Farmer, Dean's and Donna's father, had always lived in the shadow of his older, more successful brother, a banker and connoisseur of the arts. The brother had become a man of the world; adventurous, outgoing, and popular, he had done many interesting things and met interesting people. Mr. Farmer, in contrast, had turned into a restricted bureaucrat. Throughout most of his adult life he spent his days adding up figures in a big office while enviously musing upon the adventurous careers and opportunities he had missed. In his first interview he spoke admiringly of Dean and Donna as being much like his older brother and different from himself. Whereas he saw himself as shy and timid, he saw Donna and Dean as daring, extroverted, and experimentative. As it turned out, they were experimentative with a vengeance. Whether it was experimenting with sex or drugs, with new life styles (such as living in communes), with being in the forefront of protest movements, Dean and Donna always seemed to be "where the action was." Not quite 16, Dean could boast of having become acquainted with more facets of life than his parents ever had or would. These experiences, many of them gained during his runaway episodes, included various delinquencies such as breaking into people's houses, pushing drugs, having sexual relations with black girls, associating with homosexuals, Black Panthers, taking part in gunfights, etc.

The self-observation and self-confirmation of the parents—the second superego function to be discussed—is served when adolescents, while running away, provide that living contrast of badness the parents need so that they can view themselves as good and virtuous. This was the situation between Tracy and her father. Wherever runaway adolescents let themselves be enlisted as living screens for their parents' punitive projections, they serve this parental self-observing superego function.

Finally, I found in many of our crisis runaways the dynamics of parental guilt expiation by proxy. It seemed to me no accident that several of the runaway adolescents who tried to get away from home by means of a car (usually stolen) promptly created accidents. Other runaways seemed to have a knack for being quickly apprehended by the police (often on charges of possessing or handling drugs), when a minimum of circumspection could have avoided such fate. In contrast to the loyalty-bound adolescents described earlier, these crisis adolescents seemed to invite punishment, not so much because they betrayed their primary loyalty to their parents, but because they, like Tracy, made it their mission to externalize and invite punishment for their parents' disowned "bad" impulses. One can therefore say that these runaway delegates remained loyal as targets for punishment by proxy.

THE MODE OF EXPELLING

In the expelling mode, again, the parents contribute to a distorted separation. And, as in the two earlier-described modes, they do so because they try to cope with their developmental crises.

The crucial element here is that the parents, in trying to solve *their* crises, come to view their adolescent children as hindrances. Whether these parents want to make new starts in life—for example, seek new partners, new jobs, new emotional investments—or simply want to find peace, their children, instead of being viewed as living assets that can be bound or delegated, appear burdensome and expendable. Therefore, these parents accelerate the centrifugal momentum inherent in the adolescent process, as they seem to have everything to gain and nothing to lose by pushing their children's early and definitive separation. These parents, in other words, expel their children because, in contrast to the binding and delegating parents, they *do not want* these children.

Expelling can be viewed as a "sending out" minus the retracting, binding component inherent in the delegating mode. Expelling reflects an extreme centrifugal momentum, and the binding mode an extreme centripetal momentum, whereas the delegating mode occupies an intermediate position, comprising centrifugal as well as centripetal elements.

When the expelling mode prevails, parents rebuff and neglect their children. Either in a busy or in a withdrawn way, they seem so preoccupied with themselves and their own projects that they let their children run loose, as it were; they seem unconcerned when the children spend endless hours in front of the television set, experiment with drugs or precocious sex, skip classes, or roam around with delinquent gangs. In German, many of these children would be called *verwahr-lost*, which has a somewhat different meaning than being merely deprived and neglected. These children are unduly left to themselves and constantly get the message: "You are expendable, the earlier you leave the home the better." Because the children are predominantly seen as nuisances, the emotional climate in these families differs from the one found in binding and delegating families. There is lacking the ongoing though often conflicted and exploitative investment in the child that gives the latter a sense of being important to his parents.

Runaways and the Expelling Mode

Adolescents who are exposed to an enduring expelling mode run away early and casually, without much ado. Realizing they are neither cared for nor wanted, they take to peer groups and alternate adults early and easily, to the extent that their interpersonal skills equip them to do so.

It seemed unlikely that our sample of adolescents and families would yield many runaways who bore the imprint of the expelling mode, for I assumed that enduringly rejecting and neglecting parents are ordinarily not motivated to seek ongoing psychiatric help. There were, however, a few runaways in our sample who seemed to fit the above dynamics and typology rather well. These belonged to the group I have called "casual runaways." One of them was George.

George was difficult to handle, and when his parents tried to control him, he threw tantrums and became obnoxious. For the sake of peace, his parents allowed him to "get away with murder." They just gave up control and, eventually, interest. George, bent on mischief, ran away from home, first for hours, then for half days, then for days. He ran away for several days at about the age of 14, after he had stolen some jewelry that he subsequently sold. His departures then became ever more casual and occasions for delinquent activities—usually carried out with buddies from his tough motorcycle gang. By then his parents no longer seemed to care. Eventually he was arrested for taking part in a burglary that netted several thousand dollars' worth of jewelry.

There were other cases in my sample who, though not as blatant as George, revealed neglectful and unconcerned parents. Rather typically, I needed to become enduringly acquainted—through psychotherapy and ongoing observation—with an adolescent and his family before I could appreciate the extent of the parents' insidious expelling and neglecting behavior. I have already mentioned the examples of Dean and Donna, whom their father enlisted as delegates in the service of his ego ideal and who became precocious separators and experimenters. In addition to using these children as delegates, the parents were neglectful and hence insidiously expelling. The father's presence as an executive, caring parent was almost nil, for he tended to gulp a few martinis before dinner and then, dreamily dozing, would withdraw from family life for the rest of the evening. He seemed unaware or unconcerned when Dean and Donna had sex and drug parties in their bedrooms or when they engaged in delinquencies. The mother, in spurts, tried to take the father's place as the family's limit-setter and organizer, but her parenting remained inadequate also. Much of her energies and time were taken up by unending hassles with her passive husband, whom she despised. She spent little time at home herself. Despite the fact that there were five children in the family—two of them below the age of ten—she had a full-time job that kept her away from home from eight in the morning until five in the evening. During this time, she left the care of the children to their schools, to makeshift arrangements, and to themselves. When she came home, she was tired, angered by her husband's alcoholic withdrawal, and quickly exhausted by the unsolvable task of checking on the children's accumulative delinquencies, absences, or passive-active avoidance of household duties.

As I have indicated, families with "casual" runaways seem more frequent in the larger population than my sample suggests. Presently it is estimated that approximately 40 to 60% of so-called street people (permanent precariously adjusted runaways who live on welfare, handouts, shorttime jobs, the sales of drugs, etc.) have been rejected by parents who refuse to resume contact with them. Most of these runaways have probably been exposed to insidious neglect and rejection. The case of Mary Ann, although perhaps not quite typical, seems to illustrate the family dynamics that operate in the expelling mode here under discussion.

Mary Ann's story was reported by B. J. Phillips in *The Washington Post* of May 29, 1970. A follow-up story, written by Haynes Johnson, appeared in that same newspaper on March 21, 1971. Mary Ann, a 14-year-old runaway from a suburb north of Miami, became instantly famous when she was photographed crying beside the dead body of a student killed by National Guardsmen during the Kent State unrest earlier in 1970. Much of her parents' energies, instead of being channeled into the care of their children, seemed consumed by marital hassles. According to the policeman who handled Mary Ann's case in the juvenile court, her father "has been hot-tempered enough to go to jail for breach of the peace in Opalaka. The mother several times had sworn out peace warrants against her husband for disputes between themselves." Mary Ann's father worked as a carpenter and private contractor. He was quoted as saying, "I worked one hundred fifty hours a week for my family," indicating his unavailability as a father. All the other children in the family had become runaways with the exception of the youngest, who was three. A son, 20 at the time of the report, was serving a jail sentence for auto theft; another son, 16, the father of a four-month-old son, had been arrested for possession of marijuana. Mary Ann, while never having been charged with serious crimes, had begun to run away frequently and was regularly breaking the town's curfew from the age of 13. According to police, she had been on the fringe of adolescent drug use in Opalaka. Although the lengthy newspaper report gives many clues to parental neglect and rejection in the intended meaning here, the mother is quoted as saying, "Mary Ann wasn't neglected. She had the best clothes and all she could eat and she could go wherever she wanted to go. It was the school, not us." The very fact, though, that Mary Ann was always allowed to go where she wanted to indicates to me that the parents lacked the kind of caring, limit-setting investment I have tried to emphasize.

Expulsions via enduring rebuff and neglect must be distinguished from those dramatic expulsions that chiefly reflect the dynamics of a binding or delegating mode. It is only in expulsions of the first type that we may speak of an expelling mode proper.

Dramatic expulsions of the second type may occur when the balance of modes in a family shifts. I indicated earlier that transactional modes may blend and that one mode may become more or less dominant over time. Dramatic expulsions, according to my observations, may signal a switch away from a binding or delegating mode. A binding or delegating parent, usually after agonizing inner turmoil and ambivalence, has decided here to get rid of his ill-begotten child for good.

Such a dramatic expulsion, while reflecting binding and delegating transactions that have reached a critical climax, may also reveal the additional long-standing operation of an expelling mode proper. Insidious, though covert, rejective parental tendancies may then come to the fore in such dramatic expulsion of adolescents who, till now, appeared mainly bound or delegated. Most frequently, however, dynamics such as the following seem involved.

The dramatic, climactic expulsion that follows prolonged binding or delegating parental efforts resembles the manner in which marital partners of long standing may try to separarate. These partners, feeling trapped in suffocating ambivalence, can liberate themselves only by unleashing onto each other such an onslaught of rejecting hate and bitterness that they erase all chances for future reconciliation.

An expulsion that thus reverses a prevailing binding or delegating mode must be made to stick, and hence must be backed up by some unmistakable and irreversible rejecting parental action. I observed such action, for example, when one father made up his mind to get rid of his 20-year-old daughter whose seductive wiles he had so far ambivalently encouraged. In exasperation, he finally threw her down the stairs and forbade her to ever come back. He stuck to this decision despite the girl's pleading, wailing, and underhanded attempts to return home. Realizing that her father meant business, she eventually moved into another town where she made herself independent. This father, it may be added, could more easily adopt an uncompromising expelling stance because a younger daughter, no less attractive than the older one, was ready to fill her sister's vacated position. Another expelling father, after much ambivalent wavering, finally rallied his energies to get his son enlisted in the army. In so doing, he too tried to make sure that his expulsion would stick.

When an expelling mode proper prevails, the final expulsion seems by comparison undramatic. This expulsion appears, then, the logical sequence to ongoing parental rebuff and neglect, i.e., lack of concern and involvement. The child represents here for the parents some piece of cheap living furniture that can easily be used, abused, and finally discarded. When he seems useful he is, on the spur of the moment, cajoled, bribed, and manipulated; when he seems not useful he is cursed, kicked, and pushed out of sight. Much anger and hate may be expended between these parents and their children, but the anger and hate do not have the enslaving sadomasochistic, erotized quality we frequently find in the binding mode, nor do they express deep disappointment and disillusionment due to the child's not living up to his parents' expectations or image. Instead, this anger and hatred are usually shallow and aroused by immediate, situational frustrations. Typically, such a parent beats his child because he left his bycycle standing in front of the parent's car, while he passes over unnoticed and unpunished the child's drug taking or disruptive behavior in school.

This difference between expulsions within, on the one hand, the binding and delegating mode, and, on the other, the expelling mode proper, also affects the runaway picture.

Dramatically expelled adolescents, according to my observations, will often run away (either abortively or for longer periods of time) in ways that suggest that they try to forestall, anticipate, or provoke the parents' expulsion of them. Larry and Gerald, two 16-year-old boys, serve as examples.

Gerald had a tortured, ambivalent relationship with his alcoholic father. This father badly wanted to spend time with Gerald in order to find solace for his alcoholic misery and loneliness. He pleaded with his son to stay with him, spoiled him with numerous gifts, and tried to bribe him. Gerald was tempted to give in to the father's binding stratagems but, at the same time, found himself wooed by his mother, thus suffering a conflict of loyalties. His mother viewed her husband as weak, contemptible, and a hindrance to her ambivalently coveted freedom. She succeeded in winning

Gerald over as her ally and caused him to share her disparaging view of his father. The boy would ridicule, tease, and exasperate his father, thus nourishing the latter's resolve to get rid of the boy for good, painful as the operation might be. As time went on, the father's threats to expel Gerald became more ominous and the boy became more afraid, and hence more prone to run away. Gerald finally paved the way for his expulsion when he ran away for ten days. The father took this as a final proof of Gerald's incorrigibility and, by arranging for his hospitalization in another city, expelled him.

Larry, even more than Gerald, engaged his father in an intense sadomasochistic battle. Whatever father and son tried to do, they found themselves at once deadlocked in their bittersweet struggle. Larry, who was able to devise ever new ways of ridiculing and humiliating his father, ran away several times, each time in ways that enraged his father further. For example, Larry publicly smoked hash, thereby causing his father, a prominent figure in his community's antinarcotics program, to look ridiculous to his colleagues. Yet while away from home, Larry neglected his health so alarmingly that his father felt compelled to rescue him, and Larry, under protest, allowed himself to be rescued. Back at home, the sadomasochistic transaction resumed promptly until Larry, worn out and ambivalent, ran away again. This transactional pattern escalated over a period of two years to a point where the father finally evicted Larry, who then moved in with his mother—who was separated from her husband. After Larry broke off all contact with his father and settled down to live with his mother, he no longer ran away. Later, when he was approaching 18, he left his mother in order to enter a hippie commune. Both Gerald and Larry belong to the group of crisis runaways. The crisis with which they had to cope was one of an intensifying ambivalence experienced by parent and child that engendered an expelling momentum. Once this crisis was resolved through their definitive expulsion, they no longer needed to run away.

In contrast, where a more insidiously rejecting parental attitude—i.e., a truly "expelling mode"—prevails, the runaway phenomena appear different as, I believe, the earlier examples of casual runaway show. In these examples, the children seem more to drift than to run away. If there is crisis and struggle in the family, these efforts are relatively shallow and short-lived. What is overriding is the parent's enduring wish to get rid of his child.

NOTES

1. I am indebted to Dr. K. Ravenscroft, Jr., for this formulation.

2. Binding on the affective level, as described here, relates to the psychoanalytic concept of fixation. In defining this concept, O. Fenichel (1945) suggested intertwining transactional and intrapsychic dynamics. Transactionally, fixations (of drives) denote a history of either excessive gratification, excessive frustration, or abrupt alternations between both modes. Intrapsychically, "fixations are rooted in experi-

ences of instinctual satisfaction that simultaneously gave reassurance in the face of some anxiety or aided in repressing some feared impulse. Such simultaneous satisfaction of drive and of security is the most common cause of fixations" (p. 66). The concept of binding can be seen as explicating the ongoing transactional dynamics that either sustain or give rise to such fixations.

3. This characterization of the dynamics of runaways agrees only partly with that offered by R. Jenkins (1971), who was influential in including the "runaway reaction" in the *Diagnostic and Statistical Manual* of the American Psychiatric Association.

REFERENCES

Baldwin, J. M. *Genetic theory of reality*. New York: Putnam, 1915.

Bateson, G. "Double Bind, 1969." Paper presented at the Symposium on the Double Bind, Annual Meeting of the American Psychological Association, Washington, D.C., September 2, 1969.

Bateson, G., Jackson, D., Haley, J., and Weakland, J. Toward a theory of schizophrenia. *Behavioral Science*, 1956, *1*, 251–264.

Bateson, G., Jackson, D., Haley, J., and Weakland, J.: A note on the double bind. *Family Process*, 1963, *2*, 154–161.

Boszormenyi-Nagy, I. "The Concept of Change in Conjoint Family Therapy." In A. S. Friedman, et al. (Eds.), *Psychotherapy for the whole family*, pp. 305–319. New York: Springer, 1965(a).

Boszormenyi-Nagy, I. Loyalty implications of the transference model in psychotherapy. *Archives of General Psychiatry*, 1972, *27*, 374–380.

Bruch, H. Conceptual confusion in eating disorders. *Journal of Nervous and Mental Disease*, 1961, *133*, 46–54.

Bruch, H. Falsification of bodily needs and body concepts in schizophrenia. *Archives of General Psychiatry*, 1962, *6*, 18–24.

Bruch, H. "Eating Disorders and Schizophrenic Development." In G. L. Usdin (Ed.), *Psychoneurosis and schizophrenia*. Philadelphia: Lippincott, 1966.

Fenichel, O. *The psychoanalytic theory of neurosis*. New York: Norton, 1945.

Freud, S. "New Introductory Lectures." *Standard Edition, 22*, 57–80. London: Hogarth Press, 1964 (1933).

Haley, J. The family of the schizophrenic. A model system. *Journal of Nervous and Mental Disease*, 1959, 129:357–374.

Hartmann, H. Comments on the psychoanalytic theory of the ego. *Psychoanalytic Study of the Child* (1950), *5*, 74–96.

Jenkins, R. The runaway reaction. *American Journal of Psychiatry*, 1971, *128*, 168–173.

Johnson, A. and Szurek, S. A. The genesis of antisocial acting out in children and adults. *Psychoanalytic Quarterly*, 1952, *21*, 323–343.

Koestler, A. *Darkness at noon*. New York: Macmillan, 1941.

Laing, R. D. *The self and others: Further studies in sanity and madness*. London: Tavistock Publications, 1961.

Laing, R. D. "Mystification, Confusion, and Conflict." In I. Boszormenyi-Nagy and J. L. Framo (Eds.), *Intensive family therapy*. New York: Harper & Row, 1965.

Reiss, D. Personal communication, 1970.

Reiss, D. Varieties of consensual experience: Contrast between families of normals, delinquents, and schizophrenics. *Journal of Nervous and Mental Disease*, 1971, *152*, 73–95.

Singer, M. T. and Wynne, L. C. Though disorder and family relations of schizophrenics. III: Methodology using projective techniques. *Archives of General Psychiatry*, 1965, *12*, 187–200. (a)

Singer, M. T. and Wynne, L. C. Thought disorder and family relations of schizophrenics. IV: Results and implications. *Archives of General Psychiatry*, 1965, *12*, 201–212. (b)

Schatzman, M. Paranoia or persecution: The case of Schreber. *Family Process*, *1971*, *10*, 177–207.

Stierlin, H.: The adaptation to the "stronger" person's reality. *Psychiatry*, 1959, *22*, 143–152.

Stierlin, H., Levi, L. D., and Savard, R. J. Parental perceptions of separating children. *Family Process*, 1971, *10*, 411–427.

Wynne, L. C.: Personal communication, 1971.

Wynne, L. C.: "The Injection and the Concealment of Meaning in the Family Relations and Psychotherapy of Schizophrenics." In D. Rubinstein and Y. O. Alanen (Eds.), *Psychotherapy of schizophrenia*, pp. 180–193. Amsterdam: Excerpta Medica, 1972.

Wynne, L. C. and Singer, M. T. Thought disorder and family relations of schizophrenics: I. A research strategy. *Archives of General Psychiatry*, 1963, *9*, 191–198. (a)

Wynne, L. C. and Singer, M. T. Thought disorder and family relations of schizophrenics: II. A classification of forms of thinking. *Archives of General Psychiatry*, 1963, *9*, 199–206. (b)

Wynne, L. C., Ryckoff, I. M., Day, J., and Hirsch, S. I. Pseudo-mutuality in the family relations of schizophrenics. *Psychiatry*, 1958, *21*, 205–220.

20

Central Issues in the Construction of Sibling Relationships

GERALD HANDEL

My purpose in this chapter is to present a systematic way of thinking about sibling relationships. Reviews of the literature have concluded that the study of sibling interaction and sibling relationships has been neglected. In a well-known paper that was perhaps the first to make the point, Irish (1964) contrasted the great amount of study of marriage and of parent-child relationships and noted: "The interactions between and among children in the home . . . seem to have been given relatively little heed" (Irish, 1966, p. 149). Fifteen years later, Schvaneveldt and Ihinger (1979, p. 453) concluded that "with few exceptions . . . research and theory have not been expanded beyond Irish's early formulation."

Schvaneveldt and Ihinger sought to move beyond Irish's formulation. They conceptualize the family as a system and, after examining relevant literature, they state, "We have attempted to glean and mold propositions. . . . Our focus has stressed the importance of the sib subsystem in the greater family system, and the importance of siblings in the socialization process" (1979, pp. 464–5). This chapter shares the impulse to rectify the omission described by Irish. This author agrees that sibling relationships are important.

The viewpoint of the two papers differs significantly.

1. *They speak of the family as a system.* I prefer to think of the family as a group, which is one type of organization. The interrelatedness of activity among humans is a basic assumption in social psychology; the concepts of group and organization capture the fundamental qualities of collectivity and interrelatedness. The importation of the concept of system from engineering, astronomy, and biology is both gratuitous and misleading. Gratuitous because superfluous. Misleading because to speak of the family

367

as a system exaggerates the inevitability and determinateness of interaction within it. It generates an analogy of family members as machine parts or nonvolitional elements, pulled in sequences by forces totally outside their control, as gravity pulls the planets in the solar system or as temperature regulates the interplay between thermostat and furnace. But humans, although subject to forces outside their control, are interpreters of those forces, as of those within their control. They are not pulled dumbly into activity like a furnace or like planets in a gravitational path. They construct their lives in interaction.

They create and cognize norms and not infrequently deviate from them. They disagree about what the norms are or, if agreed, about what the norms require in practice. They bargain and negotiate. They persuade—and fail to persuade. They order and obey—or refuse to obey. They act out of pride, embarrassment, anxiety, self-sacrifice, and dozens of other sentiments that affirm their ties to those they care about. They worship and curse forces beyond their control. To try to encompass all these phenomena in the concept of system is to vitiate the concept, to show how inappropriate it is. To ignore them in order to cling to the concept is to show how sterile it is in this context. (No cooling furnace ever cursed its feedback loop.) The sterility of the systems concept in other social science realms has already been amply documented in studies that family systems theorists ignore (Hoos, 1972; Lilienfeld, 1978). An examination of the concept's use in family study (Broderick and Smith, 1979) fails to establish any gain in understanding that has been or would be attained by thinking of a family as a cybernetic system rather than as a group of members mutually—and tortuously—engaged in constructing a family world.

2. *They presume that there is only one "correct" way to originate research.* Families are groups or organizations. The social scientist tries to think in a systematic way about them, which is not at all the same as saying that they are systems. One seeks to end up with orderly knowledge even about disorderly situations, but the intermediate thought processes on the way to that result are not necessarily entirely orderly or systematic. The system theorist wants rigid order from beginning to end. Thus, Schvaneveldt and Ihinger criticize the many sibling studies that focus on birth order because, "For the most part this research has been ex *post facto*, disjointed, tangential, and motivated by curiosity rather than theory." I find regrettable their denigration of research motivated by curiosity. The insistence that research must always begin from preexisting theory is a *de facto* call for suppression of imagination and confinement of thought, a press toward a complete desiccation of research.

The research presented here is motivated by curiosity, not by theory. The question I wonder about is: Why do siblings in some families grow up to be friends and in other families not? I believe the question is important because I believe the outcomes of sibling interactions are important in themselves and also bear on life chances. Further, I believe the question that puzzles me is one that is deeply embedded in our culture. So I want to set the problem of this research by first considering the idealization of sibling relationships in our cultural history. I want to explore the themes of brotherhood and sisterhood as ideals in juxtaposition with some examples of failure of the ideals. I will then turn to selected items in the social science literature that bear upon the question motivating me. Finally, I will suggest a conceptual framework—derived from analysis of and reflection upon qualitative interviews and illustrated with quotations from those interviews—that prepares the way for studies that can answer my question. The fruit of this study is thus not an answer to my question (although occasional pieces of an answer are suggested along the way), but a much clearer grasp of what one has to know to get an answer and a firmer idea of how to think about the prospective data that could lead to answers.

BROTHERHOOD AND SISTERHOOD: IDEALIZATION AND DISILLUSION

The ideal of brotherhood is ancient in origin and recurrent in appeal. In Western society, the Judeo-Christian idea that one God is the Father of all mankind propagated the correlative idea that, though they be members of separate earthly families, all are also members of one heavenly ordained family. Whatever divisions separate men as they adhere to their narrow interests and delimited consciousness of kind, they are bonded together in a universal brotherhood that transcends mundane distinctions. Usually ignored, this ideal never disappeared into total obsolescence. It manifests a certain tenacity, and it has proved to be a kind of renewable resource, serviceable in diverse contexts.

Many of the contexts in which the brotherhood ideal has proved serviceable were, paradoxically or not, strife-ridden. In these contexts, the universalism of the original ideal was reduced from all mankind to all those in a particular situation. While the ideal thus became sectarian rather than universal, it remained an ideal nonetheless because its leading advocates summoned their fellows to reach beyond their customary restricted loyalties to a wider loyalty. Men were asked to join together in brotherhood to protect and advance a common interest against a common enemy. Success in the struggle was believed to require the kind of unity that is found most naturally among consanguineous brothers in actual families.

The tension between the universal and the sectarian conceptions of brotherhood is present from the origins of the ideal in Judaism and persists in the Christian conception. The word brother is used in the Old Testament in several senses: (1) son of the same father and mother; (2) tribesman or one belonging to the same nation, (3) kindred tribesmen; (4) friends who had concluded a covenant; (5) a person who experiences brotherly sentiment upon perceiving distress in another person; (6) a fellowman as son of the same God and Father ("Brother," 1906). From its apparently original meaning of son of the same human parents, the concept of brother was extended outward on a widening scale of loyalty and compassion—from fellow tribesmen, to related tribesmen, to all mankind. But there was a basic tension between the universal and the tribal-sectarian versions of the ideal. One theologian who has analyzed this tension points out that the Israelite idea of brotherhood was based on the idea of a common Father who was both God of Israel and the one and only God. He was the Father of all peoples through Creation and, in addition, Father of Israel through election. "But this special situation was the free disposition of God and it could therefore be altered at any time. This brought an element of uncertainty into any tendency to separate off the brotherly community of Israel too rigidly" (Ratzinga, 1966, p. 29).

The tension between the universalistic and sectarian conceptions of brotherhood also occurs in Christianity. Christ used the word brother in three main senses: (1) A coreligionist; (2) New People of God, starting with the disciples; (3) all those in need, without differentiation (Ratzinga, 1966, p. 45). Early Christian brotherhood was fervent:

> Christians were 'holy brothers,' 'beloved brethren' . . . They constituted a spiritual brotherhood. . . . The wonder of the New Testament age was how slaves and masters became brothers beloved in the church of the living God, and how 'from every tribe and tongue and people and nation' (Rev. 5:9) Christ was calling men and women into a redemptive society for which the word 'brotherhood' was no unfitting title. (Johnston, 1962, p. 469)

But while Christian brotherly love seems universal, it is also sectarian:

> Christians are a family, a brotherhood in the service of Christ (Matt. 23:8) commanded to love one another in imitation of Him. . . . For their brotherly love is intense, because of their common covenant, faith, and hope; but it is comprised within that perfect love, *agape*, which is universal in its range. Since it is inspired by Jesus, and his Spirit, it is gentle, kind, patient, pardoning, self-effacing, and sacrificial. (Johnston, 1962, p. 470)

From its religious origins, the idea of a brotherhood that transcends mundane kinship has diffused into political and social contexts of many kinds. A comprehensive survey of them is a larger task than I have attempted. Taking note of a few significant instances is sufficient to document the tenacity of the ideal.

The most celebrated enunciation of brotherhood in the modern world is undoubtedly in the slogan that emerged from the French Revolution—Liberty, Equality, Fraternity. The provenance of "Fraternity" in this slogan is something of a mystery. Leading historians of the French Revolution furnish detailed analyses of the growing insistence on liberty and equality, but they are vaguer on how fraternity emerged as an expression of revolutionary aspiration. Nevertheless, the slogan incorporating all three ideals is said to have taken firm hold by 1791. The Constituent Assembly worked from 1789 to 1791 developing the principles of a new order in French society.

They closely joined equality to liberty, and by bringing the resounding collapse of privileges and feudalism the popular revolution highlighted equality as the Anglo-Saxons had not done. The revolutionaries and even the bourgeoisie valued the attainment of equality above all else. (Lefebvre, 1962, p. 146)

It was from this shared purpose that the feeling of brotherhood emerged:

Equality of rights was proclaimed, and each man was left to find the means to enjoy those rights. Disenchantment was soon to set in. But concentrated capital did not yet govern the economy; not all those without inheritance at first despaired of the future. Further, the Third Estate's solidarity in face of the aristocracy entertained a sense of unity and fraternity that partly disguised the deeper antagonism of its classes. Liberty and equality thus worked irresistible charm upon imaginations. (Lefebvre, 1962, p. 148)

The fraternity that held the Third Estate together did not last. As revolutionary turbulence continued, a population grouping known as the *sans-culottes*—a mixture of small shopkeepers, self-employed artisans, journeymen workers, marginal workers—pressed for greater revolutionary change than the more substantial middle class controlling the Revolution wanted. Paris was divided into 48 districts known as sections, each with an assembly of all citizens for decisionmaking, and these became the arena of a more narrowly sectarian brotherhood.

. . . In order to prepare for the supreme moment and lacking any official central organ, the sans-culottes perfected the communications system: they invented fraternization.
    For the sans-culottes, unity obviously implied fraternity; the words are to be found most frequently linked in documents dated 1793 and the year II. *Fraternity* meant not only bonds of friendship between citizens, but also implied equality. . . . Fraternization had an emotional content and took on a mystical aura. . . . Fraternization united only those who were attracted to the sans-culottes; it was concerned with immediate action; it was a weapon against the moderates. . . . The sans-culottes fraternized in bodies; if a section was threatened by moderates, the general assembly of the neighboring section would move in en masse; in the name of fraternity, the two assemblies became one, united by the mystical bond of the oath and of the fraternal kiss, and decisions were made collectively. Fraternization was a pact of mutual assistance which . . . united all sans-culottes. (Soboul, 1962, p. 153)

The imagery and sentiments of brotherhood helped to increase the unity among the heterogeneous sans-culottes and fortified them in their political struggles. But, "When moderantism in the Paris sections was crushed, fraternization disappeared from popular political practice." (Soboul, 1962, p. 156).

Brotherly sentiments and imagery form part of the heritage of western society. They are in abeyance much of the time, but seem to be revived and renewed by groups passing through political or social events that have a decisive significance for the group's future. The need to shape those events requires the mobilization of concerted social effort and stimulates the renewal of the fraternal ideal. The most recent major instance was the development of soul brotherhood among blacks in the course of the civil rights movement and black power movement of the 1960's and early 1970's. The term "soul" arose in the 1950's to refer to a style of musical performance that evolved out of the blues. It became a term designating an affirmative and distinctive valuing of blackness.

> 'Soul brother' certainly derives, with many aspects of soul music, from Negro religious style; 'Soul' in the religious sense is self-apparent, but with 'brother' we see a church becoming the institutional model for the cooperative life. . . . The use of 'Soul' in black parlance drives . . . toward a sense of ethnic unity based on some innate, irrational sense of community, brotherhood. (Abrahams, 1970, pp. 146–149)

Soul brotherhood did not express an established sense of unity among blacks. Rather, it represented an ideal toward which they should strive, an ideal of overcoming their differences and identifying with one another on the basis of a shared heritage as they passed through trying times that were also times of promise. Swedish anthropologist Ulf Hannerz attributed the emergence of the rhetoric of soul to changes in race relations that made social barriers to achievement less impermeable to ghetto blacks. This presumption of increased opportunity generated uncertainty, and the rhetoric of soul brotherhood was a response to this uncertainty.

> . . . The motive of the 'soul' vocabulary, I believe, is above all to reduce self-doubt by persuading 'soul brothers' that they are successful. Being a 'soul brother' is belonging to a select group instead of to a residual category of people who have not succeeded. . . . By talking about people who have 'soul', about 'soul music' and about 'soul food', the 'soul brother' attempts to establish himself in an expert and connoisseur role; by talking to others of his group in these terms, he identifies with them and confers the same role on them. Using 'soul' rhetoric is a way of convincing others of one's own worth and of their worth; it also serves to persuade the speaker himself. . . . The soul vocabulary has thus emerged from the social basis of a number of individuals, in effective interaction with one another, with similar problems of adjustment to a new situation. (Hannerz, 1970, p. 203)

The French Revolution and the more limited change in American race relations had this similarity: in a time of trial and transformation, people drew upon the sentiments and imagery of brotherhood to strengthen one another. Nor was the black social movement of the 1960's the only social movement of the time to conceive of close sibling ties as a model for improving social life. A small but noticeable movement of young people to establish new forms of settlement called communes also drew upon the idealization of sibling relations. A student of some 20 of these communes in Northern California reports that "most of the communes regard themselves as extended families, not only consciously using the term but in one case actually adopting a common surname. And a typical mode of trying to settle disputes among children is through the appeal by adults to the children's sense of kinship, that is, 'Janey is your sister, don't abuse her' " (Berger et al., 1971). In the communes, then, were people whose efforts to establish a new way of life included trying to put into practice a wider kinship than that of the nuclear family or even the traditional extended family. Efforts were made to utilize brotherhood and sisterhood as models for harmonious social relations.

The ideal of sisterhood appears to be of more recent origin than that of brotherhood. Suffice it to note for our present purposes that it was a flourishing concept in 19th-century America. A historian of the women's movement notes that the sharp separation of men and women in social participation in the 19th century created new bonds of sisterhood among women. He states that:

> At least six distinct types of sisterhood flourished during the 19th century, all closely related, each gaining support from and nourishing the other forms. Two bonds of sisterhood were traditional: ties within families and those between close friends. The sisterhood of family members, existing through generations of mothers, daughters, sisters, and cousins, persisted despite frequent separations due to migration. The sisterhood of friends, involving close and long-term personal commitments, gained strength from 19th-century ideas of woman's sphere and the relevance of sentimental romanticism. Taylor and Lasch use the term 'sorority' to refer to this ideal of pure friendship based on shared sensitivity.
>
> New categories of sisterhood reinforced the traditional ties. As young women moved away from their homes to be instructed at female academies and seminaries, they formed close connections with classmates which often developed into permanent intimate friendships. A fourth form of sisterhood receiving unprecedented emphasis in the 19th century derived from the religious movement known as the Second Great Awakening. This was a sisterhood of converted women, or those seeking conversion, who thought of themselves as one in their allegiance to the Savior and who shared their anxieties and exultations of faith. Growing out of this religious drama was a fifth kind of relationship among women, binding together those who engaged in voluntary good works for religious and benevolent causes. Finally, there was another sort of sisterhood felt by women who were entering new occupations—industrial work in textiles, shoemaking and other trades—or schoolteaching. . . .
>   . . . Strong ties of sisterhood developed among young women who were able to attend the new schools open to them after 1800. . . . At Mount Holyoke and most other female seminaries where boarding facilities existed, the

family structure served as a model for organization and discipline. Hence the concept of sisterhood was relevant indeed. (Medler, 1977, pp. 30–33)

The ideal of sisterhood came into new prominence in the renewed and revitalized women's movement of the 1960's and 1970's. An anthology of writings from the movement was entitled *Sisterhood is Powerful* (Morgan, 1970). A student of the contemporary women's movement explains the meaning and significance of the slogan:

> Just as in the black power movement the slogan 'Black is beautiful' gives courage and pride to its users, so the motto 'Sisterhood is powerful' encapsules for the women's movement the new excitement over belief in themselves and in each other that women are experiencing. The phrase shows up on lapel buttons and posters, meets instant recognition in meetings and publications, and has become a symbolic rallying point for experienced as well as fledging feminists. . . .
>
> The slogan 'Sisterhood is powerful' has both personal and collective meaning. Women individually or in groups have again and again had flashes of insight that their experience of being a woman is not their sole, lonely province but the common lot and bond of women, the potential unifying force for solidarity and support among half of humankind. . . . Sisterhood means female solidarity, respect for women as women, support for all women by women.
>
> Sisterhood is part ideal and part reality in contemporary feminism. For some feminists, it is genuinely experienced as a new and fresh way of living. It is also postulated as what ought to be. . . .
>
> . . . The first step to sisterhood is self-affirmation.
>
> Second, Sisterhood must be based on an understanding that all women are in it together. All women are sisters. . . . No significant divisions among women need exist—prostitute or bunny or wife, black or Chicano or white, old or young, married or single, educated or dropout, reformist or revolutionary. (Yates, 1975, p. 101)

The expected power of sisterhood is indeed strong, the power to create solidarity among such diverse women. The parallel to the presumed power of early Christian brotherhood is notable.

As ancient as the ideal of brotherhood is the awareness that earthly brotherhood can be a nasty experience. The ordinary world of ordinary brothers must be a scene of rampant rage, deceit, and abuse of power, if the earliest portrayals at all reflected everyday events in a reportorial way. The first brothers, in western tradition, were Cain and Abel. The murder of Abel by Cain stands as one model of horror: the first violent crime recorded in western history is the murder of a brother. The relations among later Biblical brothers are slightly less awful. Esau and Jacob do not turn jealousy into murder, but their relationship does not, in any evident way, inspire hope that universalizing the brotherly relationship leads to the attainment of desirable ends. The sale of Joseph into slavery by his older brothers is remarkable not for the feelings that animate them but for the unique course of action they had available for expressing their feelings. Whether Joseph's rise to good fortune after being sold into slavery should be regarded as an argument for generalizing the brotherly relationship is a question with various answers from which one may choose according to one's taste for irony.

That brothers can be mean to each other is ancient wisdom. The ideal of brotherhood is therefore taken with a large grain of salt. A somewhat popular singer in the 1950's, Tom Lehrer, gained celebrity with his songs that satirized cant and mocked hypocrisy. One of these he entitled "National Brotherhood Week", and it ridiculed the diminution of this ideal into a ludicrously confined time period, during which the ideal was also not being pursued. But he had an easy mark, for who now expects that anyone seriously pursues this ideal in ordinary times.

That sisters can be mean to each other is perhaps not yet ancient wisdom. In the context of the contemporary women's movement, the ideal of sisterhood is taken seriously. And so there are disappointments. Under the title, "Trashing: The Dark Side of Sisterhood," a writer active in the women's movement writes in *Ms.*, the most prominent magazine to emerge from the movement:

> It's been a long time since I was trashed. I was one of the first in the country, perhaps the first in Chicago, to have my character, my commitment, and my very self attacked in such a way by Movement women that it left me torn in little pieces and unable to function. . . . Trashing is a particularly vicious form of character assassination which amounts to psychological rape. It is manipulative, dishonest, and excessive. It is occasionally disguised by the rhetoric of honest conflict, or covered up by denying that any disapproval exists at all. But it is not meant to resolve differences. It is done to disparage and destroy. . . .
>
> The Movement seduced me by its sweet promise of sisterhood. It claimed to provide a haven from the ravages of a sexist society; a place where one could be understood. It was my very need for feminism and feminists that made me vulnerable. I gave the movement the right to judge me because I trusted it. And when it judged me worthless, I accepted that judgment.
>
> For at least six months I lived in a kind of numb despair, completely internalizing my failure as a personal one. In June 1970, I found myself in New York coincidentally with several feminists from four different cities. We gathered one night for a general discussion on the state of the Movement, and instead found ourselves discussing what happened to us. We had two things in common: all of us had Movement-wide reputations, and all had been trashed. . . .
>
> Thus Ti-Grace Atkinson's memorable adage that 'Sisterhood is powerful: It kills sisters' is reaffirmed again and again. (Joreen, 1976, pp. 49, 92)

The ideal of sisterhood is not animating in all circumstances. Rivalry and destructiveness can shove it aside. Perhaps in time it will be recognized that there are no grounds for surprise. Actual sisters can be rivalrous and destructive, just as can actual brothers; wider sisterhoods must also be expected to succumb at times.

SIBLING RELATIONSHIPS IN THE SOCIAL SCIENCES

The social sciences (including here psychology and psychiatry) have focused the greatest attention on the hostility between siblings. The most fully developed concept pertaining to sibling relationships is sibling rivalry. The long established psychological focus on sibling rivalry has in recent years been supplemented by sociological investigations of violence between siblings, part of a larger inquiry into violence in families. The leading students of violence in families inform us that sibling violence is the most frequent type of family violence; it occurs more often than either violence of parents toward children or violence between spouses. They report that 53 of every 100 children attack a brother or sister in a year by kicking, biting, punching, hitting with objects or "beating up." "That means well over 19 million attacks which would be considered an assault if they occurred outside the family" (Straus et al., 1980, p. 82).

In a study of 40 firstborn children whose mothers gave birth to a younger sibling when the firstborns were between 18 and 43 months old, Dunn and Kendrick report that "by the time the firstborn children were six years old, their discussion of their feelings about the sibling and their views on what kind of person the sibling was were dominated by descriptions of fighting and aggression . . ." (Dunn and Kendrick, 1982, p. 181).

When we consider the powerful Biblical stories of hatred between brothers, together with the psychological and sociological studies of sibling rivalry and violence, we may wonder how it was possible for an ideal of brotherhood or sisterhood to develop at all. Are these ideals pure fantasies, without foundation in any real families?

Anthropologist David Schneider and sociologist Elaine Cumming argue that sibling solidarity is a characteristic of the American kinship system. In their study of aging adults 50 to 80 years old, perhaps they came upon one of the foundations of the ideal of brotherhood. They found that among aging men, morale is higher among those who have siblings nearby than among those who do not. Among women, the situation is more complicated, but what can be said is that among married women, the presence of siblings ameliorates low morale (Cumming and Schneider, 1961). Marvin B Sussman (1974) found, in a sample of lower middle- and working-class adults, that about 47% of them had given some form of help to a sibling in the preceding month and 49% had received some kind of help from a sibling in the preceding month. These figures are no doubt influenced by the geographical availability of siblings but also perhaps by the wish to help or not. Perhaps some who lived near did not give help because they did not want to or would not even have been asked, while some gave help to geographically distant siblings. The study does not probe deeply enough to deal with these questions, nor does any study that I know of.

In a study of 75 adults (but not of their siblings), investigators found that "the most powerful contributor to feelings of closeness between individual siblings was the framework of the family in which siblings grew up. The sense of belonging to the family, and of being close to particular siblings, was, for most subjects, permanently affected by experiences shared in childhood. . . . Participants who felt close to their families and to their siblings recalled an emphasis on family unity and believed that democratic child-rearing practices further encouraged its development. Especially important among these recollections were practices which stressed expectations for harmony, absence of favoritism, recognition of individual talents and accomplishments and—less frequently— the teaching of strategies for getting along and using conflict constructively" (Ross and Milgram, 1982, p. 229). This is a useful exploratory study, but it raises many questions that must be answered before closeness can be understood. To cite just one or two: Does an emphasis on unity always lead to it? Could not siblings develop a unity among themselves though their parents were mired in discordant conflict?

Cicirelli (1982, p. 281) reports that ". . . most siblings feel close affectionally to each other, with the least closeness between brothers and the most between sisters. It is clear that siblings are capable of true intimacy and extraordinary understanding of one another's problems, although most sibling relationships do not attain this level. . . . Overt sibling rivalry appears to diminish in intensity as people get older. . . . However, there is evidence that rivalry may be dormant and can be reactivated in such situations of adulthood as caring for aging parents, questions of inheritance, and so on." These findings, useful as they are, still leave open the question of why rivalries over inheritance or caring for aging parents are reactivated among some siblings and not among others. Nor does this study suggest any way of conceptually attacking such issues.

Bank and Kahn (1982) have examined strong positive bonds between siblings. They conclude that intense sibling bonds that exert a formative influence on personality result from deprivation of reliable parental care. The fact that their work is based entirely on patients in therapy justifies the inference that they have uncovered no more than one basis for enduring sibling ties, not the universal basis. One may raise other questions: How is the influence of sibling ties related to their enduringness? Is powerful influence always associated with lifelong friendship? Can siblings remain lifelong friends without necessarily powerfully influencing each other's personality? A deficit theory of strong positive sibling bonds, such as Bank and Kahn's, leaves one skeptical as to its completeness. They have done a service in opening up the subject of positive sibling bonds, but one cannot concur in their view that they have successfully concluded the discussion.

Surely the ground that we have covered thus far points to some issues that call for deeper probing into the nature of sibling relationships. We live with an ancient heritage of brotherhood as an ideal, one that has inspired cohesive action under some circumstances. The modern women's movement has been animated by an ideal of sisterhood. Yet, although we know that some adults benefit in some ways from continuing sibling relationships, we have only very fragmentary knowledge of how cohesive sibling relationships are constructed in actual families. Our most profoundly understood and most fully documented aspect of sibling relationships is sibling rivalry. We understand a great deal about jealousy, envy, and hatred among siblings. We don't know much about how some children solve these problems more easily than others. We do not know why some siblings not only help each other in adult life but are close friends, while others grow up to be indifferent or inimical.

To address these questions we need to examine the texture of sibling relationships, the many issues that enter into their construction. As Dunn and Kendrick note, "One of the challenges posed by the study of the relations between young siblings is that there are no accepted 'global' psychological dimensions that are considered to be relevant, beyond those of jealousy and rivalry" (Dunn and Kendrick, 1982, p. 85). Their comment is as applicable to older children and, indeed, to the sibling relationship as it develops over the life span. Efforts to formulate such a set of dimensions are therefore timely, as well as intrinsically important. Although the dimensions formulated here were developed from study of siblings ranging in age from 6 to 18, a consideration of Dunn and Kendrick's data in the light of them indicates that the framework offered here is serviceable for the younger ages.

In the balance of this paper I propose to begin to construct a framework for analyzing sibling relationships in childhood. I suggest an initial series of issues in childhood sibling relationships that have emerged from study of interviews of parents and children in 33 families, supplemented with some material from a life history interview obtained from a working-class man. The issues I have identified will be illustrated with brief quotations from the interviews. I do not undertake to delineate in any detail the ways in which the sex and age of the individual child or the combination of these characteristics in the sibling set affects the ways in which issues emerge and are handled. Nor do I endeavor here to work out the ways in which family organization and interaction processes as a whole affect the sibling issues. The goal of this chapter is to contribute to an empirically grounded conceptualization of sibling relationships, which will make it possible to study them in the context of family organization and family interaction processes. The questions we have raised—as well as evaluation of the adequacy of the Bank and Kahn theory—can ultimately be dealt with only by studying sibling relations within the psychosocial interior of their families.

The underlying assumption of the approach taken here is as follows: Every social situation is in some sense problematic for the participants. The situation of siblings in a family is problematic, to themselves and to their parents. First I shall identify the conditions that make the sibling relationship problematic for the participants, and then discuss the ways in which it is so, the issues that must be dealt with. When we understand what problems siblings and their parents are working on, we can understand the sibling-related significance of children's activity and the differences among families in both defining the problems and developing strategies for dealing with them. The problems are intrinsic to the family; they are fundamental, defining characteristics of any family that has at least two children.[1]

PROBLEMATIC CONDITIONS IN SIBLING RELATIONS

There are essentially four conditions that make for problematic relations between or among brothers and sisters. The first and most fundamental is the fact of shared parentage. There is a general social expectation that parents have an obligation to give care to the children they have begotten and that each of their children has a rightful claim upon this care. The children who have the same mother and father come to know that they have a relationship with each other that they do not share with children who have other mothers and fathers. They learn this from their parents who usually teach it, and they learn it from outsiders who define them as brothers and sisters.

Shared parentage is problematic for two reasons: (1) because each child sees the same persons as vital for providing the resources the child wants and requires from others; (2) because the parents define the children's shared parentage as a basis for solidarity between or among the children. Thus, children of the same parents come to find themselves under pressure to feel affection and/or to act with consideration or moderation in relation to someone who is also competitive for parental affection and time and other benefits.

The second condition that makes the relations of siblings problematic is that they are of different ages. Thus, a second basis of strain is found in the contrast between pressures toward solidarity that derive from shared parentage and the differences in social expectation directed toward children of different chronological ages.

A third condition that makes the relations of siblings problematic is that each has a psycho-socio-biological individuality along with their shared parentage. Each newborn presents himself or herself as a unique configuration of characteristics. Each evokes a somewhat individualized response from each parent. The extent of one sibling's perceived differences from an earlier-born may be great or small, but some consequential difference is likely to be perceived by parents who may later try to eradicate, minimize, or foster it. In any event, these perceived differences will enter into the inter-active histories of the family members. The significance of the differences will become part of the ground for interaction and establishment of rela-tionships within the family.

Finally, if siblings are of different sex, this fact becomes a fourth condi-tion that makes the relationships among them problematic. The difference in sex is met with different expectations concerning sex roles. Brothers and sisters learn to deal with each other in ways that are conditioned by the fact of their being of opposite sex, while also expecting that as children of the same parents they have the right to be treated "equally" by their par-ents.

The issues that arise among siblings and in parental handling of the sib-ling situation derive from these problematic conditions built into family structure in our culture. The conditions that make sibling relationships problematic in intact families exist in somewhat modified form in blended or reconstituted families composed of remarried parents with children pos-sibly from his and her earlier marriages as well as from the current one. Disparate parentage imposes added strains among siblings, as Rainwater found in his study of lower-class black families:

> In families which contain varying mixtures of illegitimate and legitimate children, each child's legitimacy affects the meaning he has for his parents and his siblings. In addition, many families contain the children of several different fathers, whether legitimate or not. Each child carries as part of his social iden-tity a designation as a particular man's son or daughter, even though he may not carry that man's name if he is illegitimate. These elements of personal bi-ography are usually taken for granted within the family and openly discussed when they are relevant to family life, with the result that most children early learn their own genealogy and that of their siblings. In some families, however, efforts are made to conceal genealogical information, so that when the child later learns 'the truth' it may come as a shock to him and cause some social disorientation until he absorbs his 'correct' identity and learns the meanings it will have for him. (Rainwater, 1970, p. 217)

ISSUES IN SIBLING RELATIONS

Equity

Perhaps the most pervasive, most fundamental issue in sibling relation-ships is the issue of equity. A child is not likely to be indifferent to how a sibling is treated by parents. Commonly, children are sensitive to the way parents treat them and their siblings. They will be attentive to and make comparisons between rewards and punishments distributed to self and sib. Parents will ordinarily feel some obligation within themselves to be fair to their children, to reward and punish in ways that satisfy both themselves and their children that they are neither excessively harsh nor excessively indulgent toward one as compared to the others. When parents do show favoritism, they may be under some external pressure from the adversely affected child if from no other to modify this unfairness. The child who feels treated persistently unfairly and who feels defeated in efforts to modify the practice of inequity may become troublesome in ways that cause him to be diagnosed as emotionally disturbed (Vogel and Bell, 1960).

Parents must deal with the problem of equity in a number of different contexts:

1. Unequal Performance. When two children perform differently in relation to some parental expectation, the parents must work out some strategy for dealing with the problem. They may reward good performance and punish unsatisfactory performance; they may reward only; they may only punish the unsatisfactory, or they may construct a more complex strategy. Mrs. GG wrestles with this problem in relation to the school performance of her two children. Grace, age eight, gets good grades; Gregory, age seven, does not. Asked, "Did you do anything about it?" Mrs. GG answers:

> No, we tried, that was one thing we tried to not do was, I mean, it was difficult because we wanted to praise Grace because she did, and yet we could see the reasons for Gregory's low grades so what we made more of an issue of was the fact that he'd get checks for talking and not keeping profitably busy and things like that. We made more of that point than of his low grades. And then we tried to give him any incentive to do better.

The dilemma Mrs. GG is here wrestling with is how to be fair to one child without having a damaging impact on the performance of the other. Related is the issue of whether similar performance can in fact be expected from both children. Each child is an audience for the interaction between parent and sibling. As parents wrestle with questions of expecting similar performance from different children and with consequences of responding to differential performances, the children are engaged in defining the parental behavior as fair or unfair.

2. The Application of Conduct Rules and Standards. A second context in which issues of equity arise is in the application of conduct rules and standards. A particularly candid recognition of this problem was provided by Mr. GG. When the interviewer asked, "Which of the children do you find it easiest to handle, would you say?" he responded:

> Well, I think that, uh, in most cases I, uh, think that maybe the girl has a certain, uh, preference as far as my tenderness is concerned. She's the firstborn, and the fact that she's a girl, I know I give her the benefit of a lot of doubts. I've been inclined at times to be more severe on the boy, only to look at him later that night or something and realize that, uh, he's only a little fellow and that, uh, maybe I shouldn't have been mean to him. And the fact that he idolizes me so, it only makes it that much harder.

Grace clearly recognizes her father's disposition:

> *Interviewer:* What kind of a person is your father?
>
> *Grace:*   Very nice and kind. . . . When I'm in trouble he takes care of the other person I'm in trouble with and that person is usually my dear little brother.

Her seven-year-old brother's interview does not yield a clear comment that bears on this issue of equity. It would be a mistake, however, to assume that the differential treatment is without impact on him; the absence of relevant data is more likely due to difficulty in eliciting statements that are specifically informative on this point.

There is some evidence to suggest that a perception of being equitably treated contributes to a feeling of solidarity between siblings. Consider the R family with two sons, Ralph, 15, and Russell, 12. In the course of a series of questions relating to other members of the family, Ralph was asked, "Do your parents treat Russell any different from you?" Ralph answered, "We both get a fair break." During an earlier interview Ralph was asked, "What do you like to do best?" His answer:

> There's three things, fishing, dating, and camping. I like to spend as much time outdoors as I can. And then Russell and I like to have a vision. He wants to be a naturalist of some kind and live in a small town. I'm going to be a lawyer, and as soon as I have my degree I'm going to the same town. And then when my dad retires they will come out there, too. We can do a lot of fishing and hunting together.

Ralph's vision should not be interpreted to mean that the brothers never fight or feel antagonism; the interviews provide abundant evidence of fighting and anger between them. But the vision of a shared future accommodating disparate occupations bespeaks a feeling of solidarity, and I suggest as a reasonable hypothesis that the sense of being fairly treated by parents is one of the factors—perhaps a necessary factor—that contributes to that sense of solidarity.

Parents are considered to be unfair when they are perceived to apply rules or standards unevenly. Thus, in the Q family, 14-year-old Quentin says that he gets mad at his mother because she sticks up for his sister when she's wrong. His sister, in turn, complains that her brother is allowed to get away with things that she does not get away with.

From the examples cited, it is evident that a certain amount of the work that goes on in families is work to arrive at interpretations of fairness and unfairness. Is this event equivalent to that? Does it call for the same or different handling? Is this way of handling situation X equal in meaning to the handling of earlier situation W? What allowance does fairness demand should be made for a girl that is not made for a boy? Why do you treat my brother/my sister more leniently than you treat me? Why don't you notice the error of his/her ways as consistently as you notice mine?

3. Resolution of Disputes. A third context in which the issue of equity arises is in the resolution of disputes. These situations are of various kinds. In one type, a parent intervenes to break up a quarrel or fight. Both children receive the same treatment, but one may feel this is unfair because the other started it. To this child, the equal treatment (based on a parental presumption that both are culpable) is unequal.

Another type of situation is one that two siblings may want to control themselves. In the P family, 12-year-old Paul says of his older sister, "If she wouldn't tease me, I wouldn't tease her." For him, fairness necessitates retaliation. He must make his sister uncomfortable if she makes him uncomfortable. Otherwise, he would allow himself to be treated unfairly by her. Equity here means "getting even." A related type of situation is one in which getting even is not handled by the siblings alone but draws the parents in as punishers. Thus, in the Z family, 14-year-old Zachary reports his 8-year-old sister's misdoings to their parents. He explains, "I tell on her because she has told on me." Equivalent victimization is Zachary's solution to the fairness problem presented by Zelda's initiatives.

4. Scarcity. A fourth context in which the issue of equity arises is the context of access to scarce resources. An obvious type of instance is when two children, with one TV set, want to watch different programs at the same time. How can this scarce resource be apportioned so that both children feel fairly treated?

Different as their interests may be, children in the same family may nonetheless be attracted to or feel they have need for or use for some possession of a sibling. They may not necessarily, however, accept the notion of equal access. Thus, Zelda complains that her brother will not let her touch his things, particularly his model airplanes, which she doesn't like because he touches her things. Equal access seems only fair to her.

In some families, equal access to parents' time and attention becomes an issue of enduring significance. In the L family, an interviewer with 16-year-old Larry elicits his views of his father's treatment of him and his 12-year-old sister Lisa. Toward the end of a series of questions on ideal family members, he is asked what an ideal son is and how he feels he measures up. He answers:

> I don't suppose I measure up either, but that's because they aren't ideal parents. . . . (How about Lisa?) Depends on what you consider ideal. If it's someone who does everything you are told to do and never grunt, then she's ideal. Of course, I think they have been more ideal with her than with me. She's gotten more attention, usually what the younger child gets. (Have you ever felt jealous?) I don't anymore. I used to feel jealous of the attention she'd get. I'm satisfied now.

Although Larry says he is no longer jealous, he also believes that the inequity in attention made him a less ideal son than he might have been.

Interview statements bearing on issues of equity are clear in some fam-

ilies, less clear in others from whom interviews were obtained. Nevertheless, it seems useful to assume that every family in which there are at least
two children must deal with such issues. Pressure toward fairness emanates
from several sources, while the structure of life presents challenges to realizing such a standard. Fairness is a norm in western culture, and parents
are likely to experience some inclination to live up to it with regard to their
children. But when that inclination is minimal or nonexistent, one or more
of the children themselves are likely to press toward such a norm, or despair that it is attainable. In any event, the equity issue presents itself and
is consequential. At the same time, equity is necessarily elusive. Children
of different ages, sex, and potentiality present their parents with ambiguities and uncertainties that must be translated into equivalencies that will
satisfy all concerned: this punishment of this misdeed is equivalent to that
other punishment of the sibling's misdeed. This reward is equal to that other
reward and is not a sign of favoritism. The siblings themselves must work
out some kind of modus vivendi. They may or may not agree that each is
being fair to the other or being fairly treated by parents, but one way or
another they will confront the issue of fairness between or among themselves.

Maturity

One of the factors making difficult the attainment of equity among siblings is the fact that they are of different ages. In western society today, as
Philippe Ariès (1962) emphasized, fairly fine age differences in childhood
constitute the basis for different expectations. As children grow and get older,
they are expected to cast off behavior acceptable at earlier ages and to
conduct themselves in ways that increasingly approximate adult ways. These
expected changes are presented to children by their parents and by others,
and children themselves take over these expectations as standards for judging themselves. Sibling relationships are to some extent shaped by these
concerns, which we may refer to generically as the issue of maturity in sibling relations.

1. Power. One fairly common way in which differences in maturity enter into sibling relationships is the tendency of older siblings to attempt to
exercise power over the younger. In the M family, one of the things that
makes 12-year-old Morton angry is the fact that when he and his 16-year-
old brother Mark are watching TV and the TV set requires adjusting, Mark
always asks Morton to do it. Morton feels Mark could do it as easily. He
resents his brother's use of his age status as a resource for exercising power.

Power is perhaps most commonly exercised by older over younger sibling, but not inevitably. There are situations in which the younger may attempt to gain control over the older, sometimes with some success. In the
V family, both 12-year-old Vance and 9-year-old Victor seem to agree that

Victor has the upper hand in their relationship. When asked about differences between his parents on how the children should be treated, Vance says, "My father thinks Victor should be punished when he's bad. Mother doesn't. I agree with father. Victor is always trying to make trouble, he's happy making trouble. Between any of us. . . . (What things do you do that make Victor mad?) Take all the blankets off him. He doesn't like that. He reaches over and takes all mine. I'd like to have a sister instead, a younger one who I could boss around. . . . Victor tries to act too smart-alecky all the time."

In response to a question about fighting with his brother, Victor says, "I like to fight with him. I don't have to be mad at him, but he gets mad at me. I can handle him by putting a leg lock on him." If we had only Victor's statement, we might be tempted to dismiss it as boasting; when juxtaposed with Vance's, we find that the two statements have correlative meaning; they are parts of a whole that illuminate each other. Our understanding of and conviction about each is increased by considering it in conjunction with the other (Handel, 1967).

Efforts of a younger sib to control or dominate an older are not always successful. A relatively benign instance appears in the Ecks family. When 13-year-old Edward is asked what things he does that make his 8-year-old sister Emma mad, he replies, "Well, she has a habit of trying to set down rules for me and I break them and she yells at me." The only clue to what those rules might be come in her reply to a question concerning what she and her brother fight about: "Mostly we fight about what we're going to look at on TV or something else, often about things that I don't understand on TV, or I ask what does a word mean, and I make him tell me. That's a hard job. He doesn't always want to." Emma does not seem intent on dominating Edward merely for the sake of superiority, of overcoming the power that derives from his age. Rather, she seems to want to control him just long enough to share some of his knowledge.

2. Knowledge. The example of Emma and Edward suggests that in some families, at least, younger siblings assign some responsibility to older ones, responsibility for helping them grow up. Older siblings are often seen as having knowledge they can and ought to share freely.

An older sib's maturity can be alternately respected and denigrated by the younger. In the EE family, 12-year-old Elizabeth says of her 15-year-old sister Eileen:

> She bosses me around too much at times. Other times we'll be awfully close. I used to be very neat and she wasn't and that would make me mad. When she's with older kids, she acts superior. But I go around with older kids, too. (What do you do that makes her mad?)
> I can't think. Maybe I pester her sometimes so she gets provoked. I ask her things over and over again. . . .
> (What characteristics about each person in the family do you like best?)

Eileen, she's understanding compared to other sisters. She'll have confidence
in me and vice versa. . . .
(Who do you usually go to with problems?)
My sister. She usually gives me good advice. We talk over problems. I've helped
her, too, like persuading Mother to let her stay out later.

The suggestion from this example, even more than from the preceding,
is that older siblings may be perceived by younger as links to adulthood,
people who know some of adulthood's secrets and should be willing to
share them because they are also still kids themselves. The younger makes
a claim upon the older as child to child, sib to sib, but does so because
the older's greater maturity results in knowledge and understanding that the
younger believe should be transferred. Even so, the older may be seen as
sometimes taking her maturity too seriously, lording it over the younger with
excessive self-importance.

Some of the secrets of maturity are sexual and sex-role-related, and so
may have a particular fascination for a younger sibling of opposite sex. In
the FF family, 9-year-old Florence is asked about her 16-year-old brother:

(What things does Frank do that make you mad?)
Over TV programs. He wants his way and he teases me and hits me.
(And what do you do that makes him mad?)
I'm under the bed and I listen to him and his friends, and once I put a pin on
his chair and he sat on it. Sometimes I read his comics and forget to take them
back, and I hang around when he's talking to his friends. That makes him real
mad.

Younger children's efforts to learn from their older siblings seem to be
quite easily defined by the latter as some form of pestering. The efforts are
perceived as excessive, or not timely, or burdensome, or inappropriate. They
may be defined also as an effort to diminish the hard-won greater maturity
of the older. If, after all, the secrets, the knowledge, the information, the
know-how is freely passed over to the younger, then older and younger are
less distinctive than they were. Under what circumstances do older brothers become willing teachers to younger sisters? To younger brothers? Older
sisters willing teachers of younger sisters? Younger brothers? We don't know.
We only know that it can happen, that Eileen, despite being provoked by
Elizabeth's pestering, can give her advice that Elizabeth values, and that it
happens often enough that Elizabeth not only values the advice but defines
the relationship as one in which the two sisters have confidence in each
other. We do not know under what circumstances pestering remains the
most salient feature of the sibling relationship and under what circumstances the relationship becomes significantly characterized by teaching and
learning in a context of mutual support.

Loyalty

Membership in a family imposes on its members multiple and conflicting loyalties. All the members are expected to be loyal to the family, and each is expected to be loyal to each other member. But these loyalties cannot remain fixed in place all the time. They are subject to stresses, so that one loyalty may be temporarily weakened by another. A child may prefer the way something is done in a friend's family over his own. A sibling may make a demand that conflicts with a parental demand. Family members have conflicting claims on each other; responsiveness to one claim strengthens the loyalty in that relationship. Disregarded claims loosen loyalty. The strengthening and loosening of loyalties are continuing processes. Fluctuations may take place within a narrow or wide range. Loyalty of one sibling to another is manifested and tested in certain kinds of recurring contexts and expressed through characteristic conduct.

1. Availability. Even as siblings pursue their own individual interests and form individual associations with playmates or friends outside the family, they also often want the other sibling(s) to be available on demand. This availability is desired for support in a particular situation, for advice, or, particularly among younger children, for companionship in play. The situation of Elizabeth and Eileen, discussed above, is an example of availability for advice. Such availability is an exemplification of the kind of loyalty that a younger sib seeks and can receive from an older. It involves an attempt by the older to understand and respond to the needs and concerns of the younger, at the younger's behest most often, but undoubtedly also often at the older's initiative. Elizabeth reciprocates loyalty by advocating maturity privileges for Eileen. She makes herself available as a supporter.

A younger version of availability is provided in the GG family. In response to the opening interview question, "What are the important things about your family?" Eight-year-old Grace answers:

> Like my mother, father and brother and my other relatives, our house and our car and all that stuff. We couldn't live without my mother. She sews and washes and changes our beds, and my father makes the money and if we didn't have a car he couldn't make any money. And my brother, well he's important to play with just to have someone around when I need him.

Later in the same interview, Grace gives an illustration of the value of *her* availability to her brother:

> Sometimes on Sunday I like to watch TV instead of looking for new houses. I like to go but I like to watch TV. And one time when my brother was sick I was forced to stay home and they said they'd be home at four-thirty and they didn't come home until six-thirty. He was crying and everything but I finally made him some crackers and cheese and calmed him down.

In distress, or perplexity, or boredom, siblings turn to each other for or with appropriate manifestations of loyalty.

They do not always respond. In the W family, when 16-year-old Wendy is asked about her 13-year-old brother, "Do you ever get mad at Walter?" she says, "Sometimes, like when I get home from work and I want to go out and he won't help with the dishes. He just won't do a thing." Wendy clearly makes the unspoken assumption that, as members of the same family, she has a justified claim on her brother's support. Loyalty to the family ought to obligate him to assist her with her chore when she is short of time, but he does not live up to her expectation. Her wish for sibling support is revealed further, when she continues, "He acts like a baby sometimes and runs to Pop, but he's young anyway. I'd rather have an older brother." Her volunteered comment expressing a wish for an older brother suggests the hypothesis that sibling relationships tend to generate expectations of sibling loyalty, and when those expectations are not fulfilled, fantasies of a more idealized sibling relationship to replace the disappointing one are produced. Here, then, may be another clue to the ideals of brotherhood and sisterhood: these ideals may partly represent compensatory fantasies for disappointing sibling relationships, the disappointment being grounded in expectations of loyalty more or less inevitably intrinsic to the relationship.

2. Sharing. One child in a family may have possession of an item the other values. If feasible, there will often be an expectation by at least one of the siblings that it should be shared. A certain amount of interaction among siblings is devoted to constructing rules for sharing. Those rules are often incomplete or ineffectual, and a fairly frequent complaint in these interviews is that one sibling takes or borrows something from another without asking. The taker or borrower is almost certainly acting on a presumption that the taking or borrowing is justified by shared family membership; it is unlikely that most of the borrowers would borrow equally freely from friends, without asking. Shared family membership imposes on siblings an obligation to share possessions that is presumptively more compelling than obligations to share with outsiders.

When an expectation of sharing is not fulfilled, the disappointed sibling can become aggressive and evoke an aggressive response. This happened in the K family, with 11-year-old Kenneth, as his 13-year-old brother Karl tells it:

> My little brother is fat and jolly. He's too jolly. Couple nights ago I had a piece of candy in my jacket and he kept nagging, 'Give me some,' and I told him 'No,' and he kept trying to get in my pocket and we were wrestling around and he got in and so I hit him.

3. Handling Information Appropriately. At some early age—it is not clear just when—children begin to understand the importance of information as something that can be managed. They recognize that information manage-

ment has some significant dimensions and that it has diverse consequences, depending upon the nature of the information and the persons
who have it.

One dimension is incrimination. Information can be incriminating. A child
may find himself or herself in a situation in which he or she feels that such
information that may be known to a sibling should, for loyalty's sake, not
be shared with the parents. In short, one's brother or sister should not tattle
to one's parents about something one has done. That information in the
hands of parents can lead to unpleasant consequences. A sibling ought to
understand and respect the consequences of information mismanagement.
In the C family, 12-year-old Caroline expresses her exasperation with her
6-year-old sister:

> My mother is more often on Cynthia's side because both of us (Caroline and
> 10-year-old brother) are against Cynthia and Cynthia is such an innocent an-
> gel. If you ask her to promise not to tell my mother and father something, she
> promises and then she tells.

The problem is made difficult when issues of maturity are confounded
with issues of loyalty. Thus, when 14-year-old Zachary, in pursuit of equity, "tells" on his sister because "she told on me," he knows what his
way of managing information can lead to but he seems unprepared to consider that his 8-year-old sister may not appreciate the consequences. He
does not want to insist on a maturity gap here; he wants her to understand
that loyalty requires that she not tell. Here is a type of situation where the
older child would like to see the younger grow up in a hurry; that would
strengthen loyalty.

Another dimension of information is its status value. At some unknown
age children become aware of secrets, and they come to recognize that
those who share in a secret have more status than those who are excluded
from it. The self is enhanced when one is deemed fit by others to be en-
trusted with a secret. Thus, in the B family, in specifying what she likes best
about each member of her family, 12-year-old Barbara says of her 10-year-
old sister, "My sister, if anything happens, she always tells me about it. She
doesn't keep anything from me."

4. Protection. Sibling loyalty is often put to a test outside the family,
when one child is in conflict with peers. When neighborhood children give
a child a hard time, that child is fortunate who has an older, tougher sib to
back him up. Nine-year-old Doreen makes clear that she is the protector
of her eight-year-old brother:

> (Who do you usually go to when you feel worried or get into trouble?)
> Nobody. I worry about my own troubles, but if I did something—. I beat up
> my brother for fighting two little girls. I settled it. I did not tell my mother. I'll
> probably end up telling her if she is in a good mood. And if my little brother

gets into trouble or if somebody is beating him up, he'd come to me. He said, 'Boy, my sister can beat you up.' I can beat him up so he thinks I can beat everybody. I can.

Doreen evidently sees herself as a protector of the underdog, which sometimes makes her an enforcer against her brother, but when he is in the underdog role she is his loyal protector.

Individuality

Even as much as siblings are involved with each other, expecting and seeking loyalty, they are endeavoring at the same time to become separate individuals capable of limiting the claims that others can make on them. They do not want the claims of loyalty to be limitless. One way of setting limits to loyalty claims is to establish a realm of privacy.

1. Privacy. Each child in a family wants jurisdiction over his or her own space and possessions and wants siblings to accept rules for entering and operating within that jurisdiction. The widespread complaint of one sibling about another—"He borrows my things without asking"—is an effort to set limits to what may be claimed on the basis of family loyalty. The child seeks to maintain a realm of privacy, a realm of space and possessions that he or she has control of and from which he or she can exclude siblings at will. There is a dialectical opposition between privacy and loyalty, a constant tugging back and forth between the sibling who wants access on the basis of loyalty and the sibling who wants to deny access on the basis that "it's mine."

A related issue arises when one sibling is with his own age-mates. Another sibling may experience this as a temporary betrayal of loyalty and seek to be included in a way that also expresses resentment for initially having been excluded. Something like this happens in the K family, where 13-year-old Karl complains about Kenneth, his 11-year-old brother:

Oh, he's too nosey. Like today I was showing a friend some valuable stamps. He came in and said they were fakes and was teasing. He butts in.

The importance of this activity to Kenneth is suggested in his interview. He has been asked what he does on Sunday:

Go to church. Then I ride my bike or do my homework. I work with clay or watch TV.
(What does Karl do?)
He keeps it a deep dark secret. I guess he trades stamps and coins. Oh, I guess some of the time I play with my stamp collection.

Will Karl and Kenneth grow up to become feuding stamp dealers, continuing into adulthood an unresolved entanglement that both brings them together and keeps them apart? The evidence we have is scarcely sufficient to justify such a prediction. Karl's effort to pull away and Kenneth's to dog his steps might be factors leading toward such an outcome, but they are insufficient in themselves—and Kenneth does not really seem that interested in stamps. But we don't know much about what makes this kind of entanglement recede and disappear in some families and remain enduringly significant in others.

The effort to maintain an arena and occasions of privacy is an effort by one sibling to limit the claims that other siblings, as well as parents, may make on the basis of the loyalties implied in shared family membership. It is a way of maintaining some control over those claims.

2. Self-Demarcation. In addition to its importance as a way of limiting the control of others over one's own circumstances, the insistence on privacy and personal ownership of possessions is one way of demarcating the self. Without at this point addressing the question of whether a clearly individuated self is a necessary requisite for effective human functioning in all societies, it indubitably is in western societies, at least for the last few hundred years. The formation of that individuated self begins in the family. The children in a family come to recognize, with greater or lesser ambivalence, that they share an identity as members of that family. So long as the family members inhabit a common household—and often long thereafter—their lives are intertwined and somewhat consequential for each other. But each child enters into the family in his or her own way. Each is initially individuated on the basis of birth order; the fact of having a unique position in the sibling birth order is sufficient basis for the initiation of an individuated self within the shared family identity. If the children are of different sex, they are additionally distinguished from each other on that basis as well. Beyond these categorical markers, which parents regard and act upon as individuating, each child discloses distinctive features of physiognomy and activity that parents and other observers interpret as individuating.

Proceeding from these initial distinctions, each child comes to regard himself or herself as marginally or significantly different from his or her siblings, and to regard them as different. Even close siblings endeavor to keep some distance from each other in order to maintain some sense of an individual boundary.

Self-demarcation can be done more or less matter-of-factly, as exemplified by the way Kenneth compares himself with Karl and his 9-year-old sister Kathy when he is asked, "How are you different from the other people in the family?"

> I make so much noise. Nobody else hardly does. I think I like more fiction books. I like geography: only my Mom does. She likes Russian geography.
> (How are you different as a personality?)
> I ask silly questions all the time.

(How are you different from Karl?)
Smarter. When he was in my grade he got lower grades and everything. I'm a little better-tempered than he is.
(And from Kathy?)
I was just trying to think of that. I can't. She's just about like me. She likes dolls. Well, I'm a little dumber than she is. She got all A's and A pluses. I got B's.

Sometimes the sense of self involves derogation of the sibling, as when 15-year-old Harvey replies to a question about how he is similar to and different from his 9-year-old brother Howard:

I don't think we're alike except our interests run the same. I'd say I'm physically better. I have a mental jump on him, too, in grades. He's just the opposite. I try to do things in their order. He's just so sloppy in everything. It's pitiful. He doesn't care what he does.

Harvey's statement suggests an interesting and potentially significant process in sibling relationships. He begins by saying that he and his brother are not alike except that their interests run the same. After dismissing the similarity of interests as of no importance, he emphasizes the differences. It is a reasonable presumption that Howard has developed his interests by modeling himself on Harvey. Harvey's activities were attractive enough that Howard wants to be like him in what he does. But Harvey all but repudiates this attempted identification, as though to say, "You may want to be like me, but you're not like me. I'm very different from you." How deep this repudiation runs in this particular instance is not clear. When Howard was asked in what ways he acts like Harvey, he replied, "He teaches me gymnastics," an answer that suggests that Harvey's sense of sibling loyalty at least partially offsets his repudiation. But in other cases, repudiation may run deeper and amount to "trashing" within the family, with significant consequences for the life course of the trashed sibling.

Younger children in a family make their way in the world partly by attending to, learning from, modeling themselves on, and identifying with older siblings. If an older sibling is "idolized," the younger may endeavor to be as much like the older as can humanly be managed. When there are several older siblings, a younger is faced with the task of sorting them out as models. This point may be illustrated by material from the life history of a 56-year-old construction worker I shall call Larry McGuire. He is the sixth of nine children. He speaks of two older brothers, Tommy, the eldest, and Willie, and of a younger brother, Ernie.

Well, my older brother was spoiled. He used to buy these bags of buns. You know, you'd get four buns for a nickel, and he'd put them up on the table. He was spoiled. He always had to have the extra one. I guess the basic reason was not only was he older but my mother had lost her first child, and he was the second one, and naturally she felt overenthused and blessed that here she had something that she molded in life. And she never let up on him. He was, like I say, a playboy and wasn't serious in life. My father tried to do things to straighten him out, but he couldn't do it. . . . My mother did spoil him with the buns or anything else; he always got the extra piece of meat. . . . But I liked my brother Willie. . . . Willie was like a more serious fellow. . . . He was a down-to-earth man. He knew his responsibilities even though he drank. . . . (What do you remember of him when you were both kids? What did he mean to you then, when you were growing up?)

He meant more of a guardian to me than my older brother, who I didn't take to and respect. Like I say, he was favored. Willie was just one of me in the house. . . . We used to do some petty thievery. . . . And one day a truck is coming up First Avenue, and I grabbed a couple of bottles of milk off the truck, and Willie seen me. He beat the hell out of me, and when I get the ,nilk in the house it was all sour milk. But my brother seemed almost like my second father. And it was through him that I took up boxing. . . . We had things in common. Willie and I would sit down and talk for hours. I can't do that with my brother Ernie and I couldn't have done it with my brother Tommy. It's an odd deal about life. . . . They didn't think like Willie and I as far as being fairly restrained."

DISCUSSION

The four issues or sets of issues that I have delineated can usefully be regarded as standing in dialectical pairs. That is, the first issue, the issue of equity, is concerned with treating siblings in such a way that they feel they have not been treated significantly differently. Significantly different treatment by parents tends to be regarded by one or more as inequitable. Similarly, privileges granted by one sibling to another—such as free access to the latter's possessions—are construed by the grantor as inequitable when the grantee does not reciprocate.

But the issue of maturity introduces contrary considerations. Greater age results in presumed greater competence and hence in greater status. Greater age is something the older is glad to have and the younger can hardly wait for because it is used to justify greater privilege or other differential treatment. Thus, solutions to the problems of sibling equity are made difficult by the issues of differential maturity. Solutions to problems of differential maturity are likely often to be regarded as dangerously close to approved inequity. The parent who is less stringent with a younger child on the ground of immaturity may arouse the older to a sense of injustice at being held to a more stringent standard. The privileges of greater maturity may seem too insubstantial to compensate. Or a greater privilege to an older may seem unjust to a younger who cannot discern the grounds for judging a maturity difference.

The issues of loyalty and individuality similarly are dialectical opposites in their implications. Loyalty provides the basis for making claims upon the other, while individuality provides the basis for resisting such claims. Loyalty strains develop when one child wants to borrow something that a sibling does not want to lend. The would-be borrower loses some faith in the loyalty of the obdurate nonlender, while the latter loses some faith in the value of sibling loyalty. If they turn to a parent for support—"Please tell him that I just want to borrow it for a little while," versus "Please tell him that it's mine and I don't have to lend it"—they present the parent with a fundamental issue of family structure.

This chapter identifies and delineates some fundamental generic issues in sibling relationships. I do not presume that I have presented a complete and exhaustive list, nor have I addressed questions of the range of societies within which an analysis such as this would be applicable, or, except briefly in passing, the ways in which these issues would be affected by different types of family organization within our own society. I do not assume that this analysis applies to families other than white middle-class and working-class families, since the analysis was derived from studying only such families. But I do believe the issues discussed make it possible to think more systematically about sibling relationships. It should be possible to move to more focused and detailed studies of how sibling relationships are constructed in the context of family relationships. It should be possible to follow the course of sibling relationships over time and to trace the changing salience of the various issues. It should be possible to study more systematically the impact of sibling relationships on social, affective, and cognitive development of children.

Sibling relations have yielded enduring metaphors of human aspiration. Brotherhood and sisterhood are ideals that have called forth great human effort. Yet the kinship relations to which these ideals metaphorically refer are scarcely known and understood. No social scientist today of any persuasion can tell us why some siblings develop the kind of loyalty that leads to enduring trust and friendship among them while other siblings do not. Few have even asked the question. Yet if rivalry is an aspect of relations between or among siblings in all families, it surely seems worth knowing why it is overcome in some and not in others, or even among some sibs but not others in the same family.

ACKNOWLEDGMENTS

For helpful comments on an earlier draft I thank Francesca Cancian and Norbert Wiley. Collection of data was supported by Research Grant M-543 from the National Institute of Mental Health and Research Grant RO 3 MH 25067 from the Small Grants Branch of the National Institute of Mental Health.

NOTE

1. This statement might have have to be qualified in the case of an age spread of more than, say, 15 years. It would be a matter of empirical study to determine the age spread at which an older sibling loses all the social characteristics but formal kinship status as a sibling to a younger one.

REFERENCES

Abrahams, Roger. *Positively black.* Englewood Cliffs, N.J.: Prentice-Hall, 1970.

Aries, Phillippe. *Centuries of childhood* (Robert Baldick, trans.). New York:Knopf, 1962.

Bank, Stephen, and Kahn, Michael. *The sibling bond.* New York: Basic Books, 1982.

Berger, Bennett, and others. Child-rearing practices of the communal family. In Arlene S. Skolnick and Jerome H. Skolnick (Eds.), *Family in transition.* Boston: Little, Brown, 1971.

Broderick, Carlfred, and Smith, James. The general systems approach to the family. In Wesley Burr, Reuben Hill, F. Ivan Nye, Ira L. Reiss (Eds.), *Contemporary theories about the family,* Vol. 2, pp. 112–129. New York: Free Press, 1979.

"Brother." *The Jewish encyclopedia.* New York: Funk and Wagnalls, 1906, Vol. 3, pp. 396–397.

Cicirelli, Victor. Sibling influence through the life span. In Michael E. Lamb and Brian Sutton-Smith (Eds.), *Sibling relationships.* Hillsdale, New Jersey: Lawrence E Erlbaum Associates, 1982.

Cumming, Elaine and Schneider, David. Sibling solidarity: A property of American kinship. *American Anthropologist,* 1961, *63,* 498–507.

Dunn, Judy, and Kendrick, Carol. *Siblings.* Cambridge, Mass.: Harvard University Press, 1982.

Editorial Board. Brother. *The Jewish encyclopedia* (Vol. 3, pp. 396–397). New York: Funk & Wagnalls, 1906.

Handel, Gerald. Analysis of correlative meaning: The TAT in the study of whole families. In G. Handel (Ed.), *The psychosocial interior of the family* (1st edition). Chicago: Aldine, 1967.

Hannerz, Ulf. The rhetoric of soul: Identification in Negro society. In Robert V. Guthrie (Ed.), *Being black: Psychological-sociological dilemmas.* San Francisco, Canfield, 1970.

Hess, Robert D. and Handel, Gerald. *Family worlds.* Chicago: University of Chicago Press, 1959.

Hoos, Ida R. *Systems analysis in public policy: A critique.* Berkeley, California: University of California Press, 1972.

Irish, Donald. Sibling interaction: A neglected aspect in family life research. *Social Forces,* 1964, *42,* 279–288. Reprinted in Bernard Farber (Ed), *Kinship and family organization.* New York: Wiley, 1966.

Johnston, G. Brotherhood. In George A. Buttrick (Ed.), *The interpreter's dictionary of the Bible.* New York/Nashville: Abingdon, 1962.

Joreen. Trashing: The dark side of sisterhood. *Ms. IV,* April 1976, 49–52, 92–93.

Lefebvre, Georges. *The French Revolution* (Vol. I, From its origins to 1793, Elizabeth Moss Evanson, trans.). New York: Columbia University Press, 1962.

Lilienfeld, Robert. *The rise of systems theory: An ideological analysis.* New York, Wiley, 1978.

Melder, Keith. *Beginnings of sisterhood.* New York: Schocken Books, 1977.

Morgan, Robin. *Sisterhood is powerful.* New York: Vintage Books, 1970.

Rainwater, Lee. *Behind ghetto walls.* Chicago: Aldine, 1970.

Ratzinga, Joseph. *The open circle: The meaning of Christian brotherhood* (W. A. Glen-Doeple, trans.). New York: Sheed & Ward, 1966.

Ross, Helgola G. and Milgram, Joel I. Important variables in adult sibling relationships: A qualitative study. In Michael E. Lamb and Brian Sutton-Smith (Eds.), *Sibling relationships.* Hillsdale, New Jersey: Lawrence E. Erlbaum Associates, 1982.

Schvaneveldt, Jay D. and Ihinger, Marilyn. Sibling relationships in the family. In

Wesley R Burr, Reuben Hill, F. Ivan Nye, Ira L. Reiss (Eds.), *Contemporary theories about the family* (Vol. I). New York: Free Press, 1979.

Soboul, Albert. The *sans-culottes* (Remy Inglis Hall, trans.). Garden City, New York: Doubleday Anchor, 1962.

Straus, Murray A., Gelles, Richard J., and Steinmetz, Suzanne K. *Behind closed doors: Violence in the American family*. Garden City, New York: Doubleday Anchor, 1980.

Sussman, Marvin B. The isolated nuclear family: fact or fiction? In Marvin B. Sussman (Ed.), *Sourcebook in marriage and the family* (4th ed.). Boston: Houghton, Mifflin, 1974.

Vogel, Ezra F., and Bell, Norman W. The emotionally disturbed child as the family scapegoat. In Norman W. Bell and Ezra F. Vogel (Eds.), *A modern introduction to the family*. Glencoe, Illinois: Free Press, 1960.

Yates, Gayle Graham. *What women want*. Cambridge, Mass.: Harvard University Press, 1975.

VII

Stress, Crisis, and Separateness/ Connectedness

Since human activity is interpretive and constructed, there is a sense in which every human situation is problematic. Every situation must be interpreted and dealt with. Some problems come to be defined as routine, and the strategies for dealing with them tend to fall within a certain range that is recognized as standard. "What to buy for dinner" is a daily or weekly problem for those who have that responsibility, but it is a routine problem for those with the means, and solutions are easily arrived at within a framework of established food preferences and budgetary options and constraints. When the major contributor to the budget loses his or her job, what to buy for dinner is transformed by a stressful event into a nonroutine problem. The family faces a crisis. Reuben Hill defined a crisis as "any sharp or decisive change for which old patterns are inadequate" (Hill, 1949, p. 51). Such a crisis usually presents a family with a challenge to its existing organization. As Hansen and Johnson note, however, not all such challenges come from a single, sharply defined event: "crisis is endemic to some families" (Hansen and Johnson, 1979, p. 584). The chapters in this section sample a range of family crises originating from a variety of stressful sources, and show how the crises affect separateness-connectedness patterns.

In a study of families with an emotionally disturbed child, Ezra F. Vogel and Norman W. Bell found that the child was a scapegoat for the family, and particularly for the parents. Marital conflict between husband and wife was a source of continuing stress. For various reasons that the authors explore, the couple were not successful in resolving the conflict within their own relationship. The family's psychosocial interior is reconstructed so that the child is made to seem a separate—and major—source of the family's troubles.

Lee Rainwater analyzes the consequences of racism for separateness-connectedness patterns in black lower-class families. Although there is a growing black middle class in the United States, the continuing existence of a victimized black lower class makes Rainwater's analysis as relevant today as when it was published in the late 1960's (*Note to reader:* Rainwater's article was written shortly before the term "black" came into common usage.) In fact, since he wrote, a new term has come into use: "permanent underclass" refers to those people, primarily black and Hispanic, who seem to be without any good prospects for raising themselves or assisting their children into the stable working class or into the middle class. Racism and poverty are such enduring and overpowering stressors as to create inimical family interiors.

Edward J. Speedling studied a more delimited type of crisis, the impact of heart attacks in eight men on their families. As soon as it was medically practicable, he interviewed the men in the hospital Intensive Care Unit, as well as their wives and children during and after hospital visits. He interviewed and did participant observation on the Intensive Care Unit, then on the general medical ward when the men were transferred, and finally in the homes when they were released. Speedling found three types of families: (1) divergent families valued, in some important way, separateness over connectedness; (2) convergent families emphasized group interests over individual; by requiring role differentiation, they ensured that members had to be interdependent; (3) discordant families were unable to work out a stable balance of separateness and connectedness. In the selection presented here, Speedling examines the different family types' ways of handling the stress of reorganization that occurs when the men return home from the hospital.

The stress generated by the transformation from a two-parent to a single-parent family has become increasingly familiar. Death of a parent has been decreasing, but divorce has been sharply increasing for a number of years. In the final selection in this volume, Robert S. Weiss explores the kinds of stresses the single-parent family is likely to experience and the new kinds of separateness-connectedness patterns that have to be constructed.

REFERENCES

Hansen, Donald A., and Johnson, Vicky. Rethinking family stress theory: Definitional aspects. In Wesley R. Burr, Reuben Hill, F. Ivan Nye, Ira L. Reiss (Eds.), *Contemporary theories about the family* (Vol. I pp. 582–603). New York: Free Press, 1979.

Hill, Reuben. *Families under stress*. New York: Harper, 1949.

21

The Emotionally Disturbed
Child as the Family
Scapegoat

EZRA F. VOGEL AND
NORMAN W. BELL

The phenomenon of scapegoating is as old as human society. Sir James Frazer, in *The Golden Bough*,[1] records numerous instances reaching back to antiquity of public scapegoats, human and other. He views the process of scapegoating as one in which " . . . the evil influences are embodied in a visible form or are at least supposed to be loaded upon a material medium, which acts as a vehicle to draw them off from the people, village, or town."[2] The scapegoat's function " . . . is simply to effect a total clearance of all the ills that have been infesting a people."[3] Frazer was dealing with the phenomenon at the level of a society, tribe, village, or town. It is the purpose of this chapter to examine the same phenomenon within families, by viewing an emotionally disturbed child as an embodiment of certain types of conflicts between parents. This pattern is a special case of a common phenomenon, the achievement of group unity through the scapegoating of a particular member. It is, perhaps, more widely known that a group may achieve unity through projection of hostilities to the outside,[4] but there are also a large number of cases where members of a particular group are able to achieve unity through scapegoating a particular member of that group. Thus, the deviant within the group may perform a valuable function for the group by channeling group tensions and providing a basis for solidarity.

Reprinted with permission of Macmillan, Inc. from *A modern introduction to the family*, edited by Norman W. Bell and Ezra F. Vogel. Copyright © 1960, 1968 by The Free Press, a Division of the Macmillan Company.

Ezra F. Vogel is Professor of Sociology, Harvard University. Norman W. Bell is Professor of Sociology, University of Toronto.

The notion that the family is in large part responsible for the emotional health of the child is a compelling one in contemporary behavioral science. By and large, however, the research has focused largely on the mother–child relationship, and the independent variable by which the mother–child relationship and the child-rearing practices are usually explained is the personality and developmental history of the mother. Recently, an attempt has also been made to treat the father–child relationship, again largely in terms of the personality and developmental history of the father. While in clinical practice there is some awareness of family dynamics, in the literature the family has largely been treated simply as a collection of personalities, and the child's personality development has been seen almost exclusively as a direct result of the separate personalities of his parents.[5] Rarely is the interaction of parents treated as a significant independent variable influencing childhood development. Even when broader cultural patterns have been considered, childhood development has been related to child-rearing practices and socialization into the culture, with little consideration of the family as the mediating unit.

Data for this chapter are derived from the intensive study[6] of a small group of "disturbed" families, each with an emotionally disturbed child, and a matched group of "well" families without clinically manifest disturbances in any child. Of the nine families in each group, three were Irish–American, three Italian–American, and three old–American. The families were seen by a team including psychiatrists, social workers, psychologists, and social scientists. The disturbed families, on which this paper is based, were seen weekly in the offices of a psychiatric clinic and in their homes over periods ranging from one to four years. Detailed information was gathered about the members' developmental histories and character structure, but even more specific data were obtained about current processes.

This chapter is concerned with how a child in the family, the emotionally disturbed child, was used as a scapegoat for the conflicts between parents, and what the functions and dysfunctions of this scapegoating are for the family.

In all the disturbed families it was found that a particular child had become involved in tensions existing between the parents.[7] In the "well" families used for control purposes, either the tensions between the parents were not so severe or else the tensions were handled in such a way that the children did not become pathologically involved. In general, both parents of the emotionally disturbed child had many of the same underlying conflicts, but in relationship to each other they felt themselves to be at opposite poles, so that one spouse would act out one side of the conflict and the other would act out the other side of the conflict. They had developed an equilibrium in which they minimized contact with each other and minimized expressions of affect, particularly hostility, which they strongly felt for each other, and this made it possible for them to live with each other.[8]

But this equilibrium had many difficulties, the most serious of which was the scapegoating of a child.

SOURCES OF TENSION THAT LEAD TO SCAPEGOATING

It is our contention that scapegoating is produced by the existence of tensions between parents that have not been satisfactorily resolved in other ways. The spouses in the disturbed families had deep fears about their marital relationship and about the partner's behavior. They did not feel they could predict accurately how the other would respond to their own behavior. Yet, the other's response was of very great importance and was thought to be potentially very damaging. The partners did not feel they could deal with the situation by direct communication because this might be too dangerous, and they resorted to manipulations of masking, evading, and the like. This atmosphere of tension has several sources. One of the sources was the personality problems of each spouse, but in the present analysis the focus will be on the group sources of the tension. These tensions usually have several sources. At a very general level, one of the main sources of tension was conflict in cultural value orientations.[9] Value orientations are abstract, general conceptions of the nature of human nature and man's relationship to it, of man's relation to man, of the most significant time dimension, and of the most valued type of activity. All societies have preferences and alternative preferences to these basic dimensions; these preferences are expressed within a wide range of phenomena. In complex ways, they are related to personality and social structure and to more specific values. When people are in the process of acculturation, as was the case with the families of Irish and Italian backgrounds, many possibilities for value–orientation conflict arise. Any one individual may have been socialized into conflicting or confused patterns, and may be unsuccessful in bridging the gap. Marriage partners may have been socialized into different patterns and may be working on different assumptions. All our disturbed families had problems of these sorts. Some were trying to shift quickly to a set of orientations they had not thoroughly internalized, and without having neutralized previous orientations. Others were trying to live by conflicting orientations.[10]

A common example of the cultural value conflicts was the conflict centered around the problems of individual performance. There were considerable pulls toward the American middle-class achievement patterns. In families that had partially internalized both sets of value orientations, it was impossible to live up to both sets of values, and whichever the family chose, this meant that certain conflicts would result.

Another source of tension was the relations between the family and the larger community. Disturbed families usually had problems in this area, rejecting and/or being rejected by the community. In some cases, a family had very severe disapproval of a very close-knit ethnic neighborhood directed at them. In other cases, families had moved from ethnic neighborhoods to more fashionable suburbs and suffered in their own eyes by comparison to their new neighbors. Consequently, their social relationships with these neighbors were often minimal; when they did exist they were usually strained, or else one spouse had fairly good relationships with some friends and the partner had poor relationships with these friends. All families, to a greater or lesser extent, had problems in their relationships with families of orientation. Typically, the wife was strongly attached to her parents and antagonistic toward her husband's family, while the husband was attached to his parents and antagonistic to his wife's family. If either spouse was critical of his in-laws, the partner typically defended his own parents and became more critical of his in-laws. If one spouse was critical of his own parents, the partner was often friendly to them. The unbalanced attachments to parents and parents-in-law was not resolved. Changes usually produced more tension, but the basic sources of strain remained unchanged.[11]

THE SELECTION OF THE SCAPEGOAT

The tensions produced by unresolved conflicts were so severe that they could not be contained without some discharge. It is not surprising that some appropriate object was chosen to symbolize the conflicts and draw off the tension. Conceivably, some person or group outside the family could serve in this capacity. However, in these disturbed families, the parents had by and large internalized the standards of the surrounding community sufficiently so that they had great difficulty in finding a legitimate basis for scapegoating outsiders. In addition, most of these families had very tenuous ties with the community, and since they were very concerned about being accepted, they could not afford to antagonize their associates. While some of the families did, at times, have strong feelings of antagonism toward various members of the community in which they lived, they could rarely express this antagonism directly. Even if at times they were able to manifest their antagonism, this usually led to many additional complications, and the family preferred to scapegoat its own child.[12]

Channeling the tensions within the family did not lead to difficulties with the outside, but usually the latent hostilities between the husband and wife made it very difficult to deal with problems openly between them. There was always danger the partner might become too angry, which would lead to severe and immediate difficulties. A number of factors made a child the most appropriate object through which to deal with family tensions. First of all, the child was in a relatively powerless position compared to the parents. While he was dependent on the parents and could not leave the family, he was not able effectively to counter the parents' superior power. Although the parents' defenses were fairly brittle in comparison with those of well parents, still their defenses were much stronger than those of their children. Because the child's personality is still very flexible, he can be molded to adopt the particular role the family assigns to him. When the child does take on many of the characteristics the parents dislike in themselves and each other, he becomes a symbolically appropriate object on which to focus their own anxieties. Since the person scapegoated often develops such severe tensions that he is unable to perform his usual task roles, it is important that those family members performing essential, irreplaceable functions for the family not be scapegoated. The child has relatively few tasks to perform in the family, compared to the parents or other elders, and his disturbance does not ordinarily interfere with the successful performance of the necessary family tasks. The "cost" in dysfunction of the child is low relative to the functional gains for the whole family.

In all cases, with partial exception of one family, a particular child was chosen as the scapegoat, while other children were relatively free of pathology. The selecting of a particular child is not a random matter; one child is the best symbol. Just as a dream condenses a variety of past and present experiences and a variety of emotional feelings, the scapegoat condenses a variety of social and psychological problems impinging on the family.

Who is selected as the scapegoat is intimately related to the sources of tension. Where value-orientation conflicts existed, the child chosen was the one who best symbolized these conflicts. For example, if the conflicts revolved around achievement, a child who failed to achieve according to expectations could become the symbol of failure. Alternatively, a child might be an appropriate object because he was achieving independently and thus violating norms of loyalty to the group.

The position of the child in the sibling group frequently became a focus for the unresolved childhood problems of the parents. If the parents' most serious unresolved problems were with male figures, the child chosen to represent the family conflict was usually a male child. Similarly, sibling order could be a strong factor. If one or both parents had difficulties with older brothers, an older boy in the family might become the scapegoat.

In two cases, the sex or sibling position of the child seemed to be particularly important in the selection of a particular child as the family scapegoat. In one of these cases, the mother was the oldest of three siblings and had considerable feelings of rivalry with her next younger sister which had never been effectively resolved. Although the father had two older siblings, they were so much older that to him they were a separate family. In his effective family environment, he was the older of two children and had considerable feelings of rivalry toward a younger brother who displaced him and for whom he subsequently had to care. This couple has three children, and there was an unusual amount of rivalry between the oldest and the second sibling. Both the parents sided very strongly with the oldest child. They were continuously conscious of the middle child bothering the older,

for which they severely criticized this middle child. There are many striking parallels, even to small details, in the relationship between the parents
and their next younger siblings and the relationship between their oldest
child and the next younger sibling.

Another pattern revolved around the identification of a child with a parent whom he resembled. This was found in all families, sick and well, in
one form or another; but in the disturbed families the child was seen as
possessing very undesirable traits, and although the parent actually possessed the same traits, the focus of attention was the child and not the parent. In one family in particular, this pattern was striking. The father and the
eldest son had very similar physical characteristics; not only did they have
the same first name, but both were called by the same diminutive name by
the mother. At times, the social worker seeing the mother was not certain
whether the mother was talking about her husband or her son. The wife's
concerns about the husband's occupational adequacy were not dealt with
directly, but the focus for her affect was the child and his school performance. In fact, the son was criticized by his mother for all the characteristics that she disliked in her husband, but she was unable to criticize her
husband directly for these characteristics. She channeled all her feelings,
especially anxiety and hostility, to the child, although her husband had similar
problems. Furthermore, in order to control her feelings toward her husband, she remained very aloof and distant and was not able to express to
him her positive or negative feelings. While she channeled many criticisms
and anxieties through the child, she also expressed many of her positive
feelings to the child, thereby leading to severe oedipal conflicts. The husband was not happy about his wife being so aloof from him, but on the
other hand he found that by cooperating with his wife in criticizing the
child he was able to keep the burden of problems away from himself. He
thus joined with the wife in projecting his own difficulties and problems
onto the child and in dealing with them as the child's problems rather than
as his own.

In three of the families the scapegoat had considerably lower intelligence than did the other children in the family. In all these families there
were serious conflicts about the value of achievement, and the parents had
great difficulty themselves in living up to their own achievement aspirations. In all these cases the parents were unable to accept the fact that their
children had limited abilities, and they continually held up impossible
standards for them. Although all three children had I.Q.'s in the 80's or
below and had failed one grade or more, all three mothers stated that they
intended their children go to college. At the beginning of therapy, one of
the mothers hoped her son would attend medical school and become a
doctor; another had begun to put away a small amount of money from a
very tight budget for her daughter's college education, even though the
daughter's intelligence was that of a moron. At the beginning of therapy,

none of the parents was able to deal directly with his own difficulties in achievement. In contrast, in one of the families there were two children who had very low intelligence, one of whom had failed a grade in school, but the family scapegoat was a boy who had normal intelligence. In this case, the parents, who had average intelligence, had resolved their conflicts about achievement by denying that they were interested in achievement and accepting their social position. This child of slightly higher intelligence and greater physical activity was seen by them as a very aggressive child who was always doing too much, and the parents were continually worried that he was "too smart." [13]

In a number of cases the disturbed child either had a serious physical disease when he was young or a striking physical abnormality, such as a hare lip, bald spots in the hair, or unusually unattractive facial features. The mere existence of some such abnormality seemed to draw attention to one particular child, so that if there were some sorts of anxieties or problems in the family at all, the child with the physical peculiarities seemed to become the focus of the family problems. Here again, however, it was not the mere existence of a physical defect but its meaning [14] in the life of the family that gave it its significance. For example, in some families there was a feeling that they had committed certain sins by not living up to their ideals, for instance by using contraceptives. This was a very common problem, since many families could not possibly live up to the two opposing sets of ideals they had at least partially internalized. The child's physical abnormality became a symbol of the family's sin of not having lived up to some partially internalized values, and the malformed child was seen as a sinful child who was not living up to the standards of the group. Since the family's relationship with the community was often tenuous, the fact that one of their children had physical abnormalities that made the child the focus of neighborhood ridicule served to make the parents increasingly ashamed of the child's physical characteristics and to focus increasingly more attention on this child. For example, one of the main concerns of the family with the unusually ugly child was that other children were continually teasing her about her appearance. However, the concern was less for the child herself and more for the whole family. Her problems symbolized the parents' past and present problems with the neighborhood; rather than sympathize with the child, they abused her all the more. In another case in which a female child's physical illness became a focus of the family's problems, the parents were extremely concerned about her saftey, which was again related in part to the potential dangers in social relationships with the outside world. As a result of the girl's illness, the family became much more cautious than was necessary, and on some occasions they were even reluctant to accept medical advice that she could participate in certain activities without danger to her health. The continual contacts that the child had with middle-class professional personnel through hospitalization and clinic visits led her to accept certain middle-class American values more than did the rest of the family, and the family was continually expressing the feeling that she had different attitudes after hospitalization and contact with hospital personnel. The disliked attitudes ascribed to the child were in general those of middle-class American culture.[15] Not only abnormalities but general body type could become the symbol to call forth scapegoating. In two families, the spouses had many problems in their sexual life. Rather than face these maladjustments directly, the problems were expressed through concern about the masculinity and normality of a slender, graceful son.

While the general process of symbolization of a scapegoat is very similar to the dream symbolization, there is one problem in the family selection of a scapegoat that is not met in the selection of a dream symbol, and that is the problem of availability. While in dreams, any symbolic representation is open to the dreamer, in the family only a very small number of children are available as the potential scapegoats. Hence, when there is a serious family problem and no child is an appropriate symbol of the problem, there must be considerable cognitive distortion in order to permit the most appropriate one available to be used as a scapegoat. For example, in one family that was very concerned about the problems of achievement, the focus of the family's problems was the eldest son. Although he was receiving passing grades in school, whereas the parents had had poor school records, the parents were critical of his school performance. Because of this pressure, the child worked hard and was able to get somewhat better marks on his next report card. However, the mother stoutly maintained that her son didn't deserve those grades, that he must have cheated, and she continued to criticize him for his school performance.

The other aspect of the problem of availability resulted from the fact that the parents apparently have had tensions since early in marriage. As nearly as it was possible to reconstruct the marital history, it appeared that the spouses had selected each other partly on the basis of the fact that they shared many of the same conflicts and understood each other quite well. Not long after marriage, however, they seemed to have become polarized in their conflicts, so that one parent represented one side of the conflict and the other represented the other side. This seems to have given each of the spouses a way of handling his own conflicts and allowed each to remain fairly consistent and well integrated by projecting difficulties onto the partner. However, it also led to very severe difficulties in the marital relationship and created many tensions that were quickly displaced onto the first available and appropriate object, very often the first child. Since the eldest child was the first one available for scapegoating, he often seems to have been assigned this role and, once assigned, has continued in it. Perhaps because of his prior availability and his closer involvement in the adult world, he is a more appropriate object for the scapegoating.[16] In the one case in which a child was able to escape the scapegoat role by decreasing his attachment to the home, the next most appropriate child was used in the scapegoat role.

INDUCTION OF THE CHILD INTO THE SCAPEGOAT ROLE

If the child is to be a "satisfactory" scapegoat, he must carry out his role as a "problem child." The problem behavior must be reinforced strongly enough so that it will continue in spite of the hostility and anxiety it produces in the child. This delicate balance is possible only because the parents have superior sanction power over the child, can define what he should or should not do, and control what he does or does not do. This balance necessarily requires a large amount of inconsistency in the ways parents handle the child.

The most common inconsistency was between the implicit (or unconscious) and the explicit role induction.[17] In all cases certain behavior of the child violated recognized social norms. In some instances stealing, fire-setting, expressions of hostility, or uncooperativeness affected the child's relationships with people outside the family. In other instances bed-wetting, resistance to parental orders, or expression of aggression to siblings affected relationships in the family. But in all instances, while the parents explicitly criticized the child and at times even punished him, they supported in some way, usually implicitly, the persistence of the very behavior they criticized. This permission took various forms: failure to follow through on threats, delayed punishment, indifference to and acceptance of the symptom, unusual interest in the child's symptom, or considerable secondary gratification offered to the child because of his symptom. The secondary gratification usually took the form of special attention and exemption from certain responsibilities. While the parents had internalized social norms sufficiently to refrain from violating the norms themselves, they had not sufficiently internalized them to prevent giving encouragement to their children for acting out their own repressed wishes. The wish to violate these norms was transferred to the child, but the defenses against this wish were never as strong in the child.[18]

Another type of inconsistency seen was that one parent would encourage one type of behavior, but the other parent would encourage an opposing type of behavior. The result again was that the child was caught in the conflict. This also permitted one spouse to express annoyance to the other indirectly without endangering the marital relationship. For example, in one case the father objected to the son's leaving toys lying around and would violently explode at the child for such behavior, implying that the mother was wrong in permitting him to do this. The mother realized that the father exploded at such behavior and did not stop the father since she "knew he was right." Nevertheless, she often indicated that the child need not bother picking up the toys, since she felt that he was too young to have to do such things by himself and that the father was too strict. If the mother's encouragement of the behavior annoying to the father was explicit, there would be danger that the father's hostility would be directed at the mother rather than the child. By keeping the encouragement implicit, the mother was able to deny that she had encouraged the child. The father was usually willing to accept this denial, even if he did not believe it, rather than risk an explosion with his wife. In some instances, however, the other spouse was angered or felt compelled to criticize the other for not handling the child properly. Then the encouragement of the child to behave in a certain way would have to become more subtle to avoid criticism of the other spouse, another delicate balance to maintain. A parent had to give sufficient encouragement to the child to perform the act without making it so obvious that his spouse felt obliged to criticize him.

In addition to the inconsistent pressures resulting from the difference between explicit and implicit expectations and from the differences between the expectations of the two parents, the child also had to deal with changes in each parent's expectations. From the parent's conscious point of view, this inconsistency resulted from an attempt to reconcile two conflicting desires: teaching the child to behave properly and not being "too hard on the child." When a parent was consciously attempting to teach the child proper behavior, he was extremely aggressive and critical.[19] At other times, the parent felt he had been too critical of the child and permitted him to behave in the same way without punishment, and would be extremely affectionate and supportive. While the explanation given for this inconsistency was that he wanted to teach the desired behavior without being "too hard on the child," its latent function was to prevent the child from consistently living up to the ostensibly desired behavior and to preserve the disliked behavior. The period of not being "too hard on the child" served to reinforce the disapproved behavior and the period of "being firm" permitted the parents to express their anxieties and hostility. This balance was also very delicate, since it was always possible that negative sanctions would become so severe that the child would refuse to behave in such a way that parents felt he could legitimately be punished.

The delicacy of this balance was perhaps best exemplified by the problem of bed-wetting. Parents complained about bed-wetting, but at the same time they could not bring themselves to do anything to alter the child's behavior. If the therapists could get both parents to be firm at the same time, the child would usually stop bed-wetting. Very soon, however, by putting a rubber sheet on the bed, or buying special night clothes "just in case he wets," the child was encouraged again to wet. One mother succeeded several times in finding methods to stop her son's wetting, but immediately stopped using them "since he's stopped now." In several cases, the parents would alternate in being concerned and trying to be firm and being unconcerned and implicitly encouraging the behavior, at all times remaining inconsistent, one with the other. It seemed clear that whether or not the child wet his bed was a relatively sensitive index of just where the balance of rewards from the parents lay. In general, however, the implicit demands carried the greater sanction power and the child continued with the behavior of which the parents unconsciously approved and consciously disapproved. Presumably, the sanctions of the parents against bed-wetting would increase as the child grew older, and the balance would become delicate only at that later time.

Since these conflicting expectations existed over a long period of time, it is not surprising that the child internalized these conflicts. Once a child was selected as a deviant, there was a circular reaction that tended to perpetuate this role assignment. Once he had responded to his parents' implicit wishes and acted in a somewhat disturbed manner, the parents could treat him as if he really were a problem. The child would respond to these expectations and the vicious cycle was set in motion. Both the child and the parents, then, had complementary expectations. The particular role assigned to the child was appropriately rewarded. It is difficult, if not impossible, to distinguish just at what point the parents began treating the child as if he were a problem and at what point the child actually did have internalized problems. There does not seem to be any sudden development of the child's problems; rather, it is a process occurring over a period of time. By the time the family was seen in the clinic, the vicious cycle was well established, and the child had internalized his disturbed role to such an extent that it was difficult to effect change only by removing external pressures. This was, of course, particularly true for older and more disturbed children. The fact that the child becomes disturbed adds stability to the role system, so that once set in motion, scapegoating did not easily pass from one child to another. In the well families, when scapegoating did take place, it was less severe and did not become stabilized, with one child as a continual scapegoat.

THE RATIONALIZATION OF SCAPEGOATING

When a scapegoating situation was established, a relatively stable equilibrium of the family was achieved. However, there were difficulties in maintaining the equilibrium. Parents had considerable guilt about the way they treated the child, and when the child was identified as disturbed by neighbors, teachers, doctors, or other outside agencies, pressure was brought to bear for some action to be taken. When called upon to explain, parents did not have much difficulty in stating why they were so concerned about the child, but they did have great difficulty in rationalizing their aggressive and libidinal expressions to the children.

One way in which the parents rationalized their behavior was to define themselves, rather than the children, as victims. They stressed how much difficulty there was coping with all the problems posed by their child. For example, mothers of bed-wetters complained about the problems of keeping sheets clean and the impossibility of the child staying overnight at friends' or relatives' homes. Such rationalizations seemed to relieve some of the guilt for victimizing the children and served as a justification for continued expressions of annoyance toward the children.

Another way was to emphasize how fortunate their children really were. For most of these parents, the standard of living provided for their children was much higher than the standard of living they enjoyed when they were children. One of the central complaints of these parents, particularly the fathers, was that the children wanted too much and got much more than the parents ever got when they were children. This was seen by the parents as a legitimate excuse for depriving their children of the toys, privileges, and other things they wanted, and for refusing to recognize the children's complaints that they were not getting things. A closely related type of rationalization stems from the change of child-rearing practices over the past generation. The parents felt that their parents were much stricter than they were with their children and that children nowadays "get away with murder." Many of the parents had acute conflicts about how strict to be with children and when the parents did express aggression to the children, they often defined it as beneficial strictness and "giving the child a lesson." Since their own parents were much more severe with them, their own children don't realize "how good they have it."

The parents also used various specific norms to justify their behavior. Even though the parents may be giving implicit encouragement to break these norms, the fact that these social norms are explicitly recognized gives the parents a legitimate basis for punishing the children. As long as the permission for disobeying the sanctions is implicit, it is always possible for the parents to deny that they are really giving it. In general, these parents were reluctant to admit that their child had an emotional disturbance or that he was behaving the way he was because of certain inner problems. They generally interpreted the disturbed child's behavior as willful badness. They felt that the child could behave differently if he really wanted to. Hence, what was needed, in their view, was not consideration, advice, and help, but a "lesson" in how to behave, i.e., severe reprimands and punishment; but even this they could not give. At times, the parents attempted to deny completely that they were scapegoating this particular child. They insisted very rigidly that "we treat all the children just the same." At other times, the parents insisted that this one particular child was just different from all others, implying that this child deserved punishment and that they were good parents since their other children have turned out so well.

Frequently, the mothers expressed, although inconsistently, unusually strong affection for a son. They justified this almost invariably in the same way: the child had problems and difficulties and thus needed more help and care than the other children. However, what they considered care and protection far exceeded the usual limits. This can be seen for example, in the mother who carried her 12-year-old son from the bed to the bathroom so that he could avoid bed-wetting, in the mother who continually fondled her adolescent son and called him "lovie," and in the frequent slips of the tongues by a variety of family members that identified the mother and son as spouses. Fathers, on the other hand, often had special attachments to, and fondness for, daughters.

All these attempts of the parents to rationalize their behavior had a very defensive quality and showed the difficulty these parents had in reconciling their own behavior with general social norms about child-rearing. In the more severely disturbed families, the pressing nature of their problems required serious distortion of social norms, but in the mildly disturbed families, more attention was given to the social norms, and attempts were made to express emotions in more acceptable ways. In any event, much energy was required to keep the balance stable, a state required coordination of many subtle and inconsistent feelings and behaviors. It was, in effect, an "armed truce," and the danger of an explosion was constantly present.

FUNCTIONS AND DYSFUNCTIONS OF SCAPEGOATING

Functions

Although the present chapter has been concerned with the dynamics of the family as a group in relation to an emotionally disturbed child, some comments should be made on the functions that scapegoating serves for the parents individually and for external social systems. For the parents, scapegoating served as a personality-stabilizing process. While the parents of these children did have serious internal conflicts, the projection of these difficulties onto the children served to minimize and control them. Thus, in spite of their personality difficulties, the parents were able to live up to their commitments to the wider society, expressing a minimum of their difficulties in the external economic and political systems. Most of the parents were able to maintain positions as steady workers and relatively respectable community members.

While the scapegoating of the child helped the parents live up to their obligations to the community, often they did not live up to their obligations as adequately as other families, and the whole family became a scapegoat for the community. Then the same mechanisms existed between the outer community and the family as between parents and child. The families, like their children, seldom fought back effectively; instead, they channeled their additional frustrations and tensions through the child. Once established, many forces may play into the scapegoating situation. Though the child suffered additional burdens, through the medium of the family he helped drain off the tension of the broader community in relation to a particular family.

From the point of view of the family, the primary function of scapegoating is that it permits the family to maintain its solidarity. In all the disturbed families, there were very severe strains that continually threatened to disrupt the family.[20] Very serious dissatisfactions between spouses came to light during the course of therapy, which were much more severe than those found in the well families. In the two families with the most severely disturbed children, when the scapegoating of the child eased up during therapy, the explosions between parents became so severe that there was serious fear the family might break up. In the one case in which the problems between spouses remained relatively latent throughout therapy, marital problems emerged more clearly after the termination of therapy, and this led to serious anxiety attacks of the father. Yet, considering these internal strains, all of these families have shown surprising stability. Only in one family had there been a brief period of voluntary separation between the parents, and it had occurred before their first child was born. By focusing on one particular child, the families were able to encapsulate problems and anxieties that could potentially disrupt various family processes. There seemed to be an added solidarity between the parents who stood united against the problem child. The fact that it is a child who is disturbed permits the parents to continue to perform the tasks necessary for household maintenance with relative stability. Since the child is in a dependent position and contributes relatively little to family task activities, his malfunctioning does not seriously interfere with family stability.

Dysfunctions

While the scapegoating of a child is effective in controlling major sources of tensions within the family, the onset of a child's emotional disturbance leads to secondary complications that are, however, generally less severe than the original tensions. One dysfunction is that certain realistic problems and extra tasks are created for the family. The child does require special care and attention. If, for example, the child is a bed-wetter, then the family must either wake him up regularly, or wash many sheets and take other precautions. This becomes particularly acute when traveling, visiting, or attending camp. Often the child cannot be left alone, and someone must continually look after him. If the child is to receive treatment, then the parents must expend time and money in providing this.

In addition, while the child is responsive to the implicit sanctions of his parents, he, too, may develop mechanisms of fighting back and punishing his parents for the way they treat him. Often the child becomes very skilled in arousing his parents' anxieties or in consciously bungling something his parents want him to do. Of course, the mother, being present during most of the day, experiences more of this counteraggression, and this in part accounts for her readiness to bring the child in for treatment. In most of these families it was the mother who took the initiative in seeking treatment. It would appear that as long as she can carefully control the amount of hostility the child expresses to her, she can tolerate this dysfunction, but when hostility rises above a certain point, she is willing to seek outside help.

While the functions of the scapegoat within the nuclear family clearly outweigh his dysfunctions, this is typically not the case with the child's relationship outside the nuclear family. While the family gives the child sufficient support to maintain his role in the family, the use of him as a scapegoat is often incompatible with equipping him to maintain an adjustment outside the nuclear family. This problem becomes particularly acute when the child begins important associations outside the nuclear family, in relationships with peers and teachers at school.[21] It is at this time that many referrals to psychiatric clinics are made.[22] While the child's behavior was perfectly tolerable to the parents before, his behavior suddenly becomes intolerable. While he may still be performing the role the family wants him to play in order to be a scapegoat, this comes into conflict with his role as a representative of the family. The family is thus in conflict between using the child as a scapegoat and identifying with the child because of his role as family representative to the outside. Both sides of this conflict are revealed most clearly in the one family that carried on a feud with the outside and alternated between punishing the daughter for her poor school behavior and criticizing the teachers and children in school for causing problems for their daughter. In nearly all of these disturbed families, school difficulty was a crucial factor in the decision to refer the child for psychiatric treatment. While the child's behavior was rewarded at home, it was not rewarded at school, and while the family could tolerate the child's maladaptive behavior at home, the fact that the school took special note of the child's behavior proved embarrassing and troubling to the parents.

This problem in relation to the outside world is perhaps most striking in the case of the school, but it is also true, for example, in relationships with neighbors and relatives. Neighbors and relatives are likely to be very critical of the family for the child's disturbed behavior, and it is often at such times that the family makes the greatest effort to get rid of the child's maladaptive behavior. In those families that alternated between punishing and rewarding the child's behavior, difficulty with the outside was often a cue to the family to move into the stage of punishing and criticizing the same behavior.

While, as a whole, the child's disturbance served to relieve family tensions, it often led to further family tensions. To the extent that outside norms or standards by which the child does not abide are considered legitimate, inevitable frustrations arise. While the parents made strenuous efforts to interpret this as a result of the child's behavior and not of their own behavior, this effort was never completely successful. In accordance with modern child-rearing theory, to which they are at least exposed, they consider themselves at least partly responsible for the disturbance of the child, and this seems to have been particularly true at the time of therapy. Thus the child's disturbance feeds back into the problems that must be faced by the parents, and the marital pair often project the responsibility for the child's disturbance onto each other. The mother will say, for example, that the father doesn't spend enough time with the children, and the father will say that the mother doesn't manage the children properly. While this was thus dysfunctional to the marital relationship, it never became so prominent that the parents ceased using the child as a scapegoat. The predominant direction of aggression was still toward the badly behaved child rather than toward the other spouse.

While the disturbed behavior leads to some dysfunction for the family, it is the personality of the child that suffers most as a result of the scapegoating. Any deviant or scapegoat within a group feels strong group pressure, which creates considerable conflicts for him.[23] While other groups may also maintain their integration at the expense of the deviant, in the nuclear family this can be stabilized for a long period of time and result in far more serious personality impairment of the child assigned to the deviant role. The development of the emotional disturbance is simply part of the process of internalizing the conflicting demands placed upon him by his parents. While in the short run the child receives more rewards from the family for playing this role than for not playing this role, in the long run this leads to serious personality impairment. In short, the scapegoating mechanism is functional for the family as a group but dysfunctional for the emotional health of the child and for his adjustment outside the family of orientation.

NOTES

1. Sir James Frazer, The golden bough (abridged ed.). New York: Macmillan, 1927.

2. Ibid., p. 562.

3. Ibid., p. 575.

4. In addition to Frazer, op. cit., see also Emile Durkheim, Deux lois de l'évolution pénale. L'Année Sociologique, 1899, 45–95; Henri Hubert and Marcel Mauss, Essai sur la nature et la fonction du sacrifice. L'Année Sociologique, 1897, 29–138; William Robertson Smith, The religion of the Semites. London: A. and C. Black, Ltd., 1927; Roger Money-Kyrle, The meaning of sacrifice. London: Hogarth Press, 1930; George Herbert Mead, The psychology of punitive justice. American Journal of Sociology, 1918, 23, 577–620; Ruth S. Eissler, Scapegoats of society. In Kurt R. Eissler (Ed.), Searchlights on delinquency. New York: International Universities Press, 1949, 228–305; and Clyde Kluckhohn, Navaho witchcraft, Papers of the Peabody Museum of American Archaeology and Ethnology, Harvard University, Vol. XXII, 1944.

5. This is not to deny relevance of psychological aspects. The same facts can be related to a number of different theoretical systems, but here focus is on the group dynamics.

6. For other reports of this research, see John P. Spiegel, The resolution of role conflict within the family. *Psychiatry*, 1957, *20*, 1–16; Florence Rockwood Kluckhohn, Family diagnosis: Variations in the basic values of family systems. *Social Casework*, 1958, *39*, 1–11; and John P. Spiegel, Some cultural aspects of transference and countertransference. In Jules H. Massermann (Ed.), *Individual and family dynamics*. New York: Grune and Stratton, Inc., 1959. A more inclusive statement of the conceptual framework will be published in the near future as, John P. Spiegel, *The structure and function of social roles in the doctor-patient relationship.* Lectures delivered at Tulane University, 1958

7. It should be noted that only families that had never been separated or divorced were included in the present sample. Of course, there are also cases of emotionally disturbed children where only one parent is living with the children and cases in which one parent is living with other relatives. Hence, tensions between parents cannot be the universal cause of emotional disturbance. A more general hypothesis would be that the emotionally disturbed child is always the focus of primary-group tension.

8. This is spelled out in more detail in Ezra F. Vogel, *The marital relationship of parents and the emotionally disturbed child.* Unpublished Ph.D. thesis, Harvard University, 1958.

9. See Florence R Kluckhohn, *loc. cit.;* and F. Kluckhohn, Fred L. Strodtbeck and others, *Variations in value orientations.* Evanston, Ill.: Row, Peterson & Co., forthcoming.

10. Well families, by contrast, had bridged the gap between the orientations of different ethnic or class groups. They had succeeded in neutralizing old orientations before taking on new ones. Usually such families were changing in a slower and more orderly fashion.

11. Discussed at length in Norman W. Bell, *The impact of psychotherapy upon family relationships.* Unpublished Ph.D. thesis, Harvard University, 1959.

12. The one family that did occasionally express antagonism directly to outsiders was the most disturbed family in the sample. The expression of hostility to neighbors was filled with such conflicts and added complication that the expression inevitably proved inadequate and the family returned to the scapegoating of their child.

While many members of these families did express prejudice toward minority groups, this prejudice did little to drain the severe tensions within the family. Perhaps the minority group was not symbolically appropriate for the handling of any of the family conflicts, or perhaps they were not sufficiently available to serve as a continual focus of family tensions.

13. While in virtually all these families there were considerable problems about achievement, another family seen by one of the authors as part of another investigation was very closely tied to the traditional ethnic patterns and had not yet seriously begun to incorporate American achievement values. In this family, there was one child, seriously substandard in intelligence, with very ugly physical features, who had epileptic seizures. There were also some children who were above average in intellignece. This family had no serious conflicts about achievement, and none of the children were scapegoated.

14. Alfred Adler, *Understanding human nature.* New York: Greenberg, 1927; and Alfred Adler, The cause and prevention of neurosis. *Journal of Abnormal and Social Psychology*, 1928, *23*, 4–11.

15. In the well families, there were cases of comparable physical illness that did not result in the same type of anxieties in the family.

16. No adequate large-scale studies are available to provide an estimate of the proportion of emotional disturbances found in the eldest child. Many small-scale studies have been made, but they are inconsistent and contradictory. See John P. Spiegel and Norman W. Bell, The family of the psychiatric patient. In Silvano Arieti (Ed.), American handbook of psychiatry. New York: Basic Books, Inc., 1959. In the present study, slightly more than half were eldest children, a finding similar to that in another small sample of emotionally disturbed children: Sydney Croog, The social backgrounds of emotionally disturbed children and their siblings. Unpublished Ph.D. thesis, Yale University, 1954. It has also been noted that eldest sons are more likely to be involved in problems of inheritance and rivalry, and are more likely to be adult-oriented. See such diverse studies as George Peter Murdock, Social structure. New York: Macmillan, 1949; Sigmund Freud, Moses and monotheism. New York: Alfred A. Knopf, 1939; and Charles McArthur, Personalities of first and second children. Psychiatry, 1956, 19, 47–54.

17. The way the parent gives the child implicit approval to act out his own unconscious wishes has already been well described for the relationship between a single parent and a single child. Adelaide M. Johnson, Sanctions for superego lacunae of adolescents. In Kurt R. Eissler (Ed.), Searchlights on delinquency. New York: International Universities Press, 1949. Melitta Sperling, The neurotic child and his mother: A psychoanalytic study. American Journal of Orthopsychiatry, 1951, 21, 351–64. For a more detailed account of family role-induction methods, see Spiegel, The resolution of role conflict within the family, op. cit.

18. Here again, the analogy to the individual personality system is instructive. Just as Freud's hysteric patients expressed a belle indifference to their symptoms and a surprising reluctance to change them, so did these parents have a belle indifference to the symptoms of their children. Just as the individual's symptom represents an expression of his own unconscious wish, so does the child's symptom represent an expression of his parents' unconscious wishes.

19. While the control imposed by parents in well families sometimes appeared to be extremely aggressive and punitive, this aggression was not such a massive critical attack on the child and did not carry the threat of such severe sanctions as did the aggression by the disturbed parents. In the well families, the punishment of the child was not regarded by the child as so damaging, and there was oridnarily the possibility of escaping further punishment by behaving in a different, desired way. There were few possibilities for the child to escape this hostility in the disturbed family.

20. In one well family, when there was considerable marital tension it was handled in a very overt fashion, and marital problems were not dealt with through the child.

21. At adolescence, the time when more demands for independent existence are made, a large number of acute disturbances appear. Many who were adequately adjusted to the roles they were assigned within the family were unable to meet the new adjustment outside the family. See, for example, Nicholas J. Demerath, Adolescent status and the individual. Unpublished Ph.D. thesis, Harvard University, 1942. A large number of acute psychoses also occur as soon as the army recruit leaves home and enters military service. Under ordinary circumstances, the socialization of the child prepares him for the social demands of external society. See, for example, Talcott Prasons, The incest taboo in relation to social structure and the socialization of the child. British Journal of Sociology, 1954, 5, 101–17; and David Aberle and Kaspar Naegele, Middle-class fathers' Occupational roles and attitudes toward children. American Journal of Orthopsychiatry, 1952, 22, 566–78.

22. The importance of difficulties with the associations outside the nuclear family in directing the family for psychiatric treatment has long been recognized by clinicians. See, for example, Anna Freud, Indications for child analysis. In *The psychoanalytic study of the child* (Vol. I). New York: International Universities Press, 1954.

23. See, for example, the analysis of the case of Long John's nightmares in William F. Whyte, *Street corner society*. Chicago: University of Chicago Press, 1943; and a report of Asch's experiments in Solomon E. Asch, *Social psychology*. New York: Prentice-Hall, 1952.

22

Crucible of Identity: The Negro Lower-Class Family

LEE RAINWATER

But can a people . . . live and develop for over three hundred years by simply reacting? Are American Negroes simply the creation of white men, or have they at least helped create themselves out of what they found around them? Men have made a way of life in caves and upon cliffs, why can not Negroes have made a life upon the horns of the white man's dilemma? . . . American Negro life is, for the Negro who must live it, not only a burden (and not always that) but also a discipline just as any human life which has endured so long is a discipline teaching its own insights into the human conditions, its own strategies of survival. . . .

For even as his life toughens the Negro, even as it brutalizes him, sensitizes him, dulls him, goads him to anger, moves him to irony, sometimes fracturing and sometimes affirming his hopes: even as it shapes his attitude towards family, sex, love, religion; even as it modulates his humor, tempers his joy—it conditions him to deal with his life and with himself. Because it is his life and no mere abstraction in someone's head. He must live it and try consciously to grasp its complexity until he can change it; must live it as he changes it. He is no mere product of his socio-political predicament. He is a product of interaction between his racial predicament, his individual will and the broader American cultural freedom in which he finds his ambiguous existence. Thus he, too, in a limited way, is his own creation.

Ralph Ellison

As long as Negroes have been in America, their marital and family patterns have been subject to curiosity and amusement, moral indignation and self-

Reprinted by permission from *Dædalus, Journal of the American Academy of Arts and Sciences*, 1966, 95, 172–216. Copyright © 1966 by the American Academy of Arts and Sciences.
Lee Rainwater is Professor of Sociology, Harvard University.

congratulation, puzzlement and frustration, concern and guilt, on the part of white Americans.[1] As some Negroes have moved into middle-class status, or acquired standards of American common-man respectability, they too have shared these attitudes toward the private behavior of their fellows, sometimes with a moral punitiveness to rival that of whites, but at other times with a hardheaded interest in causes and remedies rather than moral evaluation. Moralism permeated the subject of Negro sexual, marital, and family behavior in the polemics of slavery apologists and abolitionists as much as in the northern and southern civil rights controversies of today. Yet, as long as the dialectic of good or bad, guilty or innocent, overshadows a concern with who, why, and what can be, it is unlikely that realistic and effective social planning to correct the clearly desperate situation of poor Negro families can begin.

This chapter is concerned with a description and analysis of slum Negro family patterns as these reflect and sustain Negroes' adaptations to the economic, social, and personal situation into which they are born and in which they must live. As such it deals with facts of lower-class life that are usually forgotten or ignored in polite discussion. We have chosen not to ignore these facts in the belief that to do so can lead only to assumptions that would frustrate efforts at social reconstruction, to strategies that are unrealistic in the light of the actual day-to-day reality of slum Negro life. Further, this analysis will deal with family patterns that interfere with the efforts slum Negroes make to attain a stable way of life as working- or middle-class individuals and with the effects such failure in turn has on family life. To be sure, many Negro families live in the slum ghetto, but are not of its culture (though even they, and particularly their children, can be deeply affected by what happens there). However, it is the individuals who succumb to the distinctive family life style of the slum who experience the greatest weight of deprivation and who have the greatest difficulty responding to the few self-improvement resources that make their way into the ghetto. In short, we propose to explore in depth the family's role in the "tangle of pathology" that characterizes the ghetto.

The social reality in which Negroes have had to make their lives during the 450 years of their existence in the western hemisphere has been one of victimization "in the sense that a system of social relations operates in such a way as to deprive them of a chance to share in the more desirable material and nonmaterial products of a society which is dependent, in part, upon their labor and loyalty." In making this observation, St. Clair Drake goes on to note that Negroes are victimized also because "they do not have the same degree of access which others have to the attributes needed for rising in the general class system—money, education, 'contacts,' and 'know-how.' "[2] The victimization process started with slavery; for 350 years thereafter Negroes worked out as best they could adaptations to the slave status. After emancipation, the cultural mechanisms Negroes had devel-

oped for living the life of victim continued to be serviceable as the victimization process was maintained first under the myths of white supremacy
and black inferiority, later by the doctrines of gradualism that covered the
fact of no improvement in position, and finally by the modern northern system of ghettoization and indifference.

When lower-class Negroes use the expression, "Tell it like it is," they
signal their intention to strip away pretense, to describe a situation or its
participants as they really are, rather than in a polite or euphemistic way.
"Telling it like it is" can be used as a harsh, aggressive device, or it can be
a healthy attempt to face reality rather than retreat into fantasy. In any case,
as he goes about his field work, the participant observer studying a ghetto
community learns to listen carefully to any exchange preceded by such an
announcement because he knows the speaker is about to express his understanding of how his world operates, of what motivates its members, of
how they actually behave.

The first responsibility of the social scientist can be phrased in much the
same way: "Tell it like it is." His second responsibility is to try to understand why "it" is that way, and to explore the implications of what and
why for more constructive solutions to human problems. Social research
on the situation of the Negro American has been informed by four main
goals: (1) to describe the disadvantaged position of Negroes; (2) to dis-
prove the racist ideology that sustains the caste system; (3) to demonstrate
that responsibility for the disadvantages Negroes suffer lies squarely upon
the white caste that derives economic, prestige, and psychic benefits from
the operation of the system; and (4) to suggest that in reality whites would
be better rather than worse off if the whole jerry-built caste structure were
to be dismantled. The successful accomplishment of these *intellectual* goals
has been a towering achievement, in which the social scientists of the 1920's,
1930's, and 1940's can take great pride; that white society has proved so
recalcitrant to utilizing this intellectual accomplishment is one of the great
tragedies of our time, and provides the stimulus for further social research
on "the white problem."

Yet the implicit paradigm of much of the research on Negro Americans
has been an overly simplistic one concentrating on two terms of an argument:

$$\text{White cupidity} \rightarrow \text{Negro suffering}$$

As an intellectual shorthand, and even more as a civil rights slogan, this
simple model is both justified and essential. But, as a guide to greater understanding of the Negro situation as human adaptation to human situations, the paradigm is totally inadequate because it fails to specify fully
enough the *process* by which Negroes adapt to their situations as they do,
and the limitations one kind of adaptation places on possibilities for subsequent adaptations. A reassessment of previous social research, combined

with examination of current social research on Negro ghetto communities, suggests a more complex, but hopefully more veridical, model:

White cupidity
creates
structural conditions highly inimical to basic social adaptation (low-income availability, poor education, poor services, stigmatization)
to which Negroes adapt
by
social and personal responses that serve to sustain the individual in his punishing world but also generate aggressiveness toward the self and others,
which results in
suffering directly inflicted by Negroes on themselves and on others.

In short, whites, by their greater power, create situations in which Negroes do the dirty work of caste victimization for them.

The white caste maintains a cadre of whites whose special responsibility is to enforce the system in brutal or refined ways (the Klan, the rural sheriff, the metropolitan police, the businessman who specializes in a Negro clientele, the Board of Education). Increasingly, whites recruit to this cadre middle-class Negroes who can soften awareness of victimization by their protective coloration. These special cadres, white and/or Negro, serve the very important function of enforcing caste standards by whatever means seem required, while at the same time concealing from an increasingly "unprejudiced" public the unpleasant facts they would prefer to ignore. The system is quite homologous to the Gestapo and concentration camps of Nazi Germany, though less fatal to its victims.

For their part, Negroes creatively adapt to the system in ways that keep them alive and extract what gratification they can find, but in the process of adaptation they are constrained to behave in ways that inflict a great deal of suffering on those with whom they make their lives and on themselves. The ghetto Negro is constantly confronted by the immediate necessity to suffer in order to get what he wants of those few things he can have, or to make others suffer, or both. For example, he suffers as exploited student and employee, as drug user, as loser in the competitive game of his peer-group society; he inflicts suffering as disloyal spouse, petty thief, knife- or gun-wielder, petty con man.

It is the central thesis of this chapter that the caste-facilitated infliction of suffering by Negroes on other Negroes and on themselves appears most poignantly within the confines of the family, and that the victimization process as it operates in families prepares and toughens its members to function in the ghetto world at the same time that it seriously interferes with their ability to operate in any other world. This, however, is very different from arguing that "the family is to blame" for the deprived situation ghetto Negroes suffer; rather, we are looking at the logical outcome of the operation of the widely ramified and interconnecting caste system. In the end we will argue that only palliative results can be expected from attempts to treat directly the disordered family patterns to be described. Only a change in the original "inputs" of the caste system, the structural conditions inimical to basic adaptation, can change family forms.

Almost 30 years ago, E. Franklin Frazier foresaw that the fate of the Negro family in the city would be a highly destructive one. His readers would have little reason to be surprised at observations of slum ghetto life today:

> . . . As long as the bankrupt system of southern agriculture exists, Negro families will continue to seek a living in the towns and cities. . . . They will crowd the slum areas of southern cities or make their way to northern cities where their families will become disrupted and their poverty will force them to depend upon charity.[3]

THE AUTONOMY OF THE SLUM GHETTO

Just as the deprivations and depredations practiced by white society have had their effect on the personalities and social life of Negroes, so also has the separation from the ongoing social life of the white community had its effect. In a curious way, Negroes have had considerable freedom to fashion their own adaptations within their separate world. The larger society provides them with few resources but also with minimal interference on matters that do not seem to affect white interests. Because Negroes learned early that there were a great many things they could not depend upon whites to provide, they developed their own solutions to recurrent human issues. These solutions can often be seen to combine, along with the predominance of elements from white culture, elements that are distinctive to the Negro group. Even more distinctive is the *configuration* that emerges from those elements Negroes share with whites and those that are different.

It is in this sense that we may speak of a Negro subculture, a distinctive *patterning* of existential perspectives, techniques for coping with the problems of social life, views about what is desirable and undesirable in particular situations. This subculture, and particularly that of the lower-class, the slum Negro, can be seen as his own creation out of the elements available to him in response to (1) the conditions of life set by white society and (2) the selective freedom that society allows (or must put up with given the pattern of separateness on which it insists).

Out of this kind of "freedom" slum Negroes have built a culture that has some elements of intrinsic value and many more elements highly destructive to the people who must live in it. The elements whites can value they constantly borrow. Negro arts and language have proved so popular that such commentators on American culture as Norman Mailer and Leslie Fiedler have noted processes of Negroization of white Americans as a minor theme of the past 30 years.[4] A fairly large proportion of Negroes with national reputations are engaged in the occupation of diffusing to the larger culture these elements of intrinsic value.

On the negative side, this freedom has meant, as social scientists who have studied Negro communities have long commented, that many of the protections offered by white institutions stop at the edge of the Negro ghetto: there are poor police protection and enforcement of civil equities, inadequate schooling and medical service, and more informal indulgences that whites allow Negroes as a small price for feeling superior.

For our purposes, however, the most important thing about the freedom whites have allowed Negroes within their own world is that it has required them to work out their own ways of making it from day to day, from birth to death. The subculture that Negroes have created may be imperfect, but it has been viable for centuries; it behooves both white and Negro leaders and intellectuals to seek to understand it even as they hope to change it.[5]

Negroes have created, again particularly within the lower-class slum group, a range of institutions to structure the tasks of living a victimized life and to minimize the pain it inevitably produces. In the slum ghetto these institutions include prominently those of the social network—the extended kinship system and the "street system" of buddies and broads that tie (although tenuously and unpredictably) the "members" to each other—and the institutions of entertainment (music, dance, folk tales) by which they instruct, explain, and accept themselves. Other institutions function to provide escape from the society of the victimized: the church (Hereafter!) and the civil rights movement (Now!).

THE FUNCTIONAL AUTONOMY OF THE NEGRO FAMILY

At the center of the matrix of Negro institutional life lies the family. It is in the family that individuals are trained for participation in the culture and find personal and group identity and continuity. The "freedom" allowed by white society is greatest here, and this freedom has been used to create an institutional variant more distinctive perhaps to the Negro subculture than any other. (Much of the content of Negro art and entertainment derives exactly from the distinctive characteristics of Negro family life.) At each stage in the Negro's experience of American life—slavery, segregation, de facto ghettoization—whites have found it less necessary to interfere in the relations between the sexes and between parents and children than in other areas of the Negro's existence. His adaptations in this area, therefore, have been less constrained by whites than in many other areas.

Now that the larger society is becoming increasingly committed to integrating Negroes into the mainstream of American life, however, we can expect increasing constraint (benevolent as it may be) to be placed on the autonomy of the Negro family system.[6] These constraints will be designed to pull Negroes into meaningful integration with the larger society, to give up ways that are inimical to successful performance in the larger society, and to adopt new ways that are functional in that society. The strategic questions of the civil rights movement and of the war on poverty are ones that have to do with how one provides functional equivalents for the existing subculture before the capacity to make a life within its confines is destroyed.

The history of the Negro family has been ably documented by historians and sociologists.[7] In slavery, conjugal and family ties were reluctantly and ambivalently recognized by the slaveholders, were often violated by them, but proved necessary to the slave system. This necessity stemmed from both the profitable offspring of slave sexual unions and the necessity for their nurture, and the fact that the slaves' efforts to sustain patterns of sexual and parental relations mollified the men and women whose labor could not simply be commanded. From nature's promptings, the thinning memories of African heritage, and the example and guilt-ridden permission of the slaveholders, slaves constructed a partial family system and sets of relations that generated conjugal and familial sentiments. The slaveholder's recognition in advertisements for runaway slaves of marital and family sentiments as motivations for absconding provides one indication that strong family ties were possible, though perhaps not common, in the slave quarter. The mother-centered family with its emphasis on the primacy of the mother-child relation and only tenuous ties to a man, then, is the legacy of adaptations worked out by Negroes during slavery.

After emancipation this family design often also served well to cope with the social disorganization of Negro life in the late 19th century. Matrifocal families, ambivalence about the desirability of marriage, ready acceptance of illegitimacy, all sustained some kind of family life in situations that often made it difficult to maintain a full nuclear family. Yet in the 100 years since emancipation, Negroes in rural areas have been able to maintain full nuclear families almost as well as similarly situated whites. As we will see, it is the move to the city that results in the very high proportion of mother-headed households. In the rural system the man continues to have important functions; it is difficult for a woman to make a crop by herself, or even with the help of other women. In the city, however, the woman can earn wages just as a man can, and she can receive welfare payments more easily than he can. In rural areas, although there may be high illegitimacy rates and high rates of marital disruption, men and women have an interest in getting together; families are headed by a husband-wife pair much more often than in the city. That pair may be much less stable than in the more prosperous segments of Negro and white communities, but it is more likely to exist among rural Negroes than among urban ones.

The matrifocal character of the Negro lower-class family in the United States has much in common with Caribbean Negro family patterns; research in both areas has done a great deal to increase our understanding of the Negro situation. However, there are important differences in the family forms of the two areas.[8] The impact of white European family models has been much greater in the United States than in the Caribbean both because of the relative population proportions of white and colored peoples and because egalitarian values in the United States have had a great impact on Negroes even when they have not on whites. The typical Caribbean mating pattern is that women go through several visiting and common-law unions but eventually marry; that is, they marry legally only relatively late in their sexual lives. The Caribbean marriage is the crowning of a sexual and procreative career; it is considered a serious and difficult step.

In the United States, in contrast, Negroes marry at only a slightly lower rate and slightly higher age than whites.[9] Most Negro women marry relatively early in their careers; marriage is not regarded as the same kind of crowning choice and achievement that it is in the Caribbean. For lower-class Negroes in the United States marriage ceremonies are rather informal affairs. In the Caribbean, marriage is regarded as quite costly because of the feasting that goes along with it; ideally it is performed in church.

In the United States, unlike the Caribbean, early marriage confers a kind of permanent respectable status upon a woman, which she can use to deny any subsequent accusations of immorality or promiscuity once the marriage is broken and she becomes sexually involved in visiting or common-law relations. The relevant effective status for many Negro women is that of "having been married" rather than "being married"; having the right to be called "Mrs." rather than currently being Mrs. Someone-in-Particular.

For Negro lower-class women, then, first marriage has the same kind of importance as having a first child. Both indicate that the girl has become a woman, but neither signifies that this is the last such activity in which she will engage. It seems very likely that only a minority of Negro women in the urban slum go through their child-rearing years with only one man around the house.

Among the Negro urban poor, then, a great many women have the experience of heading a family for part of their mature lives, and a great many children spend some part of their formative years in a household without a father-mother pair. From Table 22.1 we see that in 1960, 47% of the Negro poor urban families with children had a female head. Unfortunately, cumulative statistics are hard to come by; but, given this very high level for a cross-sectional sample (and taking into account the fact that the median age of the children in these families is about six years), it seems very likely that as many as two-thirds of Negro urban poor children will not live in families headed by a man and a woman throughout the first 18 years of their lives.

One of the other distinctive characteristics of Negro families, both poor

Table 22.1. Proportion of Female Heads for Families with Children by Race, Income, and Urban-Rural Categories

	Rural (%)	Urban (%)	Total (%)
Negroes			
Under $3000	18	47	36
$3000 and over	5	8	7
Total	14	23	21
Whites			
Under $3000	12	38	22
$3000 and over	2	4	3
Total	4	7	6

Source: U.S. Census: 1960, PC (1) D. U.S. Volume, Table 225; State Volume, Table 140.

and not so poor, is the fact that Negro households contain a much higher proportion of relatives outside the mother-father-children triangle than is the case with whites. For example, in St. Louis Negro families average 0.8 other relatives per household compared to only 0.4 for white families. In the case of the more prosperous Negro families this is likely to mean that an older relative lives in the home, providing baby-sitting services while both the husband and wife work and thus further their climb toward stable working- or middle-class status. In the poor Negro families it is much more likely that the household is headed by an older relative who brings under her wings a daughter and that daughter's children. It is important to note that the three-generation household with the grandmother at the head exists only when there is no husband present. Thus, despite the high proportion of female-headed households in this group and despite the high proportion of households that contain other relatives, we find that almost all married couples in the St. Louis Negro slum community have their own household. In other words, when a couple marries it establishes its own household; when that couple breaks up the mother either maintains that household or moves back to her parents or grandparents.

Finally, we should note that Negro slum families have more children than do either white slum families or stable working- and middle-class Negro families. Mobile Negro families limit their fertility sharply in the interest of bringing the advantages of mobility more fully to the few children they do have. Since the Negro slum family is both more likely to have the father absent and more likely to have more children in the family, the mother has a more demanding task with fewer resources at her disposal. When we examine the patterns of life of the stem family we shall see that even the presence of several mothers does not necessarily lighten the work load for the principal mother in charge.

THE FORMATION AND MAINTENANCE OF FAMILIES

We will outline below the several stages and forms of Negro lower-class family life. At many points these family forms and the interpersonal relations that exist within them will be seen to have characteristics in common with the life styles of white lower-class families.[10] At other points there are differences, or the Negro pattern will be observed to be more sharply divergent from that of the family life of stable working- and middle-class couples.

It is important to recognize that lower-class Negroes know that their particular family forms are different from those of the rest of the society and that, though they often see these forms as representing the only ways of behaving given their circumstances, they also think of the more stable family forms of the working class as more desirable. That is, lower-class Negroes know what the "normal American family" is supposed to be like, and they consider a stable family-centered way of life superior to the conjugal and familial situations in which they often find themselves. Their conceptions of the good American life include the notion of a father-husband who functions as an adequate provider and interested member of the family, a hard-working home-bound mother who is concerned about her children's welfare and her husband's needs, and children who look up to their parents and perform well in school and other outside places to reflect credit on their families. This image of what family life can be like is very real from time to time as lower-class men and women grow up and move through adulthood. Many of them make efforts to establish such families but find it impossible to do so either because of the direct impact of economic disabilities or because they are not able to sustain in their day-to-day lives the ideals they hold.[11] While these ideals do serve as a meaningful guide to lower-class couples who are mobile out of the group, for a great many others the existence of such ideas about normal family life represents a recurrent source of stress within families as individuals become aware that they are failing to measure up to the ideals, or as others within the family and outside it use the ideals as an aggressive weapon for criticizing each other's performance. It is not at all uncommon for husbands or wives or children to try to hold others in the family to the norms of stable family life while they themselves engage in behaviors that violate these norms. The effect of such criticism in the end is to deepen commitment to the deviant sexual and parental norms of a slum subculture. Unless they are careful, social workers and other professionals exacerbate the tendency to use the norms of "American family life" as weapons by supporting these norms in situations where they are in reality unsupportable, thus aggravating the sense of failing and being failed by others that is chronic for lower-class people.

Going Together

The initial steps toward mating and family formation in the Negro slum take place in a context of highly developed boys' and girls' peer groups. Adolescents tend to become deeply involved in their peer-group societies beginning as early as the age of 12 or 13 and continue to be involved after first pregnancies and first marriages. Boys and girls are heavily committed both to their same sex peer groups and to the activities that those groups carry out. While classical gang activity does not necessarily characterize Negro slum communities everywhere, loosely knit peer groups do.

The world of the Negro slum is wide open to exploration by adolescent boys and girls: "Negro communities provide a flow of common experience in which young people and their elders share, and out of which delinquent behavior emerges almost imperceptibly."[12] More than is possible in white slum communities, Negro adolescents have an opportunity to interact with adults in various "high life" activities; their behavior more often represents an identification with the behavior of adults than an attempt to set up group standards and activities that differ from those of adults.

Boys and young men participating in the street system of peer-group activity are much caught up in games of furthering and enhancing their status as significant persons. These games are played out in small and large gatherings through various kinds of verbal contests that go under the names of "sounding," "signifying," and "working game." Very much a part of a boy's or man's status in this group is his ability to win women. The man who has several women "up tight," who is successful in "pimping off" women for sexual favors and material benefits, is much admired. In sharp contrast to white lower-class groups, there is little tendency for males to separate girls into "good" or "bad" categories.[13] Observations of groups of Negro youths suggest that girls and women are much more readily referred to as "that bitch" or "that whore" than they are by their names, and this seems to be a universal tendency carrying no connotation that "that bitch" is morally inferior to or different from other women. Thus, all women are essentially the same, all women are legitimate targets, and no girl or woman is expected to be virginal except for reason of lack of opportunity or immaturity. From their participation in the peer group and according to standards legitimated by the total Negro slum culture, Negro boys and young men are propelled in the direction of girls to test their "strength" as seducers. They are mercilessly rated by both their peers and the opposite sex in their ability to "talk" to girls; a young man will go to great lengths to avoid the reputation of having a "weak" line.[14]

The girls share these definitions of the nature of heterosexual relations; they take for granted that almost any male they deal with will try to seduce them and that given sufficient inducement (social, not monetary) they may

wish to go along with his line. Although girls have a great deal of ambivalence about participating in sexual relations, this ambivalence is minimally moral and has much more to do with a desire not to be taken advantage of or get into trouble. Girls develop defenses against the exploitative
orientations of men by devaluing the significance of sexual relations ("he
really didn't do anything bad to me"), and as time goes on by developing
their own appreciation of the intrinsic rewards of sexual intercourse.

The informal social relations of slum Negroes begin in adolescence to
be highly sexualized. Although parents have many qualms about boys and,
particularly, girls entering into this system, they seldom feel there is much
they can do to prevent their children's sexual involvement. They usually
confine themselves to counseling somewhat hopelessly against girls becoming pregnant or boys being forced into situations where they might have
to marry a girl they do not want to marry.

Girls are propelled toward boys and men in order to demonstrate their
maturity and attractiveness; in the process they are constantly exposed to
pressures for seduction, to boys "rapping" to them. An active girl will "go
with" quite a number of boys, but she will generally try to restrict the number with whom she has intercourse to the few to whom she is attracted or
(as happens not infrequently) to those whose threats of physical violence
she cannot avoid. For their part, the boys move rapidly from girl to girl
seeking to have intercourse with as many as they can and thus build up
their "reps." The activity of seduction is itself highly cathected; there is
gratification in simply "talking to" a girl as long as the boy can feel that he
has acquitted himself well.

> At 16 Joan Bemias enjoys spending time with three or four very close girl-
> friends. She tells us they follow this routine when the girls want to go out and
> none of the boys they have been seeing lately is available: "Everytime we get
> ready to go someplace we look through all the telephone numbers of boys we'd
> have and we call them and talk so sweet to them that they'd come on around.
> All of them had cars you see. (I: What do you do to keep all these fellows
> interested?) Well, nothing. We don't have to make love with all of them. Let's
> see, Joe, J.B., Albert, and Paul, out of all of them I've been going out with I've
> only had sex with four boys, that's all." She goes on to say that she and her
> girlfriends resist boys by being unresponsive to their lines and by breaking off
> relations with them on the ground that they're going out with other girls. It is
> also clear from her comments that the girlfriends support each other in resist-
> ing the boys when they are out together in groups.
>
> Joan has had a relationship with a boy that has lasted six months, but she
> has managed to hold the frequency of intercourse down to four times. Initially
> she managed to hold this particular boy off for a month but eventually gave
> in.

Becoming Pregnant

It is clear that the contest elements in relationships between men and
women continue even in relationships that become quite steady. Despite

the girls' ambivalence about sexual relations and their manifold efforts to reduce its frequency, the operation of chance often eventuates in their becoming pregnant.[15] This was the case with Joan. With this we reach the second stage in the formation of families, that of premarital pregnancy. (We are outlining an ideal-typical sequence and not, of course, implying that all girls in the Negro slum culture become pregnant before they marry, but only that a great many of them do.)

Joan was caught despite the fact that she was considerably more sophisticated about contraception than most girls or young women in the group (her mother had both instructed her in contraceptive techniques and constantly warned her to take precautions). No one was particularly surprised at her pregnancy, although she, her boyfriend, her mother, and others regarded it as unfortunate. For girls in the Negro slum, pregnancy before marriage is expected in much the same way that parents expect their children to catch mumps or chicken pox; if they are lucky it will not happen but if it happens, people are not too surprised and everyone knows what to do about it. It was quickly decided that Joan and the baby would stay at home. It seems clear from the preparations Joan's mother is making that she expects to have the main responsibility for caring for the infant. Joan seems quite indifferent to the baby; she shows little interest in mothering the child although she is not particularly adverse to the idea so long as the baby does not interfere too much with her continued participation in her peer group.

Establishing who the father is under these circumstances seems to be important and confers a kind of legitimacy on the birth; not to know who one's father is, on the other hand, seems the ultimate in illegitimacy. Actually Joan had a choice in the imputation of fatherhood; she chose J.B. because he is older than she and because she may marry him if he can get a divorce from his wife. She could have chosen Paul (with whom she had also had intercourse at about the time she became pregnant), but she would have done this reluctantly since Paul is a year younger than she and somehow this does not seem fitting.

In general, when a girl becomes pregnant while still living at home it seems taken for granted that she will continue to live there and that her parents will take a major responsibility for rearing the child. Since there are usually siblings who can help out and even siblings who will be playmates for the child, the addition of a third generation to the household does not seem to place a great stress on relationships within the family. It seems common for the first pregnancy to have a liberating influence on the mother once the child is born in that she becomes socially and sexually more active than she was before. She no longer has to be concerned with preserving her status as a single girl. Since her mother is usually willing to take care of the child for a few years, the unwed mother has an opportunity to go out with girlfriends and with men and thus become more deeply involved in the peer-group society of her culture. As she has more children and perhaps marries she will find it necessary to settle down and spend more time around the house fulfilling the functions of a mother herself.

It would seem that for girls pregnancy is the real measure of maturity, the dividing line between adolescence and womanhood. Perhaps because of this, as well as because of the ready resources for child care, girls in the Negro slum community show much less concern about pregnancy than do girls in the white lower-class community and are less motivated to marry the fathers of their children. When a girl becomes pregnant the question of marriage certainly arises and is considered, but the girl often decides that she would rather not marry the man either because she does not want to settle down yet or because she does not think he would make a good husband.

It is in the easy attitudes toward premarital pregnancy that the martifocal character of the Negro lower-class family appears most clearly. In order to have and raise a family it is simply not necessary, though it may be desirable, to have a man around the house. While the AFDC program may make it easier to maintain such attitudes in the urban situation, this pattern existed long before the program was initiated and continues in families where support comes from other sources.

Finally, it should be noted that fathering a child similarly confers maturity on boys and young men, although perhaps it is less salient for them. If the boy has any interest in the girl he will tend to feel that the fact that he has impregnated her gives him an additional claim on her. He will be stricter in seeking to enforce his exclusive rights over her (though not exclusive loyalty to her). This exclusive right does not mean that he expects to marry her but only that there is a new and special bond between them. If the girl is not willing to accept such claims she may find it necessary to break off the relationship rather than tolerate the man's jealousy. Since others in the peer group have a vested interest in not allowing a couple to be too loyal to each other, they go out of their way to question and challenge each partner about the loyalty of the other, thus contributing to the deterioration of the relationship. This same kind of questioning and challenging continues if the couple marries and represents one source of the instability of the marital relationship.

Getting Married

As noted earlier, despite the high degree of premarital sexual activity and the rather high proportion of premarital pregnancies, most lower-class Negro men and women eventually do marry and stay together for a shorter or longer period of time.

Marriage is an intimidating prospect and is approached ambivalently by both parties. For the girl it means giving up a familiar and comfortable home that, unlike some other lower-class subcultures, places few real restrictions

on her behavior. (While marriage can appear to be an escape from interpersonal difficulties at home, these difficulties seldom seem to revolve around
effective restrictions placed on her behavior by her parents.) The girl also
has good reason to be suspicious of the likelihood that men will be able to
perform stably in the role of husband and provider; she is reluctant to be
tied down by a man who will not prove to be worth it.

From the man's point of view the fickleness of women makes marriage
problematic. It is one thing to have a girl friend step out on you, but it is
quite another to have a wife do so. Whereas premarital sexual relations
and fatherhood carry almost no connotation of responsibility for the welfare of the partner, marriage is supposed to mean that a man behaves more
responsibly, becoming a provider for his wife and children even though he
may not be expected to give up all the gratifications of participation in the
street system.

For all of these reasons both boys and girls tend to have rather negative
views of marriage as well as a low expectation that marriage will prove a
stable and gratifying existence. When marriage does take place it tends to
represent a tentative commitment on the part of both parties with a strong
tendency to seek greater commitment on the part of the partner than on
one's own part. Marriage is regarded as a fragile arrangement held together
primarily by affectional ties rather than instrumental concerns.

In general, as in white lower-class groups, the decision to marry seems
to be taken rather impulsively.[16] Since everyone knows that sooner or later
he will get married, in spite of the fact that he may not be sanguine about
the prospect, Negro lower-class men and women are alert for clues that the
time has arrived. The time may arrive because of a pregnancy in a steady
relationship that seems gratifying to both partners, or as a way of getting
out of what seems to be an awkward situation, or as a self-indulgence during periods when a boy and a girl are feeling very sorry for themselves.
Thus, one girl tells us that when she marries her husband will cook all of
her meals for her and she will not have any housework; another girl says
that when she marries it will be to a man who has plenty of money and
will take her out often and really show her a good time.

Boys see in marriage the possibility of regular sexual intercourse without
having to fight for it, or a girl safe from venereal disease, or a relationship
to a nurturant figure who will fulfill the functions of a mother. For boys,
marriage can also be a way of asserting their independence from the peer
group if its demands become burdensome. In this case the young man seeks
to have the best of both worlds.[17]

Marriage as a way out of an unpleasant situation can be seen in the case
of one of our informants, Janet Cowan:

> Janet has been going with two men, one of them married and the other single.
> The married man's wife took exception to their relationship and killed her hus-
> band. Within a week Janet and her single boyfriend, Howard, were married.

One way out of the turmoil the murder of her married boyfriend stimulated (they lived in the same building) was to choose marriage as a way of "settling down." However, after marrying the new couple seemed to have little idea how to set themselves up as a family. Janet was reluctant to leave her parents' home because her parents cared for her two illegitimate children. Howard was unemployed and therefore unacceptable in his parents-in-law's home, nor were his own parents willing to have his wife move in with them. Howard was also reluctant to give up another girlfriend in another part of town. Although both he and his wife maintained that it was all right for a couple to step out on each other so long as the other partner did not know about it, they were both jealous if they suspected anything of this kind. In the end they gave up on the idea of marriage and went their separate ways.

In general, then, the movement toward marriage is an uncertain and tentative one. Once the couple does settle down together in a household of their own, they have the problem of working out a mutually acceptable organization of rights and duties, expectations and performances, that will meet their needs.

Husband—Wife Relations

Characteristic of both the Negro and white lower class is a high degree of conjugal role segregation.[18] That is, husbands and wives tend to think of themselves as having very separate kinds of functioning in the instrumental organization of family life, and also as pursuing recreational and outside interests separately. The husband is expected to be a provider; he resists assuming functions around the home so long as he feels he is doing his proper job of bringing home a pay check. He feels he has the right to indulge himself in little ways if he is successful at this task. The wife is expected to care for the home and children and make her husband feel welcome and comfortable. Much that is distinctive to Negro family life stems from the fact that husbands often are not stable providers. Even when a particular man is, his wife's conception of men in general is such that she is pessimistic about the likelihood that he will continue to do well in this area. A great many Negro wives work to supplement the family income. When this is so the separate incomes earned by husband and wife tend to be treated not as "family" income but as the individual property of the two persons involved. If their wives work, husbands are likely to feel that they are entitled to retain a larger share of the income they provide; the wives, in turn, feel that the husbands have no right to benefit from the purchases they make out of their own money. There is, then, "my money" and "your money." In this situation the husband may come to feel that the wife should support the children out of her income and that he can retain all of his income for himself.

While white lower-class wives often are very much intimidated by their husbands, Negro lower-class wives come to feel that they have a right to give as good as they get. If the husband indulges himself, they have the right to indulge themselves. If the husband steps out on his wife, she has the right to step out on him. The commitment of husbands and wives to each other seems often a highly instrumental one after the "honeymoon" period. Many wives feel they owe the husband nothing once he fails to perform his provider role. If the husband is unemployed the wife increasingly refuses to perform her usual duties for him. For example, one woman, after mentioning that her husband had cooked four eggs for himself, commented, "I cook for him when he's working but right now he's unemployed; he can cook for himself." It is important, however, to understand that the man's status in the home depends not so much on whether he is working as on whether he brings money into the home. Thus, in several of the families we have studied in which the husband receives disability payments, his status is as well-recognized as in families in which the husband is working.[19]

Because of the high degree of conjugal role segregation, both white and Negro lower-class families tend to be matrifocal in comparison to middle-class families. They are matrifocal in the sense that the wife makes most of the decisions that keep the family going and has the greatest sense of responsibility to the family. In white as well as in Negro lower-class families women tend to look to their female relatives for support and counsel, and to treat their husbands as essentially uninterested in the day-to-day problems of family living.[20] In the Negro lower-class family these tendencies are all considerably exaggerated, so that the matrifocality is much clearer than in white lower-class families.

The fact that both sexes in the Negro slum culture have equal right to the various satisfactions of life (earning an income, sex, drinking, and peer-group activity that conflicts with family responsibilities) means that there is less pretense to patriarchal authority in the Negro than in the white lower class. Since men find the overt debasement of their status very threatening, the Negro family is much more vulnerable to disruption when men are temporarily unable to perform their provider roles. Also, when men are unemployed the temptations for them to engage in street adventures that affect the marital relationship are much greater. This fact is well-recognized by Negro lower-class wives; they often seem as concerned about what their unemployed husbands will do instead of working as they are about the fact that the husband is no longer bringing money into the home.

It is tempting to cope with the likelihood of disloyalty by denying the usual norms of fidelity, by maintaining instead that extramarital affairs are acceptable as long as they do not interfere with family functioning. Quite a few informants tell us this, but we have yet to observe a situation in which a couple maintains a stable relationship under these circumstances without a great deal of conflict. Thus, one woman in her 40s who has been married for many years and has four children first outlined this deviant norm and then illustrated how it did not work out:

> My husband and I, we go out alone and sometimes stay all night. But when I get back my husband doesn't ask me a thing and I don't ask him anything. . . . A couple of years ago I suspected he was going out on me. One day I came home and my daughter was here. I told her to tell me when he left the house. I went into the bedroom and got into bed and then I heard him come in. He left in about ten minutes and my daughter came in and told me he was gone. I got out of bed and put on my clothes and started following him. Soon I saw him walking with a young girl and I began walking after them. They were just laughing and joking right out loud right on the sidewalk. He was carrying a large package of hers. I walked up behind them until I was about a yard from them. I had a large dirk which I opened and had decided to take one long slash across the both of them. Just when I decided to swing at them I lost my balance—I have a bad hip. Anyway, I didn't cut them because I lost my balance. Then I called his name and he turned around and stared at me. He didn't move at all. He was shaking all over. That girl just ran away from us. He still had her package so the next day she called on the telephone and said she wanted to come pick it up. My husband washed his face, brushed his teeth, took out his false tooth and started scrubbing it and put on a clean shirt and everything, just for her. We went downstairs together and gave her the package and she left.
>
> So you see my husband does run around on me and it seems like he does it a lot. The thing about it is he's just getting too old to be pulling that kind of stuff. If a young man does it then that's not so bad—but an old man, he just looks foolish. One of these days he'll catch me but I'll just tell him, "Buddy you owe me one," and that'll be all there is to it. He hasn't caught me yet though.

In this case, as in others, the wife is not able to leave well enough alone; her jealousy forces her to a confrontation. Actually seeing her husband with another woman stimulates her to violence.

With couples who have managed to stay married for a good many years, these peccadillos are tolerable although they generate a great deal of conflict in the marital relationship. At earlier ages the partners are likely to be both prouder and less inured to the hopelessness of maintaining stable relationships; outside involvements are therefore much more likely to be disruptive of the marriage.

Marital Breakup

The precipitating causes of marital disruption seem to fall mainly into economic or sexual categories. As noted, the husband has little credit with his wife to tide him over periods of unemployment. Wives seem very willing to withdraw commitment from husbands who are not bringing money into the house. They take the point of view that he has no right to take up space around the house, to use its facilities, or to demand loyalty from her.

Even where the wife is not inclined to press these claims, the husband tends to be touchy because he knows that such definitions are usual in his group, and he may, therefore, prove difficult for even a well-meaning wife to deal with. As noted above, if husbands do not work they tend to play around. Since they continue to maintain some contact with their peer groups, whenever they have time on their hands they move back into the world of the street system and are likely to get involved in activities that pose a threat to their family relationships.

Drink is a great enemy of the lower-class housewife, both white and Negro. Lower-class wives fear their husband's drinking because it costs money, because the husband may become violent and take out his frustrations on his wife, and because drinking may lead to sexual involvements with other women.[21]

The combination of economic problems and sexual difficulties can be seen in the case of the following couple in their early 20s:

> When the field worker first came to know them, the Wilsons seemed to be working hard to establish a stable family life. The couple had been married about three years and had a two-year-old son. Their apartment was very sparsely furnished but also very clean. Within six weeks the couple had acquired several rooms of inexpensive furniture and obviously had gone to a great deal of effort to make a liveable home. Husband and wife worked on different shifts so that the husband could take care of the child while the wife worked. They looked forward to saving enough money to move out of the housing project into a more desirable neighborhood. Six weeks later, however, the husband had lost his job. He and his wife were in great conflict. She made him feel unwelcome at home and he strongly suspected her of going out with other men. A short time later they had separated. It is impossible to disentangle the various factors involved in this separation into a sequence of cause and effect, but we can see something of the impact of the total complex.
>
> First Mr. Wilson loses his job: "I went to work one day and the man told me that I would have to work until one o'clock. I asked him if there would be any extra pay for working overtime and he said no. I asked him why and he said, 'If you don't like it you can kiss my ass.' He said that to me. I said, 'Why do I have to do all that?' He said, 'Because I said so.' I wanted to jam (fight) him but I said to myself, I don't want to be that ignorant, I don't want to be as ignorant as he is, so I just cut out and left. Later his father called me (it was a family firm) and asked why I left and I told him. He said, 'If you don't want to go along with my son then you're fired.' I said O.K. They had another Negro man come in to help me part time before they fired me. I think they were trying to have him work full time because he worked for them before. He has seven kids and he takes their shit."
>
> The field worker observed that things were not as hard as they could be because his wife had a job, to which he replied, "Yeah, I know, that's just where the trouble is. My wife has become independent since she began working. If I don't get a job pretty soon I'll go crazy. We have a lot of little arguments about nothing since she got so independent." He went on to say that his wife had become a completely different person recently; she was hard to talk to because she felt that now that she was working and he was not there was nothing that he could tell her. On her last pay day his wife did not return

home for three days; when she did she had only seven cents left from her pay check. He said that he loved his wife very much and had begged her to quit fooling around. He is pretty sure that she is having an affair with the man with whom she rides to work. To make matters worse, his wife's sister counsels her that she does not have to stay home with him as long as he is out of work. Finally, the wife moved most of their furniture out so that the husband came home to find an empty apartment. He moved back to his parents' home (also in the housing project).

One interesting effect of this experience was the radical change in the husband's attitudes toward race relations. When he and his wife were doing well together and had hopes of moving up in the world he was quite critical of Negroes; "Our people are not ready for integration in many cases because they really don't know how to act. You figure if our people don't want to be bothered with whites then why in hell should the white man want to be bothered with them? There are some of us who are ready; there are others who aren't quite ready yet, so I don't see why they're doing all of this hollering." A scarce eight months later he addressed white people as he spoke for two hours into a tape recorder, "If we're willing to be with you, why aren't you willing to be with us? Do our color make us look dirty and low down and cheap? Or do you know the real meaning of 'nigger'? Anyone can be a nigger, white, colored, orange or any other color. It's something that you labeled us with. You put us away like you put a can away on the shelf with a label on it. The can is marked 'Poison: stay away from it.' You want us to help build your country but you don't want us to live in it. . . . You give me respect; I'll give you respect. If you threaten to take my life, I'll take yours and believe me I know how to take a life. We do believe that man was put here to live together as human beings; not one that's superior and the one that's a dog, but as human beings. And if you don't want to live this way then you become the dog and we'll become the human beings. There's too much corruption, too much hate, too much one individual trying to step on another. If we don't get together in a hurry we will destroy each other." It was clear from what the respondent said that he had been much influenced by Black Muslim philosophy, yet again and again in his comments one can see the displacement into a public, race relations dialogue of the sense of rage, frustration and victimization that he had experienced in his ill-fated marriage.[22]

Finally, it should be noted that migration plays a part in marital disruption. Sometimes marriages do not break up in the dramatic way described above but rather simply become increasingly unsatisfactory to one or both partners. In such a situation the temptation to move to another city, from South to North, or North to West, is great. Several wives told us that their first marriages were broken when they moved with their children to the North and their husbands stayed behind.

After we couldn't get along I left the farm and came here and stayed away three or four days. I didn't come here to stay. I came to visit but I liked it and so I said, 'I'm gonna leave!' He said, 'I'll be glad if you do.' Well, maybe he didn't mean it but I thought he did. . . . I miss him sometimes, you know. I think about him I guess. But just in a small way. That's what I can't understand about life sometimes; you know—how people can go on like that and still break up and meet somebody else. Why couldn't—oh, I don't know!

The gains and losses in marriage and in the post-marital state often seem quite comparable. Once they have had the experience of marriage, many women in the Negro slum culture see little to recommend it in the future, important as the first marriage may have been in establishing their maturity and respectability.

The House of Mothers

As we have seen, perhaps a majority of mothers in the Negro slum community spend at least part of their mature life as mothers heading a family. The Negro mother may be a working mother or she may be an AFDC mother, but in either case she has the problems of maintaining a household, socializing her children, and achieving for herself some sense of membership in relations with other women and with men. As is apparent from the earlier discussion, she often receives her training in how to run such a household by observing her own mother manage without a husband. Similarly, she often learns how to run a three-generation household because she herself brought a third generation into her home with her first, premarital pregnancy.

Because men are not expected to be much help around the house, having to be head of the household is not particularly intimidating to the Negro mother if she can feel some security about income. She knows it is a hard, hopeless, and often thankless task, but she also knows that it is possible. The maternal household in the slum is generally run with a minimum of organization. The children quickly learn to fend for themselves, to go to the store, to make small purchases, to bring change home, to watch after themselves when the mother has to be out of the home, to amuse themselves, to set their own schedules of sleeping, eating, and going to school. Housekeeping practices may be poor, furniture takes a terrific beating from the children, and emergencies constantly arise. The Negro mother in this situation copes by not setting too high standards for herself, by letting things take their course. Life is most difficult when there are babies and preschool children around because then the mother is confined to the home. If she is a grandmother and the children are her daughter's, she is often confined since it is taken as a matter of course that the mother has the right to continue her outside activities and that the grandmother has the duty to be responsible for the child.

In this culture there is little of the sense of the awesome responsibility of caring for children that is characteristic of the working and middle class. There is not the deep psychological involvement with babies that has been observed with the working-class mother.[23] The baby's needs are cared for on a catch-as-catch-can basis. If there are other children around and they happen to like babies, the baby can be overstimulated; if this is not the case, the baby is left alone a good deal of the time. As quickly as he can move around he learns to fend for himself.

The three-generation maternal household is a busy place. In contrast to working- and middle-class homes it tends to be open to the world, with many nonfamily members coming in and out at all times as the children are visited by friends, the teenagers by their boyfriends and girlfriends, the mother by her friends and perhaps an occasional boyfriend, and the grandmother by fewer friends but still by an occasional boyfriend.

The openness of the household is, among other things, a reflection of the mother's sense of impotence in the face of the street system. Negro lower-class mothers often indicate that they try very hard to keep their young children at home and away from the streets; they often seem to make the children virtual prisoners in the home. As the children grow and go to school they inevitably do become involved in peer-group activities. The mother gradually gives up, feeling that once the child is lost to this pernicious outside world there is little she can do to continue to control him and direct his development. She will try to limit the types of activities that go on in the home and to restrict the kinds of friends that her children can bring into the home, but even this she must give up as time goes on, as the children become older and less attentive to her direction.

The grandmothers in their late 40s, 50s, and 60s tend increasingly to stay at home. The home becomes a kind of court at which other family members gather and to which they bring their friends for sociability, and as a by-product provide amusement and entertainment for the mother. A grandmother may provide a home for her daughters, their children, and sometimes their children's children, and yet receive very little in a material way from them; but one of the things she does receive is a sense of human involvement, a sense that although life may have passed her by she is not completely isolated from it.

The lack of control that mothers have over much that goes on in their households is most dramatically apparent in the fact that their older children seem to have the right to come home at any time once they have moved and to stay in the home without contributing to its maintenance. Though the mother may be resentful about being taken advantage of, she does not feel she can turn her children away. For example, 65-year-old Mrs. Washington plays hostess for weeks or months at a time to her 40-year-old daughter and her small children, and to her 23-year-old granddaughter and her children. When these daughters come home with their families the grandmother is expected to take care of the young children and must argue with her daughter and granddaughter to receive contributions to the daily household ration of food and liquor. Or, a 20-year-old son comes home from the Air Force and feels he has the right to live at home without working and to run up an $80 long-distance telephone bill.

Even aged parents living alone in small apartments sometimes acknowledge such obligations to their children or grandchildren. Again, the only clear return they receive for their hospitality is the reduction of isolation that comes from having people around and interesting activity going on. When in the Washington home the daughter and granddaughter and their children move in with the grandmother, or when they come to visit for shorter periods of time, the occasion has a party atmosphere. The women sit around talking and reminiscing. Though boyfriends may be present, they take little part; instead, they sit passively, enjoying the stories and drinking along with the women. It would seem that in this kind of party activity the women are defined as the stars. Grandmother, daughter, and granddaughter in turn take the center of the stage telling a story from the family's past, talking about a particularly interesting night out on the town or just making some general observation about life. In the course of these events a good deal of liquor is consumed. In such a household as this little attention is paid to the children since the competition by adults for attention is stiff.

Boyfriends, Not Husbands

It is with an understanding of the problems of isolation older mothers have that we can obtain the best insight into the role and function of boyfriends in the maternal household. The older mothers, surrounded by their own children and grandchildren, are not able to move freely in the outside world, to participate in the high life they enjoyed when younger and more footloose. They are disillusioned with marriage as providing any more secure economic base than they can achieve on their own. They see marriage as involving just another responsibility without a concomitant reward—"It's the greatest thing in the world to come home in the afternoon and not have some curly headed twot in the house yellin' at me and askin' me where supper is, where I've been, what I've been doin', and who I've been seein'." In this situation the woman is tempted to form relationships with men that are not so demanding as marriage but still provide companionship and an opportunity for occasional sexual gratification.

There seem to be two kinds of boyfriends. Some "pimp" off mothers; they extract payment in food or money for their companionship. This leads to the custom sometimes called "Mother's Day," the tenth of the month when the AFDC checks come.[24] On this day one can observe an influx of men into the neighborhood and much partying. But there is another kind of boyfriend, perhaps more numerous than the first, who instead of being paid for his services pays for the right to be a pseudo family member. He may be the father of one of the woman's children, and for this reason makes a steady contribution to the family's support, or he may simply be a man whose company the mother enjoys and who makes reasonable gifts to the family for the time he spends with them (and perhaps implicitly for the sexual favors he receives). While the boyfriend does not assume fatherly authority within the family, he often is known and liked by the children. The older children appreciate the meaningfulness of their mother's relationship with him—one girl said of her mother's boyfriend:

> We don't none of us [the children] want her to marry again. It's all right if she wants to live by herself and have a boyfriend. It's not because we're afraid we're going to have some more sisters and brothers, which it wouldn't make us much difference, but I think she be too old.

Even when the boy friend contributes 10 or 20 dollars a month to the family he is in a certain sense getting a bargain. If he is a well-accepted boyfriend he spends considerable time around the house, has a chance to relax in an atmosphere less competitive than that of his peer group, is fed and cared for by the woman, yet has no responsibilities which he cannot renounce when he wishes. When women have stable relationships of this kind with boyfriends, they often consider marrying them but are reluctant to take such a step. Even the well-liked boyfriend has some shortcomings— one woman said of her boyfriend:

> Well he works; I know that. He seems to be a nice person, kind hearted. He believes in survival for me and my family. He don't much mind sharing with my youngsters. If I ask him for a helping hand he don't seem to mind that. The only part I dislike is his drinking.

The woman in this situation has worked out a reasonably stable adaptation to the problems of her life; she is fearful of upsetting this adaptation by marrying again. It seems easier to take the "sweet" part of the relationship with a man without the complexities that marriage might involve.

It is in the light of this pattern of women living in families and men living by themselves in rooming houses, odd rooms here and there, that we can understand Daniel Patrick Moynihan's observation that during their mature years men simply disappear; that is, that census data show a very high sex ratio of women to men.[25] In St. Louis, starting at the age range 20 to 24 there are only 72 men for every 100 women. This ratio does not climb to ninety until the age range 50 to 54. Men often do not have real homes; they move about from one household where they have kinship or sexual ties to another; they live in flophouses and rooming houses; they spend time in institutions. They are not household members in the only "homes" that they have—the homes of their mothers and of their girlfriends.

It is in this kind of world that boys and girls in the Negro slum community learn their sex roles. It is not just, or even mainly, that fathers are often absent, but that the male role models around boys are ones that emphasize expressive, affectional techniques for making one's way in the world. The female role models available to girls emphasize an exaggerated self-sufficiency (from the point of view of the middle class) and the danger of allowing oneself to be dependent on men for anything that is crucial. By the time she is mature, the woman learns that she is most secure when she herself manages the family affairs and when she dominates her men. The man learns that he exposes himself to the least risk of failure when he does not assume a husband's and father's responsibilities but instead counts on his ability to court women and to ingratiate himself with them.

IDENTITY PROCESSES IN THE FAMILY

Up to this point we have been examining the sequential development of family stages in the Negro slum community, paying only incidental attention to the psychological responses family members make to these social forms and not concerning ourselves with the effect the family forms have on the psychosocial development of the children who grow up in them. Now we want to examine the effect that growing up in this kind of a system has in terms of socialization and personality development.

Household groups function for cultures in carrying out the initial phases of socialization and personality formation. It is in the family that the child learns the most primitive categories of existence and experience, and that he develops his most deeply held beliefs about the world and about himself.[26] From the child's point of view, the household *is* the world; his experiences as he moves out of it into the larger world are always interpreted in terms of his particular experience within the home. The painful experiences that a child in the Negro slum culture has, therefore, are interpreted as in some sense a reflection of this family world. The impact of the system of victimization is transmitted through the family; the child cannot be expected to have the sophistication an outside observer has for seeing exactly where the villains are. From the child's point of view, if he is hungry it is his parents' fault; if he experiences frustrations in the streets or in the school it is his parents' fault; if that world seems incomprehensible to him it is his parents' fault; if people are aggressive or destructive toward each other it is his parents' fault, not that of a system of race relations. In another culture this might not be the case; if a subculture could exist that provided comfort and security within its limited world, and the individual experienced frustration only when he moved out into the larger society, the family might not be thought so much to blame. The effect of the caste system, however, is to bring home through a chain of cause and effect all of the victimization processes, and to bring them home in such a way that it is often very difficult even for adults in the system to see the connection between the pain they feel at the moment and the structured patterns of the caste system.

Let us take as a central question that of identity formation within the Negro slum family. We are concerned with the question of who the individual believes himself to be and to be becoming. For Erikson, identity means a sense of continuity and social sameness, which bridges what the individual "*was* as a child and what he is *about to become* and also reconciles his *conception of himself* and his community's recognition of him." Thus, identity is a "self-realization coupled with a mutual recognition."[27] In the early childhood years identity is family-bound, since the child's identity is his identity *vis-à-vis* other members of the family. Later he incorporates into his sense of who he is and is becoming his experiences outside the family, but always influenced by the interpretations and evaluations of those experiences that the family gives. As the child tries on identities, *announces* them, the family sits as judge of his pretensions. Family members are both the most important judges and the most critical ones, since who he is allowed to become affects them in their own identity strivings more crucially than it affects anyone else. The child seeks a sense of valid identity, a sense of being a particular person with a satisfactory degree of congruence between who he feels he is, who he announces himself to be, and where he feels his society places him.[28] He is uncomfortable when he experiences disjunction between his own needs and the kinds of needs legitimated by those around him, or when he feels a disjunction between his sense of himself and the image of himself that others play back to him.[29]

"Tell It Like It Is."

When families become involved in important quarrels the psychosocial underpinnings of family life are laid bare. One such quarrel in a family we have been studying brings together in one place many of the themes that seem to dominate identity problems in Negro slum culture. The incident illustrates in a particularly forceful and dramatic way family processes that our field work, and some other contemporary studies of slum family life, suggest unfold more subtly in a great many families at the lower-class level. The family involved, the Johnsons, is certainly not the most disorganized one we have studied; in some respects their way of life represents a realistic adaptation to the hard living of a family 19 years on AFDC, with a monthly income of $202 for nine people. The two oldest daughters, Mary Jane (18 years old) and Esther (16) are pregnant; Mary Jane has one illegitimate child. The adolescent sons, Bob and Richard, are much involved in the social and sexual activities of their peer group. The three other children, ranging in age from 12 to 14, are apparently also moving into this kind of peer-group society.

> When the argument started, Bob and Esther were alone in the apartment with Mary Jane's baby. Esther took exception to Bob's playing with the baby because she had been left in charge; the argument quickly progressed to a fight in which Bob cuffed Esther around, and she tried to cut him with a knife. The police were called and subdued Bob with their nightsticks. At this point the rest of the family and the field worker arrived. As the argument continued, these themes relevant to the analysis that follows appeared:
> 1. The sisters said that Bob was not their brother (he is a half-brother to

Esther, and Mary Jane's full brother). Indeed, they said their mother "didn't have no husband. These kids don't even know who their daddies are." The mother defended herself by saying that she had one legal husband and one common-law husband, no more.

2. The sisters said that their fathers had never done anything for them, nor had their mother. She retorted that she had raised them "to the age of womanhood" and now would care for their babies.

3. Esther continued to threaten to cut Bob if she got a chance (a month later they fought again, and she did cut Bob, who required stitches).

4. The sisters accused their mother of favoring their lazy brothers and asked her to put them out of the house. She retorted that the girls were as lazy, that they made no contribution to maintaining the household, could not get their boyfriends to marry them or support their children, that all the support came from her AFDC check. Mary Jane retorted that "the baby has a check of her own."

5. The girls threatened to leave the house if their mother refused to put their brothers out. They said they could force their boyfriends to support them by taking them to court, and Esther threatened to cut her boyfriend's throat if he did not cooperate.

6. Mrs. Johnson said the girls could leave if they wished but that she would keep their babies; "I'll not have it, not knowing who's taking care of them."

7. When her 13-year-old sister laughed at all of this, Esther told her not to laugh because she too would be pregnant within a year.

8. When Bob laughed, Esther attacked him and his brother by saying that both were not man enough to make babies, as she and her sister had been able to do.

9. As the field worker left, Mrs. Johnson sought his sympathy. "You see, Joe, how hard it is for me to bring up a family. . . . They sit around and talk to me like I'm some kind of a dog and not their mother."

10. Finally, it is important to note for the following analysis that the labels "black-assed," "black bastard," "bitch," and other profane terms were liberally used by Esther and Mary Jane, and rather less liberally by their mother, to refer to each other, to the girls' boyfriends, to Bob, and to the 13-year-old daughter.

Several of the themes outlined previously appear forcefully in the course of this argument. In the last year and a half the mother has become a grandmother and expects shortly to add two more grandchildren to her household. She takes it for granted that it is her responsibility to care for the grandchildren and that she has the right to decide what will be done with the children since her own daughters are not fully responsible. She makes this very clear to them when they threaten to move out, a threat they do not really wish to make good nor could they if they wished to.

However, only as an act of will is Mrs. Johnson able to make this a family. She must constantly cope with the tendency of her adolescent children to disrupt the family group and to deny that they are in fact a family—"He ain't no brother of mine"; "The baby has a check of her own." Though we do not know exactly what processes communicate these facts to the children, it is clear that in growing up they have learned to regard themselves as not fully part of a solidary collectivity. During the quarrel this message was reinforced for the 12-, 13-, and 14-year-old daughters by the four-way argument among their older sisters, older brother, and their mother.

The argument represents vicious unmasking of the individual members' pretenses to being competent individuals.[30] The efforts of the two girls to present themselves as masters of their own fate are unmasked by the mother. The girls in turn unmask the pretensions of the mother and of their two brothers. When the 13-year-old daughter expresses some amusement they turn on her, telling her that it won't be long before she too becomes pregnant. Each member of the family in turn is told that he can expect to be no more than a victim of his world, but that this is somehow inevitably his own fault.

In this argument masculinity is consistently demeaned. Bob has no right to play with his niece, the boys are not really masculine because at 15 and 16 years they have yet to father children, their own fathers were no-goods who failed to do anything for their family. These notions probably come originally from the mother, who enjoys recounting the story of having her common-law husband imprisoned for nonsupport, but this comes back to haunt her as her daughters accuse her of being no better than they in ability to force support and nurturance from a man. In contrast, the girls came off somewhat better than the boys, although they must accept the label of stupid girls because they have similarly failed and inconveniently become pregnant in the first place. At least they can and have had children and therefore have some meaningful connection with the ongoing substance of life. There is something important and dramatic in which they participate, while the boys, despite their sexual activity, "can't get no babies."

In most societies, as children grow and are formed by their elders into suitable members of the society, they gain increasingly a sense of competence and ability to master the behavioral environment their particular world presents. But in Negro slum culture growing up involves an ever-increasing appreciation of one's shortcomings, of the impossibility of finding a self-sufficient and gratifying way of living.[31] It is in the family first and most devastatingly that one learns these lessons. As the child's sense of frustration builds he too can strike out and unmask the pretensions of others. The result is a peculiar strength and a pervasive weakness. The strength involves the ability to tolerate and defend against degrading verbal and physical aggressions from others and not to give up completely. The weakness involves the inability to embark hopefully on any course of action that might make things better, particularly action that involves cooperating and trusting attitudes toward others. Family members become potential enemies to each other, as the frequency of observing the police being called in to settle family quarrels brings home all too dramatically.

The conceptions parents have of their children are such that they are constantly alert as the child matures to evidence that he is as bad as everyone else. That is, in lower-class culture human nature is conceived of as essentially bad, destructive, immoral.[32] This is the nature of things. Therefore, any one child must be inherently bad unless his parents are very lucky indeed. If the mother can keep the child insulated from the outside world, she feels she may be able to prevent his inherent badness from coming out. She feels that once he is let out into the larger world the badness will come to the fore, since it is his nature. This means that in the identity development of the child he is constantly exposed to identity labeling by his parents as a bad person. Since as he grows up he does not experience his world as particularly gratifying, it is very easy for him to conclude that this lack of gratification is due to the fact that something is wrong with him. This, in turn, can readily be assimilated to the definitions of being a bad person offered him by those with whom he lives.[33] In this way the Negro slum child learns his culture's conception of being-in-the-world, a conception that emphasizes inherent evil in a chaotic, hostile, destructive world.

Blackness

To a certain extent these same processes operate in white lower-class groups, but added for the Negro is the reality of blackness. "Black-assed" is not an empty pejorative adjective. In the Negro slum culture several distinctive appellations are used to refer to oneself and others. One involves the terms "black" or "nigger." Black is generally a negative way of naming, but nigger can be either negative or positive, depending upon the context. It is important to note that, at least in the urban North, the initial development of racial identity in these terms has very little directly to do with relations with whites. A child experiences these identity placements in the context of the family and in the neighborhood peer group; he probably very seldom hears the same terms used by whites (unlike the situation in the South). In this way, one of the effects of ghettoization is to mask the ultimate enemy so that the understanding of the fact of victimization by a caste system comes as a late acquisition laid over conceptions of self and of other Negroes derived from intimate, and to the child often traumatic, experience within the ghetto community. If, in addition, the child attends a ghetto school where his Negro teachers either overtly or by implication reinforce his community's negative conceptions of what it means to be black, then the child has little opportunity to develop a more realistic image of himself and other Negroes as being damaged by whites and not by themselves. In such a situation, an intelligent man like Mr. Wilson (quoted earlier) can say with all sincerity that he does not feel most Negroes are ready for integration—only under the experience of certain kinds of intense personal threat coupled with exposure to an ideology that places the responsibility on whites did he begin to see through the direct evidence of his daily experience.

To those living in the heart of a ghetto, black comes to mean not just "stay back," but also membership in a community of persons who think poorly of each other, who attack and manipulate each other, who give each other small comfort in a desperate world. Black comes to stand for a sense of identity as no better than these destructive others. The individual feels he must embrace an unattractive self in order to function at all.

We can hypothesize that in those families that manage to avoid the destructive identity imputations of "black" and manage to maintain solidarity against such assaults from the world around, it is possible for children to grow up with a sense of both Negro and personal identity that allows them to socialize themselves in an anticipatory way for participation in the larger society.[34] This broader sense of identity, however, will remain a brittle one as long as the individual is vulnerable to attack from within the Negro community as "nothing but a nigger like everybody else" or from the white community as "just a nigger." We can hypothesize further that the vicious unmasking of essential identity as black described above is least likely to occur within families where the parents have some stable sense of security, and where they therefore have less need to protect themselves by disavowing responsibility for their children's behavior and denying the children their patrimony as products of a particular family rather than of an immoral nature and an evil community.

In sum, we are suggesting that Negro slum children, as they grow up in their families and in their neighborhoods, are exposed to a set of experiences—and a rhetoric which conceptualizes them—that brings home to the child an understanding of his essence as a weak and debased person who can expect only partial gratification of his needs, and who must seek even this level of gratification by less than straightforward means.

Strategies for Living

In every society complex processes of socialization inculcate in their members strategies for gratifying the needs with which they are born and those which the society itself generates. Inextricably linked to these strategies, both cause and effect of them, are the existential propositions members of a culture entertain about the nature of their world and of effective action within the world as it is defined for them. In most of American society two grand strategies seem to attract the allegiance of its members and guide their day-to-day actions. I have called these strategies those of *the good life* and of *career success*.[35] A good-life strategy involves efforts to get along with others and not rock the boat, a comfortable familism grounded on a stable work career for husbands in which they perform adequately at the modest jobs that enable them to be good providers. The strategy of career success is the choice of ambitious men and women who see life as providing opportunities to move from a lower to a higher status, to "accomplish something," to achieve greater than ordinary material well-being, prestige, and social recognition. Both of these strategies are predicated on

the assumption that the world is inherently rewarding if one behaves properly and does his part. The rewards of the world may come easily or only
at the cost of great effort, but at least they are there.

In the white and particularly in the Negro slum worlds little in the experience individuals have as they grow up sustains a belief in a rewarding
world. The strategies that seem appropriate are not those of a good, family-
based life or of a career, but rather *strategies for survival.*

Much of what has been said can be summarized as encouraging three
kinds of survival strategies. One is the strategy of the *expressive life style,*
which I have described elsewhere as an effort to make yourself interesting
and attractive to others so that you are better able to manipulate their behavior along lines that will provide some immediate gratification.[36] Negro
slum culture provides many examples of techniques for seduction, of persuading others to give you what you want in situations where you have
very little that is tangible to offer in return. In order to get what you want
you learn to "work game," a strategy requiring a high development of a
certain kind of verbal facility, a sophisticated manipulation of promise and
interim reward. When the expressive strategy fails or when it is unavailable
there is, of course, the great temptation to adopt a *violent strategy* in which
you force others to give you what you need once you fail to win it by verbal and other symbolic means.[37] Finally, and increasingly as members of
the Negro slum culture grow older, there is the *depressive strategy* in which
goals are increasingly constricted to the bare necessities for survival (not as
a social being but simply as an organism).[38] This is the strategy of "I don't
bother anybody and I hope nobody's gonna bother me; I'm simply going
through the motions to keep body (but not soul) together." Most lower-class
people follow mixed strategies, as Walter Miller has observed, alternating
among the excitement of the expressive style, the desperation of the violent
style, and the deadness of the depressed style.[39] Some members of the Negro slum world experiment from time to time with mixed strategies that also
incorporate the stable working-class model of the good American life, but
this latter strategy is exceedingly vulnerable to the threats of unemployment or a less than adequate pay check, on the one hand, and the seduction and violence of the slum world around them, on the other.

Remedies

Finally, it is clear that we, no less than the inhabitants of the ghetto, are
not masters of their fate because we are not masters of our own total society. Despite the battles with poverty on many fronts we can find little
evidence to sustain our hope of winning the war, given current programs
and strategies.

The question of strategy is particularly crucial when one moves from an
examination of destructive cultural and interaction patterns in Negro fam-

ilies to the question of how these families might achieve a more stable and
gratifying life. It is tempting to see the family as the main villain of the piece
and to seek to develop programs that attack directly this family pathology.
Should we not have extensive programs of family therapy, family counseling, family-life education, and the like? Is this not the prerequisite to enabling slum Negro families to take advantage of other opportunities? Yet,
how pale such efforts seem compared to the deep-seated problems of self-
image and family process described earlier. Can an army of social workers
undo the damage of 300 years by talking and listening, without massive
changes in the social and economic situations of the families with whom
they are to deal? And, if such changes take place, will the social-worker
army be needed?

If we are right that present Negro family patterns have been created as
adaptations to a particular socioeconomic situation, it would make more
sense to change that socioeconomic situation and then depend upon the
people involved to make new adaptations as time goes on. If Negro providers have steady jobs and decent incomes, if Negro children have some
realistic expectations of moving toward such a goal, if slum Negroes come
to feel that they have the chance to affect their own futures and to receive
respect from those around them, then (and only then) are the destructive
patterns likely to change. The change, though slow and uneven from individual to individual, will in a certain sense be automatic because it will
represent an adaptation to changed socioeconomic circumstances that have
direct and highly valued implications for the person.

It is possible to think of three kinds of extra-family change that are required if family patterns are to change; these are outlined below as pairs
of current deprivations and needed remedies (see tabulation below):

Deprivation effect of caste victimization	Needed remedy
I. Poverty	Employment income for men; income maintenance for mothers
II. Trained incapacity to function in a bureaucratized and indus- trialized world	Meaningful education of the next gen- eration
III. Powerlessness and stigmatiza- tion	Organizational participation for aggres- sive pursuit of Negroes' self-interest Strong sanctions against callous or indifferent service to slum Negroes Pride in group identity, Negro *and* American

Unless the major effort is to provide these kinds of remedies, there is a very
real danger that programs to "better the structure of the Negro family" by
direct intervention will serve the unintended functions of distracting the

country from the pressing needs for socioeconomic reform and providing an alibi for the failure to embark on the basic institutional changes that are needed to do anything about abolishing both white and Negro poverty. It would be sad, indeed, if, after the Negro revolt brought to national prominence the continuing problem of poverty, our expertise about Negro slum culture served to deflect the national impulse into symptom-treatment rather than basic reform. If that happens, social scientists will have served those they study poorly indeed.

Let us consider each of the needed remedies in terms of its probable impact on the family. First, the problem of poverty: employed men are less likely to leave their families than are unemployed men, and when they do stay they are more likely to have the respect of their wives and children. A program whose sole effect would be to employ at reasonable wages slum men for work using the skills they now have would do more than any other possible program to stabilize slum family life. But the wages must be high enough to enable the man to maintain his self-respect as a provider, and stable enough to make it worthwhile to change the nature of his adaptation to his world (no one-year emergency programs will do). Once men learn that work pays off it would be possible to recruit men for part-time retraining for more highly skilled jobs, but the initial emphasis must be on the provision of full-time, permanent unskilled jobs. Obviously it will be easier to do this in the context of full employment and a tight labor market.[40]

For at least a generation, however, there will continue to be a large number of female-headed households. Given the demands of socializing a new generation for nonslum living, it is probably uneconomical to encourage mothers to work. Rather, income maintenance programs must be increased to realistic levels, and mothers must be recognized as doing socially useful work for which they are paid rather than as "feeding at the public trough." The bureaucratic morass that currently hampers flexible strategies of combining employment income and welfare payments to make ends meet must also be modified if young workers are not to be pushed prematurely out of the home.

Education has the second priority. (It is second only because without stable family income arrangements the school system must work against the tremendous resistance of competing life-style adaptations to poverty and economic insecurity.) As Kenneth Clark has argued so effectively, slum schools now function more to stultify and discourage slum children than to stimulate and train them. The capacity of educators to alibi their lack of commitment to their charges is protean. The making of a different kind of generation must be taken by educators as a stimulating and worthwhile challenge. Once the goal has been accepted they must be given the resources with which to achieve it and the flexibility necessary to experiment with different approaches to accomplish the goal. Education must be broadly conceived to include much more than classroom work, and probably more than a nine-month schedule.[41]

If slum children can come to see the schools as representing a really likely avenue of escape from their difficult situation (even before adolescence they know it is the only *possible* escape), then their commitment to school activities will feed back into their families in a positive way. The parents will feel proud rather than ashamed, and they will feel less need to damn the child as a way to avoid blaming themselves for his failure. The sense of positive family identity will be enriched as the child becomes an attractive object, an ego resource, to his parents. Because he himself feels more competent, he will see them as less depriving and weak. If children's greater commitment to school begins to reduce their involvement in destructive or aimless peer-group activities, this too will impact positively on the family situation, since parents will worry less about their children's involvement in an immoral outside world and be less inclined to deal with them in harsh, rejecting, or indifferent ways.

Cross-cutting the deprivations of poverty and trained incapacity is the fact of powerlessness and stigmatization. Slum people know that they have little ability to protect themselves and to force recognition of their abstract rights. They know that they are looked down on and scapegoated. They are always vulnerable to the slights, insults, and indifference of the white and Negro functionaries with whom they deal—policemen, social workers, school teachers, landlords, employers, retailers, janitors. To come into contact with others carries the constant danger of moral attack and insult.[42] If processes of status degradation within families are to be interrupted, then they must be interrupted on the outside first.

One way out of the situation of impotence and dammed-up in-group aggression is the organization of meaningful protest against the larger society. Such protest can and will take many forms, not always so neat and rational as the outsider might hope. But, coupled with, and supporting, current programs of economic and educational change, involvement of slum Negroes in organizational activity can do a great deal to build a sense of pride and potency. While only a very small minority of slum Negroes can be expected to participate personally in such movements, the vicarious involvement of the majority can have important effects on their sense of self-respect and worth.

Some of the needed changes probably can be made from the top, by decision in Washington, with minimal effective organization within the slum; but others can come only in response to aggressive pressure on the part of the victims themselves. This is probably particularly true of the entrenched tendency of service personnel to enhance their own sense of self and to indulge their middle-class resentment by stigmatizing and exploiting those they serve. Only effective protest can change endemic patterns of police harassment and brutality, or teachers' indifference and insults, or butchers' heavy thumbs, or indifferent street cleaning and garbage disposal. And the goal of the protest must be to make this kind of insult to the humanity of the slum-dweller too expensive for the perpetrator to afford; it must cost him election defeats, suspensions without pay, job dismissals, license revocations, fines, and the like.

To the extent that the slum dweller avoids stigmatization in the outside world, he will feel more fully a person within the family and better able to function constructively within it, since he will not be tempted to make up deficits in self-esteem in ways that are destructive of family solidarity. The "me" of personal identity and the multiple "we" of family, Negro, and American identity are all inextricably linked; a healthier experience of identity in any one sector will have repercussions on all the others.

NOTES

1. This chapter is based in part on research supported by a grant from the National Institute of Mental Health, Grant No. MH-09189, "Social and Community Problems in Public Housing Areas." Many of the ideas presented stem from discussion with the senior members of the Pruitt-Igoe research staff—Alvin W. Gouldner, David J. Pittman, and Jules Henry—and with the research associates and assistants on the project. I have made particular use of ideas developed in discussions with Boone Hammond, Joyce Ladner, Robert Simpson, David Schulz, and William Yancey. I also wish to acknowledge helpful suggestions and criticisms by Catherine Chilman, Gerald Handel, and Marc J. Swartz. Although this paper is not a formal report of the Pruitt-Igoe research, all of the illustrations of family behavior given in the text are drawn from interviews and observations that are part of that study. The study deals with the residents of the Pruitt-Igoe housing projects in St. Louis. Some 10,000 people live in these projects, which comprise 43 11-story buildings near the downtown area of St. Louis. Over half of the households have female heads, and for over half of the households the principal income comes from public assistance of one kind or another. The research has been in the field for a little over two years. It is a broad community study that thus far has relied principally on methods of participant observation and open-ended interviewing. Data on families come from repeated interviews and observations with a small group of families. The field workers are identified as graduate students at Washington University who have no connection with the housing authority or other officials, but are simply interested in learning about how families in the project live. This very intensive study of families yields a wealth of information (over 10,000 pages of interview and observation reports), which obviously cannot be analyzed within the limits of one article. In this article I have limited myself to outlining a typical family stage sequence and discussing some of the psychosocial implications of growing up in families characterized by this sequence. In addition, I have tried to limit myself to findings that other literature on Negro family life suggests are not limited to the residents of the housing projects we are studying.

2. St. Clair Drake, The social and economic status of the Negro in the United States. Dædalus, Fall 1965, p. 772.

3. E. Franklin Frazier, The Negro family in the United States. Chicago: University of Chicago Press, 1939, p. 487.

4. Norman Mailer, The White Negro. San Francisco, Calif.: City Light Books, 1957); and Leslie Fiedler, Waiting for the end. New York: 1964, pp. 118–137.

5. See Alvin W. Gouldner, Reciprocity and autonomy in functional theory. In Llewellyn Gross (Ed.), Symposium of sociological theory. Evanston, Ill.: 1958, for a

discussion of functional autonomy and dependence of structural elements in social systems. We are suggesting here that lower-class groups have a relatively high degree of functional autonomy *vis-à-vis* the total social system because that system does little to meet their needs. In general, the fewer the rewards a society offers members of a particular group in the society, the more autonomous that group will prove to be with reference to the norms of the society. Only by constructing an elaborate repressive machinery, as in concentration camps, can the effect be otherwise.

6. For example, the lead sentence in a *St. Louis Post Dispatch* article of July 20, 1965, begins "A White House study group is laying the ground work for an attempt to better the structure of the Negro family."

7. See Kenneth Stampp, *The peculiar institution*. New York: 1956; John Hope Franklin, *From slavery to freedom*. New York: 1956; Frank Tannenbaum, *Slave and citizen*. New York: 1946; E. Franklin Frazier, *op. cit.*; and Melville J. Herskovits, *The myth of the Negro past*. New York: 1941.

8. See Raymond T. Smith, *The Negro family in British Guiana*. New York, 1956; J. Mayone Stycos and Kurt W. Back, *The control of human fertility in Jamaica*. Ithaca, N. Y.: 1964; F. M. Henriques, *Family and colour in Jamaica*. London: 1953; Judith Blake, *Family structure in Jamaica*. Glencoe, Ill: 1961; and Raymond T. Smith, Culture and social structure in the Caribbean. *Comparative studies in society and history* (Vol. VI). The Hague, The Netherlands: October 1963, pp. 24–46. For a broader comparative discussion of the matrifocal family see Peter Kunstadter, A survey of the consanguine or matrifocal family. *American Anthropologist,* February 1963, 65(1), 56–66; and Ruth M. Boyer, The matrifocal family among the Mescalero: Additional data. *American Anthropologist,* June 1964, 66 (3), 593–602.

9. Paul C. Glick, *American families*. New York, 1957, pp. 133 ff.

10. For discussions of white lower-class families, see Lee Rainwater, Richard P. Coleman, and Gerald Handel, *Workingman's wife*. New York, 1959; Lee Rainwater, *Family design*. Chicago, 1964; Herbert Gans, *The urban villagers*. New York, 1962; Albert K. Cohen and Harold M. Hodges, Characteristics of the lower-blue-collar-class. *Social Problems*, Spring 1963, 10(4), 303–334; S. M. Miller, The American lower classes: A typological approach. In Arthur B. Shostak and William Gomberg, *Blue collar world*. Englewood Cliffs, N. J.: 1964; and Mirra Komarovsky, *Blue collar marriage*. New York: 1964. Discussions of Negro slum life can be found in St. Clair Drake and Horace R. Cayton, *Black metropolis*. New York: 1962, and Kenneth B. Clark, *Dark ghetto*. New York: 1965; and of Negro community life in small-town and rural settings in Allison Davis, Burleigh B. Gardner, and Mary Gardner, *Deep south*. Chicago: 1944, and Hylan Lewis, *Blackways of Kent*. Chapel Hill, N. C.: 1955.

11. For general discussions of the extent to which lower-class people hold the values of the larger society, see Albert K. Cohen, *Delinquent boys*. New York: 1955; Hyman Rodman, The lower class value stretch. *Social Forces*, December 1963, 42(2), pp. 205 ff; and William L. Yancey, *The culture of poverty: Not so much parsimony*. Unpublished manuscript, Social Science Institute, Washington University.

12. James F. Short, Jr., and Fred L. Strodtbeck, *Group process and gang delinquency*. Chicago: 1965, p. 114. Chap. V (pp. 102–115) of this book contains a very useful discussion of differences between white and Negro lower-class communities.

13. Discussions of white lower-class attitudes toward sex may be found in Arnold W. Green, The cult of personality and sexual relations. *Psychiatry*, 1941, 4, 343–348; William F. Whyte, A Slum Sex Code. *American Journal of Sociology*, July 1943, 49(1), 24–31; and Lee Rainwater, Marital sexuality in four cultures of poverty. *Journal of Marriage and the Family*, November 1964, 26(4), 457–466.

14. See Boone Hammond, *The contest system: A survival technique*. Master's

Honors paper, Washington University, 1965. See also Ira L. Reiss, Premarital sexual permissiveness among Negroes and whites. *American Sociological Review*, October 1964, *29*(5), 688–698.

15. See the discussion of aleatory processes leading to premarital fatherhood in Short and Strodtbeck, *op. cit.*, pp. 44–45.

16. Rainwater, *And the poor get children, op. cit.*, pp. 61–63. See also, Carlfred B. Broderick, Social heterosexual development among urban Negroes and whites. *Journal of Marriage and the Family*, May 1965, *27*, 200–212. Broderick finds that although white boys and girls, and Negro girls, become more interested in marriage as they get older, Negro boys become *less* interested in late adolescence than they were as preadolescents.

17. Walter Miller, The corner gang boys get married. *Trans-action*, November 1963, *1*(1), 10–12.

18. Rainwater, *Family design, op. cit.*, pp. 28–60.

19. Yancey, *op. cit.* The effects of unemployment on the family have been discussed by E. Wright Bakke, *Citizens without work*. New Haven, Conn.: 1940; Mirra Komarovsky, *The unemployed man and his family*. New York: 1960; and Earl L. Koos, *Families in trouble*. New York, 1946. What seems distinctive to the Negro slum culture is the short time lapse between the husband's loss of a job and his wife's considering him superfluous.

20. See particularly Komarovsky's discussion of "barriers to marital communications" (Chap. 7) and "confidants outside of marriage" (Chap. 9), in *Blue collar marriage, op. cit.*

21. Rainwater, *Family design, op. cit.*, pp. 305–308.

22. For a discussion of the relationship between Black Nationalist ideology and the Negro struggle to achieve a sense of valid personal identity, see Howard Brotz, *The Black Jews of Harlem*. New York: 1963, and E. U. Essien-Udom, *Black nationalism: A search for identity in America*. Chicago: 1962.

23. Rainwater, Coleman, and Handel, *op. cit.*, pp. 88–102.

24. Cf. Michael Schwartz and George Henderson, The culture of unemployment: Some notes on Negro children. In Shostak and Gomberg, *op. cit.*

25. Daniel Patrick Moynihan, Employment, income, and the ordeal of the Negro family. *Dædalus*, Fall 1965, pp. 760–61.

26. Talcott Parsons concludes his discussion of child socialization, the development of an "internalized family system" and internalized role differentiation by observing, "The internalization of the family collectivity as an object and its values should not be lost sight of. This is crucial with respect to . . . the assumption of representative roles outside the family on behalf of it. Here it is the child's family membership which is decisive, and thus his acting in a role in terms of its values for 'such as he.' " Talcott Parsons and Robert F. Bales, *Family, socialization and interaction process*. Glencoe, Ill.: 1955, p. 113.

27. Erik H. Erikson, Identity and the life cycle. *Psychological Issues*, 1959, *1*(1).

28. For discussion of the dynamics of the individual's *announcements* and the society's *placements* in the formation of identity, see Gregory Stone, Appearance and the self. In Arnold Rose, *Human behavior in social process*. Boston: 1962, pp. 86–118.

29. The importance of identity for social behavior is discussed in detail in Ward Goodenough, *Cooperation and change*. New York: 1963, pp. 176–251, and in Lee Rainwater, Work and identity in the lower class. In Sam B. Warner, Jr., *Planning for a nation of cities*. Cambridge, Mass.: (1966). The images of self and of other family members is a crucial variable in Hess and Handel's psychosocial analysis of family life; see Robert D. Hess and Gerald Handel, *Family worlds*. Chicago: 1959, especially pp. 6–11.

30. See the discussion of "masking" and "unmasking" in relation to disorga-

nization and re-equilibration in families by John P. Spiegel, The resolution of role conflict within the family. In Norman W. Bell and Ezra F. Vogel, *A modern introduction to the family*. Glencoe, Ill.: 1960, pp. 375–377.

31. See the discussion of self-identity and self-esteem in Thomas F. Pettigrew, *A profile of the Negro American*. Princeton, N. J.: 1964, pp. 6–11.

32. Rainwater, Coleman, and Handel, *op. cit.*, pp. 44–51. See also the discussion of the greater level of "anomie" and mistrust among lower-class people in Ephraim Mizruchi, *Success and opportunity*. New York: 1954. Unpublished research by the author indicates that for one urban lower-class sample (Chicago) Negroes scored about 50% higher on Srole's anomie scale than did comparable whites.

33. For a discussion of the child's propensity from a very early age for speculation and developing explanations, see William V. Silverberg, *Childhood experience and personal destiny*. New York: 1953, pp. 81 ff.

34. See Ralph Ellison's autobiographical descriptions of growing up in Oklahoma City in his *Shadow and act*. New York: 1964. The quotations at the beginning of this article are taken from pages 315 and 112 of this book.

35. Rainwater, Work and identity in the lower class, *op. cit.*

36. *Ibid.*

37. Short and Strodtbeck see violent behavior in juvenile gangs as a kind of last resort strategy in situations where the actor feels he has no other choice. See Short and Strodtbeck, *op. cit.*, pp. 248–264.

38. Wiltse speaks of a "pseudo depression syndrome" as characteristic of many AFDC mothers. Kermit T. Wiltse, Orthopsychiatric programs for socially deprived groups. *American Journal of Orthopsychiatry*, October 1963, *33*(5), 806–813.

39. Walter B. Miller, Lower class culture as a generating milieu of gang delinquency. *Journal of Social Issues*, 1958, *14*(3), 5–19.

40. This line of argument concerning the employment problems of Negroes and poverty war strategy more generally is developed with great cogency by James Tobin, On improving the economic status of the Negro. *Dædalus*, Fall 1965, and previously by Gunnar Myrdal, in his *Challenge to affluence*. New York: 1963, and Orville R. Gursslin and Jack L. Roach, in their Some issues in training the employed. *Social Problems*, Summer 1964, *12*(1), 68–77.

41. See Chapter 6 (pages 111–153) of Kenneth Clark, *op. cit.*, for a discussion of the destructive effects of ghetto schools on their students.

42. See the discussion of "moral danger" in Lee Rainwater, Fear and the house-as-haven in the lower class. *Journal of the American Institute of Planners*, February 1966.

23

Reconstructing Separateness and Connectedness During Home Recovery from Heart Attack

EDWARD J. SPEEDLING

In the early home care period following a heart attack there was little tendency for the family members to engage together in discussions of patient activity. Questions of what the patient could and could not do rarely came up. At home, the patient simply did as little as possible. As Mr. Ambrosio put it, "When in doubt, do nothing." Everyone subscribed to this orientation.

Agreement over the means of coping with the management of the recovery process, which characterized the early days of home care, began to break down as soon as the husband—patients made their first tentative moves toward activity.

At first, the men undertook simple activities like cleaning the dinner dishes or setting the dinner table, changing light bulbs, and the like, and when they discovered they could accomplish these activities without discomfort, they attempted slightly more substantial tasks, for example, carrying a bag of garbage from the kitchen to a pail in the pantry. It is important to note that these were done without prior consultation with either physician or spouse. The men, it seemed, were attempting quietly to test their stamina against what they thought were fairly safe activities.

Usually the first significant task attempted involved something that was clearly identified with their normal role at home and that others, even in divergent families, did not normally share. Two men went down to the basement to check the heating system. One of them, Mr. Stein, told me

Reprinted by permission from Edward J. Speedling, *Heart Attack*. New York: Tavistock, 1982, pp. 98–134.

Edward J. Speedling is Assistant Professor of Sociology, Department of Community Medicine, Mt. Sinai School of Medicine and in the Graduate School, City University of New York.

that even though he realized his wife had been handling this chore successfully in his absence, he felt he had to check it for himself. "I must see that you are doing it right," he said to his wife when she objected to his going down the stairs. Mr. Ambrosio felt he had to check on a small crack in his basement wall to determine if it needed repair. With this goal in mind he went down a flight of steps for the first time in spite of his wife's objections.

At this time, these recently discharged patients took steps to be less visible to their spouses, who were becoming increasingly concerned over the subtle but certain turn of events. Earlier, the men tended to stay in places where they could easily be observed—the kitchen or the living room. All social establishments, Goffman (1959) tells us, have norms that govern what behavior is acceptable in the various spatial settings that comprise it. In most homes, for example, the living room is set aside as a place of rest. The husband–patients' presence there reflected their felt need for a protective environment. Dens, finished basements, and attached workrooms where the men might have chosen to repose in the days immediately following hospital discharge do not have the same symbolic value, nor would they have provided the same ready access to those who were performing nurse-surrogate roles.

Once men opted to become active, they changed location within the home. For example, now when he rested, Mr. Ambrosio chose the den where he had a desk, and which was situated near the front door. He could bring in the mail and newspaper before his wife knew they had arrived. Seated at the front window he could greet his neighbors as they came home from work. He also could look out over his garden and mentally prepare his spring planting. Mr. Stein likewise relocated from the living room to a corner of the kitchen where he stored the material he used to make stock market calculations. Responding to her husband's preference, Mrs. Polski agreed to move the site of convalescence from the city to their country home. While these spatial changes were accompanied by some alteration in behavior, the symbolic value to the men of being in proximity to elements of their normal world underscores an important psychological shift in attitude toward physical activity.

These beginning steps, however small, radically altered the social and emotional climate in the homes. For the first time since prior to the illness, family conflict erupted. The wives and children, concerned and, in some cases, frightened, agreed that the men were displaying serious lack of judgment. They went to considerable lengths to halt the trend, including becoming uncharacteristically forceful. Mrs. Stein, who preferred to be non-involved in her husband's affairs, became "hysterical" and "shrill" when she learned that her husband had smoked a cigarette at home. When she discovered that he stood on a chair to change a light bulb in the kitchen during her absence, she "hit the ceiling," and demanded that he not do such a thing in the future. Some tried physically to stop the men when they attempted to carry out the garbage or to walk out of doors. In so doing they were acting upon their felt obligation to control the patient's environment and prevent situations from occurring that would threaten his health and safety. The perspective of the husbands who were in fact apprehensive about what they could and could not safely accomplish was expressed by one of them this way:

> You just can't sit around for the rest of your life. I would not want to sit around for three months and all of a sudden start to move around. I don't believe that the doctors mean for you to do that anyway. They would rather see you move around gradually. That's my feeling on it anyway.

We see in this conflict the expression of differences in attitudes that originated during the earliest phase of hospitalization. The approach to activity of the husband—patients was in keeping with what they had experienced earlier. They saw the necessity to act and perceived dangers in extended passivity. Yet when they did so their uncertainty was apparent and was seized upon by spouses and children as a reason to postpone activity until such time as a safe course of action could be determined. They viewed such activity as misguided and an expression of impatience, tension, frustration, and the like; understandable but not worth the risks involved:

> The things he is doing, it is just to do something. Doing the dishes, and I notice how he is eating. He used to be more relaxed . . . now he is eating and doesn't know what he is eating. I think he is very tense. He gets up and tries to do the dishes right away. He wants to do something, keep doing.

For the first time different perspectives on the nature of the illness and the requirements of care and treatment brought forth a confrontation between the spouses. Previously, different viewpoints existed but were not openly acknowledged. Patients and wives were not totally unaware that they held discrepant definitions of the situation, but the extent or basis of the differences was never explored.

The conflict over the activity of the husband—patient may also be conceived of as a struggle between conflicting claims to legitimacy in representing the medical point of view in the home. Each spouse felt more equipped than his or her partner to decide how best to give specific meaning in everyday terms to what the physician or nurse had said about "taking it easy." The husband—patients argued that their wives interpreted the medical regimen too strictly, while the wives felt they were morally obliged to prevent the men from engaging in what they perceived to be potentially harmful behavior.

In pressing their respective claims for control of decision-making with regard to patient care, the spouses faced certain dilemmas. The wives saw themselves as essential to the preservation of the hospital-like atmosphere. They felt they could not simply withdraw from their role as medical surrogate. However, they realized that by continuing to insist that the men act as if they were still acutely ill, there was the very real possibility of upsetting them. This, in itself, would disturb their repose. For their part, the husbands had no way to demonstrate that they could safely perform the activities they were now proposing to do and were not merely disobeying medical advice. There were no visible signs marking the transition from one state of health to another. They had no proof they were fit to leave the sick role for one more compatible with rehabilitation. This is the reverse of a problem chronically ill patients in a later stage sometimes experience; that is, convincing persons unfamiliar with their condition that they actually have a disabling condition—like heart disease—which, while it does not show, prevents them from full role participation (Kassebaum and Baumann, 1972).

In contrast to the earlier perception within the families that their troubles emanated from external sources, the present difficulties were seen to be directly related to ill-advised behavior of individuals inside the family. Thus, rather than closing ranks against an outside threat, the family members struggled with one another. The result was a noticeably decreased family harmony in all the homes, marking the beginning of a new stage in the family experience: The Early Period of Internal Stress.

FAMILY STRUCTURE AND PATTERNS OF REHABILITATION ROLE ORGANIZATION

While interpersonal conflict generated by discrepant expectations with regard to home-care role performance was a problem each of the families had to deal with shortly after the end of the Period of Extension of Hospitalization, the ways of problem solving varied according to important group values.

Adaptation to the current period of stress took three forms.

1. *Coercion.* Family members attempted in various ways to force the husband–patient into compliance with the definition of the situation held by the wife and children.

2. *Disengagement.* The strategy was to disengage from previous roles and to allow each person a greater share in decisionmaking responsibility, with no one person monopolizing the management of the home care.

3. *Reorganization.* Families in this case reached a mutually acceptable understanding that the wife would retain the major input into the organization of the recovery process.

Each mode of adaptation had a specific effect on the affective climate in the home. Where *coercion* was the means used to settle differences with regard to home-care behavior, affective relations between the husband–

patient and others who now were his adversaries were marked by frequent hostility and antagonism. As defined by Spiegel (1957, p. 403), coercion involves "manipulation of present and future punishments. Thus it ranges from overt attack to threats of attack in the future, and from verbal commands to physical force. . . . If it is successful, the role conflict is settled through submission in which ego accepts the complementary role enforced by alter." By attempting to coerce the husband into submitting to a role of seriously ill patient, two negative consequences for the family sometimes surfaced: When the husband defied the others, conflict ensued; when he did submit, the result had alienationlike effects: the individual perceived that the family no longer fulfilled his goals or provided the outcomes he valued (Rosenstock and Kutner, 1969).

Where family members choose to *disengage* from previously held role definitions, each party accepted somewhat less autonomy than he or she desired. Something like Spiegel's (1957, p. 407) concept "role reversal" seemed to apply, whereby "ego proposes that alter put himself in ego's shoes, trying to see things through his eyes." This was a pragmatic attempt to stabilize relationships that had become conflict-ridden due to discordant role expectations. However, stress was still present because each person was behaving in less than complete harmony with his or her desires.

Where reorganization occurred, family members experienced a heightened sense of togetherness. Spiegel (1957, p. 402) uses the term "role modification" for this situation, meaning that "the change in role expectations is bilateral, and modification techniques are based on interchanges and mutual identifications of ego with alter." In this case, the wife was able to fully actualize her expectations with regard to her and her husband's home-care role behavior. The husband, in this stage of his patient career, was willing to accept a strong nurse-surrogate role on the part of his spouse.

DISENGAGEMENT: THE MODE OF ADAPTATION IN DIVERGENT FAMILIES

Although it is difficult to know precisely when and how the disengagement mode of adaptation began, it appears that the first steps to reduce the hostility were taken by the wives, who diminished the level of their opposition to their husband's behavior and disengaged, in part, from the nurse–surrogate role. Each backed off from the initial expectation of full control.

Mrs. Stein, who had earlier described her response to some of her husband's behavior as "shrill" and "like a shrew," explained that she just could not cope with the ill feeling generated by her attempts to coerce her husband. Besides, she felt it was having a negative influence on her own physical and emotional health as well. Her husband, Mr. Stein, described the change in her approach: "On certain things I get bawled out. I mean endearingly."

In place of strident arguing, these four wives turned to persuasion as a means of influencing their husband's behavior. They also compromised. For example, if Mr. Asti firmly stated his intention to descend the basement steps, his wife only insisted that he go very slowly, support himself on the railing, and allow her to help. The Astis' daughter, Rose, explained that since her father became angry whenever anyone tried to interfere with his plans, her response was to be helpful but not interfering. She explained, "I would not keep asking 'Do you want this, or this, or this?' I would just do what is necessary." In other words, she remained involved, but at a judicious distance.

The wives tried to remain vigilant of their husbands, often suggesting that they rest or postpone some activity until a later time. I asked Mr. Polski, shortly after he and his wife had gone to their country home, how often his wife reminded him to slow down his pace. He replied, "Well, she leaves that up to me. But she's after me. Like, I wanted to do a little, but this morning she said, 'Don't knock yourself out.' She was after me from three o'clock to knock it off, because the day before I had gotten chest pains."

By remaining close at hand, wives not only hoped to persuade the men to do less, but actually to assist them and thus lessen the burden of activity. Mrs. Polski explained, "Yesterday he was rushing around so much, I swept the basement so he could get done quicker. If he does it, he'll never come up." Mrs. Warren, who before the illness rarely engaged in joint activity with her husband, now sat with him so she could be available to perform small services like turning the TV dial, bringing in the newspaper, getting a cup of tea.

Mrs. Asti learned that while she could sometimes assist her husband with his activities, there was also the chance that her actions would be interpreted as interference and lead to quarreling. Therefore, she began to ask relatives to "drop by" and provide some assistance when her husband was planning to make some household repair. He was less able to refuse offers of help from others. However, in order to utilize this strategy most effectively, Mrs. Asti had to follow her husband's activities closely. While she tried to be noninterfering, they both realized that she remained highly aware of his whereabouts and plans.

In playing a modified nurse–surrogate role, the wife was still able to communicate her views to the man and was a restraining influence on his behavior.

In each of these divergent families there was evidence that the husband–patients felt obliged to respect wifely advice. Moreover, the men indicated that this input could be valuable in preventing them from misjudging their real limitations. Mr. Polski said, "I think it is good to have my wife reminding me of what to do rather than have someone who didn't care. If she didn't, I'd probably be doing something I shouldn't. It's like in the hospital where you have a nurse after you all the time." While the patient–husbands perceived their limitations in a less restrictive fashion than their wives did, most were still convinced they had a serious medical problem; one that could become dangerously worse if they overexerted themselves. They were willing to be active and even test the limits of their present strength, but doubts about their health and uncertainty about recovery still remained. Prior to his first medical examination since leaving the hospital, Mr. Asti commented, "I want to ask if there is any difference in my physical being; if I'm doing alright. Am I coming along as expected or not?" When I asked how he thought he was doing at this point he replied, "I have no way of knowing." This was doubtlessly instrumental in his susceptibility to persuasion by wife and children. When I asked about his decision to go outside the house for the first time he replied, "My wife didn't want me to do anything. So being the doctor said take it easy, I figured I'd let another week go by before I tried anything else."

In contrast to those occasions when wifely admonition would cause a man to reevaluate his intended behavior from the standpoint of his own safety, there were times when he seemed to agree with her solely out of respect for her feelings. On a number of occasions, when asked to give examples of disagreements the men had with their wives over how to interpret the medical regimen, the men would describe occasions on which they started to do some activity but stopped after wives raised objections. When asked to explain, they might reply, "Oh, what's the use of arguing," or "I don't know, I just didn't bother."

Willingness occasionally to adhere to the perspective of the wife, along with tolerating her constant advice and admonition, also seemed to be the reciprocal response of the husband—patient to his wife's disengagement from actively seeking a controlling nurse-surrogate role in the home care. It recognized the right of the wife to have some input into the recovery process without controlling it. It gave her a sense of responsibility and allowed her to feel successful in carrying out her felt obligations to keep the man from hazardous circumstances. Without some input into the home care, the wife might have no option but to demand a share in decision-making, precipitating a hostile response. It also left the patient—husband fairly free to choose when to comply with the wife's interpretation of the medical regimen.

On the other hand, the men could be forceful in rejecting wifely attempts to control their behavior. They only selectively followed their wife's counsel. Concerning his smoking, Mr. Stein demanded that his wife never speak to him about it. He told her that it was something he would handle in his own way. He never attempted to conceal the fact of his smoking. Openness rather than subterfuge was characteristic of men in divergent households. They did not pretend to others that they were doing less than they actually were.

Limitations in the strategy of disengagement were evident, particularly when the wives perceived the men's activity as especially arduous, or when the men had episodes of angina. This would compel the wives to act forcefully in pressing their opinion on the men. The specter of marital conflict made this a difficult choice, as Mrs. Stein's statement clearly demonstrates:

> When we get to the doctor at the center, there is a tremendous walk from where he parks the car to the doctor. Will he be able to maneuver that, will he be able to manage it? Should I call in advance and have somebody meet him there with a wheelchair or something? I don't know if he will want that. He's apt to blast me with his tongue out of creation.

Another source of stress to the family members during this stage of adjustment, which points up a further limitation of the disengagement mode of dealing with problems, was the fact that the real depth of personal concern was not shared. The husband who felt discomfiture in his chest did not feel free to express his concern to his wife or children, lest they feel obliged to intervene. In order not to add to the patient's problems, wives and children deliberately refrained from revealing the full extent of their own fears and doubts.

Against the remarkable similarities in their ways of handling the immediate posthospital days and subsequent shifts, there were, of course, individual differences in levels of group tension, conflict, and disorganization. Factors associated with adaptation in divergent families were the perception within the home of the state of the patient—husband's health, and the fit between the nurse-like role the wife was able to play and her perception of her husband's need for external control.

If the patient appeared to be showing signs of improving health and was taking some precautions, a limited nurselike role was sufficient for the wife, who, in keeping with normal family preferences, was not used to imposing her will on others in the family. She could begin to pursue activities that normally provided important satisfaction in her life. Likewise, the husband could begin to resume some familiar activities that were important to him. On the other hand, declining health, or even lack of perception of improvement, tended to produce marital discord and intrapersonal stress because the wife was not satisfied that her efforts on the patient's behalf were sufficient to produce the desired healthful atmosphere in the home.

During this stage, The Early Period of Internal Stress, the Polskis experienced the least disruption of normal routines and interpersonal relationships. Shortly after Mr. and Mrs. Polski returned to their country home, he began doing what he described as "light work." This involved cleaning up, sorting his tools, etc. He was, however, taking two naps a day, something he rarely did before the illness. When he experienced any pain in his chest he took a nitroglycerine tablet and stopped working. Significantly, both attributed discomfiture to his need for rest, not to any abnormality in the heart itself. In other words, they believed he was progressing normally. The pain was perceived as a warning to stop working, not an inherent danger sign in and of itself. Their confidence in his improvement seemed to be justified by his increasing tolerance for work. By the second week he was able both to increase the length of time he could work and to do more strenuous labor: he cut his naps down to one and worked until 4:30. On weekends he and his wife began to resume a bit of socializing. On these occasions, he found that he could violate the dietary requirements without any noticeable aftereffects.

Mrs. Polski continued to remind her husband about the need for caution and restraint, but she did not often feel obliged to challenge him or to press her viewpoint against his wishes. She said that although it troubled her when he took nitroglycerine, he seemed to be getting stronger, and this tempered her disapproval of his activities. Several times she began telling of projects she tried to discourage, only to say eventually, "Well, I can see his point too."

Because of this perception, Mrs. Polski felt free to pursue many of her own activities. When asked, "How about yourself, are you as busy as you normally are?" she replied:

> Oh, yes, I don't know where the day goes—I can't understand how some women can say they are lonesome, or they are bored. I could never say that. I can't seem to catch up. I have so much to do. I'm either knitting something or fixing something. The day is not long enough to accomplish what I want. My husband is the same way. The days go so fast.

When asked, "Is your routine the same or different than before your husband became ill?" she replied, "The same. It is just the same."

Even the fact that she was not taking her normal trips into the city to visit her friends and go to club meetings did not seem to cause her very much disappointment. She accepted this limitation on her freedom as part of her obligation to her husband during his recovery. She felt she had a role to play in reminding him to be cautious and in helping him with his chores. She anticipated that without her presence, Mr. Polski would tend to do more than he was doing at present. She felt she had an effective voice in the recovery process.

On each of the factors outlined above, the Polskis measured up favorably. Mr. Polski's health was perceived as growing better steadily. In spite of occasional excesses, it seemed to his wife that he did demonstrate a willingness to change normal behavior in favor of more cautious "sick-role behavior," which was consonant with his perceived health status. His wife was able to play a nurse role she felt was adequate in view of his needs and was still able to pursue her own activities.

At the opposite end of the spectrum of response in the second stage were the Steins. They experienced intense and sustained interpersonal strain as well as a good deal of individual emotional stress. Each spouse was dis-

appointed with the role behavior of the other. There were regular arguments, which created an atmosphere of hostility in the home. Conflict was
ignited easily.

Mr. Stein began to have chest pain soon after returning from the hospital. Pain, sometimes intense, came without exertion, and both partners were,
not surprisingly, concerned about this. After several days home he began
to violate aspects of the medical regimen in blatant ways. For one thing he
resumed smoking and, in a further violation of medical orders, drove to the
store to get his cigarettes. Mr. Stein made no attempt to hide this fact from
his wife, who associated smoking with the heart attack. Mr. Stein himself
called what he was doing, "my own form of suicide." His wife, bitterly
opposed to his actions, accused him of "driving nails into your coffin."

Her reaction to his behavior was a combination of frustration at not being
able to control events and dreaded anticipation of continuous conflict, which
was the cost of taking the aggressive stance she felt was required of her.
Caught by conflicting needs, the couple had frequent arguments followed
by periods of somber withdrawal.

An additional factor behind Mr. Stein's refusal to allow all but a minimal
nurse role for his wife was that he believed she did not have sufficient
knowledge to make decisions affecting his care. She made what he called
"bad judgment mistakes." Examples he gave of this included inviting relatives to visit when he was not feeling well and, particularly, her lack of
adequacy in the area of food preparation. Prior to his illness her lack of
cooking skills was a source of amusement. Now, because the diet was the
part of the regimen Mr. Stein valued most, it became a source of antagonism. His wife remarked on this problem, "Now when I come home I get
arguments from him: 'What supper are you going to ruin tonight? What are
you going to feed me tonight that I am not going to like? What chemicals
are you going to give me tonight?' I never had that with him before." Although Mr. Stein began to seek out information himself on matters such as
nutritional supplements and recipes for cooking the bland food he was now
required to eat, his wife did not become involved in this task.

In interviews, she acknowledged her lack of information and blamed this
on the medical staff at the hospital:

> I haven't been told a thing about what to expect: physically, sexually, or brain-
> wise. On TV it said that sex is the best thing after a heart attack. How do I
> know that's so? Suppose he gets an attack when we are having relations? What
> then? I don't even know who his doctor is that took care of him in the hospital.
> [E.S.: "What gives you the idea that he can't, for example, walk out on the
> porch and take the air?"] I don't know. I have no idea. (Yet she was opposed
> to this activity.)

What was especially upsetting to Mrs. Stein was that during the first week
at home life had been pleasant. Her advice was accepted and her cooking

tolerated. She longed for a return to the easy tranquillity the couple had known when together in the past.

Since coming home from the hospital, Mr. Stein was beset with a series of upsetting experiences: pain, fevers, flu symptoms. He fought depression by trying to become involved in his hobbies and doing some chores around the house. "I don't want them thinking of me as an invalid," he declared in reference to his wife and married daughter. "I'm taking a positive approach. I'm looking ahead to getting back to work." At worst, he looked upon his wife's attempts to play a nurse role as detrimental to his recovery. Most of the time he just thought she could not contribute much. I asked him, "How much is your wife involved in your activities at home?" He replied simply, "What can she do?"

The experience of the Asti family in coping with home care adjustments fell between the two that I have just described. Mr. Asti did not have chest pain or take nitroglycerine, but he still considered himself in fragile health. He tended to be cautious and unsure of himself. Yet he was willing to begin some minor activities, even though he worried as he did them. Lack of confidence in his recovery made him tense and unsure of how to go about what he thought was required of him: i.e., gradually increasing activities. He was anxiously awaiting news of his condition.

For weeks he only attempted to do small chores like drying the dishes, carrying garbage bags to the pail, picking up papers from the yard. His wife was inclined to try to discourage most of these activities. He said that he often had to tell her, "I feel alright. I want to do it now. I can't sit down for the rest of my life." He did, however, let her help him in some of these activities.

Mrs. Asti had more of a substantial role in managing the convalescence than did either Mrs. Polski or Mrs. Stein. She was completely in charge of the preparation of the food. She claimed that the hospital did not provide her with a diet to follow, so she developed her own set of guidelines by remembering what he was given to eat in the hospital. Her other resources were her own "weight watchers" diet and the diabetic diet her own mother had been on. Mr. Asti seemed pleased that his wife was handling this, and in matters related to food he gave his wife full recognition. For example, he often said things like, "My wife is trying to keep me on a low-calorie diet as much as possible." Or, "My wife thinks I ought to lose some weight." He also seemed to rely on her to remind him of when to take his medication. Prior to his heart attack he had been diagnosed as a diabetic, but had stopped taking the medication when he felt better. Now he was using his wife to ensure against this happening again. In contrast to the previous example, Mr. Asti perceived his wife as competent in at least this important aspect of his recovery.

It was evident during this period that each of the members of the family was making an effort to avoid confrontation. Rose said she tried to be helpful around the house, and during this time did more chores to help her mother than she normally did. Mrs. Asti appeared adept at knowing when she could express her own opinions about the medical care requirements and when she should maintain her distance from her husband's affairs. For his part, Mr. Asti tolerated suggestions, and when he did not want interference, generally was firm but nonhostile.

Yet occasions when the members clashed could not be avoided completely. Balancing a sense of obligation to have the patient–husband do less with strongly held family norms of noninterference and individual autonomy created tensions. At times Mrs. Asti could not restrain her need to express her views forcefully, and sought support for her position from her daughter. However, Rose did not agree. In contrast to her earlier stance, it became Rose's opinion that her father should be left to follow his own inclinations. Occasionally this different approach to the problem created heated exchanges between mother and daughter.

Aside from occasional episodes of interpersonal conflict, most of the tension in the Asti family was intrapersonal. Neither Mr. nor Mrs. Asti was comfortable resuming normal activities, and as a consequence were often in each other's presence. Prior to the illness, Mrs. Asti spent many afternoons with her friends. Now she mainly stayed at home to be near her husband. Seeing him do more than she thought was wise upset her. Yet she knew that she had to be judicious about expressing opposition to his activities. The novelty of having his actions scrutinized by his wife was something Mr. Asti tolerated but did not enjoy. In spite of being in close proximity for long periods of time, the couple did not seem to develop more of an active companionship.

If we examine the adjustments made in the second stage of the home care in light of pre-illness family patterns, certain explanations for this coping style suggest themselves. Individuals ordinarily expected to have much discretion in the performance of their daily activities. Social organization allowed for flexibility in role performance. This was related to the high value placed on separation as opposed to togetherness, both in activity in the home as well as in activity with external groups and interests.

For a short time after hospital discharge, a role-differentiated division of labor prevailed in each of these homes. Separation from the hospital temporarily constrained the husband–patients to seek a sense of security in a passive–dependent patient role and encouraged wives and children to assume highly dominant nurse–surrogate roles. However, as soon as the husbands regained a sense of security in their surroundings their preference for deciding for themselves what daily activities should consist of asserted itself. After a period of struggle, the couples, recognizing a need to adopt a strategy to mediate their interpersonal conflicts, attempted to strike a new balance based on mutual participation without interference. Wives continued to give advice, but withdrew from active opposition in the face of continued insistence on the part of the men to behave according to their own interpretation of the medical regimen. The husband—patients in various ways recognized the right of wives to participate in the home care management. In effect, the couple attempted to fit the management of the recovery to the pre-illness pattern: each person participates, neither is excluded, but the norm of noninterference in personal choice necessitates that the husband— patient has the final word in determining his own behavior.

For the wife to have continued to act as if it were her role alone to manage the recovery process, she would have acted in a nonprecedented way given the family's structure and value climate. She would have risked upsetting the basis on which marital stability rested had she tried to impose a role-differentiated order in a family that valued role exchange. It was no more in the wife's interest to do this than it was for the husband. Being a full-time nurse—surrogate would have increased the chances of marital disharmony with no corresponding rewards. In other words, there were no social gains to be had for the wife by increasing her control over her husband's behavior. She did not gain by increasing her role in the family, nor did she value the closeness a husband—patient, wife—nurse relationship would bring. On the contrary, what she valued was her own independence and her own separate life style.

Home Care Adjustment in Convergent and Discordant Families

The advantages and limitations of the disengagement mode of problem solving are exemplified in the case histories presented above. While consistent with family values, its fit with the everyday requirements of home-based recovery from heart attack was more problematic. The promise it offered of achieving a balance between the needs of the recovering heart patient and the psychosocial well-being of the conjugal unit was not always fulfilled, and in one case was thoroughly shattered.

In other families, wives responded to the husband—patients' attempts to increase autonomous behavior with more, not less, intense and active opposition of their own. Their efforts withstood a short period of challenge by the men who, for the next six to eight weeks, had their activities supervised and planned by others in the family. While not always in agreement, they seemed to accept the dominant role of wife and child in the home care.

In two cases, involving Mr. O'Shea and Mr. Goldberg, the men returned home from the hospital very fearful and confused. Mr. O'Shea believed he was better off in the hospital than he was at home and for weeks did little more than sleep or sit by the window in his pajamas. Before either man attempted any activity, he checked with his wife. An active wife—nurse was desired by these two men.

In contrast, Mr. Grasso and Mr. Ambrosio accepted control of their behavior by others in the family less willingly. Yet, for the most part, they complied with the direction given by the wives and/or children. Mr. Grasso "argued over terms," but usually Mrs. Grasso's interpretation of the regimen prevailed. Mr. Ambrosio sometimes objected to the restrictions his wife placed on him. He gave the following example:

> So we folded the laundry and put them in the position she wanted them and that was it. But she wouldn't let me take the basket up [here, he slammed his hand on the table]. See, to me this is wrong, I just feel that sooner or later I'm just going to do it and she won't say boo. [His voice rises in anger.]

Nevertheless, it was over a month before Mr. Ambrosio would openly challenge her authority in these matters.

The four men in convergent and discordant relationships seemed to rely on their wives' knowledge of the medical regimen. Explaining why he refrained from going out of doors, Mr. Grasso explained, "Well, I think it would be alright. My wife seems to feel that the doctor says I should stay inside the house. She remembers my routine should be confined inside the house." Mr. Ambrosio, in response to a similar question, answered, "I knew she was being briefed all the time she was in that hospital. She would be getting Dr. J.'s ear [the medical director of Group Hospital] or whoever's ear she could grab." Mrs. O'Shea, when asked why her spouse followed her advice now, since before the illness he often did not, explained, "I'm known as the doctor without the shingle in this family."

Mr. Grasso and Mr. Ambrosio did increase their activities somewhat during the weeks following homecoming. But they were not as active as their counterparts. Moreover, the kinds of activities they performed were, for the most part, unrelated to their former role activities. Mr. Ambrosio channeled his activities into crafts like painting, ceramics, hooking rugs. At his wife's urging, Mr. O'Shea did not call his friends on the phone. Likewise, Mrs. Grasso insisted that her husband not examine the records or daily receipts of their business or help plan the purchasing for the store during this period. She and her son Anthony assumed these functions entirely. The O'Shea family was in the midst of preparing for their daughter's wedding when the heart attack struck. Mrs. O'Shea and her daughter, not wanting him "to get excited," insisted that he refrain from involving himself with planning for the event. She and her daughter assumed this entire function. All claimed that under normal circumstances, he would have been involved a great deal.

For a period that lasted up to two months, the wives, with the help of children, made almost all the decisions with regard to the care, and handled all family business. As a consequence, husbands in convergent and discordant families were less active and farther away from resuming normal social functions than were the others at the same point in time.

Wives especially carried out their expanded functions with exceptional zeal. The claim they made to full control of the nurse function was compatible with the normal family values and life style (or that which wives had been pushing for before the illness). That is, when any task is assigned, it is expected to become the responsibility of a particular family member. Others are obliged to reciprocate with appropriate behavior of their own. These reciprocal roles and obligations are ordinarily not interchangeable among the family members. When, after hospitalization, the task of patient supervision fell to the wife, she did not expect to share it with her husband.

Change in the balance of influence over family affairs brought opportunities for social gain. This is due to the fact that the family was the major source of need fulfillment and emotional gratification for the members who had an interest in making the behavior of others congruent with their own expectations. Being a nurse—surrogate, the wife could now organize the day-to-day family life so that even more than before the illness it was compatible with her own interests and aspirations. Normally, she shared control over the content of family life with her husband. Both had their own spheres of influence, which made them interdependent. In some areas of their life together, there had been disagreement and disharmony. Now the wife had a chance to alter the patterns she found particularly disagreeable.

The wives who had the most to gain by controlling the recovery were the two from discordant families—Mrs. Ambrosio and Mrs. O'Shea. Their pre-illness disappointments over the content of home life had been great. In contrast to their present positions, before the illness they had little success at influencing their husband's behavior.

An indication of how successful their wives were in establishing the legitimacy of their claim to home-care control was that when husbands did deviate from wives' instructions, they did so *in secret*. When the couple was together, the husband—patient sometimes complained but almost never went directly against the wife's wishes. The wives were prepared to act forcefully to meet any deviation from their policies, and the men reported that they were aware of the conflict that could follow when they did not follow orders. This is illustrated by the following exchange between Mr. Ambrosio and the interviewer:

> (Interviewer) I saw that big branch was gone. (Mr. Ambrosio) I have a saw. No sweat, only I had to do it when she wasn't around. (Interviewer) I guess she noticed. (Mr. Ambrosio) No, and I haven't said a word either. [I did it] little by little . . . it could have led to a divorce.

Along with the similarities I have described, the emotional climate during this second stage of home care was not the same for the discordant families as it was for the Grassos, where prior to the illness both spouses actively supported a role-differentiated family structure. While elements of coercion were present in both convergent and discordant homes during the period we are addressing, this mode of adaptation lasted longer in the Grasso family. In the two discordant homes, Mr. Ambrosio and Mr. O'Shea adopted attitudes of restraint and passivity that are consistent with the sick role.

Ironically, couples who prior to the illness were unable to reach a consensus on conjugal roles managed to do so during the initial stages of home care.

The Honeymoon Period in Discordant Families—Reorganization in the Ambrosio and O'Shea Families

The restrictions the regimen placed on the men and that their spouses reinforced brought immediate gains to the wives. Mrs. Ambrosio explained it this way, "I always felt my husband did many things that I could do that he wouldn't let me do, and I feel so stupid in so many things. I feel that now he should let me." She took over as many household chores as she could manage to do: food shopping every day, even though there are only two of them, preparing all the meals and then doing the dishes, shopping for her husband's clothing and selecting what he would wear during the day—all things she wanted to do before but could not because her husband did them first. She was finally in control of the household. Whenever I saw or spoke to her during the weeks of the second stage, she appeared happy and spoke enthusiastically of her daily routine. "I never felt better in my life. [My younger sister] is always saying on the phone, 'Are you resting? Are you resting?' But when she came she said, 'My God, you look wonderful.' " The chores she was so happy doing were "wifely" chores, ones that prior to the illness she wanted to be in charge of. "It's a nice feeling getting up early, it's dark, and I get the breakfast ready, put the shades up to let the light in. *Then I wait on him."* Mr. Ambrosio was both surprised and impressed with his wife's energy. He told me:

> Like this morning, she said she got up at four AM. I said, "What the hell did you get up at four?" She said, "I want the floor washed." I really want to know why you get up so early, what is the advantage?" [She said] "I'm suddenly finding out: it is peaceful, quiet, there is no interruption, telephone or other duties."

Mrs. O'Shea reported the same type of rewarding experience during this part of the home care. She was able to actualize her wishes for an orderly home in which activities followed a definite routine:

> We eat on time now. My life doesn't revolve around the Knights of Columbus or anybody. It revolves around me. . . . I hated that. I wanted to eat at a certain time, I'd get a phone call [from her husband], 'I'll be a half hour late,' and a half hour would go into an hour. . . . I got like a hound dog . . . I have the say now. I don't get, "Well, this is my job . . . if you don't want to wait, don't wait. . . ." Everything is me, what I have to say, no more what he has to say. . . . Now [he says] what do *you* think, not, "I'm going to do it this way."

Both women utilized the inability of their husbands to participate outside of the home to increase their own closeness—to substitute themselves for their husband's separate friends and interests. This was something these women had wanted to accomplish prior to the illness but could not. Before, Mrs. Ambrosio and Mrs. O'Shea were denied it, but now the situation enabled them to have it. Mrs. O'Shea related, "I was always around. Now I have a companion. It is better for me. . . . It is for my benefit for a change. He checks the programs for us to watch. . . . We talk back and forth. Normally, I would be staring at the television with no one to talk to." Mrs. Ambrosio, who had a very active life outside the family prior to the illness, ceased all of these involvements and was glad of it. She claimed that what she was doing now at home pleased her more than church and community activities. She liked reading to her sick husband, talking with him, helping him with his hobbies, and most of all providing nurturance and service.

Mrs. O'Shea's advice to her husband seemed designed to separate him from those external forces that she blamed for his separation from the family. She blamed his friends, "bad guys" she called them, for his past neglect of her wishes, and now during the convalescence she used her influence to make his medical condition appear incompatible with his former friends and activities. She discouraged his friends from visiting him. She told me, "I have not let anybody come up here. He will want to be the host. . . . If friends do come I'm not afraid to say, 'Jim has to go to bed now' or 'I can't allow smoking around Jim now.' " Yet, at the same time, she portrayed them to her husband as unfaithful friends. "People he was very friendly with have never called. I say, 'I told you so, I never liked that person.' Then I'm in my glory."

When Mr. O'Shea began to feel well enough to go out for brief walks, Mrs. O'Shea sometimes used who he was likely to meet as her criteria for approving or discouraging the activity. For example, her argument against his going to church service was, "You know everybody is going to talk to you. It isn't that you are going to go and come back, everybody will grab you in the back of the church." On the other hand, during this same period she encouraged him to go to a wedding of her relatives, even though he said he did not feel up to it. In this case, she argued that "talking to people will do him good." In other words, she encouraged him in activities that they would do together and discouraged him from those that involved his friends. She substituted for his friends.

In time Mr. O'Shea began to look forward to his wife's company. When his wife came home from work he was openly glad to see her and, in a switch of patterns, got angry if his wife went out in the evening to visit her friends. As the rehabilitation progressed, closeness between Mr. and Mrs. O'Shea increased markedly. They developed a new ritual. In the afternoon, as soon as he saw her step off the bus (he looked out the window around the time she should be arriving), he would start brewing a pot of tea and make her a snack. Then they would eat and talk. He started driving at his wife's urging—she needed to be driven home from her daughter's shower. This was prior to the doctor giving approval for this activity. For several weeks thereafter he picked her up from work in the afternoon and then drove her shopping. Formerly, she did these chores alone.

One of the reasons Mr. Ambrosio was pleased to have his wife close by was that he perceived her as having a positive effect on his progress toward health. Mr. Ambrosio admitted that even though there were times he wanted to disagree with his wife and do more than she allowed, "she is right in many respects." He seemed pleasantly surprised at how much she could accomplish around the house, and how adroitly she managed his care. His wife reflected on his sentiments during the first month of the home care: "I think he has a little more confidence in what I'm doing. . . . He told me he owes his life to me. In letters he writes, people tell me: I give him tender loving care. If it wasn't for me he wouldn't have made it."

Under her supervision, Mr. Ambrosio felt confident that his health was improving. He said, "I've learned what foods to eat. . . . I can feel an infusion of energy into my body. Because now for the first time I'm eating like I should be eating. . . . I would have pancakes piled up to here. Clara would not follow through. Now, if I do she is right on me with a baseball bat."

Neither Mr. O'Shea nor Mr. Ambrosio gave indications that their present passive role challenged the security of their self-images. In the normal course of their day-to-day lives prior to the illness, neither person was concerned about sex role boundaries. Both were willing—even anxious—to do activities traditionally ascribed to females in our society. Having their wives temporarily substituting for them was not intrinsically threatening to them. Mr. Ambrosio reflected on the role that his wife was currently playing and seemed willing to accept the change in their relationship, at least for the present:

> She said like a schoolteacher: "Don't you worry about a thing, you just do as you are told." (E.S.: Is that something characteristic of her, to give you an admonition like that?) No, there it points out—I think this is characteristic of all women—the motherly instinct comes out. Not the wifely instinct, per se. First the motherly instinct: "You are the little person, you are sick and I have to treat you like an invalid . . . and you are going to listen to me."

With Mr. O'Shea not working, the financial burden of the family was the sole responsibility of Mrs. O'Shea. While the decrease in income troubled Mr. O'Shea, the fact that he was not the family breadwinner was not in itself a problem to him. He hoped that the promotion and raise his wife was scheduled for would make him less worried about the family's finances. It also pleased him very much when his married son offered to give him a sum of money whenever he needed it.

Comparing life in the Ambrosio family during the second stage of home care with what it had been like before the illness, one cannot fail to notice the remarkable improvement in the wife's morale and self-image. Moreover, the marital relationship itself was noticeably more harmonious. There was little of the former arguing between the spouses over who should take responsibility for household tasks. Mr. Ambrosio, for the most part, appeared content to play a passive patient role, which he perceived as necessary for full recovery later on. Occasionally, he verbalized impatience and even acted against his wife's wishes by going to the mailbox in the rain or walking farther than she wanted. But when his wife corrected him, he resumed a compliant posture without becoming hostile. His wife seemed to thrive on nurturing him. She liked reading poetry to him, selecting what clothing he should wear, and deciding what and when he should eat.

It is difficult to exaggerate Mrs. Ambrosio's happiness over her role. Doing everyday mundane chores seemed to delight her. After she salted down the sidewalk after a frost, she remarked to her husband and me that she felt like a young girl on her parents' farm feeding the chickens. With a sense of self-discovery she discussed a book she had just read about the positive aspects of being middle-aged. "It is truly wonderful," she exclaimed.

In spite of present harmony, there were some signs that the future would not be as harmonious as the present in the Ambrosio household. Mr. Ambrosio perceived the present state of affairs as temporary. I asked him if he thought he would ever again resume all of his former activities, many of which his wife was now taking delight in. "Oh yeah, I want it that way. This is my job. . . . This I expect to do. I know damn well that she will literally have to hold me down . . . these things I want to do myself; take the car out, take the garbage, go shopping. . . ." This was not the impression Mrs. Ambrosio conveyed, however. While she did not expect to continue to do quite as much as she was now, she perceived the illness as having brought a permanent change in the marital relationship. Her understanding of the consequences of the heart attack was that the husband would never be able to go back to a highly active life style. She recalled that one of his doctors had told her he would never be able to do anything as strenuous as changing a tire on his car. The couple, however, never discussed future adjustments. They concentrated their interaction on the present.

The Burden and the Promise of Coercive Role Adjustment— The Grassos

The experience of the Grasso family demonstrates that the second stage of home care can be a troubled time for a family, in spite of the increase in control by the wife.

Mr. Grasso was displeased by the restrictions on his activities, and he particularly resented being subject to the authority of his wife and son. He argued, complained, and criticized the present state of affairs. Mrs. Grasso, however, was unrelenting in her insistence on making all the decisions regarding her husband's activity. In the past when she tried to influence others' behavior, she did so in a quiet way. Now, however, she pressed her position and argued, as she said, in "an unladylike way." She told me, "I nag him all the time: What did you eat? Are you allowed? Did you go down the stairs? He gets annoyed, but that's how I play my role."

Having his wife and son plan and operate the family business and do his household chores bothered Mr. Grasso. He felt deeply about his masculine breadwinner role and was unable to adjust to a passive patient role, which he felt was humiliating. He said to me one day, "It used to be that she waited by the window for me to come home. Now, I'm waiting for her to come home. It is not easy. . . . I'm not being chauvinistic, but it is not easy for a man to do."

Anthony was ambivalent about the role he felt obliged to play in the home now. Criticizing his father's behavior seemed out of character, even though he felt it was needed. His father gave an illustration of his son's conflict: "I lit a cigarette the other day. I shouldn't and he caught me smoking. He chewed me out as much as a son would dare to chew a father out. He was embarrassed." (E.S.: Why was he embarrassed?) "The fact that he caught me doing something wrong. He walked out of the room mad, but he didn't say anything angry to me. I felt so bad; I threw the cigarette away immediately." The requirements of illness had altered the basic structure of parent–child relations. Father and son both disliked it. Anthony and his father had always formed a coalition in which they attempted to influence the direction of certain family matters to which Mrs. Grasso was opposed. The strong bond between father and son was something each family member reported. Anthony seemed especially gratified by it. However, his present role in the rehabilitation was stressful to him because it resulted in a coalition between mother and son *vis-à-vis* father. Yet, Anthony felt that this was what the situation required.

Mr. Grasso, in describing his first trip to the doctor since homecoming, illustrated his new isolated position in the family:

> Anthony came with me, not so much for company, but I think for—they play games with me. They want to be sure I don't lie to them, if when I ask the doctor if I can go to the store [business] I would say yes, when in fact he had said no. My wife feels that I abuse the doctor's warnings. I'm pretty sure that's the only reason Anthony was there.

Unlike many of the other men at this time, Mr. Grasso had serious doubts about ever getting well—even if he conformed to a very conservative regimen. He stated:

> But somehow I feel that sometime I'll go back there again, not with a terminal attack, but I'll have reason to go back to the hospital with some kind of heart attack again . . . one of the doctors said it . . . my wife thought that was very silly but I don't think it was silly. I feel that way . . . whatever conditions put

me there the first time still prevail and it is not a matter of eating too much chocolates or smoking too many cigars either. It's just a condition that is within my constitution that just does not leave by cutting out sugar and smoking."

At home he did stop smoking (for a short time at least), and for the first three weeks generally followed Mrs. Grasso's advice, although with reluctance. He said in our first talk at home, "I feel very well, very good, just restless. I feel strong enough. I have no worry about being able to walk a block or two. I'm afraid because the doctors didn't say that I could. I'm trying to do the right thing. Whether or not I think it is right or wrong I guess doesn't matter." Moments later, he indicated that he felt a responsibility to cooperate with his family, who he saw as suffering because of his illness. "I say the problem, whatever put me there, will never be cured. . . . I can't change that by eating different. I'm trying to be calm. I'm going to try to change. *I promised. I owe it to them to change.*"

Without this felt obligation to subordinate his own preferences to the demands of the group, which is required under the values of convergence, Mr. Grasso's rejection of the institutional definitions and prescribed procedures to cure, control or minimize the effects of the illness would probably have led to a "retreatist" behavioral response. Merton (1968, p. 242) defines the retreatist mode of adaptation as follows:

> Retreatism seems to occur in response to acute anomie, involving an abrupt break in the familiar and accepted normative framework and in established social relations, particularly when it appears to individuals subjected to it that the condition will continue indefinitely . . . it often obtains in those patterned situations which "exempt" individuals from a wide array of role obligations, as, for example, in the case of "retirement" from the job imposed upon people without their consent. . . .

Yet, Mr. Grasso made an effort to conform to a set of expected behaviors even though he failed to see the usefulness of them and experienced psychological stress in carrying them out. The evidence is that the weight of the family's collectivity orientation created a sense of obligation on the part of the patient to conform with the expectations of the group. However, the discontinuity between his subjective feelings and the demands of social obligation made conformity difficult, and there were lapses in it. His inner tension was expressed in aggressiveness, anger toward his wife and son, and depression—all of which contributed to the overall family climate during the second stage of home care.

In playing her role, Mrs. Grasso had to deal with these tensions. Anger on her husband's part did not diminish the extent of her attention to the details—large and small—of his care. She determined whether the doctor's order to rest at home meant that the husband could not sit on the porch in the sun for a few moments. She determined when he was able to see his friends and to join in the card games. To her husband's chagrin, she even answered for him when friends inquired about his treatment regimen.

According to Mr. Grasso, his wife derived a measure of satisfaction over her success in controlling his behavior. She discussed her role with friends and he listened in: "You overhear: 'Is he resting?' 'Yes, I won't let him do anything. He wants to go outside. He wants to work. I won't let him,' my wife would say proudly. She refused to let me outside, and it's a feather in her cap."

Mrs. Grasso paid a personal price for her nurse role. She reported that overseeing her husband's care left her little time for much else. She was up late doing housework. When she came home from work she had to do the bookkeeping for the store and the planning for the next day. She was forced to eliminate activities such as going to the beauty parlor and watching television. She claimed she hardly had time to prepare her clothing for work. The fact that her scrupulous attention to her husband's behavior was not appreciated by Mr. Grasso troubled her. Nevertheless, she showed no inclination to reduce her involvement in the care. When laboratory results showed that Mr. Grasso's condition was improving, the wife felt justified in her actions and strengthened in her will to continue as home-care supervisor.

The adjustments made in the Grasso home following hospitalization interfered with the normally close emotional ties the family enjoyed. Mr. Grasso was "left out" of normal family affairs to a very considerable degree. There was an awkwardness to interpersonal relations. Home-care roles were in the familiar role-differentiated style, but they did not now facilitate companionship and communication. Mrs. Grasso had control, but Mr. Grasso was isolated.

The following example of a not untypical evening in the home during the second stage of the home care illustrates the strain from the role adjustment. (It was constructed from my conversations with each family member.):

> After dinner the books and papers relating to the store's operation were brought to the dining room, and Anthony and Mrs. Grasso began discussing the day's receipts and planning for the upcoming Thanksgiving holiday. Decisions had to be made about how much new stock to order, how to display it, and whether or not to open early during the week of the holiday. Mr. Grasso was sitting in the living room about 20 feet away and was turned toward the television. He could see and hear his wife and son through the wide passageway separating the two rooms. Mr. Grasso said nothing, but later each person would report being highly conscious of his exclusion. Outwardly, all was calm. But this belied the tension each felt. While Mr. Grasso seemed to ignore events in the next room, he was tuned in. When the others went to bed, Mr. Grasso returned quietly to the dining room and examined the books and order forms. He was unaware that his son was watching him.

To review, at the start of home care, each family faced hard problems. The most worrisome arose from lack of confidence that the home environment could protect the recovering heart attack victim from relapse. Without the direct supervision of medical experts, wives, children, and patient—husbands were afraid to make independent judgments to interpret the medical care regimen. Instead, they took what was felt to be the safest course, i.e., having the patient adopt a routine modeled on the Intensive Care Unit. As difficult as this period—The Extension of Hospitalization—was, the source of family problems was seen by the members to be outside. The illness was conceived as an external threat, and the members joined forces to protect themselves from its effects. Consequently, interpersonal family relationships were generally harmonious. Working together seemed to bring a measure of well-being to families under the threat of crisis.

The nature of the problems families faced changed in a qualitative way, however, once the patient—husbands decided to become more active. Since their decisions were based on definitions of the recovery process that were not shared by their spouses, the tendency was for wives to oppose the actions of the husbands. Now family members blamed each other for thwarting the chances for recovery. Family problems centered on conflict between members.

Discrepancies in families in understanding the nature of the threat of illness and the requirements of the recovery process originated during hospitalization. The consequences of this lack of consensus, however, only surfaced a week or two after hospital discharge. Because there were no organized mechanisms at Group Hospital to allow definitions of the situation to emerge, the families were not able to work through their differences at a time when professional social service or psychiatric personnel could have helped. Instead, family members had to cope alone in a situation already tense and worrisome. The fact that lack of coordination in the hospital between patient and family experiences produced problems when the patient arrived home had no way of being fed back to the hospital staff for system correction. Since a large part of the social and psychiatric services available to patients and their families are allocated on the basis of referrals made by hospital medical and nursing staff, one can see how many families that could profit from professional counseling go undetected and unserved.

We saw from the analysis made in this chapter that strategies for managing the home care reflected the organization of the family. Whether the family's structure and value climate would have played such an important role in organizing the home care had the medical care system played a more active role is hard to assess.

People in divergent family systems were the first to disengage from acute care roles adopted at the start of homecoming. As a result, patients in these families began the process of resuming pre-illness roles earlier than their counterparts in the two other types of families. Their early mobilization was aided by the general feeling of discomfort in their families with the type of interaction fostered by a patient–nurse surrogate relationship. Segregating members into highly reciprocal interdependent roles was antithetical with the arrangements that were valued and practiced prior to the onset of the illness. With an aim toward avoiding conflict, which had surfaced when wives tried to play controlling nurse–surrogate roles to husbands' passive patient roles, the couples opted for a home-care division of labor that allowed each partner to participate. Their strategy for dealing with home-care management was basically a way of balancing the requirement of the recovery with the demands of family norms and mores.

People in convergent and discordant family systems remained in patient and nurse–surrogate roles for a longer period, and the men had fewer opportunities to test their abilities to resume activity. We saw that for couples that had been in conflict over role expectations and performances prior to the illness, the reorganized home-care role arrangement brought a significant degree of harmony to marital relationships. There was social gain from the illness in these families.

The Grassos, a convergent family, experienced considerable strain in relationships. Home-care roles were maintained by coercive efforts of wife and son against a patient who, while accepting the principle of a role differentiated division of labor, had considerable difficulty accepting the limitations the sick role posed to his sense of self. The son, too, was emotionally shaken by the role he felt obliged to play in controlling his father's behavior. The wife, deeply committed to maintaining the form if not the substance of the conjugal pattern, perceived herself as having no choice but to hold tightly the reins of home-care management. Motivated by her felt obligation to guide her husband safely to recovery and by her concern for stabilizing valued family patterns, she accepted short-term social and emotional costs for long-term benefits.

Given a context for rehabilitation in which family structure and culture influences how people behave after hospital discharge, it is significant that the medical care system left rehabilitation decision making so exclusively in the realm of the family of the patient.

REFERENCES

Goffman, E. *The presentation of self in everyday life*. Garden City, N.Y.: Anchor, 1959.

Hill, R. Generic features of families under stress. *Social Casework*, 1958, *39*, 2–3.

Kassebaum, G. and Baumann, B. Dimensions of the sick role in chronic illness. In E. G. Jaco (Ed.), *Patients, physicians, and illness: A sourcebook in behavioral science and health*. New York: The Free Press, 1972.

Merton R. K. *Social theory and social structure*. New York: The Free Press, 1968.

Rosenstock, F. and Kutner, B. Alienation and family crisis. In J. R. Eshleman (Ed.), *Perspectives in marriage and the family.* Boston: Allyn and Bacon, 1969.

Spiegel, J. P. Resolution of role conflict within the family. In M. Greenblatt, D. Levinson, and R. Williams (Eds.), *The patient and the mental hospital.* New York: The Free Press, 1957.

24

A Different Kind of
Parenting

ROBERT S. WEISS

A SPECIAL INVESTMENT

All parents care about their children. But single parents who were previously married have special reason for devotion to their children: their children are all that remain of their families. In addition, single parents who are divorced may hope that success in parenthood can partially compensate for their failure in marriage, while single parents who are widowed can find in commitment to their children an opportunity to demonstrate continued fidelity to their marriages. Single parents who were not previously married will already have committed themselves to their children, first when they decided that they would not abort, and again when they refused to relinquish their children for adoption.

Children give meaning to the lives of all single parents. For many of them, especially those with neither work they care about nor an adult partner, the children alone give meaning to their lives:

> I lived alone before I got married. I got married when I was twenty-six. And for all those years I made it on my own. One thing that I know very definitely about living alone is that after a while there is no reason to get out of bed in the morning. There is no reason to do a goddamned thing. And because of that, I think, I value the chance to be living for my kids. That is a reason to get

Reprinted by permission of Basic Books, Inc., Publishers, © 1979 from Robert S. Weiss, *Going it alone: Family life and social situation of the single parent.* New York: Basic Books, 1979, Chap. 4.

Robert S. Weiss is Professor of Sociology, University of Massachusetts, Boston. He also conducts a research program in the Department of Psychiatry, Harvard Medical School.

out of bed in the mornings. It is a reason to care what my hair looks like. It's a reason to do everything. And that keeps me from committing suicide.

To be sure, all parents' feelings toward their children are ambivalent. A single parent may blame the children not only for the usual burdens of child care, but also for the restrictions and distresses associated with raising chil- dren alone. This is particularly likely among those whose children remind them of a mistaken relationship. But ambivalence is often resolved by re- doubled commitment, and parents who could find emotional justification for resentment of their children may end by displaying determined devo- tion to them.

Raising their children successfully—providing them with care, protect- ing them from danger, trying to ensure that their homes are happy—tends to become the most important goal for single parents. It is easier for them to focus their attention on their children's needs just because their familial obligations are obligations only to their children. As one divorced mother said, "I'm not a housewife anymore; I'm a housemother." Some single par- ents take caring for their children as their lives' mission. Another divorced mother said:

> My children are my life. I have my own life, but everything stems from my children. . . . You could become anything you want to be, and if your chil- dren don't turn out well, it's lost.

Focus on the children's well-being sometimes expresses itself in over- protectiveness, which may be particularly likely when the single parent has resisted other opportunities for emotional investment and there is no other adult to whom the single parent is close. It may also occur when the single parent is, perhaps with justification, aware of the fragility of security. The following comment was made by a widowed mother of four children, the youngest a daughter, aged nine:

> I think I tend to be more cautious with the children since I've been alone. I'm more fearful for them. I'll think twice before I let them do things. I would rather take them somewhere than have them walk somewhere. Cecelia has these softball practices and I just have a fit and a half if she isn't home by a certain time. So I would just as soon go and wait.
> I just feel that if something ever happened to one of my kids it would be the end of me. I feel that I've gone through all the emotional strain that I can go through, and I don't think I could take any more than I've had. I can't re- member being quite so overprotective when I was married, and I don't like to be so overprotective now, but I know I am.

Decisions are made with the children in mind. Often the children's needs, or what are thought to be the children's needs, are given priority over the parent's. Another divorced mother said:

> When push comes to shove and it's a financial thing, the kids come first. I moved into the neighborhood I'm in for the children, not for me. I probably would have been happier in the city where there are more single people. And I joined a church for the children, not for me. I made a lot of decisions for my children.

After several years alone the single parent may be able to say with some pride, "I've learned not to put my children's needs first all the time. I don't always put myself first, but I don't always put my children first either." But this willingness to give occasional priority to the needs of the self comes only after children have grown older and persistent self-sacrifice has begun to seem pointless. In the early years of parenting alone, especially if the children are small, single parents can rationalize their constant concern over their children by seeing them as unjustly deprived. The children, after all, were not responsible for what befell them:

> It wasn't their fault that they came into the world. They didn't ask to come into the world. And it wasn't their fault that my husband and I split up.

Single parents may try to provide their children with whatever the children would have had under better circumstances, even if this requires sacrifice. One mother, for example, bought new clothes for her daughters rather than a needed new dress for herself, so that the daughters would not be penalized by her separation from their father. Another mother said:

> I don't want them to go without the necessities of life, not anything, shoes, a new winter coat. I don't feel that they should suffer for what has happened in our marriage.

Clothes, toys, and housing as good as that of their friends, and, in upper income brackets, private schools as well, can all be provisions to which single parents feel their children are entitled and that they will try as hard as they can to obtain for them. The sense of obligation to ensure that the children not suffer materially for their parents' errors increases the single parent's discomfort with reduced income and becomes one more motivation for the divorced mother's insistence that her former husband provide support at a high level. In addition, single parents are concerned that their children not be deprived of emotional security by the loss of one parent from their homes. Single parents who believe their children cannot count on their former partners may strive to assure their children that they, at least, can be counted on:

> I love my kids very much, and, while I don't try to make it up to them for not having a father, it is important to me that they know that I love them above anything else.

Like all parents, single parents become alarmed if their children seem to be troubled. But more than other parents, single parents may feel they have reason for concern. The children are likely to have been subjected to upset and stress in connection with the ending of the parents' marriages. Now the children live in households different from others'. The children may have been asked to assume unusual levels of responsibility for themselves and for younger children. For all these reasons the parents are alert to indications that their children are not doing well. Any questionable behavior—daydreaming, attention-seeking, unwillingness to go to bed at night—becomes a reason for worry. As one mother put it, "You are constantly looking for pathology." Some parents find themselves monitoring the extent to which their children display what could be interpreted as symptoms of loss:

> My son has really come out of it beautifully. He still, like when he goes to bed at night, he'll say he loves me three times, but it used to be ten times, you know.

Single parents find it profoundly reassuring to be told that their children seem no different from any other children. It was with the tone of having come through an accident unscathed that one single parent said, "You know, they are normal little kids." On the other hand, evidence that a child is troubled is deeply disturbing to the parent. One widowed mother of four, the youngest a boy of ten, said:

> My youngest might say something about somebody who was in the yard with his father. And he might make a remark, "I wish we had a Daddy." If I'm in the right mood, it's like a knife going through me.

Separated or divorced parents may examine their children's reactions for evidence regarding the soundness of their decision to end their marriages. One mother found that her son blinked repeatedly, and worried that this was connected to her husband's absence: was her son, perhaps, holding back tears? Had she injured her son by insisting that her husband leave? Other parents find support for their decisions to separate if their children seem to be functioning well at home and in school, and even more if they seem to be functioning better than when the parents were married:

> He started his sophomore year just after my husband left, and his work at school just changed. I mean, all his schoolwork was better. His grades are higher. Now whether that could be attributed to the fact that his father was gone and there wasn't any more conflict between them, I don't know. But he kept up his work and he is still keeping it up.

Often parents do not know whether they should explore the children's reactions to the new household situation with them or be tactful and permit the children to keep their thoughts to themselves. Some parents believe that children's memories are short and their attention easily distracted, and the less said, the better. Other parents ask leading questions—and sometimes encounter emotions for which they are not prepared. The following was reported by the mother of an 11-year-old girl:

> I picked up something that was bothering my daughter. She looked very unhappy one afternoon. I said, "Are you upset about the divorce?" And she just looked at me. And I said, "Do you think if we had tried harder we could have made our marriage work?" And she sort of nodded. And I said, "You know, maybe you're right. I have to admit the possibility." And at that point she ran out of the room screaming, "Don't say that. Don't say that."

In any event, single parents tend to be alert, sometimes hyperalert, to their children's emotional states. They want their children to have lives no less secure, no less protected, and no less gratifying than those of other children. And since they feel their children may have been exposed to special stress, they monitor their children's responses. They may ask the children directly, perhaps hoping the children will say—as an adolescent boy said to his father after the father finally separated from the boy's alcoholic mother—"What took you so long?" Or they may only wonder what may lie beneath their children's apparently untroubled exteriors. A mother of a school-aged only son said:

> I am more aware of his emotional development than I am of anything else. I guess I'm very concerned about him, wanting him to be secure, to feel secure emotionally as well as every other way, and that just because he's without a father, it doesn't mean that he's a strange person or that there is something he did. I'm hoping that in years to come he will understand the situation, because I think it is difficult for him now. I think he knows we both love him. And yet he never questions, "Well, if you love me, why aren't we all together?"

Some single parents whose marriages have just ended believe it is helpful to their children if they inform the children's teachers. They may ask the teachers to join them in monitoring their children's responses:

> I've kept in close contact with the school because I figure even if I couldn't notice something at home the school would pick it up.

Other single parents, however, do not want their children to be stigmatized in the classroom and do what they can to discourage teachers and others from anticipating that their children will be different. One mother went to some pains to hide her status as a single parent from her children's teachers for fear that the teachers would begin to see her children as "products of a broken home."

Single parents who work may fear that their children are being hurt by their absences. Sometimes guilt for not always being accessible to the children persists, even though the children show no sign of having been damaged. One woman, older and with grown children, had worked from the time her children were small. Although her children seemed perfectly fine, she still worried:

> I should have been with them more. I should have participated more in Boy Scouts and Girl Scouts. They never said, "Why don't you? Every other mother does." They never said anything, even to this day. But there may have been a void there that I didn't see.

Another mother, separated for two years, worried that her small son had been deprived of something important by having spent his days in a neighbor's home while she was at work:

> It was a very hard decision to leave my son with somebody else before he was three. I wanted to go back to work but I didn't want to leave him at that young age. I feel sometimes as if he's been gypped. The other kids always had me here. I guess he's none the worse for it—not yet, anyway.

It is understandable that working single parents should choose jobs that make it easier for them to respond to their children's needs, jobs near their homes, especially. Indeed, mothers of small children who had not been employed at the time their marriages ended may not seek employment thereafter because they are unwilling to be separated from their children for any part of the day. Their children, in their view, have already suffered the loss of one parent, and they will not impose on them the partial loss of the second.

CLOSER TO THE CHILDREN

One compensation for being a single parent is that there is opportunity to be closer to the children. There is no second adult in the household with whom parenthood must be shared, to whom loyalty is owed, who distracts the parent's attention and discourages the development of separate understandings with the children. Now there is just the one parent and the children. A mother of three, two not yet teenaged, said:

> Dealing with another person in your life, your mind is going to that person, it's dwelling on him, so that you are not as close to the kids. I've gotten closer to the kids since the separation.

Another mother said, "When I was married I never felt any real relationship with my children, but now I do." A man whose two school-aged sons spent half the week with him said this about his relationships with his children:

> It's weird, but we are much closer than we would have been if I had stayed married. We just couldn't be tighter. It shows itself in lots of ways. They are

able to be more relaxed with me, more open with me, tell me about secrets, do things with me that show they are more at ease. And I'm much more open with them, more relaxed with them.

It is easier, when a parent is alone, for the children to win the parent's attention for their talk about friends and games. And, because it is only the children with whom the parent now lives, it becomes natural for the parent to discuss with the children what is to be cooked for dinner, what they will do on the weekend, where they will go on vacation. Now parent and children keep each other company, watch television together, provide an audience for each other's stories.

In a two-parent household, mother and father can bring their tensions and uncertainties to each other. In a one-parent household, the parent has only the children to turn to. And although the children's reactions are sometimes childlike, the children *do* react. Having them to talk to permits the parent to put words to a problem, to formulate it, and so to objectify it and make it available for examination. While talking to the children may not be the same as talking to another adult, it is better than talking to no one. And, as children become more aware of parental feelings, they become more capable of helpful response.

> Because I'm open with my kids, they're like two little adults. You know, I've shared my feelings with them, and I've shared my hurt with them. And they have seen me hurt. They have seen me cry. And they have said, "Gee, Mom, are you ever going to be happy again? Are you ever going to stop crying?" And I said, "Yes, someday, I suppose, I will."

As one consequence of this increased closeness, the single-parent family may develop a sense of common cause and of strong family boundaries not often seen in two-parent families. A widower with two small children described this feeling:

> My family is a very tight-knit group, a very closed shop. By closed shop I don't mean that it is forever closed, that it will not ever allow anybody else in, but for now it is closed. We're in there, the three of us, and we are terribly close.

The increased closeness between parent and children in the single-parent family is not necessarily the product of increased time spent in each other's presence. Rather it comes about as a result of a broader sector of interchange, as well as increased parental accessibility during those times when parent and children are together. Indeed, in households in which the parent is newly working or in which a separated parent has agreed that the children will live part time with the other parent, increased closeness between parent and children may actually be accompanied by a reduction in shared time.

In some single-parent families there is an increase in closeness in the parent's relationships with only one or two of the children. The older children, perhaps, become companions and confidantes of the parent, while the younger children are treated as children are in two-parent families. Or one of the children maintains a position of withdrawal or antagonism that effectively confounds the parent's overtures:

> The kids don't have someone else to relay their problems to, so you hear the whole thing. They can't go to the other parent. But closeness—closeness depends on the type of relation you have with your kids. I have two daughters. With one of them I'm very close. With the oldest one I've never been able to get close. We're like fire and water. There is no way. I think it's the character. There are just certain characters that you cannot get along with.

Some parents and children are, for any of dozens of reasons, unwilling to be open with each other. Single parents and their children are not close in every case. Nor is the increased closeness found within most single-parent families incompatible with occasional tensions; on the contrary, the greater mutual responsiveness and increased mutual reliance of parent and child in the single-parent family makes it more likely that disappointments and disagreements will be painful and reactions sharp.

THE ENDING OF PARENTAL ECHELON

The one-parent family tends to be different from the two-parent family not only in the greater closeness of its members to each other but also in its structure and in the way it works.

Everyone understands how a two-parent family works, or at least how it ought to work. Mother and father are supposed to agree on how things should be done. The children need not be consulted; even adolescents may have little voice in deciding mealtimes and bedtimes and the chores that will be expected of them. Indeed, Blood and Wolfe, in their examination of household decision-making in two-parent families, gave no role to the children.[1] The children may be permitted to organize and decorate their own rooms, but the parents jointly run the family.

Because the parents are jointly responsible for the family's direction, each feels pledged to support the other. Should there be no prior agreement on a particular issue, each parent is expected to respect any position assumed by the other, at least while they are in the presence of the children. In reality, one parent may countermand the other's directives or collude with the children to frustrate the other's wishes, but behavior of this sort is understood as irresponsible and, perhaps, hostile in intent. In a well-functioning two-parent household, parents can count on each other.

An example may make the point clear. We will draw on our interviews with Mrs. Sherman, a nonworking married mother. The Shermans had three daughters, the middle one Laura, aged five and a half. One afternoon Laura damaged some furniture, and Mr. Sherman prescribed as her punishment a mealless evening. Mrs. Sherman did not agree but would not openly dispute her husband's decision:

> Laura hadn't had any lunch and I couldn't see a child going to bed without supper. I could see spanking her, but not starving her. Well, we all ate, and Laura never asked for supper. She can be just as stubborn as anybody. After we finished eating I said, "George, do you think we could give her a little bit of supper, because she had no lunch?" And he said, "Do you think she deserves supper? And I said, "No, I don't think she deserves supper, but I think I ought to give her a little and make sure she eats it. What do you think?" And he said, "Okay."

As it happened, Mr. Sherman was scheduled to go out that evening. Our interviewer asked Mrs. Sherman why she had not waited until her husband left the house since then she could feed her daughter without opposition. Mrs. Sherman was shocked at the idea: that would have been going behind her husband's back.

Erving Goffman has given the name "echelon structure" to an authority structure in which an implicit partnership agreement exists among those on a superordinate level, so that anyone on the higher level has authority in relation to anyone on the lower level.[2] The army maintains this sort of authority structure; so do hospitals; so do two-parent families. One-parent families do not. Without at least two members on the superordinate level, an echelon structure will not be formed; without the second parent in the home, the echelon system of the two-parent family collapses.

The absence of parental echelon permits, although it does not require, a parent's relationships to the children to undergo change. In particular, it permits the development of new relationships between parent and children in which the children are defined as having responsibilities and rights in the household not very different from the parent's own. Children now can be asked not only to perform additional chores—this would be possible within an echelon structure—but also to participate in deciding what is to be done.

The actual consequences of the collapse of the echelon structure of the two-parent household may vary with the level of demand for task performance to which the single parent must respond. If the parent is not employed, or has only one child and a job that is not especially pressing, the parent may not be forced to share task responsibilities. A working single parent, on the other hand—especially if there is more than one child—is likely to feel quite unable to do without the children's help. And since the absence of echelon makes it possible for the parent to redefine family roles and responsibilities, the parent is likely to decide that the children must not only perform a greater share of the family's tasks but also accept responsibility for seeing to it that the tasks are performed. The parent wants to be able to rely on the children as fully participant in the functioning of the family.

Many parents report having called their children into a family council in which they announced that now, with only one parent in the household, the family would have to be run in a new way, with every member of the family assuming a full share of responsibility. By earning the family's living the parents were doing their part; they would do more, of course, but the children would have to do their parts too. A substantial minority of the single parents we talked with indicated that a speech of this sort marked the beginning of the new structure of relationships within their households. The following report is from an interview with a mother of four children, ranging in age from about ten to about sixteen:

> As soon as I was on my own I sat down with the children—I always had a good rapport with the children—and I told them, "Now things are different. Instead of more or less being a family of mother and four children, we're all one family with all equal responsibility, and we all have a say, and we're all very important. And if it is going to work right, we all have to be able to co-operate with each other."

This is, in a way, a single parent's Inaugural Address. It establishes just how things will now be different. Here is another version, a speech made by a mother of three school-aged children just after she began work:

> I told them that I felt I was working full time and they had to help. And they weren't going to get paid for the jobs they did. It was just that everybody had to contribute. We were either going to sink or swim, and that was it. And everybody had to do their part.

Even if parents would like things to remain as they had been when they were married, they are likely to find that working full time forces them to require their children to share responsibility for home management. One woman, after separating from her husband, was left to care for five children, four boys aged nine to sixteen and a girl aged three. She did not work the first few months and during that interval asked rather little of her children. But after a few weeks of working she realized that her children would simply have to pitch in, and like other working single parents she insisted that responsibility be shared:

> That first month I was working, I would walk in from work and they would all want this and that done, and I had left the house in a mess in the morning and I had to start getting supper. And I would be tired and I would get upset and might cry. And then the boys would say, "What's the matter?" Well, we had to sit down and talk about it. I said, "I'm tired. I'm doing more right now than I feel I can handle. You're going to have to help out. There are things you are going to have to do. You can set the table while I'm getting supper. You can help with the baby."

Once children accept the increased responsibility, it becomes natural for the single parent to consult the children regarding household decisions. If the family has to move, the children might be asked what they think of the new apartment; if they are very much against it, the single parent might look further. The children almost certainly will be consulted about when meals should be scheduled and what should be served; it is so much easier to consult the children than to argue with them later. The children, in short, become junior partners in the management of the household. One woman, mother of two girls aged seven and five, said:

> We all make decisions together as far as . . . where we're going, what we're going to eat; or, if they go with me to the store, they help make decisions as far as things that I buy for the house. They make decisions on their own clothes, of course.

This parent later added, "Sometimes they dislike things I want them to get and I force it on them. But usually we agree." At least until the children become adolescent, single parents can become authoritative when they believe the issue demands it. Single parents generally try to get their children to behave properly by cajoling and nagging, but they can shift into firmness if necessary. As one mother put it, "My voice changes, and it's like, 'This is your *mother* talking!'" If the single parent has up until that point been treating the children as partners in the household enterprise, it may require something approaching desperation for the parent to become heavy-handed. Still, it is understood by all family members that the single parent is first among equals, the Chairman of the Board. It is to the single parent that the children direct their protests when they think the allocation of chores has been unfair, and it is the single parent who decides, ultimately, what the family will do. The single-parent family is hardly a perfect democracy. It is only more nearly one than the two-parent family. One mother said:

> I would have family conferences with the three kids and we would discuss whatever was coming up. I started that five years ago when we moved because we couldn't have this and we couldn't have that, and so we'd discuss what we *could* do. But my boy says to me that sometimes I didn't listen, that I always thought I was right.

The parent continues to carry ultimate responsibility for the family and to carry it alone. This may mean that the parent has to say that some issues are not family decisions—whether the parent should work, for example. But even when the parent makes the decision, the parent is likely to discuss the issue with the children and to do what is possible to reduce their objections. The mother of the two little girls, quoted above, described another incident that displayed the quality of parental leadership in joint decision-making:

> Nellie is the older. During New Year's we decided to go visit my family, and we had this big discussion. Nellie wanted to ride in an airplane, but Helen was afraid. And so we sat down and we let Nellie use her calculator, and we figured out how much it would cost if we all took the airplane and how much it would cost if we took the bus. And Nellie said, "Well, it's cheaper if we take the bus." And I convinced her that if we did take the bus we would have more money to spend when we were there.

In most instances, single parents move quite far toward sharing responsibility for family management with their children. The allocation of chores ordinarily is decided by children and parent together. Here is how the allocation of chores was dealt with by one woman and her three children, a girl of fourteen, a boy of twelve, and a girl of ten:

> I said, "This is your house too. What do you want to do about the way it is run?" So we outlined the jobs that were reasonable for them to do and I said what I would do and then I left it to the three of them to carve up who did what. I let them do their own arranging.

To someone accustomed to the management style of two-parent households, single-parent households may appear extremely permissive. The parents give greater weight to the children's wishes than is customary in two-parent households, while the children, as befits junior partners, are less deferential toward their parents.

The parents are often unaware of how the structure of their household has changed. They may recognize that they are closer to their children and rely more on their children than they had when they were married, but they are less likely to recognize that their family is no longer hierarchical, and that they have shared with their children some of their decision-making responsibilities as well as responsibilities for specific chores. They may, therefore, be uncertain how to respond to others who say that they overindulge their children, that they are too permissive, that their children are not deferential enough. The criticism seems to them unfair, but they do not know how to combat it. Here, for example, is one mother's report:

> My sister told me that she thought I was too permissive with my children. I got very angry with her when she said this. Then I realized that I am a lot more permissive with them when I'm alone with them than when there is another person in the house.

And yet the nonhierarchical single-parent family is very different from an overpermissive two-parent family. In the latter, the parents retain authority and responsibility while requiring little contribution to family functioning from the children. In the one-parent family, authority and responsibility are more nearly shared, and at the same time much is required of the children. Indeed, the indulgence of children's immaturity, which is one aspect of overpermissive two-parent families, is the very opposite of the insistence in single-parent families that the children assume genuine responsibility.

Not every single parent moves toward sharing decisionmaking responsibilities with the children. A few retain full authority, just as they would have had their marriages continued. To accomplish this, they must be able to maintain an image of what must be done without relying on anyone else in their families for support; it may help if they possess a certain rigidity of character. Here is a statement by a man who had been a strong family head before his wife left him, and who remained firmly in charge of his home as a single parent. It might be noted that he, like other single parents, required his children to assume new responsibilities. He was distinctive in the extent to which he retained the right to say what should be done and who should do it.

> As long as the children are here, they are going to go by my rules. And I'm a very hard man to get to change the rules. They have a little more responsibility now that their mother isn't here. I think that is a good thing, because they have to grow up someday and they might as well start learning a little responsibility now. But my children usually do what they are told.

Most single parents are not nearly so authoritative. They may have difficulty in defending to an outsider their practice of working things out with their children, but they have found that doing so is the only sensible way of managing their households.

WORKING PARENTS AND NONWORKING PARENTS AND THE MEANING OF THE CHILDREN'S TASKS

Because working single parents realize that only if their children help can their households function, they are likely to have little guilt about expecting their children to assume responsibility.

> Now I am working a forty-hour week, and I come home in the afternoon and supper is on. I have the oldest doing it. And I find I don't feel any guilt at all making them do these things. I think it's great for them. They are a lot more responsible.

Whatever the children do is one less job for the parent. Even very young children can make significant contributions to the household. Children of only three can keep their toys in order. Children of four and five can make their own beds—although they may complain that the beds will only have to be unmade in the evening. Five-year-olds can help with the dishes. Eight-year-olds can vacuum floors and clean up a kitchen. Ten-year-olds can cook. A man with three daughters, aged four to nine, described how they helped during the breakfast rush:

> Each of the kids has a chore. Patsy makes her bed in the morning when she gets up. Shirley gets the cereal down if we are having cereal. Lenore clears the table and puts the dishes in the dishwasher. While one is in the bathroom the others have something to do. By the time we leave the house in the morning, the beds are made, the table is cleared, and the dishes are put away in the dishwasher.

One way in which a single parent may share responsibility with a child is by having that child care for younger children in the family. The following comment was made by a widow:

> My older son, even though he's only fourteen, realizes the difficulty, and he's very good in helping with the little one. He's a very conscientious, very sensitive kid and it helps. He does a lot with his younger brother. It doesn't take the place of his father, but it does help.

If the parent works full time, this delegation of parental responsibility may happen even though the older child is still quite young. Another widow said:

> Shirley was only seven when her father died. I went back to work right away. Then she was only nine when I first had to leave Glenn with her a couple of times on a Saturday, as much as I didn't want to. My mother would come down halfway through the day or something, but Shirley was forced into responsibility quicker than she might have been, sooner than I would have wanted her to be under ordinary circumstances.

Children appear to have mixed feelings about looking after younger siblings. Some resent giving up time they could otherwise use for their own affairs. A 15-year-old girl, the oldest of three children, noted with some resentment, "I feel as though I spent my childhood taking care of my younger brothers." And a 13-year-old boy is reported to have balked at babysitting for his younger brother because that task, if no other, was his mother's responsibility. But there are attractions in the role of quasi-parent to younger siblings. There is reassurance in being able to provide security for another, and increased self-esteem as a result of being the one in charge. There is also a temporary besting of sibling rivals. Indeed, sometimes single parents have to limit the prerogatives of an older sibling who is too inclined to be bossy.

Single parents who are *not* employed outside their homes are often willing to care for their children just as they would have had they remained married. Indeed, in the absence of anything else to fill their days, they may take on additional tasks around the house. One mother of two school-aged girls said:

> I think I do more of the things around the house now. I was the one that cut the grass this summer. My husband used to do it sometimes, or one of the girls would do it, but the girls were busy with schoolwork and their friends, and I found I had the time, so why not do it? It wasn't that hard to do. So I did it.

Children in single-parent households very much prefer it if their parents remain home to care for them rather than go off to work. And yet, if parents share authority with their children—decide with the children, for example, when supper should be served—while retaining responsibility for performance of the task, the parents may risk feeling themselves to be the children's servants: the children decide what is to be done and the parents then set about doing it. The following story was told by another mother of school-aged children:

> They would complain about the laundry not being done or supper not being perfect or whatever else kids complain about. Then one day Lillian put it in front of me. She came into the kitchen and asked me to do something. I said, "I don't have to drop what I'm doing to do it for you, and I'm not going to do it." I've forgotten what it was. It was something or other. She said, "Well, you should! That's your job! You're the housemaid!" She meant to say "housewife" because she saw the little housewife on TV and in her mind that's what I was supposed to do. She forgot the word. And I started laughing because of the word "housemaid." Well, she was ready to pick a fight. She said again, "You're the housemaid!" I said, "I'm not the housemaid."
>
> I went out and got a job. Now they understand that I am not the housemaid. I have another job and I have to earn a living so that we have food on the table and we have a roof over our heads.

Some single parents who are without paid employment, like many parents in two-parent households, assign tasks to their children not because they need the children's contributions but because they believe that the children will benefit by responsibility. They want to foster in the children a sense of family citizenship together with a capacity for cooperative work. A child in any situation is likely now and again to slough off a task. When the parent has not truly been dependent on the child's contribution, the parent may be upset by the child's apparent indifference to responsibility but will not be dismayed because the task remains undone. The parent can always do it. Here, for example, is a report by a mother without paid employment of her reaction to a daughter's avoidance of a chore. The daughter was about seven.

> One thing I try to have the children do is make their beds, just to give them a taste of a little bit of responsibility. That hasn't worked out with Barbara be-

cause she forgets conveniently. There are days when she says, "Oh, I forgot to make my bed." And I know that she is full of malarkey, that she remembered, but she didn't want to be bothered. So I have told her that I will make a deal with her. She can have a nickel if she remembers to make her bed.

The mother here is skeptical but nevertheless patient and encouraging. Her reliance on bribery as a socialization technique might be questioned, but she clearly is as concerned with teaching her daughter work habits as with getting the bed made. One can easily imagine the mother deciding that it is too much trouble and letting the matter drop.

Single parents who have full-time jobs respond differently to situations in which children fail to help. Imagine a working single parent coming home after a tiring day, having stopped at a grocery so that there will be bread and milk for the morning's breakfast. The living room has not been picked up as she requested, but the real shock is the kitchen. The children have fixed themselves milk shakes and left the unwashed glasses on the kitchen table along with their school books and homework assignments. Some single parents would try to check their dismay and simply tell the children to get the kitchen clean. One mother at such times called her children together to contemplate her work-worn hands. Many, perhaps most, parents would blow up. They would shout that the children must do what they have been asked to do, that the parent cannot do it all.

Sometimes these blowups are half-calculated displays intended to impress on the children that they must do their share. Sometimes the blowups are entirely genuine, quite uncontrolled releasings of accumulated tensions. In any event, the children learn, vividly, that they have been asked to help not in order to improve their characters but because their help is essential. The following report, although it described a response not so much to a responsibility unmet as to a new task created, suggests the potential intensity of parental reactions:

> With four kids it's not too easy to keep a house picked up. The kids do their share, but not overly so. They manage to keep things picked up, not like you would like it, but they have schoolwork and social things and so forth, so I don't push. But I hate with a passion coming into a dirty kitchen. It is just my thing. If a kitchen table isn't cleared, I loathe that. If I come in and the kitchen is a mess, I'll scream bloody murder. I'll raise Cain. I'll say, "Can't I at least come home to a clean kitchen? That's all I ask!"

If there is only one child in the household, a working single parent sometimes can forgo the child's help. Parents of only children may even discourage the children from helping out. They say that it is easier for them to do things themselves than to wait for the children to get around to doing them. This may be especially the case when the parent is the mother and the child a boy. Then by discouraging her son from contributing to the household's functioning, the mother can play a wifelike role, with her son a complementary figure from whom little household work is expected.

THE CHILDREN GROW UP A LITTLE FASTER

The ending of the parental echelon makes it possible for children to deal with their parent as a near-equal. Responsibility and authority may have been shared. The parent may occasionally have called on the children for companionship, understanding, support, or advice. In addition, if the parent is working full time, the children will have been on their own a good deal; the parent may have been available to them only evenings and weekends. Even children of nonworking parents occasionally will have been left in the care of sitters or relatives while the parents attended to family responsibilities or went out with friends.

The result is that children in single-parent households often become surprisingly self-reliant and adult in their manner. Single parents sometimes describe one of their children as "nine going on forty-nine." Their children are young, yes, but they appear mature. Adolescents, especially, may interact with adults almost as if they were themselves adult. One woman said about her relationship with her 15-year-old daughter, "We talk on a very adult, one-to-one basis, because she *is* an adult. She is fifteen going on fifty." And another woman said:

> My son is thirteen, and, although I don't very often have adult conversations with him, there are times that we have conversations, about VD or something, that I would never, never have thought I would be able to have with a child.

Single parents sometimes say that their children have had to "grow up a little bit faster." Generally the parents think this a good thing: a kind of precocity deserving of respect. Indeed, the single parent may couple the expectation that the children will assume increased responsibility for the household with an expectation that the children will also become more self-reliant, more responsible for themselves. A mother of teenagers said:

> I think what happens to single parents is that they become more mature people, and they look at their children and they say, "Listen, you've got to do the same thing. You've got to grow up and you've got to be a mature person and learn to take care of yourself."

The absence of parental echelon permits the single parent to be more open with the children about the parent's uncertainties. And should the children's failure to understand the parent's concerns threaten to make matters worse, the parent may simply explain what the problems are. This is particularly true should the children want something for which there is no money.

> You're hit with these bills and who can you talk to about it but the kids? They're the only other people that you can really talk to. You have to have someone to share it with, and so you share it with the people that you're doing it for. And, every so often, if they're bugging me for something that costs too much

money, that's out of proportion to what I can afford, I take the bills out and
show them the bills, show them what we get in monthly, and say, "Now you
make sense out of it. If you can do it and get that amount of dollars that you
want, fine; do it!" And then they'll shut up for a while.

By the time the children reach adolescence they may be thoroughly familiar with their parents' worries about money. Sometimes the children become worried themselves. One adolescent girl spoke of checking the food
pantry to reassure herself that starvation was not an immediate prospect;
she was both chagrined and relieved to find the shelves well stocked. Where
there is in reality too little money for the family's needs, children may contribute to their families' income, often paying for some of their own ex-
penses from part-time, after-school work. Or they may join with their parents in economizing. The following story was told by the mother of a 13-
year-old boy:

A lot of times we live off what Danny makes on his paper route. After I pay
the mortgage, the gas, the telephone, the food, buy the clothes, that's the money
we have to live off. And Danny is really a super kid; he doesn't really mind.
    We had no money yesterday, absolutely zilch. I had twenty-three cents.
Payday is Friday. And Danny wanted to go for an ice cream. I said, "Well,
why don't we first go down to the store to buy some soap because I have a lot
of wash to do." So we went down to the store for soap and we found the
cheapest box of soap we could find. We got to the checkout; he had a dollar
thirty and I had the twenty-three cents. And the soap came to a dollar fifty-
three. I said, terrific, we have just enough. So then we went to another grocery
down the way because I needed milk, and I had some food stamps so I was
going to get the milk, and we found a box of soap that was cheaper. So I said,
"Why don't we return it? Danny, go get the soap, it's out in the car, and take
it back." So that's what he did. He got to buy a doughnut with the difference.

Children of separated and divorced parents are often aware of conflicts
between their parents over money. Some children report that their fathers
complain to them about their mothers' financial demands while their mothers
complain to them of their fathers' unwillingness to help. The mothers may
ask them to persuade the fathers to contribute more to their households or
the fathers may ask them to tell their mothers to be more reasonable. One
adolescent girl said of the way things had been different in her growing up:

You don't have—not necessarily the childhood—but you don't have the freedom of not worrying about things, of not worrying about money.

Yet adolescents seem to be pleased, on the whole, that their parents have
acknowledged, even fostered, their capabilities for maturity. And they display enhanced self-esteem for having learned to manage by themselves—
though they may regret having had to. The daily intervals of freedom from
adult supervision they are likely to have had since they were nine or ten

or eleven have allowed them to develop, along with a sort of responsible independence, feelings of self-sufficiency. Here is a comment by a 16-year-old girl:

> My mother works days, and I have to make sure that I get home when I say I will. And I do my share of the housework. Not as much as my mother would like, maybe, but enough. I have become very independent. I am an independent person. I'm a loner. So is my brother; we both are loners. I can probably get along by myself if I have to. Not completely, but if my mother died and I did not have to live with my father, I would probably go live with my aunt. And I'd be crying, but I could get along. I think it's because I already do a lot of things by myself. I suppose if I had both parents I wouldn't have to.

Contributing further to the self-esteem of adolescents, particularly girls, in single-parent families may be a sense of having developed skills not possessed by other children. In contrast to other children, they can cook, clean a house, care for themselves, and care for others. They may be slightly contemptuous of children who have not been required to meet the same challenges. Here is a comment by a 19-year-old girl:

> Where there is a father off working and a mother home taking care of the house, the kids never learn to do anything for themselves. It seems that they become very dependent on the mother to do everything. I think of my friends, like Bobbie. At least I've learned to cook a little bit and I've had to cook, like in high school, when mother wasn't here at night. But they've never had to do anything like that. And then when they have to do something like that, it's "Oh, my God, I don't know what I'm doing."

Indeed, some adolescent children of single parents see friends from two-parent families as having had an indulged and pampered life. Here is a comment by a 16-year-old girl:

> I get very angry at times, like, when I hear this girl. She said, "My mother yelled at me this morning because I didn't make my bed. And I am so upset today." And I just think, "You little twerp! I have to make my bed, my mother's bed; I have to clean the whole house; I have to cook the dinner; I have to take trash out!" And I was just so angry!

Even the most mature child is liable now and again to be childish. Single parents are sometimes surprised when children who have been functioning as young adults suddenly act their age. A widowed mother of three children, the oldest about 14, said:

> I tend to treat them as older. We'll sit down and we'll discuss something together or we'll talk together or something. Then they act like they should for their age and I have to get after them. And they're only doing what they should be doing.

Whether there is something lost to children in growing up faster is very difficult to say. Children who have had more to do than their contemporaries do sometimes regret the absence of a more nearly carefree childhood. And some children who have had to look after themselves from the time they were small may harbor unmet needs for nurturance. It may be that when these latter children become parents themselves they will be made uncomfortable by the dependence of their own children. But at least in the short run, as most single parents observe, there seems nothing wrong in growing up a little faster.[3] A mother of three children, the oldest not yet in his teens, described in this way the consequences for her children of living in a single-parent family:

> I have not seen any adverse effect. In fact, they have become a little more in-
> dependent and more mature. Since I started working, they have had to pitch
> in a bit. Before that, I waited on them hand and foot, and that's not good for
> any child.

ROLE REVERSAL AND OTHER ROLE CHANGES IN THE SINGLE-PARENT HOUSEHOLD

The changes in family functioning thus far described have involved modification in the roles of parents and children rather than fundamental change in those roles. The parents continue to be devoted to the care of the children, although they may skimp on time spent with them; the children continue to rely on the parents as guarantors of their security, although they may be more on their own than are other children of their age; and the parents continue to be ultimately in charge of the household, despite sharing responsibility and authority with their children. But the single-parent family can also experience fundamental changes in the assumptions underlying the relationships of parents and children.

Single parents, when they feel unhappy or upset, often make their distress evident to their children. Sometimes they rely on the children for sympathy or support. And sometimes the children go beyond simply feeling sad because the parent is sad and feel that they must assume responsibility for helping the parent to recover. The children become care providers for their parents, supportive or nurturant or directing in the way that parents ordinarily are when trying to be helpful to children. This is role reversal.

Role reversal may be especially likely to occur during the troubled months immediately following the ending of a marriage, for it is then that single parents are most in need of comfort and reassurance, and when they may also be most dependent on their children for companionship. One mother of two boys, aged four and six at the time of her divorce, said:

> At the time of my emotional instability I stayed with the kids and I really did
> draw from them a lot of strength. I'm not sure that was good for them or for
> me, but that was what I did.

Role reversals can be seen in parents' relationships with children as young as three and four. Here is an instance reported by a widower as having occurred a few months after the death of his wife. The child was four years old at the time.

> A lot of times in the beginning my son was like a father and I was like a son. One night we were sitting in the house watching television. I had kept him up late because I didn't want to be alone. And he said to me, "Daddy, let's play a game." And I said, "Okay." He said, "You be the Mommy and I'll be the God." I said, "Okay." And then he said, "Okay, you knock on my door." So I knocked on the door. He opens up the door and says, "Who is this at my door?" He's got the deep voice and everything. I said, "It's Mommy."
>
> And he brightened all up and he said, "Mommy, come in." And he pulled me in by the hand. And he says, "I've been waiting for you." And I said, "What is there for me to do here?" And he said, "Oh, we have baseball games, barbecues, picnics, birthday parties, and everything. And we're going to have a birthday party for you." So we had this imaginary cake and we had to blow out the candles and then at the end of it he just looked at me and he put his arms around me and he told me he loved me.

Role reversals may be encouraged by parents who are made anxious by the awareness that they are now solely responsible for the well-being of their families. One woman established a pattern of looking to her son for reassurance:

> If my fourteen-year-old sees me getting upset about something, he'll come over and say, "Now, Mom, calm down. I'll take care of it." And I really love that. When he does that I really feel good.

Sometimes children display concern for a troubled parent quite without the parent's encouragement. One mother had sent her two little girls to live with their father because she was so depressed. After the girls returned to live with her, the mother discovered that they had become alert to her moods and extremely solicitous. She told the following story:

> I picked the children up at day care and brought them home, and when we got home they immediately both went into the bathroom and I heard them saying, "She's in a bad mood." One is six and the other is five! Until I heard that I hadn't realized I was putting this trip on them. So I said to them, "I'm in a bad mood because I'm having troubles at work." And they proceeded to want to help me fix the troubles.

Occasionally a parent is disconcerted by a child's uninvited attempt at role reversal. This may especially be the case should the child try to take the role of admonitory adult. The boy in the following story was not quite ten.

> I called my house and Mark said, "When are you coming home?" And I said, "Pretty soon." And he said, "Ma, it's a quarter of eight. Now you had better

get home here quick." And I said, "Okay, Mark. I'm just having drinks with a few friends." And he said, "Well, don't drink too much and be home soon." And I said, "All right, give me about an hour." And he said, "Are you sure?" And I said, "Yes, about an hour." And I got off the phone, and I said, "I did this with my mother when I was a kid! I'd call up and have to give these excuses! I'm still doing it and I'm twenty-nine years old!"

We do not know the effects on children of persisting role reversals. Children seem to take role reversals of brief duration entirely in stride. They seem to recognize that their parents will soon be back to normal and that it is just a matter of getting them through a temporary incapacity. There also is reassurance to a child in being able to take over the role of parent when the real parent appears to be lost in sorrow or paralyzed by anxiety; at least there is still a functioning parent somewhere.

More persistent than role reversals may be shifts from parent-child complementarity to a complementarity more appropriate in a husband-wife relationship. A change of this sort occurs when a single mother relies on her son to take on the responsibilities of man of the house—to care for the family car, to be in charge of household repairs, or to help in the care and management of the other children. Or it can happen when a single father relies on his daughter to act as woman of the house—to be in charge of housekeeping, to act as the hostess for his friends, or to help in the care and management of the other children. The shift is potentially more persistent because neither parent nor child may feel pressed to return to more usual parent-child understandings. Here is a widowed mother describing an instance of complementarity:

> I expect my seventeen-year-old son to understand that even if his friends don't explain to the plumber what happened, that in his particular situation he should do it, because a plumber will pay more attention to another male.

A child's playing a complementary role makes it possible for the parent to function within the role the parent may have become accustomed to in marriage. At the same time, it provides the child the gratification of earning the parent's respect, and the reassurance of being not only loved but also indispensable. But because it can work so well for both parent and child for the child to play a complementary role, there are risks in the arrangement. One risk is that the child will be ambivalent about moving off into an independent adult life; the home situation can be too gratifying, and leaving it—and the parent—would make the child feel too guilty. And the parent may be reluctant to see the child leave. One boy who had long played the role of man of the house finally made his departure by joining the Navy. His mother said:

> Bill was really the man of the house around here for years. Any kind of physical labor that I couldn't do, he would always just do it for me. When he went into the service I missed him more than I had missed my husband.

Another risk is that children with whom parents have established complementary relationships, or who themselves seek to establish such relationships, may impose themselves on their siblings in ways the siblings find unpleasant:

> My oldest son has taken on that role of being a parent, telling the others what they should do and what they shouldn't do and how he will send so-and-so to bed if so-and-so doesn't do this or that. He'll take on all kinds of responsibilities. I don't think it's good for him, because he's only eleven.

Quite intolerable for parents is a development in which their children act toward them as might a demanding spouse. At that point a parent is almost certain to say that complementarity has gone too far. The following story was told by the mother of four, the oldest a 16-year-old boy:

> Unconsciously I was asking my oldest, "Would you fix that for me?" Or, "What would you like for supper?" But then one time he was working after school and he said to me, "I expect my meals on the table when I come in from work." I said, "Who the hell do you think you are? You are my son and you will eat when I put it on the table!"

Instead of role complementarity, a child may display role competition and may attempt to displace the parent as the leader of the household. The parent is apt to feel threatened—and angry. A mother of three children, the oldest a 13-year-old boy, said:

> I find my oldest boy getting very bossy with the other kids, and I have to stop this. I have told him that when he is the babysitter they have to listen to him, but other times, no. But when I am reprimanding one of the other kids he will come out of his room and butt in.

Sometimes it is hard for a single parent to distinguish between a child who only wants to be helpful and a child who wants to take over the parent's role. But generally a parent will limit the extent to which one child can act in a bossy fashion toward another, even if the parent is not sure what is going on. A mother of three daughters, the oldest just entering her teens, said:

> In the beginning my oldest girl would get after the other kids and say, "Pick this up," "Do that." And when the baby would be outside, she'd say, "Get in here." And I would say, "Leave her alone. It's not your responsibility. I will handle it."

These developments in parent-child relationships—role reversal, complementarity, competition for familial leadership—are made possible by the structure of single-parent households. With no parental echelon to hold parents to their parental roles, with children becoming, in limited ways, both the parents' companions and their partners, there is no barrier to still further modifications of parent-child understandings. Some of these may be entirely acceptable to both parents and children as continuing arrangements; others are acceptable only briefly; still others are troublesome from the first.

PROBLEMS OF MANAGEMENT AND CONTROL IN THE ONE-PARENT HOUSEHOLD

The structure and mode of functioning of the single-parent household make for distinct problems in management and control. Some single parents do say that their families are easier to manage just because there is no other parent with whom to argue about what the children are to do, and no opportunity for the children to play divide and manipulate. A divorced man who had custody of his two school-aged children said:

> Single parent means that there is only one person to discipline. They only have the one person to answer to, and that is me. They can't play me and Mommy against each other, because Mommy isn't here.

But this single parent was not nearly as authoritative as he presented himself. Like other single parents, he often found himself caught up in negotiations with the children. Since children in a one-parent household carry more responsibility than children in a two-parent household, they want to have more voice in family decisions. Indeed, decision-making is likely already to be shared with them. And if the children have been used by the parent as confidantes, if the parent has now and again turned to them for understanding and support, it will be doubly difficult for the parent suddenly to assume the voice of command.

Shared decision-making seems to be an appropriate management style for single-parent homes; it provides parents with the assurance of children's understanding of what is to be done and their acceptance of arrangements; it facilitates cooperation within the household. But it does give rise to characteristic problems.

Single parents may have to insist that certain decisions are theirs to make or risk the children's taking over by force of numbers. If everyone has an equal vote on television programs, the set will always be tuned to the children's programs. Parents may have to insist that they can choose shows under some circumstances—or get two sets, one for themselves and one for the children. And parents may have to insist that their taste in home decoration will govern, except within the children's rooms:

> Trying to redecorate a room with the kids is terrible, because if I do what I want and they don't like it, well, it's their home, too, and they have to live in it, so why wouldn't they get to pick the wallpaper?

Acknowledging children's equal rights in the household can sometimes result in the parent's relinquishing claims to common space. One mother was effectively moved out of her living room by her adolescent children. When her husband had lived with her, she and her husband would often sit together in the living room, chatting, reading, or listening to records. After her husband's departure, she felt she could not prohibit the children from playing their rock music on the living room stereo only so that she might be in the living room alone. So she regularly retired to her bedroom after dinner and left the living room to the children.

Children may question a parent's right to special privilege. If a parent intends to stay up late to watch a movie on television, the children may ask, "If you can do it, why can't we?" The children may expect that the parent will observe the same rules they observe, even though the rules were designed by the parent to govern the children's behavior.

> We were having supper and the phone started ringing. Larry answers. He says, "I'm sorry, my mother can't talk. We're having supper." Because that was his rule, and he figured that the rule applied to me, too. It was my girlfriend, Linda, so I said, "Okay, Larry, tell Linda that we have a rule and it applies to me, too." But I would have talked if he hadn't answered the phone.

Or the children may ask why the parent is not included in the distribution of chores. A mother of three daughters reported:

> Marcia said, "One of us always has to do the garbage. Why don't you ever do the garbage?" And I started thinking, actually there isn't any reason why I shouldn't do garbage too and rotate my jobs with them.

The absence of a second parent not only produces a situation in which children feel justified in negotiating rules and chores, but also, since the parent is without obligation to another parent to hold to a particular line, makes it possible for the parent to participate in the negotiating. Some children, recognizing this, seem determined to negotiate every request the parent makes, and parents are then left frustrated and helpless. A divorced mother said:

> I can't handle discipline. I think that's probably why I have problems with my son. My daughter, who is eleven, doesn't give me that much of a problem. But my son, who is nine—it seems like no matter what I say, he's got to argue with me. And it just drives me crazy. I can't say one thing to him and have him accept it! He's got to come back and say, "Well, how about this, how about that, and the other thing?" And I'm just about ready to blow my mind!

Yet parents' dependence on their children as well as devotion to them makes the parents try to understand the children's point of view and to be accommodating if they can be. So, although the children may argue about chores, about when to come in at night, about baths and bedtimes and which pajamas to wear, the single parent may try to remain patient and reasonable. One mother of two boys aged eleven and eight said:

> As a single parent you have to negotiate an awful lot with the kids. My mother was up this week taking care of the kids and she said I negotiate too much. "Don't talk. Just hit them." That's her cure for everything. Well, if there were two parents in my house I could make the guy the heavy. I'd tell him they've been bugging me, and maybe he'd give them a licking. I don't do it. Once in a while, when they really push me, I'll lay into them. But I negotiate more with my kids than I ever would with an adult. I always take the kids' feelings into consideration. And it's negotiation, negotiation, negotiation.

The absence of a second parent permits the single parent to accept children's proposals that, had a second parent been present, would have been dismissed out of hand. But now there is no one else to review the single parent's agreements, and so, sometimes against the single parent's better judgment, the child can gain the parent's assent to proposals of dubious merit:

> I was in the kitchen when I realized I had no cigarettes. I thought I would try to do without them. But after about fifteen minutes I couldn't anymore. I was just going out of my mind for a cigarette. Larry was there, doing his homework, and I said, "Larry, would you go to the store and buy me a package of cigarettes?" And he said, "Well, what's in it for me? Can I have a candy bar?" I said, "Yeah, if you want to rot out your teeth you can have a candy bar." "And a Coke?" He was trying to get the most for this run, right? He was working his way up to a car. I agreed to the candy bar and the Coke. I would have agreed to anything. I would have agreed to a car.

Single parents, like other parents, are likely to feel that parents are not supposed to enter into negotiations with children as though the children were equals. They are supposed to be firm, though kindly; they are supposed to maintain clear standards of appropriate behavior, establish rules, and set limits, so that the children have the security of always knowing what is proper and of knowing, too, that the improper will not be permitted. As single parents observe themselves failing to behave as parents are supposed to behave, they feel guilty. They say uncomfortably, "Sometimes I let them get away with too much. It's harder when you are by yourself. You give in to them."

But conflict with the children may impose a higher price on a single parent than the single parent is willing to pay. Here is a story of one woman's conflict with her nine-year-old son over the boy's refusal to do an assigned chore. The woman never did learn why her son would not take out the garbage on his return home from school. Perhaps he felt that because his age-mates did not have to do this, it was unfair for him to have to. The woman tried punishment, and the turmoil that followed was more than she could tolerate. It was easier for her to take out the garbage herself.

> Matt is a hard person for me to motivate to do any chores. I don't know how to go about it. I guess I should be very severe and go through this spanking thing, but I don't. I don't like to yell and scream and have temper tantrums and go through all that with my kids. Sally, I ask her something once and she does it, and there's never really a whole lot of argument. Maybe sometimes there's some discussion, but it isn't a flare-up thing.
>
> But Matt, the first week I said, "You take out the garbage. You're supposed to take the garbage out after school." And he said, "I can't do that." And I said, "You can and will." And he said, "I won't." And I said, "Well, you get a spanking!" And then I spanked him, and then he had a temper tantrum because I spanked him. He goes upstairs and he slams his door, and I go running up the stairs and he locks his door, and I say, "Don't you lock that bedroom door on me! I'm going to take off your lock!" And he refuses to open his door.
>
> How long can you sit out there and stew? You can tear the door down, or when he comes down you can spank him again and stand over him and walk out with him to the garbage. But I can't. I'm not in the mood for that when I get home from work. I'm tired. It's easier for me to do it myself. I know it's a mistake. I really should be handling it differently. But I don't, and that's all.

When there is only the one parent, fights with the children can take so much of that parent's energy that it may seem to the parent preferable to avoid them. And the single parent may wonder whether punishing the children is really the right way to manage them; there is no other parent with whom to discuss the issue and come to some shared decision. Beyond this, punishing the children dissolves the sense of partnership with them that is so important for the single parent. It isolates the parent from the children. It means that for a time the single parent will have to act alone, without the children's support; the parent may, instead, have to cope with their resentment. The single parent, as a result, is likely to learn to overlook whatever can be overlooked. A mother of three school-aged children said:

> There are a lot of things I overlook, because if I didn't, I'd be constantly disciplining them, constantly punishing them. So there aren't many things that get me uptight. When they are noisy or they do something foolish and it was an accident, what am I going to do? Take a baseball bat and beat them over the head with it? It's not a case of letting them get away with murder. It's just, what the hell am I going to do?

Women who were previously married sometimes say that since the ending of their marriages they have had problems disciplining their children. They may not recognize that the single-parent situation itself—in which the parent, without an adult ally, has become closer to the children and more dependent on their help—makes it more difficult for the parent to act authoritatively. Instead, they may feel that their gender is to blame, that boys, in particular, just don't listen to their mothers as they might to their fathers. One divorced mother of two boys not yet adolescent said:

> When Warner was there, the kids behaved better. I guess they feared him a little bit. They're not brats; they're not bad kids. I don't have any real problems with them. But if Warner said, "Shut up," they shut up. When I say, "Shut up," they say, "Oh, yeah? Make me!" There's a lot of things the kids do now that they couldn't do when Warner lived here, because they knew they couldn't get away with it, like giving me fresh answers.

Research as yet has little to say about whether women are right to feel that their gender makes it difficult for them to command their children's respect. A recent study by Hetherington, Cox, and Cox suggests that mothers on their own have only limited success in gaining their children's acceptance of authoritative directives, but whether fathers on their own would have less difficulty remains an open question.[4] It may be significant that few of the men we spoke with in our various studies considered disciplining their children to be a very serious problem, and at least one felt that discipline was less of a problem for him than it had been when he was married.

It does appear that single mothers may have a somewhat more difficult time controlling some children, perhaps adolescent boys in particular, than single fathers would. But all single parents, fathers as well as mothers, may be less controlling—and less capable of being controlling if they wanted to be—than parents who are partnered. The single-parent situation inhibits parental authoritarianism.

On the other hand, many parents, both single and married, believe that physical punishment is appropriate with younger children to make them behave or "mind." But single parents (and married parents, under some circumstances), unable to call on another parent for relief and made desperate by a child's opposition, can find themselves suddenly frenzied, with the result that the punishment is oversevere or is accompanied by harsh verbal rejection. A mother of an only son, six years old, said:

> My son would do something bad and I would punish him, and he would pout or he would have temper tantrums. Or he would try to be loving, and I would not want him to be loving, so I would push him away. And then I would feel guilty. You know, I am rejecting him and he's going to feel it. Then I would get angrier and it would be just a vicious circle of anger and guilt. And after a while I would start screaming at him and saying awful things that I wouldn't say to anybody. You know, "I can't stand you. I don't want you near me. I don't like you. I don't want you." That's a horrible thing to say. But at the moment I mean it. At that moment I don't want to see his face. Later I realize I don't really mean it. I apologize and say I was tired or I didn't feel good. And I tell him that I was wrong. But it doesn't help. It has been said. He is still hurt.

The sequence of rage and remorse described here is one that could occur in almost any single-parent household in which the children are not yet adolescent. The children play so large a role in the parent's world that when things go badly, one or more of them tends to be identified as part of the cause, perhaps the only part within reach. Parents of small children may avoid punishing their children physically for fear they will lose control of themselves; parents of older children may forgo punishment entirely rather than risk rage and remorse. And when children are sharing responsibility for the household, meting out punishment to them may simply make no sense. But just as husbands and wives can turn on each other when a reason for misadventure must be found, so can single parents turn on their children.

If punishment is two-edged, hurting the parent along with the child, how can a single parent ensure that a child meets the responsibilities the child has been assigned? One approach is to nag. Here is the mother of an 11-year-old only daughter:

> I find myself saying to her, "You've got to help me out. I have no one else who can help me." She's been given a lot more to do, and although she's accepted it a lot more, she's not fully accepted it. It really is a hassle if I have to nag her. And I have become a nag. She's been complaining that I pick on her.

Single parents may appeal to their children's consciences: "Look how much *I'm* doing for *you*." Or they may repeatedly remind their children that with one fewer adult in the household the children have to help. A father of four children, their ages stretching from primary school to nearly adult, described keeping his children aware of how badly needed their help was:

> Sometimes the kids can't understand why they should clean the garage or why they should clean the yard. One will say, "Well, he doesn't do it; I'm not going to do it." I say, "Hey, that's not the way the ballgame goes. Either we all work together or nothing gets done, because one person just can't do it all."

Many parents ask children who balk at a chore assignment what would happen if the parent decided not to do what he or she was supposed to do. Who would earn the living? Manage the household? Be there for the children?

One mother did go on strike. This woman's three daughters were all teenagers, but still she felt it took some courage to absent herself as fully as she did from managing her family.

> Laundry was piling up and the dishes hadn't been done and it was chaos. Rather than get mad, I put a sign up on the kitchen door that I was on strike until the following things were done. And I listed all the things that weren't done and

had to be done. I said I wouldn't do any cooking and that they would have to clean up any messes they made in the kitchen and that I wouldn't listen to any bickering. I also said I would come off strike only if they got all the work done and didn't fight about it.

At first they thought it was marvelous, cooking their own meals. But after three days somebody wanted to be driven to a birthday party and I said, "No deal." So then they got together somehow and they got the work done. It took three days. I did it a second time, but then they knew I was serious about it, so they did their jobs instantly.

Because single parents are so dependent on their children's coopera-tion, they have management problems different from those of parents in two-parent households. What are they to do when the children are less than helpful? Punishment can be disruptive, except when used in limited amounts. Parents can nag or cajole or point out to the children how much they themselves are doing. But perhaps most effective in gaining children's co-operation is the children's realization of how much their help is needed. (This means, incidentally, that children are most likely to be cooperative if the tasks clearly need doing.) The strength of the single-parent household lies in its shared recognition of interdependence.

NOTES

1. Robert O. Blood, and Donald Wolfe, *Husbands and wives.* New York: Free Press, 1960.

2. Erving Goffman, *Asylums.* New York: Doubleday, 1966.

3. Other comments on early maturity among children in single-parent situations may be found in Victor George and Paul Wilding, *Motherless families* (London: Routledge and Kegan Paul, 1972), p. 73; and Richard A. Gardner, *Psychotherapy with children of divorce,* New York: Aronson, 1976, p. 169 ff.

4. E. Mavis Hetherington, Martha Cox, and Roger Cox, "Divorced Fathers," *The family coordinator* (October 1976), pp. 417–428. On page 425 the authors say, "The divorced mother tries to control the child by being more restrictive and giving more commands which the child ignores or resists. . . . However, by the second year her use of negative sanctions is declining. . . . The divorced mother decreases her futile attempts at authoritarian control and becomes more effective in dealing with her child over the two year period." Children in this study were attending nursery school at the time of the parents' divorce. The "second year" referred to here is after *divorce,* not after separation.

Index